SOCIOLOGY
A Critical Approach

SOCIOLOGY
A Critical Approach

KENNETH J. NEUBECK
University of Connecticut

DAVITA SILFEN GLASBERG
University of Connecticut

McGraw-Hill, Inc.

*New York   St. Louis   San Francisco
Auckland   Bogotá   Caracas   Lisbon   London
Madrid   Mexico City   Milan   Montreal   New Delhi
San Juan   Singapore   Sydney   Tokyo   Toronto*

SOCIOLOGY
A Critical Approach

Photo Credits appear on pages C-1 to C-2 and on this page by reference.

This book is printed on acid-free paper.

2 3 4 5 6 7 8 9 0   DOC   DOC   9 0 9 8 7 6

ISBN 0-07-046315-8

This book was set in Trump Mediaeval by The Clarinda Company.
The editors were Roberta Meyer, Jill S. Gordon, and Sheila H. Gillams;
the designer was Karen K. Quigley;
the production supervisor was Leroy A. Young.
The photo editors were Barbara Salz and Safra Nimrod.
Quebecor Printing/R. R. Donnelley & Sons Company was printer and binder.

Cover photo: Ken Sherman/Graphistock.

Library of Congress Cataloging-in-Publication Data
Neubeck, Kenneth J.
    Sociology: a critical approach / Kenneth J. Neubeck, Davita
Silfen Glasberg.
        p.   cm.
    Includes bibliographical references and indexes.
    ISBN 0-07-046315-8
    1. Sociology.   I. Glasberg, Davita Silfen.   II. Title.
HM51.N45   1996
301—dc20   95-2208

ABOUT THE AUTHORS

Kenneth J. Neubeck is Associate Professor of Sociology at the University of Connecticut–Storrs. His articles have appeared in such journals as *Social Problems, Social Policy,* and *Teaching Sociology,* as well as several anthologies. Much of his work has focused upon issues of social and economic justice, covering such topics as the politics surrounding income maintenance programs, cultural values supporting economic inequality, and the relationship between central city downtown development and local neighborhood decline. The author of *Corporate Response to Urban Crisis* (Lexington Books) and *Social Problems: A Critical Approach* (McGraw-Hill), he is currently conducting research on the impact of racism on U.S. welfare policy.

Davita Silfen Glasberg is Associate Professor of Sociology at the University of Connecticut–Storrs. She has published extensively on issues of bank hegemony, the state in finance capitalism, and political economy, including *The Power of Collective Purse Strings: The Effects of Bank Hegemony on Corporations and the State* (University of California Press). She is currently working on an examination of corporate welfare and the welfare state in a study of bank deregulation and the savings and loan bailout, a study of the effect of bank political action committees (PACs) on bank deregulation and the bailout, and a collaborative study (with Kathryn Ward) on the effects of global debt on development and on the status of women in the world system.

To Gig, Michael, Kara, and Christopher Neubeck
To Cliff, Gillian, and Morgan Silfen Glasberg

CONTENTS
IN BRIEF

CONTENTS

PREFACE

We share the excitement of those who have looked forward to our completion of *Sociology: A Critical Approach.* Our goal in writing this text is to encourage students to develop, in the words of C. Wright Mills, a "sociological imagination." The text does this by acquainting students with the core concepts of sociology and demonstrating how these concepts can be used to understand (and perhaps change) features of society that help shape the trajectory of their own and others' biographies.

In this text we are particularly concerned that students gain new knowledge of the ways in which global intersocietal relations, societal membership, institutional functioning, class position, race, gender, age, state of able-bodiedness, and sexual orientation affect individuals' life chances. Our "critical approach" to sociology means that we raise analytical questions and explore issues that shed light on features of society that harm people and get in the way of their individual and collective fulfillment, suggesting the need for social change.

Sociology: A Critical Approach opens with an introductory chapter in which we discuss the importance of the sociological imagination and the core sociological concepts upon which this imagination relies. We review the major research methods sociologists use to generate knowledge essential to the exercise of the sociological imagination, commenting upon political and ethical concerns to which sociologists must be sensitive when conducting research.

In the first part of the text, students are introduced to core sociological concepts that most sociologists consider to be at the heart of the discipline. We stress the significance of these concepts for analyzing the organization and operation of society, covering topics ranging from the most "macro" (the importance of a society's position in the world-system) to the most "micro" (the impact of socialization on individuals).

The second part of the text focuses on six institutional spheres that are central to the cumulative experiences of society's members. Here students are exposed to bodies of research literature pertaining to social structures with which they have come into contact, but about which most students have thought very little. In this part of the text we show students how the sociological imagination can be put to work to shed new light on how the institutions they often take for granted affect them—for better or worse.

We close the text with a final chapter on emerging issues—recent problems or trends that people are beginning to confront—which challenge the sociological imagination. In closing the text in this way, we wish to encourage students to utilize their sociological insights and discover that the study of sociology can help them to understand and respond in an empowered way to changing societal conditions they will encounter in the future.

FEATURES

Integration of Race, Class, and Gender Issues   Our interest in issues pertaining to race, class, and gender led us to integrate materials on these and related topics into virtually every chapter. Consistent with this approach, Chapter 6 ("Systems of Inequality") moves beyond the conventional chapter-length treatment of class-based social stratification found in most texts. In Chapter 6 we not only discuss class inequality; we give equal attention to systems of race and gender inequality, as well as systems of inequality based on age, state of able-bodiedness, and sexual orientation.

Chapter 7 ("Intersection of Race, Class, and Gender")   This unique chapter flows logically from our treatment of various systems of inequality. In this chapter these systems are viewed as a matrix within which most individuals are simultaneously members of socially dominant and socially subordinate groups. Topics treated in this chapter (such as the ways in which our system of sex inequality affects women who are privileged by virtue of their class and race) increase students' awareness of the diversity of people's experiences with inequality, a diversity that traditional treatments of stratification tend to ignore.

Coherence of Chapters   Each chapter in this text is organized around a central set of questions that guides the chapter's coherence. Concepts are introduced as vehicles or sociological tools to address these questions. Thus we avoid presenting students with a text that reads like a dictionary of terms. Instead, students see how sociological concepts and perspectives can be usefully mobilized to expand their understanding of social life, the world around them, and their own position and experiences in that world.

Social Issues/People's Lives   Each chapter contains a boxed reading in which an individual speaks of life experiences that reflect, to use C. Wright Mills' terms, "public issues" rather than "personal troubles." These readings, which we chose to call "Social Issues/People's Lives," help to ground sometimes abstract concepts and ideas in terms that are easier for students to grasp. For example, in Chapter 1 a middle-class family confronts difficult times due to corporate layoffs. In Chapter 3, a young man of mixed racial ancestry describes his struggle to establish his racial identity. In Chapter 4, students will read the words of a military academy cadet who realizes he is gay; and in Chapter 8 a working mother who once needed welfare evocatively recalls others' views of recipients.

Thinking Critically Each chapter ends with a series of provocative questions that are intended to promote discussion, debate, and exercise of the sociological imagination. The questions, under the heading "Thinking Critically," encourage students to consider the implications of facts outlined in the chapter and often call upon them to relate these facts to their own lives.

Suggested Readings, Key Terms, Glossary To assist students in pursuing interests they develop while reading the chapters, annotated suggested readings are provided. In addition, each chapter contains a list of key terms that are defined in a glossary at the back of the text.

Graphics Tables and figures provide data that are useful and relevant to the text discussion. Figures are carefully captioned to assist student understanding.

ACKNOWLEDGMENTS

Many people have contributed to the successful completion of *Sociology: A Critical Approach*. Our appreciation goes to the staff at McGraw-Hill, with special thanks to Phil Butcher, Jill Gordon, Roberta Meyer, Sheila Gillams, Karen Quigley, Safra Nimrod, and photo researcher Barbara Salz. The following McGraw-Hill reviewers also deserve our thanks for their helpful comments and suggestions: Ben Agger, SUNY–Buffalo; Julie V. Brown, University of North Carolina–Greensboro; Walter E. Clark, St. Louis Community College–Florissant Valley; B. Keith Crew, University of Northern Iowa; Rita Duncan, Tulsa Junior College; David L. Ellison, Rensselaer Polytechnic Institute; Sondra Farganis, Vassar College; Mark Gottdiener, SUNY-Buffalo; Linda Grant, University of Georgia; Charles Green, Hunter College; Charles E. Hurst, The College of Wooster; Ray Hutchison, University of Wisconsin–Green Bay; Peter Kivisto, Augustana College; Beth Mintz, University of Vermont; F. Dale Parent, Southeastern Louisiana University; Brenda Phillips, Texas Women's University; Ellen Rosengarten, Sinclair Community College; Beth A. Rubin, Tulane University; Brian T. Smith, University of Southern Mississippi; R. Dale Spady, Northern Michigan University; Kenrick S. Thompson, Northern Michigan University; Lee Van Dorsten, Colorado State University; Ira M. Wasserman, Eastern Michigan University; and Stuart A. Wright, Lamar University. Our colleagues at the University of Connecticut have been very supportive of this project; we especially wish to thank Myra Marx Ferree and Ronald Taylor for their ideas and help.

We are greatly indebted to graduate students who have provided research assistance: Rachel Levy, Julia McQuillan, Denise Anthony, and

David Nielsen. David was a long-term participant in our project, and we are most thankful for the contributions he made to the very end.

We would also like to thank our respective families for their love and support, patience and good humor: Gig, Michael, Kara, and Christopher Neubeck, and Cliff, Gillian, and Morgan Silfen Glasberg. It is to them that we dedicate this book.

Last, but not least, the authors would like to thank one another. It's been "real"!

Kenneth J. Neubeck
Davita Silfen Glasberg

SOCIOLOGY
A Critical Approach

THE SOCIOLOGICAL IMAGINATION

*W*hen we glance at the newspaper headlines or tune in the nightly news, we are exposed to the troubles that many people confront in their day-to-day lives. In all corners of the world, we see people's lives affected by political turmoil, military actions, economic breakdowns, and natural disasters. Our own lives may seem calm and predictable in comparison to those portrayed in the mass media. Yet each of us, along with our friends and family members, periodically faces problems that—while not necessarily newsworthy—affect us in

1

important ways. We may, for example, have difficulty landing a decent-paying job or find ourselves living in a tension-filled home. In many instances our troubles leave us crying out for relief and calling for change.

The discipline of sociology can be useful in understanding the sources of people's troubles and what might be done about them. **Sociology** *is the study of people as participants in and creators of society. Sociologists examine the social conditions that affect people's behavior, as well as those that give rise to movements for change. The knowledge provided by sociologists can help each of us place our personal troubles in a larger context. Sociological knowledge is also useful to politicians, planners, policy makers, journalists, intellectuals, and social workers and reformers concerned with existing social conditions and their impacts.*

You may have noticed we named this textbook Sociology: A Critical Approach. *The subtitle reflects our view that sociology should go beyond merely accumulating knowledge about the world humans have constructed. We feel that sociology should also use that knowledge to (1) help people make decisions about which social conditions can and should be changed, and (2) help people figure out how to go about making the changes. This view requires that the discipline ask questions that will often be quite critical of the status quo. We might, for example, go beyond asking "What is poverty and what are its effects?" to inquiring "Why does poverty exist? Is it necessary and inevitable? If not, what are the obstacles to its elimination? How can these obstacles be overcome?" Such questions clearly imply taking a critical approach toward prevailing, often taken-for-granted patterns of economic inequality. Such an approach is crucial to the public debate that must precede decisions about social change.*

As you study sociology, expect it to differ from other social sciences you may study. The discipline of psychology, for example, focuses on the internal mental functioning of individuals and its relationship to their behavior. In contrast, sociology is concerned primarily with the social context surrounding individuals. Sociologists want to understand why and how people's thinking and behavior are influenced by their group membership, their relations with others, and the conditions under which they work and live (Berger, 1963).

Psychologists and sociologists often share the insights of their disciplines. For example, some sociologists and psychologists share common interests in the specialized area of social psychology, which focuses on such topics as attitude formation and change, the behavior of people in small groups, and the socialization process through which people learn to participate in social life (see Chapter 5). But in general it is correct to say that sociologists are more prone than psychologists to focus on the "big picture."

Sociologists also trade ideas with their social science colleagues in economics and political science. Sociologists, however, view economic and political systems as only two of many types of "social institutions" central to the functioning of society. The family, education, and religion are also of interest to sociologists. Finally, there is a good deal of common ground between sociology and anthropology in their concepts and research concerns. But anthropologists have historically emphasized the study of non-Western, preliterate societies, particularly their cultural characteristics, while sociologists have tended to emphasize analysis of the organization and operation of Western industrialized societies.

In this chapter you will learn how sociology can help you develop a very useful way of thinking about society and its problems. This way of thinking has been called the "sociological imagination." We shall identify some of the core concepts and major research methods used in sociology that contribute to the sociological imagination. We shall also address some of the ethical and political issues that arise for anyone engaged in sociological research. Through your exploration of these topics, we hope you will come to share our own sense of excitement and enthusiasm about the field of sociology.

PERSONAL TROUBLES
VERSUS PUBLIC ISSUES: DANA'S STORY

To move us toward discussion of the sociological imagination, we begin with a story about Dana, a sincere and pleasant young woman of 19. Dana grew up in a middle-class neighborhood with her parents and two younger brothers. She was a relatively good student in high school, although she was the first to admit she coasted whenever she could. To provide the family with basic necessities, Dana's parents both worked. They gave up vacations in order to put a small amount of money aside each month to help pay for their children's college expenses. Dana and her brothers found part-time jobs to pay for their personal expenses. There were few luxuries. Dana's family was proud last year when she went off to a public college that had a good reputation. It was just affordable with Dana's summer earnings and a modest boost from the financial aid office. She was on track. But now her world is falling apart.

Dana's father has been out of work for over six months. He was laid off when his employer, an industrial firm where he had worked his way up to a middle-management position, "downsized" its labor pool. To his dismay, he found little interest from other employers. He wondered how much his being middle-aged had to do with it or if his physical disability, the result of a car accident, counted against him. He took it for granted that his dark skin was a liability. Dana's mother had been working ever since her youngest child was old enough to care for himself after school. But her salary as a clerk-typist in an insurance company was not sufficient to support the family much above the poverty level, let alone contribute to Dana's college expenses. When Dana asked for more financial aid, the college aid office told her that the federal government had tightened the eligibility rules and it couldn't give her anything more. Even with the part-time jobs she was holding down, Dana could not afford to stay at college.

When Dana arrives home, she finds her family in turmoil. The stress seems to be ripping apart her parents' marriage. Mutual hostility and periodic outbursts of physical abuse mar their relationship. Dana's father was

People out of work may view their unemployment as their own personal trouble. But the long lines at unemployment offices, such as this one in New York City, remind us that the lack of jobs for those who wish to work should be treated as a public issue.

always strict but fair with his children. Now he behaves unpredictably. Her brothers seek refuge with their friends and try to avoid their father. They are also beginning to get into trouble at school; her mother is receiving a stream of calls and notes from school authorities. Dana spends a lot of time in her room, anxiety-stricken and chronically depressed by the overwhelming facts of her difficult situation. Away from her friends, and too frightened to approach her parents, Dana suffers alone.

If Dana and her family were part of a small handful of people in our society facing crises associated with unemployment and family discord, we might simply suggest that they all get counseling and wish them well. It would be logical to conclude they were just suffering from what sociologist C. Wright Mills called **personal troubles,** that is, matters involving a person's character and his or her relations with others. Personal troubles typically can be resolved in local environments by those directly involved (Mills, 1959). But a substantial body of social science research suggests that the kinds of crises and challenges confronting Dana and her family are extremely widespread (Neubeck, 1991).

Mills made a distinction between personal troubles and **public issues.** Public issues "have to do with matters that transcend these local environments of the individual" (Mills, 1959: 8). When millions of men and women in our society are involuntarily unemployed, as is the case today, their unemployment is a public issue. The individuals involved cannot correct their joblessness by an act of will. Rather, we must look at the economy as an institution and determine what steps can be taken to improve employment opportunities.

Dana's father is caught up in a situation that he may be experiencing as his personal trouble, but it is really a reflection of a larger public issue. Job loss due to changes in the economic environment in the United States is now a fact of life (Bluestone and Harrison, 1982; Eitzen and Zinn, 1989b). Between 1987 and 1992, 5.6 million U.S. workers who had been with their employers at least three years, many of whom worked in the manufacturing sector, lost their jobs because of plant closings, business failures, and similar reasons. As of 1992, over a third of these workers were still jobless. Of those who found new positions, half earned less than they did on the jobs they lost (U.S. Bureau of Labor Statistics, 1992b: 1).

The plight of Dana's family reflects other public issues that go beyond personal troubles and resist individual solutions. As we shall see in Chapter 6, millions of adults face discrimination in the labor market on the basis of their skin color or age. Some 36 million Americans suffer disabilities; they often must combat prejudices on the part of employers. Women across our society continue to face pressures to carry the bulk of child-care and domestic responsibilities. This situation, combined with sex discrimination in the work force, makes it difficult for women to perform successfully as sole providers of the family income (see Sidel, 1990). Unemployment has been shown to have a damaging impact on personal and family life, fostering tensions and even contributing to family violence (Liem and Rayman, 1982; Bensman and Lynch, 1987; Newman, 1989).

Sociology can help us become sensitive not only to the difference between personal troubles and public issues but also to the connections that often exist between the two. It is common for people like Dana's father to view unemployment as their own personal trouble and to accept the burden of responsibility for it. They blame themselves, and may be blamed by others, for their plight. But when the blame lies with social and economic forces beyond the individual's control, it is more appropriate to treat difficulties like unemployment as a public issue. The sociological imagination allows us to make these distinctions and connections.

THE SOCIOLOGICAL IMAGINATION IN ACTION

C. Wright Mills coined the term **sociological imagination** to refer to a way of thinking that enables individuals to understand how they are affected by broad features of the society in which they live. In *The Sociological Imagination* (1959), Mills noted that we tend to get so caught up in our own "personal orbits" of everyday life that we ignore what is happening in the broader environment. Family, school, work, and personal relationships absorb much of our attention, time, and energies. Yet our personal orbits are very much open to influence by larger trends and events.

According to Mills (see box), exercise of the sociological imagination involves striving to understand (1) how our society is presently structured, (2) how and why it seems to be changing, and (3) how our own personal "biographies" or life experiences fit within and are affected by the present structure and flow of change. Mills believed this knowledge gives power to anyone possessing it because it allows individuals to identify circumstances they share with others, circumstances over which they may seek to capture some control (Johnson, 1991: 14). Let's look briefly at Dana's father's situation. How would the sociological imagination have been of use to him and his family?

People like Dana's father are losing their jobs because of shifts in the global capitalist economic system. The dominant economic position occupied by the United States since World War II is undergoing challenge by Japan, members of the European Union, and a host of other capitalist nations that are successfully competing to provide manufactured goods for the world market. To deal with the competition and meet their profit goals, firms in the United States have been taking steps to reduce production costs and increase efficiency. Often this means trimming the ranks of management and other white-collar staff, substituting automated machinery for blue-collar workers, and moving some production activities to low-wage plants abroad.

As we shall discuss in Chapter 11, many of the manufacturing-sector jobs that have disappeared in the United States have been replaced by jobs in the service sector. But high-level service jobs often require skills that former industrial workers do not possess, and many less-skilled service jobs pay less than the jobs that are disappearing. Some argue that the pace at which U.S. manufacturing jobs are being lost will increase as new economic relations with Mexico and Canada (under the North American Free Trade Agreement, or NAFTA) are implemented. Both world and domestic economies are undergoing a major historic reordering, and all U.S. workers are likely to feel the effects.

Using a sociological imagination, we can evaluate Dana's father's predicament more constructively. We can gain a richer understanding of the processes presently producing joblessness, processes that affect work opportunities for all of us. We can also assess the utility of possible strategies, such as joining with others to demand needed political and economic solutions to unemployment on both the state and the national level. Finally, as we come to understand unemployment as a public issue, we would see that unemployed people like Dana's father need support and encouragement. If they can correctly analyze the wider causes of their unemployment, they are more likely to resist self-blame. Those who understand that solutions require a changed environment may feel empowered to play a role in collective efforts to help bring that about.

Our goal in this book is to help you develop a sociological imagination. The sociological imagination can help you act to affect history and thereby influence the series of life experiences that constitute your biography. It can liberate each of us from placing blame on ourselves and others for situations we did not create (see Ryan, 1976). It can redirect our attention toward more productive and appropriate analyses and strategies for social change (Johnson, 1991).

In order to develop this imagination, you must draw upon a number of core concepts used by sociologists, in particular the concepts that are discussed in Part 1 of this book. These core concepts help us analyze features of our environment. They give us a language to use in formulating questions that will help us take a deeper look at this environment. Armed with facts from such research, we are in a position to determine what, if anything, we might hope to change.

The core concepts used by contemporary sociologists derive from or reflect the influence of intellectual traditions within the discipline. We will now address the origins of sociology, its main intellectual traditions, and some of the core concepts that flow out of these traditions.

SOCIOLOGY: ORIGINS, INTELLECTUAL TRADITIONS, AND CORE CONCEPTS

The origins of sociology can be traced to the late eighteenth and nineteenth centuries, a time when rapid changes were occurring in Western societies, particularly in Europe (see Turner et al., 1989: 2–7; Ritzer, 1992: 5–10). Social movements, like the one that led to the French Revolution in 1789, challenged and undermined hierarchical social relationships between the aristocratic classes and the common people. These relationships had long been taken for granted as part of the natural order of things. Advances in science opened up alternative ways of thinking about the natural and physical worlds, providing exciting new ideas and discoveries. The increasing stature of science threatened the traditional monopoly over truth and knowledge held by the church.

Research and technological innovations fostered new means of producing goods as well as advances in transportation and communication. These

In his classic work, The Sociological Imagination, *C. Wright Mills exhorts us to develop a "quality of mind" that will enable us to view our lives and the lives of others within their larger historical and social context. While Mills's language refers only to "men," thus seeming to exclude women, it is clear that he intended his words to be a call to all humanity.*

Nowadays men often feel that their private lives are a series of traps. They sense that within their everyday worlds, they cannot overcome their troubles, and in this feeling, they are often quite correct: What ordinary men are directly aware of and what they try to do are bounded by the private orbits in which they live; their visions and their powers are limited to the close-up scenes of job, family, neighborhood; in other milieux, they move vicariously and remain spectators. And the more aware they become, however vaguely, of ambitions and of threats which transcend their immediate locales, the more trapped they seem to feel.

Underlying this sense of being trapped are seemingly impersonal changes in the very structure of continent-wide societies. The facts of contemporary history are also facts about the success and the failure of individual men and women. When a society is industrialized, a peasant becomes a worker; a feudal lord is liquidated or becomes a businessman. When classes rise or fall, a man is employed or unemployed; when the rate of investment goes up or down, a man takes new heart or goes broke. When wars happen, an insurance salesman becomes a rocket launcher; a store clerk, a radar man; a wife lives alone; a child grows up without a father. Neither the life of an individual nor the history of a society can be understood without understanding both.

Yet men do not usually define the troubles they endure in terms of historical change and institutional contradiction. The well-being they enjoy, they do not usually impute to the big ups and downs of the societies in which they live. Seldom aware of the intricate connection between the patterns of their own lives and the course of world history, ordinary men do not usually know what this connection means for the kinds of men they are becoming and for the kinds of history-making in which they might take part. They do not possess the quality of mind essential to grasp the interplay of man and society, of biography and history, of self and world. They cannot cope with their personal troubles in such ways as to control the structural transformations that usually lie behind them.

Surely it is no wonder. In what period have so many men been so totally exposed at so fast a pace to such earthquakes of change? That Americans have not known such catastrophic changes as have the men and women of other societies is due to historical facts that are now quickly becoming 'merely history.' The history that now affects every man is world history. Within this scene and this period, in the course of a single generation, one sixth of mankind is transformed from all that is feudal and backward into all that is modern, advanced, and fearful. Political colonies are freed; new and less visible forms of imperialism installed. Revolutions occur; men feel the intimate grip of new kinds of authority. Totalitarian societies rise, and are smashed to bits—or succeed fabulously. After two centuries of ascendancy, capitalism is shown up as only one way to make society into an industrial apparatus. After two centuries of hope, even formal

provided the basis for the Industrial Revolution, which dramatically changed many people's lives. The expansion of trade with European colonies and other nations, along with changes in domestic production, meant that fewer people were needed to work the land and more were needed to work in factories. Increasing numbers of families had no choice

> ## "The sociological imagination enables us to grasp history and biography and the relations between the two within society."

democracy is restricted to a quite small portion of mankind. Everywhere in the underdeveloped world, ancient ways of life are broken up and vague expectations become urgent demands. Everywhere in the overdeveloped world, the means of authority and of violence become total in scope and bureaucratic in form. Humanity itself now lies before us, the supernation at either pole concentrating its most co-ordinated and massive efforts upon the preparation of World War Three.

The very shaping of history now outpaces the ability of men to orient themselves in accordance with cherished values. And which values? Even when they do not panic, men often sense that older ways of feeling and thinking have collapsed and that newer beginnings are ambiguous to the point of moral stasis. Is it any wonder that ordinary men feel they cannot cope with the larger worlds with which they are so suddenly confronted? That they cannot understand the meaning of their epoch for their own lives? That—in defense of selfhood—they become morally insensible, trying to remain altogether private men? Is it any wonder that they come to be possessed by a sense of the trap?

What they need, and what they feel they need, is a quality of mind that will help them to use information and to develop reason in order to achieve lucid summations of what is going on in the world and of what may be happening within themselves. It is this quality, I am going to contend, that journalists and scholars, artists and publics, scientists and editors are coming to expect of what may be called the sociological imagination.

The sociological imagination enables its possessor to understand the larger historical scene in terms of its meaning for the inner life and the external career of a variety of individuals. It enables him to take into account how individuals, in the welter of their daily experience, often become falsely conscious of their social positions. Within that welter, the framework of modern society is sought, and within that framework the psychologies of a variety of men and women are formulated. By such means the personal uneasiness of individuals is focused upon explicit troubles and the indifference of publics is transformed into involvement with public issues.

The first fruit of this imagination—and the first lesson of the social science that embodies it—is the idea that the individual can understand his own experience and gauge his own fate only by locating himself within his period, that he can know his own chances in life by becoming aware of those of all individuals in his circumstances. In many ways it is a terrible lesson; in many ways a magnificent one. We do not know the limits of man's capacities for supreme effort or willing degradation, for agony or glee, for pleasurable brutality or the sweetness of reason. But in our time we have come to know that the limits of "human nature" are frighteningly broad. We have come to know that every individual lives, from one generation to the next, in some society; that he lives out a biography, and that he lives it out within some historical sequence. By the fact of his living he contributes, however minutely, to the shaping of this society and to the course of its history, even as he is made by society and by its historical push and shove.

The sociological imagination enables us to grasp history and biography and the relations between the two within society. That is its task and its promise.

Source: C. Wright Mills, *The Sociological Imagination,* New York: Oxford University Press, 1959, pp. 3–5.

but to leave rural farms, estates, and villages and seek out a livelihood in the new factories and growing urban centers. In these centers a rising class of capitalist business owners and merchants was accumulating political and economic power and aggressively using this power to further its interests in profits and growth.

It was a disruptive and unsettling era, as more and more people experienced the loss and transformation of their traditional ways of life. It was also an era in which many people—including the intellectual elites of the day—worried about high rates of crime, widespread poverty and squalor, and street rioting and threats of rebellion by workers in the burgeoning cities. This, then, is the context within which sociology emerged.

The European scholars who pioneered in the development of sociology did so out of deep concern over the societal conditions they observed (Zeitlin, 1990). Impressed by breakthroughs in many fields through the use of scientific methods, these scholars believed it was possible to scientifically study society as well. The knowledge generated, early sociologists believed, could be used to help solve social problems and guide social progress. Almost from the very beginning, however, sociologists found it difficult to agree on how to approach the study of society and its problems (Zeitlin, 1990). What concepts should be used to analyze the workings of society? What were the societal problems that needed to be solved? Disagreements about such issues gave rise to two intellectual traditions within sociology whose impact on sociological thinking lingers even to this day. The two traditions are often characterized as the order perspective and the conflict perspective (Ritzer, 1992).

The evolution of the **order perspective** is associated with French thinker Auguste Comte (1798–1857), who actually coined the term "sociology," and later with his fellow countryman Émile Durkheim (1858–1917). This

During the late eighteenth and nineteenth centuries dramatic social change occurred in Europe. During the French Revolution of 1789 the common people rose up against members of the aristocratic class, refusing to remain poor and hungry while the aristocrats lived in luxury and had privileged access, even to bread.

perspective posits that human society is a naturally stable, harmonious social system held together by a culture made up of values, rules, and practices that are widely shared. People become participants in society through a learning process known as socialization. This process includes learning how to occupy existing social positions and to perform necessary social roles in major societal institutions, such as the family, the economy, and the political system. These institutions serve critical functions for society as a whole.

Should individuals fail to be adequately socialized, their behavior is likely to depart from shared values, rules, and practices. Social positions and roles may not be adequately performed, and this may interfere with institutional functioning. Thus, deviant behavior that goes unchecked can be highly disruptive to societal stability. It can lead to conflict or otherwise undermine the order necessary for social progress to occur. From the order perspective, there is a constant need to exert social control over deviants and to ensure that others do not enter into deviant behavior. This must be done for the good of society.

Thinkers like Comte and Durkheim thus encouraged an intellectual tradition within sociology in which core concepts such as culture, institutions, socialization, social roles, deviant behavior, and social control are stressed in order to help us understand the workings of society. In the chapters that follow, we shall define and flesh out these core concepts, and show how contemporary sociologists have continued to utilize them in their scholarly work. We shall see aspects of the order perspective reflected when, for example, we discuss the functions of different institutions (Chapter 2), the impact of culture (Chapter 4), and views on socialization (Chapter 5).

Like the order perspective, the **conflict perspective** represents an intellectual tradition within sociology whose roots go back to late-eighteenth- and nineteenth-century Europe and the changes underway at that time. Thinkers within this tradition focused on the social *divisions* that often characterize human society. Jean Jacques Rousseau (1712–1778) found class inequality in pre-Revolutionary France to be unnatural and in violation of human nature. In Germany Karl Marx (1818–1883) concluded that European industrial capitalism would produce economic and political inequalities so severe as to call forth social movements that would lead to capitalism's downfall. Both were concerned with the unequal distribution of life chances that systems of inequality promote and maintain.

The conflict perspective accepts the notion that human society is naturally harmonious and stable, but it sees the creation of systems of inequality as producing outcomes that are contrary to social order. Social movements may arise among the disadvantaged as people at times refuse to submit to unjust and harmful conditions within systems of inequality from which they see no escape. Conflict is to be expected as groups or classes holding little power or privilege struggle to improve their lot and the advantaged strive to protect what they have. From the conflict perspective, social progress often requires social conflict. Those who refuse to yield to the existing order are generally viewed not as poorly socialized deviants but as people alienated from a social system that fails to meet their human needs.

Thinkers like Rousseau and Marx helped launch an intellectual tradition within sociology that encouraged sociologists to utilize such core concepts as capitalism, class, power, systems of inequality, and social movements in their efforts to understand the workings of society. These core concepts will also play a prominent role in the chapters that follow. You will see evidence of the conflict perspective when sociologists, for example, attempt to shed light on aspects of capitalism (Chapters 2 and 3), analyze various systems of inequality (Chapter 6), and address different types and sources of social movements (Chapter 9).

We have presented the order perspective and the conflict perspective as distinct intellectual traditions. Some contemporary sociologists have tended to lean toward one or the other of these traditions in their attempts to understand the workings of society. Others have moved back and forth between the two over the course of their careers. Today it is increasingly common for sociologists to borrow core concepts from both intellectual traditions, although they may find some concepts more useful than others in their analyses. Much of the diversity and creativity within sociology has come with the discovery of new ways to think about and use the discipline's core concepts, whatever the intellectual traditions with which they are associated.

We have addressed some of the core concepts that help guide sociologists in their thinking about society, and we have indicated the intellectual traditions in sociology that have nurtured and stressed these concepts. Let us turn to how contemporary sociologists conduct research. What methods do they use? How do they make use of core concepts in their research?

RESEARCH METHODS

Social scientists are trained to use a variety of different research tools and methods to establish facts about the social world. Sometimes these research methods are used to gather information relevant to a **hypothesis.** This is a carefully formulated proposition that may be either verified or discarded on the basis of the examination of relevant data. For example, a sociologist may formulate a hypothesis that states, "Episodes of interracial conflict in large cities are most likely to occur when unemployment rates are on the rise."

At other times the methods used are aimed at investigating **open-ended questions.** Such questions may be very exploratory, leaving the sociologist a great deal of flexibility in deciding what he or she will consider relevant data. For example, a sociologist may ask, "Why do some societies have high rates of sexual violence against women while others do not?" The choice of which method of research to use depends upon just what it is that the researcher wishes to find out.

In our everyday lives, we often fail to distinguish opinion and fact. Social scientists make special efforts not to fall into this trap. They tend to be skeptical about ideas that people may take for granted as true, and they seek to base conclusions on facts that have been established through objective investigation (see Berger, 1963). When social scientists report their research findings, they also describe the methods that produced them. This permits other researchers to assess the validity of the results.

Sociological research thus proceeds through a series of steps. First, the researcher determines the hypothesis to be tested or the research question to be pursued. This first step will help determine the choice in the next one. Second, the researcher chooses a research method. The method selected depends, in part, on the hypothesis or research question. Some methods will be more appropriate than others for the researcher's investigation. Third, he or she gathers data relevant to the hypothesis or research question. The data can take many forms, depending upon the research method chosen. Fourth, the researcher analyzes these data and interprets the results. Finally, he or she prepares a report that includes the purpose of the research, the method used, an explanation of how the data produced were analyzed, the findings, and the conclusions reached. Often, the report also includes recommendations for further research. If the research was commissioned by a sponsor (for example, a government agency or business), the sociologist will give the report to the sponsor. Sociologists may also submit reports on their research for publication in professional journals in sociology and other social sciences.

To illustrate the principal methods used in sociological research, we shall examine the relationship between schooling and class inequality (a topic to be pursued in Chapter 12). This area of research has been of particular interest to sociologists concerned with the ways in which systems of inequality limit people's life chances, a concern central to the intellectual tradition known as the conflict perspective. As we shall see, different questions about this relationship, explored with various research methods, have led social scientists toward valuable insights. We shall look at experimental research, field research, survey research, and historical research (see Baker, 1988; Babbie, 1992).

Experimental Research

Most of us are familiar with **experimental research** from school science courses. In the natural sciences, experimental research may be conducted to find out how a particular organism or object is affected by different types of treatment selected by the researcher. Sociologists and other social scientists likewise find this research method useful, even though experimentation with humans imposes far greater practical and ethical limitations. Like other scientists, social scientists often conduct their studies in laboratories where they are able to maximize control over experimental procedures and conditions. The basic principles guiding the experimental research method are much the same in both laboratory and natural settings.

Researchers begin by establishing at least two groups to be studied. The first is called the **experimental group.** The research is designed to determine the effect of special treatment given to this group. The second group, the **control group,** is not subjected to the same special treatment. The control group serves as a baseline of comparison to the experimental group. If the experiment is well designed, differences in thinking and behavior between the two groups should reflect the differences in their treatment. The cause of the differences, if any, is assumed to stem from researcher-designed conditions. Experimental research is typically used to test specific hypotheses. Unusual experimental outcomes may lead to new ideas to explore, and thus to further hypothesizing and experimentation.

Researchers using this method try to design their research so as to avoid biasing the results. Avoiding bias begins with the way subjects are assigned to the experimental and control groups. Typically, researchers assign subjects randomly so that possible sources of bias in assignment will be extremely small. If there is a known bias, researchers will be sure to account for it. For example, if some of the subjects in the study have unique characteristics, the researcher will make sure they are equally (and randomly) assigned to each group.

Avoiding bias also requires the researchers to take care that only members of the experimental group receive the special treatment whose effect is being investigated. Moreover, researchers must be prepared to assess the effects of unexpected factors that may influence what occurs in the experimental or control group. Such cautions are necessary if other social scientists, repeating the same experiment, are to come up with the same findings.

Laboratories provide researchers with maximum control over an experiment because they impose artificial conditions on the two groups. But people do not live in laboratories, nor are the conditions to which they are normally subjected as neatly timed and delineated as they are during laboratory experiments. Laboratory research may thus produce findings that are reproducible by other laboratory researchers but that do not necessarily apply to people's thinking and behavior in the real world. Hence it is desirable to conduct experimental research in natural settings when possible.

Obviously, there are many natural settings that are not easily replicated or that cannot even be imitated in a laboratory. A public school is such a setting. Yet, oddly enough, schools actually resemble research laboratories in some ways. For example, school staff members provide students with an "experimental treatment" in the form of teaching, and they expect this treatment to have a certain outcome in the form of learning. In the example of experimental research we shall describe, researchers manipulated the treatment of students by school staff.

For many years studies have found that students from poor and working-class backgrounds, on average, get lower scores on intelligence quotient (IQ) tests and other tests of achievement than do students from the middle and upper classes. In the mid-1960s many people believed that this fact was principally a function of **cultural deprivation** within low-income families. It was said that such families failed to provide children with the knowledge and intellectual skills needed to do well on achievement tests, largely because the adults in these families lacked such knowledge and skills. In this sense, the families, and thus the children, were culturally deprived.

Researchers Robert Rosenthal and Lenore Jacobson raised an alternative thesis: Perhaps the lower achievement was due to low expectations on the part of teachers toward such children. Perhaps children from low-income families could perform better in school if their teachers' views of them were more positive. The researchers thus set out to test the following hypothesis: "Within a given classroom those children from whom the teacher expected greater intellectual growth would show such greater growth" (Rosenthal and Jacobson, 1968a: 61). Were this hypothesis to be verified, the implication would be that the schools themselves play a role in generating lower achievement from low-income children.

The researchers conducted their experiment in a public elementary school located in a West Coast urban setting. The school's 650 students came for the most part from low-income families. One-sixth of the children were Chicanos (of Mexican descent); almost all the remainder were non-Latino whites.

Rosenthal and Jacobson began by giving the children in all six school grades a standard test of intelligence. The school's eighteen teachers were not told it was an intelligence test; rather, they were led to believe the test would predict which students would spurt ahead, or "bloom," intellectually in the current school year. Afterward, the teachers were given a list of the students who should be expected to do well. The list included 20 percent of the school's population. The researchers had actually made up the list by random selection. This meant that the "difference between the special children and the ordinary children . . . was only in the mind of the teacher" (Rosenthal and Jacobson, 1968a: 175). The so-called special children comprised the experimental group, and the other 80 percent comprised the control group. Members of the experimental group would, presumably, be subject to different treatment by their teachers under the expectation that they would intellectually spurt ahead.

At the end of the year, each student was given the same intelligence test again, and the gains made by the experimental and control groups were compared. The students in the experimental group did, in fact, bloom. For example, while 19 percent of first- and second-grade control-group children gained 20 or more points on the test, 47 percent of the experimental-group children did so. A similar, but slightly smaller, difference was found between the two groups in higher grade levels. In the second year of the experiment, all the children moved on to new teachers who had not been given any special expectations for particular children. When retested after this second year, the younger experimental-group children lost their initial test-score advantage over the control-group children, but the experimental-group children in the higher grades actually increased their advantage. The researchers concluded that the younger students may have needed continued contact with the teachers having high expectations in order to keep their test-score advantages, while the older students were more easily able to maintain and even increase theirs on their own (Rosenthal and Jacobson, 1968a: 175–176).

The experimental-group students not only experienced intellectual growth (at least as measured by a test) but also displayed positive behavioral characteristics (at least as perceived by their teachers). The researchers summarized the teachers' assessments of the classroom behavior of these students:

For many years educators argued that students' own deficiencies best explained their failure to do well in school. Sociological research has helped to underscore the importance of the behavior of school staff in encouraging both student success and failure.

The children from whom intellectual growth was expected were described as having a better chance of being successful in later life and as being happier, more curious and more interesting than the other children. There was also a tendency for the designated children to be seen as more appealing, better adjusted and more affectionate, and as less in need of social approval. In short, the children for whom intellectual growth was expected became more alive and autonomous intellectually, or at least were so perceived by their teachers (Rosenthal and Jacobson, 1968b).

Hence, the "treatment" in this experiment—the way teachers treated students they expected to grow intellectually—resulted in a **self-fulfilling prophecy.** Expected to grow, students did. Some controversy surrounds this study because of mixed results in efforts to replicate it. Still, Rosenthal and Jacobson's experiment made a major contribution in questioning the assumption that family background was the sole cause of students' poor school performance. Here were data suggesting that the cultural deprivation argument could be faulted. The nature of teachers' interactions with students, not simply the character of students and their families, needs to undergo critical inquiry.

To summarize, then, experimental research methods are modeled after methods used in the natural sciences. When experimental and control groups are carefully chosen and all safeguards against biased results are put in place, experiments can provide important insights into people's thinking and behavior. Experiments have several advantages: They can demonstrate causal links between experimental treatments and predicted outcomes; they provide researchers with a high degree of control in order to exclude sources of error; and they can be used to study changes in people's thinking and behavior over time. Disadvantages include the sometimes artificial character of experimental settings, the possibility that people involved in the experiment may adjust their behavior with this knowledge in mind, and practical limits to the size of samples for many experiments. The latter may limit the generalizability of findings.

Many policy makers find experimental research in natural settings useful. For example, experiments have been used to evaluate governmental "pilot programs" to determine if they should be implemented on a wider scale. This type of experimentation has taken place in such areas as education, health-care delivery, job training, and welfare reform.

Field Research

In the experimental research described above, Rosenthal and Jacobson did not study the student-teacher interaction directly. Rather, they concluded that this interaction was the critical factor in the experimental group's superior test-score gains and in the positive teacher comments about these students. When researchers go directly into classrooms to find out what teacher-student interaction looks like firsthand, they are conducting **field research.**

Field research utilizes different techniques of inquiry. **Direct observation** may be the best technique when little is known about a group or particular type of social setting or when enough is known to warrant hypotheses about the group. In the first case, the social scientist may enter the research site with few preconceptions and observe the entire situation just long enough to draw some conclusions about group members' thinking and behavior. When the social scientist already knows enough to have formulated a testable hypothesis, direct observation will be much more limited in its focus; only observations pertaining to the hypothesis will be of interest to the researcher.

The researcher may also engage in **passive observation,** recording the events he or she sees for later analysis and interpretation. Or the researcher may play a much more active role, to the point of becoming an actual participant in the group or social setting under study. In this case, known as **participant observation,** the social scientist is often attempting to understand matters from the position and viewpoint of the individuals being studied.

Whichever observation technique is used, researchers must decide how to handle the issue of *identity*. Should the observations be done covertly or overtly? Should subjects know they are being studied? Would this influence behavior and events in ways contrary to the researcher's objectives? There is also the issue of *privacy*. What rights to privacy do those being studied have? Are there times when people deserve the opportunity to give their informed consent to be research subjects? Thinking back, you will no doubt see ways in which such questions could be readily discussed in regard to the experimental research of Rosenthal and Jacobson.

Field research tends to take place in one particular site, within a given time period, and with a specific sample of people. How do we know whether the findings based on observations of one group at one site will be applicable to other people and other settings? We may be more confident if other researchers come up with similar findings elsewhere. Unfortunately, sometimes the research situation studied is so unique that the research may not be repeated easily. Because those reading field researchers' findings have not been observers, they must place a great deal of trust in the researchers' honesty, observation skills, and interpretive judgments.

Field research—while often rewarding—is also highly labor-intensive. Investigators may have to devote a great deal of time, often over long periods, to gathering observations. This was certainly the case in the study we have chosen to illustrate the use of this research method.

Researcher Ray C. Rist was interested in the fact that the United States is characterized by vast economic inequality. At the extremes there are very rich and very poor people, and the gap between the two groups is not narrowing. (As we shall see in Chapter 6, "Systems of Inequality," it has been widening.) Rist wanted to determine whether schools play a role in nurturing this situation. He wanted to know just how there came to be both "winners" and "losers" among those exposed to schooling, and why the latter so often seem to come from the economically deprived end of the continuum (Rist, 1973). In contrast to Rosenthal and Jacobson, Rist chose to pursue his investigation through direct observation of teacher-student interaction in the classroom.

Rist gained permission to conduct his field research in an urban elementary school in the Midwest. He decided to observe a single classroom group of children, following them with two visits each week from the time they entered kindergarten until they completed the first half of their second-grade year. Rist committed himself to this long-term study, known as a **longitudinal study,** because he felt it was the best way to understand the impact of schooling on each of the children in the classroom group chosen for the research. In longitudinal research, the investigator studies the same people over an extended period of time.

The school in which Rist conducted his observations was located in an inner-city neighborhood. It went from kindergarten through eighth grade and had about 900 students. Many were from low-income backgrounds; over half came from families on welfare whose incomes were well below the federal government's official poverty line. Other children in the school were from families that were economically middle-class. All the children and all members of the school staff were African American.

First, Rist looked at each child's preenrollment information, which was available to the kindergarten teacher. This proved to be mostly "social information." For example, the school social worker reported which children came from welfare families. Other teachers had informally commented on experiences with the children's brothers and sisters. A preenrollment interview with each child's mother elicited medical data and any motherly concerns about the child's behavior. Rist noted that none of this social information directly related to the children's academic potential. Yet, armed with this information and firsthand observation of the appearance and demeanor of each child, by the eighth day of kindergarten the teacher had established permanent seating assignments. These assignments, as Rist would quickly discern, reflected the teacher's assessment of each child's academic capabilities and potential. By the eighth day of their school career, the students were already identified in a way that would have profound effects on their level of motivation and achievement. Rist observed and recorded this process in action.

Seated at Table 1, closest to the teacher, were the better-dressed children in the classroom. None came from welfare families. Table 1 children seemed most at ease in the school setting, interacted confidently with the teacher and their peers, and tended to speak standard American English. At Tables 2 and 3 were less well attired children. They were more likely to be from welfare families, appeared restrained in their interactions, and were likely to speak in street dialect, if they spoke at all. In Rist's words, the Table 1 children

> . . . were continually being called on to lead the class in the Pledge of Allegiance, read the weather calendar each day, come to the front for "show and tell" periods, take messages to the office, count the number of children present in the class, pass out material for class projects, be in charge of equipment on the playground, and lead the class to the bathroom, library, or on a school tour (Rist, 1970: 419).

The seating arrangements and the distribution of privileges and responsibilities mirrored the teacher's opinion of the students' capabilities. Without the benefit of formal testing or any other type of systematic inquiry, the teacher was able to tell Rist on the eighth day of school that the students she had placed at Table 1 were her "fast learners," while those at the remaining two tables "had no idea of what was going on in the classroom" (Rist, 1970: 422).

Watching the process of differential treatment of the children unfold, Rist concluded that those the teacher had earmarked for school success were the children who most approximated—in their background, appearance, and behavior—offspring of the educated middle class. Apparently, middle-class status was sufficient to qualify a child as a fast learner in her eyes. Once she had made this determination, she focused most of her time, attention, and affection on Table 1 children and effectively wrote off the children at Tables 2 and 3 as unteachable. The latter were alternately ignored or subjected to discipline when they "acted out" by talking out of turn or quarreling with one another. It was not long before the children at Table 1, picking up on the teacher's cues, began subjecting the other children to taunts and ridicule. In their first experiences with school, the Table 2 and 3 children found not only the teacher but also their own peers seemingly aligned against them.

The class-biased judgments made by the kindergarten teacher began to translate into different patterns of academic achievement. Children who are not taught and not encouraged to grow intellectually usually do not test well either. Hence, it was not surprising to Rist that formal tests of IQ and reading skill that were used to sort students into "ability groups" in the first and second grades produced groupings that closely replicated the kindergarten teacher's table placements. Table 2 and 3 students academically lagged behind their more fortunate peers from the start.

Rist asks the rhetorical question, "Given the treatment of low-income children from the beginning of their kindergarten experience, for what class strata are they being prepared other than that of the lower class?" (Rist, 1970: 448–449). Children who are treated as losers find schooling an alienating and hurtful experience. It is understandable if they opt out of school at the earliest possible opportunity.

Critics of Rist's research might argue that perhaps the Table 2 and 3 children did not have the potential to academically succeed in the first place. Or perhaps they were seriously hampered in the ability to express their potential—say, by malnourishment or illnesses stemming from their living conditions. Rist's concern is that these low-income children's true abilities were not assessed, given their teacher's apparent prejudice against them. Perhaps most or all of the Table 2 and 3 children would have succeeded if they had received teacher encouragement. Rist's research thus pointed to the need to examine the role of the school in generating student failure, rather than just focusing on disadvantages students may bring with them into the classroom.

Field research takes the sociologist out of his or her office and into direct contact with people whose thinking and behavior is of interest. Its advantages include the ability of researchers to observe behavior as it occurs, to be flexible in determining what to consider as data, and to obtain information about people in natural settings. Disadvantages lie in the difficulties the researcher may face in gaining entry to and cooperation from a group, the possibility that personal limitations or prejudices may bias the researcher's observations, practical difficulties in recording and analyzing what can be substantial amounts of data, and problems in establishing the reliability of observations when two or more researchers must alternate in field research of long duration.

Rist's research on student-teacher interaction can serve as an example of the kinds of challenges field research often presents. Rist is white. All the subjects involved in his investigation were black. Rist had to assess whether this difference might affect his own perception of the subjects he was observing or the behavior of students and teachers in response to their awareness of him. He kept these possibilities in mind as he conducted his research, but he ended up confident that in this case racial differences between the field researcher and those studied did not affect the findings.

Sociologists who conduct field research must be constantly on guard to prevent their individual perspectives, values, and prejudices from biasing their observations. Race, gender, and class membership can all introduce bias into the research process, and ways must be found to avoid this.

Sociologists have used field research to gather data in a wide range of settings, including poverty-stricken neighborhoods, college dormitories, tattoo parlors, racetrack stables, factory assembly lines, communities in suburbia, nude beaches, hospital emergency rooms, working-class bars, the headquarters of religious cults, and homes of the wealthy. Field research has vastly increased our knowledge of the social conditions affecting human behavior and has challenged many stereotypes and false assumptions about different populations.

Survey Research

Perhaps you have been asked to fill out a written questionnaire or answer a series of questions over the telephone or in person. If so, you have participated in a **survey.** When social scientists use surveys to investigate a topic, they must follow strict procedures. The most important is choosing a sample. It is usually impractical for researchers to survey every single person in the population under study. Care, then, must be taken to use proper techniques to choose a sample that is representative of the population about whom the researcher is seeking to generalize. To avoid bias, the researcher selects randomly from this population. For example, researchers wishing to study views on people of color moving into a close-knit white suburban neighborhood may decide to seek interviews at every third home on each block.

The wording used for questions must be as neutral as possible. Frequently, researchers will pretest their survey questions and rephrase any that seem biased. Both sample selection and survey-question development are carried out in accordance with rules designed to minimize sources of bias and error that might cast doubt on the results.

Surveys may be undertaken simply to gain descriptive information or to gather data relevant to previously formulated hypotheses. In the example we present here, the goal was largely exploratory. Students were asked to describe and assess their school experiences.

In *Keeping Track: How Schools Structure Inequality* (1985), Jeannie Oakes explores the connection between secondary education and class inequality as expressed in tracking. At the secondary level—junior and senior high school—most schools in the United States have formal school-wide policies of **tracking.** Tracking affects the school curriculum in two ways. First, schools may divide course offerings into academic (college-bound) and one or more vocational (employment-bound) tracks to prepare students for what teachers, counselors, and school administrators believe they should be doing after graduation. Second, schools may subdivide various academic subjects into separate classes designed for different ability levels. Students are assigned, often after formal tests and teacher recommendations, to a given ability level. Oakes found that there is a great deal of variation in how schools actually conduct tracking, but in general the principles on which they are based are much the same: students are grouped for instruction on the basis of the presumption that their past classroom performance and standardized test scores are valid indicators of their ability and potential.

Oakes drew on data that were part of a large-scale survey of schooling practices at 38 schools (see Goodlad, 1984). She chose 25 schools located in 13 different communities. Each had been carefully selected by the researchers to represent the population of students in U.S. secondary schools. This meant taking into account factors such as geographic location; racial, ethnic, and class composition of the community; and school characteristics (for example, per pupil expenditures, student/teacher ratio, range of curricular offerings). It took more than 150 researchers and data collectors a year to gather the information in this large-scale study.

Oakes describes the objective of the particular segment of the overall research project on which *Keeping Track* reports:

> We were interested in learning the content and process of classrooms under tracking systems. We wanted to know what actually goes on in classes at different track levels and how they are similar or different from one another. . . . Essentially we wanted to know details about what different classes were like for students and how students felt about being in them (Oakes, 1985: 61, 62).

To gain this information, Oakes and her colleagues focused on a representative group of classes in mathematics and English. The classes were categorized as "high," "average," or "low" track in terms of the ability levels that each class was intended to serve.

Oakes's findings pointed to distinct patterns of placement in tracks. Students from poor backgrounds and students of color were found to be disproportionately present in the lower tracks. Once students were placed, the organization of the curriculum called for students in different tracks to be exposed to very different course content. Using Oakes's terminology, those in high-track classes were presented with "high-status" knowledge similar to that which they would later encounter in college and university courses. In the low-track classes, students were exposed to extremely basic materials or "low-status" knowledge requiring little more than rote learning. This was revealed not only by documents and interviews with school staff but also through surveys of students. For example, students were asked in questionnaires, "What is the most important thing you have learned or done so far in this class?" Here are some sample answers from the high-track students (Oakes, 1985: 67–70):

- "Learned to analyze famous writings by famous people, and we have learned to understand people's different viewpoints on general ideas."
- "Learning to change my thought processes in dealing with higher mathematics and computers."
- "Inductive reasoning."

In contrast, here are some answers from low-track students (Oakes, 1985: 70–72):

- "To spell words you don't know, to fill out things where you get a job."
- "How to do income tax."
- "Learned to fill out checks and other banking business."
- "I learned that English is boring."

Using the survey data in conjunction with other information gathered from the 25 secondary schools, Oakes found that students in low tracks are not being given the opportunity to learn any of the content and skills found in the high-track courses. Segregation into tracks means many teenagers are simply denied access to high-status knowledge that their peers are assumed to deserve and need.

Oakes's research results led her to criticize tracking policies. Students from economically disadvantaged backgrounds, particularly students of color, were likely to be channeled away from knowledge and high school credentials that could facilitate future upward mobility. In this sense, Oakes suggests, schools act as **gatekeepers:** they open up different doors of opportunity for different populations. In Oakes's view, being placed in the lower tracks discourages the aspirations of many young people who might thrive under different educational conditions. As we saw in our example of field research in the elementary school classroom, the process of discouragement can begin well before students confront formal tracking policies in the secondary schools.

Surveys are advantageous when one wishes to learn about the thinking and behavior of large populations, such as secondary school students in the United States. Since the ability to sample means that everyone in the population does not need to participate in the survey, costs can be kept down. People who are widely dispersed geographically can easily be reached by mail or phone if necessary. Respondents to phone or mail surveys often accept assurances of anonymity, which may make it easier to gain information about sensitive topics. Sampling and data analysis may often be done quickly and efficiently with the aid of computer technology.

There can also be disadvantages to survey research. A survey usually provides us with information about people's behavior and thinking only at a given point in time. Arranging and conducting surveys using face-to-face interviews can be time-consuming and require special interpersonal skills. The quality and dependability of survey results hinge on the representativeness of the sample chosen to be surveyed, the care with which questions are constructed, and the degree to which respondents are cooperative and truthful. But even with these disadvantages, surveys have become an important source of data for sociologists and other social scientists, as well as for decision makers in business and government. We may have escaped being part of someone's experiment or field research, but few of us have escaped being surveyed.

Historical Research

We have seen how research from the experimental, field, and survey approaches has in each case made a different kind of contribution to our understanding of the relationship between schooling and class inequality. Our next example of a research method shows that social scientists may also look at the historical record in order to understand the workings of society.

Most research in the social sciences deals with contemporary phenomena. But many researchers are concerned with establishing facts about the past. This approach is known as **historical research.** Sociologists using this method may want to gain more understanding of contemporary behavior by comparing it with that of an earlier era. Or they may want to determine origins of present-day practices. The motivation for historical research may be to understand patterns of continuity as well as change in society over time. Frequently, two or more of these motivations operate at the same time.

Historical research may help test a strictly defined hypothesis, but it may also be used to answer questions that are open-ended. Usually, the questions pursued go beyond "Who?" "What?" "When?" and "Where?" Social scientists go one step further and want to know *why* history looks like it does. Social scientists use this analytical approach to history to help shed light on the virtues of particular theories about the world humans have constructed, as well as to generate new theories and additional research questions.

Historical research involves using available data to re-create the past. Data may be found in **primary sources,** such as original records and diaries, official documents, and eyewitness accounts. In recent years a great deal of attention has been given to the use of *oral history* as a primary source: people are interviewed and asked to recount perceptions and make observations about earlier life experiences. This source of data may be particularly useful when written sources are inadequate or lacking. Data may also be found in **secondary sources,** such as the publications of scholars.

The desire to better understand the present-day relationship between schooling and class inequality informs *Schooling in Capitalist America* by Samuel Bowles and Herbert Gintis (1976). These researchers were interested in the historical origins of tracking policies in public schools. They wanted to study why tracking systems were originally established in order to better understand their contemporary significance. Bowles and Gintis, using secondary sources for the most part, trace the origins of these policies back to the beginnings of mass public education in the United States over 100 years ago.

Industrialization, urbanization, and large-scale immigration were a source of rapid social change and conflict at that time. Members of the lower strata often militantly pressed for improvements in working conditions and other reforms that would increase their opportunities and raise their standard of living. Political and economic elites of the day often found themselves struggling to forestall or control these demands, with limited success. At the same time, they were concerned about how to build and motivate the kind of obedient and disciplined work force that was necessary to maximize profitability and expansion of production in the new industrial era.

In this context, elites and (to a lesser degree) poor and working-class people viewed mass public education as offering some solutions. Educators portrayed public schooling as a "meritocracy," a system in which achievement, success, and rewards would be based on individual merit, rather than on one's nation of birth or class membership. In effect, the promise of schooling was the promise of a route upward to economic well-being and social respect for those who earned it.

The upper classes from the start maintained control over mass public education, just as they oversaw the administration of education at the college level. They organized mass public education in accordance with what

Bowles and Gintis call the *correspondence principle*. There was to be a direct correspondence between life in school and life on the job. To experience schooling was to experience performing tasks in a group setting, learning to be obedient and docile in the face of demands from higher authority, accepting others' rules pertaining to use of private property, getting accustomed to restriction of physical movement and the "tyranny of the clock," bowing to the legitimacy of the existing political order and its leaders—in a word, schooling involved being "drilled" to be an ideal worker and compliant citizen. In Bowles and Gintis's words,

> By attuning young people to a set of social relationships similar to those of the work place, schooling attempts to gear the development of personal needs to its requirements (Bowles and Gintis, 1976: 131).

But the world of work then, as today, was a hierarchy of varying levels, each requiring different degrees of skill and allowing for different amounts of autonomy, responsibility, and privilege. At each level—from worker to supervisor to manager to chief executive—there were different economic rewards. A key function of schooling was, from the very beginning, that of gatekeeper. Schools guided individuals toward these different levels.

In order to carry out this gatekeeping process, it was necessary to organize systems for differentiating children into various curriculum tracks. Such systems were rationalized as the most efficient way to make sure

From its beginnings, mass public education has emphasized respect for authority, private property, and the state. The elementary school teachers in this early twentieth-century class have their students salute the flag.

each child received a school experience appropriate to his or her potential. However, biases in track assignments destined many poor and working-class children for the lower rungs of the occupational ladder, while children of the more privileged middle and upper classes usually received quite a different education and hence quite different occupational trajectories.

Systems of tracking continue to be common in U.S. public school systems (see Chapter 12). Seeing this historical data on the origins of tracking, we must ask if the objectives of those who organized mass public education in the nineteenth century are still being played out today. In Bowles and Gintis's view this is indeed the case: schooling is expected to serve the needs of the workplace hierarchy. Indeed, much recent public debate about the quality and effectiveness of U.S. public schools stems from employers' desire to increase productivity at different levels of this hierarchy.

Historical research, then, helps us shed light on a variety of different social phenomena. For example, this research method has been used to better understand the relations between developed and underdeveloped nations, the factors producing revolutions and other movements for social change, the effects of technology on the workplace, the origins of the modern welfare state, the changing nature of the health-care system and the medical profession, and approaches to the definition and handling of crime, mental illness, and other forms of "deviant behavior."

Perhaps the key disadvantage of historical research is the possibility of inaccuracy and bias in the sources. Primary sources such as eyewitness accounts may exaggerate or fabricate reality, contain errors of fact, or be intentionally self-serving. Documents are often not intended for research purposes, and their content may be built around a presentation of reality that departs from actual events. Secondary sources are written from a scholar's point of view. The selection of source material and the meaning the scholar derives from his or her selection must be assessed critically. Anyone conducting historical research thus must be satisfied with the closest approximation of reality possible, based on review of all available information. Social scientists are obligated to be meticulous in documenting the origins of their historical data, for others must be able to judge the credibility of the research.

The principal advantage of historical research is its helpfulness in understanding not only the past but also the present: knowledge of history provides a unique context within which we can better assess present-day issues. Indeed, Jeannie Oakes's interpretation of the significance and implications of tracking in today's secondary schools was clearly assisted by the historical research on the origins of tracking published earlier by Bowles and Gintis.

While we face many issues today that are new and unprecedented, most of the issues we grapple with are not. Contemporary phenomena such as school failure, unemployment, poverty, substance abuse, different forms of criminal behavior, discrimination, and family-related problems—to mention just a few—may be rendered less mystifying and more open to change when viewed within a historical context (see box). Moreover, we may find out that certain strategies for addressing these phenomena have never worked and thus be more open to thinking about new approaches.

Craig Miller and his family live in a suburban community in Kansas. Reduced profits led his company to lay him off, along with hundreds of other highly skilled, well-paid workers. To support his family, Mr. Miller is driving a school bus and working the counter at a fast-food outlet, his income and pride seriously undermined. The sociological imagination can help us understand how and why his biography—along with that of millions of others—is being negatively influenced by important social changes. And with understanding may come new social policies.

With two cars in the garage and a swing set in the backyard, Craig Miller and his family fell easily into the suburban rhythms of Johnson County.

He was a sheet-metal worker for T.W.A. His middle-class status was stamped on the pay stub: $15.65 an hour. And the shopping mall clerks didn't care if the paying customer wore steel-toe boots or tasseled loafers.

But the airline was troubled, and it laid Mr. Miller off in the summer of 1992. When he began to search for another job, he quickly learned the market value of a blue-collar worker with a strong back and a good work ethic but few special skills: about $5 an hour.

Mr. Miller, a 37-year-old father of four, now works behind the counter in a McDonald's, hustling orders for Quarter Pounders and chicken fajitas and deferring to teen-age customers with "Yes, sir" and "Thank you, ma'am."

Mr. Miller also drives a school bus. And on the side he has started a small business, changing furnace filters. He printed up cards for the venture, "Sani-Max," but there has not been much demand for his service.

For the last eight years his wife, Susan, 34, has worked part time as a stock clerk at Toys R Us at night, when her husband can watch the children. She recently got a raise and now makes $5.95 an hour.

New Jobs, but Not Enough

Throughout the country, some two million new jobs were created last year. But for people like Craig and Susan Miller, who lack college degrees as well as coveted skills, the statistics on an increasing number of jobs offer little comfort.

"Sure, we've got four of them," Mr. Miller said, managing a chuckle. "So what? So you can work like a dog for $5 an hour."

In nearly three years since the 1990–91 recession, employers nationwide have taken on three million workers, but that is less than half as many as they hired after the 1981–82 recession. And many of the new jobs are part time or temporary.

At the same time, the number of manufacturing jobs has fallen 8.3 percent from 1989 through February 1994. Tens of thousands of jobs have moved abroad; advances in technology have taken others.

As the Millers gaze into the future from their brick-and-frame house in Overland Park, Kan., they see an employment landscape shaped like a barbell. At one end are bankers and lawyers and accountants exulting in the high-flying stock market; at the other end are countermen at fast-food franchises and clerks at big discount stores struggling to pay the bills. The solid, working-class middle ground, where the Millers once stood, has meanwhile grown narrow—and slippery.

Counting all their part-time jobs, the Millers will make about $18,000 this year, less than half what Mr. Miller earned as a union sheet-metal worker. They have found the fall difficult to fathom, and even harder to accept. They could probably qualify for food stamps but refuse to consider applying.

"We're middle-class people," Mr. Miller said. "It's just that we have a lower-class income."

The Daily Routine

The work day starts in darkness. Mr. Miller, an Army veteran, crawls out of bed about 6 A.M., careful not to wake his youngest child, 3-year-old Amanda, who shares her parent's bedroom. By 7 A.M. he is behind the wheel of a school bus, stopping and going along tree-lined suburban streets of Overland

(*Continued*)

Park. He will do it again in the late afternoon. The daily pay is $35, no benefits.

After completing the morning bus route, he stops back at his house to change into his blue McDonald's uniform with his "Craig" nameplate pinned onto it. His restaurant job starts at 9:30 A.M., in a strip mall on Highway 69.

The pay in a fast-food restaurant is low, but the work is relentless. Customers are often lined up six deep. Mr. Miller, a man who once fixed dents in the fuselages of jets and felt pride in his craft whenever a plane soared overhead, darts between the counter and the food pickup shelf, back and forth, a hundred times a day, careful not to misfill an order. . . .

When he took the job, Mr. Miller expected to be the oldest worker at McDonald's. He was surprised to find several people past 30.

Still wearing the McDonald's uniform, he climbs back in the school bus at 2:30 P.M. for the afternoon run. About 5, he arrives home.

Dinner is served right away, often pasta with ground turkey. The Millers never buy beef anymore.

Just before 6, Mrs. Miller leaves for her job, six hours of bending and lifting to stock the shelves with toys. It will be midnight by the time she returns home. She also works one day a week at the same McDonald's as her husband.

Battle with Bills

Every time the telephone rings, the Millers instinctively fear that a bill collector is calling. They are $3,000 behind in medical bills. Mrs. Miller's part-time job provides health benefits, with the company paying 80 percent of medical bills and the employee 20 percent. But with four children, even paying just 20 percent adds up. And one child recently had surgery.

When a bill collector got huffy on the phone the other day, Mrs. Miller told him wearily, "Oh, get in line."

The couple buy one newspaper a week, for the food coupons, and only one light burns in the house at a time. When a child forgets to flip off the switch,

Mrs. Miller chides gently: "Have you got stock in the electric company? Well, neither do I."

Not so long ago, such worries would have seemed absurd. The Millers were saving so they could exchange their rented house for one of their own. At backyard barbecues and church picnics they moved comfortably in a social circle that included college graduates, people who wore suits to work and were therefore deemed "professional" but who often earned no more than the Millers.

When a child in school boasted of a parent who was a doctor or a lawyer, 7-year-old Peter Miller was known to reply, "My daddy can fix planes so they can fly high in the sky."

A quarter century ago, Mr. Miller remembers feeling the same kind of pride in his own blue-collar father. But the rules and rewards were simple then: if a man wasn't afraid to sweat, he could succeed.

Mr. Miller had watched his father make good on the bargain, a factory worker who provided a two-story house, a decent savings account and summer vacations to the California redwoods and Yellowstone National Park.

"I Miss It a Lot"

That was the kind of life that Mr. Miller had always planned for his own family. But now there doesn't seem to be much point in even talking about it.

"Oh, yeah, I miss it a lot," he said, referring to the old job, and perhaps to the old rules.

He clings to the hope that the fortunes of T.W.A. will improve and that the company will then re-call him and others who were laid off. . . .

Mrs. Miller said she and her husband should have seen the writing on the wall. But when times were good, they seemed like they would last forever. Now she has scant hope that those days will ever return.

"For people like us," she said, "I'm afraid the good times are gone for good."

Source: Dirk Johnson, "Family Struggles to Make Do after Fall from Middle Class," *New York Times,* March 11, 1994, pp. A1, A14.

The Ethics of Research

The different types of research methods illustrated above provide facts that help us exercise the sociological imagination. Yet the conduct of social science research and the reporting of findings do not take place in a vacuum. Under certain circumstances, unless care is taken, research may cause harm to people. Researchers have an obligation before they even begin an investigation to consider the ethical and political implications of what they are about to do (Beauchamp et al., 1982; Babbie, 1992: chap. 18). Failure to do so not only may be harmful to others but is likely to make it more difficult for future researchers to obtain the cooperation and legitimacy they need to pursue their own inquiries. This is not to say that researchers must avoid controversy: newly discovered facts are often controversial, if only because they may be differently interpreted depending upon one's personal or group values. Rather, social scientists must be reflective and ready to take responsibility for the impact of their research undertakings.

A classic case of research generating widespread debate over ethics is Laud Humphreys's work, published under the title *Tearoom Trade* (1970). Humphreys was interested in a subject about which very little was known as recently as the mid-1960s, namely, male-to-male sexual behavior. He decided to investigate the sexual behavior and social backgrounds of about 100 men who visited public restrooms for mutually consenting, but anonymous and highly impersonal, sexual encounters. Humphreys's research exploded the popular stereotype that such men lead very deviant lifestyles in general. Most of the men were married, had families, and were respected members of their communities. They came from all walks of life, occupations, and professions. Few were exclusively homosexual in their sexual orientation.

In Humphreys's view, widespread prejudicial attitudes against individuals who depart from heterosexual behavioral norms are largely based on negative stereotypes about such persons' social worth. It has been widely assumed that those who are attracted to others of the same sex are disturbed individuals who cannot possibly be making any positive contributions in their daily lives. In this context, Humphreys felt his research was justified: it contributed to the elimination of misperceptions about a part of the population that is subject to harassment and repression.

The facts uncovered by Humphreys were indeed important—they helped shed new light on the diversity of people's sexual orientations. Yet, when Humphreys reported his findings, the facts were forced to compete with a torrent of debate about the ethics of his research procedures. Let us briefly describe what he did that raised debate.

Humphreys gathered his data using the field research technique of participant observation. His research took place in a park located in a major midwestern city. To observe the sexual behaviors of the men in question, he offered to play the role of lookout at the park's public restrooms, warning of the arrival of possible intruders (including the police). Besides systematically keeping track of the patterns of sexual behavior he observed, Humphreys also managed to take down the automobile license numbers of the men. Using friendly contacts in the local police department, but telling them only that he was performing some kind of "market research," Humphreys located the home addresses of his subjects. Using a disguise to avoid being recognized as the restroom lookout, Humphreys interviewed the men as part of a survey he said he was conducting on the health of males in the community. In this way he was able to gather a wide variety of information on their backgrounds.

One of the ethical issues Humphreys's procedures raised was that of individuals' rights to privacy. Some researchers argued that the subjects' privacy rights were invaded by Humphreys, both in his participant observation and through the interviews. Others argued that Humphreys had rights as a scientist to pursue and to disseminate new knowledge. Another issue was that of deceit; he had pretended to be a lookout at the restrooms, a market researcher at the police station, and a survey interviewer at the subjects' residences. Some researchers argued that deceit was often the only way to gain access to groups who are likely to reject being studied. Others argued that this type of activity spawned distrust among citizens and violated fundamental values about what kinds of behavior were just and fair.

But Humphreys's critics went beyond the issues of privacy invasion and deceit. They pointed out that he risked doing harm to the subjects by seeking out their identities and places of residence. If, despite safeguards that Humphreys had established, their identities had somehow leaked out, the lives of these men could have been ruined. As it was, once the research findings and debate over his methods entered the public domain, some of the men—clearly panicked—privately sought reassurance from Humphreys that their anonymity was not in jeopardy. Perhaps others, who chose not to contact him, lived in a state of fear. Psychologically, one could argue, harm at some level was done.

The debate over the ethics of Humphreys's research methods was useful because it helped make social scientists aware of their responsibilities to their subjects. The American Sociological Association has adopted a Code of Ethics that includes this passage:

> The process of conducting sociological research must not expose respondents to substantial risk of personal harm. Informed consent must be obtained when the risks of research are greater than the risks of everyday life. Where modest risk or harm is anticipated, informed consent must be obtained (American Sociological Association, 1989: 3).

The Code of Ethics addresses the principle of keeping information provided by research subjects confidential, even if the researcher is given information about illegal activities. The code states:

> Confidential information provided by research participants must be treated as such by sociologists, even when this information enjoys no legal protection or privilege and legal force is applied (American Sociological Association, 1989: 3).

Although unusual, adherence to the code's principles of confidentiality may place a sociologist in conflict with legal authorities. Rik Scarce, who does research on animal rights and environmental activists, was jailed for almost six months in 1993. Scarce had refused to answer a federal grand jury's questions about research interviews he conducted with members of a group called the Animal Liberation Front (ALF). In 1991 ALF members allegedly broke into a research laboratory at Washington State University, released mink, coyotes, and mice that were being used for experiments, and did $150,000 worth of damage. Police were unable to locate the suspects. Scarce, jailed under a charge of civil contempt, took the position that he would not breach any guarantees of confidentiality he might have made to the subjects of his research. As he put it:

> I am concerned that activists in the environmental movement may refuse to speak to me if I testify. . . . Other social scientists might find themselves less able to gain the trust of sources. . . . [Social scientists] also would be less willing to go out and do research which in some instances does require of us that we grant promises of confidentiality (Monaghan, 1993).

The Politics of Research

Research does not just raise ethical issues. The fact that research is conducted within a larger political context raises political issues as well (Beauchamp et al., 1982). While most ethical issues revolve around research methods and the handling of data, political issues arise more from the substance of the research and the uses to which findings might be put. Such political issues often accompany research requested and paid for by a sponsor, such as a government agency or private corporation. While social scientists generally agree over rules governing ethics, there are really no rules that address the political implications of conducting certain kinds of research.

In theory, social scientists are to be objective and not be influenced by personal political biases. In reality, the choice of what social phenomenon to study and what kinds of research questions to ask can hardly escape such influence. Social scientists may be able to achieve objectivity in the sense that others—using the same methods and data sources—should come up with the same findings. But beyond this, research is embedded in politics beginning with its inception and continuing to the uses made of its results.

A classic case in point is the controversial Project Camelot. In 1964 the U.S. Department of the Army made a request of a social science research institute at American University in Washington, D.C. The Army wanted to have social scientists develop a model "which would make it possible to predict and influence politically significant aspects of social change in the developing world" (Horowitz, 1967: 47). In other words, the Army wanted researchers to provide knowledge that would help it control what was going on in poor nations that interested government and industry.

At the time, Latin American nations were the focus. In many of these nations, sections of the population were rebelling against strong, often brutal dictatorships. The Army wanted a model that would help it predict where armed rebellions were most likely to occur and provide ideas on how to head them off. The idea behind the research was to buttress regimes whose policies were judged to serve the interests of the United States, regardless of the nondemocratic nature of the regimes or the justification for rebellion. It was, in short, research aimed at helping the powerful remain powerful. Those social scientists who agreed to participate in Project Camelot accepted, whether consciously or not, that political bias.

Project Camelot was to cost millions of dollars over a three-year period and was to draw upon social science expertise across the United States and in Latin American nations. Yet less than a year after Project Camelot was initiated the Army dropped the whole idea. The U.S. government was embarrassed when word about it leaked to the media. Governments and scholars around the world condemned the United States for this planned intrusion into other nations' internal affairs.

The controversy surrounding Project Camelot helped alert social scientists to the importance of understanding the interests of their sponsors, the implications of the questions they pursue, and the intended uses of the research results. Social scientists must be aware that sponsors may use these results to harm people. In our view social scientists have an obligation—much like that of medical researchers—to pursue knowledge that will aid in reducing human suffering and enhancing human potential. By that criterion, research like Project Camelot should simply not take place.

U.S. political elites historically have supported harsh military dictatorships in Latin American nations where there were U.S. corporate investments. In Chile, the U.S. Central Intelligence Agency helped General Augusto Pinochet seize power in a 1973 coup that overthrew Chile's democratically elected, reform-minded government.

CONCLUSION

In this chapter we addressed the following questions:

1. What is the difference between an individual's *personal troubles* and social conditions that are more properly understood as *public issues?*
2. What is the sociological imagination? How will it enable a person to make the distinction and understand possible connections between personal troubles and public issues?
3. How can the core concepts and research methods of sociology contribute to developing a sociological imagination?
4. What sorts of ethical and political issues arise for any sociologist who wishes to engage in research?
5. What, in fact, is sociology good for?

Early in the chapter, we presented the story of Dana, a young woman confronted with a series of crises and challenges in her personal and family life. Dana is understandably confused and under a great deal of stress. She may well be asking, "Why me?" But if she is able to understand which of her troubles are, in fact, shared by many others, and thus not subject to personal blame, Dana may be able to identify positive strategies for dealing with them.

Dana might seek out counseling opportunities and support groups for herself and family members, look for ways to assist her family financially, keep pursuing her educational goals by going to a local college part-time, and become involved in political activities bearing on the plight her family shares with so many others. Making the distinction between personal troubles, over which she can exert some direct control, and public issues, which need to be addressed in the larger political and economic arena, can help relieve her paralyzing depression.

The state of consciousness that can help people like Dana empower themselves is a way of thinking we have been calling the sociological imagination. Each of us, through the systematic search for knowledge about how our society is presently structured, and how and why it seems to be changing, can gain strength—not only to cope but also to play an active role in influencing the directions our biographies are likely to take. The choice is ours. We need not simply be passive objects to whom life happens; we have the capacity to be energetic actors with some influence over our life courses. History provides innumerable examples of such people, many of whom came from the most humble, socially undistinguished backgrounds.

Sociologists use certain core concepts and research methods, such as experiments, fieldwork, surveys, and historical research, to help generate the knowledge crucial to the sociological imagination. In the course of their activities, researchers have a special obligation to conduct themselves in ways that avoid exacerbating unjust situations or bringing harm to others. This means being fully aware of the ethical and political implications of one's work, including the unintended uses to which it might be put.

In essence, sociology's promise rests with its ability to provide us with a systematic, evidence-based understanding of the world humans have constructed. At its best, sociology does more than simply identify obstacles to change. It points to contradictions within society that are potential change levers, suggests issues around which people can organize, and stimulates continual assessments of the status quo. In sum, sociology is meant to be done, studied, and used for the betterment of humanity.

THINKING CRITICALLY

1. When a couple's marriage ends in divorce, it is usually dismissed as their own personal trouble and a matter of their individual failings. Yet the divorce rate is very high; some 50 percent of all marriages end in divorce. How might our understanding of the causes of divorce be enriched were we to view it as a public issue?
2. C. Wright Mills believed that the sociological imagination would be empowering to anyone possessing it. A counterargument might hold that the accumulation of knowledge about how the surrounding social world affects us could prove to be overwhelming, even paralyzing. Where do you stand in this argument?
3. Assuming that you had the education, training, skills, and resources, which aspect of society would you most like to study and why? What, specifically, would you want to find out? How would you go about doing so? What research methods do you think you would use? What kinds of problems do you think you would run into in doing your research?
4. In order to gain access to groups that are likely to resist being the objects of sociological research, sociologists sometimes conceal their professional identities and intentions. What issues does this raise in your mind, and where do you stand on them? Are there situations where people's rights to privacy must come before the sociologist's right to freedom of scientific inquiry? What would be an example?
5. In this chapter we discussed research which suggests that U.S. public schooling may be structured so that it denies equal educational opportunities to children from the lower classes. We also mentioned research which suggests that men who have sex with other men come from all walks of life and that many are married men with families. Sociological research findings like these may make some people uncomfortable. In your view, is this good or bad?
6. In a boxed insert, Craig Miller describes his descent from a well-paid sheet metal worker to a poorly paid employee in a fast-food outlet. In C. Wright Mills's terms, is Mr. Miller's present economic plight a personal trouble or the expression of a public issue? Why? Where might the solution to his plight lie?

KEY TERMS

sociology, *2*
personal troubles, *5*
public issues, *5*
sociological imagination, *6*
order perspective, *10*
conflict perspective, *11*
hypothesis, *12*
open-ended questions, *12*
experimental research, *13*
experimental group, *13*
control group, *13*
cultural deprivation, *14*

self-fulfilling prophecy, *16*
field research, *17*
direct observation, *17*
passive observation, *17*
participant observation, *17*
longitudinal study, *18*
survey, *21*
tracking, *21*
gatekeepers, *23*
historical research, *23*
primary sources, *24*
secondary sources, *24*

SUGGESTED READINGS

Earl Babbie, *The Practice of Social Research*, 6th ed. Belmont, CA:
Wadsworth, 1992. A comprehensive overview of sociological research
methods, including some not covered in this chapter, along with consideration of the ethics and politics of social research.

Peter Berger, *Invitation to Sociology: A Humanistic Approach*. Garden
City, NY: Anchor Books, 1963. A classic statement on the value of sociology, emphasizing how it can help debunk erroneous assumptions
about human conduct and demystify the workings of the social world.

Allan G. Johnson, *The Forest for the Trees: An Introduction to Sociological
Thinking*. San Diego, CA: Harcourt Brace Jovanovich, 1991. An introduction to core concepts and theoretical frameworks in sociology that
shows the reader why it is worth the effort to think sociologically.

C. Wright Mills, *The Sociological Imagination*. New York: Oxford University Press, 1959. Mills's classic statement of the benefits to be gained
from studying sociology. His opening chapter, "The Promise," is especially worth reading.

George Ritzer, *Sociological Theory*, 3d ed. New York: McGraw-Hill, 1992.
An in-depth review of the key thinkers and schools of thought within
sociology, from its origins to the present, showing the diverse approaches
sociologists have taken and the progress they have made in developing
theories about the workings of society.

CORE SOCIOLOGICAL CONCEPTS

SOCIAL STRUCTURE: MACRO-LEVEL

*L*ook at the labels inside the clothes you are wearing. Where were the garments made? If you drive a car or own a stereo, where was it manufactured? And have you or has someone you know been sent as a member of the U.S. military to another country to participate in an armed conflict (perhaps in Kuwait), to deliver medical and food supplies to an embattled nation (maybe in Somalia), or simply to be part of an ongoing presence (in Europe or Asia)?

Your answers to these questions should illustrate to you that we are not isolated from the rest of the world. On the contrary, we are part of a world-system, linked to other countries through the economic and political relationships forged between countries. Moreover, we are linked to our own society through our participation in its central institutions, including the family, education, religion, economy, and the state. We can best understand the shaping of our lives in terms of how we are positioned within these three levels of social structure: the world-system, our society, and its institutions. These are the three levels of what sociologists refer to as macro-level social structures, and they will be the focus of this chapter. We also can affect these macro-structures through our actions, thereby introducing flexibility and change into such structures. We shall explore this notion in more depth at the end of the chapter and throughout the book.

SOCIAL STRUCTURE

When we speak of **social structure,** we refer to the means of organizing recurring patterns of relationships within a social system. **Macro-level social structures** are large-scale mechanisms that organize and distribute individuals in an entire society, as opposed to small-scale, or interpersonal, structures (on the mid- or micro-level—see Chapter 3). Note that we are not talking about individuals and their personalities; rather, we are talking about how the positions that individuals occupy in society are organized and related. Social structure is analogous to an apartment building in which tenants may come and go but the building itself remains intact. Some members of the social system die or leave, new ones are born or migrate into it, but the social structures remain to organize the positions that these individuals fill. For example, national and international labor markets are large-scale structures that organize tasks of production and distribution of goods and services in our society and around the world; they also operate as a sorting mechanism, distributing individuals into jobs to carry out these tasks.

The patterns produced by the organization and distribution of individuals in society are beyond any single individual's control, but they remain powerful and significant forces in contouring our existence. They shape our experiences, our possible alternatives for action, our world view, and our feelings about ourselves. What, then, are these macro-level social structures, and how do they contour our individual daily lives?

Let us begin by considering how we may be affected by events and relationships in other countries. How is it possible for issues and problems to affect individuals across oceans and continents? How do we influence what happens in our nation and around the world? In what ways are all people members of an organized world-system? How is this relevant to individual experience?

WORLD-SYSTEMS

All nations are connected to each other in a **world-system.** This is the most complete macro-level structure, as it encompasses all other levels of social structure. A world-system is an international social system of "cultural, normative, economic, political, and military relations"; these are organized around the exchange of goods and services (Chase-Dunn, 1989: 348). In a world-system, nations may trade goods and services, share common goals in international treaties, allow foreign productive facilities and military bases to locate within their borders, share a common history or heritage, or exchange labor. Such relationships are not necessarily between equal partners, nor need they produce equal or mutually beneficial outcomes. Indeed, they often do not.

Let's consider, for example, the role different countries play in producing the world's goods and services. Some countries may be classified as **core nations,** in which production is based on technology that relies more on machinery than on human labor and in which human labor is relatively skilled and highly paid. While such countries tend to be wealthy, most of the people who live in them are not. Examples of core nations include the United States, Great Britain, Japan, and Germany.

In **peripheral nations,** production is based on technology that relies more on cheap human labor than on expensive machinery. Such countries are typically quite poor; however, not everyone who lives in the periphery is poor. Elites in peripheral nations tend to be wealthy compared with the poverty of the masses. Examples of peripheral nations include Bangladesh, Sri Lanka, Nicaragua, Zaire, and Lesotho.

Finally, still other countries may be classified as **semiperipheral nations.** These are countries in which production is based on a mixture of intermediate levels of machinery and human labor and in which human labor is semiskilled and paid intermediate levels of wages. Such countries are neither as poor as peripheral countries nor as wealthy as core countries. And as with core and peripheral nations, wealth and poverty coexist. Examples of semiperipheral nations include India, Mexico, Egypt, Kuwait, and South Africa (see Wallerstein, 1974; Chase-Dunn, 1989).

In the international division of labor, peripheral and semiperipheral countries provide the raw materials needed for production and manufacture more and more consumer goods, which the core nations consume. Meanwhile, the economies of core nations increasingly revolve around service sector operations, such as finance, management, sales, and information processing. How do these global patterns and relationships affect individuals' lives?

Global Patterns and Personal Consequences

The position of peripheral countries in the world-system's division of labor affects the life chances of everyone living in these nations, from birth on.

Both the land and the resources are controlled by a small privileged class, an elite group interested primarily in generating private profits by trading with large corporations in the core. Much of the land is thus used to produce cash crops and luxury commodities (such as sugar, coffee, and cocoa), rather than the food needed for survival by most of the people in the peripheral country itself. As a result, chronic malnutrition or undernutrition and poor health severely limit the life chances of the vast majority of people living in these countries.

Additionally, the cultivation of a limited number of cash crops for many years requires the use of chemical fertilizers to replenish lost minerals and pesticides to protect the crops. After years of exposure to these chemicals, many workers suffer from debilitating and life-threatening diseases. Moreover, when countries emphasize cash crops grown for profit, they must increasingly rely on technology to make production more efficient and raise profits. This displaces human labor and provokes widespread unemployment. Unemployment, malnutrition, and lack of control of fertile land combine to undermine the life chances of working people in the periphery. In particular, women and children suffer most.

Statistics show a stark gap between life chances in wealthy core nations and those in poor peripheral ones. As Table 2.1 indicates, adults can expect to live decades longer and infants have a far greater chance of survival in the core nations. In many core countries the number of children who die in the first year of life is less than one in a hundred. In contrast, in some peripheral countries in Africa and Asia, one in five infants dies before the first birthday. Moreover, it is relatively rare for children in the core to die before age 5 (1 per 1,000 people in the total population). Those who do die are usually victims of accidents. In contrast, *half of all deaths in peripheral countries are children under 5 years old,* and the typical cause of their deaths is not accidents but disease (Eckholm, 1982; United Nations Children's Fund, 1988; *Economist Book of Vital World Statistics,* 1990). In peripheral nations malnutrition severely increases children's susceptibility to diseases; when water supplies are contaminated, intestinal irritations like diarrhea become deadly. Indeed, diarrhea is one of the major causes of death among these children. The poor distribution of food and unequal control over arable land often impose a death sentence on children in peripheral countries.

In many peripheral and semiperipheral countries multinational corporations based in core nations conduct manufacturing for export. But the people they employ do not derive many benefits. For example, in electronics factories in the Philippines, young women who work for eight to twelve hours per day peering into microscopes strain their eye muscles and endanger their eyesight. Their general health also deteriorates, as their extremely low wages are hardly enough to subsist on, much less support families. While the average hourly wage for factory workers in the United States in 1990 was $14.83, it was $4.16 in South Korea, $3.98 in Taiwan, $2.79 in Brazil, and $1.85 in Mexico (U.S. Department of Labor, 1990). In some of these nations' factories, exposure to toxic chemicals and fumes causes lung and respiratory diseases, miscarriages, cancer, and other life-threatening diseases, as the boxed reading describes. Some corporations respond to

Table 2.1

GLOBAL CONTRASTS: WEALTH AND SURVIVAL

NATION	PER CAPITA GDP*	INFANT MORTALITY (PER 1,000 LIVE BIRTHS)	LIFE EXPECTANCY	
			MALES	FEMALES
United States	$22,470 (1991)	10	72	79
Japan	$19,000 (1991)	4	77	82
France	$18,300 (1991)†	7	74	82
Sweden	$17,200 (1991)	6	75	81
Germany	$16,700 (1991)†	7	73	79
Yemen	$545 (1991)†	118	49	52
Pakistan	$380 (1990)	105	56	57
Mali	$265 (1990)	110	43	47
Nigeria	$250 (1990)†	110	48	50
Bangladesh	$200 (1991)†	112	55	43
Afghanistan	$200 (1989)†	162	45	43

*GDP (gross domestic product) is defined as the sum worth of all goods and services produced within the borders of a given country in a given year, including those produced by foreign companies inside that country.
†Estimate.
Source: "Foreign Economic Trends and Their Implications for the United States," in Central Intelligence Agency, *The World Factbook 1992* (Washington, D.C.: U.S. Government Printing Office, 1992); U.S. Department of Commerce; and International Trade Administration.

complaints of these conditions by automating, replacing people with technology. This only increases unemployment, poverty, and hunger among workers in the periphery and semiperiphery. Since these workers do not own or control the corporations they work for, and since they are typically not unionized, changing production arrangements to improve their life chances becomes impossible.

In a global system, core countries aren't immune from hardship either. When peripheral countries' economies are in crisis, these nations may sharply increase their exports to core countries like the United States. These cheaper goods then compete with more expensive products made in the States, undermining sales of domestic goods. Declines in sales of domestic products may produce widespread layoffs and unemployment in affected industries, such as textiles, garments, computers, and electronics.

Peripheral and semiperipheral countries play the role of cheap labor sources for manufacturing in an increasingly global division of labor. Because of the pivotal role of business in the structure of the U.S. economy, the federal government was persuaded to pursue the North American Free Trade Agreement between the United States, Mexico, and Canada, a treaty that will enhance corporate interests in profit making by supporting the global division of labor. But each country has its own labor and environmental policies, so manufacturers can relocate to countries with the most lax policies. Since the treaty was negotiated without any attempt to standardize these policies, effects of the global division of labor will likely continue to differentially affect workers in each country. Here we see the effects of this division of labor on individuals' personal lives. How might this treaty, and the global division of labor, affect yours?

To see Luz Elena Corona Calderón climb the Tijuana hillside separating her shanty from the factory where she used to work is to see in one sweep both the promise and the failure of trade relations between the United States and Mexico. On one side, Corona can peer down to the 11-by-18-foot handmade structure she, her husband, their three adolescent daughters, and seven-year-old son call home. It is a monument to ingenuity, pieced together from scraps of old tires, corrugated tin, and fragments of old clothes. On the rise in front of her: the luminous towers of the Parque Pacífico industrial compound, part of the free-trade zone where factories (or *maquiladoras*) owned by U.S. companies have been exploiting Mexican workers and polluting the border area under little scrutiny for 29 years.

Not until debate over the North American Free Trade Agreement (NAFTA) heated up . . . did the attention of most U.S. politicians, business leaders, and environmental and labor activists turn toward the *maquiladoras,* which crowd most of the 2,000-mile U.S.-Mexico border. NAFTA, which was passed by Congress in [1993], phases out tariffs inhibiting the movement of goods between Mexico, the U.S., and Canada. Its opponents have pointed to cities like Tijuana as microcosms of what the rest of the country will look like now that U.S. corporations can move into Mexico without restrictions.

Here on the border, the legacy of unchecked U.S. investment is palpable: workers labor in production rooms with few accessible fire exits and almost no ventilation, often spraying industrial lacquer and soldering with hazardous substances that are illegal in the U.S. Menstrual irregularities and miscarriages are common. In one factory, employees describe bathrooms without water, where human excrement covers the floors. In Tijuana alone, industrial accidents have killed at least ten workers in the last year—two after they were sent to clean a chemical-laden canister emitting fumes that mixed fatally with the hundred-degree summer heat. Managers flout labor laws requiring breaks and sick and vacation days, while draconian worker manuals stipulate that employees can be suspended for refusing to work overtime. Many women work near-double shifts and then must care for husbands and children at home.

Close to 70 percent of the *maquiladora* workers are female, as a common highway sign in Tijuana illustrates: *Se Solicita, Sexo: Femenino,* or Help Wanted, Women Only. Employers prize female personnel for their supposedly delicate musculature and their willingness to work for lower wages than men. One manager explained to social anthropologist Patricia Fernández Kelly, who worked undercover in a *maquiladora* from 1979 to 1980, that the distribution of fatty tissue in women's derrieres predisposes them to long hours of sitting.

Hourly *maquiladora* wages range from 70 cents to $1.25, which can buy about a quart of oil or a couple of eight-ounce cans of condensed milk. In one makeshift grocery store in a Tijuana shanty, prices can approach those on the "other side," as the U.S. is called. Here, a canister of salt costs 47 cents; a bar of soap, 60 cents, toothpaste, 90 cents. "In Tijuana, we say there is 'opportunity' for women because they pay more than minimum wage

"Mexico's elite may be getting richer but the maquiladora worker still can't feed and shelter her family."

[around 60 cents]. But you can't live on it," remarked Tijuana labor activist Cármen Valadez, who is trying to forge cross-border alliances among women workers.

Even double-income border families can afford no better than shanties, usually with no heat, electricity, or running water; clean water must be bought from unreliable trucks that sell it for prices so high that many choose to bathe in the canals, where the sewage and factory runoff flow freely. In company-owned barracks, young single workers—often a hundred women—will share one double-burner hot plate for cooking.

For the 80 percent of Tijuana's 8,000 female *maquiladora* workers who are mothers, child care costs an average of $60 a week—equaling a week's total wages for most. Since the majority of women have parted with their extended families in other parts of the country, many are forced to leave small children locked in shanties to fend for themselves during work hours. Others sacrifice food to afford uniforms and books for parochial schools (public schools are distant and dangerous).

Along the border a number of communities surrounding the *maquiladoras* are plagued by near-epidemic rates of anencephaly—a birth defect that causes an infant to be born without a brain and to die immediately. Preliminary research has linked this phenomenon to the rivers of raw chemical waste known as *aguas negras*—literally, black waters—that flow from bluffs dense with *maquiladoras* and trickle down to worker *colonias,* or barrios, covering the hillsides and valleys below. Among Mexico's border population, studies have found high rates of skin diseases, respiratory illnesses, and anemia. In one Tijuana community, a mother and her teenage daughter describe collective outbreaks of rashes among residents, and they speak of children and old people constantly afflicted with fevers and eye conditions.

U.S. companies have been feeding off this region since 1965, when the U.S.-Mexico Border Industrialization Program established a limited free-trade zone to discourage immigration to the U.S. by creating jobs for Mexicans (also one of NAFTA's

most trumpeted selling points). In the last three decades, some 2,000 U.S. factories set up shop here, providing half a million Mexican jobs. Thus, part of the pro-NAFTA argument has been borne out: free trade, by opening up Mexican markets to U.S. goods and encouraging U.S. investment in Mexico, stimulates economic growth and creates jobs. That Mexico has seen the rise of 11 new billionaires in the last two years has also bolstered the case of NAFTA's proponents.

But for many of Mexico's poor, the last 29 years of U.S. investment in their country has not meant rising wealth; *maquiladora* wages have dropped by half over the last decade. Mexico's elite may be getting richer but the *maquiladora* worker still can't feed and shelter her family. And among most of the workers and their advocates in Mexico's border communities, there is little faith that NAFTA will either raise wages or improve working and living conditions, as its supporters have promised. "Labor conditions are getting worse, and we'll see if NAFTA just continues the trend," says Patricia Mercado, of Mexico's Mujeres en Acción Sindical (Women in Labor Action).

In Tijuana, there was a fateful synchronicity to the fact that just as the NAFTA debate reached the general public in the U.S., life in this border city took a drastic turn. . . . In January 1993, Tijuana endured three weeks of heavy rains, floods, and mud slides; hundreds of residents died when workers' shanties washed off the *colonia* hillsides. *Maquiladora* operators fired another several hundred workers for refusing to brave the often fatal torrents—"soups of rocks" as people called them—to get to work. "With the floods people just lost faith," recalls Lucila Conde, a Tijuana native who now works out of San Diego as a cross-border labor organizer. The Mexican government failed to intervene when employees were fired or were refused pay as a result of lost work, Conde says. "People realized the companies don't care about us. The government doesn't care about us. The United States doesn't care about us."

During the floods Luz Elena Corona Calderón was earning $7 a day at Plásticos Bajacal, a factory owned by Carlisle Plastics, a Boston-based manufacturer of coat hangers and garbage bags. As she tells the story of what happened to her community, Corona punctuates every third fact with a habitual *"¿Crees?"*–"Can you believe it?"—a verbal tic revealing her growing indignation. Corona's rage stems in part from a series of events that unfolded a few months before the floods, starting when she witnessed an on-the-job accident in which a drill bit split, spitting a piece of hot metal into a coworker's eye. The man lost his eye; Plásticos refused to cover the portion of disability that Mexican social security laws demand of an employer. No one in Carlisle management would comment for this story.

The same week the floods began, Corona and 11 coworkers had planned a meeting to discuss forming a union that would respond to the accident and other abuses—among them, the company's failure to provide adequate safety equipment despite employees' close contact with carcinogens and lung irritants such as benzene and formaldehyde. The workers were among a small but growing number who have shunned Mexico's ineffective government-affiliated unions and tried, often unsuccessfully, to demand accountability of U.S. companies

and the Mexican government by organizing independently.

In the United States, the six plants owned by Carlisle Plastics can be counted among the self-styled "progressive" factories of the 1990s. The company's majority owner, William Binnie, professes an entrepreneurial appreciation of the "green" or ecology-minded market. Carlisle's "environmentally sensitive" trash bags now sell under in-house labels in stores from Thriftys to Kmart. In a laudatory profile in *Forbes* last year, Binnie brought a reporter into the workers' rest room at a Texas factory. There, he boasted: "The first thing I do whenever I visit a plant is use the hourly workers' bathroom so I can see how the company's treating them."

But observers can't get close to Carlisle's Tijuana factory, a workplace that has proven especially hostile to women. When 37-year-old Corona discovered she was pregnant for the fifth time, she asked to transfer out of the plant's operation assembly division, where she had to lift heavy boxes. In a region where many factories require quarterly pregnancy tests and fire those who test positive to avoid paying state-mandated maternity

In addition, poverty in peripheral countries produces a cheap labor pool that can be exploited by multinational corporations based in the core. When U.S. corporations move their plants to the periphery to take advantage of the cheap labor, workers in the United States lose jobs. The social structure of global relationships thus affects people in both peripheral and core countries.

The Role of Raw Materials in the World-System

Dependency on imported raw materials affects the U.S. economy, its military relations, and its population. For example, heavy dependence on foreign sources of oil leaves the United States vulnerable to political and economic shocks over which it has little control. In 1973, when the Organization of Petroleum Exporting Countries (OPEC) restricted its production and export of oil, the United States suffered a serious recession.

leave, she knew she had jeopardized her job. "They told me I was lazy and was lying to get easier work," Corona recalls. So she stayed put.

While working her habitual graveyard shift a few weeks later, Corona felt cramps and knew that she had begun to bleed. At 3:30 A.M., buckling with pain, she asked permission to go to the bathroom, but her supervisor turned her down. (The company workers' manual lists "undue" visits to the bathroom as cause for suspension.) Corona asked to switch positions to one where she could sit but was refused again. Finally, she pleaded to be taken to a hospital but was told that the company had no way to transport her and that there was no one to replace her. When Corona's shift ended five hours later, her husband took her in a taxi to a nearby hospital, where what she already knew was confirmed: she'd miscarried.

Plásticos denied Corona disability payments and docked her wages for time off after the miscarriage. Soon the company fired her and the coworkers with whom she had organized the union. "I've been angry, desperate about my future. But it's made me feel more powerful too. I tell my daughters, 'You're never going to set foot in a *maquila*,'" says Corona, who is now on staff at a local labor advocacy organization. "All the *maquiladoras* are is deception. They have me on a blacklist and I can't find work in another factory. *¿Crees?* It doesn't matter. I'd never go back anyway."

In the Tijuana neighborhood of Chilpancingo, many are just as bitter. This community has seen the births of six anencephalic infants since 1991. "Nobody has to tell us about the problems," notes resident Graciela Villalvazo García, who attributes her one-year-old son's hydrocephalus (a birth defect that causes brain atrophy) to the chemical streams near her house. "Newcomers don't know the problems, and you see them bathing in the canal," she says. "The contamination is everywhere. The waters run all the way to San Diego. Where am I to live? The contamination may go all the way to the moon."

Source: Elizabeth Kadetsky, "The Human Cost of Free Trade," *Ms.*, January–February 1994, pp. 12–15.

Industries that relied on oil and petroleum products for production had to pay four times as much for these raw materials. Production became much more costly, raising the price of consumer goods. The resulting decline in consumption, together with the increased costs of production, caused thousands of U.S. workers to lose their jobs and left everyone suffering from dramatic inflation in prices. High inflation rates reduce the amount of goods and services that our wages are able to purchase, thereby lowering our standard of living.

Our reliance on imported oil also affects our international political relations. When Iraq's invasion of Kuwait in 1991 threatened U.S. access to Mideast oil, President George Bush mobilized the most massive military force since the Vietnam war. As a result, thousands of people found their employment and education disrupted and their lives at risk when their reserve units were sent to the Middle East. In many families, income dropped sharply while wage earners were away at war. And, of course,

Inequalities in the global division of labor have encouraged core factories and assembly plants to relocate to peripheral and semiperipheral countries. There, owners take advantage of cheaper labor and lax or nonexistent government regulations. These women work in sweatshops in Mexico's *maquilas*, where wages, conditions, and benefits for workers are far worse than they were when the plants operated in El Paso, Texas.

some Americans lost their lives, many others suffered injuries, and still others endured the emotional turmoil of being captured as a prisoner of war. It is unlikely that the United States would have cared so deeply about the invasion of Kuwait had oil not been involved. Note, for example, that the United States did not mobilize military forces when the Soviet Union invaded Afghanistan in the 1980s or when the Bosnian Serbs slaughtered Muslims in their "ethnic cleansing" campaign in the 1990s.

The war in Iraq also caused outbreaks of political conflict in the United States. Many people questioned whether U.S. troops should be sent to war to protect access to Mideast oil. But those who protested against the war often found themselves labeled unpatriotic by powerful political elites and by members of the public who supported the war. Thus, economic and trade relations between countries can seriously affect the social and political relations within them.

In addition to protecting U.S. trade interests, the military often facilitates international production. A strong U.S. military presence in or around countries in which multinational corporations have a stake helps secure the political environment. This military presence often requires treaties and leases to forge political interrelationships between countries. Such arrangements involve an unspoken understanding that issues like human rights violations may be overlooked in the interest of preserving the agreements. For example, for many years the United States did little to acknowledge the beating, torture, and killing of dissenters in the Philippines, in part because the Philippine dictatorship had been avowedly anti-Communist, a position consistent with U.S. economic and political interests. International relations in the world-system, then, affect the structure and experiences of whole nations and the people in them.

To sum up, where people live in the global division of labor strongly influences their lives. Factory workers all over the world live less well than corporate executives, but factory workers in Mexico and the Philippines are far more poverty-stricken than their counterparts in the United States.

It is important, too, where people are located within the society that links them to the world-system. Just as there is differentiation *between* nations, there is differentiation *within* them. What is the relationship between the individual and the larger society of which he or she is a member?

SOCIETIES

The world-system is a network of many nations and societies. A **society** is an organization of people who share a common territory, govern themselves, and cooperate to secure the survival of the group. Not all societies are nations; there may be several societies within a single nation. For example, in the United States the many surviving groups of Native Americans constitute societies within the national boundaries of the country. Similarly, before its breakup, Yugoslavia contained within its boundaries several societies, including Serbs, Muslims, and Croatians; Spain contains a society of Basques; and Iraq, Iran, and Turkey share the society of Kurds. Sometimes the presence of many societies in a single nation can produce diversity, richness of history, and gradual change. Other times, the presence of many societies within a single nation can become a source of serious conflict and sometimes war. In Iraq, Iran, and Turkey, for example, Kurds are persecuted and Shiites and Sunni Muslims clash for dominance and control. And in Yugoslavia in 1991, Serbs, Muslims, and Croatians resumed old conflicts in a struggle for control of land.

Nations are political entities with clearly defined geographic boundaries usually recognized by neighboring nations. Nations are generally characterized by the viewpoint and interests of their dominant societies. Thus, although nations may contain several societies, not all these societies are necessarily equal in power or benefit equally from social, political, and economic arrangements. For example, the Kurds in Iraq are being oppressed by a more powerful prevailing society under Saddam Hussein. And although blacks in South Africa are now in the political majority, for many years they were exploited and oppressed economically, socially, and politically by the dominant white society in that country. In the United States, Native Americans do not share the political or economic power of the nation's white-dominated society. Indeed, the dominant legal system may render aspects of Native American culture illegitimate. For example, federal laws prohibit Native American groups from using substances in

Sometimes diversity of societies within a single nation becomes a source of conflict and violence. In Bosnia-Herzegovina, Muslim refugees fleeing the terror of Serbian assaults in their town of Srebrenica are temporarily sheltered in a sports center, where they are subjected to overcrowded conditions, the fear and uncertainty of dislocation, and scarcity of food.

their traditional rituals that are deemed to be illicit drugs, despite the fact that such substances may have been an integral aspect of those rituals for centuries.

Two Views of Social Structure

Some sociologists adopt a **structural functional perspective,** in which they view societies as adaptive social structures that help human beings adjust to their physical, political, economic, and social environment (Parsons, 1951). When changes or challenges occur in that environment, the structure of a given society becomes the mechanism for organizing responses, adjustments, or preemptive strategies. For example, our use of fossil fuels has contributed to the **greenhouse effect,** a phenomenon that occurs when carbon dioxide released and trapped in the atmosphere by the burning of fossil fuels raises the earth's temperature. Structural functionalists would argue that U.S. society has made structural adaptations so that it can continue to survive. Our political structures have enacted and enforced clean-air and recycling laws, and our economic structure has made fossil fuels more expensive to discourage unnecessary use. Thus, our society functions to help us adapt to the greenhouse effect. In this sense, society's structure is functional or beneficial in meeting our needs.

However, other sociologists offer a **critical analysis** of social structure. They challenge the assumption in the functionalist analysis that all of society's members benefit from the way society is structured and from the ways it adjusts to its environment. Moreover, they argue that such policies are often driven by power struggles, not by a logical adaptation to the environment. These critics point out that some groups enjoy advantages and privileges that allow them to impose their views on others and to influence the adaptive strategies society may adopt. In this analysis, the way we are organized as a society significantly affects not only how (and if) we alter our lifestyle in response to environmental challenges but also who benefits and who is hurt by the strategies chosen (see, for example, Durning, 1994; Lowe, 1994).

Let us use critical analysis to examine the forces that might influence decisions concerning energy policy. In the United States, the power of large-scale corporations, particularly energy and utility corporations, greatly influences that policy. The nation's energy policy today emphasizes an increasing reliance on nonrenewable potentially hazardous sources of energy such as nuclear power plants. After the United States had gone to war to protect its access to cheap foreign oil in 1991, President Bush put forth a national energy policy that reflected a corporate agenda. The proposal called for a renewed investment in nuclear power generation as an alternative to reliance on oil and other fossil fuels; it made no provision for the development of less hazardous renewable sources of energy (such as solar, wind, or geothermal energy) or for conservation measures. Such a policy largely benefits the energy corporations, and their wealthy stockholders, that own the nuclear power plants, at the expense of the rest of society.

In many underdeveloped countries, global inequalities in the world-system encourage policies that favor the wealthy elites and may intensify environmental challenges. Large landowners in countries like Brazil cut down millions of acres of rain forest a year to export wood or to create more land for cattle grazing in order to export beef to industrialized nations. Since trees are the natural consumers of the carbon dioxide released by burning fossil fuels, massive deforestation in peripheral countries contributes to the greenhouse effect (Durning, 1994). Thus, the structural position of countries in the world-system affects policies that in turn can affect the earth's environment.

Notably, even political and economic power cannot protect corporate executives from the personal effects of global warming. At some point, it would seem, health issues should outweigh the profit motive in steering energy policy. For example, certain rare medicinal plants used to treat cancer can be found only in the rain forests now undergoing destruction. Thus far, however, health issues have not been connected to energy policy changes. People tend to address the greenhouse effect in terms of personal lifestyle issues (such as whether to buy large, fuel-inefficient cars, whether to carpool to save gas usage, and whether to invest in solar energy for one's own home). Framed this way, the hazards are analyzed as personal problems of lifestyle rather than as public issues of energy policy driven by profit motives.

Societies respond to the need to adapt to their environment in many ways, *always influenced by their social structures.* Thus, there is no single, universal response to a given problem. For example, some societies may respond to the threat of the greenhouse effect by outlawing the burning of fossil fuels altogether. Others may attempt to reduce the use of fossil fuels for some purposes but not for all. Still others may ignore the threat, seeing it as minimal in the near future.

The strategies we develop to respond to some environmental challenges affect not only our own society's survival but that of the entire world-system. For example, if we choose to rely on nuclear power as an alternative to burning fossil fuels, we run the risk of nuclear accidents that may poison the air, land, and water of other societies in the world-system. In 1986, the accident at the Chernobyl nuclear power plant in the Soviet Union contaminated a large area of land and water in that nation and the radiation drifted into several neighboring countries. On the other hand, if we insist on burning fossil fuels, we may be contributing to the growing threat of the greenhouse effect, and that will affect everyone.

How, then, do societies resolve the problem of survival, and how are individuals linked in the process of social survival? How do factors such as one's class, gender, and race affect each person's relationship to the larger society? How does society control and distribute access to important resources? These questions point to social structures called institutions, to which we now turn.

INSTITUTIONS

To survive, every society must successfully address the same fundamental social needs. Sociologists using the functionalist perspective call these **functional imperatives** (see Parsons, 1951). Talcott Parsons identified six basic functional imperatives, each of which is discussed below.

1. All societies must *organize the activities of their members* to obtain the basic goods and services necessary for survival (such as food, clothing, shelter, fuel, potable water), without irreparably upsetting a balance with the environment. We can obtain food by relying on what we find growing around us, or we can cultivate products that may or may not deplete the fertility of the soil. Alternatively, we can trade with other societies for food, or we can invade another country or society to seize its food, perhaps at a cost to our national security.

2. Societies must *protect their members* from both external and internal threats. External threats include invasion by other societies and destructive natural disasters like hurricanes, tornadoes, and earthquakes. Internal threats include crimes like robbery, murder, rape, and embezzlement and health epidemics like AIDS, measles, polio, and the flu.

3. All societies must *replace members* lost by death or emigration. We may encourage increased reproduction, as many Orthodox Jewish leaders have done to replace members lost in the Holocaust. Alternatively, we

may provide incentives to draw immigrants from other societies, as the United States did in the 1800s to mid-1900s to attract the large labor force needed for industrial expansion. Another way to replenish labor is to seize people from other societies, as slave traders did during the 1700s to 1800s. While slaves certainly did not officially count as members of U.S. society, they did count as greatly needed labor. As such, they filled a particular position in the social structure of plantation life, and slavery represented one strategy for replenishing diminished labor power in society.

4. Whenever societies gain new members, they must *transmit knowledge* of the rights, obligations, responsibilities, and expectations of appropriate behavior to the new members (whether they are native-born children or adult migrants). New members must also be taught the skills they will need to participate as productive members of the society.

5. All societies must *motivate both new and continuing members* to fulfill their responsibilities and conform to expected behaviors. This may be accomplished by a variety of approaches, among them providing meaning and purpose to activities and behaviors or using force and punishment.

6. Finally, societies must *develop mechanisms for resolving conflicts.* Otherwise, conflicts may disrupt a society's ability to satisfy other needs and may even destroy that society altogether.

The social structures that all known societies possess to fulfill these fundamental social needs are called **institutions.** These structures develop the standardized methods that societies use to cope with problems of survival. While most members of society accept these conventional coping mechanisms as legitimate, there may be some debate about them within a society. However, the dominant groups in society are generally able to prevail over the interests and viewpoints of the nonelite or subordinate groups in society; it is not often that organized challenges to the powerful groups' view can affect the content and operation of institutions.

Despite debates or changes in their form, institutions as social structures survive over time. Because they strongly influence our lives, they become the focus of many attempts at change. How can we view the problems experienced by individuals within the context of societal institutions? In order to answer this question, we must establish what it is that institutions do.

Five basic institutions can be found in all known societies: the *family, religion, economy, education,* and *the state.* Each institution is intended to address one or more of the basic needs determining society's survival. Sociologists call such goals the **manifest functions** of the institution. In carrying out these functions, institutions also produce unintended and often unrecognized outcomes or consequences, or **latent functions** (Merton, 1968). In addition, when institutions carry out their functions, they also sometimes inadvertently produce consequences that reduce the adaptability and flexibility of societies and hence may reduce or threaten the very survival of the society the institutions are presumably there to secure. For example, the greenhouse effect's threat to the environment is an unintended consequence of the operation of powerful economic interests.

Structural functionalists argue that, in general, the purpose of institutions is to provide for the collective or common good by attending to the survival needs of society. However, a critical analysis points out that institutions often serve some portions of the societal population better than they serve others. Institutions may even provoke or exacerbate systemic inequalities between groups within society. For example, when the United States went to war against Iraq in early 1991, the state was fulfilling its function of protecting U.S. society from external threats. Indeed, President Bush argued that it was necessary to go to war to "protect our way of life," because Iraq's invasion of Kuwait threatened U.S. access to Mideast oil. However, if we examine who actually went to the Gulf among the U.S. troops, we notice that the "way of life" of certain groups was exposed to disproportionate risk.

The troops (particularly the ground troops) were overwhelmingly from the working class. None of the chief executive officers of the nation's top 20 corporations nor anyone in the President's Cabinet had children involved in the war (Lacayo, 1990; Siegel, 1991: A31). Moreover, racial minorities were disproportionately represented among the troops in the Gulf. The percentage of African Americans and Latinos in the ground troops was much larger than their proportion in the U.S. population. Of the total troops who went to the Gulf, 30 percent were African American; more than half of the women on active duty in the Army were racial minorities. And on one Native American reservation, 70 members of a total population of 3,600 went to the Gulf (Women's International League for Peace and Freedom, 1991: 1). Why were racial minorities and working-class whites so predominant in the U.S. troops who went to war?

Economic and racial inequality and limited opportunity in the United States contributed to the disproportionate representation of African American and working-class soldiers fighting in the Gulf war in 1991.

When the United States discontinued the military draft system in 1973, the country began to rely on an all-volunteer Army. With unemployment and poverty among racial minorities running double and triple the rate among white Americans, many people of color turned to the military as one of the few sources of employment and social mobility available. Others joined the military reserves as a way to afford college tuition. An Army survey concerning recruits' reasons for joining the military found that 39 percent needed the money for college, and 26 percent needed job skills and training or income from service (DeParle, 1990: A14). Many of the women in the military cite similar reasons for volunteering: "for college money, technical training, a way out of a pink-collar ghetto filled with dead ends" (Quindlen, 1991). In many ways, poverty had led the chronically disadvantaged to become the ones who jeopardized their lives in order to preserve "our" way of life. (See Figure 2.1.) In the case of the Gulf war, the latent function of the state's actions was to reinforce inequality, while the manifest function was to protect our society from external threats to its survival.

When institutions reinforce inequalities, they are unintentionally introducing elements that may actually *erode* a society's ability to operate. For example, inequality limits the possibility that all of society's members will have an equal opportunity to develop their creative talents and skills. Inequality also may provoke hostility and distrust of society's ability to be fair or to reward hard work and accomplishment regardless of gender, race, class, age, religion, sexual orientation, or a host of other characteristics. Such distrust and hostility may weaken loyalty to the society among those who feel they have been unfairly denied rewards, and they may resist fulfilling responsibilities, obligations, and expected behaviors (Tumin, 1966). Hence, inequality as a consequence of institutions' operations may actually threaten the institutions' ability to ensure a society's survival. At the very least, inequality may lead certain members of society to disregard socially prescribed responsibilities and obligations.

It becomes important, then, to ask who benefits and who is hurt by the way institutions operate to meet fundamental societal needs. Who benefits and who is hurt by the unintended consequences or latent functions of our institutions? Keep these questions in mind as you read about institutions on the following pages.

The Family

The **family** is the institution whose manifest function is to contribute new members to society. Families also teach the new members what is expected of them, and they try to motivate members to fulfill those expectations. The family may help contain and resolve conflicts within it, including disputes over inheritance. Finally, it ideally resolves the issue of the support of members of society whose capacity to produce may be limited (such as the young, the very elderly, and the infirm). However, while the family attends to these important manifest functions, it may also produce several unintended consequences.

For example, families may reinforce race, gender, and class inequalities in the way they transmit expectations regarding appropriate behaviors and

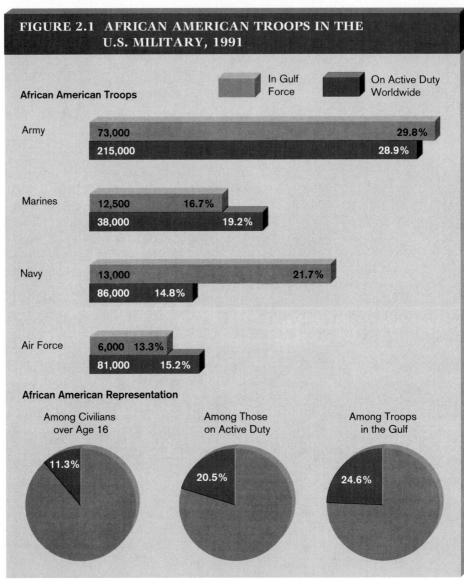

FIGURE 2.1 AFRICAN AMERICAN TROOPS IN THE U.S. MILITARY, 1991

Although African Americans are a minority of the U.S. population, a disproportionately high number are in the military and served in the Gulf war in 1991. How can you explain this? (*Source:* U.S. Department of Defense.)

goals. Girls and boys may be assigned chores that reinforce traditional gender distinctions: girls may be expected to baby-sit and wash dishes, while boys may be expected to take out the garbage or help with household or car repairs (Burns and Homel, 1989). Children of the working class may be taught behaviors and skills that are consistent with jobs requiring little or no autonomy and creativity, while children of the middle class may be instilled with expectations of autonomy, creativity, initiative, and responsibility (Kohn, 1977; Majoribanks, 1987).

Similarly, families may reinforce prejudice and discrimination on the basis of race, religion, and sexual orientation. Parents, guardians, older relatives, and siblings are important sources of such values, stereotypes, and preconceptions of superiority and inferiority of different groups (see, for example, Dennis, 1981). As families fulfill their functions, they may unknowingly perpetuate inequalities, hostilities, and unnecessarily low aspirations and goals. Over time these prejudices can undermine society's ability to develop human resources and form a consensus, both of which may strengthen a society's ability to survive.

Families can also perpetuate economic inequalities by consolidating their wealth through marriages between wealthy families or through inheritance. Kanfer (1993), for example, offers a detailed historical analysis showing how three generations of the Oppenheimer family achieved highly concentrated wealth in South Africa through their monopolistic hold over the DeBeers diamond mines, and ultimately over the world's diamond market. By the early 1990s, the Oppenheimer family controlled 90 percent of the global supply of diamonds (Kanfer, 1993: 368).

Instead of facilitating conflict resolution, families may actually produce the unintended consequence of increased conflict and violence. For example, some families in southern states were instrumental in instigating lynchings to avenge perceived injustices or insults against family members (Cutler, 1969). Their actions tended to inflame the existing conflicts rather than resolve them.

In addition, in a context of diminishing resources and increasing external pressures, family conflict in the form of domestic violence and child abuse may increase (we will discuss this in detail in Chapter 14). Domestic violence in the United States does not occur in the vacuum of family structures. Society itself provides the context for using violence to resolve conflict. This can be seen in both popular culture and political relations. For example, television graphically shows the use of violence as a method of resolving differences. Furthermore, the United States has a long history of participation in international wars to resolve global conflicts. Film footage on the U.S. labor movement (1900s–1980s), the civil rights movement (1950s–1970s), and the antiwar movement (1960s–1970s) chronicles the use of force and violence by military and police organizations to quell challenges to government policies. And private videos have recently documented police violence directed against students at the University of Hartford in Connecticut and against racial minorities in Los Angeles, California. So prevalent is the use of violence in society that it is not surprising if it comes to be accepted as a legitimate form of conflict resolution at home. One unintended consequence of the family as an institution may thus be an increase in violence, together with a diminished effectiveness of conflict resolution.

On the other hand, some families may transmit expectations of behaviors that challenge the predominant ones. Some parents, for example, argue against violence and in favor of nonviolent ways of resolving conflicts. And some children are repelled by the state-sponsored violence and war they see in news clips and by the violence they see in their own or friends' families; it may offend their sense of justice to see innocent people being clubbed or beaten, for example, or even killed. Indeed, nightly news footage of the horrors of the Vietnam war did more to raise a public outcry against the war than any debate ever could. In such instances, individual reactions to the social setting can affect the latent functions of the institution.

When families teach their children to reject certain dominant definitions of behaviors and values, or to adjust to institutional limitations, they may open the door to changing social institutions, such as the family itself. The tension between alternative and dominant expectations and behaviors in families does not necessarily indicate a breakdown of the institution. It may become a front edge of change in the structure of the family as an institution. Different conceptions of family and different needs will give rise to a variety of forms of that institution, including childless couples, gay and lesbian couples (perhaps with children), "blended" families of partners and their children from previous relationships, and so on. These variations can potentially challenge inequalities of race, class, and gender. For example, new divisions of labor may necessarily arise that do not conform to traditional gender-based divisions. Whoever is available for child care must do the baby-sitting; whoever is available may have to cook dinner if the family is to eat; and so on. Then, too, the gender construction of the household may not be conducive to a traditional division of labor: there may not be any women, or there may be only women. We will return to these issues in Chapter 14, "Family."

Religion

Structural functionalist sociologists emphasize that the institution of **religion** manifestly motivates members to comply with their responsibilities and obligations by assigning meaning and purpose to such activities. It attempts to reinforce the family's transmission of appropriate behaviors and goals to new as well as continuing members of society, and it parallels the family's role as a mechanism of conflict resolution. And religious institutions reinforce the family's legitimacy by sanctifying and protecting the family as an important institution.

However, a critical analysis suggests that religious institutions often reinforce gender inequalities by promoting notions of appropriate and inappropriate gender behaviors and reproductive roles within the family. This typically means that sexual intercourse (and therefore parenthood) is forbidden until a couple has been formally married. The father is considered the breadwinner and authority figure ("head of the family"); the mother is the caregiver, housekeeper, and child rearer and is subordinate to the father. Such interpretations of appropriate family roles imply that departures from this model are in many ways sacrilegious. Religious institutions thus often sanctify a particular family form, such as the nuclear family, and denigrate or punish others (especially homosexual family forms and heterosexual cohabitation without marriage). This reduces society's ability to adapt to changes.

Religious institutions may also underscore gender inequalities within their own power structure. For example, the Roman Catholic church does not recognize the legitimacy of women as priests. The Orthodox branch of Judaism similarly does not recognize the legitimacy of women as rabbis, nor does it allow women to be included in minions reading the Torah or leading services. Orthodox men and women cannot sit together in synagogues to pray; men who pray each morning include a passage in which they thank God they were not born a woman. Islamic religion does not recognize women as equal to men: men are dominant and superior to women. In some Islamic countries such as Iran, women must cover themselves completely when outside the home by wearing the traditional chador. Islamic women in Saudi Arabia are not permitted to drive. Whenever they wish to go anywhere, they must have a male as both a chauffeur and an escort.

Finally, religious institutions may unintentionally reinforce existing inequalities and social problems by emphasizing belief in an afterlife, when sufferers will be rewarded. This attitude may impede attempts to improve social conditions and increase society's survivability.

But despite their general tendency toward conservatism, some religious institutions challenge existing inequalities. Both Conservative Judaism and Reform Judaism recognize women as equal to men; they allow men and women to sit together in temple, encourage women to participate in prayer services, and permit women to function as rabbis. Some Christian and Jewish religious groups have begun to accept homosexuals as legitimate church members as well as leaders. Black churches in the United States were instrumental in challenging racial inequalities as part of the civil rights movement (see McAdam, 1982; Morris, 1984). And many religious groups have actively opposed inequality and have participated in antipoverty activities for decades.

Another unintended consequence of religion as an institution can be an increase in conflicts rather than the decrease of hostilities and the development of peaceful consensus. Some religions have for centuries nurtured hostilities toward one another as competitors for souls. Wars such as the Crusades have been waged in the name of God, church, and religion. People who have not conformed to the prevailing religious dogmas have been killed, as in the Salem witch trials in colonial America and in Islamic Iran. Indeed, Iran's religious political leaders issued an international death warrant against Salman Rushdie in 1989 when they decided that his book, *The Satanic Verses,* was a blasphemous attack against Islam and God. We will elaborate on these issues in Chapter 15, "Religion."

The Economy

In the United States, the institution of the **economy** includes corporations, organized markets, the banking community, international trade associations, labor unions, and consumer organizations. In noncapitalist societies, the economy might include the state-controlled production collectives, worker cooperatives, bartering and trading systems, and so on. For structural functionalists, the purpose of economic institutions is primarily to produce and distribute goods and services throughout society. They also discipline and motivate members of society to perform their role in the production, distribution, and consumption of goods and services. In a capitalist economy, workers (including managers) are motivated to do their jobs through the rewards of salaries, wages, and bonuses or the punishments of unemployment and poverty.

However, the economy is often imperfect in achieving its manifest purposes and in reality produces unintended consequences depending on how people design that institution. For example, the economy in socialist countries, where the profit motive is not the principal guide to economic activity, may not produce the consumer goods people need to survive; instead, the economy may focus on state-defined needs, such as military production. Similarly, a capitalist economy does not always produce the goods and services that people need to survive, but in this case the situation occurs because the economy focuses on profits. Grain and cheese may be warehoused and milk dumped into the ocean (despite great hunger here and abroad) because marketing too much of these products can reduce their profitability. Drugs needed to treat rare diseases, or products designed to help physically challenged individuals participate more fully in society's mainstream, may be difficult to find or very expensive because the market is considered too small to be profitable.

Yet corporations may produce many goods and services that are profitable but not needed. In spite of mounting evidence of the dangers to both smokers and nonsmokers alike, cigarettes will continue to be manufactured because of their profitability. Manufacturers are targeting younger consumers through advertisements and sponsorship of sports events and concerts. These marketing strategies are apparently working: while the percentage of smokers in all age groups has declined in the last 20 years, the decline has been slowest among 12 to 17 year olds (National Institute

As scientific and medical evidence of the health problems associated with smoking leads older people to stop smoking, tobacco companies face losses of their markets. To counter the effect of such evidence, many companies have mounted advertising campaigns to attract younger smokers by alluding to smoking as glamorous, youthful, and alluring.

SURGEON GENERAL'S WARNING: Quitting Now Greatly Reduces Serious Risks to

on Drug Abuse, 1991). Young consumers are replacing the losses among older, more educated, and health-conscious consumers. Thus, the economy as an institution provides incentives to produce harmful or useless goods and disincentives to produce important, needed goods. People often pressure the state to step in to control harmful consequences, demanding more ordinances regulating smoking in public places such as elevators, airplanes, restaurants, stores, and offices.

The economy can also reinforce class, race, and gender inequalities. When workers' wages are kept low to increase corporate profitability, the workers are less able to purchase the goods they produce. Low wages thus reduce the consumption of goods and services produced, thereby periodically provoking recessions and unemployment and aggravating class inequalities.

Seniority systems within both corporations and labor unions institutionalize racial and gender inequalities. This is because a "neutral" principle of "last hired, first fired" ensures that women and racial minorities— historically more likely than white males to be the last hired—will continue to be the most vulnerable to recessions.

Inadequate access to jobs, coupled with racial discrimination in the labor market, perpetuates class and racial inequalities by assigning different economic roles to different races and classes. In the face of dwindling opportunities, the poor and racial minorities are more likely to volunteer for military service as a job. Thus, the people who are least likely to benefit from the existing economic structure become the ones most likely to endanger their lives to protect it and the superior advantages it provides others.

In the United States the economy is supposedly based on a system of free enterprise and open competition, suggesting equal opportunity for all members of society. However, the economy actually protects the advantages of the already-privileged. Large corporations that dominate most industries prevent small businesses from entering an industry and competing successfully. For example, small mom-and-pop clothing stores and restaurants find it difficult to compete with the price advantages of large national department stores and fast-food chains; many go bankrupt as the national chains continue to grow and expand. And relatively small auto producers like the American Motors Corporation have found it impossible to remain competitive with General Motors, Ford, and Chrysler (indeed, Chrysler eventually bought American Motors).

When the economy fails to equitably and adequately produce and distribute the basic goods and services needed for survival, those members of society who are denied them may turn to other, sometimes illegal ways to survive. For example, when the Soviet Union existed, a thriving underground economy of black-market trading developed there to give consumers access to commodities (commonly at a very high price) that were unavailable to them through state-run stores. In the United States, some women consider prostitution an opportunity for employment in an economy that offers few jobs (although, to be sure, not all prostitutes make a lucrative living in a safe environment; many are exploited by pimps and work under very dangerous conditions). Drug trafficking provides a lucrative (although extremely risky) source of income. Thus, although not all crimes are the result of economic need, and not everyone with desperate economic needs commits crimes, one unintended consequence of the way we organize our economy may be increased crime.

More advantaged members of society may also receive unintended incentives for criminal behavior. Executives are more likely than assembly-line workers to embezzle corporate funds because the structure of the corporation places them in a position to do so. In the United States, for example, lack of regulatory oversight of the savings and loan institutions in the 1980s facilitated executive abuse, embezzlement, and fraud, costing taxpayers billions of dollars. In the same decade, illegal insider trading became a common practice among stockbrokers. One consequence of our economy may be that people place a greater emphasis on the value of money and personal gain than on the value of integrity and societal or collective gain.

The priority of profit making in the U.S. economy also provides incentives for corporate crimes. For example, it was profitable for the Hooker Chemical Corporation to dump millions of pounds of toxic and carcinogenic chemicals and waste products into an abandoned canal in Love Canal, New York, during the 1940s. The profit motive also prompted Hooker Chemical to sell the dump site and surrounding property to the school board and the city of Niagara Falls in 1953. The company sold the property for $1, with the stipulation that Hooker Chemical would not be liable for any injuries or damages resulting from the property's contents. Although Hooker Chemical knew what it had dumped at the site, the city did not, and it built an elementary school on the property. By 1980, almost 1,000 families had been forced to evacuate their homes around Love Canal, as toxic and carcinogenic chemicals were found in the area's soil, groundwater, and air. Among Love Canal residents (including the children who attended the school built on the dump site), rates of cancer, birth defects, and miscarriages are now much higher than expected (Brown, 1980). Hooker Chemical had maintained its profitability at the cost of human lives and at the expense of the taxpayers, who ultimately pay to clean up such sites.

These latent consequences of the economy combine to weaken its ability to ensure adequate production and distribution of basic goods and services to all. It then becomes increasingly necessary for other institutions, such as the state, the family, and religion, to redirect societal priorities so as to discourage the profit motive from overwhelming society's basic needs. We will discuss some of these issues in greater detail in Chapter 10, "The State and Capital," and Chapter 11, "The Labor Process."

Education

When structural functionalist sociologists study the institution of **education,** they see a system whose manifest function is to transmit the skills that all young members of society need to become productive members of the economy as adults. Thus, the purpose of schools is to teach basic skills such as reading, writing, and math. In the United States, free public education is available to all children up to the age of 18. The Supreme Court's 1954 decision *(Brown v. Topeka Board of Education)* that separate educational institutions based on race are inherently unequal underscored the government's commitment to equal education for all.

A critical analysis reveals, however, that in the United States, schools in fact *reproduce* inequality as an unintended consequence through a variety of mechanisms. For example, most schools fund their budgets through local property-tax revenues. This method of funding creates unequal school budgets, since school systems located in wealthy areas with high property values have access to greater tax revenues than do those in poor locales with low property values. For example, in 1990–1991 the city of Bridgeport, Connecticut, spent $6,462 per student on a student population that was 86 percent racial minorities; in contrast, the nearby affluent community of Westport spent $11,041 per pupil on a student population that was 93 percent white. Greater per-student expenditures appear to have contributed to a more advantageous environment for success in Westport: 84 percent of Westport students go on to four-year colleges compared with 28 percent in Bridgeport (Connecticut Department of Education, 1991). Why do per-student expenditures affect such outcomes as college attendance? Students who attend school in wealthy neighborhoods tend to study an enriched curriculum in well-appointed facilities with low student/teacher ratios; students who attend school in poor neighborhoods commonly study a spare curriculum in deficient facilities (including lack of adequate books) with high student/teacher ratios. The method of providing local school budgets thus re-creates past patterns of class and racial inequalities.

Moreover, our educational institutions are structured so as to place large numbers of similar-aged people in the same school or classroom. While this may be the most cost-efficient manner of imparting basic knowledge, it has the unintended consequence of serving as the largest marriage and mate-selection mechanism at the high school and college levels. By matching privileged students with one another and economically disadvantaged students with one another, schools and colleges seriously reduce the possibility that an upwardly mobile, college-educated individual will mate with someone less advantaged or less educated, whose chances of mobility are limited. Thus, the educational institution reproduces economic inequalities and unequal access to mobility.

Schools also perform the latent function of mitigating pressures on the economy during recessions by delaying the entry of students into a tight labor market. Indeed, many college graduates in the 1990s, faced with the worst job market for college graduates in more than a decade, opted for graduate school as a haven from unemployment (McFadden, 1991). Schools therefore reinforce the legitimacy of the economy by reducing the pressures that could be created on a restricted labor market if all high school and college graduates demanded jobs simultaneously.

Educational institutions can also be powerful mechanisms for social change. When skills taught by schools include independent, critical, and creative thinking, they produce the potential for challenges to society to alter inequalities and discrimination. It was to prevent such challenges that the antebellum South prohibited teaching African American slaves to read. More recently, critical thinking and the consequent challenges to institutions promoted pressures to pass and implement desegregation policies. We will return to these issues in Chapter 12, "Education."

The State

Structural functionalist sociologists conventionally view the **state** as an institution designed to protect society's members from internal and external threats. To meet this obligation, the state frequently becomes the only institution that can legitimately use force and violence, doing so through its police force and militia (Weber, 1947). Except in police states, there are controls within the state on its own power as well: when the state exceeds legitimate use of its power, even its agents can be brought to trial, as in the case of police officers who brutally beat up suspects.

The state also establishes penal and civil codes to formally define standards of acceptable and unacceptable behaviors, responsibilities, and obligations, and it specifies sanctions for violations of these standards. These codes help transmit prevailing standards and expectations and motivate society's members to comply with them. Ideally, the laws also serve to resolve conflicts through clearly defined legal processes, to be conducted in courts before impartial judges and a jury of one's peers.

Finally, the state is designed to aid the economy by developing social welfare programs that distribute goods and services to individuals the economy cannot support. By enhancing the ability of the poor to consume goods and services, such programs indirectly support the private producers and the economy.

On the other hand, a critical analysis of the state reveals activities that may reproduce race and class inequalities. When the state is controlled by interests that are already advantaged (for example, white, wealthy, corporate interests), its legitimate use of force and violence may be directed against challengers to the system. As we noted earlier, this has historically been the case in the U.S. labor and civil rights movements.

At other times, the state may become the agent of change. In the United States the state is not a single entity controlled by an absolutely powerful elite. Instead, the state is composed of several levels of government in a hierarchy that allows the federal government to act to force local governments to change. For example, the federal government used the National Guard to enforce school desegregation in southern states in the 1950s.

The state may reinforce advantages of corporations over labor and advantages of the affluent over the poor through its tax structure. A recent study by Citizens for Tax Justice reported that in 1990, as a group, the wealthiest members of U.S. society paid 81 percent less in taxes than the total paid by the poorest members as a group. This occurred because of an emphasis on regressive sales and excise taxes, as opposed to progressive ability-to-pay income taxes (*Chronicle*, 1991: 1, 7). Sales taxes are regressive in that everyone, regardless of income, must pay the same tax on purchases; this means that the poor pay a higher proportion of their income than do the wealthy on food, clothing, transportation, fuel, and so on.

Moreover, the tax structure provides the affluent with tax breaks that are not accessible to the poor, thereby reducing the affluents' share of the total tax burden. For example, mortgage interest is tax-deductible. Since far more people in the middle and upper classes than in the poor and working classes are likely to own their homes, such a deduction mainly benefits the wealthier taxpayers. Indeed, while only 17 percent of U.S. taxpayers earn more than $50,000 per year, they are the recipients of more than 52 percent of mortgage deductions. And while an income of $50,000 per year is not considered wealthy by current standards, more than four-fifths of U.S. workers earn less than that amount; thus, mortgage tax breaks are inaccessible to the vast majority of the population. A mortgage tax deduction, then, not only reduces the tax burden of the relatively privileged few; it also becomes a form of welfare for them (Mariano, 1988: 20).

This same tax policy, manifestly designed to encourage home purchases, may have the indirect consequence of stimulating job creation in the construction and supply industries (lumber, concrete, brick, plumbing, electrical supplies, durable goods, shipping and moving, and so forth). The state as an institution thus may serve the latent function of reproducing inequality while simultaneously stimulating upward mobility through the creation of jobs in high-paying industries.

The state may reinforce other inequalities as well. The Medicaid program, for example, is manifestly designed to extend health care to the poor, thereby reducing economic inequalities and promoting a healthy work force. However, since the program focuses largely on acute-care needs, it neglects the needs of the chronically ill and physically and mentally disabled, thus underscoring and aggravating such persons' problems (Tanenbaum, 1989).

Furthermore, the state may reinforce dominant ideologies in its development and implementation of laws. For example, while civil rights legislation legally ensures equal rights regardless of race, sex, ethnicity, religion, or physical ability, in fact racial and ethnic minorities, women, individuals with disabilities, and religious minorities may find their protections limited by the various ways the laws are interpreted. Moreover, some minority interests remain unprotected, even in the written policy. Homosexual rights, frequently under attack, are often defined as outside the realm of the state. Thus, one consequence of the structure and process of the American state is continued domination by a privileged minority representing wealthy, white, largely male, and often corporate interests.

The state does not always provide equal protection under the laws. Racial minorities frequently charge that they are harassed or unfairly treated by police, courts, prisons, and laws that remain insensitive to issues of discrimination. Studies in several cities have noted that prosecuting lawyers often challenge African Americans during jury-selection processes and effectively keep them off juries that are likely to hear cases involving African American defendants (Benokraitis and Griffin-Keene, 1982; Possley, 1986; *Harvard Law Review*, 1988: 1557–1587). This raises the questions of whether these defendants are being tried by a jury of their peers and whether the judicial system is neutral. Moreover, racial minorities are frequently the target of police brutality and excessive use of force on the streets, as evidenced by the disturbing video of Rodney King, an African American, shown being severely beaten by members of the Los Angeles Police Department in 1991. Racial minorities often complain that they are also the victims of denigration and excessive force and violence at the hands of their guards in prisons (Johnson, 1990; McQuiston, 1990).

Unequal protection is also manifested as a class issue. During the 1980s, the U.S. government increasingly embraced policies that favored the wealthy. The ability of the affluent to drastically reduce their share of the federal tax burden (and thus indirectly of the state tax burden) through deductions, write-offs, and loopholes has effectively meant that they have decreased their financial support of public services at all levels. Faced with reduced funding, the local levels of the state are finding it difficult to maintain adequate police forces, and the protection provided to the public is often insufficient. At the same time, however, the affluent do not suffer. Instead, they purchase their own protection by hiring private security guards. Robert B. Reich notes, "The number of private security guards in the United States now exceeds the number of public police officers" (1991: 42). Thus, the state's decision to shift the responsibility of protection to the local level, coupled with its policy of tax structures that overwhelmingly favor the wealthy, means that the state provides unequal protection to society's members on the basis of class.

Similarly, gender is an issue in unequal state protection. Women who have been raped still complain of being psychologically raped a second time by insensitive police, lawyers, judges, and other members of the judicial system who inquire about their previous relationships and their manner of dress when these women attempt to bring their attackers to justice. We still debate whether a victim's past relationships are admissible evidence during a rape trial. And many communities still treat wife abuse as a private matter of domestic dispute to be dealt with by the parties involved, rather than as a violation of the law. Fortunately, more and more communities are beginning to treat wife abuse as a crime of assault and battery, thereby opening the possibility for greater state protection of women.

However, such protection of women is still quite imperfect: once an attacker has served the specified term, the state does not typically follow up with restrictions for the attacker. For example, a Connecticut woman's estranged husband repeatedly beat her brutally. After several visits by the police, her husband was forbidden to go near her. But the state did not follow up on the injunction, and her husband finally tried to kill her. The savage attack resulted in permanent damage to her nervous system: she walks with a decided limp and sometimes has headaches and difficulty with speech. Her husband was brought to trial, found guilty, and served a prison sentence. However, in 1991 he was paroled for good behavior, and the state did not see fit to prohibit him from residing in Connecticut. The woman now lives in constant fear that, since the state did not protect her from him before, she is vulnerable to more attacks (see Park and Schindehette, 1989).

There is some evidence to suggest that a pattern defines who receives less-than-perfect protection. Those groups in society who have relatively little power, particularly women, racial minorities, homosexuals, and the poor, have found themselves to be the victims of state neglect, at best, and of violence at the hands of agents of the state, at worst. The state appears to provide the best protection to those who already benefit most from the way the state is organized and who have the power to ensure that this organization continues. In particular, the affluent in the United States, who are largely white, have historically had the power to protect the state from serious challenges and in turn have benefited from its protection of their safety, their affluence, and their position.

Institutions as Dynamic Structures

Institutions are not inexorable and unchangeable. The form and content of institutions may vary from one society to another or from one time period to another within a single society. There may also be several simultaneous alternative forms of a given institution within a single society. But the institution itself in some form or another remains identifiable as an institution everywhere. For example, there are many contrasting structural forms that may still be classified as family: nuclear families (two parents of opposite sex who are married and their offspring), extended families (nuclear families plus other related individuals, such as grandparents, aunts, uncles, cousins), single-parent families, childless couples, gay and lesbian couples, live-in couples (two people of opposite sex who are not married), blended stepfamilies, and so on. All are families, grouping individuals into a common living arrangement to obtain the necessary goods and services for survival. They all transmit to their members the knowledge and skills needed to function in society. And they sometimes replenish the population.

Institutions, then, are not set in concrete. They are dynamic structures that respond to changes and challenges. But what remain, regardless of alterations in form, are structures of organized social life that are designed to satisfy fundamental social needs and that often produce unintended consequences.

The basic institutions do not operate in isolation either. They interact and affect one another. For example, the institutions of the economy and the state affect the family and education. When the state determines that education systems must be funded by property-tax revenues, it affects schools' curricula and facilities and thus how effective these will be. In this way, decisions made by the state reinforce the schools' consequence of perpetuating class (and often racial) inequality. When the economy is in a recession, it affects the family by altering the employment status of family members. This may in turn affect gender roles as well as reinforce class inequalities, since production workers are typically the first and hardest hit in a recession. When the state awards child custody primarily to the mother (except in extreme cases) during a divorce, but does not enforce child-support payment responsibilities, it is reinforcing gender inequalities. So great are the inequalities in earnings between males and females and the gendered division of paid and unpaid (that is, housework) labor that in the first year after a divorce the mother's income typically declines by 73 percent and the father's *improves* by 42 percent (Weitzman, 1985).

The state's approach to child-custody arrangements also has the latent consequence of supporting some family forms and undermining others. Single parenthood becomes an economic liability, whereas the nuclear family becomes an asset. We will elaborate on these issues in Chapter 14, "Family."

SOCIAL MOVEMENTS: CHALLENGE AND CHANGE

Although institutions may produce inequalities, we are not powerless to affect how they fulfill their functions. **Social movements,** for example, are often large-scale organizational structures within which individuals working together may alter how institutions and whole societies operate. In Poland, workers organized in the outlawed union Solidarity were able collectively to strike, ultimately shifting the Polish communist government to one that permitted free elections of noncommunist leaders. Prior to this, elections were not part of the country's political structure, nor was participation by any party other than the Communist party.

The women's movement in the United States (which is, in fact, several movements, depending upon the kinds of changes sought) has had variable success in obtaining legislation and Supreme Court decisions designed to promote social and political rights, greater control over reproduction, and greater protection from sexual harassment. There is still a gulf between legislation and implementation, and legislation still does not guarantee equal economic rights, but the women's movement has succeeded in weakening at least some of the barriers to participation in U.S. society.

Black South Africans, organized in the outlawed African National Congress (ANC), collectively defied the white minority government, holding mass funerals and demonstrations and enlisting world support for their struggle. Together, they succeeded in forcing the white government to dismantle the discriminatory institution of apartheid. Under that system, blacks were not allowed to vote; were segregated in public as well as private facilities, housing, education, and transportation; were forced to relocate into tribal "homelands" designated by the government; and were denied the right to freedoms of assembly, speech, and movement. Such restrictive macro-structures would have been daunting for an individual to alter, but the collective pressure applied by the ANC and its international allies facilitated a change in South African social and political structures that many had thought impossible. Today the ANC holds the reins of government in South Africa after the first election in which all South Africans were able to vote.

The civil rights movement in the United States linked individuals and groups (such as churches, civic groups, student groups, and local black organizations) in a coalition to pressure and change institutions that reinforced racial inequality. Their efforts led to the Supreme Court ruling that separate educational institutions on the basis of race are inherently unequal. This fundamentally altered the structure of schools' populations, if not the manner in which schools are funded. Pressure from the move-

Social movements often successfully challenge and change social structures and institutional inequalities. In South Africa, organized resistance to the white minority government policy of apartheid led to a dramatic reversal of that policy and to an unprecedented open election. For the first time, black South Africans were able to vote.

ment also ultimately elicited civil rights legislation mandating voting rights and equal opportunity and affirmative action programs. These laws made it illegal to deny access to political, educational, or occupational opportunities on the basis of race. And while the civil rights movement's efforts have certainly not eradicated racism or eliminated the inequalities that institutions may reproduce, they have altered in some ways how institutions operate.

The disability rights movement has been somewhat less visible, but it has been fairly successful in redressing grievances and inequalities generated against the disabled by social institutions. Part of its success may be traced to the public perception that, unlike more stigmatized groups (such as gays, lesbians, and the poor), the disabled are a worthy minority. Moreover, disabilities affect all races, classes, and genders, making it likely that we each know someone personally who is disabled. Thus, the disability movement may face a less hostile public than other groups. Whatever the reason for its success, however, the disability rights movement has been able to produce important institutional changes. In many cases legislation has given the disabled greater access to public transportation (Olson, 1984). In Italy, La Lega per il Diritto al Lavero Digli Handicappati (The National League for the Right to Work of the Handicapped) has worked to eliminate architectural barriers to full participation in the labor force. The group's efforts include making professional jobs accessible for the disabled (Tudor, 1989). In the United States, such efforts have resulted in making buildings more accessible, with ramps to accommodate wheelchairs, elevators with floor indicators in Braille, and bathrooms with wider stalls, low handles, and raised seat levels. Many cities also construct sidewalks that slope at street corners so wheelchairs can negotiate the streets. And in some cities "walk–don't walk" lights emit loud signals so that visually impaired pedestrians can know when it is safe to cross the street. Most recently, efforts of the disability rights movement helped gain passage of the Americans with Disabilities Act in 1990.

This discussion of social movements suggests that changing institutions may be a very long, slow process but that change is not impossible. It also suggests how individuals may affect macro-structures. Individuals acting alone are not likely to be successful; but when people join together in a common effort, they can, in fact, collectively act as agents to alter these structures.

CONCLUSION

How do events and relationships around the world affect our everyday lives? We are all situated within a world-system, of which our own society is only one part. Changes in the relationships among the world-system's components—for example, the invasion of one nation by another—can have ramifications that reach right down into the lives of individuals in societies around the world. Our personal lives are not explicable without reference to where our own society stands within this world-system. Our nation's central position in the world-system has begun to erode in recent years as, for example, other nations successfully compete against the United States in international markets. This has affected everything in the United States, from the ability of individuals to find jobs to the quality and cost of public services upon which each of us depends.

Just as all persons are linked to the world-system through their societal membership, so are they linked to their own society through participation in its institutions. In one way or another, we all have some kind of relationship to the central institutions of family, religion, the economy, education, and the state. The functioning of these institutions influences our biographies directly, often affecting us differently depending upon our race, class, and/or gender. These factors come to be organizing principles around which institutions frequently operate. For example, in times of economic stagnation, the persons who experience the highest rates of unemployment tend to be those working in the lowest-paying jobs and are thus most likely to be individuals of color and females. In comparative terms, then, those who are white, affluent, and male are less likely to lose their jobs, and if they do, they are likely to find work sooner.

To sum up, as relationships among components of the world-system change, the operations of entire societies may be affected, and within societies the functioning of central institutions may exact costs from some people and not others. Less commonly, concerted collective actions undertaken by individuals may alter institutional and societal operations; even the world-system itself may undergo change. (Chapter 9, "Social Change and Social Movements," will investigate this process in detail.)

While it is true that each of us is part of a much larger set of structures through our participation in institutions, our society, and the world-system, we are not entirely powerless to affect how these macro-structures operate or are organized. Change occurs at all levels of this set of structures, whether out of consensus on the need for change or out of conflict over the status quo. Each of us can be involved in making change; we need not be only acted upon by society.

The discussion of social movements brings up the question of how we, as individuals, are linked to these more abstract levels of structure. Just as there are macro-level structures, there are micro-level and middle-range structures that distribute and organize individuals locally, defining positions and behaviors of individuals and linking them to the macro-structures. It is to these more local structures that we turn in the next chapter.

THINKING CRITICALLY

1. Global trade and production relationships form macro-structures that influence our daily existence. Consider the women in the boxed reading. How does the global division of labor affect them? Discuss how these relationships affect your own life.

2. Select an important and current problem facing nations all over the world (such as population growth, nuclear danger, AIDS, food shortage, homelessness). Analyze how different social structures in at least two different nations may contribute to how these nations approach the problem.

3. Examine your own family (or your religious organization or the educational system you attend) and identify the manifest and latent functions it performs. Describe how the institutions may produce the latent functions you identify.

4. At the start of the chapter we asked you where your clothing was made and where your car or stereo was manufactured. What social structures contributed to bringing these items into your possession? What are the manifest and latent functions of these structures in the manufacture of consumer goods?

5. You may know someone (perhaps yourself) who has been stationed with a military unit somewhere in the world. Identify the location of the military assignment, and discuss the social structures that may have contributed to the assignment. Discuss the manifest and latent functions of the assignment. How did the social structures affect the daily life of the individual stationed abroad? How did they affect his or her family?

KEY TERMS

social structure, *40*
macro-level social structures, *40*
world-system, *41*
core nations, *41*
peripheral nations, *41*
semiperipheral nations, *41*
society, *49*
nations, *49*
structural functional
   perspective, *50*
greenhouse effect, *50*

critical analysis, *51*
functional imperatives, *52*
institutions, *53*
manifest functions, *53*
latent functions, *53*
family, *55*
religion, *58*
economy, *59*
education, *62*
state, *64*
social movements, *68*

SUGGESTED READINGS

Hernando de Soto, *The Other Path: The Invisible Revolution in the Third World.* New York: Harper Collins, 1990. An analysis of the rise of the informal, or black-market, economy in Peru in response to inefficiencies in the formal economic institutions in that country.

Michael B. Katz, *In the Shadow of the Poorhouse: A Social History of Welfare in America.* New York: Basic Books, 1986. An exploration of the intersection of institutions of the state, the economy, and the family in creating and addressing poverty and welfare policy in the United States.

Manning Marable, *How Capitalism Underdeveloped Black America.* Boston: South End Press, 1983. A historical analysis of the effects of economic, political, and social macro-structures on the lives of African Americans.

Jerome Skolnick and Elliott Currie (eds.), *Crisis in American Institutions,* 8th ed. New York: Harper Collins, 1991. A collection of readings about structural strains and contradictions within institutions in the United States and the problems these may produce.

Kathryn Ward (ed.), *Women Workers and Global Restructuring.* Ithaca, NY: ILR Press, 1990. An anthology of the effects of the global division of labor and state economic strategies on women in the world-system.

SOCIAL STRUCTURE: MID- AND MICRO-LEVELS

Most of us spend very little time alone or in isolation from others. From birth we enter into social relationships with different people. Usually our first relationships are with members of our family, neighbors, and playmates. We develop additional social relationships as we meet people in school, in clubs, on sports teams, at places of worship, and on jobs. Any setting in which people interact—whether it be a street gang or an exclusive country club—serves as a means of developing social relationships.

Sociologists are interested in studying the nature and impact of people's involvement in different social groups and organizations. Within social groups

3

and organizations, individuals occupy different positions, or statuses, and fulfill particular roles. In this chapter we shall explore the concept of group and the kinds of social groups and organizations that are important to our lives. We shall also look at the organizational principles of bureaucracy and democracy and examine how they differ in their effects on our lives. Finally, we shall examine how individuals come to occupy various social statuses and roles and what happens when people find themselves caught up in contradictory or conflicting social roles. In short, we shall be exploring ways in which social structures at the mid-level (groups and organizations) and micro-level (statuses and roles) are important to the biography of the individual.

GROUPS AND THE INDIVIDUAL

We have all, at some time, attended a concert or sporting event. You arrive with hundreds of other people, find a seat, hopefully enjoy yourself, and participate by clapping and cheering. Such an audience is not, in sociological terms, a group. Rather, it is a **social aggregate,** a collection of individuals with no real interpersonal ties or patterned relationships.

Classrooms of college students, if they are fairly small in size, often evolve from social aggregates to something much closer to what sociologists mean by the term "group." The first day of class most people don't know one another and have little basis for interaction. As time goes on, students begin to recognize one another in and out of class, share gripes and lecture notes, study together for exams, form ties, and develop relationships. As the professor comes down the hall to enter class, she is likely to hear a lively chorus of interaction that is quite different from the relative silence that greeted her entry on the first day.

In a sociological sense, a **group** occurs only when there is regular interaction among a collection of individuals. Through this interaction people enter into orderly and predictable ties and relationships with one another. Orderliness is assisted by the formation and acceptance of rules of proper behavior, or **norms.** For example, a group norm may be "Never snitch on a friend" or "Men don't work at the office without a suit and tie." If new members join the group, they must learn and adhere to the norms. Failure to adopt these norms will make it difficult for a new member to form the social ties and relationships integral to a group.

Human beings are social animals. They rely on group memberships for everything from friendship to economic survival. Because of this, the groups in which we are involved form an important part of our personal biographies. Individuals can shape the character of their group, but the group's character also helps shape the thinking and behavior of its individual members. For example, charismatic leaders (see Weber, 1947) may give specific direction to a religious group, but participation in collective rituals and ceremonies helps members arouse one another's sense of group belonging and the desire to remain involved. Given the influence of groups, sociologists feel it is important to examine the kinds of groups in which people typically find themselves.

Primary and Secondary Groups

Sociologists generally distinguish between two different kinds of groups, primary and secondary. The term **primary group** was introduced many years ago by sociologist Charles Horton Cooley (1929). Primary groups tend to have a small number of members who interact frequently. Members share important connections that bring them together, including kinship ties, school attendance, neighborhood location, or employment at a workplace. The prototypical example of a primary group is the family. Primary groups are a source of friendship, companionship, and support, but they may also give rise to serious conflict. Because relationships within primary groups tend to be very strong, these groups play a central role in our lives.

A classic study by sociologist Herbert Gans (1982) revealed the importance of primary groups. He was interested in looking at the everyday lives of white working-class families. He chose a run-down, low-income neighborhood in Boston's West End, considered a "slum" by city officials and planners (the West End neighborhood would later be torn down and its residents dispersed as part of "urban renewal"). Gans found that the lives of working-class people in the neighborhood revolved around what he termed a *peer-group society*. In Gans's words,

> The primary group is a peer group society because most of the West Ender's relationships are with peers, that is, among people of the same sex, age, and life-cycle status (Gans, 1982: 37).

Males and females each had their own primary-group affiliations, and these in turn were roughly divided by different ages and generations.

Adult peer groups were primarily based on kinship. Members shared common interests and backgrounds (most were Italian Americans) and came together regularly. The adult peer group not only provided companionship and a sense of belonging; it was also a source of news and entertainment. It was a setting in which individuals could express their unique personalities and feel they were making a well-received contribution.

The opportunities for expression provided by the peer-group society were in marked contrast to what the adult men, for example, experienced in their low-level factory and service jobs. For them, the peer group was a place to escape to from the "outside world" of poorly paid, insecure employment. Given the nature of the jobs they could find, they viewed work in highly utilitarian terms: it was necessary, not enjoyable, and provided means to participate in the peer-group society. For example, it enabled men to play the role of hosts at get-togethers and to lay claim to the prestige associated with being successful providers and breadwinners.

All of us participate in primary groups, small groups of people who interact frequently and offer friendship, companionship, and support. These people, enjoying an Easter Sunday picnic in a city park, are primary group members who share common kinship ties.

According to Gans, for adult women the peer-group society performed other functions. The women spent most of their free time and communicated most with relatives and friends of the same sex; Gans felt that their emotional involvement with the peer group surpassed that with their husbands. He believed this was the case because of their very marginal and insecure economic position. Faced with the possibility of losing a husband through death or divorce at any time, the women looked to their peer group for support that would be available at all times.

The peer-group society Gans described also played a negative role. In some ways it encompassed and trapped its members, channeling their thinking and behavior along certain lines. For example, one norm of the peer group was that members focus on being liked and noticed within the group *(person-orientation)*. This orientation came at the expense of focusing on particular objectives such as pursuing a career or improving one's material circumstances *(object-orientation)*. Being object-oriented violated group norms because it involved detaching oneself from group life to focus time and attention in other directions. Object-oriented individuals were made to feel like traitors pursuing selfish aims. So, if a person wished to enjoy the benefits of the peer-group society, he or she had to suppress any aspirations that conflicted with the norm of person-orientation.

The peer group, therefore, was alternately a comfort and a source of oppressive confinement. Given its benefits, along with the fact that it was linked heavily to kinship, the peer-group society—as a primary group—could not be rejected lightly.

The example provided by the peer-group society may lead you to think about your own primary-group memberships. As a primary group, the peer-group society revolved around intimate, face-to-face relationships. Each individual developed strong bonds with the others and could depend upon the group for support. In return, each member had to adhere to the norms of the group. Expressing ideas not shared by others in the group could result in criticism and even rejection by the group's members. How do the features of primary groups of which you have been a member compare with those of the peer-group society? What benefits or rewards have you gained from being a member of such groups? What disadvantages or costs have been associated with your involvement? The answers to such questions will help you assess the importance of primary groups in shaping the makeup of your biography.

Secondary groups are very different social phenomena, although certainly they are as much a part of our daily lives as primary groups. Secondary groups are usually formed for a purpose, such as to accomplish a certain task (provide fire protection) or achieve a goal (make a profit manufacturing and selling cars). Examples of secondary groups include schools, government agencies, military services, corporations, and voluntary associations. (The latter are secondary groups in which members' involvement is a matter of choice, participation usually takes only a small portion of members' time, and commitment to the group and its purpose may be highly variable. The Girl Scouts and the National Rifle Association are examples.) Secondary groups vary in size from relatively few members to thousands of members. The degree and intensity of interaction and personal involvement are ordinarily less than those found in a primary group.

Note, however, that it is common for primary groups to form as people become acquainted through participation in secondary groups, as is the case when a group of people become close friends at school or in the workplace. Indeed, the impersonal nature of many secondary groups often prompts participants to form primary-group relationships for the rewards they may provide. Moreover, as we shall see later in our discussion of informal organization within bureaucracies, the formation of primary groups can affect the functioning of secondary groups.

In a secondary group, members may come and go; their emotional ties to the group are ordinarily not strong enough to make leaving a serious problem. People become members for a limited purpose and often use their membership in the group to accomplish a personal goal. Even if we are not members of particular secondary groups, we usually have some contact with such organizations; we feel the impact of their presence in our own lives and in the lives of those around us.

While employees of a large firm or members of the military tend to be a heterogeneous collection of people, members of some secondary groups often have more in common than their membership in the group. In the example we describe below, that of a voluntary association, the members happen to share a great deal in common: class position, gender, and race.

In contrast to our knowledge of "ordinary people," such as those studied by Herbert Gans, much less is known about the everyday lives of society's elites. Affluence and power enable elites to have a great deal of privacy, and such persons have little incentive to admit researchers into their personal domains. Nevertheless, the research of sociologist G. William Domhoff (1983, 1990) has provided some data about the elite (see also Kerbo, 1991: chap. 7; Gilbert and Kahl, 1993: 210–213; Rothman, 1993: 82–86). According to Domhoff, the members of a social elite in the United States interact and intermarry. Their wealth, high annual incomes, and lifestyle distinguish them from members of other strata. Domhoff estimates that this upper class makes up no more than 0.5 percent of the population (1983: 49). Upper-class activities often include membership in private clubs (for example, country clubs, men's clubs, and women's clubs).

Assisted by a chance acquaintance with a woman from the upper class, sociologist Susan Ostrander managed a rare glimpse into the world of the social elite. She secured interviews with 36 women from upper-class backgrounds who all lived in the same large midwestern city. One of the topics that interested Ostrander was how the women's group memberships—specifically, their involvement in private upper-class country clubs and women's clubs—affected their lives and the lives of others. Two of the women explained:

> The club is the place to go where you can have lunch and discuss business without having to wade through the mass of people. You want to have people who are congenial, all the same social group (Ostrander, 1984: 97).

> If I go out to the club to relax, I don't want people around I don't care about. Sameness, homogeneity—they're very pleasant. . . . I like having people like myself around, quiet, conservative, nice to their children, who don't run around with other people's wives, and are interested in the community (Ostrander, 1984: 100).

This secondary group is organized around one fundamental principal: exclusivity. Club membership is by invitation only, and in this way only those who are considered "congenial" or "compatible" gain entrance. Non-upper-class women are not considered appropriate or worthy persons with whom to interact socially.

Exclusivity is helped along by a screening process that involves current members. One woman described how this process works:

> We're full now. When people resign we take new members. We have a waiting list. Three (current) members have to write letters, and then we vote on each one. They have to be attractive, interested in civic things, art, music, friends of your friends and of your friends' friends (Ostrander, 1984: 104).

The screening process not only keeps non-upper-class women out but also effectively monitors admissions in other ways. As one upper-class woman commented when asked about admission criteria,

> Well, of course there's racial discrimination. That's the biggest. Then there're religious differences (Ostrander, 1984: 101).

No matter how accomplished they are, women of color and Jewish women are rarely invited to join.

The club is a place where members see friends, entertain outside the home, network with others in their social class, hold meetings of groups to which they belong, and even meet "suitable" marriage partners. Members use upper-class clubs to "build and maintain class traditions, networks, and associations" (Ostrander, 1984: 104).

When club members move to a new city and want to join a new club, they may present a letter of introduction from the club to which they previously belonged. In this way, members can be integrated into the upper class in other locales, a process that maintains a national upper-class network. Other institutions, such as private schools and exclusive vacation resorts, also support this network. As one woman put it,

> I'd say [the letter of introduction] is pretty typical, although we all know each other anyway, perhaps from boarding school or from having spent our summers together in Maine. I know people from all over. That's just the way it is. That's the kind of life this is. You just know people. I don't know any other kind of life and it's nice (Ostrander, 1984: 106).

Like other secondary groups, the upper-class private club provides a setting in which people may develop primary-group relations. Indeed, in this example women may get involved in the club through already-existing family and friendship ties as well as develop new primary relationships within the club.

The workings of many different secondary groups influence our biographies. In the next section we shall discuss how our experiences in these groups are affected by their structure.

GROUP STRUCTURE: BUREAUCRACY VERSUS DEMOCRACY

Secondary groups can be structured in several different ways. In this section we shall focus mainly on two organizational principles: bureaucracy and democracy. Because our lives are shaped by the structure of the organizations in which we participate, we must be able to establish the degree to which our own society is characterized by bureaucratic or democratic organizational tendencies.

Bureaucracy

The term **bureaucracy** is often used pejoratively. We think of red tape that interferes with getting things done or of inflexible employees who say things like "I just work here; I don't make the rules." Sociologists, however, use the term to refer to the way in which certain secondary groups are organized. Such groups may or may not be responsive to our needs, but that is not their defining feature.

The term "bureaucracy" was central to the thinking of German sociologist Max Weber. Weber saw the spread of bureaucracy as a dominant, or master, trend in the Western world. He identified five features of the *ideal-type*, or model, bureaucracy:

1. The organization contains a clear-cut division of labor: every member is responsible for particular tasks.
2. Authority is organized in a hierarchy: everyone (except of course the individual at the top) reports to someone whose directives are to be obeyed.
3. The activities of all members of the organization are governed by a set of formally established, written rules and regulations.
4. Members are to carry out their organizational responsibilities impartially and without the exercise of favoritism or bias toward others.
5. Recognition, rewards, and status in the organization are based upon meritorious performance (Gerth and Mills, 1968: chap. 8).

The first example of bureaucracy that may occur to you is likely to be an organization in which you have been or are working. To some extent, most work settings are organized along bureaucratic principles. In a study using the method of historical research, Richard Edwards (1979) examined the evolution of work organization in the United States. In his view, while changes in ways of organizing work have indeed occurred over the last couple of centuries, the central issue facing employers has remained the same: how to get as much work as possible out of their workers for the least amount of money. In Edwards's view, resolving this problem has required that employers deal with the issue of control.

Before the Industrial Revolution, work organizations were relatively small operations in which the "boss" ran the enterprise. Whether the owner or hired supervisors oversaw the work, power over workers was exercised personally and directly. Edwards termed this type of structure *simple control,* a form of organization that still persists today in small enterprises. In the late nineteenth and early twentieth centuries, as firm owners relied more on technologically advanced machinery and the assembly line became common, power over workers came to be exercised by the impersonal demands of technology. The machinery and other apparatus in the workplace limited the activities of each worker and dictated the pace of work. On an assembly line, for example, working too slowly quickly becomes apparent. Edwards called this form of structure *technical control.* Technical control still exists in many of today's factories, although automation and robotization are reducing the proportion of U.S. workers involved in assembly-line settings.

During the twentieth century, as work organizations increased in size and the white-collar sector grew, *bureaucratic control* became the dominant organizational structure. Bureaucratic control operates by surrounding people with rules. Employers require that their workers conform to standardized job descriptions, and they evaluate employee job performance on checklists and rating forms. Of course, it is possible to create new job descriptions, alter old ones, and make judgments about job performance, but the ability to do so is in the hands of a few persons occupying the very top positions in the organization. Thus, the individuals who make and change the organization's rules tend to be removed from the average worker. This is particularly the case in large organizations. The power wielded by such persons is masked, for it is the rules—not the top-level bosses—that workers experience as coercive and controlling. For many workers, one consequence of bureaucratic control has been dissatisfaction and alienation (Garson, 1980).

But even persons occupying managerial positions in bureaucratic work organizations are affected by the nature of the activities and relationships bureaucracy promotes. Sociologist Robert Jackall (1988) has demonstrated this in his research on corporate managers. While corporate managers hold positions of substantial responsibility and receive generous financial remuneration, bureaucracy has important effects upon their everyday lives. Here, Jackall sums up the impact of bureaucracy:

> Bureaucratic work shapes people's consciousness in decisive ways. . . . [It] regularizes people's experiences of time and indeed routinizes their lives by engaging them on a daily basis in rational, socially approved purposive action; it brings them into daily proximity with and subordination to authority, creating in the process upward-looking stances that have decisive social and psychological consequences; . . . and it creates subtle measures of prestige and an elaborate status hierarchy that, in addition to fostering an intense competition for status, also makes the rules, procedures, social contexts, and protocols of an organization paramount psychological and behavioral guides (Jackall, 1988: 5–6).

Jackall's interviews with corporate managers revealed that they were under pressure to conform to an organizational code of morality that often differed from their own. As one former corporate vice president put it, "What is right in the corporation is not what is right in a man's home or in his church. What is right in the corporation is what the guy above you wants from you. That's what morality is in the corporation" (Jackall, 1988: 6). Jackall's research suggests that conformity to an organization's code of morality is a key prerequisite for personal success in the world of corporate managers. Research on other categories of white-collar personnel in bureaucratic work organizations, such as persons in sales positions (see Oakes, 1990), has revealed similar demands for conformity.

In this century a large percentage of the U.S. labor force has come to be employed by large, bureaucratic organizations—in both the public and the private sectors (Perrow, 1986). For example, approximately 15 percent of the labor force works for agencies of government, with almost one in five of these workers being federal employees. Figure 3.1 illustrates the dimensions of the federal bureaucracy. Moreover, 20 percent of our industrial labor force is employed by sixteen of the largest U.S. corporations (Neubeck, 1991: 156, 158). Relatively few people have very much power within their own workplace. The organized labor movement, which traditionally worked to increase the power of workers vis-à-vis employers, has grown weak. Unions have been adversely affected by the loss of many unionized industrial jobs and a climate of government hostility toward their activities (Hearn, 1988: 103–119). Today, unions represent less than 17 percent of the U.S. labor force, a 50 percent drop since the mid-1950s.

The typical large work organization further discourages collective activity by workers through its reward structure: the substantial numbers of job titles, occupational levels, pay scales, and symbols of prestige that differen-

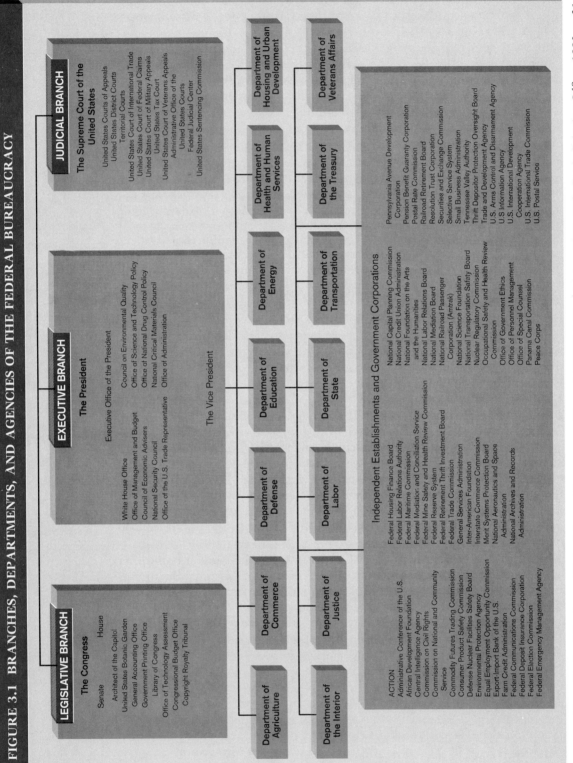

FIGURE 3.1 BRANCHES, DEPARTMENTS, AND AGENCIES OF THE FEDERAL BUREAUCRACY

LEGISLATIVE BRANCH

The Congress

Senate   House

Architect of the Capitol
United States Botanic Garden
General Accounting Office
Government Printing Office
Library of Congress
Office of Technology Assessment
Congressional Budget Office
Copyright Royalty Tribunal

EXECUTIVE BRANCH

The President

Executive Office of the President

White House Office
Office of Management and Budget
Council of Economic Advisers
National Security Council
Office of the U.S. Trade Representative

Council on Environmental Quality
Office of Science and Technology Policy
Office of National Drug Control Policy
National Critical Materials Council
Office of Administration

The Vice President

JUDICIAL BRANCH

The Supreme Court of the
United States

United States Courts of Appeals
United States District Courts
Territorial Courts
United States Court of International Trade
United States Court of Federal Claims
United States Court of Military Appeals
United States Tax Court
United States Court of Veterans Appeals
Administrative Office of the
United States Courts
Federal Judicial Center
United States Sentencing Commission

Department of Agriculture

Department of Commerce

Department of Defense

Department of Education

Department of Energy

Department of Health and Human Services

Department of Housing and Urban Development

Department of the Interior

Department of Justice

Department of Labor

Department of State

Department of Transportation

Department of the Treasury

Department of Veterans Affairs

Independent Establishments and Government Corporations

ACTION
Administrative Conference of the U.S.
African Development Foundation
Central Intelligence Agency
Commission on Civil Rights
Commission on National and Community
    Service
Commodity Futures Trading Commission
Consumer Product Safety Commission
Defense Nuclear Facilities Safety Board
Environmental Protection Agency
Equal Employment Opportunity Commission
Export-Import Bank of the U.S.
Farm Credit Administration
Federal Communications Commission
Federal Deposit Insurance Corporation
Federal Election Commission
Federal Emergency Management Agency

Federal Housing Finance Board
Federal Labor Relations Authority
Federal Maritime Commission
Federal Mediation and Conciliation Service
Federal Mine Safety and Health Review Commission
Federal Reserve System
Federal Retirement Thrift Investment Board
Federal Trade Commission
General Services Administration
Inter-American Foundation
Interstate Commerce Commission
Merit Systems Protection Board
National Aeronautics and Space
    Administration
National Archives and Records
    Administration

National Capital Planning Commission
National Credit Union Administration
National Foundation on the Arts
    and the Humanities
National Labor Relations Board
National Mediation Board
National Railroad Passenger
    Corporation (Amtrak)
National Science Foundation
National Transportation Safety Board
Nuclear Regulatory Commission
Occupational Safety and Health Review
    Commission
Office of Government Ethics
Office of Personnel Management
Office of Special Counsel
Panama Canal Commission
Peace Corps

Pennsylvania Avenue Development
    Corporation
Pension Benefit Guaranty Corporation
Postal Rate Commission
Railroad Retirement Board
Resolution Trust Corporation
Securities and Exchange Commission
Selective Service System
Small Business Administration
Tennessee Valley Authority
Thrift Depositor Protection Oversight Board
Trade and Development Agency
U.S. Arms Control and Disarmament Agency
U.S Information Agency
U.S. International Development
    Cooperation Agency
U.S. International Trade Commission
U.S. Postal Service

(*Source:* Office of Federal Registrar, *United States Government Manual, 1993/94,* Washington, D.C.: U.S. Gov't. Printing Office, 1993, p. 21.)

The term "bureaucracy" is popularly used to evoke negative images of an organization whose workers follow irrational rules and waste time, much like the worker in this cartoon. Indeed, bureaucratic work organizations often undergo periodic internal changes as managers try to increase efficiency and productivity.

tiate workers from one another. One feature of bureaucratic control, then, is the way in which it differentiates and divides people, making it very hard for workers to be aware of the things they have in common. White-collar and blue-collar workers, or professional and nonprofessional staff, fail to realize that they often share the same workplace problems, such as declining job security and difficulty getting the resources they need to do their work well.

Bureaucracy is so endemic in U.S. society that many people cannot imagine another way to organize human activity. Not only businesses but government agencies, labor unions, universities, hospitals, and many other types of secondary groups are organized along bureaucratic lines.

Sociologist Gary Fine's study of Little League baseball (1987) tells us that even the world of children's play has been subject to bureaucratization. It is coordinated by Little League, Inc., an organization with millions of dollars in assets. The organization operates under a charter awarded by the federal government. Under this charter, Little League is considered to be a quasi-governmental agency whose revenues are exempt from taxes. The charter calls for Little League to file an annual report on its finances and philosophy with the U.S. House of Representatives. Little League is also required to "shape its mission to the needs of the United States government (particularly in dealing with foreign leagues)" (Fine, 1987: 6). Presumably, this means accepting the responsibility of "promoting America" as part of its involvement in international competitions (Fine, 1987: 261).

Approximately 7,000 local Little Leagues represent more than 48,000 teams and over half a million players. Fine characterizes local leagues as "branches of a large bureaucratic organization" (1987: 7). Each league has a board of directors to oversee its operations, coaches to supervise the children and teach them how to play, umpires to interpret and enforce the official rules, and players who are expected to occupy their assigned positions and perform well. The entire operation of the game—from the length of the base paths to the number of innings to be played—is governed by decisions made by Little League, Inc. With its division of labor, hierarchy of authority, rules and regulations, and recognition based on merit, Little League baseball is an expression of the master trend toward bureaucratization.

German sociologist Robert Michels (1962) argued that bureaucratization of human activities was inevitable. The inevitability of bureaucracy was virtually a social law (much like a law of physics). In Michels's view, we are subject to an **iron law of oligarchy** in which there is always a tendency for organizations to be ruled by a few, even those that purport to be organized in accordance with democratic ideals. In the next section we shall see reason to doubt bureaucracy's inevitability and the existence of an "iron law."

Democracy

If bureaucracy involves control *of* people, **democracy** involves control *by* people. The power of a few over others that is at the heart of bureaucratic control shifts to the hands of the majority under democracy. Under bureaucracy most people have little or no power to shape the policies that affect them; in a democracy people are empowered to participate in shaping these policies precisely because they will be affected. Democratizing decision-making processes in existing organizations may be considered a radical idea in a society that is highly bureaucratized (Green, 1985). When people demand a say in decisions that affect their lives, they are demanding power. In the United States, just as in virtually every other nation in the world, such demands can be occasions for sharp conflict when made in a context where power has traditionally been held by a few.

Despite Robert Michels's view that we are subject to an iron law of oligarchy that makes bureaucracy inevitable, there *are* work organizations that incorporate principles of democratic organization. They are intriguing not only because they are uncommon but because they contradict the notion that the only way to successfully organize work is to institute a bureaucratic system or some other type of top-down control (Fischer and Sirianni, 1984: chap. 7).

Sociologists Joyce Rothschild and J. Allen Whitt have examined democratically controlled work cooperatives in the United States. Such cooperatives have a history going back to the late eighteenth century. Rothschild and Whitt suggest that since the late 1960s we have been experiencing a new wave of creation of such organizations as "alternative newspapers, arts and handicraft shops, food co-ops, publishing houses, restaurants, health clinics, legal collectives, natural foods bakeries, auto repair cooperatives, and retail stores" (1986: 11). Such cooperatives are organized at the local, grassroots level, are small in size (often 10 to 20 members), and frequently arise from members' commitment to progressive social change. Their nonbureaucratic organization typically reflects political values that view personal empowerment and involvement in the democratic process as fundamental goals.

Cooperatives are usually organized as a **direct democracy,** in which all members participate in decision-making. This is in contrast to the system of political governance in the United States, which is characterized by **representative democracy,** in which people elect others to make decisions for them. In theory, those elected represent the "will of the people." But as we shall see in Chapter 10, this is not always the case. Direct democracy is one means by which all members can express their needs and work with others in getting these needs met.

Just as the ideal-type, or model, bureaucracy described by Max Weber has certain key features, the cooperatives observed by Rothschild and Whitt had a set of common characteristics as well:

1. Power is shared within the membership as a whole, and decision-making involves discussion, negotiation, and consensus.
2. Rules are minimal; members are assumed to be capable of using discretion and common sense in conducting their activities.
3. There is a sense of community. People do not limit their interactions to the work tasks at hand but feel free to develop close relationships with one another.
4. The division of labor is minimal. Members share their knowledge and take turns rotating jobs when possible.
5. Material rewards are secondary to those otherwise derived from involvement in the group. Just as there is no hierarchy of authority, rewards are shared equally or nearly so.

From this list you might think that cooperatives are utopian forms of organization. But Rothschild and Whitt's research indicates that members must be ready to confront challenges. For example, democratic decision-making can be time-consuming. Differences among group members can at times be very intense and disturbing. Personality characteristics that may mesh well in bureaucratically controlled areas of life, such as a need for authority figures or an inability to make decisions in the face of ambiguity, may create problems when they unexpectedly emerge in a democratic setting. Majority rule under democratic decision-making is not a protection against poor decisions. And cooperatives may face external challenges— legal, economic, political, and cultural. Some fail because of internal and/or external challenges that cannot be overcome. But many do not fail, and they provide enormously rich experiences for their members.

Democratically run cooperatives need not be small. In a number of cases large-scale attempts at workplace democracy have been successful. For example, in the U.S. Pacific Northwest there are worker-owned and -managed cooperatives that produce plywood (see Jackall and Levin, 1984). Some of the most noteworthy examples of work cooperatives are outside the United States (see Bayat, 1991). The world's largest system of worker cooperatives was founded in the former socialist nation of Yugoslavia (Adizes, 1971). The cooperatives were established as state-owned industrial plants controlled and governed through a system of locally elected workers' councils. In Israel, approximately 4 percent of the population lives in 250 kibbutzim (Rayman, 1982). A *kibbutz* is a community of workers (and their families) who share ownership of its facilities and democratically determine policies concerning the production of goods and services. In the

87

Chapter 3

Social Structure:
Mid- and
Micro-Levels

Work organizations need not be bureaucratic, as demonstrated by the success of such worker-owned and democratically controlled production units as the kibbutzim in Israel. Here young workers unload materials from a truck.

Basque region of Spain, workers own and control large-scale manufacturing cooperatives in the industrial city of Mondragon; they produce stoves, refrigerators, steel, and other goods for an international market (Whyte and Whyte, 1988; Hacker, 1989: chaps. 6 and 7).

These examples once again indicate there is nothing inevitable about organizing a workplace along bureaucratic principles. The issue is really one of power—who will have it, and how it will be exercised (Whyte and Blasi, 1982; Zwerdling, 1984).

How Bureaucratic and Democratic Organizations Affect Our Lives

Persons whose lives are encompassed by highly bureaucratized organizations will behave and feel very differently than those who conduct their lives primarily in democratically organized settings. Bureaucratic organizations expect people to accommodate to their will, to become objects to whom things happen. Highly bureaucratized structures are likely to discourage spontaneity, innovative ideas, or creative group efforts that may call the status quo into question. The more a society is pervaded by bureaucracy, the more its organizational structures exert pressure on and control over the thinking and behavior of its members (Kanter and Stein, 1979).

Within democratic organizations people become subjects who make events happen. Democratic forms of organization can empower participants, providing them with degrees of freedom to decide how to conduct their own affairs. Persons who feel alienated and disgruntled when denied a say in what is going on around them may find that democratic structures open up new opportunities for the expression of their personalities and the achievement of personal goals. This is not to say that in democratic organizations "anything goes" and there are no restraints on members. Participants in democratic structures usually arrive at, if they do not start out with, some consensus as to the range of behavior and thinking they are willing to tolerate.

Today, people's lives often involve a mixture of experiences with bureaucratic and democratic organizations. You may work in an insurance company, following the office rules, fulfilling the narrow set of duties outlined in your job description, and jumping whenever the boss calls. But outside of work you may attend an evening meeting of the local parent-teacher organization, in which you serve as an elected officer; participate in a lunch-hour gathering of a free-wheeling book discussion group that you and your friends organized; accept an invitation to hear (and decide whether to support) a candidate seeking your political party's nomination; and spend a weekend hunting with fellow members of the collectively owned and operated Fish, Fur and Feather Club. While people's biographies are affected by participation in bureaucratic organizations, democratic structures may shape their biographies in important ways as well.

In nondemocratic societies, political elites use military and civilian bureaucracies to monitor and control all aspects of people's lives. In such societies, people eventually rebel and seek to create democratic organizational structures. Most nations in Latin America, a region long characterized by oppressive military dictatorships, have made a transition to greater democratic rule in recent years in response to popular movements. Eastern Europe and the Soviet Union were shaken apart by movements that were at least in part a reaction to the concentrated bureaucratic power of the state. The democracy movement in the People's Republic of China, brutally crushed in 1989 by tanks in Beijing's Tiananmen Square, will no doubt reappear. Resisting bureaucratic control is one way in which many people have sought to increase their freedom to influence their own biographies.

Informal Organization

Weber's model focused on bureacracy's formal characteristics (its hierarchy of authority, rules and regulations, and so on). Yet anyone who has worked in a bureaucratic setting knows that relationships spring up among groups of employees. Often these relationships have little or nothing to do with the bureaucratically prescribed division of labor or people's official job descriptions. They often involve people who are similar in age and of the same gender. Sociologists use the term **informal organization** to refer to social structures that emerge spontaneously as people interact in bureaucratic settings.

The importance of informal organization was first noted in research conducted in the 1930s (Roethlisberger and Dickson, 1939). Researchers at

Western Electric Company's Hawthorne Works in Chicago, where electrical components were assembled, were interested in helping the firm's management increase levels of production. The researchers assumed that one way to do this was to alter physical working conditions. They selected a group of workers and observed their reactions to changes in conditions, such as the amount of light in the workroom and the timing of rest breaks. But no matter what the researchers changed, there did not seem to be any consistent relationship between physical conditions and worker productivity.

The researchers continued their experiment. Finally they realized that the workers themselves created mutually accepted norms that guided their rates of production. According to management, these norms resulted in less being produced than was possible. The researchers tried to understand this restriction of output. It turned out that the workers were holding back their productivity out of fear. They believed that if management knew they could produce more, it would increase their production quotas without increasing their pay or would decide fewer workers were needed and lay some off. This research was taking place during the Depression of the 1930s, a time of widespread unemployment.

Within their group, the workers denounced and ridiculed those who broke ranks and produced above the norm, calling them "rate-busters" and "speed kings." At the same time, a worker who lagged too far below the norm was criticized as a "chiseler" who could possibly draw unwanted attention from management. Since most workers were concerned with earning and maintaining the respect and regard of their peers, few chose to deviate from the pressures to conform. The researchers concluded that informal relationships are important in influencing productivity levels and that the output of any individual worker should be considered a function of the informal organization in which that person participates.

Since the research at Hawthorne Electric, sociologists have conducted numerous studies in a variety of work settings and found informal organization to be operating and demanding conformity to its norms (Hollinger and Clark, 1982). At times, informal relationships actually facilitate work accomplishment, particularly when bureaucratic rules get in the way of handling problems or when established channels stifle communications that are important to organizational functioning. Workers may informally pass along knowledge that enables work to be done more safely and efficiently than bureaucratic procedures would allow (Gouldner, 1954; Kusterer, 1978). In some settings informal organization results in activities that distract workers from the mind-numbing nature of their labor and thus actually contributes to their productivity (Burawoy, 1982).

At the other extreme, informal organization has the potential of disrupting and sabotaging bureaucratic routine (see Sprouse, 1992). Let us look at two dramatic examples drawn from the auto industry. In the first example, workers actively resisted management's efforts to plan their role in production. In the second example, workers rebelled in similar ways against a new supervisor's efforts to "shape things up" and enforce previously neglected bureaucratic rules.

When Bill Watson (1971) took a temporary summer job in a Detroit auto factory, he was overwhelmed by the frenetic human activity demanded by

Informal organization is common in the workplace, since the relationships workers develop with one another often make routine jobs more bearable. These women share a laugh as they toil on the shop floor.

the constantly moving assembly line. Workers resembled robots, tied to their specialized function and place along the line. The assembly line ran inexorably at a pace that always seemed just slightly too fast. It seemed to dominate all human social interaction, or what little was possible given the incredible noise. Yet Watson quickly became aware, on the basis of participant observation in this work setting, that not all was what it seemed on the surface.

Watson found that the workers were engaged in daily and often overt struggles with management over everything from working conditions to the quality of the autos being produced. The struggles were made possible and carried out through an informal organization consisting of networks of "fictive kin": chains of friends and acquaintances across the auto plant who kept up channels of communication, did favors for one another, and looked for ways to cooperate in subverting management. The fictive-kin network extended outside the plant, through the bars surrounding it, and into local working-class neighborhoods where many of the autoworkers resided.

Workers used the fictive-kin network to establish their own rest break system. Workers in different parts of the plant would find ways to break down the assembly line at a specified hour on a given day, allowing everyone time to talk, read, or move about the plant to visit friends. When workers were asked to assemble engines out of parts known to be defective, the fictive-kin network rolled into action. Assembly workers either broke parts or misassembled the engines, and workers responsible for inspection cooperated by rejecting the engines and pulling them off the line.

The fictive-kin network made possible a great deal of organized theft. Workers would distract security guards at plant gates while peers smuggled out tools and auto parts. Similar organized distraction allowed workers to smuggle items into the plant. Chaise lounges were brought in, hoisted through ceiling traps in the bathrooms, and placed on the roof. Workers who could manage to "disappear," protected by false excuses given to supervisors by peers, were often able to escape the racket, heat, and oil-filled air by hiding on the roof for brief periods.

The heat in the plant in the summer was debilitating. Workers in one area responded by holding sporadic fire-hose fights; participants were protected by a network of lookouts who warned them whenever supervisors were coming. For a while those involved wore their wives' shower caps to work, a symbol which management could not fathom but which brought glee to coworkers across the plant.

One of management's rules stipulated that workers had to cease work ten minutes before their shift was over in order to wash their hands. Workers felt that this was a waste of time, since they could wash their hands in less than ten minutes. Using the fictive-kin network, they agreed to wash for only a few minutes, line up at the exit door, howl the sound of the shift whistle, and proceed to charge out early. For a time the supervisors were unable to mobilize enough counterforce to stop them.

Efforts to enforce conformity to bureaucratic rules among workers who have devised their own ways of accomplishing mind-numbing work may likewise foster rebellion. Ben Hamper, a riveter on a General Motors assembly line, describes workers' feisty reaction to a new supervisor's efforts in this regard:

> Enter the new boss, a self-proclaimed "troubleshooter." He had been enlisted to groom the rivet line into a more docile outpost. . . .
>
> With a tight grip on the whip, the new bossman started riding the crew. No music. No Rivet Hockey. No horseplay. No drinking. No card playing. No working up the line. No leaving the department. No doubling up. No this, no that. No questions asked.
>
> No way. After three nights of this imported bullyism, the boys had had their fill. Frames began sliding down the line minus parts. Rivets became crosseyed. Guns mysteriously broke down. The repairmen began shipping the majority of the defects, unable to keep up with the repair load.
>
> Sabotage was rather drastic; however it was an effective way of getting the point across. We simply had no other recourse. Sometimes these power-gods had to be reminded that it was we, the workers, who kept the place runnin'. . . .
>
> This new guy was nobody's dummy. He could see it all slippin' away, his goon tactics workin' against him. He pulled us all aside and suggested that we return to our old methods (Hamper, 1991: 206).

Do these workers appear irrational to you? Consider the context in which they live: Assembly-line systems of production are designed by management to leave workers with little, if any, say over what they will produce, how it will be produced, the pace of production, and the quality of the end product (Blauner, 1964). Worker dissatisfaction and alienation tend to be high. Yet, while assembly lines minimize workplace freedom, our society simultaneously values democracy and individual rights. The behavior of the autoworkers described by Watson and Hamper might be said to represent one expression of the contradiction between organizational control over workers and democratic values, in this case through the medium of informal organization. Through experiences such as these, an understanding of workers' needs and feelings has slowly become a part of management training.

Managers and workers occupy very different positions in an auto plant. As such, they have very different perspectives on the work to be done and on the respective roles each should play in the process. As we shall see in the next section, the positions we come to hold and the expectations attached to these positions are important in shaping our biographies.

STATUS AND ROLES

The term "social structure" is shorthand for the overall framework within and through which human beings relate to one another. In this chapter we have been discussing two forms of social structure in which all of us participate during the course of our lives: groups and organizations. We consider these to be **mid-level** forms of social structure, at a lower level of scale than those at the macro-level: social institutions, societies, and the world-system. In this section we shall address social structure at the individual level, or **micro-level,** and consider the concepts of status and role.

Status

We each belong to a variety of groups and organizations. In each instance membership is marked by one's **status.** The term "status" is often used interchangeably with the term "prestige." But here we are using "status" to refer to the position a person occupies in a group or organization. For example, in the family your status may be daughter as well as sister. In school your status is student. On the basketball team your status is your position and at your job your status may be salesclerk. We may occupy multiple statuses or social positions, some of which may change. A person is likely to be a daughter and sister far longer than a point guard or girl-friend. Your biography can be mapped by tracing the many statuses you occupy over time in different groups and organizations.

We assume some statuses because we possess the right combination of resources, talent, effort, and—most important of all—opportunity. An **achieved status** is one that is contingent upon the structure of opportunities open to an individual. One thus *achieves* the status of wife, truck driver, or amateur skydiver. In contrast, **ascribed status** refers to a position over which one has no control. In some cases ascribed status is linked to characteristics at birth. Sex, race, class, and nation of origin are particularly powerful forms of ascribed status present from birth. And, throughout life, sexual orientation, the presence or absence of disability, and age provide additional sources of ascribed status.

The meaning people attach to a given status may change over time and place. Thus, being female or male, African American or white, gay or heterosexual, and married or single may mean different things in different contexts. Often the outcome of power struggles between groups determines the meaning of status. Not all status positions are equally important or salient, either to the individual occupying them or to other members of society. Often one status tends to override all others, dictating how a person is likely to be treated (see box). For such cases, sociologists use the term **master status.** A female college professor may find that her sex is more salient than her occupation in determining how she is treated by others, even colleagues. Again, the distribution of master statuses in a society may reflect the outcome of power struggles.

One's master status may enhance or limit opportunities. One of the clearest examples of this involves people with disabilities. Numbering some 36 million in the United States, the disabled are the nation's largest minority group. Forty percent of adults with disabilities did not finish high school, and according to one survey, two-thirds of those between the ages of 16 and 64 are not working, even though most want to. Poverty among the disabled is much higher than it is among the able-bodied (Louis Harris and Associates, 1986). Discrimination, based on the stereotype that to be disabled is to be "defective" and less than human, is widespread.

In 1989 a committee of the U.S. Senate conducted hearings on the Americans with Disabilities Act, a civil rights bill for the disabled that

The achieved status of some African Americans generates attitudes of respect from whites that are far more positive than attitudes that people of color often experience in response to their skin shade. Toni Morrison was the first black woman to receive the Nobel Prize in literature (awarded here by Swedish King Carl XVI Gustaf), a tribute to her considerable accomplishments as a novelist.

became federal law in 1990. The hearings documented the miserable treatment that people with disabilities have faced, treatment contributing to their isolation and segregation from the able-bodied (U.S. Congress: Senate, 1989). The Senate heard from a young woman with cerebral palsy who was denied admission to a movie theater by its owner. It also learned about a zookeeper who would not admit children with Down's syndrome because he feared they would upset the chimpanzees; a disabled child whose teacher claimed he should be excluded from school because his appearance "produced a nauseating effect on his classmates"; a woman who was fired because she was caring for her son, who was suffering from AIDS; people with arthritis, cancer survivors, and others who were fired or denied jobs not because they could not do them but because of discrimination; and people who were denied equal access to public transportation and accommodations, medical treatment, and housing. The Americans with Disabilities Act is intended to provide people with disabilities with the same civil rights protections available to people of color and women, persons also often accorded a devalued master status.

Master status has a great deal to do with the distribution of power and the ability of groups to determine what is "normal." In a society in which political power is concentrated in the hands of the able-bodied, to be otherwise is to be vulnerable to stigmatization and stereotyping, common prerequisites for discriminatory treatment. This is true even though people with disabilities are members of a minority group that any person can involuntarily join. Likewise, in a society in which political power largely rests in the hands of persons who are heterosexual, gay males and lesbians are vulnerable to mistreatment. The imposition of unwanted master statuses is possible as long as men have more power than women, whites more power than people of color, the young more power than the elderly, and the affluent more power than the poor. In such a context, one's master status can sharply influence one's biography.

Roles

We have noted that each of us is liable to occupy multiple positions or statuses in the groups and organizations to which we belong. The behaviors expected of us in these positions are the **social roles** we come to play (Linton, 1936). Social roles are not rigid proscriptions, although they are often linked to prevailing social norms. Some roles are more flexible than others, permitting the role player more innovation and experimentation. For example, the role of college instructor probably allows more room for flexibility than the role of airline pilot. Some roles are subject to more severe negative sanctions than others if they are not fulfilled properly. A bank clerk who is short money from his or her cash drawer may be fired; a member of the clergy who commits a sexual offense with a parishioner is likely to be referred for counseling.

As persons attempt to fulfill the expectations attached to the roles they occupy, there are times when they experience **role strain.** Role strain refers to the distress experienced by an individual when a given role contains contradictory demands. Consider the case of a welfare mother (see

In the United States, skin color may determine one's master status, overriding other significant characteristics an individual may possess. In the extract below, a young man born of a white mother and an African American father, and raised by white adoptive parents, describes some of his struggles and confusion in dealing with a society in which race continues to be of great significance to social relations.

David Watts remembers lying in bed as a child and imagining that his brothers and sisters were Martians and he was their experiment.

A black child adopted by a white family, Watts always felt different. And while he wouldn't trade his adoptive family for the world, he firmly believes that black children should be placed with white parents only as a last resort.

The 27-year-old social worker, who grew up in Lakewood, Ohio, and now lives in New York City, has emerged as an eloquent spokesman on the long-simmering topic of whether white couples should be allowed to adopt children of color.

"My parents made great efforts to educate me about black history. They bought me books, I watched *Roots,*" he said with a smile. "I thought I knew what it was to be black."

Watts was 2 years old when he was adopted in 1968 by an Episcopalian minister and his wife, a community services worker. Watts said that his biological mother was white, but he has always considered himself black because that is the way society views him.

Watts is the third-oldest in a family of four children in his adoptive family. He remembers his adoptive father, returning from business trips, would always bring him home a book about a black author or role model. But his brothers and sisters, the biological children of his parents, got airplanes or other toys.

"I was embarrassed," Watts said. "The others were getting things to play with and I was singled out as being different."

As the only black in his high school, Watts remembered sitting silently as his friends told "nigger" jokes.

"David, we don't really consider you black," they would tell him. "You're not one of them, you're one of us."

"I took that as kind of a compliment," he said. "I wanted to fit in."

On racist behavior his parents always responded, "It's the other person's problem, not yours."

"My parents never really understood what I was talking about," he said. "I appreciated the words but at a young age I realized they hadn't gone through what I'd gone through."

White families that adopt black children often see themselves as "colorblind," he said, but they

McCrary, 1993). Out of economic desperation, women with one or more children must often turn to the state for income support. A mother on welfare is faced with role strain. She needs a minimum income to care for her children. Yet, if she remains on welfare, she is stigmatized and condemned for welfare dependence. The expectation for a welfare mother is that she will get off welfare as soon as possible. On the other hand, if she leaves her children to go to work full-time, she is likely to be criticized as a "bad mother" by those who feel that young children need their mother's daily care. Quality, affordable day care is in woefully short supply in the United States, and the result is many latchkey children, who are left on their own by working mothers. Moreover, a mother on welfare is automatically eligi-

"David, we don't really consider you black. . . . You're not one of them, you're one of us."

should be aware that while color may not matter to them, "it does matter."

It was as a teenager that Watts had the hardest time. He said that he tried to fit in by driving faster and drinking harder than his white friends. He said that he lied, too, "to make myself seem more than I was," Watts said.

Watts is protective of his adoptive parents even as he speaks out against transracial adoption. He speaks about them with love, and made it clear that they did their best. But there were things, he said, they could not teach because of their color.

"It is possible for white parents to teach history and heritage and instill in black children a positive sense of what it's like to be black," he said. "But not from a cultural aspect—you have to live in the culture to feel a part of it."

It was in New York City, where he moved after graduating from the College of Wooster in Ohio, that Watts lived and worked with blacks for the first time in his life.

"I enthusiastically jumped into black culture, trying to be as black as I could," he said. "Then I realized that while I had been calling myself black all my life, I didn't fit in. I had white, middle-class values. I was white in my clothes, the music I listened to, the way I danced."

There were subtle things that Watts had never read about in books—the nuances that define a culture as much as shared stories define a family.

"The jokes, how loud you talk, the way I walk, how close to stand," he said, all of these things were foreign to him in the black culture.

With his new friends, Watts said, he felt like a "spy."

"They thought I was black," he remembers feeling. "Sometimes I still feel like I'm acting black, that I'm an imposter and if I'm not careful my awful secret will be revealed.

"In some ways I was ashamed to have been black growing up and, as I got older, flipped and I became ashamed of being white." . . .

Once in New York, "I was working with black people, and going into black homes," he said. "It was the first time I had a chance to see what it was like to be black."

His black friends told him about how to care for his hair, how to apply hair oil—things his mother never understood.

"I remember my mother using No More Tangles and me crying, 'What have I done wrong?'"

Even in adulthood, Watts said, he sometimes still feels different.

"It takes a conscious effort for me to discover what it is to be black. It is different than absorbing it as you grow up," he said.

Source: Valerie Fineholm, "Adoption between the Races at Issue," *Hartford Courant,* January 31, 1994, pp. A1, A4.

---

ble for Medicaid, a government program of health care for poor mothers and their children. The mother who goes off welfare may lose eligibility, even though her low-paid job may not include health-care benefits. In such a situation, the rational choice of a mother concerned for her children is to stay on welfare.

Along with role strain, **role conflict** can exact costs from people. Role conflict occurs when the demands on a person from two or more of the roles he or she must fulfill are at odds. Consider, for example, the case of a college student talented enough to be awarded a scholarship to play basketball. Playing college-level ball is a dream for many young people—including low-income, inner-city youths who see few other routes to upward mobility and financial success. With few exceptions, play at this level is a prerequisite to selection by a professional team. Even though there is an extremely small statistical probability that a college player will make it into the pros, many young persons nonetheless harbor this fantasy.

Yet the role of student and the role of athlete do not necessarily coexist easily. Some of the young people recruited to play college basketball lack skills as students. More commonly, the demands made on athletes by their school's coaching staff conflict with those being made by professors. College athletes may find themselves caught in an impossible dilemma: cut back on time devoted to athletic training and draw the wrath of coaches, or cut back on time invested in one's studies and risk losing the grades necessary to maintain athletic eligibility.

Colleges vary greatly in how they react to the student athlete's role conflict. Some schools work hard to support the student role, an important consideration given how few players will turn pro. Most players will need a track record of academic success to compete for jobs when their athletic careers are over. Other schools exploit the athlete role, using whatever tricks are necessary to maintain student athletes' eligibility to play and losing interest in players when their eligibility is lost or runs out. In such settings, the graduation rate for athletes is very low.

Role conflict is very common because people must behave in accordance with a variety of different roles, not all of which are always compatible with each other. People thus must find ways to deal with the stress that arises when one or another role cannot be adequately fulfilled. The kinds of role conflicts we face, and the ways in which we handle them, constitute yet another element of our individual biographies.

CONCLUSION

If we think of social structure as the framework within and through which human beings relate to one another, it becomes clear why the groups and organizations to which we belong are so significant. It is in these settings that we interact with others most frequently. Membership in both primary and secondary groups may entail benefits and costs for the individual. The secondary groups we deal with are likely to be organized around one of two principles: bureaucracy or democracy. To the degree that organizations are bureaucratic, individuals are likely to feel that they are objects to whom things happen, as opposed to feeling like actors empowered to shape the social scene, as is often the case in democratic organizations. Informal organization within workplace settings may serve to offset bureaucracy's oppressive tendencies and even empower people to actively resist.

If groups and organizations can be conceived of as the mid-level of social structure (in contrast to the macro-level, with its institutions, societies, and world-system), the statuses and roles people occupy can be thought of as the micro-level. Statuses and roles may either sharply restrict their occupants or give them opportunities to explore their talents and capabilities to the fullest. Contradictory demands accompanying certain roles, or the competing demands of different roles, often prove stressful to the individuals involved. The struggle to live with, as well as the drive to resolve, such stresses is without doubt a major part of the tapestry of everyday life.

As we stand back and contemplate the groups and organizations into which our lives are tied, and the demands of the roles and statuses we occupy, it is easy to feel somewhat overwhelmed. Yet these forms of social structure are in actuality somewhat fragile, requiring our individual and collective acquiescence and collusion in order to persist. People can and at times do choose to challenge and change the frameworks within and through which they relate to one another.

THINKING CRITICALLY

1. Sociologists believe that the thinking and behavior of youths are strongly influenced both by their families and by the peer groups to which they belong. Use examples to characterize the influence these two primary groups have on a teenager. Does their relative influence change over time? How so?

2. Consider the features of the ideal-type, or model, bureaucracy that German sociologist Max Weber identified. Apply these features to an organization for which you have worked. How does the organization resemble the ideal type, and how does it differ?

3. We have said that bureaucracy is endemic in U.S. society. What arguments could be made for and against organizing many more of our secondary groups, such as schools and workplaces, along democratic principles? What do you see as the obstacles to doing so?

4. Think about the various social roles you occupy and the behavioral expectations associated with these roles. In what situations do you experience role strain or role conflict? How successful are you, usually, in resolving it? Why?

5. This chapter's boxed insert described the problems a young man faced because his skin color determined his master status. Do people single out a particular characteristic of yours and consider it more definitive of "who you are" than any of your other characteristics? What effect does this have on their expectations of how you should act and be treated? How does this situation affect your life?

KEY TERMS

social aggregate, 76
group, 76
norms, 76
primary group, 77
secondary group, 79
bureaucracy, 81
iron law of oligarchy, 86
democracy, 86
direct democracy, 86
representative democracy, 87

informal organization, 89
mid-level social structure, 93
micro-level social structure, 93
status, 93
achieved status, 93
ascribed status, 93
master status, 94
social role, 95
role strain, 95
role conflict, 97

SUGGESTED READINGS

M. P. Baumgartner, *The Moral Order of a Suburb.* New York: Oxford University Press, 1988. An investigation into the group norms that guide the behavior of members of an affluent suburban community, norms that allow weak social ties and produce an aversion to entering into conflicts with or assisting other community members.

Peter W. Cookson, Jr., and Caroline Hodges Persell, *Preparing for Power: America's Elite Boarding Schools.* New York: Basic Books, 1985. Research into the organization and operation of a unique type of secondary group, the prep school, that channels young people, usually from advantaged backgrounds, toward positions of success and power.

Jay MacLeod, *Ain't No Makin' It: Leveled Aspirations in a Low-Income Neighborhood.* Boulder, CO: Westview Press, 1987. A study of two groups of working-class teenagers, one white and the other black, and the role played by primary and secondary groups in shaping their aspirations and expectations for the future.

Mark Mathabane, *Kaffir Boy in America: An Encounter with Apartheid.* New York: Collier Books, 1989. An autobiographical work describing the experiences of a South African who comes to the United States to attend college and escape racist treatment under South African apartheid, only to find that many whites and people of color in this country also use skin color to define his master status; a sequel to Mathabane's *Kaffir Boy.*

Carol Stack, *All Our Kin.* New York: Harper & Row, 1974. A classic study of a poverty-stricken community that focuses upon group norms of mutual aid and sharing, norms which are crucial to its members' everyday survival but which can at times be socially confining.

CULTURE

In Western societies we marry one spouse at a time, whereas in many African and Asian societies it is common to be married to several spouses simultaneously. Children in Western societies generally live with families rather than in large communal groups. Dogs and cats are pets, not meals; cows may be food but not sacred objects, as they are in India. Women in Western societies take their freedom of movement for granted; women in Saudi Arabia are not even permitted to drive. These social practices are part of what we call culture. Where do these patterns of social practices come from, and why are they different in different societies?

4

When sociologists use the term **culture,** they are generally referring to a shared way of life among the members of a society. Culture is an agreement among a society's members about appropriate behavior, values, history and heritage, rituals that should be respected and observed, and so on. The members of a society share a way of life described by a set of blueprints that show "what must be done, ought to be done, should be done, may be done, and must not be done" (Williams, 1965: 23). These blueprints are learned understandings of acceptable and expected patterns of behaviors. But who decides what these patterns are?

Karl Marx and Friedrich Engels once noted that "the ideas of the ruling class are in every epoch the ruling ideas" (1970: 64). In their view, those who control the production of material wealth in a society also control the production of knowledge, systems of ideas (or **ideology**), and insight and in this way control the production of an entire way of life. Thus, a society is highly likely to create a culture that justifes, reinforces, and reproduces the privileges, advantages, and power of its ruling class.

Gramsci (1971) later expanded this insight with his notion of **cultural hegemony:** The ideas and values of the dominant members of society are diffused throughout society's institutions and imposed on less powerful members. Since the dominant members of society enjoy privileged access to its institutions, as well as to the media, they are in a position to promote the values that support and legitimize their privileged or dominant position. That position also enables them to tolerate only those dissenting viewpoints that do not fundamentally challenge the existing order and to squelch any views that do. The dominant members of society are thus able to defne the boundaries of debate and discussion, thereby encouraging the incorporation of their ideologies into the ideologies of subordinate members. Culture, then, can be a powerful influence on our behaviors by restricting our actions and thoughts within "safe" ranges that do not seriously undermine the existing order.

The provocative observations of Marx, Engels, and Gramsci challenge our common assumption that cultures are a blend of the shared contributions of many different groups, including those based on race, ethnicity, class, gender, religion, and so on. Their analysis, therefore, raises several questions: Is it true *that those who control wealth and production also control the culture? If so, how is diversity possible? What do all or most members of society share in common? Is there consensus concerning some values, and if so, what might those values be? Are we powerless to alter the dominant culture, or do individual and collective efforts make a difference? How successful are different groups in gaining widespread acceptance for their ideas? To what degree and in what ways can individuals and minorities resist the ideas of dominant groups within society?*

Conventionally, sociologists treat culture as a relatively static entity handed down from one generation to another with little or no significant resistance and only superficial modifications. But another way to view culture is as a dynamic process: we may challenge prevailing definitions of acceptable and appropriate behaviors and social arrangements. Who has the power to determine the elements of culture? How do the dominant groups of society convey their perspectives of culture, and how do others convey challenges to those perspectives? In this chapter we will explore these questions by examining the components of culture, including norms, values, sanctions, language, subcultures, and countercultures.

NORMS

When you come into a classroom, you generally know how to behave. You must sit down, open a notebook, and have a pen or pencil ready to take notes. You know that you should not play a boom box during class, you should raise your hand to speak, and you should not swear at the teacher or stand up and shout at friends across the room during a lecture. And you're aware that you should wear clothing to class. How do you know all this without receiving a written list of rules from each individual teacher?

Norms are standards that define the obligatory and expected behaviors of people in various situations. They reflect a society's beliefs about correct and incorrect behaviors. Once these behaviors become second-nature, members of society do not have to consciously analyze every situation and decide what their appropriate actions ought to be. Norms also can inhibit the type of thinking that might result in challenges to the dominant members of society. For example, the norms defining appropriate classroom behavior reduce the chances that a student will challenge the teacher's authority in class. Similarly, norms served for generations to inhibit the idea that women and African Americans in the United States could challenge their disadvantaged position in society (we will discuss how this situation changed later in the chapter).

On the other hand, norms also help us control inappropriate or harmful behaviors. For example, until very recently, sexual harassment of women was widely perceived as normative, something women had to learn to live with and endure. Our norms are now beginning to define such behavior as inappropriate and unacceptable. Similarly, driving under the influence of alcohol and drugs is now normatively defined as unacceptable, as are other harmful behaviors such as assault, rape, murder, and drug trafficking. And smoking in public places is increasingly frowned upon, if not defined as illegal, in some settings.

Normative indoctrination, or the teaching of norms to individuals, is so successful that we often are taken by surprise when we encounter behaviors that do not conform to prevailing norms. That is, when our unconscious expectations for behavior are suddenly violated, we experience **culture shock.** For example, we often remain unaware of our norms about physical beauty until we see someone whose face is disfigured. Such a person is considered "ugly" and "is devalued and set apart" (Stroman, 1982: 182). In some cases, people may audibly gasp, look away with revulsion, or even scream when confronted with severe facial disfigurement. In other cases, individuals with facial disfigurements are likely to be stared at, pitied, scorned, discriminated against, or made the object of derision.

Culture shock can also be seen in the way some people react to homosexuality. We are largely unconscious of the social assumption that heterosexuality is the only legitimate basis of sexual relationships. Yet, when confronted with members of the same sex kissing or openly expressing physical attraction, people may express shock, revulsion, anger, derision,

Many cultures assume heterosexuality as the norm, to the degree that displays of intimacy between two people of the same sex may provoke culture shock. This billboard in Times Square, New York, would surely be less eye-catching, provocative, and controversial if it depicted a man and a woman embracing.

ridicule, discrimination, or violence. For example, more than half of the public television stations in the United States refused to air the PBS program *Tongues Untied*, about African American homosexuals. In its listing of the broadcast, *TV Guide* warned that the subject matter was not suitable for all audiences. *TV Guide* does not always post such warnings for sexually explicit programs involving heterosexuals. Indeed, fairly explicit heterosexual interactions occur daily on network afternoon dramas, but the program listings appear without warnings.

Culture shock may be a reflection of **ethnocentrism,** in which one's own culture is held to be the standard against which all other cultures are evaluated. Here, the individual not only notices the differences between cultures but ranks them as superior and inferior, with his or her own culture as the superior one. For example, many people in the United States are unable to appreciate the fact that in India cows are sacred; no matter how hungry people might be, they may not eat cows there. To many Americans, such a status accorded to the cow even in the face of extreme hunger may indicate an inferior culture. Evaluating India as an inferior culture on this basis is an expression of ethnocentrism.

There are three types of norms, based on their level of importance to the dominant members of society: folkways, mores, and laws. The negative **sanctions,** or punishments, meted out to violators of norms vary in severity depending upon the type of norm being transgressed.

Folkways, the least formal or important norms, involve everyday conventional routines. They belong to the category of behaviors that *should* and should *not* occur, as specified by society or a social group. Folkways may include such things as how many meals we eat per day, when we eat them, and what we should eat at each one. They also include rituals of deference and public deportment, such as where to stand and whom to look at during conversations or public outings. For example, in the United States, one is expected to maintain an invisible bubble of personal space even when involved in conversations with others. Violation of personal space is tolerated only in unavoidable circumstances such as crowded trains and elevators; even then, one is expected to avoid eye contact as a means of respecting a minimum of personal space. In contrast, people in Latin America consider it rude to hoard personal space; they will attempt to get as physically close as possible to their fellow conversants. Imagine the social dance likely to develop as a person from the United States and someone from Brazil attempt to have a conversation, with the American backing away and the Brazilian advancing closer, both attempting to conform to their own folkways.

Sanctions imposed on violators of folkways are often relatively mild expressions of reprimand, such as stares, frowns, laughter, throat clearing, or tongue clucking. In our hypothetical conversation, the American may frown or stare at the Brazilian or may even laugh nervously, and the Brazilian is likely to do the same. Both are undergoing the culture shock of having a conversational partner violate the expected social behaviors defining roles and physical positions, and each may interpret the violation differently. Each may alternatively interpret the other's behavior as rude, curious, eccentric, deranged, or hostile.

Mores are more formal and important norms than folkways. They generally include behaviors defined as those that absolutely must or must not occur. Members of society view these norms as absolutes because violation of them is believed to threaten the group's ability to function or its very existence. Given the increased level of importance accorded to mores, violations of mores typically meet with more severe sanctions than do violations of folkways. These include imposition of shame and ostracism upon transgressors, and sometimes exile. Mores may include rules governing marriage-partner selection. For example, many societies require that mates be selected from the same ethnic, racial, religious, economic, political, or social group. Marriages between people from different groups are seen to threaten a group's existence by diluting its practices and its heritage. Intermarriages may be subject to a range of sanctions, including excommunication from a church, abdication of royalty, beating of the "intruding" partner, refusal to acknowledge the marriage as legitimate, and so on. Among certain groups of Orthodox Jews, the family of an individual who has married a non-Jewish partner will sit shiva, a mourning ritual. From that moment on the family will act as if the transgressor had died; many will not even permit the name of the transgressor to be mentioned, and all evidence of the person's existence, past and present, will be destroyed.

Most societies maintain mores defining heterosexuality as the only legitimate sexual orientation. Sexual relationships between individuals of the same sex are at best unacknowledged and at worst punished. In the United States, for example, gay males and lesbians are often ridiculed, chastised, denied housing and employment, subjected to violence, ignored by family members, and erroneously blamed for social problems such as AIDS or child pornography. Gay partnerships are not legally recognized as valid marriages, even though the partners may be mutually devoted for many years. As yet, few employers allow homosexuals to extend health insurance coverage to their partners, as married heterosexuals are allowed to do. Many states carry laws that make homosexual acts illegal.

Laws constitute the most formal and important norms. Laws are the mores deemed so vital to dominant interests that they become translated into written, legal formalizations that even nonmembers of the society (such as visitors) are required to obey. For example, in many communities in the United States no one may purchase alcohol before noon on Sundays; in some communities, alcohol sales are completely forbidden on Sundays, despite the fact that many people do not regard Sunday as the Sabbath. In most states, no one under the age of 21 is permitted to purchase alcoholic beverages, and that includes international visitors who may be allowed to purchase and consume alcohol at a younger age in their own country.

When laws are not firmly based on norms shared by the majority, they are difficult to enforce. The constitutional amendment prohibiting the sale of alcohol was repealed in 1933 because so many people regularly violated it. The amendment was championed primarily by the Protestant middle class, with the support of labor and socialist organizations, in an attempt to impose its norms and values on the rest of society. Today there are breaches in the social cohesion underlying laws restricting the speed limit on highways to 55 miles per hour, laws forbidding the possession of marijuana, and laws forbidding private, consensual practices by homosexuals. These are examples of laws that may be challenged in the future.

Laws concern issues that are so important to dominant interests that sanctions against violations are formalized in the written legal codes and are likely to be quite severe. Monetary fines typically penalize the poor more than the wealthy. The poor are also at a disadvantage in raising bail in order to be out of jail while awaiting trail. In addition, racial minorities pay considerably more than whites to secure their freedom before trial. In Connecticut, a survey found that African Americans and Latinos pay more than twice as much bail as that imposed on white prisoners, even when they have been charged with the same crime as whites and even though data show that they are no more likely than whites to leave town before trial (Houston and Ewing, 1992).

The most severe sanction against violations of laws is capital punishment, taking the violator's life. The death penalty sparks lively controversy. Some people oppose it on moral grounds; some find it unconstitutional ("cruel and unusual punishment"); and some question whether capital punishment is an effective deterrent to serious crimes like homicide (see Ehrlich, 1975; King, 1978; Stack, 1987). Sociologists have recently begun to concentrate on the question of bias in the implementation of this extreme form of sanction. Individuals who receive the death penalty are likely to be working-class, poor, and, disproportionately, members of racial minorities (see Radelet, 1981; Culver, 1992). For example, of those exe-

African Americans are more likely than whites to receive the death penalty. This apparent bias in the imposition of the ultimate sanction gives one pause in considering the implications of attempts to reduce the appeals process for inmates on death row.

cuted in the United States between 1977 and 1990, nearly 40 percent were African American, a figure far greater than the proportion of African Americans over age 16 in the overall population (Culver, 1992). By 1987, 44 percent of the more than 1,900 prisoners on death row were African American and members of other racial minorities. Apparently, "violent acts by blacks against whites invite executions; similar acts against blacks (whether by other blacks or by whites) are far less likely to do so" (Neubeck, 1991: 422).

VALUES

Folkways, mores, and laws are all shaped by the value system defined by the dominant members of society. **Values** are assumptions and judgments made about the goods, goals, or states of existence that are deemed important, desirable, and worth striving (or dying) for. For example, in the United States respect for private property is a fundamentally important value, as are individual rights to privacy and freedom of expression. Values shape the normative system by defining the criteria for judging which behaviors will and will not be tolerated. However, values do not necessarily *determine* our behaviors. Norms define the dominant perception of the ideal behaviors in specific situations; they are not necessarily a reflection of real or actual behaviors. Thus, although an important value in the United States is the right of individuals to privacy, it is still fairly common for children to have their personal belongings examined by their teachers and school administrators, for workers to have their private lives investigated by employers, and for individuals' credit histories to be sold to any buyer (see Rule et al., 1980, for example).

Because of the gap between ideal norms and actual behavior, societies generally feel the need to impose negative sanctions (or punishments of violations of norms). For example, jails and courts are overcrowded with hundreds of thousands of violators of society's most important norms— laws. And parents routinely talk about the need to find effective punishments for children who do not comply with family rules: Is a removal of privileges ("grounding") enough? Is a spanking too much? These examples suggest that many people violate norms, and such widespread violation indicates that norms are not necessarily shared by all. Similarly, not everyone accepts the prevailing value system advocated by dominant groups. Both the norms and values of dominant groups meet with resistance and challenge.

Furthermore, the prevailing value system may contain contradictory values that give rise to debate, challenge, and varying interpretations. For example, one of the ostensible values in the United States is the right to life. As such, laws strictly prohibit the taking of human life. In most states, killing another person, whether it is premeditated or accidental, is considered the most heinous of crimes. Yet the prohibition against taking a life is suspended during war, and some states reserve the right to take a human life in capital punishment. And some people view abortion as a violation of the right to life. Indeed, to protest the operations of abortion clinics, abortion opponents have used violence (and, in at least two cases, murder—killing of physicians performing abortions in Florida). Contradictory values may serve to help shape a normative system by generating debate and conflict. The process of developing various perspectives through debate, and of resolving the conflict, may help identify the priorities of values and the norms to which those values point us.

The Relationship between Values and Norms

Conventional wisdom holds that norms and values in the culture are the glue that binds society together as a positive, coherent unit, enabling its members to function smoothly and peaceably. However, sometimes the value system gives rise to norms that actually serve to oppress some people. We shall examine the value system inherent in a patriarchy to show this relationship between values and norms.

A **patriarchy** values male dominance as a natural, inalienable right, thereby enforcing the inferiority and subordination of women. Normative behaviors derived from this value include institutional discrimination against women in education and in the labor force, resulting in restricted opportunities, lower wages for work, and relative economic, social, and political deprivation.

Patriarchal values also encourage the treatment of women as property. This is evident in Christian marriage rituals in which the bride must be "given away" by a male (usually her father or uncle) to the male she is about to marry. Similarly, in some Jewish marriage rituals the bride's father walks her halfway down the aisle; then he turns her over to the groom, who walks her the remaining way to the rabbi performing the ceremony. At the conclusion of American wedding ceremonies the presider traditionally announces, "I now pronounce you man and wife," suggesting that the woman now belongs to the man. Many couples today prefer "husband and wife," which represents their relationship as partners rather than as a man and his possession.

While marriage rituals seem relatively innocuous, the fact that they frequently go unquestioned suggests the power of patriarchy to define our values. More extreme cases of patriarchal definitions of female inferiority involve violence against women. Even though the culture assumes that women's male partners are to be their protectors, women are more likely to suffer violence at the hands of their male partners than at the hands of strangers on the street. Domestic violence is the most common cause of injury to women in the United States. One-fifth of all emergency room visits by women are for injuries received during incidents of domestic violence. Moreover, one out of seven married women is raped by her husband, and 25 percent of abused women are attacked during pregnancy. In 1988, one-third of all female homicide victims were killed by their male partners (Monagle, 1990: 45). Date-rape statistics show similar patterns of violence against women by their partners. In one of the largest, most comprehensive studies of U.S. college campuses, 25 percent of the women surveyed reported being forced, against their will, to submit to sexual intercourse, and 84 percent of them said they knew their attackers (Warshaw, 1988). In another survey, 51 percent of the male respondents admitted they would rape a woman if they believed they could get away with it (Monagle, 1990). These survey results reflect a patriarchal value in which women become objects or possessions, a value that is all too often translated into norms of violence against women.

In spite of laws that define domestic violence as assault, many police, and indeed courts, continue to dismiss abuse of women by their partners as a private domestic affair, one in which a man must sometimes discipline a misbehaving or provocative wife (Ferraro, 1993). Many states still do not acknowledge the legal possibility of rape between marital partners. In 1993 a Virginia woman cut off her husband's penis because, she said, he had raped and abused her repeatedly. The court acquitted the husband of rape because Virginia law defines sexual relations between spouses as the normal expectation between a husband and wife, part of the agreement to which a woman enters upon marriage. Date rape, too, is often dismissed by the police, the courts, and sometimes the victims themselves as not being rape at all, because the victim consented to the date (Warshaw, 1988). Such attitudes and the consequent behaviors underscore the valuation of women as inferior to men and perhaps worthy of abuse.

India starkly shows how women can suffer from violence as a result of their treatment as property. Consumerism and patriarchy there combine to make a woman her husband's property, much as land belongs to the man and his family. The man's family can demand a very large dowry from the bride's family as payment for accepting the woman and presumably providing for her for the rest of her life. If the bride's family cannot afford the dowry payments, promised before marriage, the groom's family sometimes arranges an "accident" in which the bride burns to death, thereby allowing the man to marry again. Bride burning became rampant in the mid-1980s, especially among the middle class (Liddle and Joshi, 1986).

Bride burning is extreme, but it reflects similar values and attitudes that prevail in the United States. The fact is that many American women still endure violence at the hands of their partners. Such behavior would be less likely to occur without a culture of patriarchy in which women are seen as inferior to men and as their property. (Certainly, men do not appear to suffer similar abuse in a matriarchy.)

Some may view violence against women as simply the pathological behavior of individuals. However, many researchers point out that such behavior is better understood as an expression of the power of privilege in the context of patriarchy. For example, Ferraro notes that violence is most often condemned when it violates those who are privileged, but when those who are relatively privileged use violence against their subordinates, the behavior is generally accepted as "socially necessary and morally just" (1993: 165; see also Martin, 1976; Dobash and Dobash, 1979, 1991). Clearly, not all families are characterized by this kind of patriarchy, but statistics on wife abuse and rape suggest that it is more widespread and culturally common in the United States than we would like to believe.

Patriarchy also implies that women are objects for the sexual pleasure of males. That means women must make themselves attractive partners for sexual pleasure (as well as for reproduction). For many women, being attractive means being thin, and this value leads them to engage in various eating disorders, particularly anorexia (voluntary starvation) and bulimia (binge purging). At least 90 percent of the diagnosed cases of these life-threatening disorders are females (Gordon, 1990: 32). Both anorexia and bulimia have tended to be treated as personal troubles, that is, as psychological and medical problems of individuals. Recently, however, more and more researchers have suggested that patriarchal values combined with corporations eager to cash in on the cult of thinness have promoted eating disorders based on the notion that "one can never be too rich or too thin" (see Szekely, 1988). More than 65 million Americans annually struggle to lose weight. In 1990 profits in the weight-loss industry exceeded $32 billion, and they were expected to grow to over $50 billion by 1995 (*U.S. News & World Report*, 1990: 56). The industry spent over $285 million in 1987 to advertise and promote its pills, spas, clinics, programs, low-calorie goods, and weight-loss products, trying to convince Americans that being overweight is somehow a moral deficiency. Advertisers of these products often focus on women's weight loss as the prerequisite for being attractive and for finding or keeping one's mate. While patriarchy and advertisements do not by themselves cause such a complex problem as eating disorders, together they do form a normative context that encourages such disorders. Some researchers link eating disorders to control issues for women: in a society in which women have relatively little control over much of their existence, controlling their eating habits and body image remains a means of exercising personal power (Szekely, 1988).

Thus, far from simply organizing society into a positive, unified structure that is beneficial to all members, norms and values may create an oppressive culture for some members. Such oppression may have dire consequences for those who are victimized by the culture. But the normative system is not all-powerful; there is often resistance to the oppression that some members of society may feel. The boxed excerpt gives you an idea of how a gay man came to accept himself and resist the mores of the dominant culture. (We will also discuss resistance to the dominant culture in the sections on subcultures and countercultures.) The question we now ask is: How do societies transmit the prevailing normative system, and how do people challenge that system?

CULTURAL TRANSMISSION

Culture and Language

Culture contains prevailing knowledge, or "facts" as a particular society construes them; beliefs about the way the world works or ought to work; values defining what is important; customs and rituals; symbols; and sets of assumptions. Together, these elements are a society's **nonmaterial culture,** the body of abstractions defining the way its members live. A society's **material culture** consists of the physical artifacts that define the society, such as a flag, style of dress, means of transportation and housing, and so on.

Joseph Steffan, at the top of his class at the U.S. Naval Academy, found himself struggling with the realization that he was gay. Shortly before graduation, he acknowledged his sexual orientation when asked about it by the commanding officer, and he was immediately stripped of his rank and forced to resign from the academy. In this excerpt from Steffan's book, Honor Bound, *he describes the anguish he experienced before coming out.*

I was feeling very depressed, like nothing I had ever experienced in my life. At the heart of this depression were recurring thoughts about my sexuality. I was working so hard to ignore them, to shut them out, but I could not turn off a part of my own mind. These thoughts were always there, always resurfacing, reminding me that I was avoiding something. Our minds are so powerful, so complex, yet I thought I could control my mind and shut off a part of my being. It was a battle I was losing. On the outside I was in control as always, but inside I was self-destructing.

One night before midterm exams, I was trying in vain to study in my room. My ability to concentrate was at an all-time low, and I simply couldn't focus. There were so many pressures to deal with, so many things going on in my head. Finally, I just couldn't take it anymore. I slammed my books shut, threw on a pair of sweats, and walked down the stairs and out of the hall.

The night was pitch-black, and it was raining lightly. A heavy mist hung in the air, glowing around the dormitory, its windows completely lit, with mids studying for exams. I walked slowly across the grass practice field toward the seawall, immersed in my own churning thoughts. I finally sat down against the chain fence surrounding the field and started to cry, the rain slowly soaking through my sweats.

I was so completely frustrated. Since the first inkling of doubt about my sexuality, the first spark of attraction to men, I had resisted. I had fought, prayed, and hoped that it was just a phase, that I would wake up one morning and the attraction would be gone. But every day it was there, lingering in the background waiting to pounce.

There were times when I would forget, when I was concentrating especially hard on difficult homework or practicing with the choirs. But then something would happen to trigger my memory and the sinking feeling in my stomach would return, the feeling of dread and shame and most of all the loneliness that came from having to hide a part of myself. My family and friends had always been there to help me when I needed it, but somehow this was different. I felt so alone.

From the beginning, I had avoided dealing with my sexuality, but it didn't feel like avoidance anymore. Now it felt like a lie—a lie whose perpetuation was beginning to sicken me, to eat away at my soul. I had crossed the line between doubt and certainty months before, but I kept lying to myself. In my mind, two incompatible thoughts were waging battle: The first was my own stereotypical prejudice toward homosexuals; the second was the realization that I was one of them. For a while, I had managed to suppress this conflict by assuring myself that I was not really gay. But I could no longer deny my sexuality, and I could not continue down the path toward self-hatred. That would be a living death.

And then there was Annapolis and the military. I knew the military didn't allow homosexuals, but I had invested so much here already—so many dreams were tied to this place. How could I give them up, quit for [w]hat I knew were all the wrong

> *"Two incompatible thoughts were waging battle: . . . my own stereotypical prejudice toward homosexuals; [and] . . . the realization that I was one of them."*

reasons? I knew now that keeping gay people out of the military was wrong. I knew because I was one of them, and I had done as well as any of my classmates. I only wondered how many others there were like me, how many more silent voices in the crowd.

Deep down inside, I knew I could never leave Annapolis. The problem wasn't the academy; it was me. I had to quit running away and finally accept the fact that I was gay. I wasn't going to be able to change, and even if that meant hiding a part of myself forever, I didn't care. This place had become the focal point of my life. It meant as much to me now as anything else. No matter what, I was going to stay here and continue working toward the goals I had held for so long.

After what seemed like an hour, I finally got up and started walking back to the hall. I still didn't completely understand what it meant to be gay, or even fully accept my homosexuality. A part of me still wanted to be straight, to be "normal"—because I felt it would make my life easier. But I had taken a first crucial step toward acceptance. That step was the beginning of a long process of "coming out." It would not be my last step, and it would certainly not be my most difficult Unfortunately, it is a first step that many young gay people do not have the strength to take. They choose self-hatred over self-acceptance, and embark on an impossible path leading all too often to self-destruction through drug addiction or suicide.

For the first time in many months, I finally felt at peace with myself, and as the year went on I thought more and more about what it meant to be gay. I began examining and questioning the attitudes toward homosexuals that I had grown up with. The more I thought about them from my own perspective, the more I began to see the ignorance that lay behind these prejudices. Now, when I heard

a negative comment about homosexuals, I no longer thought, Yes, they are like that. I thought, No, I'm not like that. Despite enduring the loneliness of living in the closet, I was finally breaking away from the feelings of guilt and shame that had tormented me for so long.

That rainy night on the practice field was a great turning point in my life. I had finally stopped fighting who I knew I was and began accepting myself. I have often heard people ask why anyone would choose to be a gay, but there is no question more flawed in its misunderstanding of human sexuality. None of us, gay or straight, choose our sexualities. They are defined within us, most experts believe, by a combination of genetic and environmental factors long before we ever become aware of our feelings. Few heterosexuals who believe people choose to be gay stop to think about when they chose to be straight. That just isn't the way it works.

No one wanted to be gay less than I did. Everything in my life, from my conservative upbringing to the path in life I had chosen, was opposed to accepting my sexuality. I had a vast storehouse of negative reinforcement to back up my own prejudices toward homosexuals, and I drew upon those forces to help me ignore and evade my own feelings.

But like many gay men and lesbians, I discovered that there is no hiding from yourself. Homosexuality is simply not a choice; it is an identity. The only real choice we have is whether to continue fighting, evading, and denying that identity or to finally accept it, heal, and get on with our lives.

Source: Joseph Steffan, *Honor Bound: A Gay Naval Midshipman Fights to Serve His Country* (New York: Avon Books, 1992), pp. 103–105.

The key to the abstractions of nonmaterial culture is **language.** Language consists of patterns of written symbols, audible sounds, and gestures that convey meanings. These meanings are usually shared by the members of a society, so when some members use them, others understand the gist of what is being communicated. Through the exchange of language members of society have access to experience and history beyond their own immediate time and place. It is not necessary for us to have lived in concentration camps in 1940s Germany to know about the Holocaust and its horrors. Nor do we have to put our hands in a fire to learn that it burns. This is because language can categorize objects and events that share perceived or assumed common elements.

For example, we may categorize as wars all conflicts that attempt to resolve differences by means of weapons and bloodshed. Thus, even though we were born after the American Revolution, the Civil War, and World War I, we can comprehend them all as wars. We do not have to analyze why they occurred or who was right and who was wrong to understand that these were all wars, because we know they shared the common elements of weapons, death, and conflicting interests. And we may extend this understanding to the present day, defining as wars such events as armed disputes between urban gangs, the invasion of Kuwait by Iraq, and the extended conflict in Vietnam in the 1960s and 1970s.

Beyond just reflecting reality, language can also *construct,* or define, reality (see Berger and Luckmann, 1966). This is because the structure of language contains hidden assumptions about the world around us. For example, the English language contains many implicit assumptions about gender abilities, worth and value, and appropriate behaviors and roles (Sorrels, 1983). When we use words like "fireman," and "congressman," we are conjuring a mental image of a male, thereby constructing a reality which assumes that only men fight fires and serve in Congress. We similarly reinforce such assumptions when we use gendered pronouns, such as "the doctor . . . he" and "the nurse . . . she" or "the teacher . . . she" and "the principal . . . he." Even our use of the generic "man" to refer to all of humanity constructs our perception of a male as the embodiment of humanness. This may have the consequence of rendering females invisible and inconsequential. In contrast, when we use words like "firefighter" and "congressperson," we draw attention to the notion that females as well as males hold these positions.

The power of language to construct social reality is captured in the **Thomas theorem,** or the **definition of the situation** (Thomas, 1928): If we define a situation as real, the consequences of our definition will be quite real whether that definition is accurate or not. For example, if society accepts a definition of women as inferior to men, the consequences may be behavior that reinforces the definition as correct. Members of society, including school administrators, prospective employers, and those holding political power, may believe that women are incapable of tasks requiring intellect, independent initiative, authority, and responsibility. The all-too-real consequences set in motion by this definition of the situation may be women's economic, social, and political disadvantage and deprivation (we will discuss sexism and inequality in greater detail in Chapter 6). Because our very language suggests that men are superior to women, men are considered more qualified for leadership positions, jobs requiring skill and responsibility (which are frequently higher-paying jobs), and decision-making in politics and the home.

The idea that women are inferior in the culture is also expressed in the terminology many men traditionally apply to women—descriptive words such as "girls," "dolls," "broads," "babes," and so forth. When one executive says to another, "I'll have my girl call your girl," the statement renders both their secretaries inferior. Through one small sentence, each secretary becomes a child, her boss's possession, and his servant. Thus, the Thomas theorem describes how language and ideas reinforce each other in the social construction of reality.

Similarly, the words used to describe physical and mental impairment also construct our perception of various human conditions and the people who have them. The term "handicapped person" implies that an individual who has a physical or mental disability is a "limited person" (Stroman, 1982: 47). The use of such wording defines the person in terms of her or his physical or mental disability and precludes the understanding that the disability is merely one aspect of an entire human being. This social construction affects how people without disabilities respond to those who have an impairment. People with disabilities are frequently seen as unattractive, unintelligent, immature, incapable of competently performing jobs requiring responsibility, unable to adequately parent children, and incapable of living independently. Replacing the term "handicapped person" with the phrase "person with a disability" reorients our social construction to one in which a specific impairment is seen as only a part of a person. Stroman (1982) suggests that "handicap" be reserved to describe the limitations that culture imposes on the disabled through stereotyping and labels. In doing so, Stroman acknowledges the power of language to socially construct reality, and he suggests using that power to *resist* the prevailing social constructions. By using noticeably different words to shape our perceptions, we may call attention to the inadequacy of the words more commonly used and raise society's consciousness about the realities these words create. Thus, language can be used to challenge or change culture.

The important role of language in the social construction of reality indicates that individuals who control language have the power to control culture. Those who determine the "appropriate" words for denoting various experiences and objects can strongly influence the way we view the world around us, as well as our place and the places of others in that world. Language is the means by which we pass our culture from generation to generation and to new members of our society. But language also allows people who are less powerful to introduce change into culture. As noted above, people can alter established social constructions by deliberately using common words in new ways or by generating new concepts that heighten society's awareness of the power of existing words. Indeed, this is what sociologists frequently do when they develop new concepts or define commonly used words more precisely than is usually the case.

CORPORATE CULTURE

Where do norms and values come from? At the beginning of the chapter, we introduced the idea that powerful groups in society are in a position to define society's norms and values. In the United States, our values derive in part from the production and consumption of goods and services for profit. Cultural ideologies create relationships and structures that promote and enhance the production of private profit. We refer to this fundamental aspect of our culture as the **corporate culture.**

Corporate culture includes values based on the cult of **competitive individualism** (Cummings and del Taebel, 1978), in which members of society are taught to believe that individuals are completely responsible for their own economic conditions. As such, economic success (wealth) or failure (poverty) is the result of individual effort and competitive capabilities. Individuals who are wealthy are presumed to have earned their privileged economic position; if they did not deserve it, they would not have it. Similarly, we presume that the poor deserve their poverty because of sloth, laziness, lack of motivation or initiative, or lack of competitive capabilities. If not for these personal failures, the poor would not be poor.

The notion that the poor are poverty-stricken because circumstances have robbed them of motivation to work hard, earn a living, or gain an education is called the **culture of poverty** (Lewis, 1959, 1961, 1966). This viewpoint assumes that the poor share a value system, or normative culture, that differs from mainstream norms and values, and it implies that the poor consciously choose the value system that causes their poverty. Such an analysis does not consider the larger structural constraints that are important factors in producing poverty. For example, can valuing hard work and education ensure upward mobility for individuals if there are not enough good jobs for all the people who want them?

The success of transmitting mainstream values can be seen in public opinion polls regarding economic success issues. Table 4.1 presents the results of a 1990 survey on poverty, conducted by the National Opinion Research Center (NORC). As the table shows, 89 percent of the respondents believed that lack of effort by the poor themselves was an important explanation for poverty; 72 percent identified loose morals and drunkenness as important factors. Yet 77 percent of the same respondents recognized that an important explanation for poverty is industry's failure to provide enough jobs, and 73 percent cited failure of society to provide good schools as important. This survey reiterated attitudes from almost two decades earlier. In a 1972 survey by Peter D. Hart Research Associates, 83 percent of respondents believed that poor people are poor because they lack education, are illiterate, are lazy, have no ambition or drive, don't want to get out and work, want to be poor, and prefer welfare; only 25 percent of the respondents cited lack of opportunity as an explanation for poverty. These surveys suggest that even when a majority of people recognize the role that the economy and society play in generating poverty, most still believe that the poor are themselves to blame because of personal characteristics. This apparent contradiction indicates that the twin ideologies of

Table 4.1

ATTITUDES ABOUT POVERTY IN THE UNITED STATES

EXPLANATIONS FOR POVERTY	PERCENTAGE OF RESPONDENTS ANSWERING	
	VERY IMPORTANT	SOMEWHAT IMPORTANT
Lack of effort by the poor themselves	45	44
Loose morals and drunkenness	38	34
Failure of industry to provide enough jobs	35	42
Failure of society to provide good schools for many Americans	35	38

Source: National Opinion Research Center, *General Social Survey, 1990.* 1991.

culture of poverty and competitive individualism are powerful, pervasive, and tenacious.

These ideologies, transmitted through schools and the workplace, support an acceptance of corporate culture and inhibit any independent thinking or critical analysis that might challenge these notions. For example, is it appropriate or accurate to consider economic achievement in terms of a race that has winners and losers? Does each generation of contestants begin the race on a level playing field regardless of their parents' or previous generations' economic positions? Might such a race, in fact, be rigged at the outset, with some beginning with greater advantages to support success and others carrying heavy institutional hindrances throughout? Is individual effort the most important factor in determining economic success?

A culture of competitive individualism benefits those who are already privileged members of society. If we accept economic inequality as the fair outcome of individual effort, we will not be likely to ask to what degree the advantages of the wealthy were actually earned. And we will blame the poor for their own plight, rather than challenge the existing structure as unfair or inadequate. We are not likely to question business practices that destroy jobs and may contribute to poverty, such as automation, plant shutdowns, and exportation of production to neighboring or overseas nations. We are not likely to expect retraining and reeducation of workers to help them participate meaningfully in a changing economy. (We are more likely to assume that poor people and the unemployed are suffering from their own laziness, lack of education, or lack of motivation to improve their lives.) We are less likely to criticize the role of the state in producing tax policies that favor wealthy and corporate interests over the poor and working classes. In this way, the privileged position of the wealthy members of society and of corporate chieftains will remain relatively unthreatened. However, corporate culture is not absolute or immune to change. As more individuals articulate criticisms and organize into action-oriented groups, the likelihood increases that there will be challenges to policies such as tax structures that favor the wealthy (we will discuss social change in Chapter 9).

U.S. corporate culture is disseminated to other cultures when firms go abroad in search of profits in new markets and when the relatively better-off in many countries seek to enjoy the lifestyle that seems to be accessible to so many in the United States. That is why we find McDonald's golden arches in Russia, Mexico, Japan, India, and many European countries. Coca-Cola and Pepsi ads can be seen all around the world in dozens of languages, as can the logos of many, if not most, of the Fortune 500 corporations.

Most of these firms not only sell products in an international marketplace; they also maintain manufacturing plants abroad, particularly in underdeveloped nations where labor can be exploited cheaply. Such inroads make possible a sharing of foods, music, and material goods, but they also spread corporate culture, in which generating profits takes precedence over other cultural norms and ideologies.

Many countries encourage the presence of American corporations as part of a conscious economic development strategy, but such strategies can also have an enormous cultural impact. For example, corporate producers can disrupt agrarian cultures as land usage and labor activities shift from farming to manufacturing. Sunrises and sunsets, growing seasons, and weather patterns no longer mark the daily clock and annual calendar.

Multinational corporations often export their culture to other countries. McDonald's golden arches and its Western menu can be found in many different countries, even as the logo and menu are written in other languages and alphabets. Cultivating recognition of corporate cultural images and demand for the product can be quite lucrative in countries like China, where a population of 1.15 billion people can translate into sizable sales of Big Macs.

Instead, the day and year are organized around the assembly line, production shifts, and workweeks, all dictated by the market for material goods. Rituals and norms associated with agriculture become less meaningful in the face of corporate culture. Less visible, but no less important, is the impact on family and community structures and cultural heritages. Rural farming and fishing communities can no longer compete with the economy of scale posed by large corporate agribusinesses and fisheries, so the community members leave in search of employment in overcrowded cities.

Agents of Cultural Transmission

How is it possible for members of a large society to learn the subtle and not-so-subtle values, norms, and rituals of the dominant culture? Which members have the power to transmit and impose their cultural assumptions on others? What mechanisms and processes enhance this transmission? Do these processes produce an all-powerful, dominant culture, or is there some degree of resistance, challenge, and diversity?

Several agents combine to facilitate transmission of the dominant group's culture, most notably, schools, the media, the workplace, and the toy, game, and recreation industries. Other agents may variably reinforce this process, including the family, religion, and peers. We shall deal with the processes and agents of cultural transmission, or socialization, in great detail in the next chapter and in Chapter 12 ("Education"). Here, we focus broadly on the special role that schools and the media play in reinforcing the dominant culture.

The mass media are major transmitters of culture. Television broadcasts entertainment that reflects stereotypes of acceptable and unacceptable behaviors and values across a wide range of dimensions, including race, class, gender, age, physical and mental ability, and sexual orientation. The format of the programs often invites us to laugh at, despise, or belittle cultures other than the dominant one in the United States. For example, *The Simpsons* has a running joke that depicts Pakistani immigrants as ignorant convenience-store owners and confused taxicab drivers. While broadcasters may be showing some sensitivity to how they present diversity, they have a very long way to go.

News programmers reflect the interests of our society's major power groups—corporations and the wealthy—in the stories they select as important, the subjects they choose for interviews, and the way they treat the stories they present. This is not surprising: the media are themselves controlled by major corporate entities and the primary sponsors of programming are corporate advertisers.

Television commercials encourage a materialistic consumer mentality, regardless of the necessity, safety, or effectiveness of products. Consider, for example, the controversies over the advertisements for highly sugared cereals and junk food that children watch along with their Saturday morning cartoons. (The cartoons, themselves, are little more than half-hour commercials for toys, movies, and other merchandise related to the main characters of the shows.)

Researchers have long noted the power of commercials and the media to entice us to feel the need for products that may be unnecessary, ineffective, frivolous, beyond our means, or even harmful. The modern world is dominated, both in print and electronic media, by corporate logos, advertisement jingles and catchphrases, and visual images that create a reality that contradicts and often undermines the everyday reality of the individual (Boorstin, 1961; Ewen, 1976; Parenti, 1986).

In his examination of American culture, *Culture Against Man*, Jules Henry describes advertising as "an expression of an irrational economy that has depended for survival on a fantastically high standard of living incorporated into the American mind as a moral imperative" (1963: 45). That is, we are encouraged to believe that it is our duty to maintain a very high level of consumption in order to support the economy. Advertising creates a culture in that it defines our needs and then entices us to fulfill them by purchasing goods and services, an activity that is the lifeblood of capitalism. Indeed, referring to consumerism as a moral imperative is not so far-fetched: experts proclaim that the U.S. economy was slow to rebound from the recession of the early 1990s because consumers were not spending enough to fuel the recovery.

In *The Powers That Be* (1979), G. William Domhoff examines what he calls the *ideology process*, the use of commercials, direct mailing, television-programming productions, and full-page newspaper ads to contour public opinion and the normative system. Domhoff identifies as a major force the Advertising Council, an organization dominated by corporate interests. It sponsors conferences "where academics, journalists, and other cultural experts can brainstorm with corporate leaders about problems of ideology and public opinion," thereby helping to solidify the dominant ideology (Domhoff, 1979: 191).

The Advertising Council transmits an ideology favoring dominant interests to the rest of the population in its campaigns of advertising in the public interest. These commercial spots tend to promote the sanctity of free enterprise; to encourage voluntarism in groups like the Red Cross and United Fund (as opposed to pressing for corporate responsibility or state-funded programs); to present pollution and conservation as problems of individual behavior rather than public issues of corporate misconduct, abuse, and responsibility; and to stress the importance of religion in American life. These issues and viewpoints are ones that the "corporate-dominated boards and advisory committees [of the Advertising Council] determine to be in the public interest" (Domhoff, 1979: 183–184). Since the Advertising Council uses more than 80 percent of the public service airtime that television networks are required by law to provide, its ads, even if unsuccessful, still deprive viewers of exposure to opposing points of view.

On the other hand, when television producers are less dependent on corporate advertisers, they are freer to promote and reinforce values and norms that challenge corporate culture. For example, much of the funding for public television comes from membership dues and federal support. Therefore, it is easier for children's programs like *Mr. Rogers, Sesame*

Street, and *Barney and Friends* to promote values of sharing, acceptance of others, and racial and gender equality.

The media, as corporate entities, also tend to choose stories and present them in such a way as to manipulate public opinion about foreign policies that support corporate interests. This filtering process serves to stifle or at least marginalize dissent and to mobilize acceptance and support of corporate interests. For example, the media may define victims of violence who challenge U.S. corporate dominance as "unworthy" of coverage and victims who are supportive of that dominance as "worthy" (Herman and Chomsky, 1988; see also Elias, 1986). Thus, the U.S. media loudly protested the injustice of the murder of a Polish priest ("worthy" victim) by the Polish police, but gave scant coverage to the murders of the archbishop of El Salvador and numerous clergy ("unworthy" victims) protesting treatment of the poor by landowners in El Salvador, killed by paramilitary troops who had been trained by Green Berets at Fort Bragg, North Carolina. The amount and kind of coverage accorded stories, then, influence our perceptions of what U.S. interests are and, in turn, help "manufacture" our consent to foreign policies consistent with corporate interests.

In addition to the media, schools are cultural-transmission agents. While there is a growing and powerful movement toward a multicultural perspective in curricula, teachers and boards of education often aid the transmission of dominant culture. They determine the subject matter and perspectives to be taught and then select the appropriate textbooks for that curricula. In the United States, this policy has often meant that both the curricula and the textbooks—for political and social history, literature, and science—emphasize the dominant white, male, Western perspective, ignoring or downplaying the contributions, and, at times, the very existence, of nonwhite, female, working-class, or non-Western peoples.

The movement in the United States to broaden and enrich curricula by making them more inclusive encourages teachers and textbook writers to adopt a perspective of **cultural relativity.** This perspective considers other cultures and their points of view as worthy of respect and understanding. It treats others' cultural practices as valid within their own context. More recently, however, there has been a shift to **multiculturalism** as a critical perspective. Whereas cultural relativity focuses on the perspective of another culture, multiculturalism acknowledges the heterogeneity within societies, examines the contributions and the intersection of many different groups at crucial moments in history, and explores the factors that differentially affect the experiences of each group. For example, cultural relativism might ask us to view slavery as supporting the economy of the South and the profit "needs" of plantation owners. In contrast, a multicultural perspective would ask us to explore the roles that each group played in the larger political economy and to examine the power differences between slaves and slaveholders.

Multiculturalism has brought about a shift in the New York State public school curriculum. The new approach no longer treats Christopher Columbus and the Spanish explorers as benign heroes and native populations as violent and uncivilized. Students are now exposed to primary and sec-

Many classrooms in the United States have begun to adopt new materials to incorporate a multicultural perspective in the curriculum, an effort that is sometimes met with much resistance and controversy. These texts, designed for elementary school use, examine gay and lesbian families and identities as legitimate aspects of cultural diversity.

ondary sources describing the brutal and exploitative treatment of native populations by the explorers.

Schools in most, if not all, societies, regardless of their political or economic structure, reinforce the dominant culture of their society in addition to providing basic knowledge and skills. In their book *Schooling in Capitalist America* (1976), Bowles and Gintis describe how schools in our society have historically sought to inculcate common ideological values and perspectives under the guise of mass public education. More often than not, they argue, what is taught are the *ideals* of democracy rather than the realities. Some schools today do encourage critical thinking and discussion about the difference between political ideals and reality. However, many of them still teach that we are a government of the people, by the people, and for the people, thereby ignoring existing power structures.

Schools can also transmit culture more subtly. In the very way they are structured, schools urge students to acquiesce to bureaucratic rules, regulations, and authorities. This encourages the students to accept authority outside of school as normal and legitimate. While one can debate how much authority children should have in schools, as well as whether all institutions can or should be run on strict democratic principles, it is noteworthy how schools themselves violate the virtues of democracy they extol in their curricula. They frequently violate students' right to privacy by searching their lockers for drugs and they can restrict students' freedom of expression in student publications (Silberman, 1970: 113–157; Goodlad, 1984). Student activism, however, sometimes succeeds in challenging such contradictions of democracy. In schools where they have learned the lessons of the Bill of Rights, students protest intrusions on their rights, and sometimes they win in the courts. Thus, they see the conflicts that are inherent in democratic societies and act to confront them.

Schools and the media have recently combined as cultural transmitters. Whittle Communications, for example, introduced Channel One television, a news service, into public school systems in every state (except Nevada, Alaska, and Hawaii) and the District of Columbia (*Wall Street Journal*, 1991). The schools received free media equipment from Whittle Communications in exchange for allowing twelve minutes of news each day plus two minutes of commercials to be aired in the classroom. Critics vehemently objected to using students as a captive audience for a barrage of messages promoting consumption (Walsh and Schmidt, 1990). They also objected to the conflict of interest such programming could pose: Would Channel One run news analyses damaging to its sponsors or their interests? Can complicated news be seriously and carefully examined from a variety of perspectives in twelve minutes, without the undue influence of corporate sponsors? Might hidden advertisements masquerade as news items (Dagnoli, 1990)? For example, a news film made by General Dynamics extolling the virtues of new technologies it manufactures, aired by newscasters uncritically, could actually be an "infomercial" in the guise of an unbiased news item. Would a television station using this material also cover a story exploring how General Dynamics was able to avoid paying any federal income tax during the 1980s under the Reagan administration?

Indeed, Whittle Communications itself is a corporation, with interests more consistent with those of its sponsors than with the needs of students for objective news reporting. Many state boards of education—including those in New York, California, and North Carolina (Johnson, 1989; Mater, 1989; Walsh, 1990a), became convinced that the conflicts of interest made Channel One inappropriate and banned the broadcast from their public schools. Many other school systems, however, drawn by the attraction of free media equipment and a new medium for instruction, have invited the powerful cultural transmitter into their classrooms.

Channel One is hardly the first mechanism corporations have used to transmit corporate culture to schoolchildren. More than 3,000 large corporations regularly produce and distribute videos, films, posters, comic books, and coloring books to children in public schools (*Business Week*, 1980: 156). Teachers faced with severely tight budgets are more than happy to have the free materials. These materials, however, often carry a hidden agenda, defending the legitimacy of various industries and narrowing the critical vision of students. For example, Northeast Utilities in New England offers a comic book to grade-school children called *Let's Explore Electricity*. The book states: "Fossil fuels (coal, oil and natural gas) are burned to heat water, which makes steam. . . . A fuel called uranium may also be used. . . . This is called nuclear power" (Northeast Utilities, 1990: 6). Nowhere is the sun or wind or any other renewable source of energy mentioned as an alternative means of energy and electricity production. Children learn to assume that nonrenewable resources such as coal, oil, and nuclear power are the *only* viable sources of energy. Moreover, such materials do not question conservation policy or corporate responsibility and accountability in polluting the environment and depleting nonrenewable resources. This suggests to children that pollution and energy shortages are problems caused by individuals, not the energy and oil corporations.

SUBCULTURES

We have so far discussed culture as a single, powerful national phenomenon that we all experience. However, there are many cultures *within* our society. While there may very well be a prevailing dominant culture, we are not necessarily bound to it or forced to conform like powerless robots. Rather, we can experience a great deal of diversity within society and its dominant culture. A wide variety of groups exist whose members participate in the larger society and its institutions but who share values, norms, heritages, and rituals that differ from those of the dominant culture. Sociologists call these groups **subcultures.** Members of subcultures do not necessarily reject the dominant culture, but they embrace their own culture as valid and important.

Subcultures can be based on a variety of factors, including religion, race, ethnicity, age, and sexual orientation. Gay male and lesbian subcultures have flourished in large urban areas and in smaller towns (often university towns) where there are meeting places and organizations to support their social and political activities. A loose national network provides information about supportive, thriving gay and lesbian communities. Thus, while gay males and lesbians are active participants in the dominant culture—in jobs, educational institutions, and politics at all levels—they often also participate in a subculture containing shared norms and values that support the legitimacy of their sexual orientation.

Age subcultures also thrive in the United States. Communities of middle-class and wealthy retirees, particularly in the warmer climates of Florida and Arizona, continue to multiply. Residents' lifestyles are arranged around leisure activities and health-care issues and information. Restaurants in such communities typically provide health-conscious menus and early evening meals. Support groups abound for widows and widowers, for people with critically ill partners, and for those who are critically ill themselves. So do clubs and organizations that offer opportunities to meet other retirees, information regarding retirement benefits and entitlements, and chances to get involved in political issues affecting senior citizens. Some planned retirement communities and condominiums maintain social activities and classes and develop "blue books" of rules governing residents' behaviors, including restrictions on the minimum age of residents and on the maximum length of visits by younger people (especially if they bring young children with them).

Economic circumstances can also impose a subcultural existence on people. Elliot Liebow's study, *Tally's Corner* (1967), and that of Elijah Anderson, *A Place on the Corner* (1976), both used participant observation to examine how poverty and unemployment structured the lives of the men in two different city neighborhoods. The loss of self-esteem caused by inadequate job opportunities created the subculture of the street corner, where men gathered whose lives were characterized by shaky and failed marriages, sometimes by illegal activities, and often by shallow and fluid relationships (because of evictions from homes, prison terms, migrations in search of jobs, and so on). The men did not willingly embrace a culture of poverty. Rather, they were thrust into the street-corner subculture by poverty and by limited or nonexistent opportunities that marginalized them from mainstream society and made them appear unmotivated to settle down.

The economic circumstances of the men in Mitchell Duneier's participant observation study, *Slim's Table* (1992), were clearly better than those of the men in Liebow's and Anderson's studies, but the subculture that these middle-class men created by hanging out together at a local cafeteria was also carved out of the intersecting experiences of their work, class, race, gender, and families. Thus, while they may have had a greater sense of choice because of their more comfortable economic status than the men in the other two studies, their subculture was just as structured by economic and social circumstances.

Many ethnic and religious groups observe rituals and holidays and share foods, dances, music, and norms that are part of their ethnic heritage. For example, Jews who participate fully in American political and social life often still observe Passover and Hanukkah (Festival of Lights), as well as other Jewish holidays. Orthodox Jews observe their Sabbath even as they

Many ethnic and religious subcultures maintain their own rituals and customs even as they participate in the dominant cultures of their societies. Here, several generations of women gather to share in the candle-lighting ritual of Shabbot, a Jewish sabbath ceremony commonly performed by women.

participate in the secular world: they leave work early on Friday to get home before sundown, and they avoid the use of electricity until sundown on Saturday. Many Jewish children are bar mitzvahed (boys) and bat mitzvahed (girls) at age 13 as a rite of passage to adulthood. Participants at such events typically dance the hora, a spirited dance of joy and celebration. Each Jewish holiday and ritual is marked by a remembrance of history and custom, a reaffirmation of heritage and roots, and a recommitment to maintaining that connection. At the same time, Jews live and fully participate in the larger, non-Jewish society and culture.

It is not always easy for subcultures to maintain such clear and solid connections to their heritage. Jews in the Soviet Union had to practice their religion in secrecy or not at all. There is a long history of persecution and attempted genocide of Jews, from Jewish enslavement under Pharoah to banishment and oppression during the Spanish Inquisition to extermination during the Holocaust. And in the United States today, Jews continue to be the object of serious anti-Semitism. The results of a 1992 survey by the Anti-Defamation League indicate that 20 percent of the people in the United States harbor negative attitudes toward and stereotypes about Jews. Indeed, the survey found that since 1964 the number of people who maintain such stereotypes has steadily increased. In 1992, one-third of the respondents believed that Jews have too much power and that they are more loyal to Israel than to the United States. Half of the respondents believed that Jews stick together more than other groups in the United States and that Jewish employers go out of their way to hire other Jews (Anti-Defamation League, 1992). It is clearly difficult for the subculture of Jews in the United States to maintain its heritage in such a negative atmosphere.

Many ethnic groups have histories of oppression; two examples are Native Americans and African Americans. African Americans' ancestors were kidnapped from their tribes in Africa and sold as slaves in colonial America. Torn from their cultures, and unable to communicate with slaves from other tribes who spoke different languages, many lost their cultural connections. Only through concerted, conscious efforts by many African Americans have some threads of African culture been retrieved and nurtured. Many African Americans, for example, celebrate Kwanzaa, a festival held to reinforce and honor African heritage according to the principles of unity, self-determination, collective work and responsibility, cooperative economics, purpose, creativity, and faith. During this holiday, celebrants may wear traditional African dress; decorate their homes in the African colors of red, black, and green; arrange a table centerpiece containing the symbols of the harvest and of children; and share a feast with traditional African music and dancing in tribute to their ancestors. Some African Americans have changed their Anglo-American names to Muslim or African ones; prominent examples are writer and civil rights activist Kwame Toure (formerly Stokely Carmichael), boxing legend Muhammad Ali (born Cassius Clay), and basketball great Kareem Abdul-Jabbar (born Lew Alcindor). African crafts (such as batik), music, and dance are increasingly introduced in concert halls, community centers, and schools in African American neighborhoods as vivid reminders of the importance of the African American culture.

Native Americans have also had to work militantly to preserve their heritage, all but obliterated by the genocidal westward expansion of the dominant white population in the United States. The remaining members of the various Native American nations are recapturing the rituals, folk medicine, language, dance, norms, dress, and material aspects of their culture (such as pottery, jewelry making, textiles, and architecture).

The ability of ethnic and religious subcultures to piece together and preserve their often-threatened or lost cultural heritages is a testament to their strength and resilience. Indeed, many such subcultures are now so well preserved and maintained that their members often bring parts of their cultures with them as they participate in the larger society. Such sharing by a wide variety of subcultures diversifies and enriches the larger society. In this way, even dominant cultures can change over time. Sociologists refer to the sharing and incorporation of a diversity of subcultures as **cultural diffusion.**

We can see many aspects of this diffusion in the mainstream culture of the United States. For example, rock music popular in the 1960s youth subculture is now often used in product commercials. And fashions frequently borrow and incorporate styles from other cultures. In their 1993 line of men's clothing, designers in New York City featured the "Hassidic look": simple black suits, plain brimmed hats, and long, white, fringed scarves, which constitute the conventional dress of many Orthodox Jewish men. Foods of many ethnic subcultures have become standard American fare: pizza from Italy, frankfurters from Germany, tacos from Mexico, sushi from Japan, falafel from the Middle East, and so on. American music and dance incorporates salsa from Latin America, reggae from the Caribbean, jazz and blues from African American culture, and zydeco from the Cajuns. The noted pop and rock star Paul Simon deliberately uses the music forms and instruments of black South African groups and Latin American and Caribbean cultures in his mainstream music. And many schools in the United States have changed their Christmas parties to "winter holiday celebrations," in which children often learn Hanukkah, winter solstice, and, on occasion, Kwanzaa songs in addition to the more traditional Christmas carols. Note, however, that the cultural forms absorbed from subcultures are relatively innocuous. The norms that still prevail tend to be those established by the dominant groups in society. In order to thrive, then, a subculture must maintain its identity apart from and in addition to the mainstream culture.

Sometimes dominant groups adopt aspects of subcultures as a safety valve mechanism. Doing so reduces the probability of open hostility and challenge to the dominant culture. For example, Arizona initially refused to recognize Dr. Martin Luther King Jr.'s birthday as a state holiday. That decision evoked protest marches and boycotts, all of which stopped when the state finally reversed its position and adopted the holiday in 1992. Including King's birthday in the dominant culture of Arizona calmed race relations and reduced the probability that hostile challenges to the state would escalate.

Changes in cultures are not necessarily swift or immediate, however. There is often a lapse between the time a new subculture, technology, or idea is introduced and the time it is accepted and incorporated into the existing dominant culture. We refer to this time gap as **cultural lag.** For example, the civil rights movement has succeeded in getting legislation passed that legally protects racial minorities from discrimination. However, the notion that such minorities have the same rights as whites is still not fully accepted as part of our cultural assumptions. This is not to say that racial inequality in the United States is impossible to eradicate; but the concept of cultural lag helps us understand how the more innocuous aspects of African American culture can become incorporated into our dominant culture while African Americans themselves still struggle against racism in the mainstream.

COUNTERCULTURES

We have seen that dominant corporate and wealthy interests shape American culture, particularly its norms and values. In spite of this pervasive influence, the persistence of subcultures suggests that the power of such interests is not absolute. Even more telling is the persistence of **countercultures.** A counterculture is a specific type of subculture whose members embrace values, norms, rituals, and lifestyles that directly challenge the dominant culture. Whereas members of other subcultures participate in both the dominant culture and their particular subculture, members of countercultures reject the mainstream and challenge its pressures to conform.

The best-known, relatively recent example of a counterculture is the "hippie" movement of the late 1960s and early 1970s. Members of this loose counterculture denounced the legitimacy of the corporate culture and rejected its values of a button-down 9-to-5 work ethic and competitive individualism, its emphasis on private property and the amassing of material goods ("conspicuous consumption"), its norms of state violence and aggression as means of resolving conflicts and threats (both domestically and internationally), and its reliance on modern technologies that threaten the environment. In essence, the counterculture challenged what it referred to as "the Establishment." Many in the movement were young people who joined urban collectives and rural communes to jointly produce or buy their own food, communally raise their children, eschew the "rat race" of traditional jobs, foster cooperation instead of competition, and drastically reduce or eliminate their reliance on technology. Ironically, many communes reverted to sexist divisions of labor, relegating household chores and child care largely to women. Many also developed mainstream patriarchal power structures, with men dominating the decision-making process. While not all communes replicated mainstream sexism, its presence in some countercultural settings suggests the powerful influence mainstream norms and values can have.

Gangs can also be seen as countercultures. They tend to emerge from poverty and disenfranchisement from the mainstream's economic, social, and political opportunity structures. In the United States, where the Census Bureau indicates that 29.3 percent of African American families and 25

Gangs often function as countercultures for disenfranchised youths. Members of this Latina gang reject the dominant cultural definition of femininity as docility and adopt their own cultural code of toughness, including norms governing how to dress and use weapons, a system of gestures and body language, and violent initiation ceremonies.

percent of Latino families live below the poverty line, it is not surprising to find that 50 percent of gang members are Latino and 35 percent are African American (Spergel and Curry, 1990; U.S. Bureau of the Census, 1991b). There are also several very active Asian American gangs in New York, Los Angeles, and other cities.

Gangs come in a variety of forms, including social gangs, neighborhood street gangs, and organized-crime gangs. Our discussion here will focus mostly on the neighborhood street gangs. Many of these have spread from specific urban neighborhoods to other neighborhoods, entire cities, or more suburban areas. These gangs increasingly use illegal weapons and violence to commit crimes and control neighborhoods.

Gangs are typically organizations of alienated youths whose experiences remind them that the mainstream culture disdains and disrespects them. Gang members are frequently poorly educated and many live in substandard housing. They are chronically unemployed because urban education systems often do not provide adequate skills training and because there are fewer and fewer jobs for those without such training. Youth gangs can be seen as a countercultural response to blocked opportunities (Cohen, 1955; Kelly and Pink, 1982). They reject many of the values and norms of the mainstream and form their own often violent and predatory subculture. For example, dominant cultural norms stipulate that only the state can use force and violence to resolve disputes and that individuals must settle conflicts through negotiations or legal processes. Gangs challenge this notion by brazenly investing powers of violence with individual members. Gang violence also repudiates mainstream norms that call for deference to institutional authorities, such as those in schools and in the criminal justice system; it becomes a means of eliciting a semblance of respect, based on fear, from other gang members as well as the larger community. Gangs often respond to the unavailability of jobs in the mainstream economy by participating in drug trafficking, which can be lucrative although highly dangerous. Larceny and robbery may also be part of gang activity (Hagedorn, 1988, 1991).

Gangs reject mainstream culture in more symbolic ways as well. For example, their members' dress (such as the widespread use of bandanas as "colors" identifying gang affiliation), hairstyles, and language defy the dominant folkways. Gangs also represent an alternative to mainstream definitions of family as one's unit of procreation and parentage. The gang itself becomes an extended family providing protection as well as approval and support for delinquent and violent acts not accepted by the larger society (Kaplan, Johnson, and Bailey, 1987; Clark, 1991). (We will discuss family structures in greater detail in Chapter 14).

In a unique participant observation study of several female gangs in New York City, Campbell (1984) showed how such gangs reject the dominant culture's restrictive gender roles and establish their independence through the use of violence. While she disagreed with the notion that female gangs represent a counterculture, her descriptions of three of them suggest otherwise. For example, her findings indicate that female gangs will not accept members who are not able to "take care of themselves." Prospective members must demonstrate that they are willing and able to engage in a fight. In some instances, once the gangs have established this ability, members are initiated into the gang in a violent ritual called "jumping in." In this initiation they must endure (and perhaps defend themselves against) severe beatings by other gang members for a period of ten seconds.

Members in the gangs also form strong ties with other members; they do not allow men to come between the "sisters." Members frequently demand extreme loyalty to the gang, over and above boyfriends and even family. Female gangs thus repudiate the mainstream gender prescriptions of females as docile and dependent and as antagonistic rivals.

In some ways, gangs provide an interesting demonstration of how a counterculture can, in fact, embrace dominant cultural values while establishing very different and challenging norms. For example, gangs often accept the mainstream value of economic success and all the material comforts such success affords. But, faced with blocked opportunities, the gangs resort to their own norms for acquiring wealth, such as drug trafficking, robbery, larceny, and extortion of "protection" money from local small businesses (Clark, 1991). Some gangs have spread beyond the local "turf" battles and have organized "franchises" in many cities. These intercity franchises facilitate the movement of stolen goods and drugs. The national network this creates frustrates law enforcement agencies, which have tried in vain to control such gang activities. Gangs' countercultures thus become a parody of mainstream values, even as the gangs adopt normative behaviors that defy the legitimacy of the dominant culture.

CONCLUSION

Do people who control wealth and production also control culture? If so, how is diversity possible? Is the dominant value system fixed and inflexible, or can our efforts, individually and collectively, make a difference?

Culture is a social construction created by members of society. But not all members' viewpoints concerning values and norms are equally powerful in influencing the contours of mainstream culture. Since culture is transmitted from one generation to another, those members who have enjoyed prior privilege, advantage, and power are in a stronger position than others to impose their values and norms on everyone else. Similarly, since culture is diffused from one society to another, those societies with greater power and advantage are better able to influence the cultures of others.

Mainstream culture shapes our individual biographies by defining what is acceptable and unacceptable and what is normal and abnormal in regard to behavior and life circumstances. Our vision of legitimate alternatives becomes narrowed by these culturally defined restrictions. In addition, punishments for violations of these norms may reduce the likelihood that we will challenge existing rules and guidelines and may sometimes prevent us from even considering alternatives. Individuals who depart from the dominant culture may be marginalized and condemned by members of mainstream society.

Language, as the key to cultural transmission, is a powerful vehicle for constructing reality. Individuals who control what constitutes legitimate language usage can significantly influence the definitions of appropriate and inappropriate behaviors, viewpoints, and values. They can also shape what we consider to be real and viable and what never even occurs to us as possible.

Does this mean, then, that the less powerful members of society and of the world-system are unable to resist the imposition of dominant groups' culture? Does this mean that the forces of cultural domination and cultural hegemony are absolute and all-powerful? Hardly. Although the ideas, values, and norms of dominant groups tend to define the dominant culture, cultural diversity and resistance can still exist. The persistence of subcultures, for example, testifies to the fact that diverse values and normative systems can thrive even as the members of the subcultures participate in the mainstream culture. And the presence of countercultures illustrates the power of human effort to challenge and reject mainstream, dominant norms and values and to push at their boundaries. Moreover, while language may be the key to the social construction of reality by society's dominant members, it may also be used by the less powerful to sharpen our consciousness about that social construction and to introduce new ways of seeing the world around us.

Culture, then, is not simply a body of ideas and practices handed down unchanged from one generation to the next. It is a process of power struggles and contested constructions of social reality involving various members of society. These struggles are part of an ongoing historical process in which groups possessing variable resources and abilities strive to articulate and preserve the legitimacy of their social worlds. We will examine this process of organized struggle over the social construction of reality and cultural content in Chapter 9, "Social Change and Social Movements."

THINKING CRITICALLY

1. In the boxed excerpt, Joseph Steffan describes his internal struggle, when he was a Naval Academy cadet, with the realization that he was gay. He managed to resolve his conflict but was forced to resign from the academy as a result. If you had had the opportunity to talk with Steffan during his period of struggle, what would you have said?

2. Many variables may contribute to the development of a subculture. Consider the variety of statuses you have. Which of these might shape a subcultural existence for you? Why? Describe the elements of your subculture that depart from mainstream culture. Do these differences draw sanctions from the larger normative system? Why?

3. Think about situations you have encountered in which the norms differed significantly from those with which you are familiar. How did you react? Why? What norms did these differences define for you?

4. Consider the textbooks, ideas, and materials to which you were exposed in elementary school and high school. Make a list of the images, ideas, norms, and values focused upon in your schools. How closely did they conform to mainstream culture, and how much did they challenge it? Were you invited to debate the ideas presented in the classrooms and in the texts? How? How were uninvited challenges received?

5. Much debate has centered around the notion of "politically correct" language. What is politically correct language? What values does such language invoke? Why might there be considerable resistance to the use of politically correct language? What role does such language play in society?

KEY TERMS

culture, *104*
ideology, *104*
cultural hegemony, *104*
norms, *105*
normative indoctrination, *106*
culture shock, *106*
ethnocentrism, *107*
sanctions, *107*
folkways, *107*
mores, *108*
laws, *108*
values, *110*
patriarchy, *111*
nonmaterial culture, *113*

material culture, *113*
language, *116*
Thomas theorem (definition of the situation), *116*
corporate culture, *118*
competitive individualism, *118*
culture of poverty, *118*
cultural relativity, *123*
multiculturalism, *123*
subculture, *126*
cultural diffusion, *129*
cultural lag, *130*
counterculture, *130*

SUGGESTED READINGS

Michael Bronski, *Culture Clash: The Making of Gay Sensibility.* Boston: South End Press, 1984. An exploration of the meaning of a gay existence, including issues of gay liberation and of homophobia as cultural backlash.

Stephen Butterfield, *Amway: The Cult of Free Enterprise.* Boston: South End Press, 1985. An analysis of corporate culture through a case study of a single corporation; examines the implications of competitive individualism.

Thomas Cripps, *Making Movies Black: The Hollywood Message Movies from World War II to the Civil Rights Era.* New York: Oxford University Press, 1993. An analysis of the changing image of African Americans in film as both a creator of and reflection of larger cultural norms and ideologies about race.

Susan Faludi, *Backlash: The Undeclared War against American Women.* New York: Anchor Books, 1992. An examination of the elements in popular and political culture that resist the challenges of women to mainstream culture and a description of the economic, social, and political consequences of that backlash.

Felix M. Padilla, *The Gang as an American Enterprise.* New Brunswick, NJ: Rutgers University Press, 1992. A study of a street gang as a counterculture, analyzing the normative system that departs from mainstream culture and the social forces, including class, race, and economic and political institutions, that shape the counterculture.

SOCIALIZATION

5

*A*nswer the following questions as honestly as you can:

- *If one person of a two-earner couple has to quit work and remain home because of a family situation, how should the couple decide which person will quit?*

- *Do you believe the United States is full of opportunity for anyone willing to work hard?*

- *Would you hesitate to marry someone who is physically disabled?*

- *Would you be willing to go to war if the President asked you to, even if you didn't understand the reasons for our nation's involvement? What if you didn't agree with the reasons?*

- *You want to lease your home to tenants and you receive two similar offers, one from a female-headed family and one from a two-parent family. Which one would you rent your house to, and why?*

- *Should the school board of your child's elementary school be permitted to hire a homosexual kindergarten teacher?*

- *You are on the admissions board of a prestigious medical school, and you have one opening left. Two applicants come before you with similar grades and board exam scores. One is the daughter of an unemployed coal miner, and the other is the son of a congressperson. Which applicant will you admit?*

- *Would you buy a home in a neighborhood in which you would be a racial minority?*

- *Should legal marriage be possible for gay males or lesbians?*

- *Should capital punishment be legal?*

- *Should retirement be mandatory at age 65?*

Your responses reflect your attitudes on a number of social issues. Such attitudes are not genetically programmed; we learn them. Are your attitudes similar to or different from those of your friends, your family, or your teachers?

We know that social attitudes and behaviors are learned because of the great variability in cultural patterns throughout the world. As members of a society, we all learn and adopt social attitudes. But how does this learning occur? Who does the teaching? To what degree is the individual a passive recipient in this process? Can an individual transform the persons doing the teaching? What sorts of social roles and identities do we learn? What are the possible limitations to the process? This chapter will examine how sociologists have studied the learning process we call socialization.

139

Chapter 5

Socialization

SOCIALIZATION AS A LEARNING PROCESS

Human beings are social animals by nature. We are among the most dependent of animals at birth: when we are born, our muscles, nervous system, and digestive system are not fully developed and we cannot care for ourselves. We rely on other humans to nurture and protect us. But the need for other human beings does not end when we can walk and feed ourselves. Along the way we become members of our society. The ongoing process of learning the ways of our culture is called **socialization.** During this lifelong process, we acquire and modify our social identities. We learn, accept, reject, and modify the norms, values, assumptions, and expectations of our society. Finally, we develop the political lenses through which we view and analyze our surroundings.

Social scientists often debate the relationship between what we inherit and what we learn. We call this the **nature versus nurture debate.** Some sociologists argue that many social behaviors appear to be inherited genetically (for example, the capacity to learn, aggression or passivity, and sexual orientation) (Wilson, 1978; Caplan, 1979; Kagan et al., 1988). The study of the biological basis of social behavior is known as **sociobiology.** Other sociologists view social characteristics as primarily socially constructed, influenced by such environmental factors as power in relationships and learning. If social traits were biologically determined, they say, we would be unlikely to see such immense variation within families and societies and between cultures in social behaviors and attitudes (see, for example, Errington and Gewertz, 1987).

Yet studies of twins separated at birth and raised apart suggest that some social traits may develop independently of our social environment: such twins often exhibit surprisingly similar traits, such as shyness, in spite of very different upbringings and surroundings (Holden, 1980; Farber, 1981; Konner, 1982). How do we reconcile the contradictions of evidence in the nature versus nurture debate? Many sociologists take a middle ground. They argue that while the *potential* for expressing some social traits may indeed be inherited, striking evidence shows that social characteristics are unlikely to develop without social interaction between individuals as well as between individuals and a variety of social agents.

For example, children deprived of social contacts do not thrive physically and tend to be socially and emotionally immature. Such is often the case with institutionalized children (Spitz, 1946; Davis, 1949; Curtiss, 1977). In fact, even when infants in institutions are given the best basic care in terms of food, clothing, hygiene, and shelter, their social development is slow at best without regular play and human interaction (Bowlby,

1973). Adults who are similarly deprived, such as prisoners in solitary confinement for long periods of time, tend to regress to infantile behaviors (for example, assuming a fetal position and thumb sucking). Thus, provision of the basic physical needs for survival is not sufficient to ensure social development of the human being in the absence of human contact. Moreover, evidence suggests that children who were deprived of social interaction early in their lives improve in language, social skills, and muscle control when stimulated by increased human contact (Scarr, 1982).

These observations suggest the importance of social interaction for developing and reinforcing social characteristics. However, they do not tell us exactly *how* individuals learn to adopt certain attitudes and behaviors. In short, how do we become members of society? What is the *process* of socialization? Who participates in this process, and what role do they play?

SYMBOLIC INTERACTION PERSPECTIVE

Several theorists maintain that we develop our social identities through **symbolic interaction,** an interpersonal process using language, symbols, and sanctions. For example, Charles Horton Cooley (1902) argued that we acquire a sense of who we are by evaluating ourselves through the eyes of others, imagining how they might react to a particular behavior. He calls this identity the **looking-glass self.** We see ourselves as we believe others see us, perhaps altering behaviors we believe others disapprove of. Cooley argued that we do not need the others to be present during this process; our notion of how they are likely to react is sufficient.

Cooley's analysis of the looking-glass self did not distinguish among the various others whose perceptions we anticipate. Are the opinions of all others equally important to us when we see ourselves through their eyes? George Herbert Mead (1934) did not think so. He believed that the child's primary-group relationships were crucial to the development of the self. Harry Stack Sullivan (1953) later argued that the most important member of that primary group is the mother, who becomes the child's **significant other.** Since an infant is so dependent on its mother for nurturance and survival, he argued, the mother becomes uniquely important to the child; her judgment and approval are critical in developing the child's sense of self and identity. Recent researchers have found that fathers are also significant (Lamb, 1981; Lamb, Pleck, and Levine, 1986). In fact, anyone who functions as a child's primary caregiver may be viewed as the significant other. Such persons could be grandparents and other family members, foster or adoptive parents, day-care workers, and so on (Schaffer and Emerson, 1964).

As the child matures, the process of acquiring role identity and self-awareness extends to play. For example, children try on a variety of roles through dress-up and playacting. As they mature further, children develop a general understanding of how people around them expect them to behave and of what their place is among those people. They no longer need the actual presence of known individuals in order to understand their own roles and identities. They now evaluate their behavior through a **general-**

Children often play at adult roles during games of dress-up. Here, two children mimic the gendered adult world, where the female dresses alluringly and cares for children while the male dresses for the work world.

ized other. Such an analysis highlights play and pretend as critical elements in social development (Barnett, 1977).

Mead's analysis speaks of the process of shaping a sense of self as if it occurs only in children. In fact, many different significant others may appear throughout the life cycle. Anyone who is centrally important to us at a particular point in our lives—on-the-job mentors, for example, or coaches, advisers, or partners—may take on the role of significant other. Indeed, in many American couples, each partner refers to the other one as "my significant other." Some researchers argue that a significant other does not even have to be someone with whom the individual is intimate; nor does it have to be another person at all. For example, television may act as significant other for some people (Newton and Buck, 1985). For others, some notion of God is sufficient.

Mead's analysis of how we acquire our social identities suggests that the process of self-development is reflexive, involving the individual as an active agent rather than as a passive recipient. That is, developing a self-identity involves an interaction "between identification by others and self-identification, between objectively assigned and subjectively appropriated identity" (Berger and Luckmann, 1966: 132). Thus, socialization subjects may resist or reject the social construction of "appropriate" behaviors. However, the focus in Mead's analysis remains the socialization subject. This focus implies that the socialization process moves in one direction only: the agent socializes the subject.

More recent analyses using a symbolic interaction perspective suggest that both parties get socialized. For example, although parents and other primary caregivers may indeed teach the child about appropriate behaviors, the child may also socialize the caregivers, altering their behaviors, values, or attitudes (Peterson and Rollins, 1987). When labor and management engage in negotiations, management is certainly attempting to indoctrinate the workers about appropriate attitudes and behaviors, but the workers are also teaching management about appropriate interaction and bargaining styles, acceptable demand levels, and so forth. Both parties are in fact altering their behavior patterns. Even when one party is clearly more powerful than the other, that power is not absolute. There is usually some room for each side to modify its position.

CONFLICT PERSPECTIVE

Sociologists using a **conflict perspective** argue that socialization processes are, in fact, typified by struggles. Conflict theorists examine the internal as well as external struggles that we experience in the process of socialization. They also tend to view socialization as ongoing throughout the life cycle. As we encounter new situations and challenges in our lives, we are always shaping and reshaping our social identities. As we move from school to the work world or from single life to marriage, for example, we learn new sets of expectations, some of which may challenge previous social constructions of our selves. Even though our ascribed statuses (for example, race, sex, physical and mental capacities and capabilities) do not change, our sense of what they mean may change over time. Other statuses may actually change (such as age, family status, working status, and sexual orientation), prompting a personal reconceptualization of self and a reevaluation of expectations.

Erik Erikson's *Eight Stages of Psychosocial Development* (1963) discusses socialization as an ongoing process typified by conflict. Erikson argued that we develop our identities and our attitudes about the world around us as we resolve various developmental crises. Although he specified the life stages during which each crisis typically occurs, he argued that we may always return to earlier crises and rework them or complete unresolved ones. How we resolve these crises shapes our social identities. (See Figure 5.1.)

The basic conflict during infancy concerns reliance on others to provide food, shelter, protection, and comfort. Infants resolve this problem by developing either *basic trust* or *basic mistrust* that the world around them can be counted on to provide consistently for their needs. Toddlers encountering challenges of personal control (for example, during toilet training) resolve their crisis with either a *sense of autonomy*, if control is mastered, or a *sense of shame and doubt*, if control proves difficult to achieve. Preschool children, whose main challenge is to learn to perform basic tasks independently, develop either a *sense of initiative* born of successful attempts at mastery or a *sense of guilt* from repeated failures. Older children confront increasingly challenging academic and physical skills. If they learn that mastery of these skills involves the often frustrating process of trying, failing, and trying again, they are more likely to develop a *sense of industry* and a willingness to work through failures. If they learn that not mastering a task immediately is a personal failing and a character flaw, they are more likely to develop a *sense of inferiority*. Adolescents face the

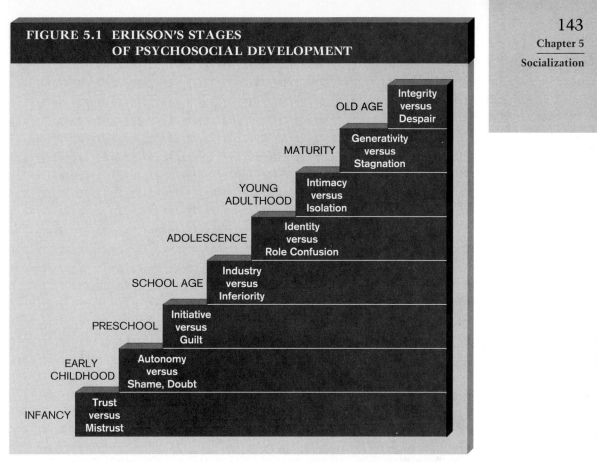

**FIGURE 5.1   ERIKSON'S STAGES
OF PSYCHOSOCIAL DEVELOPMENT**

Erikson underscored the role of culture in personality development throughout the life cycle. Consider your own personality development: Which developmental stages are you currently struggling with?   (*Source:* Adapted from Erik Erikson, *Childhood and Society,* 2nd ed. NY: W.W. Norton & Company Inc. 1950.)

challenge of establishing a clear definition of self. Success in defining "who I am" resolves the crisis with a *sense of identity;* failure to resolve the identity crisis may result in *role confusion.*

Beyond adolescence, Erikson saw three more crises. Young adults face the tension of establishing close personal relationships, many of which may not last for very long. Such crises resolve either in a *sense of intimacy* and a willingness to make oneself vulnerable to another or in a *sense of isolation* and a refusal or reluctance to risk getting close to others. Adults must resolve the crisis of maintaining a *sense of generativity,* involving productiveness and growth, or they may develop a *sense of stagnation,* of being in a rut or not being challenged or excited about their work or lifestyles. Elderly adults, particularly at retirement, resolve the crisis of identity shift either with a *sense of integrity,* feeling they have performed well and lived a good life, or a *sense of despair,* feeling they have wasted their lives or lost sight of their goals.

SOCIALIZATION AND SOCIAL STRUCTURE

Erikson's analysis introduces conflict rather than consensus as the central characteristic of the socialization process. However, it is based on the assumption that specific roles and tasks belong to particular life stages, and it defines success and failure narrowly. And because of Erikson's psychoanalytical perspective, his analysis assumes psychosocial development to be more a personal problem of individual struggles and conflicts than the result of structural restrictions. For example, if an adolescent girl is told she cannot participate in football because she is not strong enough, the feeling of inferiority she might develop would be seen as the result of a personal failure to resolve a developmental crisis. Yet it seems more likely that her inferiority would be the result of systematic discrimination and differential treatment in the social structure. Sometimes both personal and social elements are at work. Consider an elderly woman who feels a sense of despair. She may have failed to resolve some personal crises, but she also may feel the burden of a social structure that limits her opportunities, restricts her access to outlets for usefulness, narrowly defines her roles, and accords senior citizens little respect.

If we analyze socialization critically, looking at the role of both internal and external (and institutional) conflicts, we can see that the process does not necessarily produce a uniform outcome for all. Some people may, in fact, resist and reject the dominant group's definition of appropriate and inappropriate behaviors. What happens in such cases? In some instances, sanctions may be imposed to punish or correct the "inappropriate" behavior. For example, homosexuals may be ostracized or harassed, denied employment or fired. Children who display "gender-inappropriate" behaviors may be called names, ostracized by their peers, and "redirected" by guidance counselors who try to steer them to more "appropriate" behaviors and aspirations.

When informal sanctions are insufficient to alter an individual's resistance, dominant groups may sometimes attempt to reeducate, or resocialize, the transgressor. **Resocialization** is a process in which the individual's previous self is replaced with a new, more acceptable social identity (Mortimer and Simmons, 1978). This process sometimes requires removing the person from his or her environment and support networks. In some cases, the process may involve a **degradation ceremony,** in which socialization agents assail and devalue the subject's existing identity in an effort to break it down and build an entirely new one (Garfinkel, 1956).

Deprogramming of people who have joined religious cults is a commonly used method of resocialization. In his study of asylums, Goffman (1961) found that similar processes occur among prisoners and patients at state mental hospitals. These are **total institutions,** in which the individual is completely isolated from the rest of society for an extended period of time. In such environments the individual's life is carefully controlled and the process of resocialization more easily accomplished. New military recruits experience this situation in boot camp, where they undergo a fairly intense process of resocialization designed to break down civilian values of individuality, freedom of expression, and freedom of choice and replace them with new values. The recruits learn to accept orders unquestioningly, to subordinate individuality to country or troop, and to respect rank, the flag, and the uniform. They learn to accept narrowly defined conceptions of appropriate dress and hairstyles and to suspend personal opinions concerning a broad variety of issues, both personal and global.

Resocialization may also occur in more subtle ways. As we have seen, changes in life circumstances can bring about transformations of one's social identity. For example, no total-institution setting is requisite for the changes that accompany the shifts from student to worker, from childless person to parent, from worker to retiree, and so on.

At the same time that we develop a social identity, we also undergo a constant process of **political socialization.** In this process we may internalize a political identity of who we are and how we should behave in the political and economic institutions of society. Moreover, we may learn to accept the dominant social structure as just, fair, and legitimate. Socialization, then, can be a means of political control, in which the dominant group may influence and shape our perceptions of acceptable or appropriate political attitudes and behaviors (for example, voting is an acceptable way to express dissatisfaction, but rioting is not), limit our conception of valid options for action, and legitimize its rule and ideology.

Resocialization processes often involve a degradation ceremony, during which the previous identity of the individual is broken down to shape a new identity. During military boot camp training, all recruits are given the same shaved-head haircut, are provided uniforms, and are frequently the object of verbal assaults on their individuality and civilian identities.

AGENTS OF SOCIALIZATION

How do we come to be socially and politically socialized? Who or what are the agents of socialization? **Socialization agents** can be grouped into seven basic categories: family; peers; school; religion; work; media; and toys, games, and recreational activities.

We have seen how *family* reinforces "appropriate" social and gender roles. Some observers also believe that birth order acts as a passive socialization agent (Pfouts, 1980; Steelman and Powell, 1985): one's birth-order position in the family may greatly affect siblings' interactions as well as parent-child interactions. These interactions become part of our socialization experiences.

For example, firstborn children (if they are not twins) tend to be more strictly disciplined, to receive more attention, to remain in school longer, and to be higher achievers than later-born siblings. With second-born children, parents are more relaxed and tend to be less authoritative; such children may therefore have more relaxed relationships with others and be more playful than firstborns. Second-borns may also be more diplomatic negotiators than firstborns, because they are smaller than older siblings and must therefore rely more on reason and rationality than on brute strength. It is important to note, however, that these social characteristics are based on a middle-class model of the family. Birth-order characteristics may be complicated by such factors as the age and spacing of siblings and parents' differential expectations based on gender, class, ethnicity, and family structure (Kilbride, Johnson, and Streissguth, 1977).

Peer groups constitute an alternative **reference group,** a group to whom we look for approval, guidance, and role models. Peer groups may be an important factor influencing study habits, work aspirations, and lifestyle goals (Hesse-Biber, 1985). Children and adolescents often develop a greater sense of autonomy from adults by forming coalitions with peers. In extreme cases, gangs may develop to challenge authority. Adults who work together often form informal groups of peers that may counteract rules of managers or corporate culture (see Chapter 3).

People who are subject to prejudice or disapproval may form peer groups to help resist the stigma and reinforce the validity of their autonomy. For example, the many formal and informal gay and lesbian peer groups found in high schools, colleges, and urban areas serve this dual purpose. Racial and ethnic minorities frequently form cultural peer groups to reinforce their validity in the dominant culture. And women often form peer groups as a way to countervail patriarchal treatment and share information that challenges the prevailing attitudes toward women's appropriate roles, rights, and abilities.

Schools reproduce the dominant culture of society by socializing students about what is valued and appropriate in the culture and what is not (Weiss, 1986). For example, curricula and texts that stress white, male, privileged European contributions to U.S. society and ignore the legitimacy of Third World, female, and working-class contributions reproduce a limited set of cultural values. In-school celebration of Christian holidays (such as Christmas) but not of other ethnic or religious groups' holidays (such as Hanukkah, Kwanzaa, or winter solstice) makes Christianity seem more valuable and legitimate than other credos. Likewise, if schools honor Washington's and Lincoln's birthdays, but not Dr. Martin Luther King's birthday, they teach children that King's contributions to American society are less important. The celebration of the dominant groups' culture and the failure to acknowledge the importance of others may socialize whites and Christians to an identity of superiority and privilege while socializing racial minorities and non-Christians to an identity of inferiority.

Religious organizations socialize us to adopt particular attitudes and behaviors, which may or may not be consistent with the dominant culture. For example, an ideology that stresses sacrifice and asceticism, obedience to a higher authority, acceptance of one's lot in life as part of a plan of that higher authority, heterosexual love and marriage, tradition, and hard work is consistent with the values of the dominant culture in the United States. These principles contribute to a social identity based on conformity, which makes it less likely that oppressed or exploited groups will challenge the authority and privilege of the dominant groups.

On the other hand, some religious teachings stress nonacceptance of poverty, challenge of higher authorities if they are oppressive or punitive, civil disobedience, and the legitimacy of nontraditional lifestyles. This religious position has occurred as a social movement in Latin American Catholic churches, where it is referred to as **liberation theology.** This theology may pose a countervailing influence to dominant socialization forces. Indeed, in parts of Mexico, and in Central and South America, the poor are encouraged to believe that it is entirely appropriate to challenge leaders and higher authorities who see fit to oppress and starve them, deprive them of dignity and civil rights, and otherwise abuse them.

In the United States, African American churches played a pivotal role in the civil rights movement from the 1950s to 1970s. Unitarian and mainline Protestant denominational churches have come to recognize the legitimacy of women as clergy, and many Conservative and Reformed Jewish synagogues have come to accept female rabbis. Religious organizations throughout the world were often visible and vocal opponents to the Vietnam war, giving legitimacy to such opposition. More recently, churches in the United States have provided asylum for Central American refugees escaping oppression by their governments. Not only have these churches provided refugees with food, clothing, and shelter, but they have also protected them from deportation by U.S. immigration authorities. The participation of religious institutions in the antiwar and asylum movements lends institutional support to people who challenge their governments, both here and abroad. Religious doctrine, then, can contribute to a social identity that includes the entitlement to protest and challenge oppression. It can also contribute to a social identity based on a notion of social justice and altruism.

The *workplace* acts as both a formal and an informal socialization agent. For example, on-the-job training is a formal mechanism of workplace socialization, in which one is taught rules, regulations, expectations of behavior, and recognition of authority figures and status symbols. Individuals who train closely with a mentor tend to become dependent on the mentor, and therefore more susceptible to influence (Mortimer and Simmons, 1978).

Training in groups can produce a team spirit that reinforces the dominant work culture. For example, military training in boot camp emphasizes the importance of duty to country, a strong sense of "us" against "them," and the necessity of a buddy system for survival against a common enemy. Corporate softball and bowling teams similarly reinforce such principles and create a sense of family and loyalty among the workers for that firm.

Group training can, however, also produce camaraderie among trainees *against* corporate and military authority figures and become a source of resistance to the organization. For example, during the Vietnam war, there were frequent instances of apparent violent retaliation (called fragging action) by recruits against abusive or overzealous officers. (In fact, an underground newspaper that circulated among recruits during that era was called *Fragging Action.*) Assembly-line workers may develop group loyalty to one another in the face of exploitative or overly harsh management, devising ways to set more comfortable rates of productivity and, in extreme cases, sabotaging output. The classic Hawthorne studies discussed in Chapter 3 revealed how an informal group of workers punished those whose productivity exceeded the group's informally set rate. The group also covered for colleagues whose productivity fell short for various reasons (Roethlisberger and Dickson, 1939).

Some researchers have noted gender biases in on-the-job training and interaction patterns, such as mentor relationships. Employers place men in advantageous interaction systems more frequently than they do women; the men thus become part of a network tapped for promotion opportunities (Olson and Miller, 1983). Such gender differentiation in training and work opportunities serves to reproduce stereotypical gender differences.

Media are very powerful, pervasive agents of socialization. Television can play a positive role in the development of language and reading readiness skills, as well as the assimilation of basic arithmetic facts. Programs like *Sesame Street,* in particular, have been highly successful in this area. In addition, *Sesame Street* and *Mr. Rogers' Neighborhood* promote prosocial values like cooperation, helping others, sharing, and self-control (Ball-Rokeach, Rokeach, and Grube, 1984).

On the other hand, some studies have found that early and frequent television viewing is associated with increased aggression in children and teenagers (Liebert and Sprafkin, 1988; Weigman, Kuttschreuter, and Baarda, 1992; Barry, 1993; Cannon, 1993). Many observers agree that the increasing level of violence in both television programs and films teaches viewers of all ages that brute force and violence are acceptable and appropriate avenues for redressing grievances and solving problems (Pearl, 1982; Maio, 1990).

In addition to the usual components of media (such as films, television, newspapers, and magazines), *toys, games, and recreational activities* serve as socialization agents. We learn much about cultural values from the rules and concepts of various board games. For example, Monopoly rewards greed and cutthroat competition: the winner is the player who bankrupts all the other players. The game of Risk, with its goal of world domination, rewards aggression. Other games also reinforce prevailing social values. Trivial Pursuit rewards the ability to spit back odd bits and pieces of memorized information rather than the ability to present a coherent, critical analysis of a problem.

While most board games and sports tend to emphasize the concepts of competition and winning and losing, some do stress cooperation. For example, Bertel Ollman's game Class Struggle sought to deliberately counter Monopoly by rewarding cooperation and an organized struggle against capitalism that involves using principles of Marxism (interestingly, no major toy company would market the game). Group games of jump rope, particularly Double Dutch, succeed only when everyone cooperates to keep the game going by ensuring that the rope turns with a constant rhythm and accommodates the jumper. And while team sports emphasize competition between teams, they also reinforce the notion of cooperation for the common good among the team members.

Beyond a general assimilation of cultural norms and values, what specific roles do these agents socialize us to internalize? There is evidence that they work to reinforce and reproduce roles relating to class, gender, and race, as well as roles and attitudes concerning political values and norms.

CLASS SOCIALIZATION

Families, workplaces, and schools play an important part in class socialization, reproducing and perpetuating class positions and roles. Consider the different socialization processes undergone by professional, technical, and managerial workers, on the one hand, and blue-collar, clerical, and service workers, on the other. The latter operate in a work environment that requires little autonomy or creative initiative. They are rewarded for accepting orders and following directions. Professional, managerial, and technical workers, however, get rewards for exercising autonomy, independence, creativity, and initiative in decision-making and problem solving (Kohn, 1977). These differential work experiences and reward structures reproduce class differences: they affect how these workers view themselves as well as how their children perceive them as role models (Grant and Sleeter, 1988).

Class differences may persist because parents strive to prepare their children adequately for the work world they are likely to join when they become adults (Majoribanks, 1987). This preparation for future roles is what we call **anticipatory socialization** (Mortimer and Simmons, 1978). Some researchers have noted, however, that class-based differences are declining as middle-class and working-class child-rearing practices become more similar (Wright and Wright, 1976). Although some class distinctions remain, the classes increasingly share the value of developing autonomy (Alwin, 1984).

Schools also participate in socializing children for their future roles in the labor market. Teachers and guidance counselors make assumptions

Upper-class educational institutions, such as Eton, Great Britain's premier private boys' school, act as class socialization agents: they inculcate their students with the values associated with power and wealth and engage the students in anticipatory socialization through dress codes that reinforce the norms of privilege.

concerning appropriate future work roles for students and therefore appropriate curriculum tracks. The socioeconomic status, race, and gender of a student may influence school staff more than his or her actual skills and talents (Grant and Sleeter, 1988). Teachers and counselors also tend to emphasize varying degrees of obedience, the necessity to follow rules and take direction, and independent thinking (Franklin, 1986). School officials tend to reward behaviors that they see as consistent with perceptions of future work roles; inconsistent behaviors are punished. Taken together, these forces operate to perpetuate differential class roles and positions.

Differential treatment of students on the basis of class becomes a **self-fulfilling prophecy** in producing feelings of inferiority among lower-class and working-class children. Indeed, even when such children succeed later in life as Ph.Ds, they frequently express feelings of the **imposter syndrome,** of somehow having fooled those around them into thinking that they are deserving of recognition, respect, and acceptance (Ryan and Sackrey, 1984).

GENDER SOCIALIZATION

Many socialization agents are important forces in the shaping of our gender identities. They therefore contribute significantly to reproducing stereotypical gender roles.

Families may reproduce gender roles by overtly assigning different household chores along traditional gender lines: girls baby-sit, cook, and wash dishes; boys take out garbage and do yardwork (Burns and Homel, 1989). Different parental expectations for academic performance may also reinforce gender differences. Parents often send their children messages about male and female abilities and appropriate future work roles (Baker and Entwisle, 1987; Eccles, Jacobs, and Harold, 1990).

The division of household chores between parents also sends a powerful message to children about gendered domestic work roles. Studies indicate that women do the majority of domestic labor, thereby defining it as women's responsibility (Berch, 1982; Berk, 1985). Even when women work full-time outside the home, they still perform most of the household chores, a situation some observers have referred to as the **double day** or **double shift** (Hochschild and Machung, 1989). Such role models teach children that the appropriate behavior for women includes cooking, cleaning, and caring for children, regardless of the time spent working outside the home. Similarly, they imply that a man's appropriate role is that of paid worker who is not expected to assume household responsibilities.

Schools

Schools also reinforce gendered social roles. For example, researchers have documented the differential treatment accorded males and females in the classroom that reinforces a sense of inferiority and lack of initiative among female students (Frazier and Sadker, 1973; Sadker and Sadker, 1988). Boys are far more likely than girls to be given specific information that guides improvement of their performance (Boggiano and Barrett, 1991). Boys also receive greater encouragement to reach for higher standards for themselves. Girls are thus denied an important part of the education process that encourages students to strive for excellence. Instead, the vague praise girls may receive often implies that whatever they accomplish, however flawed, is "good enough," that it is not necessary for them to try for better achievement.

Gaskell (1984) found that school tracking occurs along gender lines. Girls tend to be tracked away from math and science and toward the humanities, social sciences, and secretarial studies. They are often encouraged to enter nurturing or helping professions, such as teaching (especially at the preschool and elementary school levels), nursing, social work, and clerical work. Boys tend to be tracked toward math and science, sports, and physically demanding vocations. They are pushed toward more autonomous professions, such as medicine, science and technology, law, business, engineering, and finance, or physical vocations in fields like auto mechanics and electromechanical technology (see Fennema, 1987; Peltz, 1990).

Textbooks used in schools explicitly and implicitly reinforce gender roles through both their content and their form. For example, literature texts are often dominated by the works of white males, with a few notable exceptions (such as Emily Dickinson). History texts give scant attention to the serious contributions of women in American and world history. Even in college-level sociology texts, discussions of women tend to be restricted to a single chapter on gender or sprinkled in chapters on topics such as the family and socialization, which have traditionally included women (Hall, 1988).

One study of photographs that accompany sociology texts found that only one-third of the pictures contained women of any race. Race and gender were treated as mutually exclusive categories: white women were depicted as women, while women of color were depicted for their race. Moreover, the study found that, overall, white male images dominated the textbook photographs, most particularly in the chapters on politics and economics (Ferree and Hall, 1990). The message here, in sociology textbooks of all places, is that white males are the important actors in our most crucial institutions, while women play a role primarily in the family.

Funding for high school and college athletics, including equipment, travel, and scholarships, tends to reward females less than males (with the notable exception of cheerleading). This inequality is reinforced by the lack of opportunities for women's professional sports. Even in cases where women's sports do receive some institutional support, it lags significantly behind that of men's sports. The lack of positive rewards or adequate funding to support women's sports discourages females from pursuing such activities. This reinforces notions that women are not strong and do not have physical endurance.

Work

Work roles in the paid labor market are also sharply divided along gender lines. While the gap between male and female employees has been closing since 1970 (U.S. Bureau of Labor Statistics, 1991), occupations still tend to be segregated by gender. Most occupations in industrialized societies are characterized as predominantly male or predominantly female. In the United States, almost half the women in the paid labor force can be found in fewer than 50 job categories that are predominantly female, which means that at least 80 percent of the employees doing those jobs are women. More than half the men in the paid labor force are distributed over 229 predominantly male occupations (Reskin and Hartmann, 1986). The diversity of occupations dominated by men implies that men possess a wide array of skills, talents, and intelligence. The restriction of female-dominated occupations to helping professions (such as nursing, administrative assistance, and dental hygiene) and low-prestige jobs (such as store clerk, waitress, day-care worker) implies that females' abilities and intelligence are limited. Moreover, the occupations in which women predominate tend to pay less and confer less autonomy and power than those dominated by men. The resulting differential incomes, status, and prestige reinforce the notion that men are more valuable workers than women.

Media

The media also contribute to stereotypes of gender roles. In some media, for example, stark images depict men as aggressive and dominating actors and women as docile, submissive objects (Dines, 1992). Some research shows that men who batter women tend to consume more pornographic print and video materials than other men; almost 40 percent of these battering partners also acted out the acts of pornographic violence they had read about or seen in films and videos (Sommers and Check, 1987; Page, Linz, and Donnerstein, 1990). Other studies have found that a *correlation* exists between pornography and violence, but they were inconclusive about whether pornography *caused* the violence (Vloebergh, 1979). However, research has suggested that exposure to pornographic materials does produce elevated levels of violence and aggression against women in men who already harbor anger (Gray, 1982; Fisher and Grenier, 1994). At the very least, then, pornography appears to aggravate hostility, aggression, and violence against women.

Television and films offer very limited roles for women, and those they do offer perpetuate female stereotypes and caricatures (Levy, 1989). Actresses frequently lament the scarcity of roles for strong leading women; they tend to be cast in secondary roles as prostitutes or as insecure, bitchy, or childish females. Many critics have noted a trend in films of the early 1990s: women are sold to men by other men. Such was the case in *Honeymoon in Vegas, Mad Dog and Glory,* and *Indecent Proposal.* Television reinforces this view of women as objects: the portrayal of women in videos seen on MTV, where sex and violence are often casually fused, offers teenagers a sadomasochistic perspective of women as victims (Strouse and Fabes, 1985; Maio, 1990).

Research shows that children as young as toddlers imitate behaviors they see on television and that this copying intensifies through adolescence (Comstock and Paik, 1991). Therefore, media images of gender can be powerful socializers. In children's television, very few roles are given to females. One researcher noted that the fall 1991 season of Saturday morning television was "an exclusive male preserve" (Carter, 1991: A1; see also Signorielli, 1991). The one program featuring a strong female star, *Little Rosey,* was canceled after its creator refused to comply with the ABC network's demand that she add more male characters to the cartoon. Even on the award-winning *Sesame Street* most of the muppet characters are male; only in 1994 was a female muppet (named Zoe) introduced as a main character on the show. Part of the reason for the male bias of children's programming may be that 75 to 90 percent of the writers, directors, and producers of children's television shows are men (Davis, 1990).

There are signs that some of this may be changing: the popular television series *Murphy Brown, Roseanne,* and *Grace Under Fire* all feature strong central female characters. But assertive, intelligent, in-control women are still the exception. The fact that such characters stand out reaffirms the persistence of gender stereotypes in television.

It is also the case that gender roles are depicted as appropriate only when they are heterosexual. The media, particularly television, still tend to treat gay males and lesbians as perverted oddities in overdrawn carica-tures, when they portray them at all. Indeed, a very sensitive portrayal on *thirtysomething* of two homosexual men sitting in bed discussing the hor-ror of losing friends to AIDS was never rerun because of intense objections to the scene by the network's standards and practices censors.

Hostility to depictions of homosexuality as a valid sexual orientation reached a fever pitch in a national controversy over artist Robert Map-plethorpe's photography exhibit, which included many pictures of homo-sexuals. Many people objected to what they saw as homosexual pornogra-phy. Senator Jesse Helms spoke to their fears when he called for a national campaign to rescind or deny grants for such exhibits from the National Endowment for the Arts. The campaign helped define non-heterosexual orientations as unnatural, pornographic, and unacceptable. This example shows how dominant members of a community can set standards that serve to shut off funding and media outlets for unpopular viewpoints and norms. In this role they can act as an important socializ-ing agent.

Toys, Games, and Recreational Activities

Toys and games teach children a great deal about "appropriate" and "inappropriate" gender roles. Even the packaging plays a part. For exam-ple, boxes showing girls playing with dolls and tea sets and boys playing with erector sets, or doctor kits showing a boy as the doctor and a girl as either patient or nurse, send children a message of who is "supposed" to play with these toys or who is "supposed" to assume a particular role when they play. Indeed, girls are encouraged to view the distorted body form of the Barbie doll as the ideal, while boys learn to idolize the aggression of such "action figures" as G.I. Joe, Transformers, and He-Man.

Games are subtle, but powerful, gender socialization agents. For exam-ple, Chutes and Ladders is a very popular game among preschoolers and very young elementary school children. The game very explicitly defines "good" behaviors (rewarded with advancement to the finish) and "bad" behaviors (punished with slides back toward the start). Notably, the behav-iors identified in the pictures on the game board are gender-specific: good behaviors depict girls planting flowers, baking a cake, nursing an injured dog, and sweeping the floor, and show boys mowing the lawn, rescuing a distressed cat in a tree, and finding Mom's purse. Bad behaviors show girls eating too many chocolates (girls must be careful not to jeopardize their figures) and breaking dishes by attempting to carry too many (girls are not strong enough to carry more than a few), and they depict boys reading comic books instead of the history textbook, breaking a window with a baseball, and pulling a cat's tail. Games such as Sweet Valley High and The Barbie Game teach adolescent and preadolescent girls to fit the stereotype of catty, back-biting females as they compete for boyfriends and prom dates.

Language and Gender Socialization

Language usage, particularly as it appears in media, plays an important role in gender socialization. For example, the use of the generic pronoun "he" and the term "man" to refer to any member of the human race invokes an image of a male, thereby excluding women from our consciousness as important members of humanity (Frank and Anshen, 1983; Miller and Swift, 1991). The media only reinforce this perception when they pointedly refer to a "woman lawyer," "woman senator," or "woman autoworker." Such terms as "fireman" (instead of "firefighter"), "workman's compensation" (in place of "workers' compensation"), and "manpower" (as opposed to "labor power") also underscore the power of language and media to devalue women and elevate men as the important members of society. *The New York Times,* widely regarded as the newspaper of record, resisted eliminating sexist language in its reporting for decades. Only very recently have the editors agreed to use "Ms." instead of "Miss" or "Mrs." to describe women in its articles. Why is this change important? Formal titles like "Miss" or "Mrs." clearly identify women by their relationships to men, whether these are relevant to the story or not. The term "Ms.," like the term "Mr.," makes marital status irrelevant to the story and focuses reporting on women in their own right.

Women are more likely than men to be pejoratively described by their sexuality. One study found 220 English words used to negatively describe sexually active women but only 22 describing sexually active men (Stanley, 1977). This language discrepancy reinforces the sexual double standard applied to men and women in their socialization: "nice" girls are chaste and virginal until marriage; "real" boys are sexually experienced by the time they "settle down" with a partner.

How successful are all these agents of gender socialization in reinforcing gender stereotypes of appropriate and inappropriate behavior? Gilligan, Lyons, and Hanmer (1990) studied socialization and development of adolescent girls in a girls' school in the United States, and they found striking evidence that these agents are indeed quite formidable. According to the researchers, girls tend to go through a "moment of resistance" around age 11, in which they experience a clear confidence in their abilities, insights, integrity, and potential roles in the world around them. However, as they get older, girls begin to understand and heed the restrictive messages that socialization agents in their culture send to them: they begin to realize that women are invisible and unimportant in their culture. By age 15 or 16, the girls in the study were less outspoken, less sure of their abilities and intelligence, and more docile than the preadolescents. The resistance was gone, or had at least gone "underground"; the girls were more likely to preface their statements and observations with comments such as "This may be silly," and they repeatedly said, "I don't know." The researchers' findings suggest that socialization agents are quite powerful in shaping girls' social identities to conform to gender stereotypes.

The difficulty of generalizing the findings of Gilligan, Lyons, and Hanmer stems from the fact that their study was based on an elite, gender-segregated school. Are their findings gender-specific? Or might they be age-specific to both boys and girls? A 1992 survey found that although both boys and girls do indeed suffer a decline in self-esteem as adolescents, the decline is more pronounced for girls (American Association of University Women, 1992). Another study found that while girls begin kindergarten well ahead of boys in all areas except science, they finish high school *behind* boys in almost all areas because systematic gender bias in the classroom boosts boys' and undermines girls' confidence (Sadker and Sadker, 1994).

The effectiveness of gender socialization of both boys and girls is also evident in their respective recreational activities, peer interactions, and language usage. Sex segregation in peer and play groups begins very early among preschoolers (Schofield, 1981), and it continues in school friendships as children select same-sex tablemates in the lunchroom and in the playground at recess. These groups begin to reinforce gender roles for both boys and girls. Later, schools, families, and communities support team sports as common experiences for boys, a reflection of the persistent stereotype that competitive and aggressive behavior is masculine, not feminine (King, 1991). This view is reinforced by frequent media coverage of men's professional sports and the use of male athletes in advertisements. One result of all this support is that large areas of playground space are controlled by boys playing baseball, football, basketball, street hockey, and so on. While there have been important advances in organized competitive sports for girls in many schools throughout the United States, girls usually play games such as jump rope and hopscotch, which involve turn taking and cooperation and take up relatively little playground space (Lever, 1976; Thorne, 1989, 1993).

Boys, then, dominate the "gendered turf" of the playground, where they learn that competition, aggression, and sometimes violence are "normal" aspects of being male. Such lessons extend beyond team sports, as boys'

In gendered play, boys and girls learn different notions about male and female behavior and turf: boys play an aggressive, competitive, territorially spread-out game outdoors, while girls play a game involving sharing that requires little space and takes place indoors.

interactions frequently involve contests, challenges and dares, insults, and dictated commands (Goodwin, 1980; Fine, 1986). Girls, in contrast, learn to express disagreement more indirectly, through secrets and shifting alliances (Maltz and Borker, 1983). Instead of using commands and orders, girls learn to use inclusive suggestions, such as "let's" do something (Goodwin, 1980). The gendered messages are obvious: Boys are leaders who dictate orders to others, control greater resources, and confront conflicts and challenges; girls are subordinate to boys in that they control fewer resources, follow rather than lead, and avoid or ignore conflicts.

Thus, family, schools, work, media, toys and games, and language usage operate together in the process of gender socialization, reproducing and reinforcing stereotypes of appropriate and inappropriate gender roles and behaviors. Moreover, the domination in all these agents of heterosexual images and assumptions precludes consideration of homosexuality as a viable and acceptable alternative. For such reasons, young people who know they are, or believe they might be, gay or lesbian are made to feel very negative about themselves.

On the other hand, gender socialization appears to be imperfect: many women and men transcend its powerful messages and successfully challenge them. For example, in the workplace and in educational institutions, an increasing number of women are breaking barriers considered impenetrable by previous generations. Look at the proportion of female students in your classroom. Perhaps the professor standing before you is a woman. And notice the increasing number of female executives in corporations and female politicians in Congress, the White House, and governor's mansions all over the United States. Consider, as well, the Houston Oilers football player who in 1993 refused to play in a football game because his wife was giving birth to their first child. He risked a heavy monetary fine and suspension from the team, but after a major public outcry supporting his denial of traditional gender roles and condemning his punitive coach, the team's management rescinded the sanction. Such cases depart from the norm, but the fact that they happen at all suggests that gender socialization, while powerful, is far from absolute in shaping gender identity.

RACE SOCIALIZATION

Just as the various agents play a critical role in class and gender socialization, they are vital transmitters of race socialization. Race socialization reinforces racial stereotypes and roles that legitimize racial inequality. The agents that are particularly influential here are family, schools, media, and toys.

Family

The family is an important source of values and norms of interaction for children, and it is within families that stereotypes about groups may take on added significance (Dennis, 1981). Children may go through racial rites of passage that emphasize white superiority and black inferiority (Smith,

1961). For example, Sarah Putton Boyle experienced a racial rite of passage as a white child in the South in the 1950s when she rebuffed an African American child's invitation to play. Here is her poignant description of the event:

> Crushing back my desire both for his company and for fun, I answered stiffly, "No, I can't." Then I added with proper Southern-lady courtesy, "How are you?" My mother had watched the exchange . . . [and] she said, "Mother saw and heard everything. That was a good girl" (Boyle, 1962: 22).

When families reward "appropriate" behavior regarding rules and boundaries of interracial interaction, they send a clear message to children of both races about the children's "proper" places in society.

On the other hand, some families' socialization processes may encourage resistance to prevailing racial attitudes. For example, although most families of all races want to impart to their children a sense of the children's places in the social structure and an understanding of social norms, African American families must do so in the context of racism. Unfortunately, that context may not allow their children to develop a positive self-image or pride of group membership. The challenge for people of color, then, is to stand between their children and a hostile environment to reinterpret the significance of the prejudicial attitudes and discrimination likely to confront them (see Jackson, McCullough, and Gurin, 1988). Yet not all African American families actively pursue this socialization route: one-third of African American parents in recent studies acknowledged that they do not provide racial socialization information that challenges the prevailing messages by other agents (Bowman and Howard, 1985; Thornton et al., 1990). On the other hand, among the remaining two-thirds of African American families, many reported emphasizing the right to actively confront and challenge racism and inequality (Bowman and Howard, 1985; Peters, 1985).

What factors, then, influence whether and how a family will offer racial socialization information? Research shows that the gender of the child affects the process: African American adolescent males appear more likely than females to receive cautionary messages about the racist roadblocks they will commonly confront; African American adolescent females are more likely to receive socialization information stressing racial pride (Bowman and Howard, 1985). Fathers rather than mothers, especially fathers in the Northeast as opposed to those in the South, were more likely to offer survival strategies for existing in a racially hostile environment; widows and never-married women were less likely to offer such information (Thornton et al., 1990). Apparently, gender helps determine who will deliver the messages that challenge negative stereotypes and racist barriers to achievement. Militance and challenge are more characteristic of behaviors considered appropriate for males.

This is not to say that women never receive racial socialization messages that encourage resistance to prejudice and discrimination. Just consider such women as attorneys Anita Hill and Lani Guinier and award-winning writers Alice Walker and Toni Morrison. Research does suggest, however, that men are far more likely to be socialized in this way. That such challenges occur at all underscores the role family can play as a proactive socialization agent contradicting racial messages stressed by other agents.

Schools

Schools reinforce racial inequality and race roles through a variety of mechanisms. One of these is funding. Because school budgets depend on property-tax revenues and state matching funds, much better funding is available for schools in white middle-class districts than for schools in poor, working-class, and minority districts (Pisko and Stern, 1985). Differential funding often occurs *within* districts, where school boards may allocate money unequally from school to school. A study in Detroit found that teachers' pay in predominantly white schools averaged $432 per student, compared with $380 per student in predominantly African American schools (Michelson, 1972). While teachers' salaries do not necessarily affect the quality of education provided to students, they do indicate the school board's priorities in allocating funds. They also reflect the larger class sizes in minority, urban schools, indicating the school board's failure to allocate funds for more teachers there. Funding and allocation decisions can thus produce differential educational experiences on the basis of race and class.

Texts and curricula also often contain a racial bias. As noted earlier, textbooks tend to exclude racial minorities from analyses of U.S. history. In one early study, only 8 out of 45 social science textbooks mentioned Latinos, and only 2 talked of Chicanos (Kane, 1970). Another early study found a similar sparsity of references to Native Americans in texts (Bowker, 1972). When racial minorities were mentioned, they tended to be depicted in pejorative terms (Bahr et al., 1979). Although textbook publishers have grown more sensitive to this issue (Henry, 1990), progress is still needed. Photographs of people of color are most likely to appear in chapters on race-related issues rather than being integrated throughout the book. Some disciplines' textbooks still tend to ignore race-related issues altogether. For example, two recent studies found that introductory economics textbooks ignore critical data concerning the economic difficulties facing racial minorities (Feiner and Roberts, 1990; Cherry and Feiner, 1992). Another study noted that introductory sociology textbooks fail to present information about racial minorities outside of specific chapters (such as those on race and ethnicity, family, and stratification) (Ferree and Hall, 1990).

Textbooks present a visual bias as well. For example, a study of science textbooks noted a severe underrepresentation of images of adult racial minorities in scientific occupations, which means there are few positive role models (Powell and Garcia, 1985). Another study noted that texts tend to depict all characters, regardless of race, in white middle-class roles (McCutcheon et al., 1979).

Schools reinforce racial stereotypes and roles through interactions between students and teachers. One study found that while African American female students are more likely than white female students to seek contact with and help from their teachers, the African American students are more likely to be ignored or turned away (American Association of University Women, 1992). When teachers do respond to students of color with positive feedback, the praise offered is likely to be more qualified than that offered to white students (Freiberg, 1991; American Association of University Women, 1992). Evidence also suggests that teachers' expectations of students' performances are influenced by race and class (Brophy, 1983). For example, Harvey and Slatin (1975) found that teachers had higher prior expectations of white and middle-class students' abilities than of racial minority and economically poor students.

Such prior expectations get frozen early on in the process of tracking, with the result that racial minorities are often placed in slower or non-college-bound programs of study (Alexander and McDill, 1976; Alexander et al., 1978). Such students find it difficult to earn college preparatory credits, and they enjoy fewer opportunities for educational and occupational advancement. Evidence suggests that an early placement in a slower track on the basis of race tends to become permanent and impedes academic advancement, regardless of early abilities (Brophy, 1983). Another outcome of tracking is that minority students internalize race roles to the extent that they lower their own expectations of themselves; they do not regard college as a viable alternative, even when their abilities are comparable to those of dominant-group members who do have such plans (Hauser et al., 1976).

Language also plays a part in tracking decisions. Schools tend to devalue languages other than standard English, a position that reinforces the stereotype of white superiority and minority inferiority. For example, many educators have decried the use of Black English, saying it lacks the rules and syntactical organization of standard English (see, for example, Deutsch, 1963). However, studies have shown that, while certainly different, Black English is just as regulated by rules as standard English (Baratz and Baratz, 1970). Unfortunately, teachers have more power than students to make their interpretations of language usage stick. As a result, African American students get labeled as less intelligent than white students or as slow and requiring a less advanced track of study. Other studies have found similar processes operating against many bilingual children, including Latinos (Moore and Pachon, 1985) and Native Americans (Ogbu, 1978). It is important to note that standard English is the language of high-paying occupations in the United States, so preparing minority students for these jobs must include teaching them standard English. Our point here is that, while doing so, teachers should convey that different languages are appropriate for specific circumstances (much as we teach students French or Spanish), rather than denigrating students' common usage.

Schools also reinforce race socialization through the lack of role models within their personnel. In 1988 only 8.2 percent of elementary and secondary public school teachers were African American and just 2.9 percent were Latino (National Center for Education Statistics, 1990). By the time students enter college (if they do, in fact, go to college), the proportion of minority faculty dips to 3.2 percent African American and 2.3 percent Latino (*Almanac of Higher Education*, 1993). While this does not necessarily mean that schools intentionally restrict the number of minority faculty, the decline in role models among teachers does send a visual message to all students that racial minorities are not as intelligent as whites.

Media

In addition to schools, the media are powerful transmitters of racial socialization. For example, many African American and Latino actors complain that they are typically cast as drug dealers or users, pimps, prostitutes, rapists, murderers, or muggers but are rarely given positive leading roles. Although the situation has improved somewhat and the roles have become more varied (for example, those of Blair Underwood and A Martinez on the long-running *L.A. Law*), positive minority roles are still more remarkable than typical. Moreover, television has not remained consistently vigilant about increasing the affirmative presence of racial minorities in a diversity of roles. Both television and films continue to rely heavily on racial and ethnic stereotypes and slurs. Such shows as Fox Broadcasting Company's *Martin, Living Single,* and *In Living Color* frequently make use of racial and ethnic jokes. While these shows do increase the presence of people of color on television, and may even be written or produced by people of color, they frequently do so at the cost of reinforcing racial stereotypes (Waters, 1993). One notable exception that does not rely on negative stereotypes is *Roc*, a show depicting a working-class, dual-occupation couple struggling successfully with issues confronting many African American and working-class families. But the more standard fare on television in the 1990s perpetuates racial stereotypes, reinforcing negative racial images and making people of color objects of derision.

Several studies reveal the power of media images to affect race socialization. Peterson and Thurstone (1933; see also Schaefer, 1990) found that negative attitudes toward African Americans persisted five months after respondents viewed *The Birth of a Nation*, a 1915 film that extolled the virtues of the Ku Klux Klan. On the other hand, the 1947 film *Gentleman's Agreement*, which heavily criticized anti-Semitism, reduced viewers' antagonisms and hatred against Jews (Ball-Rokeach, Rokeach, and Grube, 1984). These studies underscore both the positive and the negative influence films can have on race socialization.

Television and print news media are often swift to seize on racial stereotypes in their reporting. For example, when Carol Stewart, a young white woman, was murdered in an African American section of Boston in 1989, both the police and the press uncritically accepted her husband's insistence that she was shot by an African American in a failed robbery attempt. Later it came out that her own husband had murdered her. But the repeated emphasis in the press on the racial overtones of the case served to reinforce negative stereotypes of the violence of African American males and the danger for whites in such neighborhoods. Similar racially charged coverage marked the 1989 case of a jogger in New York City's Central Park who was brutally beaten and raped.

Toys and Games

The toys children play with may also reinforce racial stereotypes. Crayola, the leading manufacturer of crayons, has only recently discontinued identifying a peach-colored crayon as "flesh," a label suggesting that normal skin color is peach, not black, brown, yellow, or red. Dolls are also persuasive toys. In a classic study (Clark and Clark, 1947), when children were confronted with two dolls, one white and one black, one-third of the African American children selected the white doll as the one resembling themselves. Both white and African American children in the study tended to identify the white doll as good and the black doll as bad. Recent research suggests that the preponderance of white dolls available in toy stores continues to affect race socialization and perceptions of beauty and goodness. For example, 65 percent of the African American preschoolers in one study selected a white Cabbage Patch doll over a black version of the doll (Powell-Hopson and Hopson, 1988).

Toys and books do have the power to alter these preferences and stereotypes. In one study, two-thirds of both white and African American

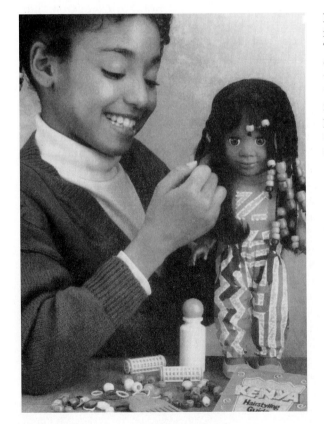

Dolls are frequently powerful race socialization agents. The preponderance of white dolls implies whiteness as the norm and color as the "other." However, availability of a diversity of dolls can provide positive models for children about race identity and heritage.

preschoolers chose the black doll after exposure to a half hour of stories containing positive images of the black doll (Gopaul-McNicol, 1988).

Thus, families, schools, media, and toys play critical roles in socialization and the reproduction of race roles and stereotypes. They also contain strong possibilities for interrupting the cycle of the self-fulfilling prophecies that these agents have more commonly perpetuated, as the boxed excerpt shows. While many agents may offer powerful messages that together reinforce traditional roles, we are not powerless to resist them. And therein lies room for change.

POLITICAL SOCIALIZATION

We have seen how socialization agents teach us about "appropriate" and "inappropriate" behaviors and expectations with regard to gender, race, sexual orientation, and class. These same agents also socialize us *politically.*

Schools

In school we learn the principles of the U.S. Constitution and Bill of Rights, concepts that facilitate our internalization of values such as the preeminence of private property, individual rights and personal responsibility for one's own fate, and civic obligations and duty to country. While in and of themselves these values may not be problematic, the implications of uncritically accepting them may be. These values lead us to believe that ours is a free and open society in which the key to upward mobility and accomplishment is simply hard work. Thus, persons who are poor, homeless, illiterate or powerless have only themselves to blame. The strong implication is that those who may be better off do not have the responsibility to shoulder the burden of the less fortunate. If we have successfully internalized these values, we may never question the adequacy of this blaming-the-victim analysis or analyze the role of political and economic institutions in producing such victims.

Schools teach us to revere the electoral process. Through elections for class officers, for example, we learn about our rights and responsibilities as voters, and we learn to value the democratic process as free and open. Along the way, however, we may also learn to accept as normal the highly competitive nature of such a process, as well as notions like "The winner takes all" and "All is fair in love, war, and politics." The process of elections in the context of principles like "one person, one vote" teaches us to validate the role of dominant groups. This is because we appear to have participated in selecting that rule, despite the fact that the candidates we choose from are overwhelmingly drawn from the ranks of the dominants to begin with.

Competitive school sports prepare us for later physical fitness training, an important aspect of our lives. But they can also prepare us to accept wars as just another sporting event characterized by team spirit and "us"

As a graduate student, Celia Alvarez collected oral histories of Puerto Rican women who worked in the New York garment industry. In this selection she reflects on the experiences in her own life that enabled her to break out of racist stereotypes and come to realize the worth of her own Latina heritage.

My mother migrated to New York in the early 1950s. . . . She was also a seamstress. She married soon after her arrival and subsequently had the three of us, one right after the other.

Raised in the projects of downtown Brooklyn near the Brooklyn Navy Yard I often wondered: What were we doing here? How did we get here? And why? Nobody said too much, however; no one wanted to talk about the poverty and pain, the family truces and secrets which clouded the tremendous upheaval from Ponce to San Juan to New York.

I grew up speaking Spanish, dancing *la pachanga, merengue,* and *mambo,* eating *arroz con habichuelas* and drinking *malta y café.* I was smart, and learned to play the chords of the bureaucratic machinery of housing, education, and welfare very well at a very young age. I translated for everyone—my mother, her friends, our neighbors, as well as my teachers. My parents kept us close to home and it was my responsibility to keep my brother and sister in tow.

It was hard to understand it all, to try to make sense of who I was as a Puerto Rican in New York, so I read everything I could get my hands on; watched the games the government would play between Afro-Americans and Puerto Ricans with social service monies; heard the poverty pimps tell their lies; watched the kids die of dope or heard about them getting killed down elevator chutes in the middle of a burglary; noted the high over-priced tags on old food being sold in the only supermarket in the neighborhood; knew of kids being raped and thrown off the roof. And I asked, "Why?"

The socially active local parish church became my refuge. It was there that I began to make connections with the poor whites, Afro-Americans, and Asians in my community, and said there had to be a better way for us all. I participated in a variety of activities including youth programs, the local food coop, and newsletter, which basically involved me in community organizing, although I didn't know you called it grassroots work then. I got swept up by the energy of the civil rights movement and wanted to go to the march on Washington but my mother said, "No!" She worried about me—didn't like me wearing my Martin Luther King button or getting involved in politics. She was afraid I would get hurt. I always liked being out on the street talking to people, however, and she knew from way back that I was not destined to stay inside. . . .

During this same period I started high school in a predominantly white school in the heart of Flatbush. I found myself desegregating the Catholic school system, one of five or six *latinas* and Afro-Americans in my class. I was known as one of the girls from the ghetto downtown and was constantly called upon to defend my race. One day it went too far. Someone said my father didn't work and that their parents supported my coming to their school. I "went off"! You just didn't talk about my family!

I never told my parents about the racist slurs—never had the heart. They were breaking their backs to send me to school; my father kept his job at a city hospital

against "them," to accept physical injuries and casualties as normal and justified, and to view as legitimate the notion that "to the winners go the spoils." Wars and competitive school sports even share a common terminology. Teams typically select warlike or aggressive figures or symbols for their names. Competitive team sports may also politically socialize us by for thirty years and took on a second job at the docks. We would all go to help him clean offices at night and on weekends after our day outings together. My mother went back to work in a paper factory down the street. Prior to that, she had taken care of the children of women in the neighborhood who worked. I've also worked since about the time I was fourteen.

Anyway, I graduated high school with honors. I had every intention of going to college—I thought it would give me the credentials to be in a position to act on the miseducation that I saw we were getting. . . .

I applied to about ten schools, got into most of them and decided to go to a new institution in New England that broke away from the traditional, predetermined academic program and was primarily based on a mentoring system between student and teacher. . . .

Ironically, it was there that I found my first Afro-American and Puerto Rican teachers. I was relieved to know someone who understood the reference points in my life without my having to explain. After pursuing some studies on Puerto Rico and the Caribbean—for the only formal mention of Puerto Rico in all my schooling up to that point had been in a geography class in which we had discussed its mineral resources—I studied questions of language planning, bilingualism and education, language, culture, and identity. I thought that knowledge of these areas would be useful to the Puerto Rican community. I always made it a point to keep my foot in both the community and academe. I have struggled to stay integrated as a human being despite the efforts of academic institutions to make me over or deny my existence.

To make a long story short, I went on to graduate school where I fought to keep my sanity and sense of self-worth in the midst of the racist sentiment that permeated my department, telling me in a variety of ways that I should not be there, let alone survive my course of study. If one were to look at their track record with regard to women of color one would see how they manage to justify their own position; for to survive requires that we deny who we are, from where we come, and where we are going as a people. . . .

Which brings me back to our oral history project. Listening to these women's stories has served as a tremendous source of inspiration and validation of my own experience as a Puerto Rican woman. They captured and brought back to life the struggles of my own socialization during the 1960s. . . .

Beyond its impact on me individually, . . . the oral history process . . . has provided a space for the collective experience and voice of Puerto Rican working women to be heard. . . . For how do we see ourselves if we are invisible, if our most courageous acts as a people go unrecognized? In order to create an authentic connection with others we must first deal with the sources of our own oppression; we must break the silence of our invisibility; but we must speak in our own voice, first to ourselves and then to each other. For in moving beyond our own individual lives we can come to appreciate the connections between us, the continuity and the change, and dispel the fears which keep us apart.

Source: Celia Alvarez, *"El Hilo Que Nos Une*/The Thread That Binds Us: Becoming a Puerto Rican Woman,*"* in Virginia Cyrus (ed.), *Experiencing Race, Class, and Gender in the United States* (Mountainview, CA: Mayfield Publishing Company, 1993), pp. 35–38.

channeling violence and aggression into an organized setting governed by rules (Elias and Dunning, 1986; Wilson, 1992; Dunning, 1993). Thus, competitive team sports become part of a "civilizing" process that teaches us it is acceptable to inflict bodily harm on players of the opposing team but not acceptable to do so to neighbors, coworkers, or authority figures. Such a civilizing process becomes easily transferable to situations of war, particularly when both settings share terminology and analytical frameworks.

Toys and Games

Our toys and games reinforce the internalization of dominant ideologies and the acceptance of war as a game. Nintendo video games are dominated by militaristic themes (including one called Contra, in which a Rambo-like figure single-handedly tries to search for and destroy guerrilla rebels). Real lives, violence, and pain become trivialized into blips on a screen, removing the horrors of war from our consciousness and developing the eye-hand coordination necessary for actual participation in war. Almost immediately following the outbreak of the Gulf war in the Middle East in 1991, G.I. Joe "action figures" in desert-beige camouflage uniforms began to turn up in toy stores. And just as quickly, Topps, the maker of baseball cards, began selling packets of Operation Desert Storm cards, with pictures of generals and weaponry replacing pictures of star ballplayers. Statistics on relative troop strengths and the capabilities of various weapon systems replaced earned-run averages and runs-batted-in statistics.

Media

The media also promote our acceptance of dominant political values (including the defense of these with our lives in war). Reporters cover wars like sporting events, using all the terminology and metaphors of competitive sports, including pep rallies, "up-close and personal" vignettes of "our" various warriors, and nightly score reports of casualties and destruction. Television news footage of U.S. Patriot missiles encountering Iraqi SCUD missiles in the Middle East in 1991 took on the quality of an innocuous video game.

We tend to accept various wars as necessary and legitimate when the media portray other countries' leaders and citizens as evil or subhuman, deserving of destruction. President George Bush repeatedly described the war against Iraq as a war of good against evil. The media frequently noted that the Iraqis "don't value human life the way we do." Such ideological broadcasts enable us to transcend our usual norms against the taking of human lives. The selectivity of media coverage may foster the impression that "we're all in this together," "we'll all benefit equally from our team effort," and "we all agree that this is right and should occur" (see MacArthur, 1992). For example, during the Mideast conflict little coverage was given to the disproportionate minority and working-class presence among the U.S. troops or to the growing opposition to the war within the United States.

In addition to socializing us to accept war as legitimate, the media may promote the legitimacy of inequality, domination, and capitalism through the stories they select and the perspective they bring to them. Project Censored annually publishes a list of the top 25 censored stories of the year. In 1990, for example, the ten most censored stories included the restricted

Media coverage influences our political socialization by conveying images that may carry subtle messages. For example, during the Gulf war, images of a casually dressed President George Bush greeting the troops implied that "we're all in this together."

media coverage of the Gulf war, which routinely downplayed opposition to the war, and the federal government's expensive and bungled handling of the savings and loan (S&L) crisis. The cost to taxpayers of bailing out the collapsed S&L industry will easily exceed $500 billion, "more than the entire cost of World War II, in current dollars and including service-connected veterans' benefits" (Utne, 1991: 61–64). That story was not widely disseminated.

Neither was the story about George Bush's critical role in the Iran-contra scandal, in which the United States illegally sold arms to Iran in order to funnel money to rebels in Nicaragua. The President repeatedly insisted that he was "out of the loop" of decision-making at the time. The media also kept mum about Bush's relationship with Panama's strong man Manuel Noriega, including Bush's role in establishing Noriega as a paid CIA informant and his role in misrepresenting the legal basis justifying the American invasion of Panama. The media also censor environmental news. While pollution and the destruction of the ozone layer continue to be portrayed as problems created by the behaviors of individuals, the roles of corporations and the military in these environmental problems are downplayed. The media squelched a report by Helen Caldicott, an internationally respected physicist, which stated that every time NASA launches a space shuttle, it releases 250 tons of hydrochloric acid, thereby contributing substantially to the destruction of the ozone layer.

These examples are just a sampling of the top censored stories of 1990. Such stories challenge the notions that government neutrally operates for the common good and that corporations do business while keeping human health and safety a priority. The censorship of news stifles critical analyses and reinforces unquestioning faith in dominant institutions and the elites who run them. As such, political socialization in general and censorship in particular reduce the information available to nonelites, making it harder for them to challenge or question the legitimacy of the dominants' rule.

This bias on the part of the media is not surprising, given that many mass-media outlets are owned and controlled by large capitalist interests. For example, the three dominant commercial television networks (ABC, CBS, and NBC) are owned and controlled by major institutional investors, the majority of which are financial institutions (U.S. Congress: Senate, 1980). Moreover, these networks directly interlock with some of the largest Fortune 500 corporations. A Senate study in 1980 found that RCA (which is owned by General Electric and which itself owns NBC) had a total of 51 direct and 300 indirect interlocks with the top 100 corporations; ABC had 30 direct and 275 indirect interlocks with such firms; and CBS had 24 direct and 270 indirect interlocks (U.S. Congress: Senate, 1980: 88, 354, 397, 582). Although these figures are now more than a decade old and Congress has not updated them, we believe that the situation has not changed (Lee and Bates, 1992; Mazzocco, 1994). The significance of the investors' and interlockers' influence over the networks is that these three networks were the main source of news for approximately 90 percent of Americans until the mid-1980s (Dye, 1983: 122). Today cable networks like Turner Broadcasting and CNN are beginning to erode the television networks' domination, but the latter still account for 70 percent of total television viewing (Dye, 1990: 121).

Newspapers and magazines are less concentrated than television broadcast media, but many of the top print media are owned and controlled by industry conglomerates. Just fifteen newspaper conglomerates account for more than half of the total newspaper circulation in the United States (Dye, 1990: 121). The conglomerates typically own several major newspapers, magazines, and local television affiliates (Dye, 1979), thereby promoting **homogenization of news.** By this we mean that we are likely to be exposed to a single perspective and a single analysis of very complex stories no matter how many different media we select as our sources of news, particularly if they are all owned or controlled by the same conglomerate. For example, Rupert Murdoch's News Corporation owns the *New York Post* and the *Boston Herald* newspapers, the Fox Broadcasting Company (television stations), *TV Guide,* Delphi Internet Services (an on-line computer service), and Twentieth Century Fox (movie-making company), all in the United States. In addition, Murdoch has similarly extensive media holdings in Australia and Great Britain (Robinson, 1993).

Concentrated control of both broadcast and print media by large corporate interests contributes to our political socialization by empowering these interests to determine what is news and how it is interpreted. Herman and Chomsky (1988) made a comparative analysis of which major news stories were covered and which were ignored: their study documented how media elites censor news to reflect and reinforce corporate and wealthy elites' interests.

Television is probably the most widely used media source of information in the United States. What effect does television have on the development of political identity? How effective is its influence in shaping this identity? A study of the impact of television found that individuals who viewed an average of four or more hours of television per day tended to become very conservative about civil rights issues. Furthermore, such viewers also tended to place a priority on their own economic well-being rather than on that of the general public (Gerbner et al., 1982). More recent studies show that television affects viewers' perceptions of what constitutes important issues and who is responsible for these issues (Lenart and McGraw, 1989; Iyengar, 1990). In Argentina, increased television viewing among adolescents correlated with antidemocratic attitudes (Morgan and Shanahan, 1991). Together, these findings illustrate that television can influence how we see the world and our places in it.

On the other hand, the media can also be an important agent in challenging the status quo. For example, film footage documenting the excesses of police against civil rights and antiwar protesters in the 1950s, 1960s, and 1970s contributed to growing public intolerance of abuses of power and the problems of racism and militarism in the United States. So did the publication of the Pentagon Papers in the 1970s, in which the role of the United States in the Vietnam war was disclosed, despite the efforts of the established elite to prevent the dissemination of these documents. More recently, journalistic pursuit of charges of sexual harassment lodged against Supreme Court Justice nominee Clarence Thomas in 1992 and Senator Robert Packwood in 1993 contributed to increased public rejection of abuses of power related to gender.

Taken together, schools, the media, and the toys and games many of us enjoy contribute to our political socialization. We often learn to accept and support the existing political and economic structures and to regard the inequalities of privilege and power produced by these structures as right, inevitable, and legitimate. This is not to say that these institutions necessarily conspire to fool us or that we are helpless robots with no ability to resist or change what may seem like "thought control." (We will discuss how people can become agents for change and resistance in Chapter 9 "Social Change and Social Movements.") The point here is that one of the identities we learn through the socialization process consists of who we are, where we fit, and how we should behave in the political and economic institutions of our society.

CONCLUSION

How do individuals become members of society? What kinds of things must be learned to become a member, and how are they learned? To what degree is the individual a passive recipient in the process, and to what degree does the individual resist and reshape the social identity created?

It is important to note that while the various agents of socialization are powerful forces in shaping our social identities and political consciousness, we are not automatically transformed into clones of one another. There is a considerable degree of individual interpretation of "appropriate" behaviors and expectations, as well as resistance to total conformity. Our individual input into the socialization process contributes greatly to a broad diversity of outcomes.

We can see personal variations in the "appropriate" behaviors suited to our genders and age groups, the challenges people make against class and race roles that they perceive as intolerable, and the resistance many people mount (against great odds) to prevailing political doctrines. We see this in the women's movement, the gay rights movement, and the civil rights movement. We see it as well in labor unions and in antiwar protests. We see it in the growing militance of senior citizens in the Gray Panthers and the American Association of Retired Persons. And we see it every day in our own personal styles.

We also see that we often change as we learn new things, collect new experiences, and meet new people with different ideas. This highlights the notion that the process of socialization is not absolute and does not flow in one direction only. It is, in fact, an interactive process (somewhat lopsided because of power differences) between the individual and the various socialization agents, a process typified by conflict and struggle, alterations, and learning.

THINKING CRITICALLY

1. Many agents participate in shaping our race, class, and gender identities. Look at the boxed excerpt by Celia Alvarez (pp. 164–165). What agents are at work in her description of her socialization experiences? How did she resist those agents? How did her subculture and the dominant, or mainstream, culture interact to help shape her identity? How would you analyze Alvarez's experiences from the symbolic interaction perspective and the conflict perspective?

2. Select one of the attitude questions at the beginning of this chapter. How did you answer this question? Now consider these questions: What values does your answer reflect? How did you acquire your attitudes and values? What agents have had a part in teaching you and reinforcing these attitudes, and how specifically did they do this? Are your attitudes the same as or different from those of your friends, your family, your teachers, your religious leaders, or the media? If they are different, how have you managed to ignore the pressures of such institutions?

3. Select a board game other than those discussed in this chapter (some good ones might be Careers, Careers for Girls, Life, Go to the Head of the Class, Couch Potato, and Stratego, but you may think of others). What are the rules and objectives of this game? What race, class, gender, or political socialization messages are contained in those rules and objectives?

4. Examine your gender, race, class, or political identity, and think about some of the agents of socialization that have played an influential role in shaping it. For example, how did your family, your school experiences, your religious training, your peer groups, or the media affect how

you see yourself? What factors influenced the socialization experiences you have had? If you are shaping an identity that challenges institutional messages, what factors influenced your ability to resist them?

5. Select a television show or movie and examine the race, class, gender, and political identity messages it contains. Does the show or movie rely on stereotypes, or does it challenge them? Be specific. How would a symbolic interaction theorist, a functionalist, and a conflict theorist analyze this show or movie? What insights might each perspective offer in analyzing the images you see? What limitations does each perspective contain?

KEY TERMS

socialization, *139*

nature versus nurture debate, *139*

sociobiology, *139*

symbolic interaction, *140*

looking-glass self, *140*

significant other, *140*

generalized other, *140*

conflict perspective, *142*

resocialization, *144*

degradation ceremony, *144*

total institutions, *144*

political socialization, *145*

socialization agents, *146*

reference group, *146*

liberation theology, *147*

anticipatory socialization, *149*

self-fulfilling prophecy, *150*

imposter syndrome, *150*

double day (double shift), *151*

homogenization of news, *168*

SUGGESTED READINGS

Judy Dunn and Robert Plomin, *Separate Lives: Why Siblings Are So Different.* New York: Basic Books, 1990. An exploration of the factors that may explain why siblings raised in the same family nonetheless may experience a very different environment and thus may be socialized differently.

Edward S. Herman, *Beyond Hypocrisy: Decoding the News in an Age of Propaganda.* Boston: South End Press, 1992. An analysis of how government's use of language and terminology and the media's presentation of these can shape political perceptions and contribute to political socialization.

Barbara B. Lloyd and Gerard Duveen, *Gender Identities and Education: The Impact of Starting School.* New York: St. Martin's Press, 1992. An exploration of how the education experience can influence the shaping of gendered perceptions of one's place in society.

Peter M. Nardi, David Sanders, and Judd Marmor, *Growing Up before Stonewall: Life Stories of Some Gay Men.* New York: Routledge, 1994. Eleven gay men tell their stories of coming to grips with their identities as homosexuals in a world in which families, friends, the state, the military, and religion provided both hostility to their identity and opportunity to explore it.

Richard L. Zweigenhaft and G. William Domhoff, *Blacks in the White Establishment? A Study of Race and Class in America.* New Haven: Yale University Press, 1991. An examination of the role prep schools play in socializing individuals for power, including how race may continue to pose obstacles to African Americans even when they attend the most prestigious prep schools.

SYSTEMS OF INEQUALITY

ECONOMIC INEQUALITY

**Functionalist Theory of
Stratification**
Critique of Functionalism

RACIAL INEQUALITY

SEX INEQUALITY

AGE INEQUALITY

SEXUAL ORIENTATION
AND INEQUALITY

ABLE-BODIEDNESS
AND INEQUALITY

CONCLUSION

Most of the things that differentiate one person from another mean relatively little in everyday life. People are unalike in characteristics ranging from eye color to style of laughter. But such differences have few, if any, implications for an individual's life chances. It is doubtful, for example, that they will affect one's educational or employment opportunities. We can think of these as **natural differences.**

Systems of inequality, on the other hand, exist on an entirely separate level and can have far-reaching consequences for the individual. They are sets of social relationships built around attributes—from wealth to skin color to sexual orientation—to which societal members accord a great deal of meaning

6

and significance in everyday life. Systems of inequality are, as we shall see, **socially constructed.**

Sociologists have long been interested in studying and understanding systems of inequality. Karl Marx (1813–1883), of course, brought attention to the economic inequalities characterizing capitalist societies, a concern that is still relevant today. But German sociologist Max Weber (1864–1920) was also highly influential (Gerth and Mills, 1968). He encouraged sociologists to analyze societies in terms of their systems of **social stratification,** *the ways in which people occupying different social positions are stratified from high to low.*

While Marx emphasized economic inequality in his writings, Weber suggested that in any given society social stratification is likely to be multidimensional. *The dimensions Weber considered most important in stratification are* class *(possession of goods, and skills to generate income),* status *(social honor or prestige), and* power *(the ability to dominate or influence others). In Weber's view the nature and relative importance of these dimensions could differ from society to society, as well as within any given society over time. Weber's notion that social stratification is multidimensional has influenced our approach to inequality in this chapter. His stratification dimensions of class, status, and power help inform our analysis of systems of inequality.*

In this chapter we shall examine six systems of inequality, focusing on the United States: economic inequality, racial inequality, sex inequality, age inequality, inequality based on sexual orientation, *and* inequality based on able-bodiedness. *These systems of inequality are human creations. As social constructions, they tend to differ from society to society and in different historical periods. For example, in the United States old age was once highly respected by society, which now venerates youth, but in China elderly persons are still treated with great respect. A society's system of production and rules of distribution determine how much poverty there is. In some societies the category "homosexual" is nonexistent, and sexual practices we might associate with homosexuality are accepted variations.*

Before looking at the six systems of inequality, we need to set them in a larger context. Not only are they socially constructed, but these systems also represent differences in power. When one group has the ability to set standards of "good" or "normal," it also has the power to impose disadvantage on others. For exam-

ple, in many societies men traditionally assume certain roles for themselves and limit women to others. In doing so, men decide what behavior is "normal" for each sex. This exercise of power and its outcome are usually justified by a system of ideas, or **ideology.**

The ideology helps keep the system of inequality going. The ideas it contains typically include the notion that the system of inequality is necessary and inevitable (Adam, 1978). When such ideologies become incorporated into a society's culture, the inequalities they foster may be accepted as the "natural order of things." The term **ideological hegemony** has been used to refer to the dominance of a set of ideas governing ways of doing things (Gramsci, 1971), to the point where the existing social arrangements are just a matter of "common sense" (Seybold, 1987: 176).

White settlers at times massacred Native Americans in the struggle to gain control over their ancestral lands, justifying their acts with the belief that the indigenous peoples being killed were inferior beings. This engraving from 1868 depicts a massacre in Idaho by white scouts, assisted by Native American allies.

For example, white people of European ancestry waged war with the indige-nous peoples occupying what is now the United States and Canada, took away their lands, and forced many to live in poverty on reservations. The conquerors justified their actions by an ideology that held whites to be racially and culturally superior to native North Americans. The latter were viewed as uncivilized "sav-ages."

Systems of inequality often give rise to conflict as some groups seek change while others fight to maintain the status quo. Our biographies are strongly influenced not only by our positions in a given system of inequality but also by the presence and outcome of movements for change. Obviously, if a person is unfavorably situated in a system of inequality—as is the case for so many people—one way to alter the system is to join or otherwise lend support to such movements.

ECONOMIC INEQUALITY

One of the enduring features of many societies is **economic inequality,** the vast difference in wealth and income that families and individuals possess. A great deal of meaning and significance is attached to the possession of such resources, principally because they can be used to improve life chances. We look briefly now at the distribution of wealth and income in the United States.

A small percentage of families owns most of the nation's personally held wealth (in the form of corporate stocks and bonds, savings accounts, real estate, cars and boats, and other types of property). The richest 0.5 percent of the population possesses over a quarter of this wealth, while the richest 20 percent owns four-fifths of the personal wealth (Kerbo, 1991: 40). There is also substantial inequality in the distribution of income (for example, from wages, government payments, and return on investments), although not as extreme as the inequality in wealth. The 5 percent of households with the highest incomes receive 20 percent of all household income; the most affluent 20 percent receive almost half (U.S. Bureau of Census, 1993b). Both income distribution and wealth distribution have become increasingly unequal in recent years (Phillips, 1990).

Another dimension of economic inequality is the extent of poverty. (See Figure 6.1.) While a few individuals possess an enormous amount of wealth, some possess practically none. In 1993, the government defined poverty for a family of four as an annual income falling below $14,763 (the figure changes depending upon family size). That year, 39.3 million people in the United States—most of whom were women and children—lived in poverty. Another 12 million persons were living in "near poverty," just above the poverty line (U.S. Bureau of the Census, 1994). Many manage to

FIGURE 6.1 NUMBER OF POOR AND POVERTY RATE IN THE UNITED STATES, 1960–1993

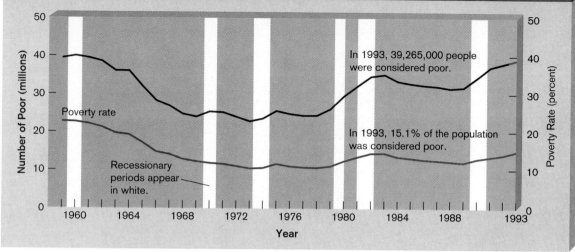

The number of people in the United States who are poor, as well as the U.S. poverty rate (the percentage of Americans who live under the federal government's official poverty line), has varied over time. After declining for almost 20 years, both the number of poor people and the poverty rate have been gradually increasing since the late 1970s. (*Source:* U.S. Department of Commerce, Bureau of the Census, *Poverty in the United States: 1992,* Washington, D.C.: U.S. Government Printing Office, 1993, p. ix, and U.S. Department of Commerce, *Bureau of the Census, Income, Poverty, and Valuation of Noncash Benefits: 1993.* Current Population Reports, Series P60–188, Washington, D.C.: U.S. Government Printing Office, 1994, table C.)

climb out of poverty, but they often don't rise very far; meanwhile, others keep plunging in. While most poor people are white (Figure 6.2), people of color are disproportionately found among the poor. Job losses in recent years, as well as a rise in the number of female-headed households because of marital breakups, have introduced poverty to many families who had assumed their middle-class status was secure (Newman, 1989).

The facts about economic inequality are open to different, often conflicting, interpretations. Let us look at one viewpoint that is very close to what most people in our society believe about economic inequality (see Kluegel and Smith, 1986). This is the functionalist theory of stratification.

Functionalist Theory of Stratification

The **functionalist theory of stratification,** whose foundations were established by early European sociologists such as Émile Durkheim (1858–1917), holds that economic inequality is the result of *beneficial* forces (Durkheim, 1964). This theory posits that different occupational levels in society *should* receive different rewards. Thus, it is not necessarily a bad

179

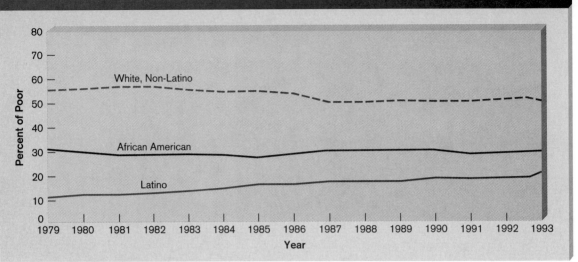

Contrary to stereotypes held by many Americans, the majority of poor people in the United States are white, while poverty has been increasing among Latinos. In recent years the proportion of the poor who are white has been declining. African Americans and Latino Americans are disproportionately represented in the poverty population. (*Source:* U.S. Department of Commerce, Bureau of the Census, *Poverty in the United States: 1992,* Washington, D.C.: U.S. Government Printing Office, 1993, p. xii, and U.S. Department of Commerce, Bureau of the Census, *Income, Poverty, and Valuation of Noncash Benefits: 1993.* Current Population Reports, Series P60–188, Washington, D.C.: U.S. Government Printing Office, 1994, table C.)

thing that the average chief executive officer of a large corporation in the United States receives an income some 100 times that of the average factory worker (Phillips, 1990: 179–180). Similar, if less dramatic, economic disparities exist throughout the occupational structure.

Why do the functionalists argue that attaching different rewards to different positions is "functional," or beneficial to society? Because, they say, this approach provides an incentive to individuals to strive for the most highly rewarded positions. Proponents argue that these positions are commonly the most important for the operation of society. It is crucial, therefore, that people who have appropriate talents, and/or who are willing to undergo the necessary training, strive to fill these positions. Otherwise, the positions could end up being filled by persons who are less competent, and society would suffer. Rewarding different positions unequally—in effect, maintaining a system of economic inequality—is thus seen as benefiting society.

Indeed, some might argue that the formerly socialist nations in Eastern Europe are now moving toward capitalism because their economic systems were not unequal enough. That is, under socialism, the similarity of rewards between the best-paid and worst-paid positions in these nations failed to provide sufficient motivation for people to work hard, be productive, and strive to move up, thus setting the scene for economic collapse. The functionalist theory, then, might be used to explain the demise of socialism and to suggest that capitalism is preferable. We'll see below that the picture is more complex than it seems.

Critique of Functionalism

The functionalist theory of stratification certainly sounds very logical. Yet the theory has been attacked as an ideology that does more to justify economic inequality than to explain it. In the United States the theory first formally appeared in sociology journals in 1945, by which time World War II had pulled the nation out of the throes of the Great Depression (Davis and Moore, 1945). During the Depression a quarter of the labor force was unemployed and sharp economic inequalities prevailed. The functionalist theory, had it appeared in the Depression years, would have counseled calm acceptance and greater individual striving, as opposed to an attack on the system of inequality itself.

Critics have assailed the theory on a number of grounds. They ask: Are the most highly rewarded positions indeed the "most important" to society? On what grounds can this be proved? Do the extremes of enormous wealth and tragic poverty have to exist? Since the talented at the bottom of the economic ladder necessarily start from a disadvantage, do we really have an open system in which all people compete on an equal footing and talent "rises to the top"?

Critics of the functionalist theory have also asked what role power, and the ability to monopolize opportunities for one's children and friends, plays in the competitive model. After all, persons who achieve economic success have resources and connections that may help others. In many trades and professions it is possible for members to limit entry, using their power to create scarcity and thus increase their own rewards. Physicians, for example, have used their power to restrict the number of accredited medical schools and so the number of doctors. This scarcity helps keep doctors' salaries high. In the past, discrimination on the basis of race and sex made it easy for white males to be admitted to most medical schools. In some cases, admissions committees gave special preference to the sons of physicians who were alumni of the schools. Such discriminatory practices undermine the open system of competition.

Finally, critics have suggested that rather than being functional, or beneficial to society, economic inequality leads to a dysfunctional situation. It harms people in innumerable ways: It results in lack of commitment to the larger society; fosters antisocial behavior such as crime and substance abuse; generates resentments, jealousies, and intergroup conflicts; and can be a very destabilizing force.

To understand the distribution of rewards in any society, we must look at where power resides. Sociologist Gerhard Lenski (1966) argues that in societies that produce a surplus—more than the minimum needed for basic group survival—the people with power will determine its distribution. In his view, "power determines privilege." We can apply this idea to see that the distribution of economic rewards is broadly influenced by state policies toward taxation of income and wealth. Do the wealthy enjoy special "breaks"? Does the system of taxation aim at mitigating or retaining economic inequalities? How much income maintenance (if any) is provided to the poor? To the degree that persons who are successful in a system of economic inequality control the state, or have influence over those who do, they can use their power to retain their privilege.

The relation between power and privilege is helpful in understanding movements for change in the formerly socialist nations of Eastern Europe. Critics of the functionalist theory of stratification are unlikely to accept the argument that these nations were on the verge of collapse because they had too little economic inequality. For example, before its breakup the Soviet Union suffered from a highly centralized *command economy* in which Communist party leaders placed emphasis on strengthening the Soviet military-industrial complex to compete in the Cold War, rather than on producing consumer goods and services needed by the citizens. The Soviet state was undemocratic and politically repressive, making it difficult for people to express their views or have any impact on decisions directly affecting them. Top Soviet officials had exclusive authority to shop in special stores offering imported goods to foreigners, rode around in expensive government autos, relaxed in luxurious state-owned vacation properties, and used political connections to get preferential treatment for their family members in regard to educational opportunities, health care, and jobs. The visibility of such privilege caused much resentment because it contradicted the egalitarian ideas accompanying socialist ideology (Parkin, 1971). People living in the Soviet Union sought its transformation

Economic injustices under Soviet socialism caused many working-class people to suffer; unlike Communist party elites, the working class had difficulty gaining access to scarce consumer goods and necessities. These forlorn people are standing in line to purchase food.

Economic inequality accompanies capitalism in the United States, to the point where many people are unable even to afford housing. Among the fastest growing groups are homeless families, like this dejected mother and her daughter, whom the state of Massachusetts is housing in a motel.

because they could no longer tolerate political and economic injustices that they believed were undermining their life chances. That transformation did not come simply because the narrow gap between the best- and worst-paid workers stifled motivation.

The economic inequality accompanying capitalism in the United States causes great suffering for many citizens. As we've noted, some 39 million people in this country live below the official poverty line. An estimated 20 million do not get enough to eat each day ("20 Million Go Hungry," 1987). Perhaps 7 million are chronically homeless (De Parle, 1994). Compared with the rates in other industrialized nations, our infant mortality rates are extremely high (U.S. Department of Health and Human Services, 1992). Rates of serious mental disorders, such as schizophrenia, are highest for poor people (Dohrenwend et al., 1980). So are deaths from infectious diseases, including influenza, pneumonia, tuberculosis, and diphtheria (U.S. Department of Health and Human Services, 1992). As we shall see in Chapter 13, poverty is a major contributor to health problems in the United States.

Economic inequality exacts enormous costs from persons who experience serious disadvantage because of it, whether a society's economy is capitalist or socialist. Society as a whole loses as well. A vast pool of potential talent is suppressed, as individuals who might make substantial contributions to the well-being of others never develop and utilize their gifts. Insofar as economic inequality stifles human potential, everyone suffers. The costs to society of increased crime, disease, and unrest can be very high.

RACIAL INEQUALITY

Relationships between peoples having different physical attributes are often characterized by misunderstanding, tensions, and conflict. Conflict is particularly likely to occur when populations with different physical attributes occupy unequal positions of advantage in the existing class structure (Steinberg, 1981). This conflict can be the basis for systems of **racial inequality,** in which some groups are subjected to discrimination and exploitation. In effect, certain groups are singled out for **minority-group** status. The term does not denote numbers but indicates status within one's society. In South Africa, for instance, blacks far outnumber whites, yet for many years black South Africans were a minority group because the dominant white group structured social institutions to ensure that blacks occupied an inferior status. (In 1994 the first elections open to all South Africans resulted in the election of a black president, Nelson Mandela.) In both South Africa and the United States, the physical trait of skin color has been used by the dominant white population as a criterion of social worth. Personal and institutional practices that adversely affect minority groups often turn their members into victims whose lives become limited by the dominant population.

Although frequently employed as a means of categorizing people, "race" is actually a meaningless concept in biological terms. We all belong to one human species. Variations in physical traits exist among members of the human species as a consequence of extremely slow evolutionary changes. These changes have evolved in response to differing demands of the various physical environments to which humans have been exposed. They are also, in part, the outcome of generations of genetic selection as different groups have come into contact with one another. Thus such features as skin color, hair texture, and shape of the eyes, nose, or lips vary among people whose ancestries lie in diverse geographic locations. Biologically speaking, these features do not really depict people of different races. *Race* is a social concept, not a biological one. Hereditarily "pure" races do not exist, and existing systems of racial categorization of people are imprecise and arbitrary (Benedict, 1959; Montagu, 1974).

Yet it is not uncommon for people to accord social significance to skin color. In the United States, for example, certain theorists have long argued that African Americans are, as a "race," biologically and psychologically inferior to whites (Gossett, 1965). Indeed, until the mid-twentieth century this was widely taken to be a scientific truth. Some scientists argued that persons of African descent had smaller brains than whites and therefore, by nature, were less intelligent. Even the famous scientist of evolution, Charles Darwin, stated:

> With civilized nations, the reduced size of the jaws from lessened use, the habitual play of different muscles serving to express different emotions, and the increased size of the brain from greater intellectual activity, have together produced a considerable effect on [whites'] general appearance in comparison with savages (quoted in Gossett, 1965: 78).

Since they were less intelligent, the reasoning went, African Americans were fit only for the low-level work whites set aside for them. This argument for racial inferiority served as part of a larger ideology justifying the enslavement of African Americans. The same argument continued to be used to justify segregated public education: mixing the allegedly less intelligent African Americans with whites in the same classroom would harm the progress of the whites.

Michael Omi and Howard Winant favor the term **racial formation** to underscore the social construction of race (1986). Racial formation is "the process by which social, economic, and political forces determine the content and importance of racial categories, and by which they in turn are shaped by racial meanings" (Omi and Winant, 1986: 61). Calling a particular population a "race" may be a first step toward singling it out for discrimination. The alleged negative characteristics of a group labeled a race are often claimed to be rooted in genetics and therefore impossible to change. This type of thinking can lead to **genocide,** the systematic extermination of a group of people by those who consider themselves racially superior.

A society in which race is socially significant is likely to be racist; there is no other reason for genetic variations to be of any meaningful concern. Systems of racial inequality are constructed around the false assumption that a link exists between features like skin color and the ways in which people are likely to think or behave. Just as humans cannot change their skin color, this view suggests, neither can they escape what it implies about their social worth.

Many people in the United States seem to believe that certain groups are inferior to others. This tendency was revealed clearly in the General Social Survey, a national study conducted annually by the University of Chicago's National Opinion Research Center (NORC). In 1990, for the first time, the NORC sought to determine the degree to which whites cling to stereotypes about African and Latino Americans. The results were sobering. The majority of whites polled held negative stereotypes. For example, 62 percent of the whites believed African Americans were less hardworking than themselves; 56 percent thought they were more violence-prone; and 53 percent felt that blacks were less intelligent. In the case of Latino Americans, 56 percent of the whites judged them as less hardworking; 50 percent said Latinos were more violence-prone; and 55 percent said they were less intelligent than whites (National Opinion Research Center, 1991a). The ability of so many whites to attribute these negative characteristics to entire categories of people, identifiable at best on the basis of physical differences, is an indication that racism is alive and well in the United States today.

Sociologists interested in the ways in which racism is expressed have identified two types of racism (Knowles and Prewitt, 1969; Feagin and Feagin, 1986). The first type, called **personal racism,** is racism expressed by individuals or small groups of people. It is an indication of prejudice toward those deemed "racially" inferior, and it may take such forms as espousing stereotypes based on alleged racial differences, using racial slurs, and engaging in discriminatory treatment, harassment, and even threats or acts of violence. In recent years, personal racism has come to be a major issue on many college campuses as people of color refuse to accept derogatory treatment from others (Bowser, Auletta, and Jones, 1993).

The second type of racism is known as **institutional racism.** As we noted in Chapter 2, an *institution* is a social structure created by people in order to accomplish certain tasks or perform certain needed functions in society. The economy and the state are examples of institutions. People of color have historically been excluded from key institutional policy-making and decision-making roles. This has contributed to institutional racism, whereby the routine operation of societal institutions fosters white privilege and advantage.

Within the economy, for example, discrimination in employment continues to be a major problem. This contributes to the income advantage whites possess (see Table 6.1). A study of Chicago-area businesses revealed the blatant racist policies of many employers toward workers from the inner city (Kirschenman and Neckerman, 1991). Employers expressed the kinds of stereotypes revealed in the General Social Survey:

> When they talked about the work ethic, tensions in the workplace, or attitudes toward work, employers emphasized the color of a person's skin. Many believed that white workers were superior to minorities in their work ethic (Kirschenman and Neckerman, 1991: 209–210).

As one employer put it,

> (According to) the energy that they put into their job and trying to be as productive as possible, I would have to put the white native-born at the high end and the Hispanic in the middle and the blacks at the bottom (Kirschenman and Neckerman, 1991: 210).

Employers, acting on these stereotypes, tried to avoid hiring minority workers. The study found that they relied on their white employees to

Table 6.1

PER CAPITA MONEY INCOME OF WHITES, AFRICAN AMERICANS, AND LATINOS, 1970–1992

YEAR	CURRENT DOLLARS				CONSTANT (1992) DOLLARS			
	ALL RACES*	WHITE	BLACK	LATINO†	ALL RACES*	WHITE	BLACK	LATINO†
1970	3,177	3,354	1,869	(NA)	10,793	11,394	6,349	(NA)
1975	4,818	5,072	2,972	2,847	12,028	12,662	7,419	7,107
1980	7,787	8,233	4,604	4,865	13,275	14,035	8,190	8,294
1985	11,013	11,671	6,840	6,613	14,360	15,218	8,919	8,623
1986	11,670	12,352	7,207	7,000	14,939	15,812	9,226	8,961
1987	12,391	13,143	7,645	7,653	15,303	16,232	9,442	9,452
1988	13,123	13,896	8,271	7,956	15,563	16,480	9,809	9,436
1989	14,056	14,896	8,747	8,390	15,904	16,854	9,897	9,493
1990	14,387	15,265	9,017	8,424	15,444	16,386	9,679	9,043
1991	14,617	15,510	9,170	8,662	15,057	15,977	9,446	8,923
1992	15,033	15,981	9,296	8,874	15,033	15,981	9,296	8,874

NA = Not available.
*Includes other races not shown separately.
†Persons of Latino origin may be of any race.
Source: U.S. Department of Commerce, Bureau of the Census, *Statistical Abstract of the United States: 1994* (Washington, D.C.: U.S. Government Printing Office, 1994), p. 474.

Personal racism is at times expressed through "hate crimes." In Howard Beach, a white neighborhood in the Queens section of New York City, three young African American men were viciously attacked and beaten by a gang of eleven white youths. One of the badly injured men, Michael Griffith, died after being hit by a car as he tried to escape across a parkway. White Howard Beach residents jeered the crowds that came to demonstrate against the violence.

refer friends and relatives for job openings, and they placed job advertisements in papers serving particular white areas and white ethnic groups. African Americans or Latino Americans who somehow made it as far as an interview would often be screened out at that point.

Institutional racism need not be as direct as in the example above. Indeed, some institutional practices have unintentional adverse effects. Take, for example, seniority rules. The most familiar is "last hired, first fired," indicating that employers will dismiss the most recent employees first when cutbacks or layoffs must occur. Since African Americans, Latino Americans, Asian Americans, Native Americans, and others who have successfully fought employment discrimination are often only recent arrivals in white-dominated work settings, seniority rules frequently work against them.

Another institution, the state, often seems less than aggressive in determining the problems people face as a consequence of racism and in enforcing the laws that do exist. At the federal level, for example, there are such vast backlogs of complaints regarding incidents of discrimination that many victims believe it is useless to file a complaint. Institutional racism in the state often takes the form of neglect, but in recent years officials have even tried to water down or retract existing state policies designed to assist victims of racism (Edsall and Edsall, 1992).

For example, the civil rights movement of the 1960s pressured the state to adopt regulations requiring that employers take **affirmative action** to stop discrimination against people of color as well as women (Hacker, 1992: chap. 7). Affirmative action meant not only that discrimination in hiring was to cease but also that employers were to take positive steps to increase the presence of people of color and women in their applicant pools, thus improving the chances that such persons would be hired if qualified. Often this required little more than improving the advertising of openings and dropping discriminatory employee screening practices. In many sectors of the labor force, affirmative action policies allowed individuals who had previously been excluded from particular workplaces to learn of opportunities and successfully compete for employment.

Political opponents of affirmative action claimed that past discriminatory practices in the workplace had largely disappeared and that affirmative action meant **reverse discrimination** against whites and males. Opponents further claimed that unqualified people were systematically being hired simply to meet race and gender quotas. Even though such claims were untrue, they fanned hostility against affirmative action among many members of the white majority, particularly males facing difficult times in the stagnating economy of the 1970s.

By the mid-1970s, while the state continued to pay lip service to the need for affirmative action, public support for it had dropped away. State pressure on employers to conform to affirmative action regulations began to wane. By the 1980s top politicians routinely distanced themselves from the issue of affirmative action in political campaigns, and some ran openly on platforms decrying "reverse discrimination." The Reagan administration (1980–1988) and the Bush administration (1988–1992) were openly hostile to affirmative action, and enforcement of regulations fell off sharply.

In large part, institutional racism in the state is a reflection of the state's composition. The fact that whites are in the numerical majority in most parts of the country has meant they could—if they wished—block members of other groups from electoral office. Moreover, at the very top levels of state bureaucracy, where crucial public policy decisions are made, positions are typically filled through political appointment. This has made it very difficult for people of color to rise as high as their talents may merit. Those who do may have to sacrifice being assertive about minority interests in return for the employment opportunity they have been afforded.

The criminal justice system is also white-dominated. The subject of law enforcement has been a particularly sensitive one for people of color (see Cashmore and McLaughlin, 1991). Civil rights laws have recently begun to have an effect, but for a long time employment discrimination in police departments was rampant. Moreover, police departments have frequently either ignored charges of police officer misconduct and acts of brutality against minorities or performed internal "investigations" of such charges with little result. Police have a monopoly over the legitimate use of force, but its misuse has led to mistrust, hostility, and occasionally civil disorder. Acts of police brutality often precipitate events, at times generating violent rebellions in ghettos, in barrios, and on reservations. Police brutality was an issue in the massive disorders in Los Angeles in 1992 that followed

The issue of brutality by white police has long generated anger in communities of color, whose members often are powerless in the face of police violence. Here, family members of an African American woman, killed by New York City police officers following a domestic dispute, protest her slaying.

the acquittal of white police officers who had been videotaped beating Rodney King, an African American.

The dominant white majority is also overrepresented among judges, prosecutors, jurors, prison officials, probation officers, and parole board members. People of color are more likely than whites to be arrested and charged with crimes, to be unable to afford bail, and to lack the funds needed to hire a private attorney. Members of minority groups are more likely to be found guilty, to receive heavy sentences, and to be denied requests for parole from prison (Petersilia, 1985). Once released, they are likely to face very restricted employment opportunities, a situation that sets the stage for possible further involvement with the legal system. For too many persons, going through the criminal justice process is like being trapped in a revolving door (Reiman, 1984).

In documenting the effects of racism, most of the attention has been given (understandably) to racism's victims. Yet it is clear that *all* of society's members lose as a consequence of racism, since the system of racial inequality stifles the potential accomplishments of millions of people. Moreover, whites are not "free" in a society in which they accord social significance to physical traits like skin color. Racists are limited in their thinking and the quality of their social relationships, duped and imprisoned by their own ideology. It is worth taking time to imagine how everyone's biography might be greatly altered by living in a nonracist society. We might also consider the invisible, unearned privileges and the costs of being a member of one group or another in a racist society.

SEX INEQUALITY

Just as systems of economic inequality and racial inequality have ideologies justifying their existence, so too do systems of **sex inequality.** Sex inequality stems from the notion that "biology is destiny," that biological differences between the sexes *require* that the sexes play very different societal roles.

Males and females obviously do differ biologically. Their genetic make-ups are not the same, anatomical differences are apparent, and their hormones perform different functions. But how much social importance should we attach to such differences? To answer this question, we must make a distinction between two concepts: sex and gender.

Sex refers to the fundamental biological characteristics that cause a person to be categorized as either a female or a male. These characteristics are genetically determined. Rarely is there ambiguity as to the sex of any given newborn once the baby's physical traits are established. Moreover, sex differences remain the same from society to society.

Gender, on the other hand, is a social construction, much like "race." Gender refers to the ways of behaving and relating to others that members of society expect of the two sexes; it refers to the different roles that males and females are expected to play. Gender is learned, whereas sex is inherited. As such, the behaviors associated with gender differ in various respects from society to society (Martin and Voorhies, 1975). For example, in some societies women are expected to be active and aggressive individuals, while in others they are expected to be passive and retiring (Frodi et al., 1977). Indeed, even within societies the role expectations for women may differ—for example, by age, ethnic subculture, or social class (Lindsey, 1994).

Nonetheless, men have used the ideology expressed in "biology is destiny" to create and maintain systems of sex inequality in which they dominate. The concept of **patriarchy** is used to refer to such systems. Not only domination but oppression and exploitation are common themes in societies characterized by patriarchy. While undergoing important changes in the last couple of decades, society in the United States is still patriarchal. Men and women are not equal sharers of power—whether it be economic, political, or social. The biology-is-destiny ideology still hovers over women, influencing male-female relationships and the trajectory of both sexes' biographies.

According to this ideology, biological differences between the sexes require that there be a **sexual division of labor,** in which men and women take on responsibility for the tasks that each sex is most capable of performing. Hence, because women bear children, female biology dictates that they are most fit for child-rearing and caretaking roles in the home. The home is said to be the best place for those whom nature has decreed the "weaker sex." It is a haven from the rough, competitive world of work and politics in which only men, biologically the "stronger sex," are able to excel. It is the men's role to provide for their dependents: women and children.

The ideology suggests that the need for the species to reproduce promulgates yet another important role for women: being sexually attractive. Women thus play an important function when they strive to be, and allow themselves to be, treated as sex objects. This is all in line with nature's grand design.

The biology-is-destiny ideology spills over into the workplace and other institutional arenas outside the home. The rigidity of the ideology has begun to erode, but most people still accept that there are "men's jobs" and "women's jobs." Few chief executive officers of the nation's largest corporations are women. But most clerks, secretaries, nurses, elementary school teachers, social workers, and domestic helpers are women. Why? According to the ideology, this division of labor simply reflects the basic biological differences between the sexes. Men are equipped to exercise power and function under demanding circumstances. Women are best suited for supportive, caretaking occupations and professions—those that call upon the particular strengths nature has given women for duties in the home.

Critics of the ideology and the restrictions it imposes on women's life chances include **feminists** and their supporters. Feminists underscore the difference between sex and gender, pointing out that the roles accorded women are largely of men's making. Women alone are capable of bearing children, but men are as capable as women in playing a nurturant role. They simply choose to allocate most of that task to women. Nor is there reason to restrict women to the home out of concern that they are the weaker sex. Given the opportunity, women can fulfill virtually any position in work and politics that is presently male-dominated. Similarly, men are eminently capable of doing "women's work" in the labor force. Finally, current social conditions make it clear that women can and must be able to support themselves. Millions of women who are unmarried, separated, divorced, or widowed—many with children—are independent by necessity or choice. The demands faced by these women, for their own survival and that of their children, often cannot be met by the earnings accorded to "women's work."

Feminists also question the notion that women must make themselves desirable to men in order to ensure reproduction of the species. Standards of beauty and attractiveness tend to be set by the dominant group. Most women are unable to meet these standards, but there are always some who can—or can at least meet them better than others. Thus, many women are raised to live in fear of rejection by men and to see other women as threats. Women's role as sex objects is not natural and inevitable but an instrument of male domination.

Patriarchy, as a system of sex inequality, finds expression through practices of **sexism.** This term refers to the systematic subordination of persons on the basis of their sex. As with racism, sexism exists both at the level of personal relationships and at the institutional level.

At the personal level, sexism typically takes the form of **male chauvinism.** Men who are chauvinistic against women express attitudes or behave in ways which suggest that males are superior to females and have a right to insist on females' subordination. Attitudes can range from sexist points of view ("Women are too emotional to be President of the United States") to extreme sexist behaviors ("I wouldn't call it rape—the way she was acting, she was asking for it"). Overt expressions of male chauvinism can be confronted, but such confrontation may be dangerous in a society in which men hold an unequal share of power. Women who challenge the sexist views and behaviors of a professor or employer, for example, may end up receiving a poorer grade than deserved, being overlooked for a promotion, or being dismissed from work. Recently the government has been pressed to provide legal protections for women who are the victims of this type of harassment.

Institutional sexism fosters male advantage through the routine operations of societal institutions. In the spheres of the economy and the state institutional sexism is pervasive, yet often less visible and less open to direct confrontation than male chauvinism. Given its far-reaching impact, institutional sexism is more of a problem—not only for women but for men as well.

Despite the biology-as-destiny ideology that stresses women's alleged biological proclivity for homemaking and child care, by 1990 almost 60 percent of all women over 16 were in the paid labor force (Renzetti and Curran, 1992: 180). Most were working out of economic necessity, either because they had sole responsibility to provide for themselves (and, in many cases, others) or because their partners were incapable of being the sole providers. Yet by all statistical indicators women get much smaller rewards for their participation in the labor force than do men, regardless of their level of education. This state of affairs is understandable only in light of institutional sexism.

The U.S. labor market is sex-segregated to the point where it is appropriate to use the term **dual labor market** to describe it (Reskin and Hartmann, 1986; Tomaskovic-Devey, 1993). As we shall see in Chapter 11, most women hold jobs in which the majority of their coworkers are female. Women are overly represented in jobs that are the least well paying, offer the least security, and have relatively low prestige—clerical work and ser-

In many societies women are relegated to the most undesirable manual occupations, forced to labor for very little money in a sex-segregated labor market. *(Left)* These women in India are hauling loads of brick at a construction site. *(Right)* In the United States, this waitress hauls dinner to her table of waiting customers.

vice occupations (such as waitresses). Conversely, women are underrepresented in the jobs highest in pay, security, and status. The median income of full-time, year-round female workers is barely over two-thirds that of their male counterparts. This dual labor market is not a reflection of educational differences between men and women; women, on average, have the edge over men in years of school completed. Rather, the dual labor market is held intact by discrimination in employment, promotion, and pay. By paying less for "women's jobs" than for "men's jobs," and by channeling women into the former, employers use the biology-is-destiny ideology to their own economic advantage.

The struggle of women to improve their standing in the labor market is relatively recent and follows upon similar struggles by people of color to end racial discrimination. (See the boxed excerpt for the stories of some women who have successfully challenged both personal and institutional sexism.) But institutional sexism in the economy is a routine matter largely because the state does so little about it. Indeed, the state itself is a locus of institutional sexism in employment. Women are poorly represented in the elected and appointed offices that make important policy decisions. Women thus have limited power in resolving major issues in which their life chances are at stake. These issues include the level of income maintenance provided to poor families, government support for affordable day care for working mothers, a national program of universal health care, and the protection of women's reproductive rights (see Sidel, 1990).

Does this system of sex inequality enhance the life chances of men? Narrow benefits for some are outweighed by much broader losses for all. Any society in which the opportunities for women—typically half the population—are channeled and restricted is a society that is limited in its development. Why should we knowingly do without the kinds of contributions women can make? Men, too, are victims in a patriarchal society in which women have to struggle against them. Working to change a patriarchy would make available a much wider range of biographies for people of both sexes.

AGE INEQUALITY

Aging is a natural biological process to which we are all subject. There is no reason why older people should be the object of mistreatment, but at times they are (Atchley, 1985). Some cultures, such as China's, interpret aging positively: they respect and venerate elderly persons for knowledge they have accumulated and share with others (Cowgill, 1986). The status of elders was extremely high in the United States until the late eighteenth century, when revolutionary turmoil prompted a shift in attitudes toward those occupying traditional roles of authority (Fischer, 1978).

Aging may also be interpreted negatively, as when the elderly are viewed as unattractive, undesirable burdens on society. This interpretation is characteristic of the system of **age inequality** that came to prevail in the United States in the early nineteenth century (Fischer, 1978). This system

Women today may not find it easy to make their way in a male-dominated world. But their chances are far better than those of women who struggled to succeed just a few decades ago. Consider the obstacles and barriers that the women described below had to overcome in the prefeminist era.

In the years that Ruth Bader Ginsburg was rejected by law firms although she had graduated first in her 1959 Columbia Law School class, Muriel F. Siebert was told that she would be hired as a securities analyst only if she wore white gloves and a hat in the elevator. At the same time, Maria Iandolo New collected rejections from medical schools because she had the temerity to marry.

[Since Judge Ginsburg's] confirmation by the Senate as a Supreme Court Justice, her long road to eminence echoes the experience of a generation of women who embarked on careers in a pre-feminist era, before they had an ideology to justify their actions and a movement to open doors that were shut to them.

Hearings Revive Memories

And many say the barriers remain formidable, although open discrimination is now illegal, thanks in part to the work of Judge Ginsburg. Ms. Siebert went on to become the first woman to buy a seat on the New York Stock Exchange, and Dr. New ended up as the first woman to head a department at Cornell University Medical College, where she is chief of pediatrics. . . .

They are among a group of largely unsung women who, for reasons they cannot even now fully explain, were driven to take an uncharted path. They were contemporaries of Betty Friedan, but they were not at first open crusaders for women's rights. Not content in the roles society deemed acceptable for women of their day, they quietly entered fields dominated by men and worked their way to the top of their professions.

They all shared a lifetime of being the first, the only, the one who stood out in the room. And they were all shaped by an era in which a lady did not do what they were doing, and certainly would never complain out loud.

Dr. New, who is 64, can still recite the letter she received from the dean of the University of Rochester's medical school in 1950 after her husband had been invited for an interview, and she had not. She had written the dean asking that he not reject her just because she was married and pointing out that she actually had the better academic record.

"You are an impertinent young lady," the dean replied, "and I am more sure than ever that we do not want you in our medical school."

Seven years later, Madeleine M. Kunin, then a student at Columbia University's Graduate School of Journalism, was offered a job in the cafeteria rather than the newsroom of The New York Times. Later, another newspaper turned down her application because, an editor told her, the last woman hired had been raped in the paper's parking lot.

Assuming the Responsibility

"You sort of took the responsibility on yourself instead of saying, 'Why don't you make the parking lot safer?'" said Ms. Kunin, who in 1984 became Vermont's first female Governor and is now, at 59, the nation's Deputy Education Secretary.

Some women faced the double bind of sex and race. When Constance Baker Motley, a young lawyer working on school desegregation cases in the early 1950's for the NAACP Legal Defense Fund, tried to enter the New York City Bar Association's library, the doorman looked her up and down. She assured him she was, in fact, a member, and told him her name.

"I carefully said Mrs. Motley, because black women were always addressed by their first name," she said.

He told her, "Oh, right this way, Constance."

Judge Motley later became the first woman to serve a full term in the New York State Senate and in 1966, the first black woman appointed as a Federal judge, to the Federal District Court in Manhattan, where she still presides. . . . But she says that for years she was not given the same opportunities as men to serve on committees or speak at conferences, activities that build judges' careers.

Bucking the Convention

As they looked back on their lives, many women said it was hard now to recapture the atmosphere of their early career years, when they were bucking the convention that women stayed at home and reared children.

"I got married at a time when it was felt that if a woman worked, it reflected her husband's failure," said Luisa Kreisberg, who is 59 and president of the Kreisberg Group, a marketing and public relations firm specializing in the arts.

Jill Ker Conway, who became the first female president of Smith College in 1975, used to pretend at parties in her native Australia in the late 1950's that she was not a young professor, but a secretary. She was not ashamed, she said, it was just "my way of saving having to spend the time explaining what I was doing."

Requirements for femininity had not changed much even by 1971, when Dr. Felicia H. Stewart arrived at the University of California at San Francisco's Medical Center as the first female resident in 12 years. An older female doctor took her aside and gave her some advice.

"No matter what time of night or day, I should be absolutely certain my hair was immaculate and my makeup was complete and my nails were perfect," said Dr. Stewart, 50, who was one of a handful of women in her Harvard Medical School class of 1969 and is now an authority on birth control.

Roadblocks for the Many

Such pressures often had the insidious effect of causing women to lower their own sights.

Nancy H. Teeters, now 63, was a promising economics student at Oberlin College in 1952, but she said she never even considered a career. "I thought I'd do what everyone else was doing: get married and support my husband through graduate school," she said. It was not until her in-laws offered to pay for her education that she began her career in eco-

nomics. Twenty-six years later, she became the first woman to be a governor of the Federal Reserve Board.

For every woman who broke through such barriers and had a successful career, there were many more who could not. Andrea Dupree, an eminent astronomer and senior scientist at the Harvard-Smithsonian Center for Astrophysics, told of several women approaching her wistfully at a reunion of her Wellesley College class of 1960. Now that they were divorced, they said, they wished they had pursued a career. One, despite her degree, was working at a discount store.

Even those women who were clearly successful in their fields had to put up with indignities, constrained in part by an ethos that women should not be confrontational.

Striving to Be Heard

"I behaved the way I was taught to behave: like a woman in the company of men," said Mildred S. Dresselhaus, 62, an engineer and solid-state physicist who became the first woman to be tenured in the engineering department of the Massachusetts Institute of Technology in 1968. "If you behaved aggressively in the company of men, they wouldn't accept you."

Many said they felt all but invisible.

"I think it is the person who is different from anybody else in the group who has a more difficult time in being heard," said Ellen A. Peters, 63, who did not receive a single job offer from a law firm despite graduating first in her class at Yale Law School in 1954. Ten years after those rejections, she became the first woman to be a tenured professor at Yale Law School. She has been Chief Justice of Connecticut's Supreme Court since 1984.

In striving to be heard, many women were labeled unfeminine. "I remember having a more senior professor say to me, 'You're almost as assertive as a man,'" said Professor Dupree, who is 53. "And that was in 1960. Now I'm shy and retiring by comparison with the younger generation."

Relatively outspoken as she might have been, Professor Dupree remembered having to gather her

(Continued)

courage to fight the one battle most commonly cited by women who managed to enter their chosen fields: being paid and promoted as much as their male colleagues. Her supervisors told her that she was paid less because she had a husband to support her.

Concessions to pregnancy and child rearing were rare. Like many other women of her day, Professor Dresselhaus hid her pregnancies as best she could and returned to work a day or two after her children were born. "The guys didn't even notice there was a change," she said.

Others negotiated part-time work and accepted that they would advance more slowly for a while. The rules at the Federal Reserve in 1959 required Mrs. Teeters, then a staff member, to resign once she was three months pregnant. Instead, she eked out a six-week maternity leave combining her sick days and vacation and worked flexible hours for several years at the Federal Reserve and elsewhere.

For many women, as for Judge Ginsburg, anger and a commitment to change conditions for the women who followed them came gradually, a slow burn that paralleled in some ways the growth of feminism. They watched, as Professor Conway put it, their private battles became public ones.

"The most amazing thing about it was that we didn't recognize these incidents to be what they were," Dr. Stewart said. "They just seemed normal. It took me a long time to find a place in my soul for outrage."

Source: Susan Chira, "Ginsburg's Spirit Is Echoed by Other Pioneers," *New York Times,* August 2, 1993, pp. A1, A16.

is organized around the expression of **ageism,** ideas and practices that have negative consequences for persons defined as old.

As with the concepts of race and gender, "old age" is a social construction. At times old age is arbitrarily said to commence with the passing of a certain number of chronological years. For example, government agencies use age 65 as the start of eligibility for certain benefits, and employers offer pensions to workers once they reach age 65. In these cases "old age" is created for the administrative convenience of the organizations.

Physical signs of aging are also used to arbitrarily define people as old. These characteristics include loss of skin elasticity, wrinkled skin, gray hair or hair loss, and physical frailty. The prevailing ideology holds that persons with such traits have entered a downward spiral of deterioration. The social construction of old age carries with it certain assumptions about the ways in which people with outward signs of aging are likely to think and behave. This social construction of old age treats women differently from men. In our society, a youthful appearance enhances a woman's image as a sex object; loss of this appearance devalues women in the eyes of many men. In contrast, as men start to age, they may be described as looking distinguished, a temporary positive assessment that is denied women. Yet even "distinguished" men eventually come to be defined as old men.

The U.S. population is aging. In coming decades there will be rapid growth in the proportion of the population that is 65 and over. This "graying of America" (discussed in Chapter 16) is taking place even while a number of myths and stereotypes about elderly people continue to prevail. These include the following:

1. *"Old people are all the same."* In actuality, our elders are as heterogeneous as the rest of the population. They differ in race and ethnicity, class, work experience, sexual orientation, political attitudes, and all the other attributes that differentiate younger people.

2. *"Old people are senile."* "Senility" is a vague term, often used inaccurately—and pejoratively—in reference to the mental state of older persons. "Senile dementia" (Alzheimer's disease) is a medical term referring to a decline of mental faculties due to deterioration of the brain. Only a small percentage of elders suffer from this condition. Most anxiety and depression among older people is not only treatable but avoidable, as is the case for the younger population.

3. *"Old people are unproductive."* It is true that many older people are not members of the labor force or actively involved in parenting. But younger people tend to be oblivious to the fact that they are reaping the benefits of their elders' many years of productive labor in the workplace and home. Older people are capable of making contributions to societal well-being in innumerable other ways, including family involvement, participation in religious activities and politics, and support of cultural affairs.

The myths and stereotypes portraying elderly people as a homogeneous, senile, unproductive, gray-haired mass in a spiraling state of physical and mental deterioration feed into **disengagement theory** (Cumming and Henry, 1961). This theory suggests that biological and psychological decline accompanies aging; thus, it is only natural that individuals, in anticipation of death, begin to remove themselves from social roles they occupied during middle age. It is considered natural not only for elderly people to withdraw but also for society itself to disengage from involvement with the elderly.

This mutual withdrawal is presented as necessary, inevitable, and beneficial to all concerned. Persons in a "deteriorating" state escape the pressures of performing a role in the labor force, thereby ensuring a more "successful" old age. Society also benefits by having the opportunity to replace the elderly with younger, more energetic, and presumably more productive workers.

Critics attack disengagement theory as an ideology justifying prejudice and discrimination against elders (Levin and Levin, 1980). It counsels elderly persons to abandon the roles they have long occupied, even if both the elderly and society may continue to draw substantial rewards from these roles. Most people remain healthy and capable of being active into their later years, contrary to the image of decline that is generally presented. President Ronald Reagan, who was 77 when he left office, is often cited as an example. Pushing people out of or away from roles they occupied in middle age may actually *cause* physical and psychological decline that might not otherwise occur, as is often the case with involuntary retirements. Nor is it necessarily the case that youth outweighs the advantages associated with years of experience in the workplace.

Many people worry about what lies ahead for them in their later years. In one national survey, adult respondents were asked what worried them the most when they thought about getting old. The worries cited most frequently were having health-related problems (40 percent), being poor or having income problems (23 percent), and being unable to take care of oneself (11 percent). Only one in ten adults could think of no worries about getting old (Princeton Survey Research Associates, 1990). These worries are made worse by ageist practices affecting elderly people today.

Consider, for example, the area of health care. While growing old does not necessarily entail a downwardly spiraling state of health, many older people do face increasing health-care requirements due to chronic, long-term problems (such as arthritis, high blood pressure, sight and hearing impairments). Some will ultimately require full-time care, although at any point in time, only about 5 percent of those 65 and older live in nursing homes.

Yet health-care costs are high, and government programs such as Medicare do not cover some services. Middle-income people who need long-term nursing-home care cannot even qualify for it under Medicare until they expend all their assets to the point of poverty. Moreover, the medical profession and its institutions are not oriented toward health needs of the aging. Too few physicians are trained in geriatric medicine; many doctors do not find the common chronic health problems of elderly people interesting or challenging; physicians often do not like to take Medicare patients (preferring the higher reimbursement usually guaranteed with private health insurance plans); and in many parts of the country hospitals and clinics are inaccessible to older persons because of distance and/or lack of adequate transportation. Finally, for elders who ultimately require nursing homes, the number and quality of these facilities remain a national scandal, as do the expenses accompanying even little more than "custodial" care. Ageism, then, is expressed in the ways state programs and the medical profession have failed to accommodate the needs of the elderly. Poll respondents have good reason to be worried about their health status as elderly citizens.

Poverty-level living and income problems are also linked to ageism. Neither the state nor the private sector acknowledges a responsibility to assist the elderly to live above the poverty line. Increasing numbers of elderly persons are forced to rely on social security for all or most of their incomes, but benefit levels remain low. Since benefits are keyed to employment and earnings history, persons who have not fared well in the labor market during their adult lives (particularly women and minority-group members) suffer the most. People who are poor when they are middle-aged are likely to continue to be so. Moreover, the state has no adequate way of compensating persons who work for firms that fail and who find themselves with broken promises and no pensions. A similar fate awaits those who have invested savings for retirement in banks and insurance companies that experience financial crises or even go bankrupt, a situation that is increasingly common in the 1990s.

In sum, the phenomenon of aging is often accompanied by victimization. Older people are subjected to myths and stereotypes, ideological justifications for mistreatment, and other forms of ageism by those who are younger. And they are victimized by ageism through the unresponsiveness of institutions to problems that severely tarnish the so-called golden years of old age. The system of age inequality that has evolved robs elderly people of their humanity and dignity, and may hasten their decline. Ironically, in the absence of a groundswell of social change, this particular system of inequality awaits us all.

SEXUAL ORIENTATION AND INEQUALITY

Sexual orientation is one of the most important aspects of our biographies. Matters ranging from who we are likely to choose as a mate to what kinds of protections we are afforded under the law will be influenced by whether we are homosexual, are heterosexual, or lean toward one orientation or the other.

Social science research on human sexual behavior indicates that both men and women occupy places on a broad spectrum in terms of their sexual interests and practices (Goode, 1984: 178–181). Moreover, many persons move around on this spectrum over the course of their lives. Because of these variations, the terms "homosexual" and "heterosexual" are rather arbitrary categories. Only at the far ends of the continuum are individuals exclusively lifelong homosexuals or heterosexuals.

Interestingly, it was not until the late eighteenth and early nineteenth centuries that the concept of "homosexual" emerged in Europe and the United States (Greenberg, 1988). Individuals who engaged in sexual activities with persons of the same sex were not seen as unique in any way apart from this behavior. This is not to say homosexual practices were widely accepted. Such behavior was condemned by Judeo-Christian religions and prohibited by law.

The concept of homosexuality emerged largely as a result of the medical profession's claim to have "scientifically" established that such behavior was abnormal and pathological, only engaged in by persons who were a separate and different human type. Despite such allegations, which continue today, no one has yet been able to definitively establish any biological or psychological traits (apart from sexual orientation) that would allow us to differentiate homosexuals from anyone else. Recent studies suggesting that homosexuality may have biological foundations remain inconclusive (Small, 1993; Wheeler, 1993). Moreover, even if the results were conclusive, there is no reason that they should be used as a basis for defining homosexuality in negative terms.

The sexual practices we associate with homosexuality have been found in many cultures and historical periods (Whitam and Mathy, 1985). In Melanesian societies, for example, such practices are ritualized as part of the pattern of relationships older men establish for brief periods with young boys. In many societies outside the West such activities are considered socially acceptable for certain members or sectors of the community (Ford and Beach, 1951). Thus, it is not unusual for practices associated with both heterosexuality and homosexuality to be part of a people's cultural repertoire.

Our own culture, however, is marked by a system of **inequality based on sexual orientation.** We tend to cling to a category—"homosexual"—and condemn those whom we perceive as fitting into it. Today, prejudicial attitudes and institutionalized discrimination are widespread against individuals labeled as homosexual. Gay men and lesbians are the daily victims of emotions ranging from disgust to fear to hatred on the part of persons who demand that everyone adhere to the dominant norm of heterosexuality. An ideology we might call **heterosexism,** which holds that homosexuality is unnatural and immoral, strongly prevails in U.S. society.

Heterosexism affects a large number of people in the United States. Pioneering studies by Alfred Kinsey and others concluded that 10 percent of the U.S. population is predominantly homosexual (Kinsey, Pomeroy, and Martin, 1948; Kinsey et al., 1953). While some would argue that this figure is too high (Billy et al., 1993; Schmalz, 1993), others believe it is an underestimate (Kirk and Madsen, 1989: 13–18). Many persons who have had or continue to have sexual experiences with members of their own sex do not see themselves as homosexual. Many call themselves bisexual, indicating that their lifestyles also allow for heterosexual practices. All these people, as well as the parents and family members of the gay population, are affected by heterosexism. Clearly, the system of inequality imposed on gay people by heterosexuals plays a role in the biographies of a substantial proportion of people in the United States.

In public opinion polls conducted in the United States, 23 percent of the adults surveyed said they have coworkers, friends, or relatives who are gay (Gallup Organization, 1993). Yet many people continue to accept the myths accompanying the ideology of heterosexism. Most do not want to know about issues of importance to homosexuals or about homosexuals' lifestyles and local subcultures. Neither the media nor educational institutions do much to encourage interest, let alone understanding.

The mistaken notions many people still believe include the following (Kirk and Madsen, 1989):

1. *"There aren't many gay people in the United States."* Since so many gay men and lesbians are forced to hide their sexual orientation, there seem to be far fewer than is actually the case.

2. *"Homosexuals are easy to identify."* In one poll, 31 percent of adults stated that homosexuals can be identified simply by their appearance or gestures (Roper Organization, 1990). But, in fact, we cannot discern a person's sexual orientation merely by observing him or her.

3. *"Homosexuality is caused by mental illness, willful perversity, or recruitment by other homosexuals."* This attitude dismisses the possibility that homosexuality is a natural inclination found in virtually every culture. Homosexuals generally are mentally healthy, do not choose their sex-

ual orientation, and come to realize their orientation without contact with other homosexuals.

4. *"Gay men and lesbians lead unproductive, dissolute lives."* This view ignores the reality that homosexuals are everywhere, in all occupations, professions, and callings. As accomplished homosexuals in medicine, the clergy, the arts, education, the military, sports, politics, and business increasingly refuse to hide their sexual orientation, the productivity and contributions of gay men and lesbians will become more obvious.

5. *"Homosexuals are terribly unhappy people, because of their affliction."* Rates of substance abuse and suicidal behavior are thought to be higher among homosexuals than within the "straight" population (on adolescents, see Gibson, 1989), but this difference may be traceable to the negative treatment homosexuals experience, not something innate.

6. *"Homosexuals are likely to give you AIDS."* In 1991, 35 percent of adults polled said that fear of AIDS was motivating them to avoid homosexuals and persons they think are gay or lesbian, as well as places where homosexuals meet (Louis Harris and Associates, 1991). Yet it is not possible to contract AIDS through casual contact.

Public opinion polls reveal extremely negative attitudes toward homosexuals. When asked how much sympathy they have for people who get AIDS from homosexual activity, 60 percent of the adults surveyed said "not much" or "none" (CBS News/New York Times, 1991). Asked whether homosexual relations between consenting adults should be legal, 56 percent of the adults polled said "no" (Gallup Organization, 1988). When asked if they would vote for a political candidate known to be gay, but whose politics they otherwise liked, 62 percent of adults said "no" (Gordon S. Black Corporation, 1989). Asked about television scenes that suggest, but do not actually show, homosexual activity, 55 percent of adults said that they should not be allowed at all, and another 35 percent would permit them only late at night (Kane, Parsons, and Associates, 1989). Finally, 69 percent of the adults polled said that gay and lesbian couples should not have the same legal rights as married couples (Gallup Organization, 1989).

Within a climate of public opinion such as this, it is understandable that gay men and lesbians not only suffer harassment and discrimination but have few rights to protection under the law. Employers discriminate in hiring. Landlords refuse housing. Insurance companies refuse to provide coverage. Consensual homosexual activity in private is rendered criminal through laws against sodomy in almost half the states. Nowhere do homosexual couples have the legal right to marriage. In cases of divorce, child-custody rights or visitation privileges are often at issue for a gay or lesbian parent. "Gay-bashing" has become a common term, denoting violent attacks on both gay men and lesbians by those seeking to uphold the heterosexual norm (see DeCecco, 1985).

According to the National Gay and Lesbian Task Force, which surveyed 119 gay and lesbian community organizations in 40 states, more than

Antigay demonstrators object to proposals that school curricula teach children to respect people who are gay, arguing that such teachings will encourage children to abandon their heterosexuality in favor of a gay lifestyle. This erroneous notion is based on the assumption that gay people choose their sexual orientation.

7,000 "hate crimes" occurred against homosexuals in 1989 (Pogatchnik, 1990). About 19 percent took place on college campuses. A survey conducted at Pennsylvania State University found that most gay male and lesbian undergraduates had suffered verbal harassment. A quarter had experienced threats of physical violence. Some had suffered serious assaults. With their expectations for future harassment and discrimination high, most homosexual students were driven to hide their sexual orientation. Some found themselves avoiding other persons who were homosexual, avoiding locations identified with homosexuals, and presenting themselves as heterosexual or "straight" (D'Augelli, 1989).

Despite this dismal picture, the system of inequality in which gay men and women are caught up has begun to change. A handful of states have passed laws prohibiting discrimination in such areas as employment and housing. Some states have passed so-called hate-crime laws that specifically outlaw and spell out penalties for violent crimes motivated by the sexual orientation of the victim. In a milestone action, President George Bush signed the National Hate Crimes Statistics Act of 1990, which requires the Department of Justice to gather nationwide statistics on crimes motivated by prejudice on the basis of race, religion, ethnic background, or sexual orientation. This was the first time a U.S. President ever signed a bill including sexual orientation as a civil rights concern—and the first time gay rights representatives had ever been invited to the White House for a public ceremony in which a bill was signed into law.

Gay men and lesbians are becoming more visible in key institutions. For example, in 1980 fewer than five elected state or local officials in the nation were openly gay. A decade later there were over 50. Shortly after assuming office, President Bill Clinton selected a woman who had publicly acknowledged her lesbianism for a key post in the Department of Housing and Urban Development and appointed a gay male with AIDS to his White House staff.

A number of major universities, including the Massachusetts Institute of Technology and the University of Wisconsin at Madison, challenged the Department of Defense policy banning homosexuals from military service, since it necessitated discrimination against gay students enrolled in campus ROTC units. Such universities were implicitly threatening to withdraw from participation in the ROTC, which is a major source of officers for the military services. Recently, the Clinton administration has worked to change Defense Department policy so as to allow homosexuals to serve discreetly in all ranks and in all military services, a policy reflecting the controversy surrounding the dismissal of many highly talented people found to be gay. Members of the armed forces will not be asked if they are homosexual and are not required to reveal their orientation. Homosexual *conduct* remains grounds for dismissal, however. While this policy is being challenged in the courts as discriminatory, it does represent an attempt to confront the issue.

Moreover, there is evidence of improvement in gay male and lesbian civil rights both in public and in corporate policy. For example, in such urban centers as Hartford, Minneapolis, and San Francisco, gay male and lesbian couples now may file at city hall for legal recognition of "domestic partnerships." Several of the nation's newspapers have abandoned their wedding and engagement pages in favor of "celebration" pages, to allow public announcement of such partnerships. A number of public and private employers have agreed to give insurance coverage and benefits to same-sex domestic partners of their employees.

Gay men and lesbians still face an enormous amount of oppression informed by ignorance and bigotry. The system of inequality based on sexual orientation has only begun to come under attack. That means gay people in the United States will undergo additional victimization as well as further courageous struggle.

ABLE-BODIEDNESS AND INEQUALITY

In 1990 President Bush signed a bill into law that was widely hailed as the most important step taken by the federal government since the 1960s to protect a group's civil rights. The Americans with Disabilities Act is intended to end discrimination against people with disabilities and to foster their participation in the mainstream of economic and social life. The specific areas of discrimination addressed include employment in the private sector, public accommodations, public services, transportation, and telecommunications (*Public Law 101–335, 1990*).

The term "disability" is open to different definitions and interpretations. The Disabilities Act uses the term to refer to any physical or mental condition that substantially limits one or more life activities of an individual. Such life activities include walking, hearing, speaking, seeing, learning, or working. Under this definition, it is estimated that some 36 million people with disabilities live in the United States. Their impairments arise from a variety of causes: illness, disease, accidents, environmental hazards, criminal victimization, involvement in war, and problems associated with prenatal development or birth. Persons with disabilities differ in the degree to which they are limited: Some have only one life activity impaired, while others are multiply impaired. And people differ in the degree to which their disability is readily discernible to others.

People with disabilities face many challenges just living with their conditions, but we are interested here in the system of **inequality based on able-bodiedness,** created by those without disabilities (Gliedman and Roth, 1980; Stroman, 1982). Once again, we have a group victimized by people who are more powerful and who justify their behavior by an ideology based on alleged inferior attributes of the victimized. In this case we are dealing with a system of inequality characterized by **ableism,** a system that treats people with disabilities as if they are defective, unwhole, or less than full human beings.

The ideology of ableism suggests that the disabling condition is all-encompassing. From this point of view, we are not dealing with "people with disabilities." The ideology subtly shifts us over to talking about "disabled people," a label implying that the disability is the only thing that matters in how they should be viewed and treated. The disability becomes a master status with a **stigma,** or a negative mark, signifying doubt as to a person's social worth (Goffman, 1963). Conceived of in this way, those with physical and mental impairments seem like members of another species, lacking the "normal" interests and concerns that occupy others of their social class, race, sex, age, and sexual orientation. In short, they are seen and treated as disabled first and as people second.

Often the ideology paternalistically suggests that this "separate species" is childlike in nature. Helplessness, dependency, inability to take on responsibility, and need for guidance are assumed to be innate characteristics of people with disabilities. In communicating with these people, the able-bodied thus often adopt an obviously conjured air of concern and kindness. Their approach is much like the one many people take when they are first introduced to a friend's dog.

On the other side of the coin, many able-bodied people are afraid of people with disabilities, so they avoid eye contact and minimize interaction. Some behave as if the disability were catching, but others are simply fearful of what they do not know. The able-bodied may question their own role: If these are "disabled people" (instead of people who happen to have disabilities), how am I supposed to know how to interact with them? What do I do? What do I say? What might the disabled person want from me? Avoidance can be a way of protecting oneself from the unknown and from the embarrassing or stressful social errors that might arise during interactions with members of this "separate species." Table 6.2 indicates the

Table 6.2

FEELINGS WHEN ENCOUNTERING PEOPLE WITH DISABILITIES

Question: When you encounter a person with a serious disability, how often do you feel *(Read List)*—often, occasionally, or never?

			AGE				EDUCATION		
							RESPONDENTS ANSWERING "OFTEN" OR "OCCASIONALLY"		
FEELINGS	TOTAL	18–29	30–44	45–64	65 AND OVER	LESS THAN H.S.	H.S. GRAD.	SOME COLLEGE	COLLEGE GRAD.
	N = 1257	342	428	318	158	138	460	320	338
Anger, because they cause inconvenience	16%	16%	14%	14%	19%	20%	16%	14%	13%
Fear, because you feel what's happened to them might happen to you	47	52	51	38	47	54	49	41	43
Awkward or *embarrassed,* because you don't know how to behave with them	58	59	65	56	50	50	57	60	67
Resentment, because they get special privileges	9	8	9	9	10	11	9	10	6
Pity, because of their situation	74	73	73	76	75	70	73	76	77
Lack of concern, because they can manage okay	51	58	52	44	48	54	52	50	47
Admiration, because they have overcome so much	92	92	93	92	91	83	91	97	96

Source: Louis Harris and Associates, *Public Attitudes toward People with Disabilities* (Washington, D.C.: National Organization on Disability, 1991), p. 20.

mixed feelings many people have when they encounter a person with a serious disability.

It was not until 1985 that any attempt was made to survey persons with disabilities and find out how they perceive their lives and opportunities (Harris and Associates, 1986). The survey focused on noninstitutionalized persons 16 years of age and older. The findings helped to buttress the arguments of groups seeking federal legislation to bring about change. The survey revealed the following statistics about the respondents:

- Forty percent had never finished high school.
- Half lived in households with incomes of less than $15,000 per year.
- Only 24 percent worked full-time; another 10 percent worked part-time.
- Two-thirds were unemployed; most of this group said they wanted a job.
- Of those not working, or working part-time, 47 percent said employers do not recognize that they are capable of working full-time.
- Fifty-six percent were prevented from getting around, socializing outside the home, or going to cultural and sporting events as much as they would have liked.

The Americans with Disabilities Act of 1990 protects the civil rights of persons who have historically suffered discrimination and thus serious disadvantage in the labor market. As ever more persons with disabilities, like this second grade teacher in Texas, enter the social and economic mainstream, many of the stereotypes and fears that help drive such discrimination will wither away.

- Those whose mobility was limited pointed to various reasons for this limitation: fear of getting hurt, sick, or victimized by crime (59 percent); lack of having someone to help them (56 percent); lack of accessible transportation (49 percent); lack of access to public buildings and bathrooms (40 percent); self-consciousness about the disability (40 percent).
- One in four of working age had encountered job discrimination because of the disability.
- Three-fourths claimed a sense of common identity with others who have a disability.
- Almost half felt they were members of a minority group in the same sense as African Americans and Latinos.
- Three-fourths believed that civil rights laws protecting minorities should also protect them.
- Fifty-seven percent believed they had been prevented from reaching their full abilities as a person.

In her testimony before the U.S. Senate on behalf of the Americans with Disabilities Act, Arlene B. Mayerson of the Disability Rights Education Defense Fund described the situation faced by people with disabilities in these terms:

> The discriminatory nature of policies and practices that exclude and segregate disabled people has been obscured by the unchallenged equation of disability with incapacity. . . . The innate biological and physical "inferiority" of disabled people is considered self-evident. This "self-evident" proposition has served to justify the exclusion and segregation of disabled people from all aspects of life.

The social consequences that attach to being disabled often bear no relationship to the physical or mental limitations imposed by the disability (U.S. Congress: Senate, 1989: 303–304).

Any of us who are presently able-bodied can, at any time, join the ranks of those who have a disability. Given the data presented above, our biographies would radically change were we to fall on the victims' side of this particular system of inequality. It remains to be seen whether the recent legislation can reverse the enormous suppression of human potential among members of the nation's largest minority group. What people have taken the initiative to build, they can equally well take the initiative to pull down.

CONCLUSION

Each of us is caught up in a complex multidimensional matrix composed of various systems of inequality. Whether the inequality revolves around class, race, sex, age, sexual orientation, or state of able-bodiedness, our biographies are shaped and tempered by where we are situated in the matrix. In each system of inequality, we may be among the oppressed, or we may be in the dominant group.

In this chapter we treated the six systems of inequality independently. But the vast majority of persons reading this book are probably disadvantaged within at least one such system, or will be at some point in their lives, and it is highly likely that many readers are oppressed within more than one. Clearly, the more positions one occupies on the victim end of these systems, the more likely it is that oppression and struggle will be part of one's biography.

Note that we enter these systems of inequality involuntarily. Persons cannot readily exert control over their social-class membership, ancestry, sex, aging, sexual orientation, or state of able-bodiedness. To perpetuate systems of inequality that subjugate and victimize people for attributes not of their own making is illogical and cruel. Individuals fighting against discrimination not only provide inspiration to others who are oppressed but often inspire those who hold membership in the dominant group. When members of the dominant group break ranks and deny the legitimacy of a particular system of inequality, that system weakens.

The systems of inequality we have presented do not all show signs of weakening. Economic inequality is actually getting worse. Sex inequality has been breaking down much faster than inequality built around sexual orientation. In the view of some, progress toward eliminating racial inequality is starting to erode. The prognosis for dismantling the system of age inequality and that involving persons with disabilities is more promising, at least at this point. If one's wish is a society in which everyone is in a position to live and contribute to his or her full potential, there is much to be done.

Finally, we should stress that systems of inequality differ from society to society. They will, for example, be different in core nations and peripheral nations of the world-system (discussed in Chapter 2). Thus, one's life chances will depend upon the society of which one is a member and one's position in the particular systems of inequality contained within that society.

THINKING CRITICALLY

1. Of the six systems of inequality discussed in this chapter, which do you feel has had the most important impact on your own life? How so?
2. While important gains in the dismantling of systems of sex inequality and racial inequality have occurred in the United States, some people would argue that a backlash against further progress for women and people of color is underway. Do you agree? Why or why not?
3. Attitudes toward the rights of people who have disabilities and people who are elderly are more sympathetic and tolerant than attitudes toward the rights of people who are homosexuals. How can one explain the differences in these attitudes?
4. Economic inequality in the United States is worsening, not getting better. Why is economic inequality not a lively public issue, compared with other systems of inequality we have described in this chapter?
5. In the boxed excerpt, talented and highly educated women talk about being pressured to avoid assertiveness and outspokenness in their professional lives, lest they be seen as unfeminine. Discuss the effects of such pressures on those who give in to them.

KEY TERMS

natural differences, *175*
systems of inequality, *175*
socially constructed, *176*
social stratification, *176*
ideology, *177*
ideological hegemony, *177*
economic inequality, *178*
functionalist theory of
   stratification, *179*
racial inequality, *184*
minority group, *184*
racial formation, *185*
genocide, *185*
personal racism, *185*
institutional racism, *185*
affirmative action, *188*
reverse discrimination, *188*
sex inequality, *190*
sex, *190*

gender, *190*
patriarchy, *190*
sexual division of labor, *190*
feminists, *191*
sexism, *191*
male chauvinism, *191*
institutional sexism, *192*
dual labor market, *192*
age inequality, *193*
ageism, *196*
disengagement theory, *197*
inequality based on sexual
   orientation, *200*
heterosexism, *200*
inequality based on able-
   bodiedness, *204*
ableism, *204*
stigma, *204*

Warren J. Blumenfeld (ed.), *Homophobia: How We All Pay the Price.* Boston: Beacon Press, 1992. A collection of articles exploring the various ways that fear and dislike of gay males and lesbians are expressed in our society and the impact such behavior has on us all.

David H. Fischer, *Growing Old in America,* expanded ed. New York: Oxford University Press, 1978. A historical account of the changing attitudes toward the elderly in the United States, showing how and why youth becomes venerated and aging becomes a social problem.

Dennis Gilbert and Joseph A. Kahl, *The American Class Structure: A New Synthesis,* 4th ed. Chicago: Dorsey Press, 1993. A review of various theories of class inequality, along with a depiction of many of the dimensions and consequences of class inequality in the United States.

Andrew Hacker, *Two Nations: Black and White, Separate, Hostile, Unequal.* New York: Scribner, 1992. An overview of the problems faced by African Americans as a consequence of continuing racial inequality in areas ranging from education to employment.

Claire M. Renzetti and Daniel J. Curran, *Women, Men, and Society,* 2d ed. Boston: Allyn and Bacon, 1992. An analysis of the significant role played by gender in virtually all institutional arenas, concluding with a discussion of the contemporary women's movement and its impact.

Joseph P. Shapiro, *No Pity: People with Disabilities Forging a New Civil Rights Movement.* New York: Times Books, 1993. A chronicle of the struggle engaged in by people with disabilities and the obstacles they have had to overcome in their efforts to be included in the American mainstream.

INTERSECTION OF RACE, CLASS, AND GENDER

PATRIARCHY IN THE
LIVES OF WEALTHY
WHITE WOMEN

WHITE WOMEN
EMPLOYERS AND
DOMESTIC WORKERS
OF COLOR

AFRICAN AMERICAN
MALES IN THE
LOWER CLASS

RACISM AND
MIDDLE-CLASS
AFRICAN AMERICANS

DIVERSITY
OF EXPERIENCES
AMONG WOMEN
OF COLOR

SPECIAL CHALLENGES
FACING WOMEN
WITH DISABILITIES

CONCLUSION

My first awareness of race was when I was about three years old, and a little white kid called me "nigger." I lived a good deal of my life more conscious of racism than sexism; for many African American women of my generation that would be the response. But the women's movement helped raise my consciousness about sexism. Once it was there, the interconnections became clear.

7

I am forever interested in talking about racism, sexism, nomophobia, ageism, economic inequality, but we also need to think a lot about the absence of all that. What kind of world do we want? If I try to imagine a world without racism and sexism, it means releasing more creativity than we can imagine. If you unleash that much creativity, of women and all folks of color, you show me a problem and I will show you that we can solve it (Johnnetta B. Cole, president, Spelman College, quoted in "Race: Can We Talk?" 1991: 36).

With this statement, Johnnetta Cole reminds us of the oppressive nature of many of the forces which help shape our biographies and which place limits on the contributions we are capable of making.

In the previous chapter we looked at a variety of distinct systems of inequality in our society: the systems revolving around class, race, sex, age, sexual orientation, and able-bodiedness. In closing, we noted that it made sense to think of these systems as together forming a complex multidimensional matrix in which each of us exists (Collins, 1990: 225–230). Our biographies are shaped and tempered by our positions in this matrix. In some of its sectors we may be among the oppressed; simultaneously, in other sectors we may be members of dominant groups.

For example, while it is true that white males are generally in a favorable position in terms of their race and gender, few white males occupy dominant positions in the class structure. The opportunities and life chances of most white males are restricted in comparison to those of their upper-class counterparts. White males can and do experience economic exploitation and insecurities; they are exposed to some of the same problems in living that confront women and people of color who occupy similar positions in our system of class inequality. Thus, we may be dominant within certain dimensions of the matrix but not others, and this relative positioning helps shape the content of our lives.

People experience the various positions they occupy in the matrix simultaneously. One does not, for example, experience life as a white person at one moment, a member of the middle class at the next moment, and a female at the next. Instead, one experiences life as a white, middle-class female. Such a person's experiences may vary substantially from those of a person who is of the same gender and class, but of a different color.

The systems of inequality comprising the matrix are not wholly static; they often give rise to tensions and conflict. At different historical moments, one or another of the systems of inequality may undergo change, thereby altering the composition of the matrix. Over the course of our lives each of us faces the personal challenge of how to contend with the multifaceted and dynamic texture of the matrix.

We shall explore some of the intersections between systems of inequality by focusing on several questions: What does occupying a position in a system of inequality like race or class mean for women? Does being male confer advantages independent of race or class? Has racial inequality declined enough in the United States that we can dismiss race as a significant determinant of one's biography? When we use such phrases as "women of color," do we inadvertently ignore diverse experiences and identities among such women? What happens when one occupies a subordinate position because of gender and must also endure the stigma of disability?

Sociologists are only just now beginning to explore the multidimensional matrix of inequality (see Andersen and Collins, 1992; Rothenberg, 1992; Cyrus, 1993). While we still have a long way to go, research shows that individuals are affected by the positions they occupy in the matrix. Let us consider the situation of persons who are clearly members of the dominant group by virtue of class and race but who are simultaneously oppressed by sex inequality.

PATRIARCHY IN THE LIVES OF WEALTHY WHITE WOMEN

The media supply much of the popular knowledge about what it means to be a member of the upper class. Television dramas such as *Dallas* suggest that even those in society's "higher circles" (Domhoff, 1970) have problems in living. But they also suggest that affluence grants members of the upper class much to comfort them in times of trial and tribulation. Through the articles in upscale magazines such as *Town and Country* and *Vanity Fair* and television shows such as *Lifestyles of the Rich and Famous,* we see a material side to life in the upper class that we might associate with royalty.

Yet the popular media are in the business of entertainment, not sociological analysis. When we look closely at the social relations within the upper class, one of the most striking facts is sex inequality. Compared with women of other classes, upper-class women may seem to "have it all," but their possessions do not enable them to escape sexism and subordination by gender. Their class membership provides them with enormous security, as does their **white-skin privilege,** a term that refers to the social advantages provided by their race (McIntosh, 1992). Nonetheless, the demands that upper-class men place on them circumscribe their life chances.

Nowhere is this clearer than in the data provided by Susan Ostrander (1984), a sociologist who conducted interviews with women of the upper class. Her sample may not be representative of all upper-class women, since it was drawn from one large midwestern city. It consists of women whom she identified through an upper-class acquaintance and who agreed to be interviewed. Nonetheless, her data provide unique insight into the otherwise hidden relations between men and women of privilege.

Ostrander was interested in the roles upper-class women play as wives and mothers, so she interviewed women who were either married and living with their husbands or recently widowed. Most of the women, ranging in age from the midthirties to the mideighties, were descendants of the oldest families in the city. Their husbands almost all held top positions in major corporations or in family-owned firms in business and law.

The women tended to be highly educated, often at exclusive private liberal arts colleges long patronized by members of their class. By many criteria, they are among the most privileged women in the world. Yet, as Ostrander found, our system of sex inequality dictates that they subordinate their interests and needs to those of their husbands.

To characterize husband-wife relations among those she interviewed, Ostrander presents the words of four women:

> He expects me to make a nice home to come to, to be a cheery companion, to be ready to go on vacations when he wants to. He expects me to go along with what he wants to do.

> My husband has never helped around the house or done anything for the children. If I were starting life over he certainly would.

> He wanted to move to the country, and I didn't so we moved to the country.

> My husband never asks me what I think. He just tells me how it's going to be (Ostrander, 1984: 37).

In the interviews the women said they were expected to play very traditional female roles, that is, be supportive, nurturant, and compliant to their husbands' needs. While perhaps not typical, the situation described in the following statement, from one of Ostrander's subjects, reveals how far such women might have to go to please:

> When he comes home in the evening the house must be perfectly quiet. I've told everyone the phone must not ring after five o'clock. He wants me to be pleasant, pretty and relaxed. I can't dare cry in front of him or show any emotion. I never bring a problem to him, except during forty-five minutes set aside on Sunday mornings for that purpose. I keep a list (Ostrander, 1984: 39).

Upper-class women are expected to run the household (which includes supervising domestic help) and in general take on all home responsibilities that would otherwise distract their husbands from full-time attention to their work. While these women are clearly capable of pursuing their own careers, most do not. Instead, they devote time outside the home to volunteer work, such as serving in leadership and fund-raising positions on boards of local charitable and health organizations and in voluntary associations that support music and the arts (see Daniels, 1988).

Obviously, upper-class women do not need to work for pay. Not only do their husbands earn substantial amounts, but many of the women have their "own money" from family trusts and inheritances (although most of Ostrander's subjects said that they had given control over their own money to their husbands). Even so, an important additional reason why the women do not pursue their own careers is that they need to be available to their husbands at short notice to organize social gatherings, entertain clients, or accompany their husbands on business travel.

The implication is, of course, that any activities these women undertake are, by definition, secondary to the activities of their partners. Indeed, when women of the upper class become too involved and successful in outside volunteer work, their husbands are likely to become jealous and resentful. The husbands see this commitment to something outside the home as a threat to their wives' role.

Women of the upper class have more material privileges than others, yet they remain subordinates within our society's system of sex inequality. The lifestyles of upper-class women often require that they be on hand to support their husbands' activities and make a good impression at exclusive social events.

Ostrander concludes:

The wives' tasks reflect not only the division of labor, or social differentiation, but also a clear subordination of the women to the men. . . . The general mode makes it difficult, if not impossible, for the women to have life agendas independent of the men (Ostrander, 1984: 49).

Ostrander points out one further irony. Since the women do not have to work, and because they often pay other women to perform the bulk of home tasks, they see little reason to challenge the sex inequality they experience. Thus, many women of the upper class may very well find it difficult to share the heartfelt commitment of other women to the women's rights movement. Their biographies are shaped not only by being members of the most privileged class and race but also by experiencing continued subordination and hence victimization within the societal system of sex inequality.

WHITE WOMEN EMPLOYERS AND DOMESTIC WORKERS OF COLOR

Although white women of the upper class may be subject to sex inequality, their race and class allow them to dominate certain other persons with whom they maintain relationships. This is also true for middle-class white women who employ domestic workers.

In many cases domestic service in the United States involves a female-to-female relationship between a white, middle- to upper-class employer and a domestic worker of color, either native-born or an immigrant from a Third World country (Rollins, 1985: 59). Here, race and class differences are played out through the subordination of one group of women by another, blurring the fact that in reality both have limited life chances as a consequence of sexism.

Within most middle-class, husband-wife households, such activities as cleaning, laundering, caring for children, shopping for necessities, and cooking are primarily considered "women's work" in the sexual division of labor. Even when married partners both have full-time jobs or careers outside the home, housework still largely falls to the woman and not to the man. Women are said to work a **second shift** involving many extra hours of domestic tasks (Hochschild and Machung, 1989). These tasks are not culturally defined as "work" in the real sense. Recognized neither by pay nor by high status, domestic tasks assigned to women reflect women's subordinate position within the existing system of sex inequality.

The work that is considered undeserving of pay or high esteem when women do it in their own homes is barely better rewarded when performed in others' homes as an occupation. Women who make a living working as domestics—cleaning other people's homes, doing their laundry, watching their children, running their errands, cooking and serving their meals—do so out of economic necessity. As with many other forms of manual labor, domestic service is poorly paid. Full-time, year-round, private-household service workers have lower median incomes than workers in any other occupational category (U.S. Bureau of Census, 1992c). In 1991, the median earnings of such workers were $7,309.

Moreover, the people who employ domestic workers provide them with few, if any, benefits. Some employers do not even bother to pay legally required social security taxes on their domestic workers' salaries (an issue that undermined the candidacy of several persons poised for high-level appointments in the Clinton administration). Domestic workers have few job protections, are nonunionized, and may be asked to work under arduous conditions (Romero, 1992). Domestic service differs from other work situations, however, in that typically a member of the subordinate gender employs a member of that same gender.

Women who take up domestic work do not usually aspire to it. Limited education, lack of language skills, or noncitizen status makes it difficult for them to enter other jobs. But they are also oppressed by the system of sex inequality that restricts job opportunities for women in general. Women of color are victims as well of the system of racial inequality that operates to "ghettoize" minority-group members disproportionately into low-wage service occupations (such as food service workers and health aides). The system of class inequality in the United States places those who are heavily dependent on income from domestic service near the bottom in class terms. Hence, women domestic workers of color are caught within intersecting systems of racial, class, and sex inequality.

Sociologist Judith Rollins conducted some unique research on the relationships between black domestic workers and white female employers in the Boston area. Rollins used a variety of techniques to gather her data: she interviewed 20 domestics and 20 employers, worked alongside domestic

Domestic workers and their employers are often of the same sex but occupy different positions in our systems of race and class inequality. The social gap between such women is dramatically expressed by this contrast of a cleaning woman standing before a portrait of then First Lady Nancy Reagan.

workers in the guise of being their "cousin," drew on her own experiences as a worker in a number of settings, interviewed personnel at agencies dealing with domestic workers, and conducted a three-hour group interview with six domestics (Rollins, 1985: 8–10).

Most of the women employers began to hire domestic workers around the time of the birth of their first child. The women's mothers often played active roles in encouraging them to get help. In some cases the mothers had their own domestics and "loaned" them to their daughters. In most cases the women were familiar with domestic workers from their childhood and thus were able to model their own employer-domestic relationships after those they had seen while growing up.

Rollins found that, besides practical needs and family tradition, other factors influenced the decision to hire domestic help. The roles and responsibilities thrust upon the employers interviewed were part of the picture. According to Rollins,

> As a result of the women's movement, the expectation of young middle-class women is that they will have careers whether there is family economic need or not. But this dramatic change in women's roles in the workplace has not been accompanied by a significant change in their attitudes towards their roles at home. The middle-class women I interviewed were not demanding that their husbands play a greater role in housekeeping; they accepted the fact that responsibility for domestic maintenance was theirs, and they solved the problem of their dual responsibilities by hiring other women to assist (Rollins, 1985: 104).

There was also the issue of prestige. Having a domestic in the house can be used as a status symbol. Some of the domestics Rollins interviewed claimed that this was one reason why their employers preferred to hire "girls" who were black: anyone would know that such a person just had to be a maid. The women employers that Rollins interviewed did not cite prestige as a reason for hiring domestics. This could mean that it is an unconscious motivating factor, if indeed it is a factor at all, or that the women considered it inappropriate to disclose prestige concerns to an interviewer.

While Rollins discovered a variety of relationships between women employers and their domestics, she believed that some overall patterns prevailed. Unlike other low-paid, low-status occupations, domestic service allows a personal relationship to develop between employer and employee. In Rollins's view, the close one-to-one interaction, carried out in the physical and social isolation of a private home, can give rise to a type of psychological exploitation. Employers are less concerned with the productivity of household domestics than with their personality traits.

For example, employers expect domestics to express deference—in everything from language ("Yes, Ma'am," "Of course, Ma'am") to behavior toward the employer's property and personal space. This deference must even be paid when the employer expresses attitudes and behaviors not deserving of respect. When the domestic worker shows deference to her mistress, she acknowledges her own subordinate status. Her deferential behavior reflects their respective positions in the systems of class and racial inequality. Domestics may be of the same sex as their employers, but race and class differences prevent them from treating each other as equals.

The employer-domestic relationship often also entails dynamics of maternalism. The women employers tend to regard their workers as child-like, in need of protection, support, and guidance. The maternalistic treatment meted out—giving gifts, offering loans, assisting with reading bills, interceding with travel plans, offering to meet male friends—must be accepted by domestic workers in the interests of survival. To reject such treatment would be to jeopardize one's job.

One domestic described the situation:

> [My employer] was always offering me bags of stuff. But if it was something I didn't want, I'd thank her, walk out of there, go around that corner and the first trash can I got to, I'd throw it in. But you take it, whatever they give. When she had a party, the next day she'd give me half dead flowers, soggy salad, and left-over Chinese food. Maybe she thought I was deprived and really needed it. But it was all just more dead weight I had to get rid of. She felt like she was really being nice (Rollins, 1985: 190).

Another woman domestic explained it this way:

> I didn't want most of that junk. But you have to take it. It's part of the job, makes them feel like they're being so kind to you. And you have to appear grateful. That makes them feel good too (Rollins, 1985: 191).

Giving places one in a position of superiority; having nothing to give back except expressions of gratitude relegates one to a position of inferiority. Thus the employers' expressions of maternalism become part of the psychological exploitation domestics must endure.

Rollins believes that the fact that both parties are women intensifies the psychological exploitation. The woman employer, like the domestic worker, holds subordinate status in this society on the basis of sex. Yet employing another woman gives her a position of power that housewives do not usually possess (Rollins, 1985: 203). In this way, the employer can attempt to compensate for the inequalities in power that she experiences in her interactions with her husband.

But the implications of the dynamics between a white, middle-class employer and her domestic servant of color are much broader in Rollins's view:

> The presence of the "inferior" domestic, an inferiority evidenced by the performance she is encouraged to execute and her acceptance of demeaning treatment, offers the employer justification for materially exploiting the domestic, ego enhancement as an individual, and a strengthening of the employer's class and racial identities. Even more important, such a presence supports the idea of unequal human worth: it suggests that there might be categories of people (the lower classes, people of color) who are inherently inferior to others (middle and upper classes, whites). And this idea provides ideological justification for a social system that institutionalizes inequality (Rollins, 1985: 203).

Rollins's research stresses the oppressive aspects of the employer-domestic relationship. Domestic workers of color must struggle to resist depersonalization, loss of dignity, and attacks on their self-worth as they go about their work (see Dill, 1988).

In the next section we shall examine the situation of lower-class African American males, persons who many whites apparently believe are inherently inferior to themselves and of unequal human worth.

AFRICAN AMERICAN MALES IN THE LOWER CLASS

The fact that women of all classes find themselves oppressed does not necessarily mean that being male makes one immune to subordination. Nowhere is this clearer than in the case of African American males. Even those who have broken through discriminatory barriers, earning success in traditionally "white" occupations and professions, find that their race continues to be salient in defining future opportunities and day-to-day relations with others (Davis and Watson, 1982; Benjamin, 1991; Feagin and Sikes, 1994).

But our focus here will be on lower-class, African American males who reside in central-city ghettos. Younger black males have begun to be referred to as an "endangered species" (Gibbs, 1988). Hearings before the U.S. Senate produced testimony revealing the following facts (US. Congress: Senate Committee, 1991):

- Official unemployment rates indicate that African American men, including those with college educations, are more than twice as likely as their white counterparts to be jobless.
- An estimated two-thirds of African American males living in poverty areas of central cities are either underemployed or not in the workforce at all.
- African American males are six to ten times as likely as white males to die from homicide.
- Most African American males who die between the ages of 15 and 24 are murdered by other black males; most of these deaths involve guns.
- Suicide rates for African American males peak among men in their twenties; for whites the rates do not peak until old age.
- African American men in ghetto neighborhoods are less likely to live to age 65 than men in the extremely poor Third World nation of Bangladesh.
- African American males are disciplined, suspended, and expelled from school at higher rates than white males, and they are more likely to be labeled by school authorities as mentally retarded or emotionally disturbed.
- African American males are less likely than their white counterparts to attend college; indeed, their college attendance rates have been declining in recent years.
- Approximately one in four African American males between ages 20 and 29 is either in prison, on parole, or on probation.

- The probability that an African American male will be imprisoned at some time during his life is 18 percent; for the general population it is less than 0.5 percent.
- More African American males are under the control of the criminal justice system than are enrolled in higher education.
- An ever-increasing percentage of arrests of African American males involve drug offenses (for example, unlawful possession and sale).
- African American males are increasingly less likely to be married; the proportion of those married dropped from 50 percent in 1960 to 30 percent in 1990. Those who are working are twice as likely to marry the mothers of their children as those who are not.

The picture that emerges from such statistics is not a pretty one. While city ghettos harbor only 10 percent of the nation's poor (Bane and Ellwood, 1991), the dense concentration of low-income people of color in these inner-city areas renders them highly visible. The problems that ghetto dwellers face are formidable. Severely limited employment opportunities, due in part to job shortages and discriminatory hiring practices, make it difficult for ghetto households to avoid chronic economic insecurities. Poverty can undermine the stability of marriages. Poverty fosters female-headed families, compels people to suffer the humiliation of relying on welfare assistance, and negates the role that adult males can play as providers and parental role models (Wilson, 1987). Poverty also encourages criminal behavior, such as property crime and substance abuse, and in general fosters a social climate that can be threatening, stressful, and conducive to impulsive acts of violence.

In the late 1960s, a presidential commission appointed to investigate widespread revolts in the nation's ghetto communities concluded, "Our Nation is moving toward two societies, one black, one white—separate and unequal." The commission went on to say:

> White society is deeply implicated in the ghetto. White institutions created it, white institutions maintain it, and white society condones it. Race prejudice has shaped our history decisively; it now threatens to affect our future. White racism is essentially responsible for the explosive mixture which has been accumulating in our cities since the end of World War II (National Advisory Commission on Civil Disorders, 1968: 1, 5).

This "explosive mixture" erupted in late April 1992. Days of street rebellion followed a suburban Los Angeles jury's decision to acquit four police officers who had been videotaped beating Rodney King, a black motorist stopped for speeding. The acquittal was widely interpreted to mean that police brutality against people of color could take place unchecked. The rebellion in Los Angeles neighborhoods involved not only African Americans but many Latino Americans and members of other minority groups as well. More than 50 people were killed and 2,300 injured, making the event the most violent civil disturbance in the United States in this century (Lacey, 1992). Property damage amounting to $1 billion also occurred, as crowds of people took to the streets to burn and loot.

People who live in racially segregated, resource-deprived urban ghettos face the constant challenge of coping with their daily environs. Using discarded tires and material from abandoned buildings, these children have constructed their own makeshift playground on a vacant lot in New York City's South Bronx.

The majority of ghetto dwellers abhor the conditions in which they find themselves trapped. They deeply resent the stereotypical view held by many whites that all African American males who live in the inner city are "dumb, deprived, dangerous, deviant, and disturbed" (Gibbs, 1988: 3). Most ghetto dwellers are deeply concerned and unhappy with the negative features of the climate within which they reside. Coping with problems of living in the ghetto is a constant, unrelenting challenge. But conditions are such that a significant minority of ghettoized African American males—especially the young—are driven or drawn into behaviors harmful to others and themselves.

Being born an African American male in one of the nation's ghettos means having one's biography conditioned by the systems of racial and class inequality that exist in the United States. Color and class disadvantages make it difficult for many African American males to escape the ghetto and a future filled with economic adversity.

Within the nation's system of sex inequality, men are encouraged to see themselves as the rightfully empowered, dominant sex. Much of the male claim to dominance rests with men's superior ability to command wages that can support a family. A "real man," so the conventional wisdom preaches, should be able to get a decent job in order to take care of a wife and children. By placing substantial barriers to doing so in the way of African American males, the system of race inequality symbolically emasculates black men. It compels many young men to seek a sense of male empowerment in other ways, including gang membership, rebellion against the authority of school and law, macho posturing, and out-of-wedlock fatherhood. Being a member of the dominant sex, but imprisoned by the treatment one receives due to color and class, may kick off a relentless search for validation of one's manhood. As the homicide statistics on young African American males indicate, that search may entail a tragically short life trajectory.

RACISM AND MIDDLE-CLASS AFRICAN AMERICANS

The popular stereotype holds that just about all African Americans are inner-city ghetto dwellers or members of the poverty population. While it is true that members of the U.S. black population are disproportionately represented in lower income brackets, there is as well a sizable black middle class (Lacayo, 1989). One-third of all African American families have solid middle-class incomes of $35,000 per year or more. One in seven black families earns an annual income of $50,000 or more (U.S. Department of Commerce, 1993: 46). The 2 million adults in these more affluent families tend to be married, middle-aged, employed, and well educated, and most own their own homes. While the majority are city dwellers, many live in suburbs or small towns (O'Hare, 1989: 25). Members of the African American middle class are far better off than the millions of whites who make up the bulk of America's poor. Even so, does being middle-class mean that one's racial-group membership becomes irrelevant? Do African Americans who occupy professional and executive positions in the labor force face racism?

In recent years a debate has raged among academics and public policy makers over the alleged **declining significance of race** (see Wilson, 1978; Willie, 1983; Landry, 1987; Willie, 1989). Some have argued that less prejudicial attitudes among whites, the passage and enforcement of civil rights laws, and efforts to promote educational and occupational opportunities have removed most barriers to black advancement. One's color, the argument goes, is no longer the key social determinant that it once was in our society. The growth of the black middle class since the 1960s is offered as evidence that the significance of race has declined. More and more African Americans are finding a place in the mainstream of society. Some social scientists even argue that lack of skills and credentials, not racism, is the sole reason for poverty among blacks (Mead, 1992).

Other social scientists have compiled data which suggest that racism continues to play a significant and determining role in the lives of African Americans, including those who are part of the nation's middle class (Farley and Allen, 1987; Jaynes and Williams, 1989; Hacker, 1992; Feagin and Sikes, 1994). African Americans are denied the unearned social advantages that whites possess simply on the basis of skin color, advantages suggested by Peggy McIntosh in the accompanying box.

When interviewed, many middle-class African Americans complain of racist treatment by service workers in restaurants and public accommodations, by police officers and strangers on the street, by people with whom they interact at work and school, and by those from whom they seek to

Regardless of sex or class, members of the white majority possess certain unearned advantages by virtue of their group's position within the system of racial inequality in the United States. In the article below, Peggy McIntosh presents many examples of these advantages. She compiled her list as she sought to answer the question, "What is it like to have white-skin privilege?" You may wish to add items based on experiences of your own.

Through work to bring materials from Women's Studies into the rest of the curriculum, I have often noticed men's unwillingness to grant that they are over-privileged, even though they may grant that women are disadvantaged. They may say they will work to improve women's status in the society, the university, or the curriculum, but they can't or won't support the idea of lessening men's. Denials which amount to taboos surround the subject of advantages which men gain from women's disadvantages. These denials protect male privilege from being fully acknowledged, lessened or ended.

Thinking through unacknowledged male privilege as a phenomenon, I realized that since hierarchies in our society are interlocking, there was most likely a phenomenon of white privilege which was similarly denied and protected. As a white person, I realized I had been taught about racism as something which puts others at a disadvantage, but had been taught not to see one of its corollary aspects, white privilege, which puts me at an advantage.

I think whites are carefully taught not to recognize white privilege, as males are taught not to recognize male privilege. So I have begun in an untutored way to ask what it is like to have white privilege. I have come to see white privilege as an invisible package of unearned assets which I can count on cashing in each day, but about which I was "meant" to remain oblivious. White privilege is like an invisible weightless knapsack of special provisions, maps, passports, code-books, visas, clothes, tools and blank checks.

Describing white privilege makes one newly accountable. As we in Women's Studies work to reveal male privilege and ask men to give up some of their power, so one who writes about having white privilege must ask, "Having described it, what will I do to lessen or end it?"

After I realized the extent to which men work from a base of unacknowledged privilege, I understood that much of their oppressiveness was unconscious. Then I remembered the frequent charges from women of color that white women whom they encounter are oppressive. I began to understand why we are justly seen as oppressive, even when we don't see ourselves that way. I began to count the ways in which I enjoy unearned skin privilege and have been conditioned into oblivion about its existence.

My schooling gave me no training in seeing myself as an oppressor, as an unfairly advantaged person, or as a participant in a damaged culture. I was taught to see myself as an individual whose moral state depended on her individual moral will. My schooling followed the pattern my colleague Elizabeth Minnich has pointed out: whites are taught to think of their lives as morally neutral, normative, and average, and also ideal, so that when we work to benefit others, this is seen as work which will allow "them" to be more like "us."

I decided to try to work on myself at least by identifying some of the daily effects of white privilege in my life. I have chosen those conditions which I think in my case *attach somewhat more to skin-color privilege* than to class, religion, ethnic status, or geographical location, though of course all these other factors are intricately intertwined. As far as I can see, my African American co-workers, friends and acquaintances with whom I come into daily or frequent contact in this particular time, place, and line of work cannot count on most of these conditions.

1. I can if I wish arrange to be in the company of people of my race most of the time.

"White privilege is like an invisible weightless knapsack of special provisions, maps, passports, code-books, visas, clothes, tools and blank checks."

2. If I should need to move, I can be pretty sure of renting or purchasing housing in an area which I can afford and in which I would want to live.

3. I can be pretty sure that my neighbors in such a location will be neutral or pleasant to me.

4. I can go shopping alone most of the time, pretty well assured that I will not be followed or harassed.

5. I can turn on the television or open to the front page of the paper and see people of my race widely represented.

6. When I am told about our national heritage or about "civilization," I am shown that people of my color made it what it is.

7. I can be sure that my children will be given curricular materials that testify to the existence of their race.

8. If I want to, I can be pretty sure of finding a publisher for this piece on white privilege.

9. I can go into a music shop and count on finding the music of my race represented, into a supermarket and find the staple foods which fit with my cultural traditions, into a hairdresser's shop and find someone who can cut my hair.

10. Whether I use checks, credit cards, or cash, I can count on my skin color not to work against the appearance of financial reliability.

11. I can arrange to protect my children most of the time from people who might not like them.

12. I can swear, or dress in second hand clothes, or not answer letters, without having people attribute these choices to the bad morals, the poverty, or the illiteracy of my race.

13. I can speak in public to a powerful male group without putting my race on trial.

14. I can do well in a challenging situation without being called a credit to my race.

15. I am never asked to speak for all the people of my racial group.

16. I can remain oblivious of the language and customs of persons of color who constitute the world's majority without feeling in my culture any penalty for such oblivion.

17. I can criticize our government and talk about how much I fear its policies and behavior without being seen as a cultural outsider.

18. I can be pretty sure that if I ask to talk to "the person in charge," I will be facing a person of my race.

19. If a traffic cop pulls me over or if the IRS audits my tax return, I can be sure I haven't been singled out because of my race.

20. I can easily buy posters, postcards, picture books, greeting cards, dolls, toys, and children's magazines featuring people of my race.

21. I can go home from most meetings of organizations I belong to feeling somewhat tied in, rather than isolated, out-of-place, outnumbered, unheard, held at a distance, or feared.

22. I can take a job with an affirmative action employer without having co-workers on the job suspect that I got it because of race.

23. I can choose public accommodation without fearing that people of my race cannot get in or will be mistreated in the places I have chosen.

24. I can be sure that if I need legal or medical help, my race will not work against me.

25. If my day, week, or year is going badly, I need not ask of each negative episode or situation whether it has racial overtones.

26. I can choose blemish cover or bandages in "flesh" color and have them more or less match my skin.

I repeatedly forgot each of the realizations on this list until I wrote it down. For me white privilege has turned out to be an elusive and fugitive subject. The pressure to avoid it is great, for in facing it I must give up the myth of meritocracy. If these things are true, this is not such a free country; one's life is not what one makes it; many doors open for certain people through no virtues of their own.

(*Continued*)

In unpacking this invisible knapsack of white privilege, I have listed conditions of daily experience which I once took for granted. Nor did I think of any of these perquisites as bad for the holder. I now think that we need a more finely differentiated taxonomy of privilege, for some of these varieties are only what one would want for everyone in a just society, and others give licence to be ignorant, oblivious, arrogant and destructive.

I see a pattern running through the matrix of white privilege, a pattern of assumptions which were passed on to me as a white person. There was one main piece of cultural turf; it was my own turf, and I was among those who could control the turf. *My skin color was an asset for any move I was educated to want to make.* I could think of myself as belonging in major ways, and of making social systems work for me. I could freely disparage, fear, neglect, or be oblivious to anything outside of the dominant cultural forms. Being of the main culture, I could also criticize it fairly freely.

In proportion as my racial group was being made confident, comfortable, and oblivious, other groups were likely being made inconfident, uncomfortable, and alienated. Whiteness protected me from many kinds of hostility, distress, and violence, which I was being subtly trained to visit in turn upon people of color.

For this reason, the word "privilege" now seems to me misleading. We usually think of privilege as being a favored state, whether earned or conferred by birth or luck. Yet some of the conditions I have described here work to systematically overempower certain groups. Such privilege simply *confers dominance* because of one's race or sex.

I want, then, to distinguish between earned strength and unearned power conferred systematically. Power from unearned privilege can look like strength when it is in fact permission to escape or to dominate. But not all of the privileges on my list are inevitably damaging. Some, like the expectation that neighbors will be decent to you, or that your race will not count against you in court, should be the norm in a just society. Others, like the privilege to ignore less powerful people, distort the humanity of the holders as well as the ignored groups.

We might at least start by distinguishing between positive advantages which we can work to spread, and negative types of advantages which unless rejected will always reinforce our present hierarchies. For example, the feeling that one belongs within the human circle, as Native Americans say, should not be seen as privilege for a few. Ideally it is an *unearned entitlement.* At present, since only a few have it, it is an *unearned advantage* for them. This paper results from a process of coming to see that some of the power which I originally saw as attendant on being a human being in the U.S. consisted [of] *unearned advantage* and *conferred dominance.*

I have met very few men who are truly distressed about systemic, unearned male advantage and conferred dominance. And so one question for me and others like me is whether we will be like them, or whether we will get truly distressed, even outraged, about unearned race advantage and conferred dominance and if so, what we will do to lessen them. In any case, we need to do more work in identifying how they actually affect our daily lives. Many, perhaps most, of our white students in the U.S. think that racism doesn't affect them because they are not people of color; they do not see "whiteness" as a racial identity. In addition, since race and sex are not the only advantaging systems at work, we need similarly to examine the daily experience of having age advantage, or ethnic advantage, or physical ability, or advantage related to nationality, religion, or sexual orientation.

Difficulties and dangers surrounding the task of finding parallels are many. Since racism, sexism, and heterosexism are not the same, the advantaging associated with them should not be seen as the same. In addition, it is hard to disentangle aspects of unearned advantage which rest more on social class, economic class, race, religion, sex and ethnic identity than on other factors. Still, all of the oppressions are interlocking, as the Combahee River Collective* Statement of 1977 continues to remind us eloquently.

One factor seems clear about all of the interlocking oppressions. They take both active forms which we can see and embedded forms which as a member of the dominant group one is taught not to see. In my class and place, I did not see myself as a racist because I was taught to recognize racism only in individual acts of meanness by members of my group, never in invisible systems conferring unsought racial dominance on my group from birth.

Disapproving of the systems won't be enough to change them. I was taught to think that racism could end if white individuals changed their attitudes. [But] a "white" skin in the United States opens many doors for whites whether or not we approve of the way dominance has been conferred on us. Individual acts can palliate, but cannot end, these problems.

To redesign social systems we need first to acknowledge their colossal unseen dimensions. The silences and denials surrounding privilege are the key political tool here. They keep the thinking about equality or equity incomplete, protecting unearned advantage and conferred dominance by making these taboo subjects. Most talk by whites about equal opportunity seems to me now to be about equal opportunity to try to get into a position of dominance while denying that *systems* of dominance exist.

It seems to me that obliviousness about white advantage, like obliviousness about male advantage, is kept strongly inculturated in the United States so as to maintain the myth of meritocracy, the myth that democratic choice is equally available to all. Keeping most people unaware that freedom of confident action is there for just a small number of people props up those in power, and serves to keep power in the hands of the same groups that have most of it already.

Though systemic change takes many decades, there are pressing questions for me and I imagine for some others like me if we raise our daily consciousness on the perquisites of being light-skinned. What will we do with such knowledge? As we know from watching men, it is an open question whether we will choose to use unearned advantage to weaken hidden systems of advantage, and whether we will use any of our arbitrarily-awarded power to try to reconstruct power systems on a broader base.

*Combahee River Collective: A group of black feminist women in Boston from 1974 to 1980.

Source: Peggy McIntosh, "White Privilege: Unpacking the Invisible Knapsack," in Virginia Cyrus (ed.), *Experiencing Race, Class, and Gender in the United States* (Mountainview, CA: Mayfield Publishing Company, 1993), pp. 209–213. ©1988 Peggy McIntosh. Permission to copy must be obtained from Peggy McIntosh, Wellesley College, MA, 02181. Longer version, from which this is an excerpt, is also available from the author at the above address.

rent and buy housing (Benjamin, 1991; Feagin, 1991a, 1991b; Cose, 1993). National surveys confirm the kinds of complaints voiced in these interviews. For example, in one survey, one-third of the respondents said they had personally been victims of racial discrimination in housing or employment; black college graduates and African Americans making over $40,000 a year were *most* likely to say they had been victims (Anti-Defamation League, 1993: 50–53).

Sociologist Raymond S. Franklin (1991) argues that many white people in the United States view all African Americans through the same lens that they use to look at black members of the lower class. As the survey findings in Table 7.1 indicate, whites are strongly disposed to perceive African Americans collectively as less hardworking, less intelligent, more prone to violence, and more likely to prefer living off government welfare benefits than are whites themselves (National Opinion Research Center, 1991a; Anti-Defamation League, 1993). Franklin believes that such ideas may derive from the fact that African Americans are "overcrowded"—that is, statistically overrepresented—in the lower class. Racist stereotypes about the character and worth of lower-class blacks, in Franklin's view, cast a "shadow" over African Americans who are middle-class. In his words,

> The shadow that is cast and generalized from the economically subordinate portion of the black population determines the attitudes and behavior of all whites toward all blacks, and, specifically, toward the more affluent and educated members of the black population who have class characteristics comparable to their white cohorts (Franklin, 1991: 122).

In other words, middle-class blacks are frequently viewed and treated as if they carried the attributes that whites stereotypically associate with lower-class African Americans.

African Americans born into or moving into the middle class quickly learn that their race remains significant (see, for example, Jones, 1986). At the same time, middle-class African Americans are very aware of resentments their elite status raises among low-income blacks who cannot move upward. Describing this dual problem, one middle-class African American woman poignantly expresses thoughts of which most whites may be ignorant:

> I am a member of the black middle class who has had it with being patted on the head by white hands and slapped in the face by black hands for my success. . . .
>
> I am burdened daily with showing whites that blacks are people. I am, in the old vernacular, a credit to my race. I am my brother's keeper, and my sister's, though many of them have abandoned me because they think I have abandoned them. . . .
>
> Some of my "liberal" white acquaintances pat me on the head, hinting I am a freak, that my success is less a matter of talent than of luck and affirmative action. I may live among them, but it is difficult to live with them. How can they be sincere about respecting me, yet hold my fellows in contempt? And if I am silent when they attempt to sever me from my own, how can I live with myself? . . .

Table 7.1

WHITES' TRAIT RATINGS OF WHITES, AFRICAN AMERICANS, LATINOS AND ASIAN AMERICANS

	PERCENTAGE OF WHITE RESPONDENTS APPLYING TRAIT TO:			
TRAIT	WHITES	AFRICAN AMERICANS	LATINOS	ASIAN AMERICANS
Wealth:				
1. Rich	2.4	0.3	0.2	1.1
2.	4.8	1.4	1.4	5.8
3.	30.6	2.8	4.6	17.3
4.	55.5	20.0	16.1	36.5
5.	6.2	38.7	40.7	23.8
6.	0.3	29.3	29.2	11.6
7. Poor	0.2	7.5	7.7	3.8
Work ethic:				
1. Hardworking	8.3	2.0	3.1	10.5
2.	18.5	3.8	5.5	16.4
3.	30.0	11.8	17.7	25.5
4.	38.0	35.7	37.0	30.8
5.	3.9	25.5	21.8	11.0
6.	0.9	15.1	12.2	4.1
7. Lazy	0.3	6.0	2.8	1.6
Welfare:				
1. Prefer to be self-supporting	16.1	1.9	2.6	9.9
2.	31.7	3.1	4.8	18.0
3.	25.9	8.3	12.8	18.0
4.	22.4	27.8	33.8	35.7
5.	2.5	24.5	26.1	12.6
6.	1.3	24.6	13.3	3.9
7. Prefer to live off of welfare	0.2	9.8	6.6	2.0
Intelligence:				
1. Unintelligent	0.8	2.0	1.5	1.1
2.	1.8	7.5	9.1	4.5
3.	3.8	21.1	21.7	9.3
4.	35.1	48.8	47.3	42.9
5.	27.6	13.8	13.5	21.5
6.	21.4	5.2	4.9	13.7
7. Intelligent	9.4	2.3	2.0	7.0
Violence:				
1. Violence-prone	0.6	8.5	4.1	1.2
2.	3.6	17.7	14	3.9
3.	12.4	27.5	24.5	14.5
4.	44.7	30.1	37.7	46.8
5.	17.4	9.3	21.8	18.9
6.	16.6	5.1	12.2	10.4
7. Not violence-prone	4.8	1.8	2.8	4.4
Patriotism:				
1. Patriotic	24.9	8.5	5.5	7.3
2.	31.1	15.8	10.7	13.3
3.	20.1	19.3	17.5	17.7
4.	21.0	38.4	39.9	40.1
5.	1.8	11.2	15.7	14.0
6.	0.9	4.7	7.5	5.1
7. Unpatriotic	0.2	2.2	3.3	2.4

Source: Lawrence Bobo and James R. Kluegel, "Modern American Prejudice: Stereotypes, Social Distance, and Perceptions of Discrimination toward Blacks, Hispanics, and Asians." Paper presented at the Annual Meetings of the American Sociological Association, Cincinnati, Ohio, August 23–27, 1991; data from 1990 General Social Survey, National Opinion Research Center; unpublished version, October 7, 1991.

I need only look in a mirror to know my true allegiance, and I am painfully aware that, even with my off-white trappings, I am prejudged by my color. . . .

As long as we are denigrated as a group, no one of us has made it. Inasmuch as we all suffer for every one left behind, we all gain for every one who conquers the hurdle (McClain, 1992: 120–122).

Class differences exist among African Americans just as they do within the white population. But the shared historical legacy of racist victimization, along with present-day experiences in a white-dominated society, help bond African Americans across class lines.

To sum up, data on the personal experiences of African Americans and on the racial attitudes of the dominant white population show that race remains highly significant in the United States. Even as more African Americans "make it" into the middle class, many whites continue to hold racist stereotypes about persons with black skin color. And many middle-class and other African Americans report experiences of discrimination. The biographies of all African Americans—including those in the middle class—are conditioned by our nation's continuing system of racial inequality.

DIVERSITY OF EXPERIENCES AMONG WOMEN OF COLOR

The contemporary women's movement has recently had to confront tensions that have developed among its supporters. For over two decades this movement has been dominated by white, middle-class women and the issues most pressing to them. Tensions have emerged because women of

There is a substantial and growing African American middle class in U.S. society, comprised of dual-career households such as the one pictured here. The financial resources of such families may undergo heavy demands, as less affluent kin at times must look to those who have made it into the middle class for assistance.

color (as well as other groups of women) have found that the women's movement has not adequately addressed their own needs and interests (hooks, 1981; Dill, 1983).

Women of the white middle class have championed the cause of enlarging female representation in professional and managerial settings, as well as in governmental bodies. They have fought hard against attacks on women's reproductive rights, including the right to choose whether to have or not have an abortion. Women of color certainly recognize the importance of such issues. But their overrepresentation in the lower and working classes often forces them to place their priority on issues of basic economic survival.

For example, heterosexual African American women need African American men to join them as marital partners and parents for their children. Yet, as we saw earlier, young African American males are becoming an "endangered species." The shortage of male counterparts makes it difficult for many African American women to form stable households. Thus, the racism that contributes to the maintenance of segregated ghettos and the troubles of their inhabitants is of pressing concern to these women. Many women of color would like to see the women's movement throw its full weight against racism and the harm it continues to do to women (Marable, 1983: 95–103). In their minds, the movement needs to be more sensitive to what it means to be both black and female.

At the same time, African American women must deal with their own treatment—as black persons, as women, as black women. Their history is unique in comparison to that of other women of color in the United States, for the ancestors of almost all African American women were held in bondage as slaves: legally owned as property, exploited for their labor, and freely sexually assaulted by white males—a dominant group in terms of class, race, and gender (Davis, 1983). Some people argue that this historical legacy continues to influence the ways in which many white males perceive and treat African American women today (Jewell, 1993). These women still live under conditions in which white males exercise society-wide dominance, and many of these males feel that they have little reason to respect women of color, on the basis of long-standing racist stereotypes about their morality and sexuality.

African American women must also contend with a system of sex inequality in which they are subordinate to African American males. Disempowered by the larger white society, many African American men seek to compensate for this condition by engaging in sexist treatment of "their" women. African American women are caught in a quandary: Should they battle with black men, whose self-esteem and self-worth are already besieged by racism? Or should they be understanding of these men, who are oppressed by racism even as they themselves are oppressed by the men's sexism? These kinds of questions came up in the wake of the controversial 1991 hearings held to evaluate U.S. Supreme Court candidate Clarence Thomas, during which he was charged with sexual harassment by black law professor Anita Hill (see Morrison, 1992). Many African American members and supporters of the women's movement have come to the conclusion that elimination of the sexism of which they are victims requires combating racism. This is an insight that may not be self-evident to a white woman.

The fact that women are not "all the same" should seem like an understatement, given the ease with which our discussion has ranged from wealthy white women to black women who are domestic workers. The tendency of the women's movement to emphasize the common experiences of women has opened it to the charge of **false universalism** (Asch and Fine, 1988: 3, 4). This term refers to the idea that all women experience life in the same ways. Yet who could experience a relationship more differently than a white woman employer and her black domestic servant? Indeed, are there any experiences common to all women that are not somehow colored by their positions in the systems of racial and class inequality? Many believe the answer is no (King, 1988; Amott and Matthaei, 1991).

Women of color, by being subordinates in two sectors of the matrix of inequality, face challenges qualitatively different from those facing white women or men of color (Spelman, 1988). But we also must keep in mind that the phrase "women of color" encompasses in itself a diverse population of women. It includes women from different **ethnic groups,** people who possess distinguishing cultural traits and a sense of community based on their shared heritage (Marger, 1991: 12–13). In the United States such groups include African Americans, Latino Americans, Asian Americans, Middle Eastern Americans, Native Americans, and many others (see Zinn and Dill, 1993).

These ethnic labels mask a great deal of further diversity. Among Latinas, for example, are included women who are U.S. citizens of Mexican descent, Puerto Ricans, and immigrants from different Latin nations in the Caribbean as well as Central and South America. Similarly, Asian Americans include women of Chinese, Japanese, Philippino, Asian Indian, Korean, Vietnamese, Cambodian, and Thai ancestry.

The heritages of women of color in the United States vary a great deal, both in terms of the women's treatment in ancestral societies and their treatment in this country (Almquist, 1979, 1989: 414–425; Amott and Matthaei, 1991). Let us illustrate this point by focusing upon women of Mexican descent, or Chicanas, the largest Latina group in the United States. Some of the ways in which Chicanas' experiences and identities as women of color differ from those of African American women will become apparent.

The history of Chicanas can be traced back to the forcible conquest by Spanish invaders of what was later to be named "Mexico" (see Almquist, 1989: 421–423). The Spanish conquistadores plundered the territory's indigenous Native American nations, engaged in genocidal massacres of many of their members, and captured or bartered for their women. The Spaniards treated native women as male property and intermarried with them freely. Their offspring, called *mestizos,* became part of a three-class system of racial inequality in this Spanish colony: Spaniards were at the top, mestizos in the middle, and the remaining Native Americans at the very bottom. Important roles that women had often played in the indigenous nations were lost. The goddesses they had worshiped were replaced by a religion oriented around male domination (Almquist, 1989: 421–422).

For three centuries of Spanish colonial rule the submission of women was promoted by the teachings of Roman Catholicism, the religion of the Spanish invaders. Women were exhorted to emulate the ideals associated with the Virgin Mary—remain pure and celibate before marriage, bear many children and be good mothers when called upon, suffer pain and sorrow with grace and dignity, pursue lives of self-denial, sacrifice, and even martyrdom.

Complementing this principle of *Marianisma* ("Mary-ism"), the cultural norm by which women's behavior was to be judged, was the Spaniards' norm for men called *machismo*. This was a Latino version of the myth of male superiority (Williams, 1990). Men were expected to be strong, sexually virile, and dominant over women while respecting and protecting their honor. Women were expected to be virgins at marriage and sexually faithful afterward, but men's "natural virility" allowed them to routinely have affairs and mistresses. Under Roman Catholicism, women unhappy with this situation could not seek a divorce.

In the mid-nineteenth century the U.S. government precipitated a war with Mexico in order to gain control over rich farmlands and natural resources. Upon winning the war, the government annexed much of what was then Mexico and incorporated this territory's inhabitants and their culture into the United States. The Mexicans who lived there lost control over their properties. The conquering "Anglos" dominated them politically and economically, exploiting their labor when needed and treating them with racist disdain. Most Chicanas today can trace their ancestry to persons living in the annexed area (Acuña, 1988).

Thus, Chicanas have long suffered subordination along the lines of race, class, and gender. As persons of Spanish and Native American ancestry, they have been the victims of their conqueror's belief in Anglo racial and cultural superiority. Chicanas' labor has been and continues to be purchased cheaply (Amott and Matthaei, 1991: 63–93). Historically, Chicanas have had lower labor-force participation than Anglo and African American women, but this has changed dramatically in the last couple of decades (Zavella, 1984). Today over half of all Chicanas in the United States are in the labor force, principally in the Southwest, where they are overconcentrated in low-paying seasonal jobs and in blue-collar, service, and agricultural settings.

Chicanas on average have very limited formal educational credentials. This is due to a combination of factors: lack of respect for their cultural heritage and language in Anglo-dominated schools; high dropout rates due to family responsibilities; and, for some, disruptions in school attendance because of family involvement in migrant labor. Their lack of formal education, coupled with racist and sexist employment practices, means that Chicanas are at a serious disadvantage in the job market (Amott and Matthaei, 1991: 63–93). Moreover, they often find themselves competing for work with other women of color, including Mexican women who have entered the United States illegally with the desperate hope of finding work.

The cultural traditions of Marianisma and machismo continue to linger among both sexes, but adherence to such traditions varies within the population. This is a key finding in interviews conducted with Chi-

Over half of all Chicanas are in the labor force; the low wages they typically receive have become an increasingly important supplement to their husbands' efforts to support their families. This Chicana, accompanied by her daughter, is laboring on a California farmland.

canas by Patricia Zavella (1984, 1987). She found that the inability of men to earn wages that will allow their wives to play their traditional roles has helped alter male-female relations. Increasing numbers of Chicanas have had to go to work to help support their families. Their entry into the job market has coincided with the rise of a service economy that has opened up job opportunities for these women. The Chicanas have, in turn, placed pressures on their husbands to take on household tasks, including child care. Their participation in work outside the home—work that the family depends on—gives Chicanas a sense of empowerment they would not otherwise have in their marital relationships. Zavella found that while in some cases this has led to serious conflict between men and women, in many cases it has contributed to more egalitarian relationships within the home. Her research demonstrates that cultural traditions alone do not drive family gender roles; these roles are subject to influences outside the family that may provoke both men and women to negotiate, experiment, and change.

Elizabeth Almquist, in comparing the situations of different groups of women of color, characterizes Chicanas in this way:

Today, Mexican-American women display equalitarian attitudes and resent any attempts to divide women from men. . . . The Chicana movement does not portray an overriding opposition between women and men; men are not pictured as the enemy or blamed for the limitations placed on women. . . . Chicana feminism places little stress on liberation for women alone; it emphasizes instead the benefits that can be obtained for Chicanos as a group (Almquist, 1989: 422–423).

Unlike African Americans, persons of Mexican descent did not become part of the United States through forced migration and enslavement of their ancestors. Chicanos were absorbed through a process similar to colonial conquest. While African Americans have long been stripped of their homeland cultures by the dominant white majority, many Chicanos have been able to hold on to language and practices that frequently reflect their dual cultural heritage—Native American and Spanish. While African Americans live an enormous physical and psychological distance from their continent of origin, persons of Mexican descent live where their ancestors lived; the proximity of Mexico and the rest of Latin America helps strengthen and renew their cultural identity. Thus, although the challenges faced by Chicanas may seem, and may indeed be, very similar to those faced by African American women, the historical and cultural contexts within which Chicanas' and African American women's biographies are forged are not the same. Moreover, as people of color, both groups of women face challenges and operate in contexts that are different from those of Anglo women.

SPECIAL CHALLENGES FACING WOMEN WITH DISABILITIES

As we noted in the previous chapter, our society has constructed a system of inequality around people's able-bodiedness. An estimated 36 million people in the United States presently possess a disability, a physical or mental condition that substantially limits one or more life activities such as walking, hearing, speaking, seeing, learning, and working. Members of this population often find themselves the objects of discrimination by the able-bodied majority.

Because people with disabilities are overrepresented in low-income and poverty circumstances, many of them experience oppression in the nation's system of class inequality as well. As we shall see, women with disabilities are particularly vulnerable to being poor. In any case, poor or not, such women simultaneously experience oppression within the system of sex inequality.

For many years social science literature concerned with the challenges confronting persons with disabilities assumed either that the gender of such persons was irrelevant or that these persons were males. The idea that women with disabilities might face special problems not faced by able-bodied women or men with disabilities was largely ignored (Quinn, 1994).

Even social movements relevant to people with disabilities have been slow to address specific issues of concern to women in this group. Disability-related organizations that have pushed for an end to discriminatory practices and for increased access to the U.S. mainstream have tended to be male-dominated. Women's voices have been largely muted within such organizations. The women's movement has primarily been concerned with fighting sexism, not ableism. The movement has been slow to incorporate concerns unique to sisters with disabilities who are supportive of its goals.

The relative invisibility of women with disabilities in the United States is now beginning to change, as research has underscored their plight. Yet most people still remain unaware of the special problems these millions of women experience. The impact on the biographies of those forced into subordinate positions on the basis of both sex and limited able-bodiedness is enormous (Browne, Connors, and Stern, 1985).

Women are more likely than men to internalize the master status of "disabled person" thrust upon them by able-bodied members of society. It is hard for many women with disabilities to see what their alternatives might be. Men are more likely to resist this master status when they can, because they possess more options and have access to more roles that it is assumed they can play. Moreover, traditional sex roles built around the notion that women are naturally weak, dependent, and in need of care match the stereotypes associated with being disabled. On the other hand, traditional male sex roles expect men to be strong, independent, and commanding. Men with disabilities who can respond to these expectations are by definition breaking with stereotypes of the disabled.

In an article that helped encourage sociological thinking about women with disabilities, Michelle Fine and Adrienne Asch argue that such women often suffer from **rolelessness,** that is, the absence of socially sanctioned roles to fill (1985: 12). This can be clearly seen in the economic arena. Women with disabilities are frequently turned away from aspiring to economically productive roles not only through rejection by employers but also through discouragement stemming from their school experiences and even their own families. Publicly funded rehabilitation and job training programs provide more services and wage-earning outcomes for men than for women (Fine and Asch, 1985: 7).

In our system of sex inequality, men are expected to work outside the home, and our occupational reward structure is tilted in favor of "men's jobs." Men with disabilities are thus more likely than women to feel encouraged to aspire to economically productive roles and to seek work. While job difficulties faced by men with disabilities are common, the situation for their female counterparts is worse. Partly as a consequence, such women often live in adverse economic circumstances.

Fine and Asch suggest that the rolelessness handicap extends to the social arena as well. Our system of sex inequality calls for women to play loving, nurturant, reproductive roles, but women with disabilities are widely viewed as unable to do so. They also typically do not meet male-generated standards for personal attractiveness. In addition, disability is stereotypically equated with being incapable of handling a family and household responsibilities, another unattractive trait to many men.

Here is how one never-married woman with disabilities assesses her life:

If you are not a cripple, you cannot possibly imagine the way the world reduces you to that condition. For a woman, especially, normality, acceptability, and marriageability depend upon looking whole. I have been in leg and arm braces since I was three. Boys never considered me fair game for dating, even though they liked me a lot to pal around with. Teachers never thought it possible that I might accomplish what others could do. Firms that I interviewed with approached me with fear and loathing.

I got through because I believed in my inner wholeness, even if my outside leaves a lot to be desired. But the world around me saw a woman without the use of her limbs, without womanliness, without a man, without children. Everything else had a cameo role (Simon, 1988: 220).

Since men can usually determine the terms on which they will interact with women, their rejection of women with disabilities in favor of able-bodied women limits the role options of the former. In comparison to able-bodied women, women with disabilities are less likely to marry and more likely to be divorced. Although far more women than men with disabilities are married, many live without a mate because of divorce, separation, abandonment, or death (Asch and Fine, 1988: 13–15). Consequently, social isolation is a chronic problem for such women.

Poor women, particularly those of color, have historically been pressured not to bear children and been subjected to involuntary sterilization (Shapiro, 1985). Yet women with disabilities have been treated in this way no matter what their race or class background. It has long been widely assumed that such women cannot mother successfully and thus have no business bearing children in the first place. Many people are surprised that women with disabilities possess sex drives and have "normal" interests

Increasingly, women with disabilities are unwilling to be handicapped by others' ignorance and mistreatment and are demanding that others accept them on their own terms. The well-being of this dignified woman is enhanced when the able-bodied act as if disability were not her most important defining feature.

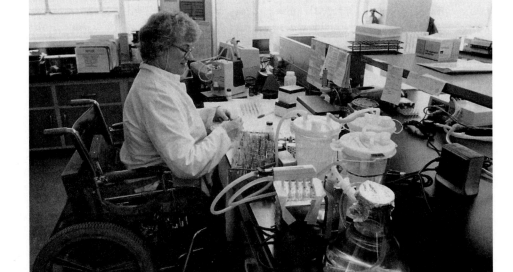

and needs that mirror those of the able-bodied population (Lonsdale, 1990: chap. 5). A lack of professional interest in these challenges faced by women with disabilities leaves the women in a vacuum when seeking appropriate advice. In contrast, men with disabilities are unlikely to be discouraged from becoming fathers (it is assumed that they have wives to take care of parenting). And what little clinical guidance exists to assist with problems of sexual functioning is principally addressed to men.

Women with disabilities are not immune from sexual abuse, assault, rape, and other forms of serious victimization (Asch and Fine, 1988: 22–23). Moreover, such women may find it more difficult than women who are able-bodied to extract themselves from exploitative and abusive relationships. Their fear of social isolation and their inability to earn a living on their own may lead many women to remain in such relationships, despite the toll they take on a woman's psychological or physical well-being.

Men with disabilities thus have certain advantages over their female counterparts in terms of involvement in the economy and the family, two central institutions affecting an individual's biography (Fine and Asch, 1985; Asch and Fine, 1988). They can use their power as members of the dominant group within the system of sex inequality to offset or overcome the stigma associated with disability. Women, as members of the subordinate sex within this system, have far less power to do the same. Consequently, they are typically viewed more negatively than are men with disabilities, and their opinions of themselves tend to be more negative than those of their male counterparts.

The Americans with Disabilities Act of 1990 protects the civil rights of all people with disabilities and encourages them to develop positive self-images. Consequently, more and more women with disabilities may arrive at what Asch and Fine call "the other end of the spectrum," where they "resist all the gender-based and disability-based stereotypes and take pride in the identities they forge" (1988: 25). Such women will seek out educational opportunities and well-paying jobs, enter into egalitarian relationships with their male or female partners, be sexually active, and make their own choices about pregnancy and motherhood. Asch and Fine suggest that we should expect women with disabilities to increasingly demand that others accept them on their own terms (1988: 25).

CONCLUSION

This chapter has highlighted the importance of the multiple memberships each of us has in different systems of inequality. One's biography is not simply a matter of being a woman or a man, a rich person or a poor one, or a person of color or a white. Where one stands in such systems of inequality as sex, race, and class is equally important in understanding the constraints on one's life chances. All women have to deal with being subordinate within the system of sex inequality in the United States. But the experiences of a wealthy white woman in this system are going to be very different from those of a working-class African American woman. Both are women, yet the nation's systems of racial and class inequality have very different implications for their lives. Likewise, all men occupy a dominant position in the sex inequality system, but not all men are the same. The wealthy white man's life is supported by class and race privilege. His life will thus be very different from the lives of lower-class men of color, despite the fact that they are of the same sex.

People usually experience their positions in the matrix simultaneously. For example, an African American female domestic experiences her race, gender, and class not one at a time but all at once. A woman with a disability is made to feel like a disabled woman, not a disabled person. Moreover, women with disabilities do not exist in vacuums; they exist within other systems of inequality that may condition how they are treated. Being a woman of color with a disability means being open to stigmatization from a variety of directions. But again, much also depends upon which color.

Our attention in this chapter has focused upon women and people of color, both heavily dominated populations within the systems of inequality discussed in Chapter 6. But it is important to emphasize that white males do not walk about unscathed. Being a member of the dominant racial group and the dominant gender does not protect white males from blocked opportunities or even poverty-level living. The notion that white males are capable of being successful by definition is a myth. Economic forces expose them to some of the same problems associated with unemployment and job insecurity that women and people of color must face. Moreover, the oppressive effects of systems of racial, class, and gender inequality rob society of important contributions from women, minorities, and the economically disadvantaged in such areas as health care, the sciences, engineering, business, literature and the arts, and law. This is a situation in which everyone—including white males—loses.

All the systems of inequality within the matrix are socially constructed and interlocking. A change in one will have important implications for the others. We saw this in our discussion of the benefits women of color see in combating racism, a condition that contributes to the sexism that also oppresses them. Likewise, racism helps perpetuate systemic economic inequality and the overconcentration of women of color in poverty. Understanding more precisely the ways in which aspects of the matrix interlock, and the implications of this interlocking for individuals' biographies, poses a provocative challenge for sociologists.

THINKING CRITICALLY

1. As you have learned in this chapter, white women of the upper class are subordinate in terms of gender but dominant in terms of race and class. For lower-class black men, the situation is reversed. What, if anything, do both groups have in common?
2. Some white males feel threatened by advances in education and employment made by women and people of color. Should white males view such gains positively? Give arguments to support your opinion.

3. In discussing some of the problems women with disabilities face, we talked in very general terms about disability itself. What difference do you think the *type* of disability makes in terms of how these women are treated? Why?
4. Identify several key stereotypes about people of color. Include some that are specific to males and others that are specific to females. How are these stereotypes fostered and maintained? What facts belie them? What functions do such stereotypes play?
5. Our boxed article lists advantages that white-skin privilege provides for whites. Prepare similar lists for males, able-bodied people, and other groups whose positions provide them with unearned advantages, and compare your lists with those of classmates.

KEY TERMS

white-skin privilege, *214*
second shift, *216*
declining significance of race, *223*

false universalism, *232*
ethnic groups, *232*
rolelessness, *236*

SUGGESTED READINGS

Teresa L. Amott and Julie A. Matthaei, *Race, Gender, and Work: A Multicultural Economic History of Women in the United States.* Boston: South End Press, 1991. An overview of the ways in which sexism and racism have historically shaped work opportunities for women of color and continue to do so today.

Patricia Hill Collins, *Black Feminist Thought.* Boston: Unwin Hyman, 1990. An exploration of the historical and contemporary treatment of African American women, underscoring problems they face and problem-solving strategies many develop in the face of oppression along the lines of race, sex, and class.

Virginia Cyrus (ed.), *Experiencing Race, Class, and Gender in the United States.* Mountain View, CA: Mayfield, 1993. A discussion of the impact of race, class, and gender on people's sense of identity, power relations, and desire for change, often presented through accounts of personal experiences.

Joe R. Feagin and Melvin P. Sikes, *Living with Racism: The Black Middle-Class Experience.* Boston: Beacon Press, 1994. A description of the everyday experiences of racism that middle-class African Americans endure even today and the psychological toll this endurance exacts from them.

Michelle Fine and Adrienne Asch (eds.), *Women with Disabilities.* Philadelphia: Temple University Press, 1988. A collection of articles exploring the various problems faced by women with disabilities and the impact of how these women are treated on their life chances.

Clyde W. Franklin II, *Men & Society*. Chicago: Nelson-Hall, 1988. An analysis of the social construction of the male sex role, masculinity and male culture, male dominance and sexism, heterosexuality and homo-sexuality, and the ways in which the roles of and relations between men and women are undergoing change.

Maxine Baca Zinn and Bonnie Thornton Dill (eds.), *Women of Color in United States Society*. Philadelphia: Temple University Press, 1993. An exploration of the diversity of life experiences found among women of color from different ethnic backgrounds.

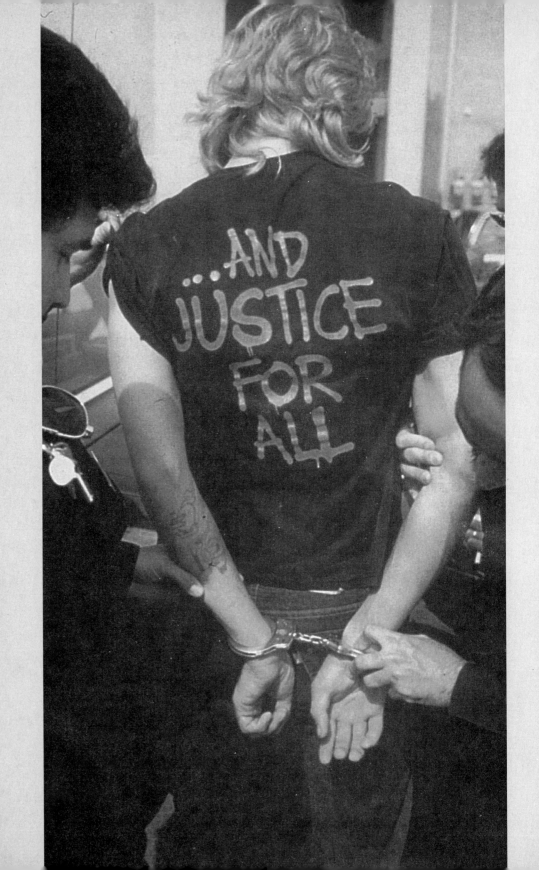

DEVIANCE, SOCIAL CONTROL, AND RESISTANCE

*C*onsider the following separate events: Members of anti-abortion groups block passage to a women's clinic where abortions are known to be performed. Students at a military academy violate their honor code by cheating on a test. A woman chooses to totally ignore her appearance, saying that how she looks is

8

nobody's business but her own. A 13-year-old's academic accomplishments allow him to begin college. Industry executives approve the production of an automobile even though they are aware that its gas tank has been known to explode if the car is hit from behind. A firefighter, who has suffered severe burn-related facial and bodily disfigurements, elects not to mask his disability in public. Using fake indentification, underage youths procure an X-rated video for their weekend beer party. A homeless woman assertively begs for money and angrily complains when passersby ignore her.

*What do all these events have in common? Each is an example of what sociologists call **deviance**: behavior that is in violation of or departs from social norms. Note that while some of the events described above involve law violations, deviance can occur without the commission of a crime. Moreover, many people think of deviance in terms of distinctively negative behaviors, but deviance is not always negative. For example, an unusually positive accomplishment (the 13-year-old's entry into college) or simply the assertion of one's right to be accepted as different (the firefighter's refusal to hide his disfigurements) may constitute a norm violation.*

In this chapter we shall explore a number of different questions: Who or what determines that certain people are "deviants"? What kinds of sanctions may befall those whose behavior is considered deviant? Are people sometimes treated as deviant on the basis of attributes other than their behavior? To what degree and in what ways do the ideas of dominant groups play a role in this process? Why do people engage in behavior that is considered deviant? Are there circumstances under which deviant behavior would be a positive force, that is, would make important contributions to society?

DEVIANCE AS NORM VIOLATION

In Chapter 4 ("Culture") and Chapter 5 ("Socialization"), we addressed the issue of what makes society possible. Through socialization into the commonly shared ideas and practices of a culture, members of society learn the boundaries of acceptable behavior. Sociologists refer to these boundaries as **norms.** Norms are standards that define the obligatory and expected behaviors of people in various situations. They are, in effect, rules.

As discussed in Chapter 4, there are different types of norms. These range from *folkways* (the least formal or important norms, involving everyday conventional routines) to *mores* (more formal and important, defining behaviors that absolutely must or must not occur) to *laws* (norms so vital, often to dominant interests, that they are translated into a written legal code and enforced by the state).

Thus, norms as folkways may pertain to mundane interactions such as replying "Hello" to a friend who has greeted you. Norms may, as mores, pertain to behaviors about which there are strong and widely held feelings, such as childhood incest among siblings. Or norms may be institutionalized and backed by state power, such as laws prohibiting evasion of taxes. Through the processes of socialization, discussed in Chapter 5, we become aware of an enormous number and variety of norms outlining acceptable behavior.

People whose behavior violates prevailing norms may be seen as being anything from odd or eccentric to annoying, disruptive, or even dangerous to the functioning of society. Since social life is possible only if people generally abide by norms, members of society must develop means of **social control,** that is, means of minimizing deviant behavior (Davis and Stasz, 1990). Some types of behavior, such as destruction of property or violence, must be checked; without order, the cooperation any society needs to function will be jeopardized.

Social control of deviant behavior can be informal, as when a teacher chides a student for misbehavior, or formal, as when an individual is brought to trial in a judicial system. Social control generally calls for the use of **sanctions,** that is, the meting out of punishments or rewards. **Negative sanctions** serve to punish norm violators and to remind others of what could happen to them if they engage in similar behavior. Such sanctions can range from expressions of disapproval by members of one's primary group (family, friends, coworkers) to imprisonment or capital punishment by the state. The nature of the negative sanction depends upon such factors as the norm violated, the importance attached to it, the circumstances under which the violation occurred, the status of the violator within society, and the remorse he or she has shown.

Positive sanctions also serve to encourage conformity, but they do so from a different direction. By rewarding persons who abide by the rules, positive sanctions reinforce their behavior and remind others of the benefits of behaving according to expected norms. The reward one receives for returning a lost wallet to its owner communicates the virtue of honesty over theft. The ceremonies honoring police officers and firefighters who heroically risk their lives in the line of duty remind everyone of the courageous work they do and encourage them to remain motivated. By seeing what is honored, we can often tell what would bring dishonor. In this case bravery is honored, and by implication expressions of cowardice in the line of duty are condemned.

How do we know what deviant behavior is? Does deviance reside in the act itself, or is it defined by society's members? Some have argued that certain acts, such as taking another person's life, are inherently deviant. Many sociologists reject this argument (Becker, 1963). In their view, determining that certain behaviors are deviant is a subjective process and one that tells us something about those making the rules (Orcutt, 1983: 222–242). According to this view, deviant behavior is *socially constructed.* Let us look at what this means.

THE SOCIAL CONSTRUCTION OF DEVIANCE

For many years sociologists focused their attention almost solely on the deviant and his or her behavior. In the last few decades, however, sociologists have explored ways in which deviance gets defined, or the **social construction** of deviance. Sociologists today readily acknowledge that deviant behavior is always defined with reference to a set of rules, or social norms. Thus, there is no act in which human beings can engage that is inherently deviant in and of itself. When a person or an act is held to be deviant in the context of a set of norms, the social construction of deviance is taking place.

For example, whether taking the life of another human being should be defined as deviant depends on the normative context. Killing a bank teller in the course of a robbery would be considered deviant by most people but not by criminals for whom killing in the course of a robbery is normative. Seeking out and killing another person—even many persons—may at times receive recognition as a positive accomplishment; an example is the killing of enemy soldiers in a war. But some people are committed to norms, based on religious beliefs or matters of conscience, that hold any killing to be intolerable. As these examples show, judgments made in the context of social norms determine whether or not deviance exists (Akers, 1985: 6–7).

If we view deviant behavior as a social construction, then, in theory, *any* act could be considered deviant by someone. The use of the term "deviant behavior" implies a social process whereby the **label** "deviance" is attached to the acts of an individual or group (Becker, 1963). From a sociological perspective no act is deviant unless people define it as such within the context of norms, be they folkways, mores, or laws.

Does this mean sociologists believe there is no right or wrong? No— sociologists, like most other people, have ethical and moral standards. Saying that deviant behavior is socially constructed is not the same as saying that everything is morally relative and that societal members should be permitted to act however they choose, even if their behavior entails genocide and other atrocities. Sociologists are merely pointing out that people regularly make decisions about what they hold to be right, wrong, moral, or immoral. Indeed, people have to make such decisions to facilitate the functioning of human societies. For this reason virtually all societies develop some kind of rule-making processes and systems of sanctions.

Since deviant behavior is a social construction, what is considered deviant may vary with time. For example, before 1973, abortion was against the law in many parts of the United States, and this law was widely accepted. Persons who did not adhere to the law, including both those performing abortions and the women having them, were subject to criminal penalties. Because their behavior violated existing norms as formalized in law, it was considered deviant. Over time, however, views toward abortion changed. More and more people came to the conclusion that women should have the right to make their own decisions about something as personal and private as childbearing. In 1973, the U.S. Supreme Court legalized abortion nationwide through its decision in the case of *Roe v. Wade.* Many people still held steadfastly to views condemning abortion and disagreed with the court's decision, but under the law abortion was no longer defined as deviant.

This example suggests another fact about deviant behavior. There may be little consensus over whether an act is deviant, and laws may express the normative views of some people but not others. In recent years, groups disagreeing with *Roe v. Wade* have struggled to reverse the decision (Luker, 1984). The Supreme Court has not acceded to the decision's opponents, but it has allowed states to restrict the ease with which abortions may be obtained. Likewise, Congress has come under pressure to deny federal funds for abortions in government health-care programs. This example emphasizes the social construction of deviance: the same act can be considered deviant by some groups and not others.

Only in small, homogeneous societies, where all members tend to share the same norms, are we likely to find considerable consensus as to what behaviors are deviant. Members of larger, more heterogeneous societies are more likely to disagree about what is deviant. In our heterogeneous society performing or having an abortion is not the only behavior on which people disagree. Consider also using marijuana, driving above the speed limit, leaving home (by young people) to join religious cults, engaging in homosexual acts (by consenting adults), and fudging on tax returns. Some people would find one or more of these acts perfectly acceptable, while other people would vigorously condemn them all.

As we saw with the example of legalizing abortion, defining deviant behavior may involve struggle and conflict. People may feel very strongly

In large, heterogeneous societies people may find it difficult to agree that certain behaviors are deviant. These people are openly using marijuana, a practice that many of their fellow citizens would condemn even as they themselves indulge in alcohol.

Although beverage alcohol is a potent drug that contributes to crime, illness, accidents, low workplace productivity, and family dissolution, its use is legal and widely accepted in our society. Here, people passing through New York's Grand Central Station pause to imbibe.

about whether a particular behavior is deviant or not, depending upon the norms by which they believe others should abide. Groups may be at such odds with one another that it is difficult or even impossible to resolve their differences. In the case of abortion, debate as to when human life begins and differing views over the right of women to control reproduction have forced opposing parties to seek relief in courts and legislatures.

Of course, what is considered deviant behavior differs not only over time and from group to group within a society. The social construction of deviance means that whole societies may also differ in what is considered deviant (Edgerton, 1978). When U.S. troops were stationed abroad during the Gulf war, they were required to avoid alcohol even when off duty because the Saudi and Kuwaiti cultures do not permit alcohol consumption. In deference to local customs, female troops at one air base in Saudi Arabia were ordered to remain completely covered at all times despite the severe desert heat. They were also housed in sex-segregated quarters, told to avoid public fraternization with male colleagues, and restricted as to when and where they could drive (M. Moore, 1990). In the heavily patriarchal Arab culture, men suppress any public expressions of female sexuality and independence by demanding strict adherence to norms pertaining to dress and conduct.

In sum, many sociologists view deviance as being socially constructed and involving a labeling process. Members of a group, a community, or a whole society may develop norms that make certain behaviors socially unacceptable. These norms take the form of folkways, mores, and laws. Norm violators are labeled deviant and subjected to sanctions intended to minimize such behaviors. In large heterogeneous societies such as our own, people not only disagree about what behaviors are unacceptable but also possess different amounts of power to define who or what is deviant. In the next section we shall look at ways in which dominant groups may impose their norms on others.

THE ROLE OF POWER IN DEFINING DEVIANCE

249

Chapter 8

Deviance, Social
Control, and
Resistance

Although societal members define deviant behavior, doing so is not a simple process of reaching a consensus or determining public opinion. For each behavior in question, some people's opinions count more than others' opinions. In short, not all individuals and groups possess equal power to determine whether a particular behavior will be considered deviant. In Chapter 6, we saw that some groups dominate others and play a strong role in influencing their life chances. One way to influence people's life chances is to maintain social control over their behaviors. Dominant groups in a society typically have the power to decide what is deviant and what is not.

Writing in his classic work on deviance, *Outsiders*, Howard S. Becker states:

> To the extent that a group tries to impose its rules on other groups in the society, we are presented with a question: Who can, in fact, force others to accept their rules and what are the causes of their success? This is, of course, a question of political and economic power. . . . Differences in the ability to make rules and apply them to other people are essentially power differentials. . . . Those groups whose social position gives them weapons and power are best able to enforce their rules. Distinctions of age, sex, ethnicity, and class are all related to differences in power, which accounts for differences in the degree to which groups so distinguished can make rules for others (Becker, 1963: 17–18).

We shall illustrate Becker's point using the case of women and deviance.

In his book *Labeling Women Deviant* (1984), sociologist Edwin M. Schur suggests that in patriarchal (male-dominated) societies many norms function to control women and keep them "in their place." Among those he identifies are *appearance norms* and *motherhood norms*. Control over behavior in such areas, Schur feels, serves "as a capsule statement of what male domination entails" (1984: 53). These norms are increasingly subject to question and change in the United States and are held more strongly by some members of our society than others. Still, the continued presence of these norms means that women who depart from them risk being labeled deviant.

In Schur's view, **appearance norms** encourage women to be preoccupied with what are, in effect, male standards of attractiveness. Most women feel an obligation to be concerned about their appearance and are conscious of how they present themselves, not only in the eyes of men but in the eyes of other women (Wolf, 1991). In the United States, advertising has long played a powerful role in stimulating and reinforcing this concern on the part of women. Whole industries—such as fashion, cosmetics and beauty aids, diet and weight control, and cosmetic surgery—thrive on it (Ewen, 1976; Barthel, 1988).

Yet the role models for female beauty typically presented in advertising, and in the media in general, cannot be emulated in real life by the vast majority of women (Glassner, 1988). No matter how hard they try, most women cannot make themselves resemble those in the annual swimsuit issue of *Sports Illustrated:* young, white, long-haired, thin, high cheek-boned, blemish-free, and perfectly proportioned, with the exception of unusually large breasts (see Sutton, 1992). From magazines to Hollywood films to MTV, the media present standards of beauty that women compare themselves to and are judged by. In Schur's view, the more a woman falls short of appearance norms, whether by choice or through an inability to conform, the more likely it is she will be labeled as deviant by males.

Behaviors among women that manifest a preoccupation with personal body shape may reflect the internalization of the appearance norms that Schur describes. Many women try to reshape themselves through cosmetic surgery; they undergo breast implants, face-lifts, nose jobs, and liposuction. Diet regimes, health clubs, aerobics classes, and jogging are only in part motivated by health concerns. For many women, these activities are part of the endless (and unsuccessful) pursuit of the "perfect body" (Glassner, 1988).

Some women will risk their health rather than fall short of appearance norms. Consider the recent controversy over the use of silicone gel implants to enlarge women's breasts. In the last 30 years, almost 2 million women underwent this cosmetic surgery in the United States. Until recently, breast implants were a $500-million-a-year business. Representatives of the American Society of Plastic and Reconstructive Surgeons called the insertion of implants a "cure" for micromastia—small breasts—which they have designated a "disease" (Ehrenreich, 1992).

Beauty contests, covered widely in the mass media, emphasize standards of physical appearance from which most women, by no fault of their own, depart. The Miss Universe Pageant provides special photo opportunities for members of the press to help publicize pageant activities with this parade of contestants.

But there is strong evidence of serious side effects associated with the implants. Among the dangers are difficulties with lactation, illnesses (including cancer), disfigurement from leaking of the chemical products, and interference with diagnostic mammograms that could provide early detection of breast cancer (Weiss, 1991). Despite these dangers, many women supported efforts by lobbyists representing plastic surgeons and health product firms to prevent the U.S. Food and Drug Administration from restricting access to such implants for cosmetic purposes (Pollitt, 1992). Such restrictions were imposed, pending further research (Hilts, 1992).

Besides appearance norms, Schur suggests that **motherhood norms** are also directly tied into the system of male dominance (1984: 81–110). Pointing to lesbian couples and heterosexual women (married and single) who choose to be childless, he argues that there is no scientific evidence for the existence of a universal, invariant "maternal instinct" in all females that drives them to childbirth and childrearing. In Schur's view, the belief that nature has equipped women with such an instinct is best understood as part of the patriarchal biology-is-destiny ideology (discussed in Chapter 6) that has justified the channeling of women into particular sex-typed roles and responsibilities.

According to Schur, motherhood norms include the notion that "normal" women get married and bear children. Married women who wish to bear children but cannot are objects of sympathy, while wives who make it known that they (and their spouses) choose not to bear children may be labeled as deviant by friends, acquaintances, and even family members. *Refusal* to mother is an act that flaunts the norm. Women who make this decision may find little social support for it and may even be stigmatized as immature, self-centered, and inclined to lead barren, unfulfilled lives.

Men can appeal to motherhood norms to pressure reluctant partners into bearing an unwanted child or more children than they really want. Males who have chauvinistic attitudes toward women, or who do not succeed in the traditional role of husband and main breadwinner, may seek to establish or gain recognition of their "manhood" through fatherhood, a situation facilitated by the existence of motherhood norms.

Schur observes that another motherhood norm is the concept of not giving birth out of wedlock. This norm may be shifting, given the growing rates of out-of-wedlock births in recent years (including an especially rapid rise in rates for white females). Still, such births meet with negative evaluations, often expressed through pejorative phrases like "unwed mother" and "illegitimate child." In one survey, 46 percent of those polled said that it was "very important" that women have children only when they are married (Yankelovich Clancy Shulman, 1992).

When a birth occurs out of wedlock, it is primarily the woman who is judged to have done something wrong. Attitudes may be changing on this notion as well. The spotlight is focusing on paternity because of recent political clamors over the costs of welfare assistance for female-headed families, the need to place more responsibility for child support on fathers from all economic levels, and technological advances that make establishing paternity easier. Still, the fathers of children born out of wedlock are not so routinely condemned as are the mothers. Until recently, many fathers simply disappeared from the picture. It is the woman who has violated the prevailing motherhood norms.

The norm against giving birth out of wedlock pressures women to marry even when they do not wish to or else to live singly with the guilt and ambivalence that accompanies the stigma of "unwed mother." Many unmarried pregnant women choose neither marriage nor unwed motherhood; they opt for abortion instead. Obviously, for many in our society abortion itself is a violation of motherhood norms.

Married women who do not wish to have children and unmarried women who do not want to bear children out of wedlock face hurdles. There is no contraceptive that is 100 percent effective. Some forms of birth control, such as the pill and certain of the intrauterine devices, can pose threats to women's health and safety. Abortion to end an unwanted pregnancy remains controversial, and access to abortion is being made increasingly difficult for women, particularly those who are poor.

Most women want to be sexually active with their partners but may end up bearing children they do not really want. Some women who become mothers unwillingly may take out their frustrations on their children; some may engage in child neglect. For such women a new label denoting deviance is waiting: "unfit mother." In Schur's view, motherhood norms not only include the notion that "normal" women marry and have children within marriage but also include expectations that women will strive toward a maternal ideal of self-sacrifice, unconditional love, and nurturance.

In recent years many single, middle-class women, including professionals with careers, have chosen not to marry but to conceive intentionally and give birth to children out of wedlock. This single mother holds her child in the fertility clinic where she underwent artificial insemination with the sperm of an anonymous donor.

Motherhood norms can also make it difficult for women who want to have children outside a conventional marriage. Heterosexual single women who intentionally conceive and give birth may be labeled as deviant. Vice President Dan Quayle's comments during the 1992 presidential campaign, condemning such behavior by the television character Murphy Brown, played upon such sentiments. But these feelings may be changing. Murphy Brown symbolizes a recent trend among single professional women to become mothers by choice.

Lesbian women who choose to become mothers are viewed as even more deviant than single heterosexual women who do so. In a 1993 court ruling in Virginia, a judge awarded custody of a lesbian's baby to her mother, reasoning that her sexual orientation made her "unfit" to raise the child. (This decision, overruled in 1994, was then appealed.) Both lesbian and single heterosexual mothers challenge the notion that adequately fulfilling the motherhood role requires dependence on a male partner. In one survey, 47 percent of the respondents disagreed with the statement, "A single mother can bring up her child just as well as a married couple" (*Washington Post*, 1991). Such popular sentiments pressure women not to choose motherhood outside marriage.

In a patriarchal society, men have the power to make and enforce rules that determine what is "normal" behavior for women. In the United States, in part due to the existence of an active movement for women's rights, that power has been challenged. Appearance and motherhood norms still exist and exert control over women, but in various ways and in various places they have been breaking down. The women's movement has inspired women to depart from gender-related norms that restrict their right to make choices.

The ability of other dominant groups in U.S. society to attach the label "deviant" to the behavior of those they oppress has also been under attack. Gay males and lesbians have been fighting against heterosexual-imposed norms that define homosexuality as deviant (Blumenfeld, 1992; Duberman, 1993). People of color have been challenging the norm that calls for them to be quietly passive and acquiesce to racist treatment by members of the dominant white majority (Omi and Winant, 1986; Williams, 1987). And people with disabilities have been using political activism to dismantle norms that have excluded them from sharing in activities engaged in by the able-bodied (Shapiro, 1993).

These examples suggest that people may reject the label "deviant" that dominant groups attempt to bestow upon them when their behavior departs from prevailing norms. In the next section we shall look closer at people's resistance to being defined as deviant.

DEVIANCE AND RESISTANCE

Deviance as Behavior versus Deviance as Being

Thus far in this chapter we have defined deviance as *behavior* that is in violation of social norms. Most sociologists would agree with this traditional definition. We have emphasized that dominant groups may use their power to determine what behaviors will be considered deviant. But it is also apparent that power allows dominant groups to define others as deviant in terms of their very *being!* Thus, being a woman, a person of color, a gay male or lesbian, a person with a disability, an elderly person, or a poor person often means being defined as a deviant by dominant groups, even in the absence of any actual behavior that violates norms.

Groups with power tend to define themselves as normal and those they dominate as "the other." Arturo Madrid describes what it is like to be defined as the other by dominant groups:

> Being *the other* means feeling different; is awareness of being distinct; is consciousness of being dissimilar. It means being outside the game, outside the circle, outside the set. It means being on the edges, on the margins, on the periphery. Otherness means being excluded, closed out, precluded, even disdained and scorned. It produces a sense of isolation, of apartness, of disconnectedness, of alienation. . . . Being *the other* involves a contradictory phenomenon. On the one hand being *the other* means being invisible. . . . On the other hand, being *the other* sometimes means sticking out like a sore thumb. What is she/he doing here (Madrid, 1992: 8)?

Persons who by their being (the other) or behavior are defined as deviant may be considered "outsiders," a term introduced by Howard S. Becker:

> But the person who is thus labeled an outsider may have a different view of the matter. He may not accept the rule by which he is being judged and may not regard those who judge him as either competent or legitimately entitled to do so (Becker, 1963: 1P–2).

Becker thus suggests that outsiders may resist efforts on the part of dominant groups to bestow the label "deviant" upon them in response to their behavior or on the basis of their being.

Resistance to Being Labeled Deviant for One's Behavior

One of the most familiar settings in which struggles take place over being labeled deviant on the basis of one's behavior is the courtroom. Each year police arrest literally millions of people and charge them with crimes ranging from misdemeanors to felonies. In many cases charges are dropped, but arrests for the most serious offenses result in a court appearance for the accused. There, a battle ensues between the prosecutor, whose job it is to prosecute the case, and the defense attorney, who is intent on achieving a positive outcome for his or her client. The accused does not want to suffer the consequences of being successfully prosecuted and will, through the medium of the defense attorney, resist imposition of the label "criminal." Ordinarily, the higher one's class position, the greater the level of resistance, as individuals in higher positions have more economic resources to bring to bear in financing a defense (Reiman, 1984).

While it is rarely pursued, despite the impression one might gain from sensational cases reported in the media, the insanity defense is another example of the struggle over labeling persons deviant whose behavior violates social norms ("Insanity Defense," 1985). In this case, the accused attempts to resist the unwanted label "criminal" by demanding to be given a substitute label: "insane." The goal is to be found not guilty by reason of insanity.

"Insanity" is a legal term, not a medical one, and states differ as to the criteria they use to judge its existence. The defense may argue that the accused was not in his or her right mind when performing the act in question; the prosecution will say that the defendant knew exactly what he or she was doing and knew that it was wrong. Each side is likely to bring in professional psychiatric experts to support its case. Only a small proportion of the attempts to substitute the label "insane" for the label "criminal" are successful. Judges and juries seem loathe to accept insanity as an excuse for serious crimes, in part because psychiatrists themselves often disagree on diagnoses (see Rosenhan, 1973, 1975).

At times, people whose behavior violates social norms are given the label "mentally ill." Once this label is bestowed, through a court process or other routes to diagnosis by mental health professionals, they may find it difficult to ever successfully resist being treated as outsiders (Link et al., 1987). According to sociologist Erving Goffman (1963), such individuals carry a negative social **stigma,** a "damaged identity" by which they are marked by others.

For example, harboring a history of mental illness may make one an undesirable candidate for such social roles as employee or spouse. Within our society, an element of fear is commonly connected with the idea of associating with the mentally ill, and it frequently results in the avoidance and exclusion of persons so labeled. Even when a person has undergone treatment and no longer has any symptoms of being ill, the label "mentally ill" may remain. Should discriminatory behavior interfere with the ability of such a person to enter and perform important roles, the stigmatization may actually contribute to mental illness. This then leads to an "I told you so" attitude on the part of those who would not let the label go.

A similar "looping" process occurs when people are released from prison. Often they have trouble finding employment because they have been labeled with the stigma "criminal." Employers expect applicants to report criminal convictions, but then they frequently refuse to hire those who do. Seeing little choice if they are to survive, former inmates frequently end up again committing crimes and, if caught, are reinstitutionalized. This pattern is reflected in statistics that show very high rates of **recidivism,** that is, the return to prison of persons who have already been there. For example, in 1989, 78.5 percent of males and 68.6 percent of females in prison had previously been sentenced to probation or jailed for other offenses (U.S. Department of Justice, 1992: 625). Their conviction for additional criminal behavior simply serves to confirm for employers the wisdom of not hiring those labeled criminal in the first place.

Resistance to Being Labeled Deviant for One's Being

Obviously, it is one thing to resist a label like "criminal" or "mentally ill" that is imposed in response to one's behavior but something else again to resist being labeled deviant on the basis of one's very *being*. As we mentioned earlier, certain categories of people are often defined and treated by dominant groups as "the other." The dominant group views itself as normal and the other as deviant by definition. Resistance to being labeled deviant often requires that persons who make up the other openly question the legitimacy of the dominant group's judgments and assertions about them.

For example, gay men and lesbians who stay "in the closet" do so largely because of the discriminatory treatment they know they otherwise will have to endure, not because they are gay. This discriminatory treatment follows a labeling process in which the dominant group—heterosexuals—defines homosexuals as unnatural creatures, freaks of nature, and perverts. Gay resistance to being considered the other, as inferiors deserving of oppression, includes questioning the accuracy and legitimacy of the dominant group's stereotypes and assertions. Gay males and lesbians are people who differ from heterosexuals only in their sexual orientation. The stigma of being homosexual is fought by emphasizing that being different is not the same as being inferior.

Likewise, people with disabilities remain socially and economically marginalized not because of their disability but because of discriminatory and exclusionary attitudes and practices on the part of the able-bodied. People with disabilities are, by definition, considered to be deviant, or the other, by many members of the able-bodied majority. From the perspective

In efforts to combat the label "deviant," many gay males and lesbians have openly demonstrated on behalf of their own and others' rights to come "out of the closet" without suffering harassment and discrimination. The marchers at a Richmond, Virginia, Gay Pride Day assert their presence and intention to remain "out."

of this dominant group, people with disabilities are less-than-whole people. They are missing important physical or mental attributes that would render them decidedly "normal" human beings. Thus, the disability rights movement has emphasized the importance of using the term "people with disabilities," as opposed to "disabled people." Such individuals are people first, just like everyone else. What they have in common with the able-bodied is far more significant than the differences associated with a disability. Again, being different is not the same as being inferior.

In the struggle to resist and overcome the label "deviant," some groups defined as the other have been more successful than others. The African Americans' civil rights movement and the women's movement have operated for some time and can cite substantial victories. The disability rights movement is much more recent, but it has made some important strides in combating discrimination, as have groups supporting rights and protections for older persons. The gay rights movement has been less successful. The ignorance and hostility of those who impose the "deviant" label are just too deep. Gay rights activists must also contend with groups who strongly oppose homosexuality on the basis of religious doctrines. But this movement too has had some notable breakthroughs.

Finally, poor people suffer more silently than most who are victimized by the "deviant" label. Despite the large size of the nation's poverty population—some 39 million people in 1993—it too is defined and treated as the other by many people in the United States. The nonpoor often define poor people as deviants whose economic circumstances alone are sufficient to call their character into question (see Mead, 1992). (A former welfare recipient describes her experiences in the accompanying box.) The magnitude and diversity of individuals who live at the economic margins, as well as the shifting membership within this group, complicate efforts to organize resistance. For many poor people, a sense of fatalism and hopelessness contributes to political stagnation; they simply accept the dominant view that they are at heart inferior by nature in comparison to their class superiors. Resistance to being defined as the other and being negatively treated thus is not as visible among poor people as it is among other groups.

EXPLANATIONS FOR DEVIANT BEHAVIOR

Why do people engage in behavior that violates norms? How can we explain deviant behavior? Sociologists and other social scientists have proposed many different types of explanations for such behavior: physiological, psychological, social-psychological, and sociological (Liska, 1987). Much attention has been focused on why people engage in illegal acts, so our discussion will emphasize criminal behavior over other forms of deviance.

Physiological, or biological, **explanations** argue that deviant behavior is rooted in some type of physical peculiarity or malfunction. Or perhaps the proclivity to engage in the behavior in question is inherited and resides in the genes. **Psychological explanations** hold that deviant behavior is an expression of psychological problems or unusual personality traits. Such

Some people are defined as deviant simply because of who they are: their very being falls outside the norms. In the article below, a young woman describes the shame and degradation she was made to feel as a "welfare woman." Many people who are not poor view welfare recipients as immoral and thus undeserving of sympathy or help. Increasingly, it seems, recipients of welfare are being treated somewhat like criminals.

In my office one morning, one of the secretaries said President Clinton should "make welfare women work for their check" instead of just "sitting around, collecting." Everyone (and there were 13 others) wholeheartedly agreed. Except me. I would like to know why a homemaker with a husband is defended as having the "hardest job in the world" while a woman on welfare with no man helping her raise the children, no man bringing home a paycheck, is just "sitting around."

Seven years ago, I was a "welfare woman"—not the nasty, racist stereotype, but more like a typical welfare recipient: a white woman in her early thirties with three children. (Actually the average aid recipient only has one.) I had married young and was abandoned after 14 years by a husband who—rather than pay child support—quit his job and left the state. I remember the move into our new "home": a ten- by eight-foot hovel with no heat, a rotting carpet, and swarms of maggots. I remember that no matter how frugal I was, by the third week of every month I ended up out of money and out of food, wondering how we would make it till the first of the month and the next meager check.

That is not me any longer. Eventually, a friend helped me break into a well-paid profession, and I've had a good job for three years now. Nobody at my office knows what I used to be. And I would die of shame if they found out.

Shame is not what I want to feel. Shame is what society wants welfare women to feel. Shame is what the intake worker wanted me to feel when she asked not "Who is the father of your children?" but "Do you know who the father of your children is?" Shame is what the grocery store patrons snickering behind me wanted me to feel as the clerk tore out my food stamps and laid them on the counter. Shame is what I felt last year when the licensing board that oversees my profession found out that I had once been on welfare. They gave me a notice saying they might dismiss me for "moral turpitude." They said I could keep working if I wrote a statement saying how sorry I was for going on welfare,

problems or traits often stem from one's experiences with family members and other persons in a position to influence psychological development.

Social-psychological explanations look at the influence of people's immediate social environment on their thinking and behavior. This environment encompasses the people with whom one associates in the neighborhood, at school, or in the workplace. While psychological explanations might view deviant behavior as evidence of a personality deficiency, social-psychological explanations might emphasize the role played by peer-group influences. Finally, **sociological explanations** examine the ways in which a society is structured and the demands it makes upon its members. Such explanations stress that the factors contributing to deviant behavior may lie well outside the control of the individuals and groups engaging in it. In this sense, the deviant may be considered to a certain degree a victim of circumstances.

"When did it become a crime to be poor?"

how it was I came to think I had to do such a thing, how I now knew it was a mistake. I wrote it.

And now the public is coming to see collecting welfare as not only immoral but *criminal.* Los Angeles County is now testing a program that would require all AFDC recipients to be fingerprinted. Two counties in New York State are *already* fingerprinting people who get other forms of public assistance. And other "reformers" back a plan to make welfare women do community service jobs—the same work that is assigned to those convicted of a crime. That's not reform, it's punishment. Why treat welfare women like criminals? When did it become a crime to be poor?

I'm not saying we don't need welfare reform. I think we do. But instead of Clinton's proposed two-year cutoff, why not allow someone to collect for six years? This would give her time to get additional schooling (should she choose to) and would allow her children to become school age. And instead of keeping welfare payments so low a woman is forced to commit what they call fraud (doing child care for neighbors or housecleaning on the side), give her enough so that she can get by without having to worry about getting thrown out on the street.

And child care. When I went on welfare I got a flier that promised subsidized child care if I got a job. I got a job. Then I found out that more than 700 families were on the waiting list. I asked a welfare worker how long it would take for my name to come up. She laughed.

I was hired at that job for $7 an hour: $4 of it went to child care, $1 went to taxes. This left a net pay of $2 an hour or $288 a month, about half of what I had been getting from AFDC. I had no choice but to quit. Every time I tried to get off welfare, I was faced with the same dilemma: low-paying jobs and high-cost child care.

I know a woman who lives with her two small children in a one-room apartment in the worst part of town. She never gets help; she can't afford a baby-sitter so she never gets out. I said to her, "You must be going nuts in here with the kids all the time with no breaks." She said, "No. I get welfare. I look at this as my job."

There you are. Why can't society look at raising children as an important job? And why can't it stop penalizing poor women who do that job?

Source: Ginna Tessier, "Whose Welfare?" *Ms.*, March–April 1994, p. 96.

In pointing out the different types of explanations and categorizing them as we have, we are oversimplifying to some extent. No single explanation can account for all deviant behavior, and none of the types of explanations is silly or irrelevant. One could argue that for each different expression of deviance, one particular type of explanation and not another will be most appropriate.

For example, certain forms of mental illness, such as schizophrenia, are thought to be linked to physiological traits. Substance abuse may in many cases be a form of psychological escapism, a way of relieving stress or combating depression. Peers not only may teach novices the skills needed to successfully commit crimes but may provide informal pressures that compel them to engage in repeated criminal acts. A society that fails to deal successfully with economic recessions and the loss of jobs will foster frustration and anger on the part of the unemployed that are reflected in high rates of spouse and child abuse. Notice how we shifted from one type of explanation to another in commenting on the possible causes of different types of deviant behavior.

Obviously, the nature of the explanation that one finds most useful for a particular form of deviant behavior will considerably affect one's approach to solutions. If higher rates of spouse and child abuse are "caused" by breakdowns in our economic system, then the way to address this deviant behavior is not simply to pass stricter laws and parcel out harsher punishments but also to improve the workings of the economic system.

There is, however, a popular tendency toward **reductionism** when most people think about explanations for deviant behavior. That is, people are quick to reduce explanations to the psychological or even the physiological level. Thus, if some individuals are assaulting their spouses and children, there must be "something wrong with them." Since most people do not abuse their family members, the deviant behavior must stem from defects or deficiencies in the abusers. Sociologists tend to be very leery of reductionist explanations when they are offered dogmatically and without reasonable consideration of other explanatory factors, such as the impact of social-group memberships or the effects of societal-level factors. In the next sections we shall consider the different types of explanations in more detail, providing additional illustrations.

Physiological Explanations

Being deviant in terms of one's behavior implies being different from others in some way. Why, then, could deviants not be different from everyone else in terms of their physiological characteristics? The search for biological traits that would distinguish persons engaging in deviant behavior from everyone else has gone on for a long time and encompassed a variety of behaviors. Social scientists have explored the possibility that the propensity for criminal behavior is inherited. They have even tried to correlate it with physical features, such as head shape and body build, or chromosomal differences (Fishbein, 1990). Physiological causes have been explored for other forms of deviance as well, including mental illness, alcoholism, homosexuality, and suicide.

A relationship does exist between physiological characteristics and deviant behavior in some areas. For example, brain damage due to aging or alcohol abuse can cause people to act in unusual ways, as in the case of Alzheimer's disease and alcoholic psychosis. There are indications that for some people heredity may play a role in acquiring an addiction to alcohol (Goodwin, 1988). A few researchers have begun to claim progress on uncovering possible physiological causes for homosexual behavior. Some perpetrators of violent crimes have suffered from brain tumors to which their behavior may be linked. But for most types of behavior that are considered deviant, physiological explanations thus far have proved inadequate.

While we no doubt will learn more in the future about the relationship between physiological characteristics and behavior, sociologists and other social scientists tend to dislike its reductionist character and are likely to point to what it leaves unexamined. People not only have bodies; they have minds. Explanations for deviant behavior must take into account people's thought processes. People also have friends, relatives, and associates whose behavior bears upon their own. People are social animals whose biographies are very much forged by their position within society and by the changing nature of society itself. Even if it can be scientifically proved that physiology is involved in some expressions of deviant behavior, is it not also likely that nonphysiological factors have something to do with the behavior as well?

Psychological Explanations

One of the most influential psychological explanations for a wide range of deviant behavior is based upon the work of Sigmund Freud (Clinard and Meier, 1992: 53–54). Freud argued that mental illness stemmed primarily from unconscious conflicts. Depending on their nature, such conflicts could lead individuals to violate social norms.

Following Freud's lead, many psychologists have searched for personality traits that distinguish the deviant from the nondeviant (Clinard and Meier, 1992: 54–57). For example, while some researchers have argued that alcoholism is a disease, possibly inherited, and thus best understood in terms of a physiological explanation, others have argued that there is such a thing as an "alcoholic personality" with distinct traits. Researchers have even reached a rough consensus on what the traits of this personality are. However, the traits in question can also be found within the nonalcoholic population.

Psychological explanations for deviant behavior often founder in the face of the fact that there do not seem to be any psychological traits that distinguish deviants from nondeviants. For example, mental illness does not seem to be any more prevalent within the population of known criminals than it is among persons not known to have committed criminal acts.

More broadly speaking, psychological explanations for deviant behavior are limited to inferences about what goes on in the minds of those defined as deviant. Such explanations are at times criticized as reductionist, since often too little attention is paid to the nature and relative importance of social influences on deviant behavior. While it is very important that researchers continue to study the role psychological factors play in various forms of deviance, they should not do so at the cost of ignoring the possible role of the social environment.

Social-Psychological Explanations

We are all constantly aware of the people around us and the fact that they are conscious of what we are doing in their presence. Social-psychological explanations for deviant behavior are based upon people's sensitivity to their immediate social environment. Such explanations suggest that others help shape the behavior that comes to be defined as deviant (Hagan, 1994: chap. 2). Let us look at some examples of social-psychological explanations.

Sociologists interested in crime and juvenile delinquency often focus on the associates of persons engaging in deviant behavior. One approach, known as **differential association theory,** posits that individuals learn to engage in deviant behavior by communicating and interacting with those already disposed to do so (Sutherland and Cressey, 1974: 75–77). Novices are taught the skills and techniques involved in committing crimes and are shown why such behavior is worthwhile, and they are encouraged to adopt others' rationalization for flaunting the law.

Take the example of marijuana use. In his now-classic research on how people become users of this drug, Howard S. Becker notes that deviant behavior does not necessarily require a preexisting psychological motivation to engage in the act (1963: 41–78). Rather, he argues, the reverse can be true: an individual may be urged into certain behavior and only then become motivated to do it again. People are usually encouraged to try marijuana by experienced users with whom they are associating. They may agree to do so simply out of curiosity. Someone who has never used the substance must first be taught the way to use it, the circumstances under which it is best used, and the kinds of sensations to watch for. The novice must also be taught to interpret these sensations as pleasurable.

An individual may have to try marijuana several times with experienced users before learning to enjoy its effects. After the initiation period, these associates continue to be important in providing access to the substance and to others who will share in behavior that is ordinarily conducted in secrecy because of its illegality. A person who does not associate with marijuana users, or who associates with people who condemn such behavior, is unlikely to ever try this particular deviant behavior. Becker's analysis thus underscores the important role group membership can play in encouraging deviant behavior. Explanations that focus only on the psychological characteristics of marijuana users would miss the importance of this factor.

Related to differential association is a second social-psychological explanation, **containment theory** (Reckless, 1961). It proceeds from this question: Why doesn't much more deviant behavior take place in society? The answer, according to containment theory, is that people encounter both external and internal controls that *contain* the temptation toward deviance. External controls are such things as community standards for behavior and the institutions that function to uphold them. Internal controls exist within the individual. They result from socialization experiences people undergo through the family, education, and religion, and they supply the individual with self-control capabilities. People who engage in deviant acts are said to do so through a lack of sufficient self-control or the absence of clear community standards and social pressures to conform to them.

Containment theory is an example of a broader body of thinking known as **control theory** (see Hirschi, 1969). This theoretical orientation stresses that deviance is due to the absence of social control or other constraints on behavior. It assumes that human nature contains flaws that lead people to act in ways that are "bad" and that it is necessary to control these innate tendencies if society is to function. Those social scientists who favor control theory tend to differ on where the most important sources of control originate. In containment theory, as noted above, the sources are both external and internal to the individual.

A different type of social-psychological explanation suggests that deviant behavior is the result of **social reinforcement.** In this view, humans, as a species, are psychologically motivated to seek out pleasure and avoid pain, but their behavior is directed by past experiences and speculations as to the likely outcomes of future behavior (Akers, 1985). If people feel that the rewards from acts of deviance outweigh the punishments (or potential punishments), they are likely to engage in such acts. From this point of view, people who commit crimes, engage in substance abuse, or take their own lives do so because this behavior has been reinforced in their minds as desirable by the calculus of punishment and rewards. The criminal or substance abuser may have found that the deviant behavior was rewarding enough to be initiated or repeated, while the suicide victim may have found that life was punishing enough to be avoided.

Social-psychological explanations consider the behavior of people within their immediate social environment. They explore the nature and relative importance of social influences. Yet social-psychological explanations have critical shortcomings. In the case of differential association, there are many forms of deviance to which the theory does not seem to apply. In most murders, for example, a person impulsively kills a relative, friend, or acquaintance. The murderer usually has never associated with others committing similar acts and has never murdered before.

Similarly, although containment theory may make a lot of intuitive sense, there seem to be many instances for which it is less than useful. For instance, a highly successful, middle-aged local business owner—a family man well known and respected throughout his community for his philanthropy and acts of community service, suddenly shoots his equally accomplished and socially involved wife and then takes his own life (Brown, 1993). How does one explain such sudden, seemingly impulsive behavior on the part of someone who by all criteria should be "contained"?

Theories of deviant behavior that stress the importance of reinforcement (through rewards and punishment) lack empirical support. They tend to be applied after the fact: "He must have done that because he found it rewarding." Such theories cannot be used in predicting who is likely to engage in deviant behavior, since people differ greatly in terms of what they are likely to find rewarding.

Nonetheless, social-psychological explanations are broader and encompass more factors bearing on deviant behavior than explanations that stop short at the physiological or psychological level. In that sense, proponents of social-psychological explanations are usually able to avoid charges of reductionism. Yet some sociologists argue that social-psychological explanations do not go far enough. They suggest that features of society itself may make deviant behavior "normal" (Hagan, 1994: chap. 2). Sociological explanations address such features of society. Let us take up these explanations next.

Sociological Explanations

Deviance and the Opportunity Structure   Perhaps the best-known socio-logical explanation bearing on deviant behavior is Robert Merton's **oppor-tunity structure theory** (1957: 131–160). Merton noted that U.S. society places enormous stress on the pursuit of material success. Indeed, he sees this success as a cultural goal that most people share in common. It is unusual for individuals to say that they have no interest in being better off economically or for privileged persons to express no interest in holding on to their economic status.

Along with the cultural goal of material success, Merton points out, there are socially approved means for pursuing this goal. These include working, saving, and investing. Most people have access to and make use of these means in their quest for material success. But what happens in cases in which the means and the goal do not coincide? In Merton's view, the stage is set for individuals to engage in a *mode of adaptation* that can entail deviant behavior.

For example, people may choose the mode of adaptation Merton called *innovation*—they make money illegally. Thus, a society whose culture stresses material success, but which offers only some members the means to pursue it, is a society in which we should expect to see deviant behavior in the form of burglaries, robberies, drug trafficking, prostitution, and other types of crime.

Still other people, faced with a gap between the cultural goal of material success and access to the means, may reject both. Choosing the mode of adaptation Merton called *retreatism*, they may adopt an alternative lifestyle as a vagrant or hobo, pursue altered states of consciousness through sub-stance abuse, or even commit suicide. Retreatism entails walking away from a reality that just does not seem workable.

In contrast to retreatism, the mode of adaptation Merton termed *rebel-lion* involves inventing new goals and new means of achieving them. The goals are likely to be quite different from, or even radically counter to, those that dominate the existing society. Persons who dedicate their lives to revolutionary organizations or transformative social movements (see Chapter 9) are adapting through rebellion.

Finally, in Merton's scheme of things, the means-goal gap may result in the mode of adaptation he calls *ritualism*. Seeing the goal of material suc-cess as hopeless, people abandon it; nonetheless, they go through the motions of working each day, rationalizing that the means are worth pursu-ing in and of themselves. Since jobs that do not pay well are often also unre-warding in other ways, this can prove to be a rather hollow rationalization.

Merton suggests that since most people are able to utilize socially approved means to pursue material success, they have little reason to engage in deviant behavior. Yet for others access to these means is prob-lematic. The opportunity structure creates conditions that pressure some people into modes of adaptation that may violate social norms. Much deviant behavior, from this point of view, originates outside the individ-ual's control. Its origins lie in the characteristic features of society itself. To reduce such deviance, society must undergo change.

Many people internalize our society's cultural goal of material success but face seemingly insurmountable obstacles when they attempt to attain it. Such persons may turn to illicit activities, such as prostitution, in a struggle to better their financial situations.

Merton's analysis is very compelling. It provides a larger context for understanding the role of social-psychological factors in producing deviance. Its critics are likely to point out, however, that it does not tell us why people adopt any one particular mode of adaptation. Why, for example, in the United States, are there so many thieves and so few revolutionaries? And why do some people of affluence, who have access to socially approved means for material success, commit financial crimes? And how do we explain criminal behavior on the part of the executives of large corporations?

Merton's theory seems to contain a bias toward deviant behavior as exhibited by the excluded and downtrodden, while saying little about deviance on the part of elites (Coleman, 1989; Simon and Eitzen, 1990). It is also highly tailored to cultural and social conditions in the United States. Nonetheless, in pointing to the influence of a society's cultural values and structure on its members' behaviors, Merton has greatly enriched sociological thinking about the origins of deviant behavior.

Deviance and Capitalism   A different, but related, type of sociological explanation for deviant behavior involves the concept of *alienation*. This explanation has its origins in the work of Karl Marx, a nineteenth-century German sociologist and economic thinker. Contemporary sociologists borrowing from his ideas can be termed neo-Marxists (McGuire and McQuarie, 1994). The focus of the **Marxist theory of deviance** is on the demands that an industrial capitalist society imposes on people.

An industrial capitalist society is one in which the means of producing goods and services (factories, farms, offices, mines, railroads, communication systems) are privately owned. Ownership tends to be concentrated in the hands of a few, a group called the capitalist class, or *bourgeoisie.* Most people, in order to survive, must sell their labor to members of the capitalist class in return for wages. Marx calls this working-class group the *proletariat.* A problem arises because the self-interests of the capitalist class and those of the working class are in opposition.

The capitalist class wants to maximize profits in order to expand its property holdings and further enrich itself. Capitalists thus hold wages down to the bare minimum and organize industrial production in ways that are often physically and psychologically costly to their workers. In contrast, the working class wants adequate wages and working conditions. But, since they are not owners, members of this class lack the power to get their needs met. Consequently, they experience a sense of **alienation,** or estrangement, from their labor. This is extremely damaging because, in the neo-Marxist view, labor is the principal vehicle through which the human species expresses itself and seeks fulfillment.

Suffering from low wages, sporadic bouts of unemployment, and a sense of alienation, members of the working class are driven into behaviors that are defined as deviant. Crimes of violence, property offenses, and drug crimes are symptoms of the economic oppression and alienation they experience. The structure and workings of society—in this case, its capitalist features—turn the majority of its members into victims. Acting out their alienation from a system that thwarts their fundamental needs, members of the working class engage in activities that are harmful to themselves and/or to others (Taylor, Walton, and Young, 1973, 1975).

Neo-Marxists find that this sociological explanation for deviant behavior fits the United States (see Quinney, 1979). The U.S. capitalist economy is characterized by chronic bouts of unemployment, poverty-level standards of living for the jobless and low-wage families, and workplace alienation, as indicated by worker tardiness, absenteeism, turnover, and acts of sabotage (Sprouse, 1992). Neo-Marxists see economic oppression and alienation as the main reason for the high incidence of crimes of violence, property crimes, and drug crimes at the lower levels of the U.S. class structure. In the neo-Marxist interpretation, capitalists' white-collar crimes, such as unethical and illegal business practices, are symptoms indicating that members of the capitalist class also experience a sense of alienation, even as they accept the logic of capitalism.

Marx argued that workers in industrial capitalist societies, when pushed to the limit, would develop a revolutionary consciousness and join in social movements to overthrow capitalism. In its place they would construct a socialist society in which the workers owned and controlled the means of production and in which goods and services were produced to serve the needs of the people, not to enrich the few. Contrary to what many Marxist analysts have predicted, socialist revolutions have not taken place in industrial capitalist societies, such as the United States. Revolutionary movements seeking to build socialism *have* arisen in some underdeveloped, agriculturally based societies. These movements were successful in such widely different settings as the People's Republic of China, Cuba, and the Soviet Union. Yet, to varying degrees, deviant behavior has been found to exist in these and other socialist societies.

Thus, while the demands made by capitalism may well drive many people into deviant behaviors, the dynamics of capitalism need not always be present for such behaviors to occur. The organization and operation of socialist economic systems may also contribute to deviance, a phenomenon that relatively little sociological research has explored.

DO SOCIETIES NEED DEVIANT BEHAVIOR?

Virtually all societies, however they may differ from one another, contain behavior that comes to be defined as deviant. In light of this fact, some sociologists have suggested that perhaps societies *need* deviant behavior. Rather than viewing deviant behavior negatively, perhaps we should see it as beneficial and functional to society. This **functionalist theory of deviance** was first put forth by the French sociologist Émile Durkheim (1964).

Durkheim pointed out that deviance is not simply found in poorly organized, unstable societies. Rather, the best of societies (using whatever criteria one wishes) contain deviant behavior. Crime of one sort or another, for example, can be found everywhere. According to Durkheim, the occurrence of crime is actually a service to society; the anger and dismay crime generates function to bring people together and strengthen their solidarity as a group. The deviance reminds people of their commonly shared morality. As a sociologist who was interested in the bases of social order, Durkheim saw deviant behavior as contributing to societal stability. Without periodic opportunities to collectively condemn unwanted behavior, it would be harder to reinforce social order. In effect, deviant behavior functions as an internal threat against which societal members must rally.

Sociologist Kai Erikson elaborated on Durkheim's thoughts in *Wayward Puritans* (1966). Erikson uses the term "boundaries" to refer to the norms that evolve in human groups:

> Human behavior can vary over an enormous range, but each community draws a symbolic set of parentheses around a certain segment of that range and limits its own activities within that narrower zone. These parentheses, so to speak, are the community's boundaries (Erikson, 1966: 10).

Since the boundaries, or norms, are not always apparent, undergo change, and yet still must be internalized by new group members, some way must exist to demonstrate what they are. In Erikson's view, deviant behavior serves this function:

> The deviant is a person whose activities have moved outside the margins of the group, and when the community calls him to account for that vagrancy it is making a statement about the nature and placement of its boundaries. It is

declaring how much variability and diversity can be tolerated within the group before it begins to lose its distinctive shape, its unique identity (Erikson, 1966: 11).

Thus Erikson sees the actions of *policing agents* as important in demonstrating where a group's norms, or boundaries, lie. Policing agents take many forms and include criminal justice systems, the psychiatric profession, military institutions, and religious bodies. These agents, confronting people who wander outside society's boundaries, show everyone where the boundaries are.

Erikson points out that much of what we call "news" in the media concerns deviant behavior and its consequences. Many of the programs that appear on entertainment television also focus on deviant behavior. In recent years a number of documentary-like programs have centered on police activities, most wanted criminals, and unsolved crimes. Erikson's argument is that the media play an important role in reinforcing societal norms by showing people repeatedly testing and enforcing them.

Erikson suggests that deviant behavior is so important to societal stability that society actually encourages it. The failure of prisons to rehabilitate and of mental hospitals to cure actually ensures a steady supply of deviants who will violate norms, generate activity on the part of policing agents, and regularly reinvigorate the majority's sense of the boundaries of socially acceptable behavior. Indeed, the segregation of deviants into such institutions ensures their continued alienation from society. Moreover, while institutionalized, deviants have the opportunity to learn new styles and techniques of norm violation from one another, an education that may assist some in pursuing a "career" of deviant behavior (Erikson, 1966: 13–15).

Erikson's ideas do not really address the sources of the behavior that violates norms, but these sources are a major concern of sociologists. Nor does his implication that deviance may be beneficial, or functional, to society address the enormous harm done by many deviant acts. But he does force us to think about whether a minimal degree of norm violation by a society's members is unavoidable if that society is to operate successfully. If we accept Erikson's ideas, then we can view deviant behavior as a positive force that makes important contributions to society.

DEVIANCE AND SOCIAL CHANGE

There is another perspective from which deviant behavior may be viewed as a positive force. People may intentionally violate norms to draw attention to societal conditions they consider wrong and to bring about or increase pressures for social change. History is filled with examples of people "going against the system" even when it meant making enormous sacrifices of their livelihoods or even their lives.

Within the civil rights movement in our society, many social activists violated norms and risked sanctions as they sought to bring about change (Williams, 1987). Consider the importance we now attach to the refusal of a Montgomery, Alabama, seamstress, Mrs. Rosa Parks, to give up her seat in a segregated city bus to a white man. On the day this occurred, in 1955, the norms governing appropriate behavior for African Americans in the nation's South included a detailed and intricate body of rules of interracial etiquette (see Doyle, 1971). African Americans, for example, had to enter the front of the bus to pay and then had to go back outside and enter the rear of the bus to sit in the "colored only" section. Violating such rules, some unspoken and others written into law, invited negative sanctions from members of the dominant white majority.

Mrs. Parks's action, and her subsequent arrest, sparked a major boycott of public transportation in Montgomery that proved successful. The buses were desegregated. The Montgomery bus boycott demonstrated to the nation that segregation could be fought by collective grass-roots action. From that point the norms governing black-white relations underwent a sustained attack, including an all-out assault on such common features of everyday life as "whites only" restrooms, schools, bus station entrances, water fountains, cemetery sections, phone booths, motels, blood banks, lunchrooms, movie theater seats, swimming pools, and beaches.

By the early 1960s African Americans and their supporters, including many whites, were flagrantly contesting the norms of segregation through peaceful marches, boycotts, and sit-ins across the South. Groups such as the National Association for the Advancement of Colored People, the Con-

Sometimes people have to defy existing norms to apply pressure on dominant groups who are resisting social change. The people in the police wagon shown here were protesting 1960s segregation policies that allowed restaurant service to Cold War leader Nikita Khrushchev of the Soviet Union but denied access to African Americans on the basis of their skin color.

gress of Racial Equality, the Student Nonviolent Coordinating Committee, and Dr. Martin Luther King's Southern Christian Leadership Conference provided leadership, legal assistance, and other resources to help advance what had become a major social movement.

Many southern civil rights workers and other advocates of the movement were targeted for negative sanctions, such as harassment, loss of their jobs, and threats or acts of violence directed against themselves and their families. Widely condemned acts of terrorism occurred, including the church bombing in Birmingham, Alabama, that killed four African American children and the murder of three young civil rights workers in Mississippi (a black state resident and two white New Yorkers). These acts were the response of whites who felt their world shattering as the civil rights movement, building on its day-by-day successes, overturned laws permitting racial segregation.

Deviant behavior that defies the imposition of norms by others occurs in many settings. The civil rights movement, for example, has helped inspire others to challenge "business as usual." The women's movement, the disability rights movement, and the gay rights movement are but three examples. Within the gay rights movement, an organization known as ACT UP became concerned with the slowness of AIDS research and drug trials and angered over the high costs of drugs used to delay the onset of AIDS. ACT UP has staged dramatic demonstrations to harass and embarrass government and pharmaceutical industry officials (Handleman, 1990).

But not all change requires a social movement. Sometimes an individual willing to take risks for what he or she believes in can have an important impact. Even if the person is unsuccessful in bringing about change, efforts in this direction can inspire others. A good example is that of **whistle-blowers** within corporate or governmental settings. These people, at great risk to their jobs and career chances, speak out to the mass media about such issues as unsafe practices, unethical and illegal acts, wasteful spending, fraudulent policies, payroll padding, and incompetence.

For example, in 1991 a technician at Tennessee's Oak Ridge National Laboratory, a federal nuclear facility managed by Martin Marietta Energy Systems, appeared on a CBS news program to "blow the whistle" about suspiciously high rates of cancer among the laboratory's workers. The technician himself had recently undergone treatment for colon cancer. In his view, the cancers were caused by unsafe working conditions that exposed workers to dangerous radiation. Managers at the facility retaliated by assigning the technician to "a room filled with toxic and radioactive chemicals" and ordering him "to perform useless work there" ("Whistle-Blowing," 1993). But he was successful in helping to draw attention to the issue of worker health and safety at nuclear facilities. He also won a legal action requiring compensation for the way he was mistreated by the laboratory's managers.

Often a battle for credibility emerges when the whistle-blower's superiors attempt to cast discredit on the disclosures and tarnish the whistle-blower's reputation (Hilts, 1993). The whistle-blower's actions violate norms that call for organizational loyalty, communication only through proper channels, and maintenance of confidentiality of internal information. Such actions reverberate in the executive suite. What if all employees got it into their heads to act like this? Hence the employers are likely to engage in social control through negative sanctions to eliminate this deviant behavior.

CONCLUSION

Sociologists have devoted considerable attention to the topic of deviant behavior. In recent years the notion that such behavior is a social construction has opened up new questions and issues. Why is some behavior considered deviant and not other behavior? Who or what determines deviancy? While there are no definitive answers, in our discussion we stressed the significance of norms as reference points against which people judge one another's behavior. We also noted, however, that in a heterogeneous society—one in which people differ along such lines as class, race and ethnicity, gender, sexual orientation, age, and able-bodiedness—norms will differ at least somewhat from group to group. As people's backgrounds, experiences, self-interests, and needs differ, so will the standards they use to define the expected and obligatory behaviors of others.

The distribution of power in society influences which behaviors will be defined as deviant. Whole social categories of people may even be defined as deviant because they differ from dominant groups in some way. Dominant groups tend to view those they dominate as "the other," as people who are deviant by their very being. For example, the poor are often defined as deviant. It is not their behavior but the very fact that they exist at all that allows the more affluent to judge them as deviant. Being materially successful is "normal"; being poor violates the norm. Since dominant groups frequently impose the "deviant" label on people who do not want it (because it portrays them as inferior people, because it is unjustified), there is often resistance to the labeling process. Again, the more powerful the group doing the labeling, the more difficult resistance becomes.

Behavior that is defined as deviant does have causes. Sociologists have long been interested in why a wide range of such behaviors occurs. For the most part, explanations that focus principally on physiological or psychological shortcomings of persons who deviate have been of limited value. Most people engaging in deviant behavior (which in theory could be any behavior defined as such) are similar to those not engaging in such behavior. It has proved impossible to find any single characteristic that distinguishes persons who violate norms from those who do not.

On the other hand, social-psychological and sociological approaches have offered more promise. Such explanations view people as existing within a context that itself is very important. They examine the influence of group memberships on people's behavior and explore how people are affected by particular features of society over which they have little control. Sociological explanations raise the question of whether there are certain societal conditions conducive to the appearance of particular kinds of behavior. Depending upon the distribution of power in a society, these behaviors may or may not then be defined as deviant.

Since deviant behavior exists in all societies (although societies differ on what behavior is deviant), there arises the issue of whether societies need deviance. Some observers argue that norm violation and its consequences remind people of what the norms are, thus encouraging necessary social stability and order. In this sense deviant behavior may make a positive contribution to societal functioning. From another angle, societies benefit from those individuals who rise up against norms that support harmful and unjust social conditions. Harsh inequalities, discriminatory practices, and other conditions often linked to the unequal distribution of power seem to call forth counterefforts. From the revolutionary to the whistle-blower, people challenge what those more powerful would prefer be considered normal (or not be the subject of consideration at all). Such forms of deviant behavior can produce, and have produced, important social changes, even while entailing significant risks for the individuals seeking to overturn the status quo.

Thus, in the sociological imagination deviant behavior conjures up far more than bizarre acts or perverted behaviors (some people confuse the word "deviant" with "deviate," a term used to refer to a person who practices sexual perversions). Deviance is a concept that deserves to be at the very center of our efforts to understand social life, since it is tied so closely to other key concepts such as social structure, culture, socialization, inequality, and social change.

Finally, you should consider the importance of the concept of deviance to an understanding of your own biography. Try asking yourself some questions: To what degree do you consider yourself a conformist? Why? What norms have you ever violated? What behaviors have you engaged in that were labeled deviant? Are you a member of a social category that is subject to treatment as "the other"? Has being labeled deviant, in response to your behavior or your being, affected your life chances? If so, how? In answering these questions, you will be using a concept important to the exercise of the sociological imagination.

THINKING CRITICALLY

1. Discuss the role played by power in definitions of what behavior will be considered deviant. Are people who have power able to "get away with" behaviors that might be considered norm violations if engaged in by the less powerful? Why? Give examples.
2. We pointed out that what is considered deviant may differ from society to society, given that societies have different norms associated with their cultures. On the basis of other courses you have taken, experiences of your friends and family members, or observations you have made while traveling, discuss some examples of these differences and speculate about why they exist.
3. In Chapter 4 we discussed subcultures. Subcultures often have their own norms, which differ in various ways from those that prevail elsewhere in society. Are there norms that must not be violated within the

college student subculture? What are they? What happens to people who violate them, and why?

4. Are there circumstances in which you have felt that you were defined and treated as deviant simply on the basis of who you are rather than because of your behavior (for example, on the basis of your sex, class, race, sexual orientation, age, or state of able-bodiedness)? How did you feel, and why? How did you respond?

5. In the boxed article, a young woman describes the experiences she encountered as a result of being forced to rely on welfare. How can you explain the fact that some groups define the poor as deviant, even to the point of implying that being poor is comparable to criminality?

KEY TERMS

deviance, *244*
norms, *244*
social control, *245*
sanctions, *245*
negative sanctions, *245*
positive sanctions, *245*
social construction (of deviance), *246*
label, *246*
appearance norms, *249*
motherhood norms, *251*
stigma, *255*
recidivism, *255*
physiological explanations, *257*
psychological explanations, *257*

social-psychological explanations, *258*
sociological explanations, *258*
reductionism, *260*
differential association theory, *262*
containment theory, *262*
control theory, *262*
social reinforcement theory, *263*
opportunity structure theory, *264*
Marxist theory of deviance, *265*
alienation, *266*
functionalist theory of deviance, *267*
whistle-blowers, *270*

SUGGESTED READINGS

Peter Conrad and Joseph W. Schneider, *Deviance and Medicalization: From Badness to Sickness*, expanded ed. Philadelphia: Temple University Press, 1992. An insightful analysis of the growing tendency to define many individual behaviors that violate social norms as "disease" conditions requiring intervention by medical doctors or mental health professionals.

Nanette J. Davis and Clarice Stasz, *Social Control of Deviance: A Critical Perspective*. New York: McGraw-Hill, 1990. An examination of dominant groups' efforts to maintain social control over deviant behavior; stresses the concept of power and the ways it is used to uphold unjust social and political arrangements.

Susan Goodwillie (ed.), *Voices from the Future*. New York: Crown, 1993. A collection of interviews—conducted on the streets, in schools, and in shelters—in which children and teenagers talk openly and poignantly about the impact of the violence that is a central part of their lives.

John Hagan, *Crime and Disrepute.* Thousand Oaks, CA: Pine Forge Press, 1994. A concise overview of contemporary sociological literature focusing on both "crime in the streets" and "crime in the suites" of business and government.

William M. Kephart and William W. Zellner, *Extraordinary Groups: An Examination of Unconventional Lifestyles,* 4th ed. New York: St. Martin's Press, 1991. An examination of the beliefs, norms, and practices of various groups that have contributed to the cultural diversity of U.S. society, from the "Gypsy" Rom to the Jewish Hasidim.

SOCIAL CHANGE AND SOCIAL MOVEMENTS

*S*ocieties and cultures rarely stand still: they are frequently involved in a process of change, slow or rapid, incremental or radical. Social scientists have always been fascinated by the rapid changes that accompanied the Industrial Revolution in the mid- to late nineteenth century. Changes generated by political revolutions such as those in France, Russia, China, and Cuba are also a source of great interest to social scientists. Some of the questions the process of change inspires include these: What is social change? Why

9

does it occur? How does it occur? What forces and factors affect the direction and magnitude of social change? Are all social changes as dramatic as revolutions? What are the consequences and ramifications of social change? Does social change provide advantages and benefits to some and not to others? What is the impact of social change on various groups in society and on world relations? Is social change inevitable, or can we affect social change?

THE MEANING OF SOCIAL CHANGE

When sociologists talk about **social change,** they are referring to significant variations or alterations in social structures and cultures over time. Social change may occur on varying levels and in varying amounts of intensity. For example, **social reforms** are adjustments in the content of cultural patterns of behavior or normative systems, adjustments that do not fundamentally alter the social structure. Alterations in the U.S. tax laws—for example, to decrease income taxes of middle-income and poor families while increasing capital gains taxes on corporations—do not change the structure of society: corporations remain in control of the production of goods and services, and federal laws are still made by Congress. **Social revolutions,** on the other hand, are fundamental and radical upheavals of existing social structures. Revolutions sometimes involve bloody battles between identifiable organizations of armies, but this is not always the case. The Industrial Revolution, for example, fundamentally altered the processes of production and the power and control workers had over those processes, and therefore it changed institutions, roles, and statuses (see Thompson, 1966; Gutman, 1977). But it did not occur on a battlefield between clearly organized armies. The battlefield was the shop floor in the factories, and the conflict was initially between individual workers and owners (although, to be sure, the struggles in the labor movement that emerged many years later were at times quite bloody).

It is also useful to consider that some social change is **manifest.** In many cases a large or powerful group (not necessarily a majority) deliberately and consciously organizes a movement for change. For example, the colonists began the American Revolution to gain independence from Great Britain. The women's movement arose when women began pressing for social, political, and economic equality.

Other social change is **latent:** it is largely unrecognized and unintended. For example, the baby boom that occurred in the United States after World War II was not recognized until it was well under way. It produced a demographic "bubble" that had many consequences. Schools became overcrowded when that age cohort entered the education system, and the situation prompted a national scramble to build more schools and hire more teachers. Competition for jobs intensified as baby boomers entered the labor market, and by the 1980s unemployment and underemployment had become a greater possibility for more people. Baby boomers became a political force in the late 1960s and early 1970s when they participated in several social movements. The antiwar movement hastened an end to the Vietnam war. Critical analyses of the war, the military draft, and the political process raised by the antiwar movement also prompted a lowering of the legal voting age from 21 to 18. The growing women's movement gained women more access to higher education and better jobs. In turn, the new opportunities for women had the unintended consequence of reducing birth rates in the United States. When baby boomers retire early in the next century, they will impose great demands on the social security system. At that time the labor force will be much smaller and perhaps be unable to support those demands.

Explaining Social Change

How do we explain social change? Is it a natural, inevitable phenomenon? How much effect can we have on it? Is a society's social change propelled by forces within that society, or do external forces contribute to changes in all societies? What are the forces of global social change? Are these forces neutral and natural, or are they social constructions in response to the interests of particular groups?

Sociologists generally agree that whether it is manifest or latent, social change is an ongoing process; it is not a singular, discrete event in a vacuum of time and place. In our discussion of the baby boom, we have already seen that an initial social change may set the stage for later changes. Beyond this fact, there is wide disagreement over how to explain social change. Several perspectives attempt to explain it as a normal, natural force that is part of a stable social system. But another perspective views conflict as the catalyst for social change.

The Cyclical Perspective   Some sociologists see social change as a natural cycle of the rise and fall of social systems. We call this analysis the **cyclical perspective** (Sorokin, 1957; Pareto, 1963). In this view, societies are likened to an organism. Every society is presumed to pass naturally and inevitably through the same age phases as individual biological organisms (particularly the human being) pass through: infancy, childhood, adolescence, adulthood, old age, and, finally, decay and death. Oswald Spengler (1926) argued that each phase lasted a definite and predictable length of time for all societies. He suggested that all societies possess an internal biological clock determining their natural life span, which he believed to be a millennium (1,000 years).

However, we can document societies that have lasted beyond a millennium (such as Egypt, China, and India) and others that seem to perish "prematurely" (such as the Union of Soviet Socialist Republics, which lasted slightly more than half a century). Even when a society perishes, it is questionable whether we are, in fact, witnessing a "natural" death from old age. The division of Germany into the Federal Republic of Germany (FRG) and the German Democratic Republic (GDR) after World War II was a political act taken by the Allied countries to ensure that Germany would never again be an international threat. And the reunification of these two countries into a single Germany in 1989, effectively causing the demise of the GDR and FRG as independent nations, was also a political, not a natural, development.

Spengler's cyclical perspective also leaves little room for an examination of the effect of external forces on a given society's life span. For example, it ignores the role that invasion, war, annexation, exploitation, or genocide inflicted by other societies may play in hastening a society's death. More recent cyclical analyses of social change have sought to correct this limitation by examining societies' rise-and-decline patterns as part of a global system. For example, Paul Kennedy (1987) argued that some societies rise economically and politically while others around them decline, in large part because the ascending societies ultimately conquer the faltering ones. This type of rise-and-decline cycle is influenced by a society's economic production, its fiscal strength, and its military strength. Rising states tend to capitalize on technological developments to enhance and increase production, which increases the production of taxable wealth. This in turn provides the state with increased wealth to support military expansion, which facilitates the ability of rising states to conquer declining states.

Although Kennedy's analysis does recognize external factors that may affect societies' cycle of social change, it overemphasizes military conquest as an important factor in the rise and decline of states. Take the example of Japan's successful competition in the global market of the 1980s. Japan had capitalized on technological innovations to increase production, but it did not invest the state's revenues in military expansion, nor did it militarily conquer anyone. One might also argue that although the Soviet Union did not exploit technological innovation effectively in the 1980s, it did invest a great deal of its state revenues in military expansion, and yet it still declined without being militarily conquered. Both cases call Kennedy's analysis into question.

The Evolutionary Perspective Other sociologists favor an **evolutionary perspective** to explain social change. They share the cyclical perspective's assumption that societies are like organisms, but the evolutionary perspective likens social change to Darwin's notion of biological evolution. Societies go through a natural series of stages based on increasing complexity, propelled toward higher, more advanced, and developed states of existence. Thus, the evolutionary perspective favors a notion of progress, wherein each new stage of development is more advanced than the one before. All societies are believed to progress through the same stages in the same order while evolving into ever-higher forms (Durkheim, 1964; Comte, 1966). But whereas the cyclical perspective sees the death of a society as the natural end to the social life cycle, the evolutionary perspective makes no such presumption. Some societies might die off, but only as a result of "natural selection." Recent analyses argue that this natural selection is governed by a society's cultural inheritance of technological innovations, which permits a society to command greater control over its environment. Only those societies that invest in technological innovation will survive

(see Lenski, Lenski, and Nolan, 1991). That is, the "fittest" societies survive. Sociologists call this last argument **social Darwinism.**

281

Chapter 9

Social Change
and Social
Movements

The problem with social Darwinism is that it does not analyze the ways
societies might differ in their access to information and technology or the
role conquest plays in the demise of societies. Furthermore, the evolutionary perspective's presumption that all societies must pass through the
same stages in the same order, and that each successive stage is necessarily
more advanced, denies the unique histories societies may have. It assumes
that all societies have access to the same resources to achieve the same
levels of evolution. Its implicit use of Western nations as models of
advanced societies leaves out the possibility that non-Western societies
may be advanced as well. Social Darwinism does not address the possibility that societies may have "advanced" by taking advantage of resources
from the "less advanced" societies. We will return to this issue shortly.

The Equilibrium Perspective   Other sociologists believe social change
occurs as societies become more and more complex. The increasing complexity demands greater and greater specialization of social structures and
societal members. This analysis, called the **equilibrium perspective,** shares
the cyclical and evolutionary perspectives' analogy of society as a biological organism (Parsons, 1951; Ogburn, 1964). Societies are likened, for example, to the human body, in which the circulatory, digestive, endocrine, and
musculatory systems are interdependent. Each system requires the functioning of all the others in order to function adequately itself. Any disturbances or alterations in one of these bodily systems prompts adjustments
in the others so that the body as a whole remains in equilibrium. Like an
organism, social systems are seen to have a natural tendency toward stability. As such, when a disturbance or change occurs in one sector of a social
system, the great interdependence of sectors prompts changes in all other
sectors to accommodate the initial change and achieve stability in the
overall system (Parsons, 1951). From the equilibrium perspective, social
change entails a series of minor adjustments, rather than fundamental
alteration of the structure of society.

The problem here lies in the question of the source of disturbances or
changes in particular sectors of the social system. What causes such
changes to occur in the first place if all the parts are integrated and harmo-
niously in balance? And if stability is the normal state of existence for a
social system, how do we explain radical social change like revolution?

The equilibrium perspective is imprecise in its notion of "social system," a central concept. It is unclear just what constitutes a social system:
Is it a block, a borough, a city, a nation, or a subculture? If the social system were to be defined as a nation, how do we take account of the economic interdependence today that in fact creates a world-system? If one
nation changes its trade relations, for example, the change affects other
nations. Economic recessions in one nation can have painful economic and
political repercussions in others. Thus, one of the difficulties of the equilibrium perspective is that it neglects the possibility that changes may
come from outside the social system.

Finally, the equilibrium perspective emphasizes how order and stability are maintained, but it ignores conflict. Critics question the failure of the equilibrium perspective to discuss the role that conflict and power differentials may play in destabilizing society (see, for example, Gouldner, 1970).

The Conflict Perspective In contrast to these perspectives focusing on change as gradual and natural, another perspective sees *conflict* as a normal, constant state of affairs that makes change ubiquitous in all social structures. We refer to this view as the **conflict perspective.** What causes conflicts to erupt and generate social change?

Karl Marx and Friedrich Engels (1967) referred to the ongoing process of social change as the **dialectic.** Every social structure begins as a **thesis,** or its current (temporary and momentary) state of existence. But every state of existence carries its own internal contradictions or antagonisms, prompting a challenge to that structure. That challenge is called the **antithesis.** The conflict that accelerates between the thesis and antithesis eventually must resolve itself into what Marx and Engels called the **synthesis.** The synthesis is a wholly new social structure carrying some elements from the thesis and some from the antithesis. This new structure eventually becomes a new thesis that carries its own antagonisms and inconsistencies, prompting the dialectic process to continue (see Figure 9.1).

For example, Marx and Engels argued that there are inherent contradictions and antagonisms in every social structure of production and that conflicts percolate between the "haves" and the "have-nots." Under capitalism, the conflict is between two classes, those who own the means of production (**capitalists**) and those who do not (**proletariat,** or workers). Sharp class antagonisms in a capitalist system arise because of contradictions between social production, in which goods and services are produced by groups of workers cooperating together, and private appropriation of this wealth by the capitalists. While capitalists pay workers a wage for their labor, workers are not paid the full value of the wealth they produce. The surplus value is taken by the capitalists, who are constantly looking for ways to increase their income at the workers' expense. Conflict takes the form of continual organized struggle between the proletariat and the capitalists over who owns the rights to the fruits of workers' labor. For Marx, social change is the outcome of the ongoing process of class struggle between these two groups. Marx saw the entire history of humanity as the history of such class struggles.

According to this analysis, order in society comes about only with conflict and change. Hence, conflict is not necessarily a negative, destructive force. Marx and Engels saw conflict as a positive, restructuring force, a prerequisite for social change and progress.

While the conflict perspective may respond to many of the limitations of other theories of social change, it does not explain social stability. If conflict and change are normal and inherent in the social structure, how is social stability possible? Is it not possible for social change to occur without conflict?

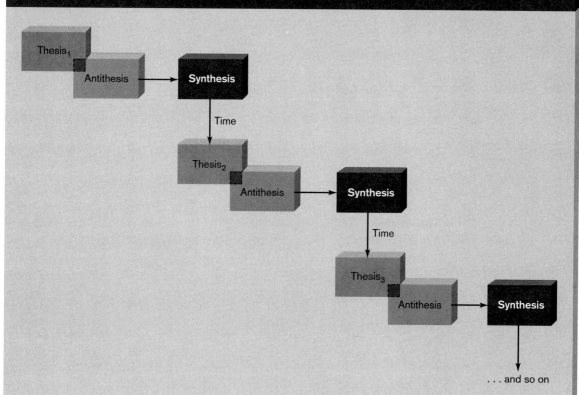

FIGURE 9.1 DIALETICS OF SOCIAL CHANGE

Thesis₁
Antithesis → Synthesis
Time
Thesis₂
Antithesis → Synthesis
Time
Thesis₃
Antithesis → Synthesis
. . . and so on

While most theories depict social change as linear or cyclical, following a single, predictable path, Marx and Engels's notion of the dialectic suggests a more complex, less predictable path. It is difficult to predict the next thesis without knowing the resolution of the contradictions between the current thesis and its antithesis.

In sum, these perspectives on social change offer some explanations for how and why individual societies may change. Each also implies some explanation for unequal development throughout the world. Is the modern world-system, marked by unequal economic growth and development, a sum total of each nation's individual social change processes, or is each nation an element of a larger, more globally interrelated process? We now turn to this question.

MODERNIZATION, DEVELOPMENT, AND UNDERDEVELOPMENT

The evolutionary perspective implies that social change entails progress and that all societies must follow the same path in their development. Poor countries are presumed to need to embrace the values and imitate the experiences of industrialized Western nations in order to become modernized and civilized (Hoselitz, 1960; Rostow, 1960; Inkeles and Smith, 1975). The poverty of some countries and their failure to modernize are attributed to their failure to adopt the "appropriate," "progressive" Western values. **Modernization theory,** a global version of the culture-of-poverty analysis, argues that the value systems of poor countries interfere with those nations' development and modernization. Such countries are therefore "less developed" or "more primitive" than the "developed" countries.

Many industrialized countries have helped poor nations improve their quality of life, but we must be careful not to confuse the sharing of expertise, knowledge, and equipment with a judgment concerning cultural values. And we must understand more clearly why a country is poor, rather than dismissing it as primitive because of its value system.

The Meaning of Development

Critics have questioned the meaning of development implied in modernization theory (Frank, 1967; Todaro, 1985). A high level of development is frequently defined as an advanced degree of urbanization and industrialization, characterized by the use of state-of-the-art technology and the generation of large amounts of wealth. This definition is simply a description of the West; it is based on the ethnocentric assumption that Western nations are the most highly evolved.

Furthermore, during the 1950s and 1960s many Third World countries achieved growth targets identified by the United Nations, suggesting that they were indeed evolving. Yet the standard of living for most people in these nations did not improve (Seers, 1969). This contradiction between the growth of wealth production and the stagnation of poverty called into question the conventional meaning of development. It showed that development existed for some people but not others in these nations. Moreover, such inequality could be found in the "developed" nations of the West as well. How, then, do we measure development?

Studies frequently measure development in terms of kilowatt-hours of electricity used per capita and gross national product per capita. The problem here is that such measures simply average out the wealth produced and the electricity generated over the entire population, thereby skirting the important question of distribution. Does everyone in the population receive an equal amount of the wealth produced? Arriving at only one statistic for an entire population implies that distribution is equal. The use of an aggregate measure, such as gross national product per capita, provides a measure for comparing the overall wealth of nations but ignores regions of poverty, patterns of inequality, and hunger and homelessness within so-called developed countries (see Figure 9.2). Likewise, it allows us to define countries such as Haiti or the Philippines as less developed while overlooking their regions of wealth and their elites.

Some critics suggest replacing the definition of development with a definition of **basic needs** (Streeten, 1981; Wood, 1986). Using this definition, we would look at how well the basic goods and services needed for survival are distributed to the entire population. Basic needs are measured

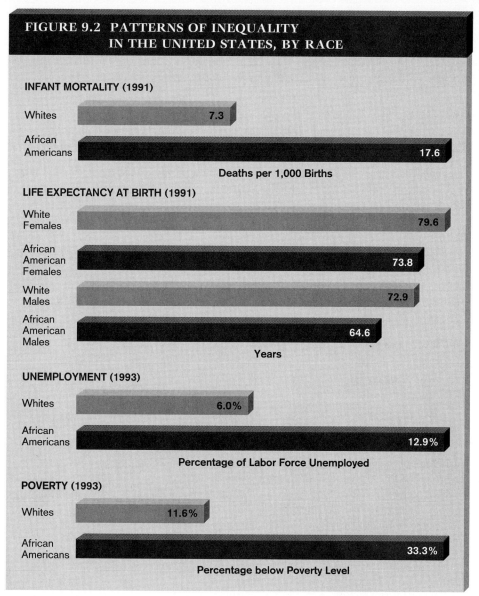

**FIGURE 9.2 PATTERNS OF INEQUALITY
IN THE UNITED STATES, BY RACE**

INFANT MORTALITY (1991)

Whites — 7.3

African Americans — 17.6

Deaths per 1,000 Births

LIFE EXPECTANCY AT BIRTH (1991)

White Females — 79.6

African American Females — 73.8

White Males — 72.9

African American Males — 64.6

Years

UNEMPLOYMENT (1993)

Whites — 6.0%

African Americans — 12.9%

Percentage of Labor Force Unemployed

POVERTY (1993)

Whites — 11.6%

African Americans — 33.3%

Percentage below Poverty Level

Statistics indicate that racial inequality produces a greater likelihood for a lower quality of life among African Americans than among whites. (*Source:* U.S. Department of Commerce, Bureau of the Census, *Statistical Abstract of the United States, 1994.* Washington, D.C.: U.S. Government Printing Office, 1994.)

in terms of health (such as life expectancy at birth and infant mortality rates), education (such as literacy rates and the proportion of the population age 5 to 14 enrolled in school), food (a proportion of minimum daily requirements for human survival), water supply (the percentage of the population with access to clean water), and sanitation (the percentage of the population with access to sewers and other sanitation facilities). The basic-needs approach to development makes it clear that even countries like the United States would have difficulty being defined as fully developed.

Critics also have argued that modernization theory looks at individual countries as if they existed in a vacuum, focusing only on internal dynamics and value systems as causal factors for development. This ignores international power dynamics and global historical processes. Each country has occupied a particular structural position and played a particular role in the development of the world-system. Countries therefore have different sets of experiences, histories, and social and economic structures, not by choice or value system but by virtue of their relationships with other countries, relationships marked by differential power and privilege (Frank, 1967; Wallerstein, 1974). For example, by the late seventeenth century India's economy was more advanced than economies in Europe: it had a large, thriving manufacturing sector that produced many luxury commodities, including textiles such as silk and cotton. Yet by the end of the eighteenth century India's economy, particularly its manufacturing sector, had declined significantly because of technological advances in Great Britain during the Industrial Revolution and "the imposition of the free trade doctrine under unequal conditions by the British" (Griffin, 1979: 82). Great

Economically poor countries are not simply in an earlier phase of development long surpassed by industrialized nations. Rather, they are products of histories of unequal trade and industrial relations between countries that have created roadblocks to their development efforts. In India, a well-established textiles manufacturing sector was destroyed by the late eighteenth century when its market was flooded with goods from Great Britain.

Britain destroyed India's textile industry by flooding India with cheaper British-made cotton in an effort to eliminate competition for its own textiles. Therefore, India's status as an underdeveloped nation resulted not from its own "primitive" value system but, rather, from its inequitable trade relationship with a more powerful industrialized country.

Poor or peripheral countries are thus not simply at an earlier stage of development and modernization already experienced by industrialized countries, and industrialized countries did not at one time take the same path now traveled by peripheral countries. Rather, peripheral countries are **underdeveloped nations.** That is, their historically disadvantageous relationships with more powerful industrialized or core nations have imposed severe limitations on development opportunities. Industrialized countries today were never *under*developed—although they were once *un*developed (Frank, 1967).

Dependency and Development

We may understand the historical dynamic of underdevelopment by examining three different types of relationships (often referred to as forms of dependency) between countries: trade dependency, dependent development, and debt dependency.

Trade Dependency   In his historical analysis of the world-system, Wallerstein (1980) traced the outcomes of trade-dependency relationships. **Trade dependency,** which dominated the world-system between the fifteenth and nineteenth centuries, is characterized by limited numbers of trade partners for peripheral countries. Typically, a peripheral country would strike an exclusive agreement with one or two trade partners from the core and focus its productive activities on a limited number of commodities, usually mineral and agricultural products. Peripheral countries exchanged these raw materials for finished consumer goods imported from their core trading partners. Initially this arrangement favored the peripheral country: it was able to concentrate limited economic resources on a few activities, rather than trying to produce everything it needed. The peripheral country also had a guaranteed market for its primary commodities.

In the long run, however, Wallerstein found that this arrangement impeded the development of peripheral countries (see also Delacroix and Ragin, 1981). Since its economic activity was concentrated on the production of primary commodities, the peripheral country developed a distorted economy rather than a diversified one. Its economy could not absorb economic shocks from trade disruptions, volatile weather patterns, and alterations in consumer demands in the core. For example, if a peripheral country focused its productive activities on sugar crops and coal, it was not able to withstand a decrease in sugar consumption in the core, destruction of the sugar crop from a season of floods, or shifts in core consumer goods production from the use of coal to other energy sources. Loss of the primary market for its goods would seriously undermine the entire economy of the peripheral country. In a country with a diversified economy, shocks to one industry can usually be offset by the health of other industries.

Therefore, a nondiversified economy produces a structural blockage to development in the periphery.

Trade dependency creates other economic troubles. Primary commodities are cheaper than finished consumer goods. Trading relatively cheaper primary commodities for more expensive finished goods creates an imbalance of trade for the peripheral country, because the nation often pays for the finished goods with the relatively low earnings generated by its exports. Throughout the world-system there has been a drain of money and resources away from the periphery to the core, which has seriously undermined the peripheral countries' ability to support their own development. The one notable exception to this trend appears to be the oil-producing countries. But these countries operated for many years in a cartel (the Organization of Petroleum Exporting Countries—OPEC), so together they had greater control over the supply and price of a basic commodity everyone needed for production. They also traded with many global partners rather than with one or two. They therefore did not suffer the restrictions imposed by trade-partner concentration.

Finally, researchers have found that trade dependency has aggravated income inequalities between urban and rural areas, between elites and masses, and between men and women within peripheral countries (Bornschier et al., 1978; Bornschier and Ballmer-Cao, 1979; Bornschier and Chase-Dunn, 1985). Local elites in the periphery cooperated with core elites to control trade arrangements, the benefits of which were rarely redistributed equally throughout the peripheral country. Income inequalities also were aggravated because male elites from the core typically awarded the trade routes to men in the periphery (Boserup, 1970; Papanek, 1979). Moreover, males in the periphery were often charged with the more lucrative cash-crop farming, mining, and manufacturing for trade, while women were left with the responsibility of subsistence farming to feed the local population (Deere, Humphries, and deLeal, 1982). For example, women in South Africa and Lesotho increasingly worked the farmlands by themselves, while the men in their families were drafted to work the mines (Mueller, 1977). In Latin America, corporations seek out Peruvian and Colombian men to work in the factories, while women are recruited into agriculture (Deere and deLeal, 1981).

Unequal power relationships within the periphery allow elites to own and control most of the arable land. They decide what will be grown on it and what market the crops will go to. Wealthy landowners typically grow cash crops and luxury items for export and elite consumption (such as sugar, coffee, and cocoa) rather than food needed for local consumption. As a result, the poor suffer hunger and malnutrition, which are often misunderstood as a problem of overpopulation. Hunger in the periphery is, more accurately, a product of the lack of local control over the land by the masses. Thus, inequitable trade relations between the core and periphery reach into the everyday lives of individuals in the periphery, particularly the peasants, the rural dwellers, and women. Their lives are impoverished not because they have not adopted the values of the West but because elites in their countries and in core nations maintain trade relationships that principally benefit themselves.

Dependent Development Over time, the peripheral nations attempted to resolve the problem of the resource drain and the unequal benefits accompanying trade dependency on the core. One strategy was to substitute locally produced goods for imported goods (**import substitution**) as well as to manufacture goods for sale abroad (**export processing**). This dual strategy is referred to as **dependent development**. Peripheral nations attempted to bring about economic development with focused and planned foreign investment in certain manufacturing sectors. This investment would enable them to manufacture the consumer goods they previously imported, thereby reducing the cost of the goods. Peripheral countries encouraged core-nation corporations to invest in them by promising a low-wage labor force, inexpensive natural resources, and large markets.

Bornschier and Chase-Dunn (1985) studied the effects of this strategy in their cross-national statistical analysis of 103 countries. They found that in the short run the capital flows led to increases in the growth of the peripheral economies. The flow of investment capital to build new plants and the generation of new jobs in the factories did stimulate the local economy. So, too, did the increase in construction activity on peripheral nations' infrastructures, such as the roads, railways, airports, sewage and electrification systems, schools, and housing required to accommodate the presence of the core nations' corporations.

In the long run, however, Bornschier and Chase-Dunn found that the presence and dominance of these corporations aggravated underdevelopment. First, most profits earned locally by the corporations flowed back to the core, where the companies were headquartered. Capital also flowed from peripheral countries to the core in payment for debts incurred by their governments to build the supportive infrastructure. Furthermore, rather than bringing in outside capital, the core corporations often used local capital, thereby limiting its availability and depriving local entrepreneurs of a capital source (Muller, 1979).

Bornschier and Chase-Dunn found that income inequality remained high in peripheral nations because the manufactured goods were affordable only for local elites rather than for mass markets. And any profits that did not drain back to the core were concentrated in the hands of the local elites. Foreign investments also often led to the decline of indigenous industries, both because the industries could not obtain local capital to survive and because they could not compete with the larger core-based corporations.

According to Bornschier and Chase-Dunn, the capital-intensive, highly mechanized forms of production that were introduced actually further distorted the economies of peripheral nations. Technological innovations and control of agriculture by core corporations reduced the number of laborers required, and many agricultural workers were left to seek new jobs. At the same time, many manufacturing corporations were using the latest capital-intensive forms of production rather than labor-intensive forms. Displaced agricultural workers, unable to find other sources of employment, were often drawn into poorly paid service jobs and informal-sector jobs, such as street vending, sweatshop production, and prostitution (see also Evans and Timberlake, 1980; Portes, 1985). Decisions made by elites in corporations and the state thus affected the daily lives of workers, altering their work choices (or their access to any work at all), as well as where they lived.

Export-oriented factories emerged in electronics, pharmaceuticals, and apparel in countries such as the Philippines, Mexico, Sri Lanka, and Hong Kong. Employers hired women rather than men because they were a more docile, cheaper labor force. However, researchers have found that wages at such jobs were typically insufficient to support the women workers and their children. Many women entered the informal sector in service, assembly, and prostitution, where they received wages but had no benefits or protective legislation (Boserup, 1970; Ward, 1987; Enloe, 1989). In fact, the economic situation for many women in peripheral countries has deteriorated to the point where they must often work a daily triple shift combining jobs in factories, the informal market, and the household (Hossfeld, 1988; Ward, 1990). Researchers have found that both trade dependency and dependent development have also increased hunger and infant mortality rates throughout the peripheral countries (Ward, 1984). World-system trade relations favoring core corporations thus have helped impoverish women and children in peripheral countries and altered their life courses, their family relations, their work, their economic and social status, and their very survival.

How do these core-periphery trade relationships affect individuals who live in the core nations? Workers in the core lose jobs, partly because core corporations relocate factories to the periphery and partly because inexpensive goods from peripheral countries flood core markets and compete with more expensive domestic goods. As core manufacturers go out of business, unemployment rises. Workers' lives in the core are, then, affected by world-system trade relations. Many people suffer from the increased unemployment; some lose their homes because they cannot maintain mortgages, and some experience poverty, hunger, and even homelessness.

Debt Dependency Governments in peripheral countries have sought to boost development with international aid and loans from core countries and international development agencies such as the International Monetary Fund, the World Bank, and the Organization for Economic Cooperation and Development (Corm, 1982; Lichtensztejn and Quijano, 1982; Dale and Mattione, 1983). We call reliance on loans for development **debt dependency.** Aid agencies provide **concessional loans,** which have below-market interest rates and are not due to be paid for relatively long periods of time. However, peripheral countries' reliance on concessional loans has dramatically declined over time.

Why? Many peripheral countries found the loans too restrictive. The funding agencies limited the use of the funds to specific projects they defined as desirable (Wood, 1985; Green, 1987). These projects, such as huge hydroelectric dams to generate power, superhighways to move goods to markets and ports, and military buildups to secure the political environment, benefited the corporations operating in the peripheral nations but did not enhance the lives of most of the residents. Nor did these projects stimulate development. Many countries were also concerned about the negative consequences of foreign investment, particularly the drain of capital from the periphery to the core. Still other countries exhausted their financing from international agencies and were forced to seek financing from private banks (Wood, 1985; Schatan, 1987).

The oil shocks of the 1970s created both new problems and opportunities for peripheral countries. The cartel of Mideast oil-producing nations (OPEC) effectively acted as a monopoly, controlling production and prices. The result was a leap in oil prices that badly hurt oil-consuming peripheral nations, already struggling to finance their development efforts. At the same time, private banks in the core accumulated huge deposits of money from OPEC nations' sale of oil (Seiber, 1982; Stallings, 1982; Schatan, 1987; Swedberg, 1987). The demand for large bank loans by corporations in the core stagnated at this time. The banks thus needed to find new investment opportunities for their burgeoning deposits, and they found them in peripheral countries.

Loans from private banks are called **nonconcessional loans.** They differ from loans made by official aid agencies in that their interest rates are much higher and payment is due in much shorter periods of time. Nonconcessional loans were attractive for peripheral countries anxious to escape the international aid agencies' control over how they chose to invest. Private banks were concerned only with whether their loans were likely to be repaid. Some peripheral states used this opportunity to increase their private-loan capital and invested the funds in their own state-controlled and -operated industries.

Unfortunately, in the 1970s and 1980s many countries found that declines in the value of the goods they produced and exported eroded their incomes and their ability to pay the high interest on their bank debts (Debt Crisis Network, 1985; Wood, 1986). Increasingly, these countries were forced to take out new loans from private banks in the core nations simply to pay off their old debts. Loans that should have helped with development now only helped the profitability of core nations' private banks.

In a cross-national statistical study of peripheral countries, Glasberg and Ward (1993) found evidence suggesting that while both concessional and nonconcessional loans initially stimulate development, over time nonconcessional loans impair development. This is not surprising. Money that is borrowed at increasingly higher interest rates to pay off old debt means that more and more money will be drained from the peripheral country. Because the vast majority of private banks providing the loans are headquartered in the core countries, the interest paid is not reinvested in the peripheral country. By the early 1980s, a chronic debt crisis existed throughout the peripheral world, a crisis that was particularly pronounced in Latin America.

When peripheral countries reach the point where they are unable to continue to pay the interest on their debt, private banks refuse to provide new loans to pay off the old ones. At this point, the International Monetary Fund (IMF) steps into the breach. The IMF's role is to get the peripheral country's house in order, restructure its economy, and make it attractive once again for investments by private banks and core corporations. The IMF does this by imposing a standard austerity program on the ailing peripheral economy in return for the promise of economic assistance.

Food riots often erupt in peripheral countries where austerity programs are imposed by the International Monetary Fund to control and reduce huge burdens of debt. Here, demonstrators in Venezuela protest sharp increases in food prices in 1992. The cost of living rose faster than wages in Venezuela that year, making food inaccessible to many people.

The austerity program typically includes (1) devaluation of the recipient country's currency, making its money worth less; (2) decreases in the amount of money the peripheral country spends on social welfare, including subsidies for consumer goods, and the elimination of price controls; (3) increases in control of labor unions, including the suppression of labor strikes for better working conditions and higher wages; (4) increases in the amount of money the peripheral country allocates to military spending (to help enforce the austerity program by suppressing labor strife, food riots, and insurrections and to secure the general political climate for core corporations' investments); (5) decreases in or elimination of state control of industry, including the selling of state-owned industries; (6) sharp reductions of imports and increases in manufacturing for export; and (7) dramatic increases in the amount of money the peripheral country devotes to paying off its debt (Debt Crisis Network, 1985). The IMF's rationale is that this program will force peripheral countries to keep their expenditures down while they pay off their debts and their economies get healthy once again.

Unfortunately, the track record of the IMF's austerity program is not very impressive. Several case studies have documented how the austerity program increasingly damages prospects for development and helps drain even more capital from the periphery to the core. For example, in a study of Mexico's 1982 debt crisis, Glasberg (1987, 1989) found that the austerity program resulted in serious declines in the value of Mexico's money and sharp reductions in the state's subsidies for food. The price of frijoles (beans that are a protein staple in Mexico) increased 250 percent in less than two weeks when state subsidies were withdrawn. Workers lucky enough to still have jobs found that their wages had been frozen or reduced; since the value of their money was much lower than it had been, and prices incredibly higher, they were increasingly unable to pay for food.

IMF demands for sharp reductions in imports seriously hurt Mexico's economy, because the country's critical petroleum industry relied on imported machinery. The petroleum industry, which was supposed to save the country economically, was unable to import the spare parts it needed to keep running and be profitable. The result of the IMF's austerity program was that Mexico was unable to recover economically and, indeed, was back in a debt crisis less than two years later. The country's mixed economic outlook today is due partly to U.S. guarantees of Mexico's debt (principally to U.S. banks) and to trade and production agreements with the United States that ultimately export U.S. production jobs to Mexico. Evidence of the long-term effects of such relationships on peripheral nations in the past should alert us to the possibility that Mexico's economic health may be an issue for some time to come.

Peripheral nations' debts to private banks are thus being paid off at the expense of the poor, the workers, women, and children, the very groups that did not benefit from previous efforts to develop. In fact, as we have seen, these groups were hurt the most by the income inequalities that accompanied inequitable trade relationships with and investments by core nations' corporations. The real winners in the economic restructuring imposed by the IMF are the wealthy elites in peripheral countries, core nations' corporations, and private banks in the core.

This discussion of trade relationships, dependent development, and debt dependency shows that development is *not* simply a matter of poor countries following the steps to modernization taken by industrialized countries. Nor are peripheral countries simply in an earlier stage of development long surpassed by industrialized countries. Rather, the historical role of peripheral countries in the world-system has meant that they have had to undergo experiences the industrialized countries have not. Underdevelopment is best understood within a global context of private profit generation, rather than as a national problem of improper value systems. Underdevelopment is a *political* process involving economic and military power differentials. It is not simply a problem of national internal dynamics or a matter of inexorable, but slow, progression toward development.

Creative strategies to address the problems of underdevelopment, burgeoning debt burdens, and global inequality have begun to link these problems with global environmental issues. **Debt-for-nature swaps** are arrangements in which debt-ridden governments agree to purchase or set aside land to conserve as state-owned parks and to protect their natural resources in exchange for a debt cancellation. The first such swap occurred in 1987 between Bolivia and Conservation International, a private U.S. organization that had purchased Bolivia's debt from Citicorp Bank. Conservation International agreed to retire the debt in exchange for Bolivia's promise to protect almost 4 million acres around the Beni Biosphere

Reserve. Fourteen other, similar debt-for-nature swaps have been arranged since 1987, involving eight countries. And while most have entailed Latin America's rain forest areas, such as those in Ecuador, the Dominican Republic, and Costa Rica, swaps have also been arranged for land in the Philippines, Madagascar, Zambia, and Poland (Passell, 1991). These swaps underscore the interdependence of countries in the global economy as well as in the environment, and they highlight the possibilities for change in the politics of underdevelopment.

TECHNOLOGY AND SOCIAL CHANGE

Many contemporary observers view technological innovation as the generator of social change. What is the role of technology in processes of social change? Where do technological developments come from? Why do some technologies develop and not others? Is technological development a neutral process, wherein "necessity becomes the parent of invention"? Who determines the meaning of necessity, and who decides what is necessary? Who benefits and who is hurt by technological development?

Energy Production

Many of us have been taught that the Industrial Revolution was a time marked by a sudden explosion of inventions that revolutionized production processes and everyone's lives, generally in a positive way. New technologies improved people's lives and made society more progressive. Those who argued against the increasing reliance on technology were often criticized as being old-fashioned or standing in the way of progress.

We learned that **inventions**—new practices and objects developed out of existing knowledge—"happened" because necessity dictated their development. For example, the steam engine was invented because people needed a large source of power to modernize industry. But who decides that a particular invention is needed? Who supports the development of particular inventions as solutions to problems? Why are some inventions developed, and others not (even though they may, in fact, be needed)?

For example, why is the technology for nuclear power generation and energy production based on the burning of fossil fuels so well developed, while the technology for solar energy remains relatively primitive and inefficient? The answer may have to do with who benefits and who is hurt by our continued dependence on certain kinds of energy production. Nuclear energy and fossil fuels are nonrenewable energy sources: they are based on resources that are mined or extracted from the earth (such as coal, petroleum, and uranium). We cannot use the resources indefinitely without depleting them, and we cannot turn them into energy without the technological help provided by energy corporations and utility firms.

Solar energy, wind energy, and geothermal energy are based on renewable resources. We can indefinitely derive energy from these resources as long as the sun shines fairly regularly, the winds blow, and the earth continues to contain warmth. While these resources still require some techno-

Our reliance on nonrenewable sources of energy may open a door of compromise in the enforcement of safety measures in energy production. In this picture, helicopters with radiation counters observe and measure the devastation produced by the accident at the Chernobyl nuclear power plant in the Ukraine.

logical aid in delivering their energy to us in usable forms, we do not need to rely on energy corporations and utilities to provide them to us. Once the technology is in place, the resources are self-sustaining in their delivery of energy.

It is not surprising, then, to find that energy corporations and utilities sponsor research to invent technologies that rely on nonrenewable sources of energy. These same companies have purchased several patents for useful solar technologies and never used them (Reece, 1980). Were we to have access to those technologies, we might be independent of the energy corporations and the utilities after the initial construction of facilities. Large corporate interests benefit greatly from our dependence on them as providers of energy; we all lose a great deal from their ability to turn that reliance into expensive (for us) and profitable (for them) energy production.

Technological Change and the Labor Process

Framing the analysis of technological development and social change in terms of who benefits and who is hurt also helps us understand the rise of the factory during the late 1800s and early 1900s as a major *social* change rather than as an inevitable, neutral result of technological progress. Prior to the eighteenth century, individuals manufactured many consumer goods in their homes, using manual labor—a system often referred to as **cottage industries.** They sewed clothing, cobbled shoes, built furniture, and created pottery using their hands and simple tools. This system allowed them to determine how long they worked on any given day, which days they worked, how much they produced, what they produced, and to some extent how much money they made. While capitalists provided them with the materials for making goods on order, the workers could determine how to maximize use of the materials, and they often kept the remnants to make goods for themselves or to sell to other buyers. Thus, the cottage industry system gave workers control over the work process and some power over distribution of the profits of their labor. This changed when production shifted to factories. Why did this change occur if workers stood to lose so much?

The conventional view is that factories developed in response to the invention of the steam engine as a central source of power. The steam engine was too expensive and too large for individual cottage industries to use. It was simply cheaper, according to this view, for workers to gather together under one roof and share use of the new centralized source of power. This would seem to make sense, until we examine the historical research on forces leading up to the development of both the factory and the steam engine.

Through his historical analysis of industry in the United States, Dan Clawson (1980) clearly establishes that there was a terrific struggle from the mid-eighteenth century to the late nineteenth century between workers in the cottage industries and capitalists wishing to exert greater control over the work process. Capitalists were dismayed by workers' retention of remnants of materials that the capitalists had paid for and by workers' sometimes erratic work hours. And they were displeased that workers could determine what the capitalists would pay for production. In order to gain greater control over the labor process, capitalists built factories and tried unsuccessfully to coerce workers into them. Workers were well aware that they stood to lose much by giving the power of managing the work process to the capitalists. Capitalists countered by using the coerced, unpaid labor of prisoners, slaves, and orphans in the factories. The use of such an inexpensive labor force began to erode the cottage industries' ability to compete with the factories' economy of scale, volume of production, and lower-priced commodities. Poverty and lack of alternatives eventually forced the cottage industry workers to join the workers already in the factories.

All this took place *before* the introduction of the steam engine. Prior to the late eighteenth and early nineteenth centuries the factory merely gathered the workers together under one roof, but the technological aspects of the production process remained essentially the same as before the development of the factory. It was *after* the factory took hold that the steam engine was introduced and became a technological justification of the factory. What workers lost in control of the work process capitalists gained. The capitalists could determine the commodities produced, the way they were produced, the hours and days worked, and the wages earned. The introduction of the steam engine, then, was stimulated by the conflict between workers and capitalists over control of the production process and the resultant profits. Use of steam power firmly tilted that struggle in favor of the capitalists, rationalizing the social change in production that had already taken place.

Technology and Reproductive Issues

While most analyses of social change propagated by technology focus on its effects on work and production, there have also been profound technologically generated changes in the area of human reproduction. Technological developments such as fetal monitors can measure the heart rate of the fetus and thus determine whether the fetus is in distress during labor. Such devices are quite useful in increasing the chances of a healthy, live birth. But critics note that they have also given more control over the birthing process to doctors and technicians. One alarming indicator of this shift is the sharp increase in cesarian births over the last decade: one-third of all births in the United States are now delivered through surgery (Rowland, 1992).

Some would argue that the increase in cesarian section deliveries represents greater knowledge about health and safety for both the mother and the baby. However, there are other, perhaps more compelling, incentives for physicians' increasing reliance on fetal monitors and other technologies to justify interventions like cesarian deliveries. Because cesarian sections are surgery, they are expensive, and the surgeon can count on being paid by the mother's health insurance company. The combination of insurance policies and the profit motive in organized medicine has prompted technological developments that invest greater control of the birth process with doctors and less with women.

Technology has also altered the process of conception and pregnancy, thereby throwing society into a storm of controversy over several ethical issues. Amniocentesis, for example, can identify genetic defects in a fetus, revealing conditions such as Down's syndrome, Tay-Sachs disease, sickle-cell anemia, and a whole host of other genetic abnormalities. It can also identify the sex of the fetus. Critics have long argued that such information could lead to the abortion of a fetus that happens to be the "wrong" sex. And, since many societies value males more strongly than females, there is an increased danger of abortion of female fetuses simply because they are females. While there is no evidence that this practice is widespread in the United States, a study found that of 8,000 fetuses aborted in Bombay, India, following amniocentesis, 7,999 were female (Rowland, 1992).

The abortion of "defective" fetuses, or those with potential disabilities, also raises an issue: When is a defect life-threatening, and when is it simply a departure from our social construction of the "perfect" human being? While the technology of procedures like amniocentesis may be very useful in early identification of fetal genetic disorders and infections in order to promote treatment, that same technology holds great potential for abuse: it allows us to identify and destroy fetuses that fail to conform to the culturally dominant image of perfection—a human being with no genetic, physical, or mental "defects."

In vitro fertilization has increased the chances of becoming parents for infertile couples or those who have had difficulty establishing a pregnancy. This technology has also made it possible for a couple to hire a third party to carry the fertilized egg, give birth to the child, and then turn it over to them for parenting. We refer to the person who carries the fertilized egg and gives birth as the **surrogate mother** (although there are some controversies concerning the very definition and identification of who is the mother, who is the surrogate, who is biological, and so forth).

The technology of in vitro fertilization raises several thorny issues concerning class dynamics. Poor women could be contracted to carry and deliver babies for middle-class and wealthy couples. Poverty could create a situation in which poor women "rent out" their wombs, much like poor and working-class families during the early twentieth century rented out rooms in their homes to lodgers to help pay the rent. Such a situation has the potential for seriously exploiting the surrogate. Sociologist Barbara Katz Rothman asks:

> What will happen if the new technology allows brokers to hire women who are not related genetically to the babies that are to be sold? Like the poor and non-white women who are hired to do other kinds of nurturing and caretaking work, these mothers can be paid very little, with few benefits, and no long-term commitment (Rothman, 1989: 236–237).

Surrogacy contracts also enable the brokers to control the lives of the surrogates, both economically and socially. The contract typically specifies behaviors that are strictly forbidden (such as drinking, smoking, drug use, and dieting) and those that are required (eating healthy foods, taking vitamins, getting plenty of sleep, and avoiding risky activities, which may include certain kinds of jobs). Like the workers in the factories Clawson studied, surrogate mothers become workers who can be carefully controlled by those who stand to profit a great deal from that control.

Clearly, the main beneficiaries of surrogacy are the lawyers who broker such contracts. Surrogacy brokering is a highly lucrative business, aided by the development of reproductive technologies that raise ethical and social questions. Meanwhile, poor and working-class women and people of color can be hurt in these arrangements. Consider that they are paid for a full nine months of their lives (and *not* merely for eight hours per day, five days per week) and factor out what they are getting paid per hour; even at a wage of $10,000 they are poorly paid.

Moreover, surrogates' bodies undergo the physical risks of any pregnancy, and they are often emotionally battered by the process of giving birth and then having the baby taken away because of a contract. While it may be relatively easy to agree to be a surrogate in exchange for more money than many of these women can earn in a year, it is not always so easy to adhere to the contract.

This discussion illustrates the tremendous changes in human reproduction that have been brought about by technological developments. But it also highlights the fact that cultural change has lagged behind the technology: although science enables these changes to occur, social and cultural processes have not yet determined whether they *should* occur or how to deal with their effects if they do (see Stephenson and Wagner, 1993). This implies that social change is not just a process made possible by technological inventions and innovations; it is also a political process.

Technological Innovation as a Political Process

Technology is not a neutral force. It is driven by many factors, including profit motives and vested interests in control over such processes as work and reproduction. Technology is not necessarily the natural response to necessity; it is a social and political response to necessity as defined by those who stand to benefit most from its development and who have the power and the economic resources to support such development.

Technological developments frequently affect the possibilities of our daily lives, enhancing some aspects and restricting others. For example, factory technology meant that workers would no longer be able to control their work or their earnings. Their life choices became more restricted as they lost control of the work process. Similarly, while reproductive technology may enhance the chances that infertile couples can have babies, it also increases the medical establishment's control over reproduction and aggravates class, gender, and race inequalities. Poor women and women of color may increasingly find themselves "renting" their wombs to wealthy white women for a fee in order to eat a healthy, enriched diet and receive otherwise unavailable medical care for nine months.

Ironically, technological developments that enhance the power of the already privileged may also introduce unintended benefits to the *disadvantaged.* For example, while the rise of the factory concentrated power in the hands of capitalists, it also made the production process more efficient than it had been under the cottage industry system. More goods were available to more people at lower costs than previously was the case. The rise of the factory also stimulated the rise of the labor movement, which enabled workers to resist capitalists' greater control and exploitation. Since workers were now engaged in the work process under one roof, they could more easily communicate and develop common viewpoints, common strategies for resistance, and more strength in their combined organized efforts to challenge capitalists' power.

SOCIAL MOVEMENTS

Are we captives of inexorable technological and social changes, or can we affect the direction and the content of social change? Since social change is a human, social construction, humans do have the ability to affect how societies change. Social change does not just happen like the weather; what we do alters the content of our social structures and sometimes alters the very structures themselves. How do we affect social change, if so much is made to happen by and for the already privileged? Must we always adjust to the changes dictated by people who are powerful and advantaged, or do we have options to counter those forces?

The key to these questions has to do with collective, organized action. As individuals, we are fairly powerless to challenge the social changes introduced by the powerful and advantaged members of society. One voice alone may not be heeded or even heard. However, organized, collective efforts by many similar-minded individuals have historically posed formidable challenges to the powerful, even if they have had variable success. For example, when factory owners introduced machinery into the stocking industry in Great Britain in the nineteenth century, workers collectively rebelled by smashing the machinery they saw as displacing their labor (Rude, 1964, 1985). While the rebellion only temporarily postponed the introduction of the new machinery, it represented collective action taken to resist the use of technology that benefited factory owners but hurt workers.

We call persistent, organized, collective efforts to resist existing structures and cultures, or to introduce changes in them, **social movements.** They often permit the less powerful members of society to effectively challenge and resist the more powerful members. Social movements also sometimes allow the relatively powerless to affect intersocietal relations. For example, the influx into the United States and several Caribbean nations of thousands of Haitians fleeing the dictatorship of their country in 1993 increased the pressure on the United States to redefine its relationship with Haiti. By 1994, the United States deemed it necessary to send troops into Haiti to "encourage" the military dictatorship to leave and to facilitate the reinstatement of Haiti's elected president. The hope was that this would sharply reduce the movement of refugees from Haiti to the United States. Social movements can be the vehicle through which individuals working together may be able to address issues that otherwise seem too big, too daunting, and overwhelming to them.

Types of Social Movements

Social movements differ in the types of change they pursue and the amounts of change they aim for (Aberle, 1966). For example, **redemptive movements** do not attempt to change society; their efforts target individuals. Many redemptive movements are religious movements seeking to convert individuals. Evangelists who preach on television and Jehovah's Witnesses who knock on doors to talk to people are engaged in similar attempts to convince individuals to convert from sinful pursuits to Christianity.

Alterative movements also seek changes among individuals. But while redemptive movements seek total changes, alterative movements focus on limited, but specifically defined, changes. Students Against Drunk Driving (SADD), an organization of high school and college students, for example, seeks to convince other students to resist the peer pressures to drive under the influence of alcohol or drugs. SADD has chapters throughout the country, but it does not try to change society. Rather, it focuses on trying to alter the behaviors of individual students.

On the other hand, Mothers Against Drunk Driving (MADD) is a **reformative movement,** in that it aims to change society. This nationally organized group actively lobbies for strict national and state legislation criminalizing driving under the influence of drugs or alcohol. What MADD seeks is a limited, but specifically defined, change in societal norms, not just in the behavior of individuals.

Similarly, the American Association of Retired Persons (AARP) is a reformative movement comprising more than 32 million members over the age of 50. The AARP lobbies legislators for better legal protection of the rights of the elderly, and it informs the rest of society about those rights through education, advocacy, and service in the community. The association also engages in voter registration drives and voter education campaigns, and it presses for attention to health-care and quality-of-life issues that concern retired persons. The AARP's goal is not to radically change the structure of society but to reform institutional politics and change societal norms toward treatment of the elderly.

The goal of **transformative movements,** like that of reformative movements, is change in society. But while reformative movements work toward limited, specific changes, transformative movements seek total change in society. Revolutions are good examples of transformative movements. Their goal is radical and total change of the social structure, resulting in a society that is completely different from the existing form. The Cuban revolution of the 1950s, for example, worked to overthrow the dominating capitalist social structure that produced gross inequalities of wealth, power, and privilege and to replace it with a socialist structure that favored collective production for the common good rather than for individual wealth.

Within large social movements several types of movements (based on their goals and strategies) may coexist (Ferree and Hess, 1994; see also Simon and Danziger, 1991). For example, the women's movement actually comprises several different movements. The liberal feminist movement, articulated by organizations such as the National Organization for Women (NOW), is a reformative movement. Its goal is to integrate women better into the existing political, social, and economic institutions, thereby increasing the equal participation of women in society. Such organizations do not question or challenge the existing social structures; they challenge the discrimination against women that occurs within those structures. Their efforts, therefore, focus on legislative lobbying, antidiscrimination suits in the courts, and public education and consciousness raising.

In contrast, the radical feminist movement defines men as the enemy and seeks to change existing institutions viewed as patriarchal. Marriage, in particular, is seen as an oppressive institution for women; radical feminists seek to redefine the structure of family to eliminate the traditional restrictive roles that inhibit women's development as independent individuals. For example, families of women living together to support one another and perhaps their children do not include men and are not based on sexist divisions of labor. Radical feminists, then, support one another's individual resistance to oppressive institutions. While the ultimate goal is to have so many women resist that the existing institutions change, radical feminists work primarily to convince individual women to alter the social structures of their personal living arrangements. In this sense radical feminists may be understood as involved in a form of redemptive movement.

Marxist or socialist feminists, however, see capitalism as the enemy rather than men per se. In their view, both men and women are victims of a system that exploits people for the benefit of the capitalist class. The conflict between men and women is viewed as a false wedge driven within the working class by the capitalist class to divide and conquer it and

The women's movement actually contains several types of movements of varying goals and strategies. The liberal feminist movement seeks to protect and enhance abortion rights and reproductive freedoms within existing social structures. Three-quarters of a million people marched in one of the biggest demonstrations in Washington, D.C., in 1992 in support of these rights.

reduce the possibility that male and female workers will organize to challenge capitalism. Socialist feminists, then, do not seek greater integration of women into the political, social, and economic institutions of society, as do liberal feminists, since that would only legitimate the existing system of oppression. Similarly, they do not define men as the enemy, as do radical feminists, because that would divert energy and attention away from the real problem of capitalism as an oppressive social structure. The goal of socialist feminists is to have women and men recognize sexism as a vehicle of capitalist oppression and join forces in working toward a socialist society. The elimination of sexism requires the elimination of capitalism first. Socialist feminists, then, represent a transformative movement; they seek total change of society.

When a social movement contains several types of movements, the diversity usually stems from disagreements among the participants on the definition of the source of a problem or on the strategy most appropriate for change. That much said, however, we are still left with the question of how social movements develop in the first place. Why do social movements occur, and how do grievances of individuals translate into efforts to bring about social change? The fact that societies are interdependent leads to another question: Do social change movements in other societies have implications for individuals in our own?

Explaining Social Movements

Absolute versus Relative Deprivation   Karl Marx and Friedrich Engels (1967) argued that the working class and the capitalist class would eventually become so polarized that the workers would suffer immiseration, or

absolute deprivation: they would be unable to purchase the simplest means of survival. According to the theory, as the capitalists became richer because of their control over the labor force and work process, the workers would be forced to work longer hours at low wages just to support their own subsistence. When the workers became so poor that they were immiserated, Marx and Engels argued, they would collectively revolt to overthrow the social structure that caused their oppression. That is, revolutions, as organized resistance movements designed to challenge and replace existing social structures with new ones, would be provoked when the workers became intolerably impoverished.

The immiseration thesis is often used to frame popular media analyses of the civil rights movement in the United States. According to these analyses, the civil rights movement was touched off by a single act of resistance: When Rosa Parks finally could not take the intolerable conditions of racist oppression, she refused to give her seat on a Birmingham bus to a white man. The use of the immiseration, or absolute-deprivation, perspective in this instance points to one of the limitations of that thesis: Not all social movements are prompted by economic deprivation. Rosa Parks may have suffered from extreme or even absolute deprivation of civil rights, but the fact that she was employed suggests that she had at least a minimum, if not middle-class, ability to purchase what she needed for basic survival.

Some sociologists criticize the use of this thesis on still other grounds. James Davies (1962, 1969, 1974), for example, argued that revolutions historically did not occur when conditions reached an intolerable or absolute low. Rather, he noted, such organized rebellions occurred in response to **relative deprivation.** Davies argued that people's understanding of deprivation is *relative* to conditions around them, conditions they expect, or conditions that previously existed but no longer do. People revolted when a gap opened, over time, between the conditions that they expected and the conditions that actually existed. Davies's relative-deprivation thesis can apply to economic as well as social and political conditions.

For example, people's expectations may gradually rise, but real conditions may gradually improve too, even if they don't quite reach expectations. In Davies's view, revolutions will not occur until real conditions begin to deteriorate somewhat relative to expectations. In this instance, real conditions do not need to deteriorate to the point of immiseration, as Marx and Engels believed; it is sufficient, according to Davies, that real conditions simply get slightly worse while expectations continue to slightly rise.

In a similar case of relative deprivation, expectations for improved conditions may rise sharply, and real conditions may also rise sharply but not quite enough to reach expectations. Revolutions will not occur until real conditions plateau while expectations continue to rise. In this instance, real conditions need not deteriorate at all; it is sufficient that real conditions stagnate while expectations continue to increase.

Finally, expectations for improved conditions may be on a sharp increase, and real conditions may be on an equally sharp incline of improvement. In this instance, revolutions will occur when expectations for improved conditions rise more sharply than real conditions. It is not necessary for real conditions to deteriorate or even stagnate; for revolutions to occur, it is sufficient, even in the face of vastly improved real conditions, that expectations dramatically increase relative to real conditions.

Resource Mobilization   Critics of both the absolute-deprivation and the relative-deprivation explanations argue that they imply a spontaneous combustion of social dissatisfaction. The theories presume that at a given point in time conditions will become absolutely intolerable, or the difference between expectations and real conditions will suddenly become intolerable, and a large group of people will revolt. This analysis ignores the question of resources. No matter how intolerable conditions become, people usually do not revolt unless they have access to resources to support their activity. They need human resources to articulate the frustration and formulate a strategy for response; leadership to organize and mobilize others; tangible resources, such as financial backing, to spread the word, support endangered or jailed participants, and communicate widely with other potential supporters; and networks of other groups of people or existing organizations to support movement efforts. Thus, revolutions and other social movements are unlikely to occur in the absence of supportive resources and the ability of people to mobilize them, regardless of how pronounced the feelings of absolute or relative deprivation might be. We refer to this explanation of social movements as **resource mobilization theory** (see Jenkins, 1983).

In his study of the civil rights movement, Aldon Morris (1984) found, on the basis of extensive interviews with activists and participants, that resource mobilization is the best explanation of the movement. Morris concluded that African Americans everywhere did not suddenly and simultaneously get frustrated enough to rebel. He documents how leaders in several African American organizations mobilized resources and combined their organizational efforts to become a powerful collective force in challenging segregation and other forms of racial discrimination in the United States.

As we noted, popular media accounts of the civil rights movement often ascribe its beginnings to a single incident, Rosa Parks's seemingly spontaneous refusal to give her seat on the bus to a white person. Morris documents that Parks was, in fact, an active member, and the first secretary, of the local National Association for the Advancement of Colored People. She had been arrested several times before that incident for the same action. Rosa Parks's famous act of rebellion was part of an organized, conscious resistance movement rather than an isolated, spontaneous reaction to racism. She herself insisted, "My resistance to being mistreated on the buses and anywhere else was just a regular thing with me and not just that day" (Morris, 1984: 51).

While many popular accounts personalized the civil rights movement in the charismatic leadership of the Reverend Martin Luther King, Jr., Morris demonstrates that the movement was much greater than one person. Dr. King was simply the most visible and stirring articulator of the issues, a person able to galvanize and mobilize great numbers of individuals. But the civil rights movement was actually the result of the collective efforts of the National Association for the Advancement of Colored People (NAACP), the Southern Christian Leadership Conference (SCLC), the Student Nonviolent Coordinating Committee (SNCC), and the Congress of Racial Equality (CORE), as well as African American churches, white religious organizations, labor unions, student organizations, and local small businesses. Their combined efforts enabled them to mobilize vast resources in support of the movement. Instead of having to organize individuals in support of civil rights, the leadership was able to tap into existing organizations of people, communication networks, and monetary resources to quickly and effectively organize boycotts, marches, voter registration drives in hostile southern states, and acts of civil disobedience such as sit-ins at lunch counters (see also McAdam, 1982, 1988).

Morris's analysis of the civil rights movement illustrates how social movements can use resource mobilization to empower people who are powerless, disadvantaged, and largely disenfranchised from the mainstream. Against overwhelming odds, the civil rights movement managed to dislodge a discriminatory social structure and rigidly racist cultural values that had denied African Americans basic civil rights.

Doug McAdam (1982), who also studied the civil rights movement, notes the role of the state as a factor in the rise and fall of social movements. For example, elimination of racial barriers to voting enhanced the likelihood of electing well-placed sympathetic elites such as John F. Kennedy and Lyndon B. Johnson. However, McAdam emphasizes that federal support for the goals of the civil rights movement came only in

Resource mobilization for social movements like the civil rights movement in the United States requires money, leadership, and people willing to invest time and to endure risk. These civil rights demonstrators suffer the power of firehoses being used against them by firefighters attempting to break up a protest in Birmingham, Alabama, in 1963.

response to insurgency and violent and nonviolent acts that subverted civil order. Similar findings on the role of the state in social movements, particularly in response to insurgent disruptions, can be seen in analyses of other movements, such as the labor movements in Brazil and South Africa (Seidman, 1993) and the antinuclear movements in the United States and Germany (Joppke, 1993; see also Meyer, 1993).

The civil rights movement has achieved only partial success in eliciting affirmative action, equal employment opportunity, and desegregation legislation. But it is important to realize that even that much was unlikely to have occurred in the absence of the pressure applied by the organized, collective efforts of the movement (see, for example, Lawson, 1990). And although the legislation represents only official policy changes, and does not necessarily alter actual practices, it is equally important to note that the movement has been less active in the past decade. That is, the gap between legislation and actual practice is not a measure of the failure of social movements to affect social change by society's relatively powerless members. It more likely reflects a cultural lag between a social change in policy and its translation into real changes in the normative system. Additional pressure from the civil rights movement will hasten a closing of that gap. This suggests that the movement needs to remain vigilant in mobilizing resources and galvanizing the politically, socially, and economically disenfranchised to continue the progress toward racial equality begun in the decades between 1950 and 1980.

Indeed, we may be witnessing a reawakening of the civil rights movement in the 1990s. For example, several organizations and groups, including the NAACP and the Rainbow Coalition, picketed the National Football League's 1994 Super Bowl game in Atlanta, Georgia, because the stadium unfurled the Georgia state flag at the game. The flag includes a replica of the Confederate flag, which many see as a strong historical symbol of racism. The state of Georgia was put under considerable pressure to change its flag before the 1996 Winter Olympics in Atlanta, under the scrutiny of the world. The increased willingness to articulate such concerns and to demand change indicates a renewed spirit in the civil rights movement and the potential for recapturing lost momentum.

If social movements require the mobilization of organizations and other resources, how do the poorest groups in society get their needs addressed? In their comparative study, *Poor People's Movements* (1977), Frances Fox Piven and Richard Cloward argued that only insurgency and mass rebellions like strikes and riots brought concessions from elites for poor people. Organizations, they argued, sapped energies, diverted attention, co-opted the poor into nonthreatening actions, and propagated the false perception that the political system was fair and responsive to their needs. According to Piven and Cloward, insurgency emerges from the mass discontent and disruption of everyday life produced by poverty and deprivation. Thus, their analysis of poor people's movements (such as the welfare rights, the unemployed workers', the industrial workers', and the civil rights movements) implicitly used a deprivation model to explain how the poor and powerless wrested change from elites: the poor rebelled, rioted, and staged strikes in massive eruptions of insurgency sparked by discontent and deprivation.

Piven and Cloward rejected a resource mobilization explanation of poor people's movements. However, Jenkins and Perrow (1977), in their study of the migrant farmworkers' movement (1946–1972), demonstrated that resource mobilization was critical to the efforts of the United Farm Workers in the late 1960s and early 1970s to win the right to unionize and secure decent working conditions. The lack of resources was a key factor in the failure of the earlier National Farm Labor Union in the late 1940s and mid-1950s. Both organizations of migrant farmworkers had outside leadership, derived initial organizational sponsorship from outside their communities, and used insurgency tactics like strikes and boycotts. But widespread *sustained* support from a coalition of liberal organizations neutralized elite resistance to the farmworkers' insurgency in the late 1970s and led to the right to unionize for migrant farmworkers. Jenkins and Perrow concluded that discontent was not enough to ignite the insurgency and the successful challenges of the migrant farmworkers' movement; persistent organizational support from outside groups that had access to resources and devoted them to a group that had little was the critical difference between success and failure.

We can also see evidence of resource mobilization in the disability rights movement, which has been organized, vocal, and visible in the last decade. "Disability" covers a wide range of conditions, including hearing and visual impairments, motor function limitations, mental disabilities, diseases such as AIDS and cancer, and physical appearances that depart from cultural definitions of normality, such as obesity, harelips, dwarfism, and facial disfigurement (see Stroman, 1982). Such a diversity of conditions could have easily led to a splintering of the disability movement into sepa-

Social movements using resource mobilization approaches often mobilize existing organizations to support their struggles. This 1990 demonstration against Greyhound Bus Company for its failure to make its buses accessible took place on Memorial Day weekend, at the height of a strike against the company by its bus drivers. Thus, organized labor and people with disabilities mobilized to support each other's struggles against the bus company at one of its busiest times.

*H*ow do you change an unjust law? The author of this article tells us that bringing about change takes determination, patience, and massive mobilization of support.

A young woman is attacked by a stranger who holds her in a viselike grip as he licks and bites her breasts through her clothes. He was caught in the act, but not sent to prison or forced to register as a sex offender. In fact, he could, if he wished, be licensed as a child care worker.

There was no law in California (or most other states) that could adequately address this insidious crime, because the victim was attacked through her clothing. Illegal touching was defined by sexual assault laws as skin-to-skin contact, or through the clothing of the attacker. It did not include touching through the victim's clothing. The only charge that applied was battery, which carries a light maximum prison sentence and therefore is rarely prosecuted.

I am the young woman who was mentioned in the beginning of this article. I was the one who was attacked. The police watch commander told me that this crime is reported every day in his precinct, and many officers—including the one who investigated my case—even underline that portion of the sexual battery law in their penal code books. They do it, he said, to show victims that there is really nothing to be done.

I could not contain my outrage, and vowed the law would change. I knew I had to get the full attention of my assemblyman (now a state senator), Patrick Johnston. But I had no idea how to, until I was at a fund-raiser for the local battered women's shelter. One of the items up for auction was a private lunch and state capitol tour with him. I made the highest bid—$125—using my travel money for Christmas.

When I met with Johnston, I came prepared. I presented him with a package of information that he said looked better than those of most lobbyists. He also told me that another assemblyman, Bill Filante, had drafted a bill, AB 674, calling for a similar legal change. He said it had been voted on once before and failed.

I found out why after I talked with a staffer for another representative. He said assemblymen were afraid that young men in college would be with a date, fondle her, and then be charged with sexual battery. They felt that a boy shouldn't be put away for "miscommunication" with a date. He told me that most of the state assemblymen had been college boys once themselves.

I contacted Filante's office. As it turned out, a staffer said that the bill had the votes to pass this time. The big problem was that the governor at the

rate powerless organizations, each attempting to apply pressure for legislative reforms addressed to its own constituency. Instead, over 80 different national disability organizations joined forces in the Consortium for Citizens with Disabilities to press successfully for passage of the Americans with Disabilities Act of 1990. This act makes full and equal participation in U.S. society more accessible to people with disabilities. The consortium elicited the support of other organizations such as the American Federation of Labor and Congress of Industrial Organizations (AFL-CIO) and the American Civil Liberties Union (ACLU). Simple acts of discontent and insurgency would not have been enough to get results for people who are so marginalized. The mobilization of the vast resources of many organizations, both within the wide-ranging community of people with disabilities and outside it, was critical.

"I asked what I could do. She said I could launch an all-out effort to change the governor's mind—if enough people got involved, maybe, just maybe, he'd sign it."

time, George Deukmejian, had privately said that he'd veto it.

I asked what I could do. She said I could launch an all-out effort to change the governor's mind—if enough people got involved, maybe, just maybe, he'd sign it.

I wrote a paper explaining the loophole in sexual assault laws that hurt me and so many other women. I wrote sample letters to the governor and made copies of them for distribution. I told every friend to contact their friends. I gave out the pack to all my coworkers, and asked them to spread the word.

I spoke at the Women's Center of San Joaquin County and disclosed that I was a survivor. The speech generated tremendous support, especially at the sexual assault center. Women there contacted other centers around the state. I called the leaders of major women's organizations and racial equality groups. Calls, letters, and even telegrams poured into the governor's office calling for passage of AB 674, the "Sexual Battery" bill.

The day slated for the governor's veto came. I called his office with apprehension. His staffer told me that the bill was postponed for further consideration. I contacted everybody I could to keep up the pace for justice. Time was running out. The governor had to make the decision about this and a thousand other bills before midnight. He had three choices. He could either sign the bill, not sign it (in which case it would automatically become law), or veto it.

The waiting became its own hell. I could not sleep. I cried. I prayed. The next morning, September 30, 1989, I called the governor's office at 8 A.M. I asked the staffer for the status of AB 674. When I was on hold waiting, tears streamed down my face. Finally, this disembodied voice said, "It became law."

The man added, "The governor even chose to sign it. That shows he now supports the bill."

I found that one determined individual has the power to change an unjust system. Somebody asked me, "Does this mitigate your attack?" Absolutely not. I still have the scars. But no woman in California need ever again endure what I did. Still, I do worry about the other states that have this loophole. I want to inspire others (that means you) to change these terrible laws. I have found that when women, along with men who share our vision, band together we can make a difference. We can change the world!

Source: Renée La Couture Tulloch, "How I Changed the Governor's Mind," in Virginia Cyrus (ed.), *Experiencing Race, Class, and Gender in the United States* (Mountain View, CA: Mayfield, 1993); originally published in *Ms.*, May–June 1991.

Our discussion of social movements suggests that less powerful people are not absolutely powerless, particularly when they work with others rather than alone as individuals. Consider the article in the accompanying box. Its author refused to be defeated by laws that frustrated her rights. Instead, she learned to marshal resources and support to alter an important and powerful institution.

External Forces   Interestingly, most explanations for social movements look at the internal dynamics of individual societies. But it is important to emphasize that societies do not exist in a vacuum, that forces supportive of social movements or against them can come from outside a given society. For example, as we have noted earlier in this chapter, debt crises have prompted the imposition of IMF-sponsored austerity programs in many underdeveloped countries. In their cross-national comparative analysis of countries with debt crises, John Walton and Charles Ragin (1990) found that the likelihood of political protest was enhanced by increased external pressures for countries to adopt the austerity programs. Such external pressures also increased the intensity of the protests. Walton and Ragin found that although deprivation and hardship of living conditions certainly contributed to people's grievances, these were not strongly related to the protests.

The gay and lesbian movement has organized forces across national boundaries, linking many national gay rights organizations in North America, South America, Asia, Europe, Australia, and Africa in the International Gay Association (IGA). The IGA helps movement organizations join forces, share experiences and information, and support one another's national agenda for gay and lesbian civil rights. The gay and lesbian movement has also organized in solidarity with other groups' movements, including those of women, labor, and people of color, drawing on shared experiences of oppression and the shared desire for change. For example, in a cross-national analysis of gay and lesbian movements, Barry Adam noted that the Mexican Gay Pride Day activities offered support to the people of El Salvador in their struggle for self-determination and, in return, the Farabundo Marti National Liberation Front in El Salvador gave its support to the international gay and lesbian movement (1987: 165). Thus, external resources may combine with internal resource mobilization to provoke and sustain social movements across national boundaries.

CONCLUSION

Social change is not a neutral, natural life force in societies. It is, rather, a political process that involves the organized struggles between the powerful, advantaged segments of society, on the one hand, and the disadvantaged and disenfranchised segments, on the other. People with power and privilege are often in a better position to define the content and direction of change in a way that preserves and enhances their power and privilege.

Development is similarly a political process, marked by unequal historical relationships among nations in a world-system. As such, countries are not advanced and less developed, as if all countries mature through a single series of steps to modernization. Rather, some countries are *under*developed because they have historically been thrust into a disadvantaged position by other countries that have exploited their resources and drained their economies.

Technological innovation as a force of social change is also the product of power inequalities: the powerful are in the best position to define technological needs according to their own interests. Technological innovations tend to enhance the power and control of dominant groups over the less powerful, whether the technology pertains to the workplace or to such personal affairs as human reproduction.

However, despite the strong sense that power inequalities direct social change in order to reinforce and reproduce those inequalities, we are not entirely powerless to affect this process. Social movements are the means through which the less powerful, the disadvantaged, and the disenfranchised can challenge and alter the status quo. And they may even be organized across national boundaries to produce larger, stronger movements with access to greater resources than otherwise possible.

What, then, do processes of social change mean for each of us in our daily lives? New technologies are introduced almost every day, many of which make our existence easier or more comfortable, such as air conditioners, dishwashers, refrigerators, and cars. Some technologies make work safer, such as robots that perform dangerous jobs. Those same technologies, however, may also cost us our jobs, as machines displace human labor. Educational technologies introduce the problem of unequal access to information, as personal computers, copy machines, and fax machines become increasingly central to the education process. Those of you who are unable to afford your own personal computers or word processors know that writing papers and other assignments is more difficult and time-consuming for you than for students who have this equipment. Reproductive technologies are making it possible for many women to conceive and give birth who might otherwise not have had the chance. But the cost of such technologies means that the hope they offer for fertility is available only to relatively affluent women. And these technologies are also contributing to a continuing battle over women's control of the birth process. Women today may have a greater chance than their mothers had to have a baby, but they will need to be highly assertive with their doctors and midwives to have the pregnancy and birth experience they want.

In addition to technological changes, global changes in trade and production also alter our existence. World-system relationships that affect development in Latin America, Asia, and Africa also affect people in countries like the United States. When corporations shift production to poor countries to take advantage of inexpensive labor, consumers in the United States may be able to purchase clothing and electronics more cheaply than before. But they may also find that their jobs disappear as a result of that shift. (We will discuss this problem in greater detail in Chapter 11.)

Finally, once we understand that social change is a political process rather than an inexorable force, we become more empowered to participate in that process. Individuals have generally found it very difficult to combat oppressive forces, but organized groups of individuals have had greater success in resisting social arrangements and institutions they saw as oppressive. This means that you have the potential to participate in the process of social change, from the social organization of the classroom to the institutional arrangements of the economy and the state.

THINKING CRITICALLY

1. We often feel powerless as individuals against the institutions of society. Yet sometimes individuals do alter how they are affected by institutions. Consider the boxed article in this chapter. How did the author manage to instigate change? What resources did she marshal on her

behalf? Did she, in fact, do this alone? Which theory of social movements best explains this case?

2. Select a recent technological innovation and discuss how it might alter society. How might it make life easier or better? What might be some of the limitations or problems generated by this technology? Now consider: Who would benefit from this technology, and who would be hurt? Why? How might this technology alter your life?

3. The early 1990s saw the breakup of the Soviet Union into separate, independent countries. How has this dramatic social change in Eastern Europe affected the United States? How has it affected your daily existence? What does this suggest about the sources of social change?

4. Select a social movement (such as the nuclear freeze, gay rights, disability rights, women's rights, labor, pro-choice, antiabortion, or fundamentalist movement or some other movement of your own choosing). Examine the successes and setbacks of this movement. What factors might account for its successes? What factors might account for its setbacks? Who benefits and who is hurt by the movement's successes? How? Which theory of social movements best explains this movement?

5. Compare your daily life with that of your parents or grandparents at your age (it might be useful and interesting to talk with them if possible and to talk to both males and females). How is your life different from theirs? Why? How is it similar? How might gender or class explain some of these differences and similarities? Which theory of social change or social movements might explain the differences or similarities?

KEY TERMS

social change, *278*
social reforms, *278*
social revolutions, *278*
manifest social change, *278*
latent social change, *278*
cyclical perspective, *279*
evolutionary perspective, *280*
social Darwinism, *281*
equilibrium perspective, *281*
conflict perspective, *282*
dialectic, *282*
thesis, *282*
antithesis, *282*
synthesis, *282*
capitalists, *282*
proletariat, *282*
modernization theory, *284*
basic needs, *284*
underdeveloped nations, *287*

trade dependency, *287*
import substitution, *289*
export processing, *289*
dependent development, *289*
debt dependency, *290*
concessional loans, *290*
nonconcessional loans, *291*
debt-for-nature swaps, *293*
inventions, *294*
cottage industries, *295*
surrogate mother, *298*
social movements, *300*
redemptive movements, *300*
alterative movements, *300*
reformative movements, *300*
transformative movements, *301*
absolute deprivation, *303*
relative deprivation, *303*
resource mobilization theory, *304*

SUGGESTED READINGS

313

Chapter 9

Social Change
and Social
Movements

Steven Buechler, *Women's Movements in the United States: Woman Suffrage, Equal Rights, and Beyond.* New Brunswick, NJ: Rutgers University Press, 1990. A comparative analysis of the women's suffrage movement from the mid-nineteenth to early twentieth centuries and the current women's movement.

Marlene Gerber Fried (ed.), *From Abortion to Reproductive Freedom: Transforming a Movement.* Boston: South End Press, 1990. A collection of essays that together make a case for expanding the abortion rights movement from its focus on a single issue to a more broadly defined, multicultural feminist movement.

Hans Haferkamp and Neil J. Smelser (eds.), *Social Change and Modernity.* Berkeley, CA: University of California Press, 1992. A collection of essays exploring social movements and social changes, including the feminist movement, the antinuclear movement, and the environmental movement in the United States and Europe.

Aldon D. Morris and Carol McClurg Mueller (eds.), *Frontiers in Social Movement Theory.* New Haven: Yale University Press, 1992. A collection of essays outlining new approaches to the study of social movements, with analyses of the relation between social movements, the state, and social change.

Peter Rachleff, *Hard-Pressed in the Heartland: The Hormel Strike and the Future of the Labor Movement.* Boston: South End Press, 1993. An analysis of the bitter strike against the Hormel meatpacking corporation and its implications for the labor movement.

Rudi Volti, *Society and Technological Change,* 2d ed. New York: St. Martin's Press, 1992. An examination of technological innovations in work, communications, and warfare and a critical analysis of the forces that encourage technological changes and the social consequences of these changes.

William Wei, *The Asian American Movement.* Philadelphia: Temple University Press, 1993. An exploration of the emerging consciousness and development of a movement among an ethnically diverse population. The analysis examines issues of ethnicity, class, and gender as the movement begins to transform itself from radical politics to the electoral process.

INSTITUTIONAL SPHERES

THE STATE
AND CAPITAL

*T*wo of the most powerful institutions affecting our biographies are the state and the economy. The term **state** refers to the organization of political positions and the structure of political relations in society. This is different from **government,** which refers to the politicians who occupy positions within the state. As individual politicians come and go, the government may change specific policies or views, reflecting individuals' personal styles, perspectives, party affiliations, interests, and so forth. However, the structure of political relations—electoral processes, policy-making processes, relations between the

government and corporations, labor, consumers, and others—remains intact regardless of the individuals who occupy the positions within the state.

The **economy** *comprises the structures, relationships, and activities that produce and distribute wealth in society. Both the state and the economy are quite influential in shaping our opportunities and our places in the larger society. These institutions do not operate in isolation from each other but, rather, intersect in various ways to affect our lives. What is the nature of the relationship between political and economic institutions within a corporate capitalist society? Can a society in which economic ownership is concentrated in relatively few hands function democratically? Is the state a neutral arbiter among competing interests, legislating in the common good? What is the relationship between the military, the state, and capital? In what ways do the needs of capital clash with the fundamental needs of people, and with what results?*

This chapter will explore how sociologists use different perspectives to examine these questions. In particular, we will focus on the corporate economy in this chapter; we will emphasize the role of labor in the economy more specifically in Chapter 11, "Work and Production." Thus, here we will look at voting patterns in the United States and at the way our economy affects how well voters can influence their elected leaders in government. We will also examine the relationship between workers, private corporations, and the state and consider how this relationship affects the functioning of government. In short, we will discuss various ways in which the state and the economy intersect. Finally, we will look at an example of how these relationships can affect our daily existence by exploring the New Federalism of the Reagan-Bush years.

PLURALISM

Some sociologists argue that the state and the economy are two separate institutions. They generally presume that the economy is a neutral entity governed by its own "laws" of the market, such as supply and demand, and they focus their analyses on how political structures affect our lives and how we affect the political process. We call this perspective **pluralism.** There are two strands of pluralist thought, interest-group pluralism and elite pluralism.

Interest-Group Pluralism

According to advocates of **interest-group pluralism** (such as Truman, 1951), our society is composed of a wide variety of competing interest groups, through which we engage in political activity and affect the workings of government. We may choose to belong to one or more of these interest groups, and many of us very likely belong to several. Each of these groups pressures the state in order to get its needs met. In doing so, the groups compete against one another, often making conflicting demands on the state. Examples of interest groups include the American Medical Association, the National Association of Manufacturers, the American Banking Association, labor unions, the National Organization for Women, the National Association for the Advancement of Colored People, and the American Association of Retired Persons.

In the view of the interest-group pluralists, the state acts as a neutral referee, or arbiter, in this scenario, weighing and balancing competing demands, evaluating the legitimacy of each, and negotiating a compromise wherever possible in order to legislate in the common good of society. In this way, the state ensures a balance of power between many groups, thereby lending stability to society.

Several other characteristics of our political system also are said to contribute to stability. For example, interest-group pluralists believe a "natural" balance of power occurs between the interest groups, because none of them is strong enough to win whatever it wants each time. This leads groups to form alliances with one another on a variety of issues. Groups also realize that each has a sort of veto power over the others: if any group did operate unilaterally against the interests of the others, the others would form an alliance against the transgressor. This interaction among groups is said to ensure the common good of society as a whole. Moreover, since members of our society are likely to belong to several interest groups, the overlapping memberships serve to create pressures that dilute each group's powers. Interest groups must compromise with others to avoid losing members who may find the conflict between their various memberships too great.

Pluralists also believe that society is balanced and stable because everyone agrees on the basic rules governing interest-group competition. This means that when we have an interest or a goal we want the state to address, we approach the state through democratic procedures, including elections, petitions to our legislators, lawsuits filed in the courts, and so on. Adherence to these procedures ensures legislation in the common good.

Finally, society is stabilized by the existence of *potential* interest groups. When existing interest groups do not address the needs or interests of people, or when the state ignores people's interests, individuals may mobilize to form a new active interest group and enter into the democratic process of appealing to the state. The possibility of such a mobilization prevents existing groups from ignoring the interests of others.

Critics argue that interest-group pluralists tend to treat all existing groups as if they had the same strength and power. But some groups have access to greater resources than others, some are larger in membership than others, and some represent more powerful constituencies. Moreover, some important interests have historically been weak and disregarded in the democratic process, such as those of children, the homeless, undocumented workers, people of color, and the poor. It is difficult to argue that all groups, both existing and potential, are equally powerful when we can see that some groups have had great success in obtaining many of their goals while others have had little success.

Pluralists would counter this criticism by arguing that the reason some groups seem more successful is that their interests and objectives are more consistent with the common good. When the state, as neutral arbiter, weighs and evaluates the competing demands before it, it legislates in the "common good." However, we must question the meaning of this term. Who defines the common good? Is it possible that what the state defines as the common good may still hinder or eliminate the ability of some groups to have their objectives met? What are the social background characteristics of those who define the common good? Interest-group pluralists assume that the state (structure) is neutral and that individuals within that structure make decisions impartially. Their analysis assumes that governmental officials have no interest-group ties of their own.

Critics of interest-group pluralism do not accept the notion that stability is necessarily a sign of social health. Some people may benefit and others be hurt by a stable system. Interest-group pluralists skirt this issue by assuming that those whose interests are being ignored will eventually mobilize and form new interest groups. For these pluralists, then, stability in society means that a wide variety of interests are being met adequately and any inequalities that may exist are minimal. But it is possible for society to be "in balance" while ignoring important interests. For example, we can have a stable and balanced economy while having a high rate of unemployment and poverty. Similarly, we can achieve racial balance in schools and workplaces while still maintaining a fairly high level of discrimination within classrooms and offices. The meaning of balance and stability is defined by the relatively powerful and advantaged groups whose existing privilege is preserved by such definitions.

Critics of interest-group pluralism also take issue with the notion of potential interest groups. How can we gauge the power of potential groups if they do not yet exist? How can we analyze the effectiveness of potential groups in altering or modifying the behavior of existing groups? Existing interest groups may, indeed, worry about challenges from others, but how much do they worry, and how much does that concern alter their pursuit of their own objectives?

Finally, critics argue that interest-group pluralism overstates the importance of groups. Because it focuses on group dynamics, it fails to address the importance of individuals. Since interest-group pluralists do not distinguish between successful and unsuccessful interest groups, they do not discuss the differences between individuals who are regularly advantaged by the political system and those who are not.

Elite Pluralism

One group of sociologists looked for a way to address the issue of individual advantage while still retaining much of the pluralist framework. They became known as elite pluralists (Lipset, 1960; Dahl, 1961; Rose, 1967). Their perspective, **elite pluralism,** focuses on the plurality of competing *elites* rather than competing groups in the political process. Elite pluralists argue that the political process operates much like the marketplace: elite politicians compete for our votes in the same way that consumer products compete for our dollars. Just as competing interest groups are balanced by the need for cooperation and alliances, competing candidates are balanced by the fact that various constituents ignored today may be needed tomorrow for coalitions and support. So politicians are constrained to legislate in the common good because their own political fate is in the hands of the electorate. If elected officials do not pay attention to certain interests, they run the danger of being voted out of office by angry constituents. If they ignore issues of concern to people who do not regularly participate in the electoral process, politicians still run the danger of being voted out of office when those individuals become politically active.

For example, elected officials have consistently ignored or attacked the interests and needs of the gay community. In response, gays have become increasingly active politically. They have organized and mobilized their resources in the electoral process to replace unsympathetic elected officials with more supportive candidates. In the 1970s there were less than 5

Social gatherings such as this tailgate party at Stanford University help to solidify class identity of the power elite. Notice that all participants in this party are white, one of the characteristics of the power elite.

openly gay elected officials in the United States; in 1990 there were more than 50 on local and state levels (Corcoran, 1991).

Critics of pluralism have argued that the shift in emphasis from groups to elites still does not explain the persistence of serious social problems such as racism, poverty, sexism, suppression of political dissent, and homelessness. If the system is balanced by the need for politicians to heed the interests of their constituents, why do so many people still seem left out? The elite pluralists' argument does not account for the many people who are not politically well represented.

POWER ELITE THEORY

Pluralism focuses exclusively on the electoral and political processes. **Power elite theory** examines some of the ways political institutions, particularly the state and the economy, intersect. Unlike pluralists, these theorists argue that the state cannot be neutral, because of the structures and processes of the **power elite** (Mills, 1957). The power elite are those people who fill the command positions of strategically important institutions, namely, the state, the corporate economy, and the military. The elite who fill these positions come from a single group and share a single world view

Although pluralists argue that elites are held in check by the electoral marketplace, critics note that not all elites in power are elected. These auto workers are trying to stop plant closings in their communities. Although they may elect their local representatives, they do not elect the corporate leaders who determine whether they will continue to have jobs.

because of three related processes: co-optation, class identity, and the interchangeability of the institutional elites.

Co-optation involves the socialization of prospective and new members of the elite so that they come to share the world view of the power elite. That is, individuals who aspire to elite positions must be willing to adopt the prevailing world view and ideology espoused by the existing elite, who select the new members of their circle of privilege. Only those who share that prevailing ideology will be selected. Once selected, new members of the elite become surrounded by that ideology, and they further internalize it.

Class identity results from the common life experiences of members of the elite, which give them a sense of being members of an exclusive group. Members of the power elite have usually attended prestigious private prep schools and Ivy League colleges, belong to exclusive social clubs, live in affluent communities, and travel in cliques. Their children tend to marry one another, thereby sealing wealth and power between families (Domhoff, 1970). In this way they are unlikely to confront views held by members of other classes that challenge those they share. They are unified in their beliefs about what is best for society and how the world works, because these beliefs are constantly reaffirmed by their experiences and their contacts.

Finally, the power elite are unified by their **interchangeability** among the three main institutions. The people who fill the top positions in the state, the corporate economy, and the military circulate easily from one sphere to another. This mingling of personnel blurs any sharp distinctions in experience, perspective, ideology, or world view such leaders may have. For example, Alexander Haig, Jr., was a president of United Technologies (a major defense contractor), a former four-star general in the U.S. Army, and secretary of state under Ronald Reagan (1981–1982). George Shultz, president of the Bechtel Corporation (another major defense contractor), was Reagan's secretary of state (1982–1989) as well as a previous secretary of the treasury and secretary of labor (Dye, 1990: 91). (Table 10.1 presents additional examples of former cabinet members and their institutional ties).

C. Wright Mills argued that the interchangeability of elites among the three most powerful institutions results in a fusion of views among leaders. They do not develop viewpoints and interests specific to one institution. When the power elite switch hats from one institutional realm to another, they bring with them their prejudices, their beliefs, and their interests. No competing viewpoints are expressed, then, among leaders. There is only one viewpoint, expressed by one group of people: the power elite. As such, the interests of Chrysler, the Pentagon, and the United States become fused into one set of common interests.

The state, then, according to power elite theorists, is not neutral or autonomous; it is heavily influenced by capital and corporate interests. Voting processes simply make the existing state *appear* legitimate; they channel our energies into relatively innocuous activities that appear to empower us. Electoral politics also distract our attention from an understanding of the relationship between the state and the economy and therefore give us the false security of believing that the state legislates for the common good.

Table 10.1

THE POWER ELITE IN THE CABINET

SECRETARIES OF DEFENSE

Thomas S. Gates (1959–1960): Secretary of the Navy, 1957–1959; chairman of the board and chief executive officer, Morgan Guaranty Trust Co.; member of the board of directors of General Electric, Bethlehem Steel, Scott Paper Co., Campbell Soup Co., Insurance Co. of North America, Cities Service, SmithKline and French (pharmaceuticals), and the University of Pennsylvania.

Caspar W. Weinberger (1981–1989): Vice president and director of the Bechtel Corporation, the world's largest privately owned corporation; a member of the board of directors of Pepsico and Quaker Oats Co.; former Secretary of Health, Education, and Welfare under President Richard Nixon; former director of the Office of Management and Budget; former chairman of the Federal Trade Commission; a former San Francisco attorney and California State legislator.

SECRETARIES OF STATE

Alexander M. Haig, Jr. (1981–1982): President of United Technologies Corporation; former four-star general, U.S. Army; former Supreme Allied Commander, NATO forces in Europe; former assistant to the President under Richard Nixon; former deputy assistant to the President for national security under Henry Kissinger; former deputy commandant, U.S. Military Academy at West Point; former deputy Secretary of Defense.

George P. Shultz (1982–1989): President of the Bechtel Corporation; former Secretary of the Treasury, former Secretary of Labor, and former director of Office of Management and Budget under President Richard Nixon; earned Ph.D. in economics from M.I.T.; former dean of the school of business, University of Chicago; former director of General Motors, Borg-Warner, and Dillon, Read & Co.

SECRETARIES OF THE TREASURY

William E. Simon (1974–1977): Director of Federal Energy Office; former deputy Secretary of the Treasury; formerly a senior partner of Salomon Brothers (one of Wall Street's largest investment firms specializing in municipal bond trading).

Warner Michael Blumenthal (1977–1979): President of the Bendix Corporation; former vice president of Crown Cork Co.; trustee of Princeton University and the Council on Foreign Relations.

G. William Miller (1979–1981): Chairman and chief executive officer of Textron Corporation; former partner in Cravath, Swaine & Moore (one of the nation's 25 largest and most prestigious law firms); a former director of Allied Chemical and Federated Department Stores; former chairman of the Federal Reserve Board.

Source: Thomas R. Dye, *Who's Running America? The Bush Era* (Englewood Cliffs, NJ: Prentice-Hall, 1990), pp. 89–92.

It is noteworthy, too, that the power elite are typically white male Protestants educated at prestigious institutions. Analyzing the Reagan-Bush era, for example, Thomas R. Dye (1990) found that less than 5 percent of the top 7,314 institutional positions in the power elite were filled by women and only 0.3 percent were filled by African Americans. He noted the findings of a study by Richard D. Alba and Gwen Moore (1982):

While white Anglo-Saxon Protestants made up less than 23 percent of the people born before 1932, they filled 57.3 percent of the top corporate positions and 53.4 percent of congressional seats.

Dye also found that 54 percent of the corporate elite and 42 percent of the state elite were graduates of the twelve most exclusive private universities (1990: 193). And more than two-thirds of the institutional elite were members of social clubs; more than one-third belonged to 1 or more of 37 exclusive clubs. Together, these data suggest a strong race, class, and gender bias among the power elite.

Given the combined processes of co-optation and class identity, it is not surprising to find evidence of an overwhelmingly white, male, relatively affluent network of individuals mentoring, supporting, and promoting new elites much like themselves. Yet there is also evidence that this network is not powerful enough to be entirely closed; it is possible for someone outside the network to break into elite ranks. Consider the women you read about in the box in Chapter 6: although they encountered formidable resistance and hostility, both to their gender and, at times, to their race, they transcended these obstacles and managed to rise to positions of significance in a variety of institutions. And while there are still few women holding executive-level positions in the powerful institutions of society, the stories presented in Chapter 6 suggest that we may expect to see more women in these positions in the future.

The experiences of such women point to a weakness in power elite theory: Mills mistakenly attributed a sense of omnipotence to the elite and therefore overlooked the dynamics of class struggle and conflict in redefining the balance of power from time to time. For example, the labor movement in the United States played a significant role in shifting the balance of power in the economy, thereby reducing the unbridled power of capitalists. In fact, Mills's view that the role of the masses was insignificant led him to specifically ignore the importance of racism in the development of elite power. Practices of institutionalized racism, including restrictions on the education and voting rights of blacks, prevented African Americans from being able to counter the concentration of power among relatively few whites. Similarly, Mills did not discuss the significance of imperialism, which gave power to the multinational corporate, military, and political elites on the global level.

In addition to these historical problems, there are some conceptual problems in power elite theory. Mills argued that resources available to the powerful—such as money, prestige, and status—are drawn from these individuals' commanding positions in the three main social institutions. But it may be that the various positions provide access to different kinds of resources in differing amounts. And, while Mills presumed that all these resources were equally important as power bases, it may be that some resources are more important than others. Similarly, Mills assumed that the three main institutions are equally significant, but he did not provide evidence supporting this equality. Nor did he provide a concrete analysis of how the main institutions of society operate together to produce an omnipotent institutional structure.

An International Perspective

Power elite theory is often criticized for consisting of myopic analyses of Western countries, particularly the United States; it does not explain much about other, noncapitalist, nondemocratic societies. However, as the boxed interview shows, there may be some aspects of other countries, such as China, that power elite theory can help us understand. As in the United States and other Western democratic countries, democracy and freedom of speech are important issues for many people in China. The struggle to attain such freedoms escalated in 1989 when thousands of students and others gathered in Tiananmen Square to voice their concerns despite intense pressure from the state to cease such activities. Finally, after the demonstrators ignored the state's demands, state leaders instructed the military to forcibly disperse them. Estimates are that between 3,000 and 7,000 people were massacred in the ensuing confrontation.

The Military-Industrial Complex

If we accept that there is a power elite, what effect do its members have on the relationship between the state and the economy? According to some social scientists, their influence occurs through the actions of the **military-industrial complex,** composed of the uniformed military, the aerospace-defense industry, the civilian national security managers, and the U.S. Congress (Pilisuk and Hayden, 1965). Each of the components of the military-industrial complex works to advance its own interests while simultaneously promoting and reinforcing the interests of the others (Barnet, 1969; Adams, 1982).

What does each of these components want? The uniformed military needs to maintain—and preferably expand—its capability to wage war. Its massive budgets enable it to conduct public relations campaigns portraying military goals as patriotic and justified.

An even more influential component of the military-industrial complex is the corporate sector, particularly the large aerospace-defense industry. This industry supports military expenditures because it benefits from huge procurement contracts. In 1991, for example, U.S. military contracts totaled $150.9 billion, 83.4 percent of which went to U.S. corporations (U.S. Department of Defense, 1992). Such sizable contracts guarantee substantial profits without the risks of the free market. Indeed, Defense Department contracts are so lucrative that they constitute the biggest proportion of business done by most of the largest firms in the aerospace-defense industry (Tobias et al., 1982). Since the end of the Cold War in the late 1980s, Congress has reduced the military budget. However, the reductions have not returned the military budget to pre-Cold War proportions. Furthermore, the Clinton administration agreed with the need to support a strong defense capability by maintaining military expenditures, pointing to the instability facing the United States and the world from Haiti, Cuba, North Korea, and the Middle East, as well as from terrorists. Thus, many corporations that enjoyed highly profitable defense contracts during the Cold War still benefit from military expenditures.

The civilian national security managers support military spending because they tie American national security to access to global resources and markets and develop foreign policy with that goal in mind. These managers are influenced heavily by their backgrounds in large corporate firms. Richard Barnet's study of the military-industrial complex found that 76.9 percent of the top national security managers between 1940 and 1967 had at one time worked for major corporations or financial institutions (1969: 88). Not surprisingly, their views on national security and foreign policy were consistent with those of corporate leaders.

Finally, members of Congress consistently grant the military a large proportion of the federal budget because doing so creates jobs for their voting constituents both in the military (on its hundreds of bases) and in the aerospace-defense industry. Furthermore, since members of Congress tend to be affluent, they are likely to be stockholders in major American corporations, including aerospace-defense contractors. And so are their major campaign contributors. The positions our representatives take, then, on defense spending may affect both their own personal wealth and their chances of getting reelected (Lens, 1970).

The primary interest unifying these components of the military-industrial complex is the protection of capital accumulation. For close to 50 years, U.S. military expenditures and foreign policy had been fueled by Cold War fears of communism. More recently, they have been influenced by fears that Third World countries will restrict or eliminate our access to crucial resources. At the same time, thousands of U.S. corporations have opened production facilities abroad, particularly in Third World countries. But those countries characterized by widespread poverty and oppression are susceptible to revolutions and socialist economic systems. These systems threaten capital-accumulation interests, because they may institute state control of production, nationalize industries, and restrict employers' exploitation of labor. Vast military expenditures have been devoted, then, to securing the political environment in which U.S. corporations operate abroad. This protection has often extended to U.S. military and paramilitary (for example, CIA) interventions in other countries, such as Nicaragua in the 1980s and Chile in the 1970s.

Why are private capital-accumulation interests so important to the state? In 1991, the top 1,000 corporations identified by *Business Week* produced sales of $3.8 trillion, with earnings of $176 billion. With assets totaling $2.97 trillion, these firms are clearly at the center of the nation's economic well-being. When they succeed in growing and in generating profits, the economy avoids stagnation, recession, or, worse, depression. Thus, as former Secretary of Defense and General Motors Chairman Charles E. Wilson once said, what's good for General Motors is good for the United States.

In order to grow, many of these firms must eventually expand their operations beyond the shores of the United States. When firms operate production and trade facilities in other countries, we call them **multinational (or transnational) corporations.** Most of the money such corporations have invested abroad has gone to the economies of developed countries where American corporations provide manufactured goods. The remaining invest-

Chai Ling was one of four widely recognized student leaders in the Chinese democracy movement. In this interview he describes a power elite in China that appears to parallel the power elite in the United States, even though the political economy in China is very different from that in our own nation. And while we may believe that stories such as those in Tiananmen Square would never happen in our own country, the fact is that history is replete with many similar stories in the American labor movement, antiwar movement, and civil rights movement.

Q: How do the masses see Tiananmen?

A: We have often heard that the masses look to the students with admiration. They identify the students with their own sons and daughters, fighting for their own interests. The transformation of the Student Movement to a Democracy Movement indicates that the Chinese people are exerting their authority, that a new China is born, one which belongs to the people.

Q: What has the atmosphere been like over the past few days?

A: There have been some management problems and some confusion; but the organization is very united, and we are confident.

Q: Do you think that [competing Chinese leaders] are making use of the Movement?

A: Naturally. Every Movement in the past has produced governmental changes. However, the present Movement has been unique in putting itself above factional struggles. We will not get involved in them, even though they attempt to use us. Such attempts are, I think, in vain; for the aim of the Student Movement is to struggle for progress towards a modern Chinese democracy. The Movement does not choose between [these leaders] for we oppose every leader who stands in opposition to the people. If, however, a leader takes a popular position, reflecting the demands and interests of the people, then he will be supported by them.

Q: You place the greatest emphasis on democracy. There are probably many Chinese who don't understand what it is. In the United States, democracy means the choice of each new President by popular vote.

A: I think that dem ocracy is a natural right. In the past, human nature in China was very restricted, and there were no rights. For example, consider the conditions in the universities. When it comes to getting a job, you must go where the party decides. Furthermore, there is no supervision over the party, the security forces, or the army. This gives rise to profiteering, corruption, decadence and all of the ills that have accompanied the last ten years of economic reform. Those who acquired wealth recently all have links to those in power. The Chinese have had an emperor to rule them for more than two thousand years. There has never been freedom of speech, freedom of the press, or personal security, and there is little hope for the future. Prior to this Movement there was a moral crisis, and nobody was interested in anything but money. Through this Movement the Chinese have regained a sense of purpose and ability to solve their own problems. We do not depend upon foreign models, but upon ourselves.

"The transformation of the Student Movement to a Democracy Movement indicates that the Chinese people are exerting their authority, that a new China is born, one which belongs to the people."

Q: Can democracy and communist-socialism co-exist?

A: I have not done any great theoretical research. My view is that democracy is a basic human need, and not contrary to the basic tenets of communism. The sort of democracy which we demand is very natural, a natural right. It is not hooked up to any specific ideology. We are fighting for control of our own lives.

Q: Do you visualise how democracy will spread in China?

A: I think that it will be a long process, possibly sixty or seventy years. My hope is that one day we might live securely in a China where people can enjoy the fruits of their labours whilst possessing the power to participate in the management of the country. We shall have power to determine the policies implemented by our leaders, feeling ourselves to be our own masters in a country that we own. It will be a powerful nation which each generation will struggle to maintain.

Q: Will your Movement have any international significance?

A: Knowledge has no barriers. Although we struggle for our own country, we can have an influence on others as members of the world community.

There has been some confusion, but the more resolute of us are now united to combat that. We have demonstrated to the world that we are orderly, reasonable and strong. I say to you from the bottom of my heart that, if this Movement fails, it will be a tragedy for the whole nation. It will mean that the people's democratic consciousness was insufficiently developed, and that it was doomed from the start. The few thousand students on the Square cannot alone prevent its failure. However, if the Movement succeeds, the victory for democracy will be a liberation of the human nature of the whole Chinese people.

Q: Do you want to see a country of equality or inequality of wealth?

A: We don't have statistics; but I would say that the disparity of wealth in China today, between the privileged and the ordinary person, is as extreme as that found in capitalist countries. I would hope that, after human nature is liberated in our society, a kind of spontaneous and harmonious regulation will occur. There will be differences. For example, those who are wise and hardworking will be better off than the lazy and incompetent. This is a natural inequality and not deliberately designed. However, today China's inequalities are deliberately produced by those in power, man-made and unnatural.

The Movement has been spontaneous and non-conspiratorial. There is no ruling theoretical framework. We just follow our feelings! It is a pure and unsullied demand for democracy. In it we see that the best and most advanced elements are students, who form a vanguard for the nation.

June 3, 1989

Source: Mok Chiu and J. Frank Harrison (eds.), *Voices from Tiananmen Square* (Montreal; New York: Black Rose Books, 1990), pp. 158–161.

ment capital has gone to Mideast countries rich in petroleum and to under-developed countries in the Third World, where corporations can capitalize on inexpensive labor and various tax breaks. While the risk is certainly higher for investments in underdeveloped countries than for those in Europe and Canada, the rate of return is also much greater. For example, the average rate of return on dollars invested in Latin America is approximately 20 percent, compared with the international average of approximately 7 percent (see U.S. Department of Commerce, 1990). Since U.S.-based multinational corporations' earnings from their foreign operations account for 50 percent or more of their annual earnings, they want to be sure that the environment in which such earnings are produced is secure. Thus, the economic well-being of the United States depends significantly on U.S. corporations' ability to do business abroad.

Not incidently, the ability of these firms to operate in other countries also gives them access to—and often control over—critical raw materials. These resources, needed in aerospace-defense industries, are inaccessible or expensive to mine in the United States. Therefore, it is in both the economic and the military interests of the state to secure the safety of U.S. corporations in other countries and enable them to continue operations in times of political unrest.

The global expansion of U.S. capital-accumulation interests has been aided, then, by congressional willingness to provide tax dollars for military expenditures and by the foreign policy devised by civilian national security managers. These managers, typically drawn from business and finance circles, formulate foreign policy that is consistent with the need to protect corporations' foreign operations. For example, U.S. national security managers have supported economic and military aid to underdeveloped countries in the Third World. Economic aid often requires the recipients to purchase goods and services from U.S. corporations. Military aid similarly requires the recipients to purchase military equipment and supplies produced by the U.S. aerospace-defense industry. This arrangement has enormous economic consequences for U.S. corporations: in 1991, sales of U.S. arms and weapons systems to both underdeveloped and developed nations exceeded $62.9 billion, more than half of the world export market (Bixby, 1992).

The Gulf War   The power of the military-industrial complex was exercised forcefully in 1991, when the United States entered into the Gulf war against Iraq. Ostensibly, American intervention after Iraq's invasion of Kuwait was based on the need to maintain U.S. access to Kuwait's vast oil reserves. Yet U.S. national security managers had previously notified Iraq's Saddam Hussein that Iraq could settle its disputes with Kuwait in any manner that it saw fit. Why, then, did the United States, with the approval of Congress, go to war against Iraq?

In the aftermath of the war, it became clear that the big winners were the components of the military-industrial complex. One was the Raytheon Corporation, the manufacturer of the Patriot missiles, which

The military-industrial complex benefits each of its components well by fusing their interests. Here, President Bush's visit to the Raytheon Corporation's Patriot missile plant during the Gulf war reflects that fusion of interests and mutual advantage among the military, the state, and defense corporations like Raytheon.

became a military symbol of U.S. strength and resolve. The profits of Exxon and other oil corporations increased by an amazing 75 percent in the first weeks of the war (Hayes, 1991). This is because the war created a disruption in oil production, thereby allowing U.S. oil corporations to sharply raise their prices. Other big winners included the military, which was facing vast budget cuts at the end of the Cold War against the Soviet Union. Finally, among the major winners were members of Congress whose home districts benefited economically from the military buildup and the prospects of future orders for military hardware from several Mideast countries. Clearly, President George Bush benefited from the Gulf war as well. His approval rating in the United States reached its highest point in his presidency, boosting his political capital a great deal. People in the United States and abroad perceived him as a strong, no-nonsense President and international leader. Many in the media characterized the Gulf war as an end to the "Vietnam syndrome," wherein political leaders hesitated to become involved in international conflicts for fear of strong criticism and resistance in the United States. All components of the military-industrial complex, then, benefited handsomely from massive expenditures connected with the war with Iraq, even if the poor, the hungry, the homeless, the working-class unemployed, women, and schoolchildren in the United States, as well as nonelites in Iraq and Kuwait, did not.

VOTING: WHO PARTICIPATES?

Our discussion of the U.S. military-industrial complex highlights an important fact: Nonelites are not central actors in that important structure. How, then, do nonelites participate politically? Pluralists emphasize the importance of elections and voting. However, power elite theorists point out that while we may elect some of the power elite, we do not elect the leaders who run the corporate economy and the uniformed military. Voters have no way to hold these elite leaders accountable. Pluralists assume that we all agree on how we are to behave politically and that the only acceptable means of affecting government is through electoral politics. But the norms of political behavior are determined by the people in power and the people who benefit most from the existing system. For example, regulations defining who may vote, based on residence qualifications, are determined by Congress, which is disproportionately populated by persons who are relatively advantaged. One must have a permanent address in order to qualify to vote. Thus, the homeless are not allowed to participate in selecting the leaders whose decision-making will affect their lives. Electoral politics may channel certain issues and problems into a controlled institutional arena, but what happens when elites consistently ignore some issues?

In any case, voters in the United States turn out in notoriously low numbers. As you can see in Figure 10.1, voting participation rates have steadily declined from an all-time high of around 63 percent in the 1960 national elections. By the 1992 presidential election, only 54 percent of the eligible voters actually participated (a slight improvement over 1988) (Pear, 1992). Participation rates are even worse in state and local elections. In fact, the United States has one of the lowest voter participation rates among industrialized capitalist democracies (only Switzerland has a lower rate) (Jackman, 1987: 409). What do such poor voter turnouts in the United States mean?

Pluralists argue that the low rates indicate the population is satisfied with the existing leadership and feels no need to participate. When the electorate becomes dissatisfied, they argue, it will mobilize and vote to unseat the unsatisfactory political elites. To pluralists, then, low voter turnout rates suggest that the system is working and that voters are happy with the current state of affairs.

Table 10.2 shows the characteristics of persons who vote. Such data make it more difficult to accept the pluralist interpretation. Overwhelmingly the highest turnout rates occur within the higher-income, higher-education, and higher-status-occupation groups. And whites, as a group, tend to turn out more than racial minorities. We might interpret these data as evidence that people who benefit most from the status quo are more likely to participate in electoral politics than people who are disadvantaged by it.

Some pluralists counter that it is good that the better-educated are the most likely to vote, since they are more likely than the poorly educated or illiterate to make intelligent choices and are not likely to be exploited by political extremists (Banfield and Wilson, 1963). Some also argue that the language skills of highly educated people and the political skills entailed in high-status occupations easily translate into the skills required to participate effectively in electoral politics. Others argue that political participation (particularly those activities that go beyond voting) requires a great deal of time, money, and energy—resources that the poor and working class are not likely to have in great quantities (Lipset, 1960).

Critics of pluralism point out that the electoral system is set up to *discourage* some people from participating. Registration and voting procedures raise mechanical obstacles to participation by the poor, the working class, and the poorly educated. Indeed, registration rates for African Americans and Latinos, as well as the poor, lag behind those of whites and more affluent groups. The lack of bilingual registration and election forms, the confusion associated with absentee ballots (for students, migrant workers, and military personnel), poorly phrased and confusing legalistic jargon on referenda, and endless primaries all serve to reduce participation rates among those groups (Piven and Cloward, 1988).

Taken together, these analyses of differential participation suggest that there are numerous reasons why the advantaged are more likely to vote than the disadvantaged. Yet, when we look at who does *not* vote, we find that nonparticipation cuts across all categories, including the more advantaged groups. What does such nonparticipation mean?

Voting is supposed to be the means by which we hold our elected leaders accountable. Yet voting participation rates in national elections since at least 1932 indicate that citizens do not flood the voting booths to make their opinions matter. Why is the turnout so low? Did you vote in the last election? Why or why not? (*Source: New York Times*, November 5, 1992, p. 34.)

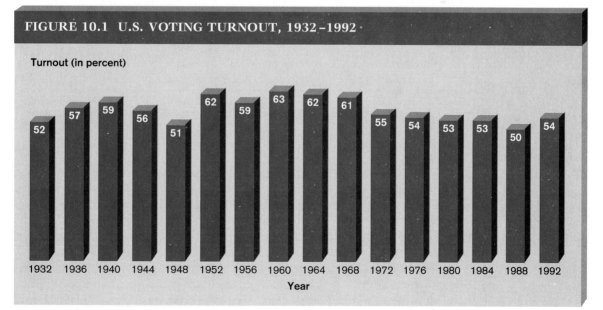

FIGURE 10.1 U.S. VOTING TURNOUT, 1932–1992

Turnout (in percent)

Year	1932	1936	1940	1944	1948	1952	1956	1960	1964	1968	1972	1976	1980	1984	1988	1992
Turnout	52	57	59	56	51	62	59	63	62	61	55	54	53	53	50	54

Table 10.2

CHARACTERISTICS OF VOTERS, 1992

CHARACTERISTIC	PERCENTAGE VOTING
Education:	
Less than 8th grade	35.1
Some high school	41.2
High school graduate	57.5
Some college	68.7
Bachelor or higher degree	81.0
Labor-force status:	
Employed	63.8
Unemployed	46.2
Occupation:	
Managerial, professional	79.0
Technical, sales, administrative support	68.0
Service occupations	52.2
Precision product, craft, repair	53.6
Farming, forestry, fishing	54.2
Operators, fabricators, laborers	46.4
Income:	
Under $5,000	32.4
$5,000–$9,999	39.5
$10,000–$14,999	46.8
$15,000–$19,999	55.7
$20,000–$24,999	62.5
$25,000–$34,999	69.5
$35,000–$49,999	75.7
$50,000 and over	79.9
Race:	
White	63.6
African American	54.0
Latino	28.9
Gender:	
Male	60.2
Female	62.3

Source: U.S. Bureau of the Census, *Current Population Reports,* Series P20-466: *Voting and Registration in the Election of November 1992* (Washington, DC: U.S. Government Printing Office, 1993).

A likely explanation for the lack of a pattern in the social background characteristics of nonvoters is that there is a great deal of disaffection and alienation among a wide variety of people within the existing political system. When Marx spoke of **alienation** as an overwhelming sense of normlessness, powerlessness, and meaninglessness, he was referring to workers' estrangement from their work (Marx, 1844/1964; see also Seeman, 1959). But alienation can also affect our political behavior. For many people, electoral politics simply does not address their interests or their needs. Why, then, should they vote? In a 1991 survey 39 percent of the respondents believed that "it is a waste of time to vote because the government can't really do what it wants to do" (ABC News/Washington Post, 1991). And a 1990 survey found that only 48 percent of the respondents strongly agreed with the statement, "My vote can make a difference" (Gordon S. Black Corporation, 1990).

Political alienation is not the same thing as **apathy.** When people are apathetic, they do not care what the outcome is. When people are politically alienated, they care about the outcome but do not feel that the process is relevant (Levin, 1960). Why are people alienated? They are alienated in part because the way the system actually works is not the way they were taught that it is *supposed* to work. Modern political history has contributed to voter alienation. The Vietnam era imbued a generation with the realization that our elected officials could conduct a war against the wishes of vast segments of the population. Several government scandals— including Watergate in the Nixon era, the Iran-Contra affair of the Reagan administration, and, more recently, the Whitewater investigation of the Clinton administration—indicated to voters that political elites are less trustworthy and ethical than one would like to believe. Thus, although people are taught that voting is the means by which they can hold elected officials accountable, and that voting is the exercise of power, their experiences suggest that voting is not necessarily an effective way to control political elites or to get them to address their concerns.

Critics of pluralism point to limitations of the power of voting. The electoral process involves far more than simply voting. Campaign formation, candidate selection, and the party agenda are important aspects of the electoral process that occur before anyone enters the voting booth in November (Domhoff, 1979). The participants at these early stages of the electoral process are likely to be persons already advantaged by the system as well as active members of one of the two major parties. Candidates have typically come up through the ranks of the party organization. The party is not likely to champion outsiders and challengers to the system because they have not invested time, money, energy, and work in the party organization.

Moreover, the huge expense of running a campaign usually means that aspiring candidates will try to articulate positions that attract the support of powerful interests. It is not surprising, for example, that Bill Clinton received the enthusiastic support of the computer industry in his 1992 presidential campaign after he forcefully advocated an expansive information superhighway. The computer and communications industries stand to gain huge profits from such a project. Thus, political elites are most likely to listen and respond to the interests of privileged groups and classes during candidate selection and campaign planning.

We can also see inconsistencies between the objectives of privileged voters and those of the masses in the kind of legislation that is passed. For example, Richard Hamilton (1972) found that during the 1950s and 1960s, most people in the working and middle classes in the United States supported the expansion of federal social welfare programs. Yet legislators consistently opposed efforts to establish such programs. Then, too, polls indicated that 63 percent of people in the United States favored the equal rights amendment (ERA), which would prohibit discrimination on the basis of sex. Yet the ERA was not passed because constitutional amendments require ratification by two-thirds, or 38, of the nation's state legislatures and only 35 states were willing to approve it (*Time*, 1982a, 1982b).

The class bias of elected officials also dilutes the power of voting. Members of the nation's political elite tend to come overwhelmingly from economically advantaged backgrounds (Dye, 1990), partly because it is very costly to prepare for and run large campaigns. These privileged persons are not likely to be sympathetic to the views of the disadvantaged, such as the poor, the homeless, and other groups considered marginal in U.S. society.

Our discussion of the limits of electoral politics suggests that the state and the economy are not actually separate, distinct institutions. What is the relationship between these two institutions in a capitalist system, and how does it affect our daily lives?

THE STATE AND CAPITALIST SOCIETY

The discussion of the power elite and the analysis of the military-industrial complex suggest significant ways in which the state and the economy operate together in a society dominated by corporate interests. Sociologists do not necessarily agree, however, on the nature and meaning of their intersection. In *The Communist Manifesto*, Karl Marx and Friedrich Engels (1967) argued that "the executive of the modern state is but a committee for managing the common affairs of the whole bourgeoisie," the bourgeoisie being the capitalist business owners. Their observation has become a centerpiece of debate among various sociologists.

Business Dominance Theory

Business dominance theory (sometimes referred to as *instrumentalism*) extends the analysis of power elite theory by arguing that the state is not a neutral arbiter of the common good because the capitalists have captured the state and use it as their instrument (Miliband, 1969). Capitalists take control of the state either by entering key leadership positions themselves (Useem, 1984; Dye, 1990) or by putting pressure on the noncapitalists who fill those offices (Neustadtl and Clawson, 1988; Allen and Broyles, 1989). Capitalists may also greatly influence the state by filling positions in key advisory, regulatory, or policy committees, such as the Council on Foreign Relations, a nationally influential private organization (Domhoff, 1990; Burris, 1992). Business dominance theorists argue that the state is not free of **capital-accumulation interests,** that is, individuals and organizations that benefit from amassing and maintaining private profits. Business dominance theorists note that the people making decisions in the name of the state are either capitalists or their representatives. They act to legitimate capital-accumulation interests. This analysis implies that it is the decisions of individuals who fill key governmental positions that determine the role of the state in capitalist society.

Structuralist Theory

Advocates of **structuralist theory** agree with business dominance theorists that the state is not a neutral arbiter of the common good (Poulantzas, 1968, 1973; Block, 1987; Jessop, 1990). But they take issue with the focus on individuals. Structuralists argue that an economy based on capitalism *forces* the state to shape its policies in ways that are consistent with capital-accumulation interests. Moreover, the fate of the state rests on the economy's health. The state needs to collect taxes for social programs to keep down unrest and make its existence legitimate in the eyes of the citizenry. But it must often legislate in favor of capital-accumulation interests rather than social programs because to do otherwise would be to damage the health of the economy on which the state depends (O'Connor, 1987). The state, then, is not simply subject to the whims of individual capitalists and their representatives who hold state offices; the structure and requirements of the capitalist economy constrain the actions of the state. Therefore, changes in personnel in political offices do not alter the types of decisions that the state makes. State decisions will be consistent with the interests of capitalists, regardless of who is elected to fill state offices.

The influence of the economic structure on the legislative process can be seen in laws passed by the state that ostensibly control the capitalist sector but may in fact function to advance its interests. For example, laws regulating the structure of corporate boards of directors stipulate that publicly owned firms must have **outside directors** in their board membership. An outside director is someone whose primary institutional affiliation is not with the firm whose board he or she serves on. An outside director may have a primary affiliation with another corporation (in the same industry or in another industry), a university, a private foundation, or even (in the unique case of Chrysler Corporation) a labor union. When a director from one corporation also sits on the board of another corporation, he or she forms an **interlocking corporate directorate** between the two firms. An interlock structurally ties the two firms together: the common director is privy to inside information about both firms and can modify decisions of each board to avoid conflicts with the interests and needs of the other. Such **direct interlocks** create informational and decision-making ties between firms. Figure 10.2 shows the interlocks at one of the largest firms in the United States.

When a director from one firm sits on the boards of two other firms, he or she forms an **indirect interlock** between the two firms. Both direct and indirect interlocks help unify the capitalist sector. Interlocks often occur between firms assumed to be competitors. For example, General Motors indirectly interlocks with Chrysler because both have board members from Chase Manhattan Bank. Such interlocks help control the amount and terms of competition between firms.

How widespread are interlocks? The largest corporations interlock more often than smaller firms and are interlocked, both directly and indirectly, with one another. For example, AT&T is interlocked with 93 of the top 130 corporations. Through a statistical analysis of the structure of corporate interlocks, Mintz and Schwartz (1985) found that in 1962, 88.2 percent

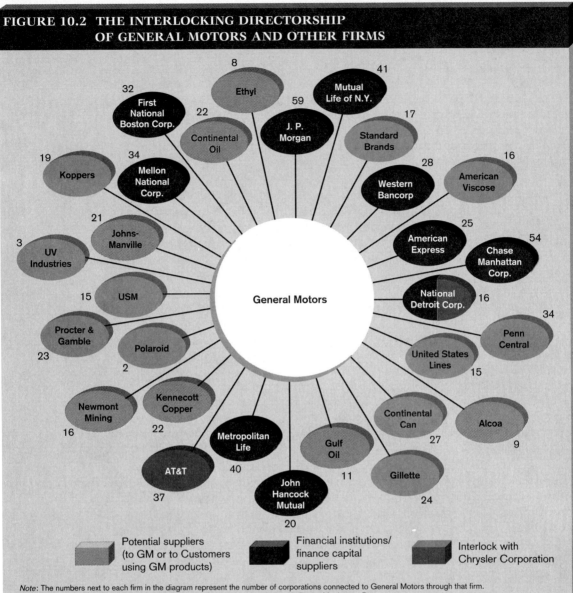

FIGURE 10.2 THE INTERLOCKING DIRECTORSHIP OF GENERAL MOTORS AND OTHER FIRMS

Potential suppliers (to GM or to Customers using GM products)

Financial institutions/finance capital suppliers

Interlock with Chrysler Corporation

Note: The numbers next to each firm in the diagram represent the number of corporations connected to General Motors through that firm. For example, GM indirectly interlocks with 54 other firms through its interlock with Chase Manhattan Corp.

Modern corporations in the United States frequently share directors on their boards, forming interlocks between two or more corporations. As this simplified diagram shows, General Motors interlocks not only with firms that may be suppliers of either materials or financing for GM's production, but also with firms that may, in fact, be competitors. What effect might this arrangement have on the economy?

of the 1,131 large firms in their sample were connected through interlocks. "Each of these 998 companies could reach every other company through a chain of shared directors. Moreover, the overwhelming majority of these chains had fewer than three links. None exceeded six links" (Mintz and Schwartz, 1985: 145). Thus, the largest corporations are linked together in a network of interlocking directorates made possible by regulations set by the state to govern firms whose stock is publicly traded.

Mintz and Schwartz (1985) also noted strong patterns regarding the types of firms that had the greatest number of interlocks. The most central corporations, or **hubs,** in the national network of interlocks were the large commercial banks, mostly headquartered in New York City. Morgan Guaranty Trust, Chemical Bank, Chase Manhattan, and First National City repeatedly turned up as the most central hubs in the network. In 1966, twelve of the thirteen most central hubs were commercial banks. The central position of banks in the national network of interlocking directorates allows them to affect corporate decision-making and helps control interfirm competition. And while there has not been a more recent study as extensive as Mintz and Schwartz's, we have reason to believe that the patterns they found remain significant today: none of the laws, regulations, and standard business practices that facilitated these patterns have changed.

Other laws and regulations ostensibly aimed at controlling corporate activity actually operate to the advantage of capital-accumulation interests. The Glass-Steagall Act of 1933, for instance, placed restrictions on banks in an attempt to deal with the Great Depression of the 1930s. The act prohibited an individual bank from lending more than 10 percent of its assets to a single borrower. In this way no bank's future could be destroyed by the bankruptcy of one firm, and no bank could "own" or take over another corporation by being a firm's only lender. Although the objective of the act was to restrain banks, Glass-Steagall actually empowered them. This is because the borrowing needs of major corporations and Third World countries are today vastly greater than the lending ability of any single bank. Banks therefore must pool their resources to satisfy their customers' borrowing needs and still comply with the legal restrictions the state established in the Glass-Steagall Act. Why is this empowering for banks?

When banks cooperate in this way, they are united in a single **lending consortium,** which enables banks to elicit greater concessions from the borrower. In addition, the lending consortium is organized by a lead bank, typically one of the large commercial banks. The lead bank invites other banks to join it in providing large loans to corporations and governments. Since such loans are lucrative business for banks, smaller banks are anxious to remain on good terms with the lead banks to ensure an invitation to join. The structure of the lending consortium allows the large banks to force smaller banks to comply with their terms.

The lending consortia are typically quite large: Chrysler Corporation's lending consortium contained over 325 banks when that firm borrowed to avoid bankruptcy in 1979; Mexico's lending consortium contained over 1,600 banks in 1982 when it sought to avoid default on its international

Pictures of stockholders' meetings such as this one at General Electric imply that millions of individuals own shares of U.S. corporations. Most people, however, are not stockholders; financial institiutions typically are the most important actors in corporations: they are the most central firms in interlocking directorates, and as pension and trust fund managers, they are the largest controllers of corporate stock.

loans (Glasberg, 1989). Such a huge number of banks in a single lending consortium serves to sharply reduce competition among banks.

The lending consortia also empower banks as a group, since together they control the flow of a unique resource: **finance capital.** Finance capital is not just money. Rather it includes stocks, bonds, loans, and pension funds—and the social relations involved in the ownership and control of these assets. Unlike the case with all other resources, there are no alternatives to finance capital. It is also the only resource used to purchase all other resources necessary for production and for operating the state. And unlike any other resource, finance capital is extended to its users by a coalition of providers. As such, banks control the purse strings of corporations and the state: any entity that refuses to comply with financial institutions' interests and objectives could find its access to investment capital shut down or could be forced into bankruptcy or default (Glasberg, 1989). Thus, the Glass-Steagall Act, which was to assist both the economy and the country by controlling the activities of the banking community, has in fact empowered banks and *increased* their ability to accumulate capital.

The objectives and interests of financial institutions are not always tied to just the financial health of their borrowers. Banks are willing to use their collective power to achieve their own interests, even when doing so damages the financial health of their borrowers. For example, in 1969 the

Leasco Corporation, a very healthy company, tried to take over Chemical Bank by purchasing its outstanding stock. Appalled that a nonfinancial corporation would break into banking circles, the banking community refused to advance any loans to the firm. More importantly, the banks sold all of Leasco's stock from the pension and trust fund portfolios they managed, causing its value to plummet. Within two weeks of stock dumping, the banks had all but destroyed Leasco: between 1965 and 1969 the value of Leasco's stock had grown by 5,400 percent to a high of $140 per share; two weeks after the takeover attempt it was $99; by the end of the year it had fallen to $7. Leasco was forced to withdraw its attempt to take over Chemical Bank (Glasberg, 1989). The collective power of the banks enabled them to significantly damage a firm, not because the firm was unprofitable or negligent in paying back its loans but because its interests and behavior did not conform with the interests of the banks. That collective power of the banks was made possible by regulatory laws passed to control them.

More recently, a law deregulating the banking industry in 1982 facilitated the enhanced concentration of that industry and prompted the savings and loan (S&L) crisis of the late 1980s. **Deregulation** is the process of removing or significantly relaxing government restrictions on industries. In the case of the banking industry, deregulation removed the structural and legal constraints that defined different markets for large commercial banks and smaller S&L institutions. As a result, the two types of financial organizations began to compete against each other, to the decided advantage of the large commercial banks. Previously, S&L institutions had been legally restricted to providing low-cost home mortgages and offering low interest rates on deposits. Following deregulation, in order to attract depositors from the commercial banks, S&L institutions offered dramatically higher interest rates on deposits but still collected low rates on old mortgages. In addition, deregulation permitted S&L institutions to engage in speculative investments that had previously been prohibited. These investments, particularly in real estate, crashed in the late 1980s. Another result of deregulation was that far fewer field supervisors regularly audited the S&L institutions' books to ensure that prudent investments were being made. The lack of supervision encouraged a great deal of fraud to occur in the industry as standard operating procedure (what Calavita and Pontell, 1991, called *collective embezzlement*).

Before long the unwise speculative investments and the shortfalls between high-interest payouts on deposits and low-interest incomes on mortgage loans caught up with the S&L institutions, creating a massive national crisis (Glasberg and Skidmore, 1992). Many S&L institutions failed and had to close down, leaving the government to cover their debts. Thus, laws passed by the state to deregulate the banking industry resulted in further concentrating the industry in fewer hands (particularly large commercial banks), undermining the sector of the banking industry intended to provide affordable mortgage loans to working people, and enhancing the capital-accumulation interests of the largest members of the industry.

Class Dialectics and the State

Some sociologists challenge both the business dominance theorists and the structuralists on the grounds that they tend to focus only on relations between elites in the state and in the economy and fail to examine how these relations affect the rest of society, especially the working class. Sociologists using a **class dialectic perspective** focus on the dynamics of conflict between the working class and the capitalist class. They point to how this conflict at times results in compromises in state policy, some of which may not necessarily be in the best interests of capitalists (Whitt, 1982; Quadagno, 1984; Levine, 1988; Quadagno and Meyer, 1989). They ask, If the state is captured, controlled, or influenced either by members of the capitalist class itself (business dominance theory) or by the structure of the capitalist economic system that favors them (structuralist theory), how is it possible that we periodically get legislation that favors workers or disadvantages capitalists? For example, how is it possible that we have laws guaranteeing workers the right to form unions and collectively bargain with capitalists? How is it that we have had policies that increased social welfare expenditures and expanded social welfare programs, such as the New Deal in the 1930s and the War on Poverty in the 1960s?

Class dialectic theorists argue that the state is the arena in which class struggles are played out. Social welfare programs and the legal protection of workers' rights are outcomes of prolonged struggles in that arena. According to class dialectic theorists, these outcomes actually exemplify the state's willingness to address working-class interests in order to protect capital-accumulation interests.

For example, during the late 1800s and early 1900s, workers in the United States began to press forcefully for the right to unionize. They faced serious challenges and concerted opposition by capital-accumulation interests. Capitalists fired workers who were active in organizing attempts and hired private police and paramilitary forces to beat and shoot striking workers. Sometimes, as in the cases of the Pullman railway workers' strike in 1893 and countless coal miners' strikes (particularly in the 1930s), the state sent in armed troops to quash workers' organizing efforts (Sexton, 1991). The state used various methods to undermine and discredit labor leaders. In a glaring case, Joe Hill, a leader in the International Workers of the World, was arrested for committing a murder that no one had witnessed; although no evidence ever connected Hill to the murder, he was incarcerated and eventually executed for the crime (Foner, 1965).

At the same time, deplorable working conditions and oppressive treatment made socialism an increasingly attractive alternative for many workers. Under socialism, workers would control their working conditions. Much debate occurred within Congress and among capitalists. Capitalists abhorred collective bargaining with workers' unions, but the threat of socialism was even more repugnant. Many understood that socialism would become much more attractive to workers who were denied the right to unionize. Collective bargaining came to be seen as the lesser of two evils. Finally, with the grudging approval of many elites in the corporate community, Congress passed the Wagner Act in 1934, guaranteeing work-

The state is hardly a neutral force in class struggles. In Harlan County, Kentucky, in 1939, 1,300 National Guardsmen arrested and shot at striking coal miners in an attempt to break a strike and force the miners back to work. The miners were demanding union representation, which the mine operators refused to grant.

ers the right to unionize (Weinstein, 1968; Zinn, 1980). Thus, workers' struggles with capitalists were fought out in the arena of the state, with the state acting not as an unbiased judge but as an advocate for the long-run interests of the capitalist class. The business dominance and structuralist perspectives would find it difficult to explain the state's behavior in these situations, unlike the class dialectic perspective.

THE STATE AND POLITICAL ECONOMY: NEW FEDERALISM

We have seen that the state may be viewed as the central arena in which struggles between the interests of labor and those of capital accumulators are acted out. As the budget process shows, since the late 1970s the state has restructured the economy in favor of business interests and to the disadvantage of labor, as well as the poor, women, children, racial minorities, and those with disabilities. (These latter groups had benefited relatively little from state policy in the past, and then only after long battles.) What came to be called **New Federalism** (or, erroneously, "Reaganomics," in some circles) was based on the conservative political philosophy that the federal government should be involved only with taxation and national defense; all else, particularly social welfare programs, education, mass transportation, and health, should be the responsibility of state and local governments. Under New Federalism battles previously won by disadvantaged groups would have to be fought again in the future.

New Federalism began quietly in the late 1970s under President Jimmy Carter. The state responded to an ailing economy by lowering federal social welfare expenditures, reducing the burden of taxes on the wealthy to stimulate increased saving and investment, and relaxing or eliminating federal regulation of corporations. The goal of New Federalism was to regulate the economy to the advantage of businesses, particularly large corporations. The assumption was that firms would reinvest their increased profits to improve productive capacity, thereby creating new jobs. President Ronald Reagan greatly expanded this approach, which came to be called **supply-side, or trickle-down, economics.** Its supporters argued that benefits to capitalists would trickle down to benefit labor; eventually everyone would benefit from New Federalism. "A rising tide raises all ships" was the supply-siders' motto.

In practice, though, some ships sank. New Federalism is a glaring example of class struggle "mediated" by the state to the distinct advantage of big business and to the disadvantage of groups that had won support from the state in previous decades (Ackerman, 1982). Supply-side economics did not achieve the goals it was supposed to. Tax cuts instituted under President Reagan greatly benefited the wealthy and large corporations. Meanwhile, the economy continued to suffer, increasing the ranks of the poor, the hungry, and the homeless. While their needs grew, some social welfare and entitlement programs originally designed to catch economic victims in a federal safety net were slashed; others' eligibility requirements were redefined to reduce the number of people the programs served. These programs included Aid to Families with Dependent Children (AFDC); Women, Infants, and Children (WIC), a nutrition program for pregnant and nursing women and young children; food stamps; unemployment insurance; Medicaid and Medicare; an employment training program for the poor; the Community Services Administration, which helps equip low-income people with the skills and knowledge needed to move out of poverty; public housing; and mass transportation (see also Piven and Cloward, 1982; Phillips, 1990).

New Federalism also hit people with disabilities. The federal government reduced its financial responsibilities by redefining eligibility standards and reformulating the budgeting for disabilities programs. For example, greater financial responsibility for the education of children with disabilities was shifted to states and local communities, whose already-strapped budgets could not make up the shortfall of federal contributions. By 1984 the federal share of community-based services for people with disabilities had dropped to 7 percent, down from 45 percent, leaving state and local governments to make up the difference. In 1984, 70 percent of total public spending on community-based services for people with disabilities came from state-level funds. Income maintenance programs for people with disabilities declined 2 percent between 1985 and 1987 (Castellani, 1987: 43). It quickly became clear that the federal safety net had gaping holes through which the poor and people with disabilities could easily fall.

New Federalism also contained a policy that Frank Ackerman (1982) called "zapping" labor. A massive program to deregulate industries and remove restrictions from management, together with budgetary cuts in existing federal programs, undermined the position of workers. The government slashed the budgets of the Occupational Safety and Health

Administration (OSHA), which oversees workplace conditions, and the Environmental Protection Agency (EPA), which acts as watchdog over industries' effects on the environment. These cuts may have reduced some of the regulatory costs to corporations, but they have also compromised the health and safety conditions of workers and the quality of the nation's air, water, and land.

Antilabor decisions began cropping up in the National Labor Relations Board (NLRB), a government body that had previously helped protect workers against unfair labor practices by corporations (Novak, 1991; Sexton, 1991). Now the NLRB was rendering decisions that effectively made labor contracts binding in one direction only—against labor. Management could, according to the NLRB, break a contract if it decided that the contract would pose a hardship for the corporation. Management could even decide to relocate a firm's operations to another county, state, or country to avoid compliance with a labor contract it did not like. Not surprisingly, firms typically relocated to areas where labor had not made significant inroads. And the corporations were not required to make public their financial accounts to demonstrate their claims. In contrast, union claims that contracts were going to create undue hardships for workers were rejected.

Union busting became a national phenomenon. Law firms specializing in such activities flourished, and unions found themselves the objects of pitched campaigns against their very existence (Sexton, 1991). Corporations sometimes welcomed strikes as an opportunity to replace unionized workers with nonunionized workers, often people who had been unemployed and hungry for so long that they were glad to have a job, unionized or not. New Federalism tolerated union-busting activities on the basis that unions had pushed wages too high and that employers were simply operating as they should in a free and open market—seeking the lowest labor cost to increase profitability.

If New Federalism budget cuts slashed programs that supported social welfare initiatives, where did the federal budget makers place their emphasis? Increases in Department of Defense spending—particularly on the now-legendary Strategic Defense Initiative (SDI, or "Star Wars" to its critics)—did not enhance the nation's defensibility against nuclear attack, but they did help increase the federal deficit by almost $300 billion—more than the *combined* deficits of all previous presidential administrations since Washington. That deficit helped fuel inflation and recession, eroding the buying power of the declining wages that labor was now receiving. SDI was supposed to zap incoming enemy missiles, but budget priorities were zapping labor, women, children, racial minorities, people with disabilities, and the poor. In 1980, expenditures for human resources (excluding social security and Medicare) accounted for 28 percent of total federal outlays, while expenditures for national defense amounted to 22.5 percent. By 1987, these two expenditure categories had traded places, with human resources dropping to 21 percent and national defense galloping to 28 percent (Phillips, 1990: 88).

By 1990, even conservative political analysts like Kevin Phillips could not deny the damage New Federalism had done, both to the national economy and to individuals (1990: 202). Deregulation of industries, relaxation of antitrust laws, and huge tax windfalls for corporations were supposed to increase productivity. Instead, they fueled more than a decade of merger mania. Between 1980 and 1988 the total value of corporate mergers and acquisitions "exceeded two thirds of a trillion dollars" (Phillips, 1990: 172). Mergers and acquisitions do not increase productive capacity, nor do they stimulate the production of any new jobs; they simply reshuffle who owns the existing production facilities. In fact, mergers often entail job loss, as the acquiring firm tries to streamline operations to help pay off its debt. While there is little documentation of the number of jobs lost through mergers, AFL-CIO Secretary-Treasurer Thomas Donahue testified before Congress that an estimated 80,000 union jobs have been lost as a direct result of mergers and another 80,000 as an indirect result (*National Journal*, 1989). His estimate is conservative, since it does not include the number of nonunion jobs lost through mergers. Corporations were using their increased profits from New Federalism policies to buy one another out, not to create new jobs. The rising economic tide was not raising all ships. Only the largest corporations were rising; smaller businesses were capsizing. Between 1985 and 1992, there were 533,000 small-business failures, a significantly larger number than in previous years (Federal News Service, 1993).

The effect of the state's twist on Robin Hood could be seen on the individual level. Overall, the economic distance between the nation's wealthy and poor widened to a gap unseen since the Great Depression in the 1930s. As Figure 10.3 shows, the average family income of the poorest 10 percent of the U.S. population declined by almost 15 percent between 1977 and 1988, while the average family income of the wealthiest 10 percent

The New Federalism of the 1980s widened the gap between wealth and poverty. The irony of this photograph captures that gap: As the early-1990s economic crisis resulting from the policies of New Federalism worsened, homeless New Yorkers sought warmth and safety by sleeping in automatic bank teller booths, where those who benefited from the policies went to retrieve their money.

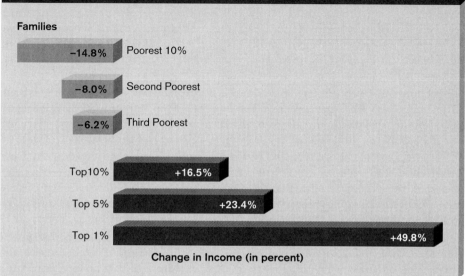

**FIGURE 10.3 THE NEW FEDERALISM AND CHANGES
IN AVERAGE FAMILY INCOMES, 1977–1988**

Families

−14.8%   Poorest 10%

−8.0%   Second Poorest

−6.2%   Third Poorest

Top10%   +16.5%

Top 5%   +23.4%

Top 1%   +49.8%

Change in Income (in percent)

Income inequality has grown since 1977. Incomes of families in the *poorest* 10 percent of the population *dropped* by nearly 15 percent, while incomes of the *richest* 10 percent *rose* by 16.5 percent. Even better off were the top 1 percent, whose wealth grew by almost 50 percent in just nine years. How did this happen? (*Source:* Based on Kevin Phillips, *The Politics of Rich and Poor* (New York: Random House, 1990), p. 17, table 1.)

increased during the same period by 16.5 percent. More strikingly, the average family income of the wealthiest 5 percent increased more than 23 percent, and that of the wealthiest 1 percent increased by almost 50 percent (Phillips, 1990: 17). New Federalism had succeeded in redistributing income from the poorest to the wealthiest.

New Federalism also impoverished women. While women's share of jobs in the labor force increased during the 1980s, their share of poverty increased quite dramatically as well. This was because the vast majority of new jobs created were minimum-wage, part-time service sector jobs with no benefits. Even if a mother of three worked full-time, year-round at the minimum wage, she would not be able to make enough on her own to rise above the federal poverty line. Working part-time guaranteed that both she and her children would be entrenched in poverty, be hungry, and possibly be homeless. If she did not have a wage-earning partner, a mother was likely to face impoverishment. Single-parent families increased from 13 percent of the total number of families in 1970 to 29.7 percent in 1992, and most of these were female-headed. While the median family income of married couples increased 9 percent between 1980 and 1993, the median income of female-headed households actually declined by 1.7 percent (U.S. Bureau of the Census, 1994). Thus, while the overall rate of poverty in the

United States in 1993 was 15.1 percent, the rate of poverty among female-headed families was an astounding 35.6 percent (compared with a rate of 16.8 percent for male-headed families) (U.S. Bureau of the Census, 1994). Given the jobs women could find, even a college education did not guarantee their economic security: in 1992, the median income of women with a college degree was less than $1,000 higher than that of men with only a high school diploma (U.S. Bureau of the Census, 1993a).

New Federalism also disproportionately hurt people of color. The poverty rate for whites in 1993 was 12.2 percent, but the rate for African Americans was 33.1 percent and for Latinos, 30.6 percent (U.S. Bureau of the Census, 1994). According to the Bureau of Labor Statistics, African Americans were more than twice as likely as whites to be unemployed in 1992, and Latinos were almost twice as likely. The gap between African Americans and whites in terms of wealth and median family income widened, regardless of education levels. Indeed, in 1991, African American men with a college degree still earned less than white men who had only completed high school (U.S. Bureau of the Census, 1992c).

Thus, the state was hardly neutral in the class struggle between capital-accumulation interests and those of workers, the poor, women, racial minorities, people with disabilities, and children. New Federalism succeeded in legislation and budgeting practices that unabashedly favored capitalists and severely disadvantaged workers by redistributing wealth from the poor and workers to the wealthy and corporations. Even conservatives like Kevin Phillips could not argue that this was in the common good.

CONCLUSION

Political and economic institutions intersect in very powerful ways in the United States, a capitalist society dominated by the presence of large corporations. The state hardly seems to be a neutral arbiter, balancing competing demands of various interest groups and legislating in the common good. Rather, it is a very active participant in class struggles and frequently legislates in favor of capital-accumulation interests. At times, when groups of the disadvantaged press for change, the state finds ways to incorporate their demands as long as capitalist interests are not adversely affected. Indeed, reforms may serve to legitimate and stabilize the capitalist system. Even voting, which would seem to be the mechanism by which everyone, regardless of race, gender, income, occupation, or education, could participate in the political economy, does not appear to level the playing field. Participants in the political process are overwhelmingly likely to be individuals who are already advantaged by the existing political economy, and their participation increases the likelihood of protecting and maintaining their advantage relative to others.

The state is not able to escape the influence of capital-accumulation interests. To undermine capital accumulation is to undermine the country's (and maybe the world's) economic health. The state is therefore constrained to make policy decisions from a very limited range of options.

However, perceptions of what is a viable option for a given problem can be influenced by the process of class struggle. That is, conflict between the relatively advantaged and disadvantaged members of society can often redefine problems and solutions so that new ways of understanding issues can develop.

The military-industrial complex is the most visible structure that shows the fusion of the state and the economy. What enriches one of the components in the complex tends to enrich all the others. The military-industrial complex operates to secure capital-accumulation interests, both in the United States and abroad, by supplying materials, personnel, and policies to protect those interests.

The clash of the requirements of capitalists and the fundamental needs of people can be seen most painfully in the outcomes of New Federalism, which redistributed wealth and power away from the disadvantaged and to large corporate interests and the wealthy. The result was increased impoverishment and suffering among women, people of color, children, people with disabilities, and the working class.

Conservative observers like Kevin Phillips now argue against the wisdom of New Federalism. The increase in poverty and suffering in the face of growing concentrations of wealth could well heighten political alienation and lead to a major backlash by the people most disadvantaged by New Federalism. Indeed, the 1992 presidential election, which denied President George Bush a second term by sending Bill Clinton to the White House, represented, in part, a repudiation of New Federalism by an electorate grown weary of the redistribution of resources from the bottom up. It remains to be seen whether that backlash will continue to support programs designed to correct that redistribution.

THINKING CRITICALLY

1. Consider the boxed interview with the student activist from China. What elements of a power elite in China did this student describe? What challenges to radical elite theory did he suggest? How well does radical elite theory explain the situation he described? Can you think of any similar situations in the United States?

2. Look in the newspaper for a situation that currently or potentially involves the presence of the U.S. military in a foreign country. What is at stake in that country for the United States? Whose interests are likely to be served by the military's presence, and why? Identify the components of the military-industrial complex, and analyze what each has at stake in this particular case. What effect might U.S. military involvement in this situation have on you?

3. Select an issue that is currently controversial (such as the North American Free Trade Agreement, reform of the welfare system in the United States, health care, abortion rights, or gun-control legislation), and sort out the various interests that are likely to be affected by that issue. Consider the different ways that such a controversy might be resolved.

Whose interests are served and whose interests are hurt by each possible outcome? How are you likely to be affected by each outcome? How might you affect the outcome?

4. The Supreme Court currently includes two women and one African American. Does their inclusion alter the kinds of decisions made by the Court, as opposed to the decisions of an all-white, all-male Court? Why or why not? Suppose *five* of the Supreme Court members were women or people of color? Would that change the decisions made? Why or why not? What if the Chief Justice were a woman or a person of color?

5. Does the existence of the military-industrial complex, the power elite, and the dominance of the state by business mean that nonelites are powerless? Why or why not? What can you point to as evidence of nonelite power or powerlessness?

KEY TERMS

state, *317*
government, *317*
economy, *318*
pluralism, *318*
interest-group pluralism, *319*
elite pluralism, *321*
power elite theory, *322*
power elite, *322*
co-optation, *323*
class identity, *323*
interchangeability of elites, *323*
military-industrial complex, *326*
multinational (transnational)
   corporations, *327*
alienation, *334*
apathy, *335*
business dominance theory, *336*

capital-accumulation interests,
   336
structuralist theory, *337*
outside director, *337*
interlocking corporate
   directorate, *337*
direct interlock, *337*
indirect interlock, *337*
hubs, *339*
lending consortium, *339*
finance capital, *340*
deregulation, *341*
class dialectic perspective, *342*
New Federalism, *343*
supply-side (trickle-down)
   economics, *344*

SUGGESTED READINGS

Donald Barlett and James B. Steele, *America: What Went Wrong?* Kansas City: Andrews and McMeel, 1992. A critical analysis of how state and economic elites altered the structure of the political economy to further advantage those already privileged, including an examination of the effects on the poor and middle classes.

Fred Block, Richard A. Cloward, Barbara Ehrenreich, and Frances Fox Piven, *The Mean Season: The Attack on the Welfare State.* New York: Pantheon, 1987. An analysis of the processes of New Federalism and its effect on the poor.

Lois Bryson, *Welfare and the State: Who Benefits?* New York: St. Martin's Press, 1992. A comparative analysis of the welfare-state policies of several countries that explores their effects on the wealthy as well as the poor, including analyses in terms of race and gender.

Dan Clawson, Alan Neustadtl, and Denise Scott, *Money Talks: Corporate PACs and Political Influence.* New York: Basic Books, 1992. A study of political action committees (PACs) and the effect campaign contributions have on electoral processes.

Peter W. Cookson and Caroline Hodges Persell, *Preparing for Power: America's Elite Boarding Schools.* New York: Basic Books, 1987. A look at the processes that prepare the children of elites for assuming their places in positions of power.

G. William Domhoff, *The Power Elite and the State: How Policy Is Made in America.* New York: Aldine de Gruyter, 1990. An analysis of the formation of coalitions within the power elite around such policies as the Social Security Act, the Wagner Act, and the Employment Act, with implications of these coalitions for state theory.

Michael Parenti, *Land of Idols: Political Mythology in America.* New York: St. Martin's Press, 1994. An examination of the meaning and source of the prevailing political ideologies and myths that dominate culture in the United States, with an analysis of their effects relative to race, class, and gender.

WORK AND PRODUCTION

11

When you graduate from college, do you expect your income to be better than, worse than, or the same as that of your parents when they were at that stage of their lives? What about your lifestyle? Are you likely to purchase your own home before you are 30 years old? Will you be able to afford to send your children to college? Will you be able to afford adequate health care? Where will you be economically in the next 20 years? The next 30? During the 1960s, a college degree was almost a guarantee of security and upward mobility. In the 1990s that security is less certain. What has changed in the last 30 years or more to alter the meaning of a college degree in the work world?

Since the late 1970s, people in the United States have begun to feel that they are working harder but falling further behind in their standard of living and their economic well-being. In a 1991 survey by the Council on Competitiveness, 60 percent of the respondents believed that the standard of living for the average U.S. family has declined over the past few years. And in a 1991 Time/Cable News Network survey, 54 percent of the respondents said they worried a great deal about having their own standard of living decline; another 30 percent said they worried at least a little. Said one jobless college graduate who was living at home with his parents since graduation: "Of the 30 or so people I graduated with and am closest to, I know of just three who have professional jobs. Others are receptionists or doing things like waiting tables" (Greenwald, 1992: 38). More and more couples, particularly those with children, are finding that both partners must work full-time to be able to afford the basic necessities of their lives. One young couple noted that they are struggling more than their parents did at their age: "We have two incomes and a 40-year-old home, and we're making it. But not as well as my parents did on one income" (Bernstein et al., 1991: 84). In a cover story, Business Week *(1991) asked the pointed question: "What happened to the American Dream?" The article noted that "the under-thirty generation may be losing the race for prosperity."*

The question of what happened to the American Dream is linked to the labor process and its place in the economy. What is the current structure of work and the economy in the United States? How has that structure changed in recent decades, and what effect do the changes have on us? What forces have prompted these changes? What consequences have these changes had on labor, family, politics, race, class, gender, the meaning of age, disabilities, and inequalities? Who benefits and who is hurt by these changes? What role have labor unions played in fostering or mitigating these changes and their consequences?

THE MEANING OF WORK

To analyze these questions, we must define what we mean by work. Generally, **work** refers to any activity "that produces something of value for other people" (U.S. Department of Health, Education, and Welfare, 1973). This activity can involve both paid and unpaid labor. That is, we need not be paid for our production of something of value in order for it to be considered work. Moreover, our efforts need not be readily visible to anyone else, publicly recognized, or performed outside the home to be considered work: as long as our activities produce something of value for someone else, we have engaged in work. So work includes paid labor (usually performed outside the home, but not necessarily), or what sociologists often refer to as the **formal labor market;** unpaid labor (both voluntary and involuntary, but excluding domestic labor), often referred to as the **informal labor market;** and **domestic labor** (work done to maintain the home and family, usually unpaid) (Glazer, 1987: 249).

Many sociological studies have examined the relationship between formal, informal, and domestic labor. Most of these studies note that it is far more common for women than for men to work in two or more of these sectors. Men more commonly work in the formal labor market, typically outside their homes. Even when women work full-time in the formal labor market, they are still primarily responsible for the domestic labor at home. Working full-time in the formal labor market does not seem to appreciably alter the domestic division of labor. Hochschild and Machung (1989) refer to the domestic labor responsibilities facing women at the end of a full day in the formal labor market as the **second shift.** This situation may be changing somewhat in some households; but the overall pattern still indicates that when women enter the formal labor market, the total amount of time spent each day at work (both in the formal and domestic labor spheres) increases substantially, while for their partners the total amount of time spent each day at work remains essentially the same.

Some middle-class and upper-middle-class women respond to the pressures of the double shift by transferring the domestic labor into the formal labor market. The typical arrangement is for white middle- and

Many women who work in the formal labor market also juggle the responsibilities of domestic labor. Here, a mother struggles to wrestle her key from her toddler as she drops her child at day care on her way to her paid job.

upper-class women to hire minority and poor women to care for their children, clean their homes, and cook their meals (Glenn, 1985, 1988). While such arrangements do provide employment for minority and poor women, they also highlight the assumption that such work belongs to women. Class advantage allows some women to shift the burden of gender exploitation to other, less advantaged women, thereby exploiting class and race inequalities (see also Rollins, 1985).

Women are more likely than men to work in the informal labor market, engaging in the invisible unpaid labor of volunteer work and bartering. Bartering may involve the sharing of car rides, child care, and errand running with other women. The volunteer work done by women may be an important aspect of class and community as well as an aid to the careers of many women's partners (Daniels, 1988). It can involve working in local libraries, schools, and museums and developing charitable resources for the less fortunate in a community. Although women's volunteer work can build visibility, social networks, and contacts vital for their husbands' success at work, it is often devalued as unimportant in large part because it is unpaid.

In many cases, participating in the informal labor market is necessary for women to survive poverty. Many women must participate in all three spheres of labor every day. The following is a description of a typical day for a woman in Peru:

> Soledad, age thirty-five, with three children and a husband who works occasionally as an electrician, rises at 4 A.M. . . . She eats a stale bun with tea and packs her merchandise for the hour and a half long ride from Villa El Salvador to the centre of Lima. . . . She is one of the thousands of *ambulantes* or street vendors who crowd the capital's major commercial districts, hawking cigarettes, candy,

magazines, lottery tickets, cheap clothing, trinkets for tourists. Before leaving around 5:30, she wakes up her teenage daughter, Manuela. She will serve breakfast for the family and make sure that her two young brothers will arrive on time at the morning shift at the local primary school. Fourteen-year-old Manuela will do some school work, but most of her morning will be spent cleaning and washing clothes at the water spigot in the shack which adjoins the house. Sometimes, she will share these tasks with her mother during the evening hours. . . . Soledad will return home sometime after noon with her morning's earnings. In her "free moments" she also knits sweaters on consignment. Since [her husband] lost his job three months ago, her work brings in the household's only regular income. Around 1:30, Soledad and Manuela will pick up the family's most important daily meal at a *comedor popular*. It is one of some 800 communal or "popular" kitchens which function in Lima today. The weekly fee is modest because Soledad, like the other women who organised the *comedor*, combine resources and take turns preparing the meals for the dozens of families served by it. Some of the women work at the *comedor* in the mornings. Soledad spends one afternoon a week cooking the snacks which will be distributed in the evening. But she is distracted and worried about what her younger children may be up to—no one is at home. . . . On Monday afternoons, Soledad and two of her neighbours from the local "Glass of Milk Committee" will go to the municipal depot to pick up their weekly ration of powdered milk. It will be distributed free by other members of her committee. . . . The daily struggle to ensure her family's survival adds up to an eighteen-hour work day. . . . She says, "I feel tired all the time" (North, 1988: 12).

Soledad's incredible day describes what is referred to as the **triple shift**: a daily juggle of work in the formal, informal, and household labor spheres (Hossfeld, 1988; Ward, 1990). While Soledad lives in an underdeveloped country, many women in the United States similarly labor a triple shift, juggling paid work in the formal labor market, unpaid housework, and the informal labor of carpooling, child care, and volunteer work connected with their children's schools and after-school activities.

How is the formal labor market structured, and how does its structure produce differential experiences, such as the triple shift, based on race, class, and gender? In this chapter we will explore that structure and how it has changed over the past 50 years. We will examine how the burdens of the changes, such as unemployment, may be distributed. We will also investigate the effect of these changes on wages and on the status of the middle class. And we will discuss the prospects for further change.

THE STRUCTURE OF THE FORMAL LABOR MARKET

The formal labor market in the United States can be seen as a combination of sectors. But sociologists differ in how they divide the market into such sectors. Some sociologists identify the activity sectors of agriculture, manufacturing and mining, and service; others define the labor market by productive sectors, such as the monopoly, competitive, and state sectors. Yet another typology emphasizes the different characteristics of the work itself, such as full-time versus part-time, minimum-wage versus higher-paying, unionized versus nonunionized, blue-collar versus white-collar, and so on. These typologies are not necessarily mutually exclusive; there is some overlap. However, it is important to realize that each typology emphasizes different aspects of the formal labor market and the economy.

Activity Sectors

If we divide the formal labor market into agricultural, manufacturing and mining, and service sector jobs, we can see some interesting patterns of distribution. In 1990, 60.6 percent of the employed population worked in the service sector, compared with only 22.9 percent in the goods-producing sector (manufacturing, mining, and construction) and 2.9 percent in agriculture, with the remainder working for the federal, state, and local governments (U.S. Bureau of Labor Statistics, 1992a). Workers in agriculture tend to be paid minimum wage; the work is seasonal, prompting many workers to migrate from region to region to follow various growing seasons. Although many migrant farmworkers have unionized, their working conditions tend to be unstable because of the seasonal nature of their work and the uncertainty of weather conditions.

Workers in manufacturing and mining are more likely than farmworkers to be unionized, although, like farmworkers, the majority are not. Compared with agricultural work, the work in this sector tends to be less seasonal and more secure, be better paid, and have greater benefits. However, even in this sector, job insecurity is not uncommon; factories and mines shut down production when the economy is slow or when corporations merge or shift production offshore.

Less than 17 percent of all U.S. workers are unionized, and workers in the service sector are the least likely to be unionized (U.S. Department of Labor, 1991a). They tend to be paid minimum wage (or less, if they are high school or college students), have few, if any, health and retirement benefits, and work part-time. Jobs in this sector are growing faster than those in either of the other two sectors.

Productive Sectors

Dividing the formal labor market into sectors defined by the structure of production results in monopoly capital (sometimes referred to as the "core"), competitive capital (sometimes referred to as the "periphery"), and the state sector (Hodson, 1978; Ward and Mueller, 1985). In the vast **monopoly sector** production is large-scale and capital-intensive. That is, production is done by large national or transnational corporations that rely more on machinery than on human labor. "Monopoly" here does not refer to an industry controlled by a single firm; it refers to industries that are not characterized by open competition. They tend to engage in price setting and wage determination by collective bargaining. The profits in this sector are generally relatively high, as are the wages; workers are more likely to be unionized in this sector than in any other, although most are not unionized. This sector comprises manufacturing and mining more than agriculture or service work, although not all manufacturing and mining companies belong in this category. The critical factor is that the companies producing in this sector are quite large and typically supply national or international markets.

Very different conditions prevail in the relatively smaller **competitive sector.** Here, wage and price competition is more prevalent. Workers tend not to be unionized, and health and retirement benefits are poor or nonexistent. Working conditions are likely to be unsafe or substandard. Productivity and profits in this sector are usually relatively low, as are wages. Production is more labor-intensive; that is, it relies more on human labor than on expensive machinery. The competitive sector includes small farms and farms employing migrant workers, small manufacturing and mining companies, and many service sector employers.

Sociologists who focus on productive sectors as a typology often include the **state sector** as the category of government employment. Here, productivity is low, but wages are high. While jobs in this sector are typically service work, conditions differ from those in competitive sector service work: because government workers are more likely to be unionized, they enjoy greater health and retirement benefits and somewhat better working conditions.

Using a productive sectors scheme, Hodson (1978) has given us some insights into the structure of paid work in the United States. He found that about half of the labor force worked in the competitive sector. He also found that earned income in the competitive sector was much lower than that in either the monopoly or the state sector, even after he accounted for factors such as race, sex, age, and education. Even more pronounced was the difference in the distribution of unemployment. Recession tended to hit workers in the competitive sector much harder than workers in either of the other sectors, and prosperity tended to benefit the competitive sector workers less. This analysis of conditions affecting half the labor force shows just how precarious work and benefits are in the formal labor market.

Other researchers (Ward and Mueller, 1985; Kaufman, 1986) found significant gender and race differences between and within productive sectors. Women and African Americans disproportionately work in the competitive sector, where wages are lower, and are more likely than men and whites to be concentrated in low-authority positions. However, this alone did not completely explain the gender and race gap in earnings: men and whites were found to gain higher benefits than women and African Americans from being in the monopoly sector and from holding higher-authority positions. Women and African Americans received lower rewards for greater increments of education and experience than men and whites in the monopoly sector. Ward and Mueller concluded that the lower earnings of women in the competitive sector reflected the characteristics and conditions of work in that sector, whereas the earnings of both women and men in the monopoly sector were equally affected by conditions in the labor market, such as unionization. Similar conditions affect the earnings of African Americans (Kaufman, 1986). Monopoly sector workers are more likely to be unionized and therefore to have somewhat greater protections against discrimination. In the competitive sector, work conditions are poorer and workers have comparatively less bargaining power. This situation makes it easier for discrimination between men and women, and between whites and people of color, to exist and to depress wages even further (see also Parcel, 1979; Parcel and Mueller, 1983).

Such a critical analysis of the effects of productive sectors on earnings challenges the functionalist view that differential earnings simply reflect the functional importance of different jobs and the investment that individuals make in their training and education (see Davis and Moore, 1945). It appears that the structure of labor markets can differentiate earnings according to gender and race, regardless of education level or job category (see Farkas and England, 1988).

THE CHANGING STRUCTURE OF PAID WORK

The structure of the formal labor market in the United States has changed over time. Look at Figure 11.1: In 1910, the formal labor market was almost evenly distributed among the agriculture, manufacturing and

The economy has undergone dramatic changes since the mid-1800s. How do these changes affect workers? How might they affect your own life chances after you graduate? (*Source:* U.S. Department of Labor, *Monthly Labor Review*, April 1984, p. 16; and U.S. Department of Labor, *Employment and Earnings*, November 1989, pp. 12, 49.)

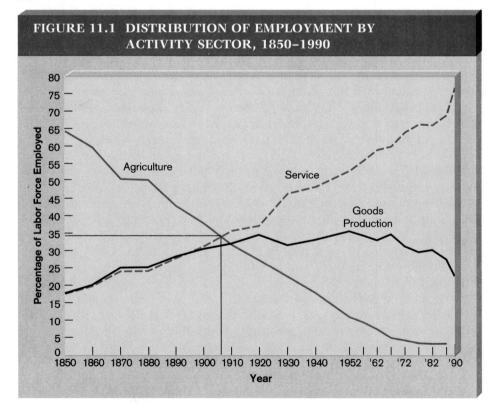

FIGURE 11.1 DISTRIBUTION OF EMPLOYMENT BY ACTIVITY SECTOR, 1850–1990

goods-producing (including mining and construction), and service sectors. By World War II, this distribution had shifted dramatically; employment in agriculture began to decline, while employment in manufacturing and service work continued to increase. After 1952, service employment kept on climbing as both manufacturing and agricultural jobs fell. Currently, employment in the agricultural sector is shrinking almost to extinction, as food production in the United States falls increasingly under the control of major food-processing corporations. The service sector is growing by leaps and bounds: almost three-fourths of U.S. workers today are employed in this sector, including those working for the government. And manufacturing activities are dramatically declining, with about one-fifth of the U.S. labor force engaged in manufacturing (U.S. Department of Labor, 1992).

Moreover, between 1979 and 1987, the greatest job growth was in involuntary part-time work: such jobs increased by 55 percent, while full-time jobs grew by only about 18 percent (U.S. Department of Labor, 1989). This means that more than half of the people who found work in the newly created jobs during those years were forced to work part-time, even when they preferred to or needed to work full-time.

Why has this structural shift and transformation of the economy occurred? Sociologists D. Stanley Eitzen and Maxine Baca Zinn pinpointed four major forces: (1) dramatic pathbreaking developments in *technology*, particularly in microelectronics; (2) an increasingly *global economy*; (3) increasing *capital mobility*; and (4) *deindustrialization* (1989a: 2). Let's look at these forces one at a time.

The formal labor market in the United States has been transformed: Whereas agriculture employs more machinery, displacing human workers, the service sector, still heavily reliant on human labor, employs more and more people.

Technology

Just as the steam engine fueled the Industrial Revolution, the computer microchip has spurred the latest structural transformation of the economy. The microchip is capable of storing, retrieving, and manipulating mountains of data quickly and accurately. Information can instantaneously be transmitted from one computer to another halfway around the world. Engineers and architects can anticipate and correct design problems quickly on computer screens, rather than spending months on costly experiments only to discover serious product defects. And microchips have enabled computerized robots to increase productivity in manufacturing. While these robots eliminate many tedious, boring, low-paying, and hazardous jobs, they also unfortunately displace human labor rather than create jobs (Oxford Analytica, 1989). Thus, microchips and the technological advancements they foster have served to increase productivity, but at the cost of higher-paying manufacturing jobs.

The Global Economy

In addition to the destruction of manufacturing jobs, the microchip has also contributed to the shift toward a global economy. The speed and accuracy of information processing between computers around the world enables managers in the United States to run production processes abroad. Prior to the development of the microchip, the sheer distance separating North America from the other continents essentially protected U.S. manufacturers from international competition for the large markets within the United States. Enormous breakthroughs in transportation and communication have reduced that protection, and products from abroad now easily compete with domestic products in U.S. markets (Dolbeare, 1986).

The success of that competition can be measured by the decreasing profits of manufacturers in the United States. Many U.S. corporations have responded to the competition by stepping up the level of automated production, thereby destroying jobs while increasing productivity. Other corporations have wrung concessions from workers, such as lower wages, moratoria on pensions, decreases in health benefits, and increases in layoffs. Corporate management responds in this way to competition from abroad because it believes it is facing overly high labor costs and declining productivity.

Capital Mobility

The globalization of the economy is related to a third force in the restructuring of the U.S. economy: capital mobility, the ability to move money and assets. Banks and manufacturers may move both financial and production resources at will anywhere they choose. They have increasingly chosen to merge their assets with other corporations and to relocate their plants abroad and invest overseas.

Overseas Investment   Over the past 40 years, overseas investment by U.S. corporations has grown dramatically, from $16 billion in 1950 to

$373.4 billion in 1989 (U.S. Department of Commerce, 1990; see also Vernon, 1986; Eitzen and Zinn, 1989a). Indeed, many of the largest U.S. corporations now receive most of their revenues from their investments abroad (*Forbes*, 1986). So much of their production and revenue has shifted abroad that such firms are routinely referred to as multinational or transnational corporations.

Why have these corporations invested so heavily abroad? Part of the reason is that labor in other countries, particularly in the underdeveloped nations of Latin America and Asia, is nonunionized and therefore cheaper than labor in the United States. Moreover, underdeveloped countries tend to have fewer and more lax environmental and worker health and safety regulations. Thus, production is inexpensive, if not safe and responsible. Decisions to invest abroad have the consequence of exporting U.S. production jobs. The loss of jobs causes a decline in the purchasing power of workers in the United States: not enough workers are employed or making enough disposable income to purchase and consume all the goods produced. Consequently, production must slow down, more of the remaining production workers must be laid off, and many small businesses fail for lack of consumer support.

U.S. corporations often decide it is profitable to relocate production and service facilities elsewhere within the United States in addition to overseas. Both forms of relocation are often referred to as **runaway shops.** Plants are typically moved to locations where labor tends to be nonunion-

U.S. corporations are not alone in closing productive facilities at home and opening factories abroad in search of cheaper labor and more lax state regulations; corporations in most core countries engage in this form of capital mobility. Here, we see the Japanese firm Honda manufacturing motorcycles in New Delhi, India.

ized and where taxes and laws most favor business interests. The pattern has been that manufacturing corporations close plants in the North and Midwest (the "frostbelt"), where labor unions have historically been strongest, and move production to the South and Southwest (the "sunbelt"), where unions have been nonexistent or weak (Rifkin and Barber, 1978). Often, such a move gives corporations the opportunity to further automate so that production can be done with less human labor.

Indeed, something of a bidding war has waged over the past two decades among states vying for plants to be relocated in their communities. That bidding war can be quite costly: states and cities may offer corporations gifts of land, long moratoria on taxes (many of which are lowered to attract business), infrastructural development (such as roads and schools), and lax regulations. For example, when Illinois "won" its bidding war with several states for the Chrysler Corporation–Mitsubishi Diamond Star Motors assembly plant, the cost to the state's taxpayers was $52,000 per job created. This cost derived from the state's gift of $10 million worth of free (prime agricultural) land to Diamond Star and a ten-year property-tax abatement of $20 million. In addition, the state spent about $300 million on infrastructural construction, including roads, streets, sanitation, sewer systems, and schools (*In These Times*, 1986). In Minnesota, the state ignored its own budget deficit of $343 million and offered Northwest Airlines $838 million in loans, loan guarantees, and grants to entice the airline to locate two new maintenance facilities there. Minnesota's "victory" will cost the state a projected $500,000 for each of the 1,500 jobs created by these facilities (Schwartz and Barrett, 1992). Politicians have engaged in this expensive, seemingly irrational bidding war because they fear the consequences of having to explain to voters why they did not try to attract jobs to their states.

Such costs make us wonder who the winners and losers are in the domestic relocation of productive facilities. The communities where plants shut down have relied on their presence for jobs and economic security; thus, runaway shops are clearly not to their advantage. But it is questionable whether the recipient communities are winners either. Some states and cities have begun to recognize that the bidding war does not work to anyone's advantage: New York City, New York State, New Jersey, and Connecticut have entered into an agreement to stop advertisements designed to entice producers to pull up stakes and relocate. And the National Governors' Association has begun to discuss similar ways to curb corporate relocators' power to instigate costly giveaways by states that can hardly afford them, all for the dubious distinction of creating relatively few jobs (Schwartz and Barrett, 1992).

Mergers   U.S. corporations also move investment capital into **mergers** with other corporations. That is, they invest in the purchase of other firms. The flurry of mergers or takeovers over the past two decades has been called **merger mania.** As Figure 11.2 shows, in the 1980s alone, thousands of mergers occurred annually: in 1990 there were 4,168 mergers, up from 1,558 mergers in 1980. Corporate purchases of other firms are quite expensive: the total cost of the mergers in 1990 was $172.3 billion, up from

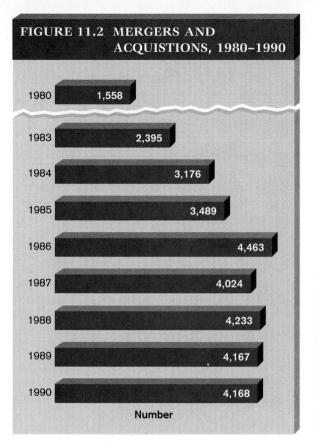

FIGURE 11.2 MERGERS AND ACQUISTIONS, 1980–1990

Year	Number
1980	1,558
1983	2,395
1984	3,176
1985	3,489
1986	4,463
1987	4,024
1988	4,233
1989	4,167
1990	4,168

Number

The number of corporate mergers increased sharply during the 1980s. What might this mean for the structure of the economy? (*Source:* U.S. Bureau of the Census, *Statistical Abstract of the United States, 1992,* Washington, DC: U.S. Government Printing Office, 1992.)

$32.8 billion in 1980 (MLR Publishing, 1991). In addition, such purchases take away from funds that might otherwise be invested in production. In some cases, investing in a merger rather than in production can lead to revenue losses that, in effect, greatly increase the price of the merger. The importance of such investment decisions can be seen in U.S. Steel's 1982 acquisition of Marathon Oil. That purchase, which cost U.S. Steel $6 billion, occurred precisely when the domestic steel industry was suffering greatly from foreign competition and desperately needed to modernize its productive facilities. So the decision to purchase Marathon Oil came at the expense of upgrading and modernizing U.S. Steel's facilities. Yet, when the steel industry's profits plummeted, corporate executives blamed the steelworkers for making the industry noncompetitive.

Mergers help restructure the U.S. economy by increasing concentration in corporate America: more and more of the country's productive capacity is being owned and controlled by fewer hands. This means less competition among fewer producers and higher prices of consumer goods. Increasing concentration of productive capacity also gives corporations greater power advantages over workers and the state. They find it easier to wring concessions from workers and to elicit favorable tax policies and relaxation of regulations from the state. Finally, mergers tend to eliminate jobs because the acquiring firm reduces duplication and streamlines its operations (Russell, 1987). Merger mania, then, has been a strong factor in restructuring the U.S. economy.

Deindustrialization

Since World War II, the economy has witnessed increasing growth in the service sector. At the same time, the United States has become more and more dependent on imported manufactured goods (*Business Week*, 1984). As a result, plants in the United States are increasingly becoming empty factories. Either they are shutting down or the workers are simply assembling imported parts into finished goods, rather than manufacturing the parts themselves and then assembling them. We refer to this process of declining domestic manufacturing activity as **deindustrialization.**

The increasing reliance on imported manufactured goods and parts has dislocated workers from the labor market in the United States. Some workers have lost their jobs (and health and retirement benefits) too close to retirement to be retrained and hired elsewhere. Other workers have relocated their families in hope of finding new jobs, only to discover that thousands of others had the same idea. What looks like a promising local job market may soon become glutted with dislocated workers in search of employment.

Some economists and politicians argue that the dislocation of workers, while admittedly uncomfortable, is temporary: as the economy undergoes its normal readjustments, new jobs will be created to replace those lost to deindustrialization. Unfortunately, research shows that more jobs have been lost than created and that the new jobs pay less than the old jobs that were destroyed (Romo et al., 1989). Moreover, recent evidence suggests that the new jobs created in the service sector have not filled the void left by deindustrialization (Nasar, 1992).

In addition to permanently dislocating workers, deindustrialization can have devastating consequences on whole communities. Towns and cities that once prospered while heavily or exclusively reliant on a single company (or a single industry) find themselves facing increased poverty and loss of population when the company moves or closes (Bluestone and Harrison, 1982). In their case study analysis of the shutdown of Wisconsin Steel on Chicago's southeast side, Bensman and Lynch (1987) noted that the steel industry employed three-quarters of the men in the community before it closed. At the time of their study, more than half of the workers in the local area were laid off. The effects of the shutdown reverberated throughout the community:

> Then steel-related businesses also began to collapse. The historic Pullman railcar factory closed its doors, idling 3,000 workers. Illinois Slag and Ballast Company also went out of business. In nearby Indiana, dozens more firms closed, cutting off any hope steelworkers might have had of finding work across the state border. In the short span of three years, the Calumet region's economy was reduced to shambles. The impact on the people of the mill communities was immediate, and often devastating (Bensman and Lynch, 1987: 92–93).

Many of the workers had been with the steel mills for almost 30 years and were near retirement. When the mills closed, they lost all or part of their pensions, their health insurance, and, in many cases, their homes. Here is one worker's story:

> I worked at Wisconsin Steel for almost thirty years. I get a partial pension of $300 a month, that's all. No other benefits. Nothing. I had a hernia. The doctor said I could die if I didn't have an operation. I didn't have any hospitalization, no money to pay for it. I tried to get a green card [Medicaid] to pay for it, but they said sell your house and car if you want it. I couldn't do that. Finally, my doctor says if you can get into the hospital, I'll do the operation. So I lied to the hospital, just went in there and told them I had insurance. I never could have imagined doing such a thing.
>
> I've been everyplace looking for a job—White Castle, Burger King, McDonald's, Sears, K Mart. I've been to hospitals and cemeteries. I went to Jays Potato Chips. They gave me a test and said, "You're overqualified." I said, "I'll tell you what, you said you're paying $5 an hour, well I'll work for $3." They still wouldn't take me. I'm a skilled electrician, plumber, a pipe fitter. But they ain't gonna hire a guy like me. I still go out every day and look (Bensman and Lynch, 1987: 93).

Changing Corporate Organizational Structure

Why has it been possible for corporations to engage in decision-making that produces deindustrialization, plant relocation, and the globalization of labor and production? The answer lies partly in the changing organizational structure of firms. Most companies were once owned and controlled by a single proprietor, who often resided in the community or close by, but firms now are owned by stockholders and controlled by managers and bankers. The change began in the late 1800s, when owners needed to raise capital to expand; they had the choice of either taking out loans and incurring debt or selling shares of ownership, or stock, in their firms. When an owner sells shares in the firm, the company structure expands to include a board of directors and potentially thousands of shareholders. Since the sales of stocks were dispersed among thousands of independent shareholders, corporate managers were able to control a corporation by owning as little as 5 percent of its stock (Berle and Means, 1932; Gordon, 1945; Bell, 1973). Burnham (1941) termed this turn of events the **managerial revolution,** in which the functions of ownership and control were presumably separated, with the power of corporate decision-making accruing to managers. Critics, however, have noted that while it may be true that the sale of corporate stock separates ownership and control, shares are not as widely dispersed as previously thought: wealthy families and banks remain the largest proprietary interests in many firms, since they hold the greatest number of shares. As much as 70 percent of all stock traded, for example, is controlled by financial institutions investing other people's money, typically from pension and trust funds (Rifkin and Barber, 1978; Herman, 1981; Glasberg and Schwartz, 1983; Mintz and Schwartz, 1985). Thus, financial institutions hold major concentrations of corporate stock, thereby replacing conventional owners without widely dispersing the stock.

How does the separation of ownership and control promote plant reloca-tion and deindustrialization? Companies that are controlled by financial institutions, corporate managers, and stockholders are not necessarily tied to the local community where the plants operate; these interests often reside elsewhere and may have little allegiance to the local community. Thus, the corporate structure of the firm becomes an important force in the structural transformation of the economy.

In addition to undergoing a change in corporate structure, modern cor-porations are no longer the individual, competitive firms they once may have been. Instead, the vast majority of the largest firms (referred to as the Fortune 500, because of their inclusion in *Fortune's* annual list of the 500 biggest corporations) are connected through **interlocking boards of direc-tors** (see Chapter 10). With large commercial banks acting as central figures in these corporate networks, it is not surprising to find boards of directors treating the corporation as an organization of chunks of financial assets to be bought and sold or relocated, rather than as a staple in the local community and an organization of mutual obligations and responsi-bilities. Corporate boards of directors may be more concerned with keeping their firms' cash flow, stock values, and dividends high. Corporate inter-locking directorates, then, may reinforce plant relocations, shutdowns, and deindustrialization.

ECONOMIC RESTRUCTURING AND LABOR-MANAGEMENT CHANGES

Some observers blame U.S. workers for the loss of jobs in the nation's manufacturing and goods-producing sector. They argue that the inordi-nately high wages of workers have made U.S. firms noncompetitive rela-tive to the wages in other industrial countries from which we increas-ingly import manufactured goods. Many U.S. corporations have used this rationale to justify relocating production to other countries. However, the evidence shown in Figure 11.3 does not support this viewpoint: in 1990, workers in the United States received hourly wages comparable to those of workers in Japan and Canada and considerably lower than the wages of workers in Germany. Workers in the United States received $14.83 per hour, while workers in Canada received $15.94 (107 percent of the wages of U.S. workers), those in Japan earned $12.84 (87 percent of U.S. wages), and workers in Germany received $21.30 per hour (144 percent of U.S. wages) (U.S. Department of Labor, 1991b). While the wages of U.S. work-ers have stagnated since 1979, particularly in the 1980s, those of workers in these other countries have steadily increased.

Only when we compare the hourly wages of U.S. workers to those of workers in South Korea do we see a decided advantage for foreign competi-tors from an industrialized country. Wages in South Korea increased slowly between 1979 and 1990; by 1990 South Korean workers were earning only $4.16 per hour, or 28 percent of the wages of workers in the United States (U.S. Department of Labor, 1991b). Other workers who are paid consider-ably less than U.S. workers are those in severely impoverished underdevel-

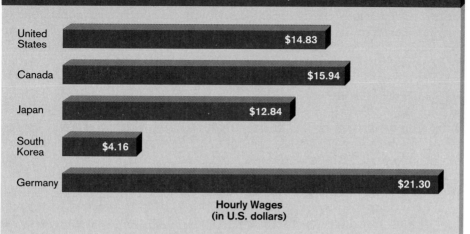

FIGURE 11.3 HOURLY WAGES FOR PRODUCTION WORKERS
IN SELECTED COUNTRIES, 1990

United States — $14.83
Canada — $15.94
Japan — $12.84
South Korea — $4.16
Germany — $21.30

Hourly Wages
(in U.S. dollars)

While many people believe that workers in the United States do not compete with workers in other industrialized countries because they demand excessive wages, this figure's data suggest that such an analysis is at best oversimplified. What else might cause jobs to be exported? (*Source:* U.S. Department of Labor, Bureau of Labor Statistics, *International Comparisons of Hourly Compensation Costs for Production Workers in Manufacturing, 1990,* Report 803, Washington, DC: U.S. Government Printing Office, 1991.)

oped countries, particularly in Latin America and Asia. Thus, the evidence does not support the argument that the U.S. economy has become non-competitive in international markets simply because workers in the United States have been overpaid relative to their counterparts in competing countries.

A more important factor in explaining the erosion of the U.S. economy and the downward slide of American industry is the decision-making by corporate executives that produces deindustrialization. It is managers, not workers, who determine the placement of factories and the level of hiring to be done; management decides its own compensation, as well as whether to invest the firm's cash flow in expansion and modernization of existing plants or in purchases of other firms. Indeed, as we have already pointed out, many of the largest firms have spent significant proportions of their investment capital on mergers and acquisitions, instead of upgrading facilities and production processes. In the early 1990s, General Motors announced that it had to lay off 75,000 workers because of serious declines in the market value of its stock. This action implied that the workers themselves were the cause; however, poor managerial investment decisions, inordinately high compensation of management, and refusals over decades to update its U.S. facilities have been the main causes of GM's decline. Yet managers did not suffer the extensive layoffs, loss of income, or loss of pension security that workers did. Unfortunately, workers are the more visible and easily blamed "causes," and they become the greatest victims of deindustrialization.

In contrast, despite the declining profits of manufacturing in the United States, corporations' chief executive officers (CEOs) have continued to prosper. Between 1965 and 1979, increases in the annual pay of U.S. production workers and the total compensation for CEOs were roughly parallel. The wages/compensation of workers as a proportion of chief executive officers ranged between 3.5 and 4 percent. However, from 1980 on, workers' pay increases slowed considerably, while the compensation of CEOs soared. By 1988, the rate was down to 2.8 percent (Phillips, 1990: 181). Total compensation of CEOs has continued to increase sharply in the 1990s, unabated by significant declines in corporate profitability and serious economic recessions.

How has this been possible? Part of the answer has to do with the power structure of work in the United States. Workers' wages are determined either by management alone or through negotiation between management and unions in collective bargaining, but CEOs' compensation is determined by a corporate board of directors. The CEO is typically a member of the board and thus is in a position to greatly influence his or her own compensation.

Another factor that heavily contributed to the rise in CEOs' compensation during the 1980s and 1990s was the restructuring of tax codes under the Reagan administration. That restructuring encouraged executives to shelter much of their compensation in ownership of their firms' stocks, which were not taxed as heavily as income. Since stock values increased dramatically in the 1980s, CEOs' total compensation soared to unprecedented heights, even as the CEOs were laying off tens of thousands of workers and demanding that workers give up benefits included in their labor contracts. Thus, while workers' salaries and purchasing power have stagnated for over a decade as a result of economic restructuring, those of CEOs have increased remarkably, regardless of the condition of their firms or the general economy (see Crystal, 1991).

Technological changes, the globalization of the economy, increasing capital mobility, and deindustrialization have combined to generate a structural transformation of the U.S. economy that differentially affects labor and management. Exactly how has this transformation affected the daily lives of workers? We now turn to an examination of its effects.

ECONOMIC STRUCTURAL TRANSFORMATION AND INEQUALITY

Taken together, the forces of the structural transformation of the economy have accentuated inequality in U.S. society. We can see this most clearly when we look at these effects: (1) structural unemployment, (2) the transformation of the formal labor market from manufacturing to service work, and (3) the declining income generated by the remaining jobs in the formal labor market (Eitzen and Zinn, 1989b).

Rising Unemployment

One indicator of the overall effect of deindustrialization and the permanent restructuring of the economy is unemployment. Between 1979 and 1983, almost 12 million workers were permanently dislocated from their jobs. Close to 5 million of these job losses were due to plant closings; the rest were caused by the elimination of jobs or shifts, the lack of enough work to sustain the existing work force, or business failures (U.S. Department of Labor, 1985; Mishel and Simon, 1988: 27). In 1992 alone, 5.6 million workers were permanently dislocated, 2.9 million of them because of plant closings (U.S. Department of Commerce, 1993). These figures suggest that deindustrialization and the unemployment it generates have been escalating. Unemployment has shown a general tendency to get deeper since the end of World War II. Whereas the unemployment rate in the United States in 1947 was 3.9 percent, by 1991 it had risen to 6.7 percent (U.S. Bureau of Labor Statistics, 1992b). But the effects of the structural transformation of the economy are specified more clearly by the patterns describing *who* the unemployed are.

In 1991, teen unemployment was 18.6 percent (U.S. Bureau of Labor Statistics, 1992a). Because teenage workers tend to be less experienced and less skilled than older workers, they are often hired for unskilled or semi-

The structural transformation of the formal labor market does not affect everyone equally in the United States. Racial minorities, teenagers, and newly hired factory workers suffer the highest rates of unemployment as the economy shifts its focus away from manufacturing and unskilled work. This pattern is evident in the faces of the people on this unemployment line in Brooklyn, New York, a line that stretched outside the building, down the block, and around the corner one day in 1991.

skilled work. Unskilled work is frequently the first to be dislocated by automation.

Even more telling is a breakdown of unemployment by gender and race, as shown in Figure 11.4. Women's unemployment rates were higher than the rates for men until 1987, when their rates became the same (U.S. Department of Labor, 1989). But this parity is, paradoxically, a result of continued sex discrimination. Men have had greater employment in manufacturing, precisely the sector that has suffered the most severe job losses. Women, on the other hand, have had greater employment opportunities in the service sector, which has shown pronounced increases in employment. Thus, for the first time the unemployment rates for men and women have come to be about the same.

Racial comparisons of unemployment show a marked pattern. Unemployment rates for African American workers have consistently remained two to three times the rates for white workers. Latino workers have fared only slightly better: their rates of unemployment have consistently run more than 50 percent higher than those of white workers. The unemployment rates for African American and Latino teenage workers have shown equally alarming patterns relative to white teenage workers: these minority teenagers are three times (and sometimes nearly four times) as likely as white teenage workers to be unemployed (U.S. Bureau of Labor Statistics, 1992a). A large part of this difference in unemployment rates is the result of institutional racism (see Chapter 6).

While unemployment is on the rise for all groups in the United States, it does not strike the working population randomly. On the basis of this graph's data, which people are more likely to lose their jobs? Why do these unemployment patterns occur? (*Source:* U.S. Bureau of the Census, *Statistical Abstract of the United States, 1992,* 112th ed., Washington, DC: U.S. Government Printing Office, 1992.)

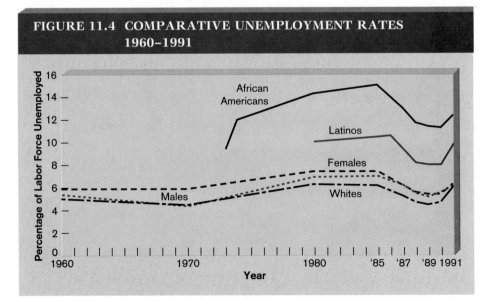

FIGURE 11.4 COMPARATIVE UNEMPLOYMENT RATES 1960–1991

This analysis of unemployment is based on the official rates of unemployment reported by the U.S. Bureau of Labor Statistics. But these rates have come under criticism for *under*reporting the real rates of unemployment. This is because of the way the Bureau of Labor Statistics defines and counts unemployment. Persons must be considered "attached to the labor force" in order to be counted as active participants in the labor market. Anyone who has been out of the labor force and has not been actively looking for a job in the previous four weeks is not counted as unemployed. Thus, people who have become discouraged and have ceased looking for work are not included in the official statistics on the unemployed. Nor are those who work at least one day per week at a part-time job, even though they would like full-time work. If we included all the uncounted people who want to work in the formal labor market but cannot find employment, the real rate of unemployment would almost double the official rate reported by the government (Mishel and Simon, 1988: 19).

The state determines eligibility for federal benefits for the unemployed on the basis of definitions and counts established by the Bureau of Labor Statistics. Persons who are attached to the labor force and lose their jobs through no fault of their own are supposed to be provided for under the federal unemployment insurance program. However, the percentage of the unemployed who actually receive unemployment insurance payments has declined since World War II. In 1989, only 33 percent of those who could not find employment were receiving benefits or payments from the program (U.S. Bureau of the Census, 1991b). This is in part because many of the unemployed could not find new jobs before their entitlement period expired. Others did not work long enough before losing their jobs to qualify for unemployment benefits. Still others worked only seasonally or part-time and thus did not qualify for such benefits. Moreover, the payments provided by the program cover no more than 50 percent of the wages earned during employment and continue only for a period of 26 weeks.

Economic structural transformation has, then, caused unemployment for significant numbers of U.S. workers. Most workers, however, are still employed. What has happened to them?

Declining Income from Existing Jobs

There has been a net increase in the number of jobs created in the United States since the late 1970s, but these new jobs do not compensate for the income that workers lost from deindustrialization. Specifically, we need to look at the incomes of the declining and growing sectors. Weekly earnings in the goods-producing sector averaged $429 in 1989; in comparison, weekly earnings in the service sector averaged $306 that same year (U.S. Department of Labor, 1990b). Thus, the greatest job growth is occurring in the sector that pays lower wages. The average annual compensation rate in the shrinking industries is more than $6,000 greater per year than the compensation rate in the expanding industries: jobs in goods production average an annual compensation of $22,308, while service sector compensation averages only $15,912 (U.S. Department of Labor, 1990a). Why is there such a gap in compensation for work in different sectors?

Part of the answer may be unionization. Workers in the service sector are unlikely to be represented by unions. Evidence shows that the collective bargaining that unions engage in has historically succeeded in raising workers' wages and benefits, including health and pension coverage (Wallace et al., 1989; Krecker and O'Rand, 1991). Thus, it is not surprising that average annual compensation is much greater in the more unionized goods-producing sector. A significant proportion of jobs in the service sector pay the minimum wage of $4.25 per hour, and many such jobs are only part-time, seasonal, or temporary work. Part-time workers typically do not receive health or pension benefits. Indeed, in 1987, 62.6 percent of workers earning less than $500 per month had no pension coverage. And making greater monthly incomes did not guarantee pension coverage: 16.9 percent of those earning $2,000 per month or more did not have any coverage (U.S. Bureau of the Census, 1991a). In 1991, 11.2 percent of full-time, year-round workers had no health coverage at all (U.S. Bureau of the Census, 1992a).

Another problem is that the value of the minimum wage has sharply declined since 1978. The minimum wage in 1988 could purchase only two-thirds of what it could purchase in 1978. This is because the minimum wage, which is established by Congress and is rarely adjusted for inflation, has not kept up with the cost of living (Mishel and Simon, 1988: 43). Workers who labor full-time, year-round on minimum wage cannot earn enough income to rise above today's poverty line of $14,763 for a family of four. In fact, the poverty rate for full-time, year-round workers over the age of 15 has increased by 8 percent since 1973: in 1990, 2.5 percent of these workers were in poverty, and 12.6 percent of heads of households with fifteen weeks or more of involuntary part-time work were in poverty (U.S. Department of Labor, 1991a). Full-time workers made up 9 percent of all poor people in the United States in 1991, and part-time workers totaled 39.8 percent of the poor (U.S. Bureau of the Census, 1992a).

The jobs the working poor are most likely to have are concentrated in the service sector, including managerial and professional positions (usually managers of fast-food outlets, convenience stores, and other retail and service operations), clerical work, sales, protective services, and private household work. Together, these jobs accounted for 55 percent of the working poor in 1987 (U.S. Bureau of the Census, 1988). Thus, even working full-time, year-round is not a guarantee that one will not be poor.

Gender and Race Inequality and the Labor Market

If we look at the race and gender distribution of workers between sectors and within sectors, we can see patterns of inequality that changes in the labor market have only accentuated. Since World War II, female labor-force participation rates have increased more sharply than those for males. But men and women do not necessarily secure employment in the same kinds of jobs, nor do they receive equal compensation for the work done. In 1990, for example, women were concentrated in clerical and service jobs, holding over 90 percent of the jobs in sewing and stitching, child-care services, typing, reception, and secretarial work. On the other hand, men were concentrated in higher-paying jobs, holding over 90 percent of the jobs in fields such as logging, construction work, mining, auto mechanics, plumbing and pipefitting, firefighting, and railroad work. These data suggest that there is a **segmented labor market** wherein women and men compete in different labor markets for different jobs (Rosenfeld, 1980). The significance of such a segmented labor market can be seen in comparative incomes: Female-dominated jobs pay median annual incomes ranging from $6,968 for child-care workers to $17,732 for secretaries, stenographers, and typists, while the median annual incomes in male-dominated jobs range from $16,276 for timber cutters and loggers to $37,232 for railroad workers (U.S. Bureau of Labor Statistics, 1992a).

What happens when men and women do the same job? If differences between men's and women's median annual incomes were attributable to the differential work they do, we should expect to find no gaps between such incomes when men and women do the same job. However, the data suggest otherwise. Regardless of whether a job is performed predominantly by women or men, women tend to make less than men. In 1990, women earned 69.9 percent of the salaries paid to men in managerial jobs, 88.6 percent of men's income in engineering jobs, 84.9 percent of that in protective services, and 66.5 percent of that in machine operation. Even in female-dominated jobs such as sewing machine operation, women still averaged only 82.7 percent of the salaries of their male counterparts; they also averaged 89.2 percent of male elementary teachers' salaries and 88.1 percent of male secretaries' salaries (U.S. Bureau of Labor Statistics, 1992a). Thus, even when men and women perform work in the same job category, men's income is higher. And this is the case in both female-dominated and male-dominated jobs. Why?

If we examine job categories more closely, we can see that they frequently contain a hierarchy of statuses, all of which are categorized as the same job. Take the occupation of baker. Female bakers are typically employed in supermarkets and similar establishments, where baking entails popping premixed dough into the oven. In contrast, men are more commonly bakers in the traditional sense: they are more likely to be employed in bakeries, restaurants, and catering services, where baking involves measuring and mixing ingredients specified in a recipe to create fresh-baked goods. Reskin and Roos (1990) found that exploring such gender discrepancies in the status hierarchy of job categories offered a powerful insight into wage discrepancies. Indeed, when wages are compared across more finely differentiated job categories, the pay differences between men and women, while real, are relatively minor.

Table 11.1 shows patterns of racial discrimination, particularly among males, in earnings. Even when they perform the same job, white males typically earn considerably more than African American males. Notably, when we compare the median earnings among females by race, the pattern reverses for all categories except precision production, craft, and repair: African American females' median incomes are higher than that of white females. Why is this so? The answer lies in the number of hours worked. African American women tend to work longer hours than white women in the United States, thereby producing higher earnings for similar work. Moreover, white women are more likely to take time off from their jobs to

Table 11.1

MEDIAN EARNINGS IN SELECTED OCCUPATIONS, BY SEX
AND RACE, 1989

	ANNUAL MEDIAN EARNINGS			
	WHITE		AFRICAN AMERICAN	
OCCUPATION	MALE	FEMALE	MALE	FEMALE
Executive, administrative, and managerial	$37,053	$21,434	$30,943	$22,030
Professional specialty	35,772	21,805	27,280	23,273
Technical and related support	27,712	18,279	24,456	19,601
Service (except private household)	8,089	5,621	8,611	6,650
Precision production, craft, and repair	22,408	14,575	18,180	12,634

Source: U.S. Bureau of the Census, *Current Population Reports*, Series P20-448: *The Black Population in the United States: March 1990 and 1989* (Washington, DC: U.S. Government Printing Office, 1991).

bear and raise children. That interruption in work histories is likely to depress incomes for white women relative to African American women (Malveaux, 1985, 1990; Sokoloff, 1992).

In addition to wage differentials based on race and gender, a **glass ceiling** faces women and racial minorities in promotions, particularly to managerial levels: such workers may rise to middle-management levels but rarely are promoted to the highest executive levels. According to a study by the U.S. Department of Labor (1991c), the glass ceiling is lower for racial minorities than it is for women, but neither women nor minorities advance very frequently into the higher ranks of management. One reason for this ceiling is that recruitment and promotion practices tend to rely on word-of-mouth referrals and networks rather than on executive-search and referral firms. Thus, an informal mentoring system in which white male executives recruit, train, and refer other white males for promotions tends to lock women and racial minorities out of the system.

The Department of Labor study also found that career-enhancing projects, educational opportunities, and credential-building assignments were often less accessible to women and racial minorities (a situation probably related to the restricted informal mentoring system). Finally, women and minorities did not always benefit from the protection of Equal Employment Opportunity Commission regulations aimed at combating discrimination. Accountability and compliance with such regulations were carefully monitored at lower levels but were highly lax for senior-level executive positions and managerial positions involving decision-making. Taken together, the forces of informal mentoring, accessibility to career-building opportunities, and lack of compliance with equal employment opportunity rules at higher levels in the corporation produced the glass ceiling for women and racial minorities. This glass ceiling helps depress median annual-income figures for women and racial minorities relative to those for white males in the United States.

Furthermore, research has shown that job displacement caused by plant closings and industrial reorganization hits women and people of color harder than males and whites (T. Moore, 1990). For example, rates of unemployment and duration of unemployment are greater for women and African Americans than for men and whites. The consequence of differential job displacement and employment and wage discrimination based on sex and race is that women and U.S. racial minorities are more likely than males and whites to be poor. In the United States in 1993, the poverty rate for whites was 12.2 percent, whereas the rate for African Americans (33.1 percent) was almost triple that for whites, and the rate for Latinos (30.6 percent) was more than twice that for whites (U.S. Bureau of the Census, 1994).

The social implications extend beyond individual workers. Families certainly are affected. Female-headed families are more than twice as likely as male-headed families to be poor: the poverty rate for female-headed families was 35.6 percent in 1993, compared with only 16.8 percent for male-headed families (U.S. Bureau of the Census, 1994). Even within these categories, there are stark racial differences, as shown in Table 11.2. Families

Table 11.2

FAMILIES BELOW THE POVERTY LEVEL, 1993

FAMILIES	POVERTY RATE (%)
All families	12.3
Married-couple families	6.5
Male householder, no wife present	16.8
Female householder, no husband present	35.6
White families	9.4
Married-couple families	5.8
Male householder, no wife present	13.9
Female householder, no husband present	29.2
African American families	31.3
Married-couple families	12.3
Male householder, no wife present	29.6
Female householder, no husband present	49.9
Latino families*	27.3
Married-couple families	19.1
Male householder, no wife present	20.2
Female householder, no husband present	51.6

*Latino family members may be of any race.
Source: U.S. Bureau of the Census. *Income, Poverty, and Valuation of Noncash Benefits: 1993,* Current Population Reports, Series P60-188 (Washington, D.C.: U.S. Government Printing Office, 1994).

of color, whether headed by a male or a female, are as much as three times more likely than white families to be poor. We can see, then, that the economic structural transformation in the United States has not only accentuated race and gender inequalities; it has also had severe social consequences, such as the impoverishment of women and children, particularly those of color.

The Declining Middle Class

The economic structural transformation of the United States has contributed to the erosion of the middle class. For the first time in our history, downward mobility has been greater than the upward mobility we have come to take for granted (Eitzen and Zinn, 1989b). Until now, members of each succeeding generation have generally been able to exceed the lifestyle their parents could afford. Now we are finding that the current generation of workers is struggling just to match, let alone surpass, that lifestyle. In a 1992 Time/Cable News Network poll, 62 percent of the respondents felt that people in the United States today cannot enjoy the same standard of living that recent generations enjoyed.

The *middle class* is loosely defined as a category of people whose income places them above poverty but below the wealthiest fifth of the population. We also may conceptualize the middle class by lifestyle. Ehrenreich defined the middle class in terms of home ownership, the ability to send one's offspring to college, and "the ability to afford such amenities as a second car and family vacations" (1986: 50). Probably the most visible and telling indicator of the decline of the middle class is home ownership. In 1980, 65 percent of American households owned their own homes; by 1986, the figure had fallen to 64.2 percent. While this percentage change does not indicate a significant overall decline in home ownership, a breakdown by age reveals serious decreases among certain groups. For younger Americans the prospect of owning a home is becoming dimmer: between 1980 and 1990, the home-ownership rate for people between the ages of 25 and 34 fell from 51.6 to 45.3 percent, and the rate for those between the ages of 35 and 44 declined from 71.2 to 66.2 percent (U.S. Department of Commerce, 1993). The middle class has clearly been losing its grip on the American Dream of owning a home.

The ability to send their offspring to college has also begun to elude more and more members of the middle class: "For a family with 1985 earnings equal to the median national income, keeping a child in a four-year private college or university would have taken 40 percent of that income, up from 30 percent in 1970" (Phillips, 1990: 22). By the 1990s, even sending a child to a state university or public college had become increasingly costly and therefore less accessible for many middle-class families. The combination of rising tuitions, rising home purchase prices, and loss of higher-paying manufacturing and service jobs has seriously eroded the lifestyle of the middle class. Its downward mobility has been described by sociologist Katherine S. Newman (1989) as a "fall from grace."

The structural transformation of the economy has thus made the American Dream less and less possible, for the first time in our history, for members of the middle class. Earlier job paths to upward mobility for the working class and the poor either have permanently disappeared or have undergone serious income erosion. The recession of the late 1980s and early 1990s has fostered the downward mobility of many members of the middle class; for the first time white-collar workers and professional and managerial workers are finding themselves unemployed. In the past, recessions generally hit blue-collar and unskilled workers. Now even those with college degrees and good skills are joining their more traditional brethren on the unemployment, food-stamp, and soup-kitchen lines. In a cartoon (in the *Philadelphia Inquirer*, December 22, 1991), a middle-class man passed by a homeless person, dropped some coins into his hat, and said, "Those people used to annoy the hell out of me—until I got laid off." That description fits the subject of the boxed excerpt, who had to undergo homelessness himself to appreciate the experiences of others.

PROSPECTS FOR CHANGE

Clearly, a major contributing factor to problems of deindustrialization and the structural shifts of the formal labor market is the lack of control by labor and communities over the work process. One possible source of increasing labor control is labor unions.

Unions provide definite benefits for workers. They have had a positive impact on wages, benefits, health and safety on the job, and the like. However, deindustrialization and global relocation have meant a loss of jobs in manufacturing, the very sector where unions had made the greatest inroads in organizing workers. Labor unions have lost significant ground since 1960 in the proportion of the labor force they represent: union membership has declined from a high of greater than 35 percent of the U.S. work force to a low in 1991 of just slightly over 16 percent (Mabry, 1992; U.S. Bureau of Labor Statistics, 1992a). Moreover, the public image of unions was tarnished by revelations of corruption in some unions and of union leaders' collusion with management against workers' interests (Serrin, 1970).

Several strategies and approaches to change are beginning to occur. First, elections in the Teamsters Union in the early 1990s brought in a leadership devoted to reform, symbolizing the new image of greater honesty sought by unions. The Teamsters have eliminated perquisites for union executives: gone are the union limousines, special jets, and luxury condominiums in Puerto Rico, as well as the unlimited paid vacations anywhere in the world for union executives. The image of less privileged union executives, along with greater democratization of unions, promises to improve workers' sense of participation in union decision-making and to enhance their perception that unions are functioning in their interests.

Unions are also increasingly coming to recognize the need to organize workers globally. It is no longer useful for workers in the United States to be unionized if their counterparts in other countries are not. Corporations can simply exploit the differences in pay and work conditions to undermine workers' standard of living both here and abroad. There are signs that

We frequently interpret the experiences we have as workers, and the experiences of others, as the product of our own efforts and motivation. This excerpt describes a man whose homelessness was not the result of poor personal choices, alcoholism, drug addiction, mental illness, or laziness. Rather, his fall from a comfortable middle-class existence was the result of losing his job when International Harvester, a major manufacturer of farm equipment, laid off more than 18,000 people.

For more than three years, Gerald Winterlin, now in his 40s, was one of the estimated 3 million homeless Americans. Forced by joblessness to live in his car or abandoned buildings, he had to cope with a sense of hopelessness and despair that could, and occasionally did, destroy others like himself.

Now he lives in a warm, modest apartment near the University of Iowa, where he's a scholarship student working on his degree in accounting and maintaining a 3.9 average. I traveled to Iowa to speak with him, hoping to understand how this bright, well-spoken, typical-seeming American could ever have hit such a deep low in his life. Just as important, I wanted to know how he fought his way back.

On the first of two long nights we would spend talking together, the burly Winterlin sat at his kitchen table and recalled an incident that still haunts him.

"I was on the cashier's line at a supermarket," he began, "behind this young, healthy-looking black woman. When her groceries were rung up, she pulled out a bunch of food stamps. I said, 'Hey, get a job. I'm tired of having money taken from my paycheck for people like you!' I expected a sharp answer, but instead she looked embarrassed and said, 'There's nothing I'd like better than a job, but nobody will give me one.' 'Bull,' I shot back, then turned away. Twenty years later, I'd love to find that lady and tell her I'm sorry. Little did I realize that what happened to her could happen to anyone. It happened to me."

Winterlin was born in an area known as the Quad Cities, encompassing Davenport and Bettendorf on the Iowa side of the Mississippi River, with Rock Island and Moline on the Illinois side. One of four children of a tool-and-die man, he graduated from Bettendorf High and eventually began work at the International Harvester plant. "I worked there about eight years," he said, "till '82, after the farm recession hit. Quad Cities is a world center for manufacturing farm equipment, and over 18,000 people, including me, were laid off."

"At first we figured the government would help," he said, adjusting his large framed glasses. "Hell, they bailed out Chrysler, right? But, instead, weeks turned into months with no work. With only two or three weeks of unemployment left, my demands dropped real fast, from $15 an hour to begging to sweep floors—anything. One day I just picked up the phone book and started with the A's. I made a list of every company I applied to. The final number

unions are beginning to take corrective action. For example, telephone technicians in New England went on strike against Northern Telecom, a company based in Canada, and the strike lasted for months. The company was not inclined to bargain with the New England workers until the Communication and Electrical Workers of Canada supported them at the bargaining table. Within days, the New England strike was over, to the satisfaction of the workers. The lesson here: Since the division of labor has become globalized, workers must also globalize their union representation.

"We're good, hardworking Americans who happened to fall between the cracks."

was 380, and I remember realizing that what few jobs there were went to younger people. Still, I'd go out all day looking."

Winterlin heaved a deep sigh and glanced out the window at the cold Iowa night. "I kept thinking there'd be a tomorrow. Late one night, I finally said, 'Well, Gerry, this is it. No tomorrow.' I packed what I hadn't already sold or pawned and walked out. I never planned on living in my car for long," he added, "but then, no one *plans* to be homeless."

What about his family—couldn't they help? "They'd have probably taken me in," he said, "but people who ask that don't understand how impossible it is to say, 'Hey, folks, here I am in my late 30s, such a pathetic loser I can't even take care of myself.' Besides, my old man had lost his own job after 25 years, just six months shy of a full pension."

I asked about welfare, and Winterlin laughed. "Don't get me started on that," he said. "Welfare is the fast route to nowhere. They give you everything except what you need—a job. Some people have no option, like women with kids, but guys like me who want just enough to get started again would rather freeze than fall into a system that gives you a roof but robs you of hope. You trade your individualism and spirit for survival, and for some of us that's not a fair trade. Homeless people are proud people too."

For months, Winterlin lived in his '60 Mercury with rags stuck in the rust holes. Finally, the car died, and he was forced to find shelter wherever he could. "Somehow I made it from day to day," he

said. "I tried to look as good as I could, to keep clean. Sometimes I did odd jobs, but never enough to put a roof over my head. I kept trying, but before I knew it, three years of my life were gone."

I noted the framed scholarship certificates displayed proudly on the wall, and Winterlin smiled, putting a hand up to conceal the spaces where he'd once been forced to pull his own teeth. "No big secret to that," he laughed. "Just plain hard work." He studies 50 hours a week, besides attending classes and working 20 hours at a part-time job. He has no friends, he admitted, and spends weekends alone. "I know it wasn't my fault, but when you're homeless you lose so much self-respect, you stay away from people." I asked if he felt his fellow Americans understood the homeless problem.

"The thing most people *don't* understand," he replied, "is that most of the folks you see huddled in doorways in Eastern cities or living in parks in Santa Monica or begging for a roof right here in America's Heartland aren't there by *choice*. I didn't ask to lose my job. None of us did. We're not bums," he said pointedly, his voice rising. "We're good, hardworking Americans who happened to fall between the cracks."

Source: Peter Swet, "We're Not Bums," in Virginia Cyrus (ed.), *Experiencing Race, Class, and Gender in the United States* (Mountain View, CA: Mayfield, 1993); originally published in *Parade Magazine,* May 13, 1990.

This suggests that U.S. workers should stop seeing their counterparts in other countries as rivals and competitors.

Another way in which unions can make an impact is by organizing workers who have not been unionized, particularly in the service sector. That sector is the least unionized of the formal-labor-market sectors. Service workers in the state sector, on the other hand, are among the most unionized of the service workers, and as a result they enjoy better wages and benefits, better working conditions, and somewhat better job security

Although in 1995 unions represented the lowest proportion of U.S. workers since World War II, they remain an important element in prospects for change in the conditions under which workers labor. These workers in Chinatown, New York City, protested work conditions and unfair labor practices, in which employers kept the tips customers left for servers and workers who protested were fired. As a result of the demonstration, several laid-off workers were returned to their jobs and employees were allowed to keep their tips.

than service workers in the private sector. While union representation in other sectors, particularly manufacturing, has seriously eroded, representation among state workers has increased by 30 percent since 1987 (Mabry, 1992). Similar progress can be made among service workers in the private sector—secretaries and clerical workers, fast-food workers, and the like.

There are other promising strategies for workers to regain some control over or voice in corporate decision-making. For example, by 1988 there had been more than 70 successful employee or community buyouts of industrial plants throughout the United States. These plants were about to be shut down and their operations relocated elsewhere (Ford, 1988: 184). The buyouts often succeeded through coalitions of community, labor, and, at times, religious organizations and municipal governments (see Kelly and Webb, 1979; Luria and Russell, 1981; Giloth and Rosenblum, 1987; Hodson and Sullivan, 1990: 166–167). Sometimes such buyouts are financed with workers' pensions or employee stock-option programs, in which workers have purchased shares of stock in their own companies (Ford, 1988). When workers pool their stockholdings in the company, they may have enough capital or clout to buy out at least the plant in their community, thereby preserving jobs and the plant's productive capacity. Once a buyout is completed, the plant may be converted to a **worker cooperative,** which is entirely owned and operated by the workers themselves (Rothschild and

Whitt, 1986). This ensures that ownership and operation remain locally controlled and eliminates the possibility of a runaway shop.

Federal programs sometimes offer useful strategies for communities and workers to prevent runaway shops. For example, the Community Reinvestment Act (CRA) offers local community organizations an opportunity to challenge banks' tendency to disinvest in the local community. Banks frequently take the deposits from local communities and reinvest that finance capital elsewhere, often supporting plant relocations. A CRA challenge is often initiated when a bank is attempting to open intercity branches or to participate in an interstate merger between banks. Such mergers tend to reinforce patterns of disinvestment in the local community. The CRA challenge prompts negotiations between the local community and the bank, frequently resulting in greater bank commitments to invest in local and regional development (Fitzgerald and Meyer, 1986). CRA challenges may, in fact, be combined with workers' buyout attempts to support retention of plants scheduled for shutdown.

Many of these challenges have produced highly encouraging results. For example, the Southern Counties Action Movement (SCAM), a local grassroots community organization in southern Illinois, used CRA in 1985 to challenge the Bank of Zeigler's poor reinvestment performance in the poverty-stricken region when the bank attempted to merge with a bank in St. Louis. The CRA challenge produced a settlement in which SCAM agreed to discontinue its objections in exchange for the bank's commitment of $5 million to the community (SCAM, 1986). Similar success stories have occurred in Cleveland (Marschall, 1979: 131–132), St. Louis (*St. Louis Post Dispatch*, 1986), Philadelphia (*Philadelphia Daily News*, 1986), and Phoenix (*Phoenix Gazette*, 1986), among many others.

These developments suggest positive possibilities for workers to become a stronger force in the reshaping of the American economy. And unions are now poised to play a more significant role in reducing gender and race inequality than they have in the past. If unions, as workers' organizations of power, are to grow once again, they must include women and people of color among their members. Unions therefore must address the issues and concerns of these workers in order to attract them as members. Through unions, women and racial minorities may be able to gain a stronger voice in what happens to them in the formal labor market.

CONCLUSION

Several factors have worked to devalue college degrees and what they can do for people who attain them. The changing structure of the economy and of the formal labor market tends to reduce workers' control over decisions affecting their jobs and their participation in the economy. The consequences of that restructuring most negatively affect lower-level workers and the poor, women, and people of color—that is, those who have historically been disadvantaged in the formal labor market. The result has been increasing inequality: a widening gap between wealth and poverty, between men and women, between whites and racial minorities. In addition, the most recent phase of the structural transformation of the economy has begun to hit the middle class and managerial workers, those who until the past decade generally enjoyed secure, protected positions and upward mobility. Higher education (when we can obtain it) no longer guarantees upward mobility.

The changing formal labor market suggests that the economy is hardly a neutral force devoid of politics. Indeed, power imbalances enable some in the economic hierarchy to make decisions that benefit themselves but adversely affect others. Workers can protect themselves by actively seeking a greater voice in decisions that affect the economy, their communities, and their jobs.

Of course, work occurs not only in the formal labor market but in the informal labor market and in the unpaid domestic labor sphere as well. Work in these three spheres is differentially distributed along race, class, and gender lines: the poor and the working class, women, and people of color are much more likely to engage in a triple shift than the wealthy, men, and whites. People in our society who are already advantaged are better able to delegate responsibility for the work done in the household and in the community to the less advantaged. Perhaps we can formulate strategies to more equitably distribute work in all three spheres, and devise ways to better reward both paid and unpaid labor.

THINKING CRITICALLY

1. Consider the boxed excerpt describing Gerald Winterlin's experiences. What institutional forces prompted his homelessness? Think about not just the immediate cause but the larger institutional forces that may have contributed to it. Was his situation hopeless? What forces made his homelessness temporary? What does Mr. Winterlin's story suggest about the structure of work?

2. We discussed Reskin and Roos's observation that within broad job categories are occupational status hierarchies. Select a job category and analyze the occupational status hierarchies that it might include. Which of these occupations might pay more, and why? Who is more likely to have each of these occupations? What does this suggest about the distribution of earnings?

3. Consider the division of labor in your family. Outline the various jobs that each member does, and identify whether these are done in the formal, the informal, or the unpaid domestic labor markets. Which of these markets does each member *primarily* work in? Is there a balance between labor markets for all members, or do some members work primarily in one market? What are the variables that might explain the distribution of work in your family? What does this suggest about the structure of work?

4. Think of industries or corporations that left or ceased operations in your state or community. Why did they leave or close? How did these shutdowns affect your local community? Your state? Your family?

What could the community and/or the state do to avoid the loss of industries or to reduce the effects of their loss?

5. The North American Free Trade Agreement (NAFTA) allows free movement of goods, services, and production between the United States, Mexico, and Canada. This means that corporations in the United States may elect to produce goods in any of the three countries without incurring import tariffs on goods produced outside the United States. Who is likely to benefit and who is likely to be hurt by NAFTA, and why? What might those who may be hurt by NAFTA do to protect themselves from possible disadvantages of the trade agreement?

KEY TERMS

work, *355*
formal labor market, *355*
informal labor market, *355*
domestic labor, *355*
second shift, *355*
triple shift, *357*
monopoly sector, *358*
competitive sector, *359*
state sector, *359*
runaway shops, *363*

mergers, *364*
merger mania, *364*
deindustrialization, *366*
managerial revolution, *367*
interlocking boards of directors, *368*
segmented labor market, *375*
glass ceiling, *376*
worker cooperative, *382*

SUGGESTED READINGS

Donald Barlett and James B. Steele, *America: What Went Wrong?* Kansas City: Andrews and McMeel, 1992. An analysis of the institutional forces (particularly political forces) that have significantly contributed to the restructuring of the economy.

Barry Bluestone and Irving Bluestone, *Negotiating the Future: A Labor Perspective on American Business.* New York: Basic Books, 1992. A look at creative alternatives in labor-management relations in a changing economy.

Jeanne Boydston, *Home and Work: Housework, Wages, and the Ideology of Labor in the Early Republic.* New York: Oxford University Press, 1990. A historical analysis of gendered notions of work as an element of industrialization in the United States, with explorations of how these notions contributed to the devaluation of unpaid domestic labor today.

Len Krimerman, Frank Lindenfeld, Carol Korty, and Julian Benello (eds.), *From the Ground Up: Essays on Grassroots and Workplace Democracy by C. George Benello.* Boston: South End Press, 1992. A collection of readings focusing on various alternatives to conventional workplace and community power structures.

August Meier and Elliott Rudwick, *Black Detroit and the Rise of the UAW*. New York: Oxford University Press, 1979. An exploration of the intersection of race and class that examines the experiences of African American autoworkers in Detroit.

Lawrence Mishel and Jared Bernstein, *The State of Working America, 1992–93*. Armonk, NY: M. E. Sharp, 1993. A highly informative exploration of the effects of economic transformation on workers, with analyses of gender and race as important variables.

Mary Romero, *Maid in the U.S.A.* New York: Routledge, 1992. An analysis of the race, class, and gender issues raised when women hire other women to perform the domestic labor in their homes.

on the graph?

$$f(x) = x^2 + 3$$

$$g(x) = x - 3$$

$$\therefore f(g(x)) = (x-$$

EDUCATION

*T*hink back to the very first days and weeks that you attended school as a small child. While everyone's memories will be somewhat different, you may recall the boisterous clamor of voices in the hallways, the odors of wet boots and clothing on rainy days, the teacher's authoritative demeanor as she

12

passed out books and new supplies, the lunchtime cafeteria smells, the sense of release and freedom accompanying recess periods, the experience of making new friends and acquaintances, and the routine of bringing your papers and art-work home for parental perusal and praise. By now those first special days and weeks are long past, and you have spent twelve or more years of your life as a student. Your cumulative experiences may be such that overall you have enjoyed school, have mixed feelings about it, or have found it just barely tolerable and best depicted by songs such as Pink Floyd's "Another Brick in the Wall."

In the United States, it is common for people to spend a substantial part of their childhood and young adulthood in school. Almost 78 percent of adults age 25 and older have completed a high school education, and 21 percent have completed four or more years of college (National Center for Education Statistics, 1992: 16). Even persons who drop out of school at the earliest legal opportunity (age 16 in most states) may have been in school for ten or eleven years. Participation in schooling is a near-universal experience for members of our society; we may find it enjoyable or not, but all of us have occupied the status of student. If you are reading this textbook, it is likely you still occupy this status. Thus, it is both appropriate and timely to ask what role educational institutions play in shaping our biographies.

Today, education has come to be seen as the answer to many of society's most serious problems—from getting rid of poverty to maintaining our competitive advantage over other industrial nations in the global economy. Unfortunately, education is not making such problems disappear. Consequently, a cacophony of voices has arisen calling for change in our nation's educational system. In the last decade or so, researchers, specially appointed commissions, and government agencies have issued numerous reports critical of education in the United States (Long, 1991). All generally agree that there is need for a drastic overhaul, even if they disagree about what that overhaul should comprise. One of the most influential and widely quoted reports, A Nation at Risk, *contained this overall assessment:*

> *[T]he educational foundations of our society are presently being eroded by a rising tide of mediocrity that threatens our very future as a Nation and a people. . . . If an unfriendly foreign power had attempted to impose on Amer-*

ica the mediocre educational performance that exists today, we might well have viewed it as an act of war. As it stands, we have allowed this to happen to ourselves (National Commission on Excellence in Education, 1983).

Most of the criticisms focus on unsatisfactory levels of student academic achievement, which often falls short of that of students in industrialized nations of Western Europe and in Japan (see Bowen, 1987; "Not Just for Nerds," 1990). Solutions offered by critics to combat this perceived mediocrity include mandatory testing of teachers for competency, greater parental involvement, increased course requirements and graduation prerequisites, and an extended school year or day. Shortcomings in student achievement tend to be seen as the outcome of inadequate effort on the part of students, their families, and school staff.

In general, the critics do not address many of the social characteristics of education that play a large role in student failure and success. In theorizing about why student performance is below standard, they ignore how such phenomena as class bias, racism, and sexism in education may affect student learning (Mickelson, 1987). Acknowledging the significance of these phenomena would require solutions that go far beyond calling upon students, families, and school staff to try harder. These solutions would include redistributing power in society as a whole, a formidable idea to which people who benefit from the status quo are likely to be hostile.

In this chapter we shall explore some of the ways in which societywide systems of class, race, and sex inequality influence education. What is the relationship between education and upward social mobility for society's members? Does education affect class, race, and sex inequalities? What are the prospects for enhancing equality of educational opportunities? These are some of the questions we shall address.

DIFFERENT FAMILY BACKGROUNDS, EDUCATIONS, AND LIFE CHANCES

Imagine two young people, both 15 years old. The first is named Christopher Lane Bond—"Kip" to his friends. His father is a successful corporate attorney with a Yale law degree, and his mother, a graduate of Smith College, is a part-time editor for a publishing firm. Kip has never attended a public school, even though the ones in the affluent suburb where his family lives are said to be excellent. Instead, through the sixth grade, Kip went to a private school near his home, and he is now a resident student at a private college preparatory school in another state.

Kip's parents are proud of the outstanding quality of the education he has received in the all-male prep school. Ivy League–educated teachers and staff provide each young man with a great deal of personal attention. His parents expect that when he graduates, Kip will attend an elite private college such as the institutions from which they both graduated. There, Kip will mingle with persons from similarly enriched educational backgrounds, choosing courses from a full range of offerings in the arts and sciences. Ultimately, Kip wants to move on to a prestigious law school and a place in his father's firm.

Then there is the other young person, Michele Josephine Mendez. "Josey's" father works for a large frozen-food company where, for the last 20 years, he has operated machinery at the loading dock. Without a high school diploma, this is the best job he can get at this company. Josey's mother works as a hairstylist in a neighborhood salon, using skills she learned at a beauty academy. Knowing how easy it would be for Josey to drop out of the large public high school she attends, they have kept a tight rein on her. Josey's parents do not want her to end up on the streets like many of her peers in their working-class, central-city neighborhood.

Affluent families may choose to send their children to private college preparatory schools, where they receive an enriched, high-quality education. While there is often some diversity in the student bodies of these exclusive schools, most attendees are from a privileged class background. These boys are attending Phillips Academy in Andover, Massachusetts.

The situation at Josey's high school is bleak. The facilities are out-moded, and the building is run-down. Shortages of books and supplies, overcrowded classes, episodes of violence, chronic drug abuse, and frazzled teachers are common. Even though it is clear that Josey is not learning very much, her parents hope conditions at the school will not lead her to drop out before graduation. When she graduates, Josey's parents expect that she will look for work to help the family pay bills. Josey's father thinks that after graduation she should try to take some evening computer pro-gramming courses at an inexpensive local community college to avoid end-ing up stuck in a dead-end job like "the old man."

We have created Kip and Josey to look at an important issue: educational opportunity in U.S. society. Agents of socialization such as schools and the mass media encourage us to think of our society as a **meritocracy,** a system in which rewards come to people on the basis of their individual merit. The concept of meritocracy assumes the existence of equal educational opportu-nity, for without it the system would obviously be unfair. With equal educa-tional opportunity, success or failure becomes more a matter of individual responsibility. If Kip and Josey receive equal educations but one goes on to a successful career and the other does not, we might think that the less suc-cessful one is less able or motivated. But Kip and Josey, by virtue of being born into a particular level of the class structure, start the competition at very different points. Kip is ahead from the beginning. In fact, the resources available to each are so different that their individual talents may have rela-tively little to do with where each one ends up.

The Importance of Cultural Capital

More broadly speaking, Kip and Josey have been endowed with very differ-ent amounts of **cultural capital.** This term refers to material and nonmater-ial cultural goods that are socially valued, such as education, important social connections, and high-status information and social skills. These goods can usher individuals into positions in which they will have social leverage over others in society (Bourdieu and Passeron, 1991). With the cul-tural capital that he is accumulating, Kip will be welcomed through doors of prestige and privilege that Josey will have little chance of even finding.

Clearly, the class position of a family is an important source of its chil-dren's cultural capital. Class position helps determine a family's power as a "consumer" of education, just as it determines a family's ability to con-sume other goods and services, from autos to health care. The consumer power of the affluent is quite a bit greater than that of the poor and work-ing class, and the quality of education that members of these groups are likely to be able to consume is not the same for each group.

The resource of family income helps determine where children, such as Kip and Josey, spend their years in elementary school and high school. A family's economic circumstances dictate where it can afford to reside, and the relative affluence of a community ordinarily dictates the resources found in the neighborhood public school system (see Renchler, 1992). In the United States, public school budgets depend heavily upon money raised by local property taxes.

Crystal Rossi is a troubled 12-year-old who is having difficulty with school. Because the central-city school Crystal attends lacks adequate financing, it is probable that she will not get the quality and amount of help that she needs. Crystal, at this early age, is on the way to becoming a school dropout with little hope for future success.

Crystal Rossi wears two streaks of bright magenta in her hair. They hang, stains of Kool-Aid, down her loose, long strands of blond like a seventh grader's twist of punk: Don't come too close. Don't mess with me. Don't tell me what to do. I'm not like you.

At her Brooklyn public school, a kaleidoscope of teen-age rage, Crystal's teachers see a young girl with an attitude. They focus on her slouch, her Kool-Aid streaks, her grunge clothes and sullen anger and see all the signs of trouble. But those vivid slashes say the most, communicating a basic paradox of adolescence, the double-edged message: "bug off" and "LOOK AT ME."

This is the time, this tender age of 12, when every major decision on the treacherous road to adulthood looms. It is also the time, in the sixth and seventh grades, when some students start a long, slow fall away from school.

"The Classes Are Boring"
On the surface, Crystal hardly seems the sort of child who would stumble.

Her family is stable. Her stepfather works. Her mother takes care of the home. Her father lives just blocks away. Her school is typical, chaotic, underfinanced and overcrowded, but it is clean and relatively safe.

But in a competition between the street and her Bensonhurst school, the street seems to be winning.

Her teachers worry that she might not even make it to her high school graduation. They already see the signs. In class she ducks competition and is losing focus. Outside of school hers is a childhood of temptations and dangers: drugs, alcohol, gangs and older kids who linger on street corners wanting everything from sex to the coat off a 12-year-old's back. . . .

At school, some teachers are trying to help. But sitting in one class, a "resource room" tailored to give troubled students individual attention, Crystal slumped on her desk. "We just sit there," she said later. "They are supposed to help you with stuff you don't understand. But I understand everything so I just sit there."

"Kids who study are all nerds," she said dismissively. "Who'd want to be like that? Everybody makes fun of them."

But the kids make fun of one another for failing, too.

"Stooopid," Crystal taunted a friend in the resource room one morning.

"No, you're stupid, stupid," the girl retorted.

"No. You. You're stupid," Crystal shot back, her head resting on her desk top.

Most days, Crystal says, she is usually happy only at lunch, when she and her friends bend over pizza and sandwiches "just talking." The time brings them together, jostling and punching and trading stories of their day. Sometimes they vanish into a bathroom and plant thick lipstick kisses—perfect O's—on one another's foreheads. Their mark of solidarity against a world too often hostile.

Of the 950 or so students at Cavallaro Junior High School on any given day, says Rose P. Molinelli, the principal, 300 or more are at risk of everything from dropping out to doping up to slashing their wrists and watching their lives literally drain

"In a competition between the street and her Bensonhurst school, the street seems to be winning."

right out of them. One of the school's seventh-grade classes last year had five suicide attempts. This year has been quieter, but the threats remain.

"You can walk out this door any afternoon and get hurt," Mrs. Molinelli said as she stooped on a busy stairwell to scoop up a bit of litter. Other pressures are subtler.

"The kids all know who is abused and who is having trouble at home and who is in a gang," Mrs. Molinelli said. "They know who gets high. They know who gets killed. It gets to them. I think all kids today are at risk. And parents are overwhelmed. A lot of kids get lost."

Three years ago Cavallaro, on 24th Avenue and Cropsey Avenue, was a place where gangs lurked in hallways and teachers lived in fear. Then Mrs. Molinelli came, the gangs were banished and a new sense of order was imposed. Today the halls are clean and orderly and, unlike the local high school where a metal detector was recently installed to screen out guns and knives, students can move about with a sense of ease and safety. A guard monitors everyone entering and leaving the building, and Mrs. Molinelli herself quizzes every child she finds wandering the hallways during class time.

Crystal glides through the environment as though untouched. When a fight breaks out in the hall, she slips around the corner. But privately, she whispers about the gangs, the kids who have been robbed or hurt or are threatened by bullies, and of friends with "troubles" at home.

"I know a kid who just got shot," she said starkly. "He got shot and he is dead."

Mrs. Molinelli changed the school hours—ending the day a half-hour earlier—to let her students out before the local high school students have a chance to victimize the younger children. Other problems are more intractable.

Classes run at or near their maximum of 30 children each, and teachers have to struggle just to keep order, much less provide individual attention. Budget cuts have whittled resources, and although Mrs. Molinelli says her teachers have come up with creative ways to compensate for the shortages, she knows the children could use more.

"We're on the edge," she said. "We're already on the edge and now they are talking about more funding cuts. Right now, we've only got one guidance counselor for 700 students. That's not enough."

Crystal's schedule includes one-on-one tutoring in a "rap class" where Cathy Searao, a school drug counselor, spends time talking with troubled students partly as a mentor and partly as a friend. Shrugging, embarrassed and monosyllabic, Crystal says she likes the program because there "the teacher really talks to you." One afternoon Ms. Searao taught Crystal and a friend how to develop film. It was the one moment in her school day when Crystal smiled. She shyly admits that she also enjoys science and a dance program she goes to after school.

Mrs. Molinelli would like to see more individualized programs in the school. But in the meantime, she fights cutbacks.

Crystal's mother wants more from the public school as well. "I feel like I try my hardest," she said, "but I still need someone there education-wise who can back me up."

Source: Catherine S. Manegold, "To Crystal, 12, the Classroom Serves No Purpose," *New York Times,* April 8, 1993, pp. A1, B7.

In an affluent suburban community such as that in which Kip's family lives, residents own expensive single-family homes and luxury vehicles, and even modest taxes on such property can generate a lot of money for their children's education. In a poorer central-city community such as the one in which Josey's family lives (and in rural areas as well), the relatively low value of the property, and the inability of many people to pay high taxes, produces tax revenues that are often insufficient to meet the educational needs of children attending the local schools. In poorer communities, children's needs can be especially great. One such child is 12-year-old Crystal, whose situation is described in the preceding box.

In affluent West Hartford, Connecticut, a predominantly white suburb bordering the city of Hartford, spending per student in 1990–1991 was $8,155. In 1991 almost 60 percent of West Hartford's children scored at or above the state's goal for mathematics performance, and 90.2 percent of the community's high school graduates took the Scholastic Aptitude Test (SAT), on which they scored an average of 962 out of a possible 1,600. In contrast, the city of Hartford, in which over a quarter of residents live below the federal poverty line and many others live just above it, spent almost $200 less per student in 1990–1991 than did West Hartford. This difference may not seem great, but Hartford also had a much more diverse and problem-plagued student population, meaning the children had a wider range of educational needs. One educator commented:

> A teacher with an average fifth-grade class of 23 children would have 3 who were born with low birth weights, 3 born to mothers using drugs, and 5 born to teenage mothers; 13 living below the poverty line, 15 living with single parents, and 8 living in inadequate housing; 21 members of minority groups; up to 12 from families in which English is not spoken, and 9 whose parents do not work (Judson, 1993).

He went on to say, "Such is the stunning constellation of social problems that will confront the members, both teachers and students, in a typical class in a Hartford public school" (Judson, 1993). Partly because the Hartford school system lacked sufficient resources for adequately serving such students, in 1991 only 12.6 percent of the city's children met the state's goal for mathematics performance, and the 57 percent of graduating seniors (excluding dropouts) who took the SAT scored an average of only 668. As we shall discuss later, these kinds of disparities in central-city and suburban school system resources and educational outcomes are found in metropolitan areas across the country.

Affluence not only allows some families to live in property-rich suburban communities and send their children to well-financed, resource-endowed public schools. It may also allow people like Kip's parents to send their children out of the local community altogether to attend private college preparatory schools. While today such schools usually try to achieve some diversity in their student enrollment, they are still quite exclusive institutions that function to reinforce the advantageous life chances of upper economic classes (Zweigenhaft and Domhoff, 1991). The high-quality education provided by private prep schools makes their graduates attractive candidates for admission to the prestigious colleges that are a stepping stone to top-ranked graduate and professional schools (Cookson and Persell, 1985).

Family income also helps determine whether a student will go on to higher education and, if so, where (see Table 12.1). The divergent educational trajectories that Kip and Josey are likely to enter upon high school graduation are not uncommon. Data show that the affluent are much more likely to take advantage of college opportunities. In 1980, only 15.5 percent of high school graduates from low-socioeconomic-status families were enrolled in a four-year college full-time, in comparison with 55 percent of graduates from families of high socioeconomic status. (Socioeconomic status was measured by parental education, family income, and father's occupation.) A large gap was also found between the two populations in their annual enrollment in all types of postsecondary education, part-time and full-time, even when the high school graduating class of 1980 was looked at each fall through 1985 (National Center for Education Statistics, 1992: 300).

It is not necessarily the case that students (such as Josey) from less affluent socioeconomic backgrounds fail to go on to college because they are less able than those who do. Social scientists have found that students from affluent families who have low measured intelligence are *more* likely to attend college than students from low-income families who have high measured intelligence (Kerbo, 1991: 375–376). This is because expectations for college attendance are different for people from different class backgrounds (Kerbo, 1991: 375). These expectations are influenced by one's socialization experiences in the family, in school, and with peers. Students from affluent families are more likely than others to *expect* to go to college, and they are also the ones whose families are most capable of affording to send them.

Indeed, the costs of college tuition increased throughout the 1980s; in 1992–1993 the costs rose an average of 10 percent, or three times the rate of inflation. During this same period the availability of student financial aid, other than debt-generating loans, dwindled. More and more students from poor and working-class backgrounds have been forced to quit college or been prevented from enrolling at all. Since the 1980s college enrollment by such students has dropped by half. They now number less than 10 percent of all college students (Oullette, 1993). For a glimpse at the challenges faced by young people from poor families, see the box about Derrick White.

Unequal Life Chances

The fact that Kip and Josey have unequal educational opportunities, and thus will have different educational attainments, will affect their life chances. Kip's law school degree and Josey's computer programming certificate will open up quite different occupational and earning opportunities. Kip and Josey will labor in vastly different realms and garner vastly different rewards (see Schwartz, 1988). For example, some years ago the federal government calculated the expected lifetime earnings for year-

Table 12.1

EDUCATIONAL ATTAINMENT AMONG 1980 HIGH SCHOOL SENIORS AS OF 1986

SOCIOECONOMIC STATUS[†] AND RACE/ETHNICITY	HIGHEST LEVEL OF EDUCATION (% OF SENIORS)*					
	NO HIGH SCHOOL DIPLOMA[‡]	HIGH SCHOOL DIPLOMA	LICENSE[§]	ASSOCIATE DEGREE	BACHELOR'S DEGREE	GRADUATE/ PROFESSIONAL DEGREE
Lower 25 percent:						
White, non-Latino	0.9	75.1	12.2	5.0	6.6	0.3
Black, non-Latino	1.4	73.0	12.7	5.1	7.7	0.1
Latino	1.6	73.9	11.8	7.8	4.9	¶
Asian	¶	53.4	17.3	15.7	12.0	1.6
Middle 50 percent:						
White, non-Latino	0.3	62.0	13.0	8.0	16.3	0.4
Black, non-Latino	0.3	67.5	14.7	6.5	10.7	0.3
Latino	1.0	67.0	14.7	6.5	10.7	0.2
Asian	¶	51.1	11.7	11.1	26.1	¶
Upper 25 percent:						
White, non-Latino	¶	44.9	8.6	6.2	38.2	2.2
Black, non-Latino	¶	56.3	12.4	5.4	25.5	0.4
Latino	0.3	60.0	11.4	9.6	18.0	0.7
Asian	¶	42.9	6.5	4.8	40.0	5.9

*Because of rounding, percents may not add to 100.
[†]Socioeconomic status was measured by a composite score on parental education, family income, father's occupation, and household characteristics in 1980.
[‡]Seniors who dropped out of high school after spring 1980 survey and had not completed high school by 1986.
[§]Includes persons who earned a certificate for completing a program of study.
¶Less than .05 percent.

Source: U.S. Department of Education, *Digest of Education Statistics, 1993* (Washington, DC: U.S. Government Printing Office, 1993), p. 305.

round, full-time workers by sex and education. In 1981 dollars, males with five or more years of college (a group Kip aspires to be in) could expect lifetime earnings of $1,503,000. Females with one to three years of college (Josey's father's hope for her) could expect lifetime earnings of less than half that (National Center for Education Statistics, 1984: 192). While part of the difference lies with gender inequality within the labor market (see Chapter 11), educational attainment is directly correlated with lifetime earnings for both men and women.

In this section we have focused on the importance of family economic background in determining one's ability to gain access to and take advantage of educational opportunities. In the next sections we shall look at ways in which systems of class, race, and sex inequality affect the quality of education that schools provide to students in the United States. Differences in students' school experiences can have a significant and lasting impact.

CLASS INEQUALITY AND SCHOOLING

Schools as Gatekeepers

In recent years much research has focused on the relationship between education and the class structure of U.S. society (see Persell, 1977; Oakes, 1985; Meier et al., 1989). While many people think of education as the "great social equalizer" and a vehicle of upward social mobility, the evidence suggests a different reality.

In fact, schools may best be viewed as **gatekeepers,** functioning to keep people at or near the class position of their families. Of course, many people have overcome the obstacles and risen above squalid conditions, but these admirable individuals are exceptions. Despite the billions of dollars spent on education in the United States each year, class inequality continues, and most people end up living in much the same way as their parents. How do schools succeed in performing this gatekeeping function?

In the 1960s, some sociologists argued that class position of the family was the key determinant of a child's achievement in school. A massive, federally funded study by sociologist James Coleman (1966) provided data in support of this view. However, other sociologists took issue with Coleman's research (see Bowles and Gintis, 1976; Dougherty, 1981), asserting that schools tend to treat low-income students *differently* than their more affluent counterparts. Today, while not denying that families also play a role, sociologists believe that the nature of the experiences schools provide for low-income children has an important impact on these youngsters' performance.

Tracking

One of the most important phenomena investigated in recent years is the system of **tracking** found in U.S. public schools (see Goodlad, 1984: chap. 5; Oakes, 1985). Tracking, in theory, offers students the opportunity to par-

Derrick White is an African American youth whose poverty-stricken family resides in a public housing project in Memphis. Despite his exceptional achievements in high school, financial difficulties have posed formidable obstacles to his ability to attend and remain in college, obstacles that don't exist for students from affluent families.

Memphis—Derrick White rides through the crumbling asphalt roads of the Hurt Village housing project where he played tag among the steel clotheslines and shot baskets through bent and wobbly hoops. He passes the trash bins where men with black plastic bags mine for cans to sell to a recycling center. He passes the "dope track," where he saw a friend shot in the neck and killed.

Beyond the project, he passes the supermarket that refused him a job interview because, he believes, his address marks him as a project kid. He passes Northside High School where he graduated 15th last year in a class of 299, third among the boys, and was king of the senior prom. He stops at a McDonald's restaurant, five miles away, where he worked 20 to 25 hours a week throughout the 11th grade.

A Graduate in the Grease Pit
Inside, he points to the spot where he grilled hamburgers. "You get tired of it," he said. "You be back there cooking and cooking." Startled, he recognizes the fellow there now, a classmate at Northside High. "Man!" he whispered. "He got a diploma and he's working at McDonald's."

Derrick White believes he has left that world behind. From his mother, Shirley White, his stepfather, Wardell Horton, and his high school counselors and neighbors who have heaped their own hopes upon him, he has soaked up the message that the safest and surest route out of welfare and the project is a good job.

Yet to go much beyond McDonald's, Derrick, who is 19, needs college. And his prospects have blurred since his dashing performance at Northside High. In September he fulfilled a dream, going to the other end of the state to attend the University of Tennessee in Chattanooga on a full scholarship. But in January, worried about fees and troubles at home, he dropped out.

A Northside counselor then steered him to a college in Memphis. But for lack of financial aid, he left in February. He says he will enroll in still another college in June. Even if he does, he will have lost a semester of his freshman year and sidetracked his progress toward a career.

Derrick is burly and 6 feet 1 inch tall, his close-shaven hair cut with the stripe of a mock part. He has a tiny fake diamond in his left ear that cost $7. His family sometimes calls him Bernard, his middle name. He is unhurried and soft-spoken, amiable but not jovial. Around Hurt Village he commands the sidewalk by merely being on it. Over the years, he said, he has had very few fights, but those few were over money.

"What makes me mad is people trying to use me," he said. "Use me as a fool, trying to play you over." He recalled a fight over whether he had repaid a man who had lent him $5.

"He pushed me," Derrick said. "That's all it took." Striking the air, he replayed the blows—a right, a left, a right. He said the fellow went off with a bloody nose.

Derrick says he wants to be a doctor, an obstetrician. On a school trip last year to colleges and medical schools, he met a black pediatric neurosurgeon in Baltimore named Ben Carson. After a childhood of poverty and delinquency, Dr. Carson won renown six years ago for successfully separating Siamese twins joined at the head.

"At least I know there's one person like me helping people," Derrick said. He cannot recall ever needing a doctor, and he does not know an obstetrician. But in a time of fewer secure and stable jobs everywhere, he reasoned: "That's a field that will never die out. Women will always have children."

Medicine also pays good money, he said. How much? "Man!" he said, as if he had to guess the distance to a star. "One hundred thousand? Two hundred fifty thousand? Probably more." With that, he said: "I'll start a bank account, get a car, get a house, a *huge* house. Put money away for my children's education. Help my mom. Give money to the church."

While he waits to return to school, he scrounges for work. In March, he earned $276 working for a radio station that put a temporary studio in Hurt Village. Since then he has been tutoring the 16-year-old granddaughter of a prominent black Memphis woman in math and science, and is paid $10 a visit.

His mother had a good factory job once, but quit when Derrick, the first of six children, was born. His stepfather has had several jobs but none for very long. Of the 1,365 people living in Hurt Village at the end of last year, only 46 had jobs. Only four of those were men, and Derrick knows none of them.

He says he just barely avoided one form of employment that entraps many young men. The summer before he started the 11th grade and his job at McDonald's, he considered quitting school to sell drugs."

"I wanted some things my friends had," he said. "I knew what they were doing to get them." He recalled a friend, Kermit Smith. "He had everything," Derrick said, "two cars, all the clothes he needed, everything."

One day Derrick, Kermit and some other boys were shooting baskets. Kermit left to buy a snow cone near the dope track.

"We heard a shot," Derrick said. "He was running. 'Boom.' Running. 'Boom.' He fell and I went to him. He said his neck was burning." Kermit was pronounced dead at a hospital. To hustling drugs today, Derrick says: "No, no, no! Look at the consequences—jail, death."

However grim the odds against him, Derrick says he will make it because of two little secrets:

"getting people behind me" and playing by the rules. . . .

During honor assemblies, Northside High erupts in catcalls when students are beckoned to the stage for awards.

"Most will not stand up," said a teacher, Josephine Young. "Derrick always would."

Derrick said: "Well, yeah. I'm a nerd."

Getting into the University of Tennessee was a coup for a kid from Hurt Village. But Derrick said he had to leave Chattanooga after the university sent him a bill for fees, $660 that he could not pay.

He might have dropped out anyway. He spent his first semester worrying because his mother went to the hospital to have gallstones removed. For part of the year his stepfather was in jail. His brother Kevin's grades were flagging under the pressure of the football season.

"She was calling me saying, 'I need help,'" Derrick said of his mother. "I was thinking, She's not going to make it on her own."

Until Derrick left for Chattanooga, he and Kevin, a junior, did homework together on the kitchen table. "I was telling Kevin, 'I don't know how you're going to get into college with grades like this,'" Derrick said. By March, with Derrick home and the football season long past, Kevin's grades had recovered to a high C.

Derrick had no clear idea about how he would get back on track to medical school. At first, he thought of going to Shelby State Community College, a junior college where yearly tuition is just $900. He could become a nurse and use that as a steppingstone to medical school.

But his career counselor from Northside, James Thompson, recommended LeMoyne-Owen, a predominantly black, private four-year college where a semester's tuition is $2,100. Mr. Thompson led him through the application process.

Derrick said he had attended classes for three or four weeks, but the scholarship he was finally granted was $1,200, leaving him $900 short. He

(Continued)

considered borrowing the money, but he said his mother had dissuaded him. "I had to stop classes," he said.

Now he wants to enroll at Memphis State University in June. It costs about $1,000 a semester, and Derrick should be able to qualify for aid for at least part of that. He says he will get a job to cover other expenses.

Derrick landed his first job, the one at McDonald's, after a friend who worked there had told him of an opening. He was interviewed on a Sunday and asked to start the next day. His pay, at the minimum wage of $4.25 an hour, usually came to $100 a week.

Since McDonald's, he has had four jobs—the two this winter, one the summer of his junior year cleaning public parks and roadsides, and one last summer as a clerk at the Memphis Health Center.

Derrick White doesn't have a real role model nearby, but Hurt Village might have one in him. He will get past his unsettled debut in college, he said.

"I know what I got to do," Derrick said. "There's so much I want, that my family wants. They see me giving up, then they think they should give up."

Obstacles are just part of the game. "It's like a hand being dealt you," he said. "You just got to play it. Get people behind me. I know I'm going to make it."

Source: Peter T. Kilborn, "Finding a Way: The Quest of Derrick, 19," *New York Times*, April 22, 1993, pp. A1, B10.

take of educational programs geared to their individual abilities. It originated early in this century, when urban public school systems sought ways to reorganize their curricula to accommodate a growing and increasingly heterogeneous school population. Today, in a system stemming from the practices begun at that time, students are placed in homogeneous "ability groups" with others who teachers and counselors have determined have similar achievement potential. Virtually all students experience some form of ability grouping during their years of schooling (National Education Association, 1990).

Most elementary schools have *in-class* ability grouping (Asher, 1992). For instance, a student may be assigned to sit with certain classmates who will read books of a similar level of difficulty during reading period. By the upper grades, school staff formalize tracking into *between-class* ability grouping (Slavin, 1990: 471–472). A student may travel with a set of peers through a year-long curriculum or track entirely separate from the track of another set of peers (Rosenbaum, 1976; Oakes, 1985). One study found that approximately two-thirds of U.S. schools have ability grouping in some or all subjects in the fifth through ninth grades (Braddock, 1990: 446). Formalized systems of tracking are most common at the middle and high school levels (Asher, 1992).

In high school, students may be assigned to a track labeled "college preparatory," "general," "vocational," "special," or "alternative." Within these tracks, students will find courses intended to correspond to different levels of ability. College preparatory courses may be labeled "high honors," "honors," and "advanced." In the general, or non-college-oriented, track, the courses may be labeled "advanced," "basic," and "remedial." The contents of these courses, and the value each carries toward earning points that will determine a student's overall class rank, are ordinarily quite dissimilar.

Educators who defend tracking claim that it is the most effective and efficient way of teaching students and justify it as being in students' interests. Tracking is said to respond to the fact that students have different needs and capabilities. Here is how proponents defend ability grouping:

> In essence, the argument in favor of ability grouping is that it will allow teachers to adapt instruction to the needs of a diverse student body and give them an opportunity to provide more difficult material to high achievers and more support to low achievers. The challenge and stimulation of other high achievers are believed to be beneficial to high achievers (Slavin, 1990: 473).

Yet a growing body of social science research suggests that track placement can have a *negative* effect on students (Meier et al., 1989; Glazer, 1990; Page, 1991; Slavin, 1990: 473–474). Tracking may do the most harm to low achievers and is thought to be a factor in delinquent behavior and dropping out of school (Wiatrowski et al., 1982). Children and youths are generally aware of their standing compared with that of other students in the tracking system. When students are consistently placed in low-level reading groups or in a collection of known "gut" courses in which little is expected of them, they are likely to develop a negative self-concept, low motivation to achieve, and limited aspirations for the future (Gamoran and Berends, 1987). Schooling can become a humiliating and alienating experience when every day one must take one's place at or near the bottom of a system of stratification built around a school staff's judgment of who has the ability to learn what.

Looking at the backgrounds of students in different tracks, we see that for the most part children and youths whose families are middle-class or higher dominate the college preparatory tracks or their equivalent, while children of poor and working-class families are by and large clustered in the lower tracks (Oakes, 1985; Glazer, 1990).

Who makes the placement decisions, and how? Teachers play a major role, as do guidance counselors, particularly in the middle and high school years. Two factors are thought to operate in the decision-making process. The first is subjective: biases about abilities and appropriate expectations for children of different class origins (see Irvine, 1990). School staff may be influenced by a child's home circumstances, dress and physical appearance, language, behavior both in and out of the classroom, and their experiences with his or her parents and siblings. These "measures" may have little or nothing to do with a child's ability to learn. But when school staff believe they do, a **self-fulfilling prophecy** is likely to be set in motion (Rist, 1970, 1973). In Chapter 1 we reviewed experimental research indicating that teachers' positive expectations can have a significant impact on students' intellectual growth (Rosenthal and Jacobson, 1968a, 1968b). School staff may likewise "create" low achievement simply by making tracking assignments that carry with them low expectations for students' performance.

The second factor that comes into play in determining track placement is the use of standardized achievement and IQ (intelligence quotient) tests. Despite widespread acknowledgment of the inadequacies of such tests and the biases known to accompany their use (Gould, 1981), they continue to be used. One problem with standardized tests is that they tend to reflect the advantages associated with a privileged class background. The resources affluent families can make available to their children from an early age give the children greater exposure to the types of knowledge and skills these tests measure. It is the affluent family that is most capable of providing enriched day-care and nursery school experiences; the stimulation of travel; educational games and a home computer; expensive books, magazines, and videos; and support for lessons and hobbies. Children from poor and working-class families generally lack such resources and, on average, perform less well on achievement and IQ tests (Lareau, 1989).

The conclusion typically, but erroneously, drawn from such test results is that poor and working-class children are less able and thus belong in a track that will demand less of them. Moreover, since in our society children of color are disproportionately found in the poor and working-class populations, and on average test less well than the predominantly white affluent population, children of color are more likely to be in classes in the lower tracks (Glazer, 1990). (See Figure 12.1.) It is not uncommon for students within a racially mixed school building to experience racial segregation along curriculum lines as a consequence of tracking (Meier et al., 1989).

Tracking, then, results in very different sets of educational experiences for children from different socioeconomic classes. Jeannie Oakes (1990) has explored the impact of tracking in mathematics and science, two areas of importance to our increasingly technological economy. Using survey data from 1,200 schools and 6,000 teachers, Oakes found that low-track students tended to have less qualified math and science teachers, lower-quality texts and laboratory equipment, less active and engaging classes, and fewer opportunities to take college preparatory math courses. She also found that the proportion of low-track math and science classes increased with the proportion of racial minorities in a school. Thus, opportunities to learn math and science differed along both class and racial lines. Familiarity with math and science is increasingly important for finding a decent job in the manufacturing and service sectors of the economy. But, as one social scientist put it, "The lower track is training for the blue-collar jobs of the '50s. Those jobs are gone" (Glazer, 1990: 749).

Tracking leads to quite different trajectories for youths from different class backgrounds. Those from more affluent families, having been exposed to the appropriate subject matter in the college preparatory track (J. Oakes, 1985, 1990), are likely to go on to a four-year college or university, with prospects for a white-collar job or postgraduate professional training. Because of their family incomes, they generally are able to afford expensive higher education. (In recent years it has been increasingly

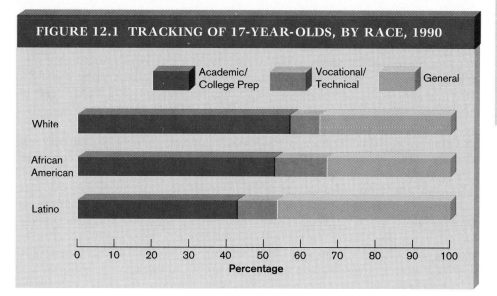

FIGURE 12.1 TRACKING OF 17-YEAR-OLDS, BY RACE, 1990

Academic/College Prep   Vocational/Technical   General

White

African American

Latino

Percentage

Among 17-year-olds in high school, whites are more likely to be in academic or college preparatory tracks than are African Americans or Latinos. The latter two groups, when compared with whites, are more likely to be in vocational or technical tracks. (*Source:* U.S. Department of Education, *The Condition of Education, 1993,* Washington, DC: U.S. Government Printing Office, 1993, p. 67.)

difficult for middle-class families to guarantee the availability of the economic resources needed for college. See Newman, 1989, and Phillips, 1990.)

In contrast, children from working-class and poverty-level families, who have been routed into and through non-college-bound tracks, end up with quite different destinations (Rose, 1989). They are most likely to go directly into the labor market, where they compete with others who possess limited skills, or to two-year community colleges or technical schools that are not selective in their admissions criteria (Zwerling, 1976; Brint and Karabel, 1989). In such colleges and schools, they may gain credentials that will enable them to enter a paraprofessional position or skilled manual trade. Earning even these credentials may take time, for these students are often forced to attend school part-time; neither they nor their families may be able to afford the costs of full-time school attendance.

Students assigned to lower tracks in high school are less likely than other students to stay through graduation (Gamoran and Mare, 1989). Young people who drop out are in the weakest position in the labor market and are likely to remain so throughout their adult working years. In 1991, 12.5 percent of persons between the ages of 16 and 24 had not completed high school and were not enrolled in school. As would be predicted from the greater representation of people of color in low-level tracks, the percentage of dropouts was lowest among whites, at 8.9 percent, while the rate for African Americans was 13.6 percent and the rate for Latinos was 35.3 percent. With the exception of a slightly lower rate for Latino females than males, dropout rates did not differ by sex (National Center for Education Statistics, 1992: 109).

Over the last three decades, U.S. society has experienced the phenomenon of *credential inflation* (see Collins, 1979). The high school diploma and more recently the bachelor's degree have steadily lost value as credibility for employment. More people than ever before have these degrees today and consequently find themselves pitted in intense competition for advancement. In response to the rising number of diploma and degree holders, employers have slowly increased the educational requirements for entry-level jobs. Being a high school dropout today means facing a future of very limited life chances.

In sum, the tracking system within education, buttressed by the fact that families in different class positions bring different resources to bear on behalf of their children, shapes our biographies. Students with the potential to learn and make important contributions are more likely to be encouraged in school if they are from families of higher class position. The class bias that ignores and suppresses the potential of people from poor and working-class backgrounds cheats society of the contributions they could otherwise make. The gatekeeping role played by education is a major factor supporting the perpetuation of class differences and inequality in the distribution of life chances within society as a whole.

While our focus in this section was on class inequality and schooling, we did mention that students of color from low-income families are disproportionately represented in low-level tracks and are more likely to drop out of school than white students. In the next section we shall address ways in which the system of racial inequality in the United States has affected and continues to affect the quality of education available to racial minorities. We shall begin with a look at racial segregation in education.

RACE INEQUALITY AND SCHOOLING

De Jure and De Facto School Segregation

As recently as 1954 it was perfectly legal for towns and cities in the United States to maintain separate schools for white children and children of color. Southern states routinely practiced segregation of students by race. The segregation of African American children was part of the "Jim Crow" strategy southern whites used to retain the sense of racial superiority they had enjoyed during the era of slavery (Williams, 1987). Millions of children of color, many of whom are adults today, went through segregated schools, which were typically less well funded, staffed, and equipped than those available to whites in the same communities. In cases where maintaining dual systems of schooling was too expensive because there were only a few children of color, these children were bused long distances to segregated schools in other communities.

In 1954, after decades of legal struggles, the U.S. Supreme Court ruled that racially segregated schools denied children of color equal rights under the law. This ruling, rendered in *Brown v. Board of Education of Topeka*

(Kansas), pulled the legal foundations from under the U.S. educational version of South African apartheid. The Court ordered offending school districts to dismantle racially separate systems and to abolish segregationist policies "with all deliberate speed." The Supreme Court ruling met with a great deal of state and local resistance, however. Little **desegregation** of public school systems in the southern states began until more than ten years later, after Congress passed the Civil Rights Act of 1964. That act gave the executive branch of the federal government the power to initiate lawsuits against school systems that refused to desegregate and the power to cut off federal financial assistance.

The federal government's attack against segregated schools was aimed primarily at the southern states, where racial separation was written into law (known as **de jure segregation**). Once this legalized segregation was ended, southern schools ultimately became the least segregated in the nation (De Witt, 1992a). This remains the case, even though segregation of southern schools is on the increase: in 1988–1989, 44 percent of African American children were in predominantly white schools in the South; by 1991–1992, the figure had dropped to only 39 percent ("New Era of Segregation," 1993).

Many southern states and communities resisted desegregating their schools even after the U.S. Supreme Court declared segregated school systems unlawful. In 1959 Prince Edward County, Virginia, closed its public schools rather than eliminate segregation. Until the federal government stepped in during the 1960s to end such practices, the county's white children were sent to well-subsidized private schools created especially for them, while African American children were left to fend for themselves. This teacher ran a school for these unfortunate children in a one-room shack.

In the Northeast, Midwest, and West, schools were segregated largely because of racial discrimination in the real estate market and in the informally enforced, self-segregation of neighborhoods by white landlords and homeowners. This is known as **de facto segregation.** Unlike the case in the South, segregation was not authorized by law, but local school boards—typically all-white—often helped create and perpetuate segregation by the ways in which they located new schools and drew boundaries. Relatively little federal executive branch pressure to desegregate was exerted on these school systems outside the South. Rather, initiatives to break down segregation took the form of an occasional court order and voluntary local plans.

Since the mid-1960s the school systems attended by children of color in the Northeast, Midwest, and West have become increasingly segregated (De Witt, 1992a). Today, children in these regions frequently attend schools that have few, if any, members of other racial and cultural groups, much like the racially segregated neighborhoods they live in. De facto segregation is most noticeable in metropolitan areas where predominantly African American and Latino school systems within central cities are surrounded by suburban school systems that are predominantly white. Among the most segregated states in this regard are Illinois and New York.

One study of big-city school systems in the United States found not only that there is widespread de facto segregation but that it has dramatically increased since the late 1960s (Orfield and Monfort, 1988). In big cities, fifteen out of sixteen African American and Latino students are in schools that have few whites ("New Era of Segregation," 1993). The Northeast is now the most segregated region of the country. There, half of all black students attend schools in which less than 10 percent of the students are white; one in three African Americans attend schools in which 1 percent or less of the students are white (Jordan, 1992). Latino students are also highly likely to attend schools in which children of color are in the vast majority (De Witt, 1992b). In contrast, Asian American students are typically integrated into white school populations (Jordan, 1992).

Segregation and Central-City Fiscal Crises

De facto school segregation reflects prevailing patterns of housing segregation. Discrimination in the rental or sale of housing has been illegal nationwide since the 1960s. Nonetheless, informal discrimination in banks' mortgage-lending policies, as well as bias in housing owners' and realtors' sales and rental practices, have channeled African Americans and Latinos into certain residential areas within cities. As these areas have grown and extended, one result has been *white flight* (the relocation of Anglo residents) into outlying suburban communities. Often these are communities that historically have not tolerated African American or Latino families. Tragically, even today the residents of many communities make residents of color feel unwelcome.

In any case, given that people of color are disproportionately represented among the poor and working class in central cities, many cannot afford the high housing costs in outlying white communities. Moreover, even those who can afford to relocate often must weigh the difficulties and costs of commuting back to central-city jobs on which incomes of family members depend. Some parents of color may worry about how they will replace the support network of family and friends that helps with child and elder care while they go to work. All must consider how they and their children will be received and treated in the new community. The difficulties many families face in moving to predominantly white communities outside central cities—from racial discrimination to the issue of their own resources—reinforce segregated living patterns. Because public education systems in the United States tend to be organized around local or neighborhood schools, which parents generally prefer, residential segregation readily translates into racially separate schooling.

The U.S. population has undergone significant changes in composition in recent years, due both to natural population growth and to immigration policies that have made it easier for people from Latin America, the Caribbean, and Asia to enter the country and gain citizenship. Because of this, public school enrollments of children of color have been growing. At present children and youths who are African American, Latino American, Asian American, and Native American account for 30 percent of the total enrollment in the nation's public schools (National Center for Education Statistics, 1992: 60). This percentage is expected to increase to a full *one-third* of public school enrollment by around the year 2000 (DePalma, 1990).

At the same time that central cities have increasingly come to house people of color, urban fiscal crises have squeezed city budgets. The aging and deterioration of central-city housing, combined with the loss or shut-down of businesses and manufacturing plants, has left cities across the United States with a weakened property-tax base. Their fiscal situations have been exacerbated by cutbacks in federal aid that state governments have not been able or willing to offset (Ornstein, 1988). City budgets are stretched to the limits, as residents have the need not only for education but for health care, police protection, and income assistance programs (Cummings, 1988). Too often the funds available for public education fall far short of what is needed to adequately staff and equip city schools. While money alone does not create quality education, many city schools are so starved for funds that they lack even the most rudimentary basics. The result is what education critic Jonathan Kozol (1991) has called "savage inequalities."

The savage inequalities to which Kozol referred are those that characterize the gap between the quality of public education cities can afford to provide and the quality more affluent suburbs can afford. On average, large urban systems spend $5,200 per student each year, while suburban systems spend an average of $6,073 (Council of Great City Schools, 1992). Gross averages, however, tend to minimize the distance between extremes. For example, in 1990–1991 predominantly white Rye High School in New York State spent $12,570 per student and had a one-to-seven teacher/student ratio. In contrast, Chicago's predominantly Latino and African American Carl Schurz High School spent $5,275 per student, with a one-to-sixteen ratio (Mitchell, 1991). Such differences in resources affect the

Children who live in affluent communities that are easily able to generate taxes for education are likely to attend schools that are well-staffed and generously equipped, like this high school classroom. Notice the small student/teacher ratio, supplies of instructional materials, and furnishings, which all encourage close teacher-student interaction.

educational opportunities of students who must attend these schools, no matter what their skin color.

Kozol's research on the differences between well-financed and poorly financed schools across the country vividly illustrated the outcomes of spending inequities. The poorer, racially segregated central-city schools tend to be physically dilapidated, overcrowded, understaffed, and ill-equipped with textbooks and supplies. Kozol even found science laboratories with no science equipment. In Kozol's view, the overall effects of attending such schools on children's educational opportunities, level of performance, and sense of self-esteem are extremely negative. The disproportionate enrollment of children of color in poorly financed central-city schools thus contributes to their limited life chances. (See Figure 12.2.)

Racial Inequalities within Schools

The internal environments of schools play an important role in segregating education and in limiting minority opportunity. In a variety of ways a school's environment—including its staff composition, patterns of teacher-student interaction, and curricular opportunities—can prove inhospitable to learning.

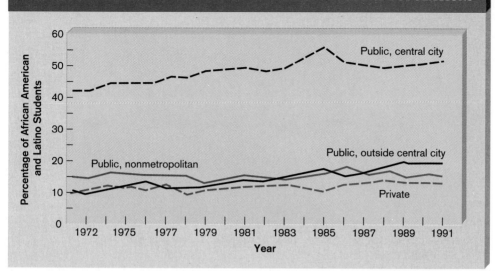

FIGURE 12.2 THE CHANGING COLOR OF SCHOOLS' STUDENT POPULATIONS

Since the early 1970s, public schools in and adjacent to central cities have been enrolling increasing numbers of African American and Latino students. In 1991 over half the students in central-city public schools were from these two groups. Student bodies in public schools just outside central cities were about 20 percent African American or Latino. (*Source:* U.S. Department of Education, *The Condition of Education, 1993,* Washington, DC: U.S. Government Printing Office, 1993, p. 117.)

School Staffing Consider, for example, the staffing of public schools. By and large, whites disproportionately dominate the staff of the nation's public schools: 97 percent of school superintendents are white; 90 percent of public school principals are white; and 89 percent of teachers are white ("Excerpts from School Poll," 1988). These percentages do not reflect the composition of the larger population or the population of public schools. Our societal system of race inequality often discourages interracial relationships, and many whites lack knowledge and harbor stereotypes about racial minority groups. White school staff can find it difficult to comprehend the needs and capabilities of children of color, to communicate effectively with them, and to fashion educational programming that will maximize their individual learning potentials. In part this is also an outcome of the inadequacies in the education and training that school staff members themselves receive (Irvine, 1990: chap. 6).

Jeannie Oakes studied three California high schools and found that students were being channeled into different tracks on the basis of racial stereotypes held by teachers and counselors (Glazer, 1990: 750). Even when their scores on standardized tests were identical, Asian Americans were far more likely to be placed in high-track classes than Latinos. Oakes is quoted as saying:

Racially segregated central-city schools are often overcrowded, short-staffed, and poorly supplied and equipped. It is amazing that despite such obstacles and limitations, many children in these schools—such as the high school students pictured here—maintain their desire to learn. This desire is nurtured and reinforced when teachers and administrators foster a positive social and academic environment.

> Even where language was a problem for both Asian and Hispanic groups, some [school officials] would say, "The Asian kids will work together and make sure each other learns . . . and we can't depend on Hispanic kids to do that." The trouble is that there are stereotypical judgments made about groups that then are applied to most children who belong to that group, whether or not it may be true in that individual case (Glazer, 1990: 750).

School staff make decisions that often have the effect of providing children of color with an education that is different from and inferior to that provided to white children. This happens to African American children even when they are enrolled in schools with whites (Irvine, 1990: xiv–xvi). According to Marion Wright Edelman of the Children's Defense Fund,

> Once a black child enters public school he or she is twice as likely as a white child to be held back a grade, three times as likely to be placed in classes for the educable mentally retarded [EMR], and twice as likely to be suspended from school. . . . A white child is twice as likely to be placed in a class for gifted students as in an EMR class; a black child is almost three times as likely to be placed in an EMR class as in a class for gifted students (Edelman, 1988: 144–145, 154).

In addition, as we saw earlier, a higher proportion of students of color are channeled into low-level high school tracks labeled "general" or "vocational," as opposed to "college preparatory" ("Racial Harm," 1990).

Cultural Differences   Jacqueline Jordan Irvine (1990) has explored factors that may help explain the problem of African American achievement in public schools. Her ideas may be helpful in understanding the plight of other racial minorities as well. One of the main factors she addresses is that of **cultural synchronization.** Irvine argues that African Americans share common cultural traits deriving from their African ancestry and from their history of racial oppression as a people in the United States (see also Kochman, 1981). These cultural traits are not possessed by the dominant "Eurocentric" majority (white Americans of European ancestry).

In Irvine's words,

> Because the culture of black children is different and often misunderstood, ignored, or discounted, black students are likely to experience cultural discontinuity in schools, particularly schools in which the majority, or Eurocentric persons, control, administer, and teach. . . . This lack of cultural sync becomes evident in instructional situations in which teachers misinterpret, denigrate and dismiss black students' language, nonverbal cues, physical movements, learning styles, cognitive approaches, and worldview. When teachers and students are out of sync, they clash and confront each other, both consciously and unconsciously, in matters pertaining to proxemics (use of interpersonal distance), paralanguage (behaviors accompanying speech, such as voice tone and pitch and speech rate and length), and coverbal behavior (gesture, facial expression, eye gaze) (Irvine, 1990: xix).

Researchers and educators point out that conflicts arising from lack of cultural synchronization between African American children and school staff occur most notably in schools serving children from poor, inner-city neighborhoods where residents are socially isolated. In poverty-stricken sections of New York City, for example, teachers and students grapple and clash over students' use of black dialect instead of standard English (Lee, 1994). While many students are, in effect, "bilingual" and can switch back and forth between the two, others do not possess skill in the use of standard English. Black dialect, which linguists suggest reflects remnants of West African languages used by slaves, is often dismissed with little respect by teachers. Under such circumstances, many students use it intentionally as a form of resistance to school authority and as a badge of in-group ethnic and class identity (Lee, 1994).

While acknowledging the presence of cultural differences, researcher John Ogbu (1991) argues that the academic performance of African Americans as well as other minority groups must be understood in the context of how they came to be incorporated into this society, their history of discriminatory treatment, and the patterns of adaptive behavior they consequently adopted. **Immigrant minorities** have come to the United States voluntarily. Examples include many immigrants from Asia, the Caribbean, and Latin America. On average, their children tend to do better in school than the children of **involuntary minorities** such as Native Americans and African Americans, groups who were incorporated into our society through colonization, conquest, or slavery.

Ogbu believes such differences in academic performance are due to a variety of factors. Immigrant minorities usually possess a positive social identity rooted in their original homeland. They have reason to be optimistic about their future life chances when comparing the opportunities before them to those they left behind. They rationalize that the problems they often face in this country—with language, discriminatory treatment, employment, housing—are temporary, and they expect to overcome such problems with time and effort. Immigrant minorities tend to trust members of the dominant group and the institutions that it controls and seek ways to use its institutions for their benefit. In sum, immigrant minorities are likely to possess a positive world view and hopes for the future that affect their children's orientation toward schooling and may be reflected in academic performance.

In Ogbu's view, African Americans' history and contemporary life experiences have encouraged many of them to adopt a negative world view and to be cynical about their future life chances. The social identity of African Americans is less likely to be positive than that of immigrant minorities, given their long history of oppression and denigration by the dominant white population. African Americans often find it difficult to be optimistic about their life chances, for the problems in living they face often look and turn out to be permanent. Their experiences with members of the dominant white majority and the institutions it controls generate wariness and distrust. Ogbu suggests that under conditions of poverty and racial isolation in a ghetto community, many African American children find it difficult to believe that societal rules for self-advancement will work for them and doubt that schooling will produce any worthwhile payoff. They have difficulty seeing how going to school will provide them with the cultural capital they need to "make it" outside their community. Affected as well by teachers' low expectations for them, many students place little value on academic performance.

Ogbu thus gives a much broader interpretation of minority academic performance, suggesting that a minority group's history, structural position, and world view contribute to how its members interact in the school setting. This may help explain why minority groups may differ in their experiences with school and why many African American students have difficulty with their academic performance. In the absence of mutual respect between students and school staff, the school environment is likely to be one of tension and even conflict. Staff members then focus their energies on maintaining order and control, and opportunities for students to learn are lost.

The in-school experiences of children of color can also be affected by how white school staff react to the community politics accompanying desegregation. For example, in early 1990 African American parents and students in Selma, Alabama, protested against the fact that many black children with high test scores were placed in the lowest tracks (Glazer, 1990: 750–751). Despite the fact that the Selma school system was 70 percent black, over 90 percent of black students were tracked low. Observers suggested that such tracking practices started in the early 1970s, when Selma public schools finally desegregated, as a way of persuading middle-class white parents to keep their children in the local public schools.

While Selma ceased to maintain separate schools for blacks and whites, its school system *re*segregated students within schools through racially biased track placements.

Selma, Alabama, is not unusual in this respect. Other school systems have segregated students by race within schools to help reduce many middle-class whites' antipathy toward having their offspring attend school with children of color. Kenneth Meier and his colleagues (1989) studied 174 large central-city school systems. They confirmed other researchers' findings: African American students were more likely than white students to be in lower-level tracks. But they also found that school systems in which whites were concentrated in the higher tracks experienced less white flight. In their view, racially biased tracking practices, while harming the educational opportunities of many children of color, had become a means by which public school officials were able to stem the flight of middle-class white families from central cities.

Given the high degree of competition for jobs today, being disadvantaged in terms of educational credentials amounts to losing the competition before it begins. Moreover, lack of school success feeds into the discriminatory hiring practices of many employers. Such employers can reject people of color for being educationally unqualified, thereby hiding the blatant racism involved in rejecting them for their skin color. Indeed, one way employers may minimize the probability that persons of color will qualify for jobs is to arbitrarily inflate the educational credentials required for the positions. (Federal affirmative action policies, largely unenforced in recent years, originated to prevent such discriminatory employer practices. See Hacker, 1992: chap. 7).

Clearly what is occurring is racism in education. Racism remains a central open wound within our society as a whole, as we saw in Chapter 6. While we may wish it were not so, our schools have not escaped or proved to be a haven from racism. Education, as one of many white-dominated and -controlled institutions, needs to be purged of racism as much as any of the others.

GENDER INEQUALITY AND SCHOOLING

Thus far we have been discussing education as if a student's gender was of no real significance. However, given that a system of sex inequality exists in the larger society, we should expect to find evidence of it in schooling. In recent years accumulating evidence shows that males and females are treated very differently in school and that their differential treatments affect educational opportunities (Wellesley College Center for Research on Women, 1992). As we shall see, the nature of the treatment girls experience structures and skews the directions in which their learning proceeds and adversely affects their sense of competence and self-esteem. In brief, girls are not encouraged to explore and develop their full potential and range of talents as much as are boys.

Suppressing Female Students' Potential

Ample research exists to show that boys receive far more teacher attention in school at all grade levels, no matter what the sex of the teacher (Wilkinson and Marrett, 1985; Jones, 1989). This is not simply because males demand more attention; teachers actively solicit males' responses more frequently within the classroom. When teachers express more interest in, and give more positive feedback to, contributions from boys, they create an environment that encourages boys to be actively engaged in the learning process while girls become passive and restrict their involvement (Wellesley, 1992: 68).

Some researchers argue that differential treatment by teachers can lead to **learned helplessness** in female students, whereby they lose confidence in their own abilities and are less likely to persevere in schoolwork that is difficult and challenging (Parsons et al., 1982; Wellesley, 1992: 69). Girls may thus abandon academic courses and programs for which they are actually well qualified.

For example, many people have commented upon the relative dearth of girls in advanced mathematics and science courses that college-bound students might profitably take (Raffalli, 1994). Jones and Wheatley (1989) point out that there are gender differences in attitudes toward science as well as differences in achievement in science by sex. Achievement differences are especially notable in chemistry, earth and space science, and physics. Differences in attitudes toward science start as early as elementary school; differ-

Too often young girls are discouraged from developing and pursuing interests in mathematics and science. This New York City school is attempting to reverse that trend by experimenting with an all-girl extracurricular program in these subjects.

ences in achievement start to show up when students reach adolescence (Jones and Wheatley, 1989: 535–536). Since no one has demonstrated that innate sex differences in science-related skills or aptitudes exist, social scientists interpret such attitudinal and achievement differences as outcomes of the ways in which males and females are treated.

Jones and Wheatley (1989), along with many others, argue that schooling often fails to encourage girls to be interested and involved in science and may actively discourage them. In observations of 30 physical science and 30 chemistry classrooms, Jones and Wheatley found that 93 percent of the wall posters and displays used males as the dominant scientific figures. Teachers in these classrooms were more likely to call on male students and to ask males to volunteer to conduct experiments and demonstrations. Female students were more likely to be relegated to the role of observers. Finally, teachers' use of language and examples showed that "teachers continue to sex type science occupations and reinforce the traditional role of the woman as the homemaker" (Jones and Wheatley, 1989: 543).

In college programs women are underrepresented in engineering and other technical fields that require an in-depth science and math background; they find their way instead into education or the humanities, fields in which such a background is not necessary (Jones and Wheatley, 1989: 535). Thus, women end up in programs leading to jobs that are less well paid than those of men. (See Figure 12.3.) In 1989–1990, women received 78 percent of the 104,715 bachelor's degrees awarded in education, but only 13.8 percent of the 82,110 bachelor's degrees awarded in engineering. While this is a major advance from the 0.004 percent of the engineering degrees they received in 1959–1960, women are still a long way from parity with men (National Center for Education Statistics, 1992: 274, 287).

The research on science classrooms addresses an aspect of the educational environment thought to bear on girls' self-esteem: the way in which women's contributions to society are handled in the formal curricula. While there have been some improvements in recent years, curricula still heavily focus on the contributions of men in such subjects as English and social studies, with attention to the role of women being negligible or token. Observing that girls' self-esteem goes *down*, not up, as they progress through school, researchers have postulated that curricular bias and omission of the contributions that women make are part of the reason:

> Lowered self-esteem is a perfectly reasonable conclusion if one has been subtly instructed that what people like oneself have done in the world has not been important and is not worth studying (Wellesley, 1992: 67).

Not all students, as we saw earlier, are bound for college or are channeled into college preparatory programs in public high schools. Most high schools have vocational education programs that serve both male and female students who are likely to enter the labor force directly upon graduation. Again, treatment is different for the two sexes, despite laws prohibiting discrimination in educational programs (Wellesley, 1992: 42–43). Girls are clustered in programs that prepare them for low-paying, dead-end, traditionally female jobs (such as secretarial work and food services), while

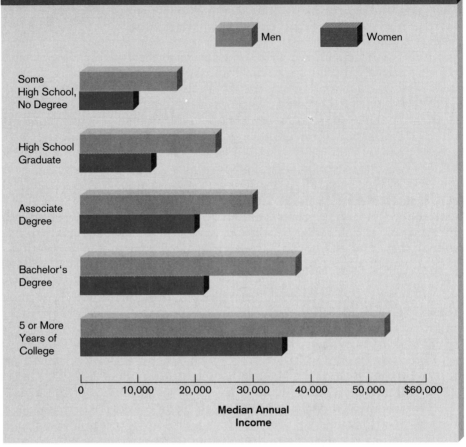

FIGURE 12.3 EARNINGS OF MALE AND FEMALE WORKERS, 1991

On average, women workers 25 years old and over have lower incomes than men, even when both have completed equivalent years of schooling. This is due, in part, to the fact that women are more likely than men to be enrolled in educational programs that do not lead to the more highly paid skilled jobs and professions. (*Source:* U.S. Department of Education, *Digest of Education Statistics, 1993,* Washington, DC: U.S. Government Printing Office, 1993, p. 388.)

boys are concentrated in programs that point toward skilled trades and occupations (such as woodworking and engine repair) in which monetary rewards and opportunities for mobility are likely to be higher.

Female teachers predominate in the courses girls take in home economics, consumer skills, health care, and office practices, while male teachers are most likely to supervise the boys whose presence dominates courses in industrial arts, agriculture, and technical occupations. Moreover, high school placement efforts and policies do not work to break down the resistance women face when attempting to enter areas of the labor market that men have tended to monopolize (Wellesley, 1992: 43).

In 1972 Congress passed legislation barring sex discrimination at institutions that receive federal funds. Title IX of the Education Amendments of 1972 states, "No person in the United States shall, on the basis of sex, be excluded from participation in, be denied benefit of, or be subjected to discrimination under any program or activity receiving Federal financial assistance." Title IX pertains not only to the formal curriculum but also to athletic activities, another arena in which one's potential and range of talents may be cultivated and displayed. Here again, while there have been some efforts to address discrimination in this area in recent years, problems remain.

For example, only 26 percent of high school girls participate in athletics, while almost twice as many high school boys do so. And the girls do not necessarily have role models who would encourage more active participation. The percentage of high school coaches who are female has been declining (Wellesley, 1992: 45). Within high schools there tends to be far less interest in and enthusiasm for girls' sports than for boys' sports. Ironically, many girls participate in pep clubs and cheerleader squads whose activities help validate this situation (Eder and Parker, 1987). The bias in athletics parallels the bias in the formal curriculum, in that women's contributions are less well acknowledged and valued.

The imbalance in men's and women's sports participation continues at the college level. For example, a 1990–1991 survey by the National Collegiate Athletic Association found that men at Division I colleges (colleges that play big-time sports) were much more likely than women to be on sports teams. Moreover, men's sports received the greatest proportion of college sports expenditures. While women accounted for more than half of the enrollment at the colleges surveyed, twice as many men as women were athletes. Men's teams received 77 percent of sports operating funds, 83 percent of the funds available for recruiting, and twice the number of scholarships available to women's teams (Lederman, 1992). Critics argue that such treatment of women athletes is fundamentally unfair and in violation of Title IX of the Education Amendments; however, the federal government has been slow to move against sex discrimination in school sports.

The School and Teenage Pregnancy

Schools also shortchange girls and narrow their life chances by the ways in which they handle teenagers who become pregnant. Today's teenagers become sexually active at an early age. The average age of first intercourse is estimated to be 16, but many children become sexually active even earlier. The number of 15-year-olds with sexual experience increased from 17 percent in 1980 to 26 percent in 1988 (U.S. Centers for Disease Control, 1991). Teenage pregnancy has become a widespread phenomenon and a problem of major importance. Indeed, the United States has a higher rate of early childbearing than almost any other industrialized society (Jones et al., 1985).

In 1990, teenagers were responsible for 31 percent of the 1,165,000 live births to unmarried mothers (U.S. Department of Commerce, 1993: 78). It is not uncommon for girls to confront the challenge of motherhood while in high school (and even in junior high school). Many of these girls face discrimination within school, both while they are pregnant and after they have their children. School staff may exert little effort to have the girls continue attending school, making them feel like second-class citizens whose presence somehow contaminates the rest of the student body (Wellesley, 1992: 39–40).

One study found that for 72 percent of teenage girls who had both conceived a child and dropped out, the conception had preceded the dropout (Polit and Kahn, 1987: 134). Such data led researchers to conclude that "the single best-documented consequence of an early pregnancy is a truncated education" (Polit and Kahn, 1987: 133). However, more recent research qualifies this conclusion. Girls who have children while enrolled in school, but who remain in school, are just as likely to graduate as those who do not become pregnant. But girls who become pregnant and drop out of school are less likely than the others to graduate (Upchurch and McCarthy, 1990). We do know that half of the families headed by female school dropouts live in poverty (Polit and Kahn, 1987: 134). The boys who father these schoolgirls' children generally do not have similar negative consequences of pregnancy on their life chances.

Clearly one of the contributors to high rates of premarital pregnancy and premature motherhood is the failure of most schools to fill the vacuum in

Having a baby when you're a teenager can do more than just take away your freedom, it can take away your dreams.

THE CHILDREN'S DEFENSE FUND

Teenagers often fail to appreciate the enormous and irreversible impact that the responsibility of parenting (especially single parenting) will have on their lives. Many people feel the media can be helpful in encouraging teens—both girls and boys—to use birth control when they become sexually active. Posters and ads like this one are becoming increasingly common in the face of high rates of teen pregnancy.

students' sex education. Their own sense of sexuality is of central interest to young people, and poses many important issues for them, yet schools suppress discourse and thus knowledge about it (Fine, 1992). Parental ambivalence and opposition, often on religious grounds, have helped keep comprehensive sex education programs out of public education.

There is no evidence that such programs "cause" young people to become sexually active who are not already so; moreover, those who are sexually active are more likely to take precautions against pregnancy if they have been exposed to a comprehensive sex education program (Zelnick and Young, 1982). The failure of schools to deal with this important topic is far more harmful to girls than boys, since the former must deal with the issue of pregnancy and parenthood. Finally, inadequate sex education contributes to the spread of AIDS and other sexually transmitted diseases, which often go undetected by those affected because of poor dissemination of information on risk factors and symptoms as they occur in women.

Sexual Harassment in Schools

Schools contain many of the same dynamics in gender relations that exist in the larger society, including sex-biased peer interactions and sexual harassment (Wellesley, 1992: 73–74). Some recent court cases in which students have sought redress for sexual harassment—from both teachers and staff, as well as from other students—have made headlines. The harmful nature of student harassment of students has long been ignored, and the damage done to girls by sexual harassment has typically been made light of and been dismissed by (predominantly male) school administrators who feel that "boys will always be boys." Insofar as male students are permitted to get away with such behavior, "the clear message to both girls and boys is that girls are not worthy of respect" (Wellesley, 1992: 73). This message has been communicated to girls through other aspects of their school experience as well.

Gaining accurate knowledge of the extent of sexual harassment is difficult: it is a sensitive subject, difficult to define, and subject to varying interpretations. The first survey undertaken of the harassment experiences of students in grades 8 to 11 found that sexual harassment in schools is widespread (Barringer, 1993; Frahm and Barger, 1993). In this survey, sexual harassment was defined to students as "unwanted and unwelcome sexual behavior which interferes with your life."

Four out of five of the students polled, including boys, said they had experienced some form of harassment; the most common forms (in rank order) were being subjected to sexual comments, jokes, gestures, or looks; being touched, grabbed, or pinched in a sexual way; being intentionally brushed up against sexually; and being shown, given, or left sexual pictures, photographs, illustrations, messages, or notes. Most of the harassment occurred in school classrooms and hallways. One in four of those victimized never told anyone. While most harassers were other students, one-fifth of the victims reported being harassed by teachers, custodians, coaches, or other members of the school staff.

The survey found that boys were more likely to be harassers and girls were more likely to be victims. Two-thirds of the boys surveyed, compared with 52 percent of the girls, said they had harassed other students. Conversely, 65 percent of the girls, compared with 42 percent of the boys, said they had been touched, grabbed, or pinched in a sexual way. Moreover, the effects on girls were found to be greater: 70 percent of girls but only 24 percent of boys said they were "very upset" or "somewhat upset" when the harassment happened. Female students were far more likely to say the harassment led to their not wanting to go to school, not wanting to talk in class, finding it hard to pay attention, making a lower grade on a test or in a class, finding it hard to study, and thinking about changing schools (Barringer, 1993).

The sex-biased interactions among peers also include harassment of male and female students perceived to be homosexual. In the survey mentioned above, almost 25 percent of the boys and 10 percent of the girls said they had been called a homosexual; this was the form of harassment boys found most upsetting. In a news account accompanying details of the survey, a student described a nightmare of chronic harassment by his peers:

> "If I had the option, I wouldn't have gone to school after the second day of sixth grade," said a 16-year-old Connecticut boy who endured years of taunts from classmates who called him gay.
>
> The boy, who said he is not gay, received mocking invitations from other boys to have sex. He was tickled, pinched, tripped, beaten and called a "fag," he said.
>
> Once, he said, "a guy screamed out across the street, 'Oh. By the way, I will be attending the orgy tomorrow night'" (Frahm and Barger, 1993: A6).

Boys called homosexuals may be told that they are "acting like a girl." When boys condemn other boys as "fags" or "queers," their homophobic comments typically include reference to alleged female traits, to which nothing but negative attributions are made. The message once again is that there is little about being female that is worthy of respect. Homophobia directed at girls seems almost contradictory, as it typically contains accusations of excessive masculinity (the stereotypical derogation of lesbian women as "bull dykes"). Such harassment makes it clear that females have no business appropriating "male traits." The underlying, unspoken premise can be phrased as a question: If even lowly females can be like us, what does it mean to be male? School personnel who permit such harassment, whether through lack of vigilance or as an outcome of their own homophobia, lend support to a system of inequality in which the status of being female is further denigrated.

Thus, our institution of education rather systematically shortchanges female students by linking the quality of their educational experiences to the societal system of sex inequality. Women's biographies are subtly shaped by the structure of their school experiences. In many subtle and some not-so-subtle ways, girls are told that they are second-class citizens best suited for the sex-typed roles awaiting them in a male-dominated society. Rather than liberating women from patriarchy, education tends to cave in to patriarchy's influences.

LEGAL CHALLENGES TO UNEQUAL EDUCATIONAL OPPORTUNITY

Our portrait of education has emphasized the role it plays in reinforcing and perpetuating the status quo—in this case, existing systems of class, race, and sex inequality. In this sense we can say that education plays a "conservative" function in society (Henry, 1963), as it helps conserve what already exists. Put another way, education contributes to the **social reproduction** of systems of inequality, facilitating their continuance over time (Bourdieu and Passeron, 1991). These systems are strengthened to the degree to which members of society accept class-biased, racist, or sexist treatment in educational institutions.

As other chapters have noted, however, these systems of inequality breed tensions that often result in challenge to the system. One of the most important vehicles of challenge is a court of law. Social science research can play an important role in documenting the harm being done by different systems of inequality and the processes through which this harm occurs. Such data have at times been of great assistance to people trying to inform and persuade the courts of injustices to be corrected, although courts do not always heed the information (see Chesler, Sanders, and Kalmus, 1988).

One would think that systems of tracking—insofar as they provide students from different class backgrounds with markedly different educational treatments—would be unconstitutional and subject to challenge in the courts. Yet, despite the accumulating evidence of harm being done, the illegality still remains very unclear (Oakes, 1985: 172–190; "Tracking and Civil Rights," 1990). Courts have called for change only in those cases where racial segregation was obviously part of the reason for instituting a tracking system and children were denied equal rights to education on the basis of their race. The courts have been reluctant to act in cases where tracking functions to deny children equal rights on the basis of their class background. This reluctance on the part of the courts stems partly from a tradition of not getting involved in the everyday administration of local school systems. Judges may also be genuinely puzzled over how to change educational practices that are so firmly tied into a societywide system of class inequality. Hence, tracking within schools will continue until some new bases or vantage points are devised from which to challenge it.

Likewise, de facto segregation of central-city schools has been relatively impervious to challenge. Recent Supreme Court actions have made such challenges extremely difficult. People who seek change through the federal courts must be able to demonstrate that the segregation occurred deliberately; that is, they must show that the school system intended to create racially homogeneous schools (Marcus, 1992). Those looking for ways to break down de facto segregation are carefully watching a 1993 state-level court case in Connecticut. The schools in the city of Hartford serve largely African American and Latino students from poor and working-class families, while school systems in the surrounding suburbs are nearly all-white and middle-class. Complainants are arguing that their rights to equal educational opportunities, guaranteed by the Connecticut state constitution, are being denied. They claim that not only de facto racial segregation but economic segregation as well is having damaging effects on the educational opportunities open to Hartford children. If this challenge at the state level succeeds, a court order will require school officials to take steps to end the de facto segregation of the schools in Hartford and those in its suburbs. Similar patterns elsewhere in the state will also have to change. A successful outcome in Connecticut's courts will no doubt be followed by similar court suits in many other states.

The situation regarding sex discrimination in education is a little more promising. While education is highly segregated along the lines of race and class, males and females are at least educated side by side for the most part. Nonetheless, the many problems identified in this chapter remain. These problems continue to be attacked today because sex discrimination remains a major public issue. Women are not allowing this issue to fade away, and efforts to combat sex discrimination through the courts, legislation, and the media continue unabated.

Some results can be seen. For example, in some schools the traditional lopsided allocation of resources to male sports teams has been reversed and policies prohibiting sexual harassment have been put into place. Of particular importance in this regard has been Title IX of the 1972 Education Amendments. However, it is clear that much work remains if the existing vestiges of unequal treatment of the sexes are to be eliminated.

CONCLUSION

In Chapter 5, "Socialization," we saw that one important function served by education was to prepare children and youths to participate in their society and culture. The socialization function of education is what usually comes to mind in answer to the question, "What do schools do?" Equally important, though most people remain quite unaware of it, is the cozy relationship between education and social inequalities that we have focused upon in this chapter.

Most of us are imbued with the idea that in the United States there is equal educational opportunity and anyone who really tries can succeed. Educational achievement is one of the routes to success in the common wisdom. Many young people are not achieving success in school, however, as various critical studies have made clear over the last decade or so. But few observers link this failure to achieve, and its impact upon the biographies of tens of millions of young people, to class bias, racism, and sexism within education.

In this chapter we have stressed that a person's educational opportunities, and hence experiences with education, will depend upon his or her class background, skin color, and sex. The systems of inequality that pervade U.S. society at large are reflected in and supported by current educational practices. Mediocrity in students' performance is in large part due to school experiences in which many students' ability and potential go at best ignored and at worst demeaned. Years of such treatment during childhood and adolescence can leave irreversible damage that helps shape one's biography in negative directions.

Some have argued that the situation can be changed. Education could be rendered free of class bias, racism, and sexism if everyone involved in schools would only work together toward that goal. Others disagree, arguing that education will never be free of these forms of injustice until the larger society is purged of them. This position holds that education is not freestanding but is an open institution subject to the influences of the society of which it is a part. The actions to be taken will depend upon where one stands in this debate, a debate to which sociology and other social sciences will surely make additional contributions.

THINKING CRITICALLY

1. Compared with that of Kip and Josey, how would you characterize the cultural capital to which you have access? What can this cultural capital do for you? What is the relationship between your cultural capital and the likelihood that you will someday occupy a position at the very top of the class structure?

2. Discuss what is meant by "credential inflation." Are there occupations or professions that you think require far more in the way of educational credentials than is really necessary? Identify them, and discuss the reasons for this situation. What are the ramifications?

3. Despite legislation and court decisions, public schools today are highly segregated along racial lines. Discuss the arguments for racial and ethnic diversity in public education. Why don't these arguments outweigh the resistance to taking whatever steps are necessary to end segregation?

4. Have you ever been subjected to sexual harassment in a school setting? What were the circumstances? What was its impact on you? What did you do about it? Why? Do you think that more attention should be paid to combating sexual harassment in schools? If not, why not? If so, what steps do you think should be taken?

5. In a boxed excerpt, you read about 12-year-old Crystal Rossi, who is having difficulty with school and is showing all the signs of becoming a dropout. If she does drop out, how do you think her life will differ from yours once she reaches the average college-going age? How similar is your life to that of 19-year-old Derrick White, whose problems affording higher education are also described in a boxed excerpt? What are some of the similarities or differences? Why do they exist?

KEY TERMS

meritocracy, *393*

cultural capital, *393*

gatekeepers, *399*

tracking, *399*

self-fulfilling prophecy, *403*

desegregation, *407*

de jure segregation, *407*

de facto segregation, *408*

cultural synchronization, *413*

immigrant minorities, *413*

involuntary minorities, *413*

learned helplessness, *416*

social reproduction, *423*

SUGGESTED READINGS

Margaret A. Gibson and John U. Ogbu, *Minority Status and Schooling: A Comparative Study of Immigrant and Involuntary Minorities.* New York: Garland, 1991. A series of case studies of the schooling experiences of different minority groups, in both the United States and other nations, and an analysis of the reasons these experiences vary.

Jonathan Kozol, *Savage Inequalities.* New York: Crown, 1992. A moving description of the scandalous conditions characterizing poorly financed and ill-equipped public schools in many cities across the country, conditions that deprive children of the opportunity for a quality education.

Annette Lareau, *Home Advantage: Social Class and Parental Intervention in Elementary School.* Philadelphia: Falmer Press, 1989. A study of the different resources and approaches upper-middle-class parents are able to bring to bear on their children's early education and of the social and economic conditions that impede working-class parents from doing likewise.

Jeannie Oakes, *Keeping Track: How Schools Structure Inequality.* New Haven, CT: Yale University Press, 1985. A study of tracking practices in public schools and the ways in which they create unequal educational opportunities for students, often along the lines of race and class.

Myra Sadker and David Sadker, *Failing at Fairness: How America's Schools Cheat Girls.* New York: Scribner, 1994. An exploration of the nature and consequence of gender bias in schools and classrooms, which, although often subtle, imposes substantial costs on female students.

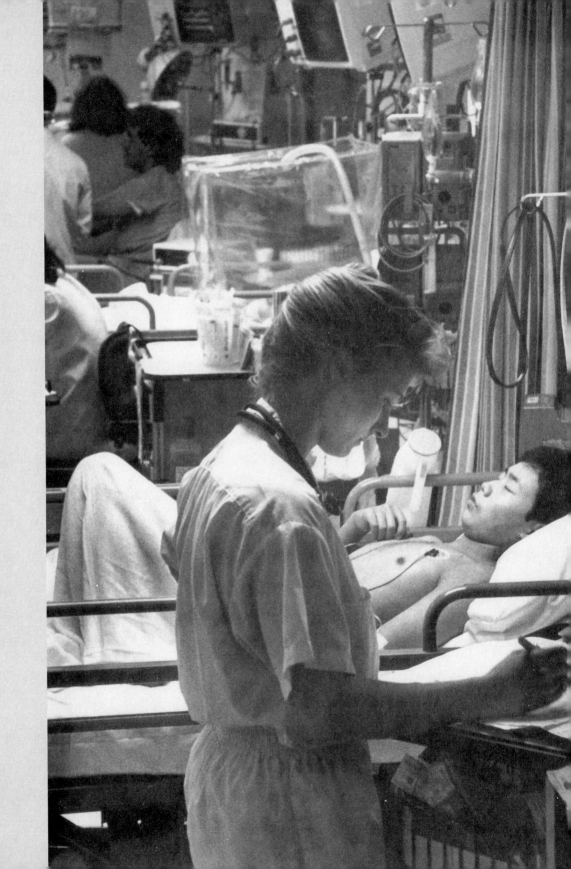

HEALTH

Imagine yourself afflicted with a progressively debilitating disease for which there is no known cure. The disease, which affects the central nervous system, can cause blindness, incontinence, paralysis, muscle spasms, dizziness, numbness, and slurred speech. Each time symptoms flare up, they may

13

become more severe. Now imagine that a new drug has come onto the market that may actually slow the course of the disease. Wouldn't you be anxious to begin using it immediately? But what if the drug was so expensive that you could not afford to buy it? What if your health insurance did not cover it? What if other people with the same disease, who are not nearly as ill as you, are able to gain immediate access to the drug while you cannot? If such a situation were to arise, you would probably conclude that you are part of a health-care system that falls far short of meeting your needs.

The situation described above is real; it reflects some of the difficulties many people in the United States are facing in obtaining the latest drug treatment for multiple sclerosis (Lewis, 1994; Stolberg, 1994). Some 350,000 people have multiple sclerosis (MS), which most often strikes young people, particularly females, between the ages of 20 and 40. A new genetically engineered drug, Betaseron, is the first medicine thought to slow the course of MS. But in order to recoup research and development expenditures and financially reward its investors, the drug's manufacturer is charging about $10,000 for a year's supply. Many MS patients and their families cannot afford the out-of-pocket cost, and health insurance cannot always help them. Costs of the drug are not covered by some private health insurers or by the major federal health-care program, Medicare, which serves persons who are elderly or disabled.

Despite its high cost, the demand for Betaseron quickly exceeded the initial supplies. Consequently, its manufacturer held a lottery to determine who would receive the drug and when. Persons suffering the most advanced stages of MS were excluded from eligibility, as they had not been part of the trials in which effects of the drug were established. Some 67,000 people with lesser, but varying, degrees of illness from MS entered the lottery. Those most fortunate in the lottery began receiving the drug, while the least fortunate entrants were told they would have to wait eighteen months or more, a period during which their health could well undergo further irreversible decline. Almost 4,000 other people with MS—some of whom were not eligible for the lottery—by luck or social connections managed to become part of research projects that prestigious medical institutions are conducting on Betaseron, and thus they bypassed any wait (Lewis, 1994).

Four out of five MS patients lack access to Betaseron because of insufficient supplies of the drug, its unaffordability, problems with health insurance, lack of social connections, or fate. This situation is a small, but symbolic, expression of the problems many people face when they confront the health-care delivery system in the United States. As we shall see, health issues are directly linked to social, economic, and political features of a society. If access to quality health care is not available or is inequitably distributed, the health status of many members of society will be adversely affected.

In this chapter we address several questions: How can we assess the health status of a society's members? What is the health status of people in the United States, one of the wealthiest nations in the world-system? What role do class, race, and gender play in our health status? What kinds of problems fuel the widespread public concern over the adequacy of our system of health care? What alternatives could improve this system? While these are difficult questions, we must pursue them if we want to enhance our own and others' life chances.

ASSESSING HEALTH STATUS

What do we mean by "health"? From one point of view, health can be defined simply as the absence of illness or disease. This view may be called the **medical model** of health, and it is the model that has come to prevail in Western nations, including the United States.

The medical model is the principal point of reference for the U.S. health-care system. This system includes practicing physicians and other medical professionals; the settings in which they practice (clinics, hospitals); the universities, research centers, and manufacturing corporations that create new drugs and medical technologies; and the organizations that regulate health care and help consumers purchase it (government agencies, insurance firms). Guided by the medical model, the health-care system focuses on responding to the problems of individuals who present themselves to it. The system is largely skewed toward *curative,* rather than preventive, activities.

Critics have suggested that the medical model provides a very narrow, and in many ways inadequate, definition of health (see Sidel and Sidel, 1983). A broader and more adequate conception would define health as the condition that exists when people are free to use their mental and physical capacities to the fullest extent possible. Anything hindering this freedom would be viewed as contributing to poor health. A health-care system built around such a definition would obviously need to respond to medically treatable problems. But in defining health much more broadly, such a system would be largely directed toward *preventive* and *protective* activities.

For example, a preventive health-care system might place high priority on making sure that everyone in a society had access to:

1. Adequate food, water, clothing, shelter, and hygiene
2. Jobs with wages that permit a decent standard of living, and the education and training necessary to perform them well
3. A guaranteed minimum income above the poverty line for those who cannot work
4. Safe, flexible, low-stress workplace conditions
5. Affordable, high-quality child care and elder care for households that need it
6. Adequate vacation and leisure time to engage in individual and group recreation
7. A natural environment cleansed of and protected against toxic and other harmful polluting substances
8. A social environment unmarred by the threat or reality of warfare, criminal assault, and other forms of violence

Such a preventive health-care system would be primarily **proactive,** aimed at enhancing people's collective well-being, rather than primarily **reactive,** aimed at responding to individual cases, as is the medical model. Few societies have made far-reaching moves to organize their health-care systems around a preventive model. (Sweden has perhaps gone the furthest in this direction. See Elling, 1986; Rosenthal and Frenkel, 1992.)

Because of the prevalence of the medical model, the most commonly used indexes of health status relate to illness and death, rather than to how well people are exercising their potential. Among these measures is **life expectancy.** This is the average number of years a group of people all born in the same year are expected to live. This statistic can vary greatly from society to society. In 1992 life expectancy in Italy was 74 for men and 81 for women, but in Sierra Leone it was only 43 for men and 48 for women (U.S. Central Intelligence Agency, 1993: 167, 306).

Another commonly used measure of health status is the rate of **infant mortality.** This refers to infant death in the first year of life and is expressed in terms of the number of infant deaths per 1,000 live births. Again there is wide variation worldwide. In 1992 the infant mortality rate was 115 per 1,000 live births in Somalia but only 7 per 1,000 in Canada (U.S. Central Intelligence Agency, 1993: 62, 312).

Finally there is the rate of **maternal mortality.** This refers to the death of a mother as a consequence of pregnancy and birthing; the rate is expressed as the number of mothers who die per 100,000 infants born. The variation is once more quite extreme. In 1988 the rate was 123 maternal deaths per 100,000 infants born in Ecuador but less than 6 per 100,000 in Austria (United Nations, 1992: 355).

Obviously, these measures only very crudely assess the health status of any given society's members. The statistics do not tell us anything about the different rates of life expectancy, infant mortality, or maternal mortality in different sectors of a society. Nor do they provide insights into why there is such variation. Social scientists find interpretation of such statistics a complex task. Not only must they account for differences in nations' fundamental characteristics, such as culture, economics, and geography, but they must also acknowledge that data gathering, record keeping, and reporting are not conducted with equal efficiency in all nations. The value of health-status statistics is therefore somewhat limited, and they have to be used with caution. With this in mind, how is the United States doing with regard to the health status of its population?

HEALTH STATUS OF PEOPLE IN THE UNITED STATES

Compared with most of the world's nations, the United States measures up well on the health-status indicators we have been discussing. Indeed, the U.S. population has undergone a marked improvement in its health status since the early part of this century. Persons who were born in 1900, for example, could expect to live only about 47 years. Today, as the twentieth century draws to a close, life expectancy is 75.

But the vast life expectancy gains in the United States since 1900 have occurred only in part because of advances in the field of medicine. Improvements in the population's diet, personal hygiene practices, and housing conditions have played a role. Perhaps most important have been improvements in public health and sanitation policies. Medical advances

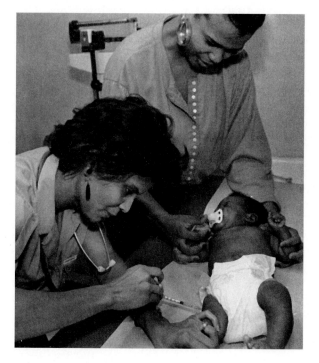

Today, most people in the United States have access to at least basic health services, such as immunization against or treatment of common diseases. This baby is being immunized against diphtheria, whooping cough, and tetanus—health problems that, in the absence of vaccines, were once widespread.

have, in fact, played a relatively minor role in increasing life expectancy (McKinlay and McKinlay, 1990).

The most important medical development was the ability to immunize against or treat common infectious diseases that frequently resulted in death. Such diseases—from tuberculosis to influenza—cause far fewer deaths in the United States today (though they remain important factors in mortality rates for the nation's poor). Spared from life-threatening infectious diseases, and living on average much longer than in the past, older Americans today are most likely to succumb to cancer or heart disease. The prevalence of these illnesses as the cause of death reflects the "graying of America."

For life expectancy at birth to have dramatically gone up, the infant mortality rate had to come down. Again, the statistics for 1900 and today provide a sharp contrast. At the beginning of the twentieth century 143 infants died for every 1,000 born live. By the 1990s the infant mortality rate had dropped to about 9 per 1,000. Likewise, the maternal mortality rate has dramatically dropped. In 1915 some 610 mothers died for every 100,000 infants born live. Today the number is down to 8.

Both infant and maternal mortality rates have been reduced in part by the same kinds of improvements in nutrition, sanitation, and so on, that have increased life expectancy. Moreover, advances in prenatal, neonatal, and obstetric medical practices have aided infants and mothers. Advances in obstetrics, coupled with changes in abortion laws, have also made it easier for women to detect problems and end pregnancies that could have been life-threatening. The maternal mortality rate in the United States dropped precipitously after the Supreme Court's 1973 *Roe v. Wade* ruling legalizing abortions. It went from 21.5 maternal deaths per 100,000 live births in 1970 to 9.4 per 100,000 in 1980 and has remained low since (U.S. Department of Health and Human Services, 1992: 172). Recent Supreme Court actions permit states to impose certain restrictions that would make it more difficult to obtain abortions. This could lead to a rise in the maternal mortality rate.

Despite the promising trends since the early part of this century, the health status of people in the United States remains for many a cause of concern. Good health is not equally distributed within the population, any more than is wealth and income. We shall take this issue up in the next sections, examining why class, race, and gender are of importance to an assessment of health status. But it is also of note that this country, which spends more money on health care than any other nation in the world, compares unfavorably with many less affluent nations on the common measures of health status.

For example, let's look at the fifteen richest nations in terms of gross national product per capita in 1989. As Table 13.1 shows, seven nations had longer life expectancies than the United States, twelve had lower rates of infant mortality, and six had lower maternal mortality rates. Among the nations that were doing better than the United States on two or more of these health-status measures were Japan, Switzerland, the Netherlands, and Finland (World Bank, 1991: 205, 259, 267). Data for the mid-1980s, examining infant mortality rates only, revealed that countries as widely

Table 13.1

KEY HEALTH-STATUS DIFFERENCES BETWEEN THE POOREST AND RICHEST NATIONS

	GNP PER CAPITA, 1989 (dollars)	LIFE EXPECTANCY AT BIRTH, 1989 (years)	INFANT MORTALITY, 1989 (per 1,000 live births)	MATERNAL MORTALITY, 1988 (per 100,000 live births)
FIFTEEN POOREST NATIONS				
Mozambique	80	49	137	800
Ethiopia	120	48	133	900
Tanzania	130	49	112	600
Somalia	170	48	128	900
Bangladesh	180	51	106	650
Lao PDR	180	49	105	750
Malawi	180	48	147	500
Nepal	180	52	124	850
Chad	190	47	127	800
Burundi	220	49	70	800
Sierra Leone	220	42	149	1,000
Madagascar	230	51	117	600
Nigeria	250	51	100	750
Uganda	250	49	99	700
Zaire	260	53	94	700
FIFTEEN RICHEST NATIONS				
Netherlands	15,920	77	7	14
Kuwait	16,150	74	15	30
Belgium	16,220	76	9	4
Austria	17,300	76	8	11
France	17,820	77	7	13
United Arab Emirates	18,430	71	24	130
Canada	19,030	77	7	7
Germany	20,440	75	8	8
Denmark	20,450	75	8	4
United States	20,910	76	10	13
Sweden	21,570	77	6	7
Finland	22,120	75	6	15
Norway	22,290	77	8	16
Japan	23,810	79	4	6
Switzerland	29,880	78	7	6

Source: World Bank, *World Development Report, 1991* (New York: Oxford University Press, 1991), and United Nations Development Programme, *Human Development Report, 1994* (New York: Oxford University Press, 1994).

divergent as Iceland, Hong Kong, Australia, and Luxembourg had rates of infant deaths lower than the United States (U.S. Department of Health and Human Services, 1989: 59).

Many factors account for such differences between the United States and other nations, but two stand out. First, as we have seen, the class structure in the United States is characterized by a distribution of wealth and income that leaves many individuals and families ill-equipped to afford basic necessities. While all Western capitalist nations are characterized by class differences, the United States has a higher degree of income inequality than many members of this group, including France, Britain, Canada, Sweden, the Netherlands, and Japan (Kerbo, 1991: 35–38). Second, unlike other Western industrialized nations, the United States does not provide a national system of health care for its citizens. The importance of the combination of these two factors for the health status of the U.S. population will become clear in the next sections.

CLASS AND HEALTH STATUS

Unlike most other industrialized nations, the United States does not routinely collect and disseminate data on mortality rates (death rates) and other health-status indicators by class (although it does do so by race, sex, and age). This, as critics have pointed out, makes it difficult to develop accurate answers to such questions as, "Do corporate executives, on average, live longer than the blue-collar workers they employ? If so, how much longer?" (Navarro, 1991a). Given the fact that the distribution of wealth and income has been growing more unequal in the United States in recent years, the nature of the correlation between class membership and health status should be of great public policy concern (Navarro, 1990, 1991b).

Class Differences

The limited data that the federal government does compile on class and health are revealing. For example, data on people's self-assessments of their own health status (see Table 13.2) indicate considerable differences among income categories. In interviews of a sample of the population, about 80 percent of individuals in affluent households ($50,000 and over in family income) reported that they were in excellent or very good health in 1990. In contrast, among those in the lowest-income households (under $14,000) only about 52 percent had such a positive self-assessment. Strikingly, only 4 percent of the best-off households reported fair or poor health, in comparison to more than 18 percent of the worst-off (U.S. Department of Health and Human Services, 1992: 202).

The correlation between class and health status suggested by such self-assessments receives further support from federal inquiries into the degree to which people feel their daily activities are restricted by illness, injury, or impairment. Persons in middle-class to affluent households report the least restrictions, while those in the lowest-income households report the most. The latter, for example, say they experience the most days lost from school or work. They also report the highest number of days in which household members were so unable to function that they had to remain in bed (National Center for Health Statistics, 1989: 113).

Finally, there are class differences in the frequency of contact with physicians and in the length of time spent in short-stay hospitals. In 1990,

Table 13.2

SELF-ASSESSMENT OF HEALTH, 1990*

CHARACTERISTIC	PERCENTAGE CHARACTERIZING THEIR HEALTH AS:			
	EXCELLENT	VERY GOOD	GOOD	FAIR OR POOR
Total	40.5	28.5	22.0	8.9
Age:				
Under 15 years	52.8	28.1	16.6	2.4
Under 5 years	53.2	28.1	15.8	2.9
5–14 years	52.6	28.1	17.1	2.2
15–44 years	43.1	30.9	20.6	5.4
45–64 years	29.2	27.1	27.7	16.0
65 years and over	17.1	22.9	32.3	27.7
65–74 years	18.9	23.5	32.6	25.1
75 years and over	14.5	21.9	31.9	31.7
Sex:				
Male	42.5	28.3	20.8	8.4
Female	38.7	28.8	23.2	9.3
Race:				
White	42.1	29.0	20.8	8.1
Black	31.1	25.3	28.5	15.1
Family income:				
Less than $14,000	28.1	24.3	28.9	18.6
$14,000–$24,999	34.6	29.6	25.0	10.8
$25,000–$34,999	40.6	30.2	21.7	7.5
$35,000–$49,999	45.9	29.7	19.1	5.3
$50,000 or more	52.1	28.0	16.0	4.0
Geographic region:				
Northeast	43.1	28.1	21.6	7.2
Midwest	41.7	29.3	21.1	7.9
South	37.3	27.8	23.8	11.2
West	42.2	29.1	20.6	8.1
Location of residence:				
Within metropolitan statistical area	41.6	28.5	21.5	8.5
Outside metropolitan statistical area	36.7	28.7	24.1	10.4

*Data are based on household interviews of a sample of the civilian noninstitutionalized populations.
Source: U.S. Department of Health and Human Services, *Health, United States, 1991* (Washington, DC: U.S. Government Printing Office, 1992), p. 202.

13 percent of families with incomes of less than $14,000 had no contact with a physician in the previous two years or more, compared with 9.4 percent of families with incomes over $50,000 (U.S. Department of Health and Human Services, 1992: 220). Yet illnesses in low-income families lead members to spend more time in hospitals. In 1990, families with incomes under $14,000 required 1,141 days of care per 1,000 population, while those with incomes over $50,000 required only 446 days of care per 1,000 population (U.S. Department of Health and Human Services, 1992: 224).

One of the few federal investigations of mortality rates by class was undertaken in 1986 and focused on heart and cerebrovascular diseases. The mortality rate for heart disease in 1986 was more than twice as high for persons employed in blue-collar jobs (as operators, fabricators, and laborers) as it was for those working in white-collar positions (as managers and professionals). The findings for class and cerebrovascular disease pointed in the same direction (Navarro, 1990: 1238–1239).

Social scientists have pieced together data from a variety of sources that support the correlation between class position and health status in the United States (Syme and Berkman, 1976; Dutton, 1986). This correlation is often based on inferences drawn from data on black and white racial differences, since African Americans are disproportionately found in poverty and low-income circumstances. Obviously, such inferences allow for rough conclusions at best, given that the data also include millions of poverty-stricken whites and middle-class African Americans. But there is little doubt that infant mortality rates are highest among the poor, as are death rates for children in general. This contributes to lowered levels of life expectancy at the bottom of our class structure.

We have noted the benefit to life expectancy of controlling infectious diseases. In comparison to the situation in 1900, a relatively small percentage of the population today dies from pneumonia, influenza, tuberculosis, or diphtheria. But persons who do die of these diseases are most likely to be poor. The incidence of tuberculosis (TB), for example, has been on the increase in recent years, rising from 22,000 cases in 1985 to over 50,000 new cases per year today. These increases tend to be concentrated in large cities with populations of 500,000 and over (Navarro, 1992: L58). Yet not all individuals in these large cities are equally vulnerable to TB. The TB rate in New York City's low-income central Harlem area, for example, is 220 cases per 100,000 people, 35 times as high as the rate in more affluent neighborhoods in the city (Cockburn, 1992: 17).

Reasons for Class Differences

Why are the poor more likely than the affluent to suffer serious health problems? Some might think that poor people simply fail to take care of themselves. But the fact is that the poor confront a daily environment containing many more health threats than the environment of the more affluent contains. Features of their workplaces, community settings, neighborhoods, and living quarters put people who are economically disadvantaged at particular risk for health problems.

Many people who live in poverty, and even more of those who live just above the official federal poverty line, hold jobs. These jobs typically involve physically taxing, stressful, and hazardous labor. Workers in manufacturing, wholesale and retail trade, services industries, construction, and transportation have the highest occupational injury rates. In addition, many workers (particularly in manufacturing) are routinely exposed to toxic fumes and substances that can cause acute and chronic illnesses and diseases. Private employers reported 6.4 million occupational injuries and over 330,000 occupational illnesses to the U.S. Bureau of Labor Statistics in 1990. Nearly half of the injuries resulted in lost workdays, assignment of lighter duties, or other restrictions in work activity. Some 3,000 of the injuries resulted in death (Personick and Jackson, 1992: 37).

Poor and working-class people often lack the power to improve health and safety conditions in the workplace, although unions and community groups have struggled successfully to bring an end to some of the most blatant abuses. Still, much remains to be done. A tragic and highly publicized reminder of this involves the chicken processing workers in North Carolina. Their work is low-paying, grueling, and injurious; chicken processing workers are, in fact, three times more likely to be injured on the job than other workers in the state. Common injuries include carpal-tunnel syndrome, an extremely painful condition affecting the nerves of the wrists, which stems from repetitive work on the processing line (Diebel, 1993). In 1991, 25 people died and 56 were injured in a fire at Imperial Food Products in Hamlet, North Carolina. As described in one press account,

> With the fire raging, many workers died attempting to flee through emergency exits, which were chained shut—supposedly because workers were stealing chickens. The dead left bloody footprints where they'd tried to beat down the fire doors in desperation (Diebel, 1993).

Despite such horror stories and the workers' struggles to put an end to them, health and safety standards and provision for their enforcement continue to remain a problem in North Carolina as well as in many other states (Diebel, 1993).

The features of their community settings, neighborhoods, and living quarters also can contribute to health problems among poor people. Older buildings, in which the poor are likely to live, may have health dangers associated with asbestos and lead paint, insects and rodents, and deficient heating and electric systems. Skyrocketing housing costs have forced low-income city dwellers to double or even triple up in apartments and houses. This overcrowding magnifies stress and facilitates the spread of infectious diseases. Many of those who are homeless are particularly vulnerable to illness, accidents, and violent episodes because of their constant exposure to life on city streets and to communicable diseases in shelters.

There may not always be enough to eat in poverty-stricken households; an estimated 20 million people in the United States do not get enough food to eat each day. Such persons are "chronically short of the nutrients necessary for growth and good health" (Brown, 1987: 37). Malnutrition lowers a person's ability to resist illness and regain health. It has been associated with anemia, tuberculosis, and osteoporosis. Pregnant women who do not eat adequately are likely to give birth to low-weight babies, who often suffer mental retardation and other disabilities. Low birth weight has also been directly linked to a higher likelihood of infant mortality. Malnutrition also frequently undermines the health of the elderly.

Some members of the poverty population suffer from living amid conditions of violence. For example, the conditions of poverty help contribute to the high rate of homicide in the United States. In low-income sections of

Hazardous housing occupied by people who are poor often poses risks to their health and safety. Children may unthinkingly ingest lead-based paint chips or come into contact with asbestos in older housing that landlords have neglected and allowed to fall into disrepair. The damage to these children's health by exposure to such toxic substances can be severe and permanent.

many cities, some residents—children as well as adults—resort to deadly weapons to protect themselves and to handle conflicts with others. Most killings are impulsive; they are individual acts involving a single victim, usually a family member, friend, or acquaintance. Yet some homicide is organized. Youth street gangs periodically engage in armed warfare with one another, and local drug dealers may commit murder to safeguard their activities and control the competition. More and more homicide victims are innocent bystanders to gang members' "drive-by killings" and to drug deals that have "gone bad." Government policy makers have come to view the high rate of death by homicide in U.S. cities as a major public health issue.

Drug abuse is widespread throughout the U.S. population, but the use of crack cocaine, heroin, and other addictive drugs is endemic in some poverty-stricken urban communities. The sale of such drugs often goes on openly, making some poor city neighborhoods resemble "drug bazaars." City hospital emergency rooms routinely treat drug users who become ill. Many users accidentally die from drug overdoses. Others contract diseases from sharing needles and syringes; rates of acquired immune deficiency syndrome (AIDS) are high for intravenous drug users, affecting African Americans most severely. The human immunodeficiency virus (HIV) responsible for AIDS is often passed by male users to female sexual partners, who, if they become pregnant, may transmit the HIV virus to their fetuses. Hospitals serving poor communities treat not only the newborns who are HIV-positive and may develop AIDS but also the "crack babies" born to women who are addicted to crack cocaine. The latter infants' exposure to cocaine prior to birth often permanently impairs their health and ability to thrive.

Finally, as will be discussed later in this chapter, the U.S. health-care system has failed to provide adequate services to tens of millions of poor and working-class people who have been without adequate health insurance coverage. Such people often find that the care they need is inaccessible and unaffordable. Consequently, they are more likely to be without the care they need altogether or to go without it for a longer period than do those who are more affluent.

Taken together, self-reports on people's health, inferences that can be drawn from official statistics on the distribution of illness and disease, and people's differential exposure to unhealthful work and living environments indicate that class position helps shape people's health status in the United States. Middle- to upper-class people are less likely than poor and working-class people to be exposed to a high volume of health risks and are better able to afford and gain access to health care. They are thus more likely to be healthy. However, we know that the class structure is not homogeneous by race. Given that U.S. society has not only a system of class inequality but also a system of race inequality, it is important to ask about the health status of people of color. Is the health status of people of color any different from that of the dominant white population?

RACE AND HEALTH STATUS

By most health-status indicators, people of color are, in general, worse off than whites in the United States (Jones and Rice, 1987; Willis, 1989). But it is important to draw attention to the fact that differences in health status along the lines of race are often *also* differences influenced by class. One cannot make sense of black and white differences in health status, for example, without understanding how these two populations are distributed in the class structure. Because African American households have average incomes and wealth holdings below those of whites, they are overrepresented in the lower reaches of the class structure. We have seen that the economically disadvantaged—whatever their racial heritage—are more likely than the affluent to have health problems. As we noted, one reason for this is that the unemployed or underemployed are less likely to have health insurance that will help them afford care when it is needed.

Yet there are two other health issues pertaining to people of color that are more difficult to tackle and have been the subject of relatively little research. First, do the daily experiences of being a person of color in a society in which race inequality is so prevalent have a negative impact on one's health? Second, are people of color offered inadequate health-care services *because* of their race? Let us briefly examine some illustrative data concerning race and health status.

The most comprehensive data compare whites with African Americans. (Government agencies have failed to collect systematic data on other peoples of color.) A good starting point is infant mortality rates. We have seen that overall infant mortality rates in the United States are high in comparison with those in many other nations. But within the United States racial differences are notable. The infant mortality rate for whites is about 8 infant deaths per 1,000 live births, while for African Americans it is close to 18 per 1,000 (U.S. Department of Health and Human Services, 1992: 141). In 1989, low weight at birth, a factor linked with infant mortality, occurred in 13.5 percent of all live births to African-American mothers but in only 5.7 percent of births to white mothers.

Life expectancy figures are likewise strikingly different by race. For example, in 1990 white women could expect to live to 79.3 years of age, while the life expectancy for African American women was 5.8 years less. For men, the difference is even more extreme: white men in 1990 could expect to live to 72.6 years; African American men could look forward to only 66 years of life, or 6.6 years less than whites. Today, life expectancy at birth for African Americans is about what it was for whites in 1950 (U.S. Department of Health and Human Services, 1992: 140). In recent years the life expectancy for young African American males has been on a *downward* trend, in part due to the high loss of life resulting from homicide or death in connection with drug abuse. Overall, in comparison with whites, African Americans have higher death rates from almost all causes in any given year (U.S. Bureau of the Census, 1992b: 85). (See Table 13.3.)

Comparable national-level data on other people of color in the United States are rare, but in the first comprehensive health survey ever undertaken among the nation's Latinos, the influence of class position on the health status of people of color was further confirmed (Thompson, 1991). The Hispanic Health and Nutrition Examination Survey compiled data on 11,000 Latinos between 1982 and 1984. Its findings indicate that Latinos' average life expectancy is not greatly different from that of whites. And while the two top causes of death for both populations are the same (heart disease and cancer), Latinos are slightly less likely to die from such causes. But they are more at risk of death from diabetes, liver disease and cirrhosis, tuberculosis, AIDS, perinatal conditions, accidents, and homicide.

Disproportionately clustered in the lower levels of the class structure, suffering much higher rates of unemployment and poverty than whites, and confronting language and cultural barriers, Latinos often find themselves without health-care services that could improve their quality of life (De La Rosa, 1989). According to the Hispanic Health and Nutrition Examination Survey, Latinos are less likely to have health insurance than any other group. Almost one-third of those surveyed lacked such insurance, compared with 10 percent of whites and 20 percent of African Americans.

Apart from the impact of class position on people of color, does racism have its own impact on health? How does one account, for example, for findings that indicate that even among the babies of African American college-educated parents, infant mortality rates are twice as high as the rates among babies of similarly educated white parents ("Racial Link," 1992:

Table 13.3

DEATH RATES, BY AGE, RACE/ETHNICITY, 1989

CHARACTERISTIC*	DEATHS PER 100,000 POPULATION	
	ACCIDENTS AND ADVERSE EFFECTS	HOMICIDE AND SUICIDE
1–14 years:		
All races	13.7	2.3
White	12.8	1.7
Black	18.9	5.4
Latino	13.0	2.3
15–24 years:		
All races	45.8	30.3
White	48.1	22.3
Black	34.9	75.2
Latino	51.3	43.4
25–44 years:		
All races	35.4	28.7
White	33.9	23.5
Black	47.7	68.0
Latino	42.5	37.8
	DISEASES OF HEART	CANCERS
45–64 years:		
All races	241.5	290.9
White	225.8	282.8
Black	409.2	399.0
Latino	158.0	160.6
65 years and over:		
All races	1,949.2	1,085.1
White	1,959.9	1,079.0
Black	2,080.6	1,269.8
Latino	1,336.0	727.3

*The race groups include persons of both Latino and non-Latino origin. Conversely, persons of Latino origin may be of any race.
Source: U.S. Department of Health and Human Services, *Health, United States, 1991* (Washington, DC: U.S. Government Printing Office, 1992), p. 155.

A12)? It would appear that something is happening to African Americans on the basis of their race more than their class.

A number of explanations are possible. Higher rates of infant mortality may be related to the accumulated and compounded social stresses many black women must endure as they function in our society. Or they may be related to the racial segregation of urban African Americans in predominantly black communities, where medical facilities providing quality prenatal, postnatal, and well-baby care are few and overburdened. Perhaps racial discrimination in employment opportunities for college-educated African Americans, something not experienced by whites, hampers their access to health insurance and their ability to afford the care needed. Or perhaps the higher rates of infant mortality have to do with the toxicity of the living environment in which many African Americans reside. As we will see in Chapter 16, evidence suggests that commercial hazardous waste facilities and other sources of pollution are disproportionately concentrated in or near black communities (Bullard, 1990; Bryant and Mohai, 1992). These are the kinds of questions that challenge social scientists as they attempt to sort out the relationship between racism and health.

A second issue is whether there is racism in the health-care delivery system. Are people of color less well served by this system than whites, simply on the basis of race? Again, the research on such questions is very limited, but what does exist is disturbing. For example, reports in the *Journal of the American Medical Association* suggest that African Americans are systematically deprived of certain high-technology medical procedures and are underrepresented in clinical trials of new drugs that could affect them differently than they affect whites (Scott, 1989; Svensson, 1989).

According to researchers, when elderly black persons are hospitalized for heart problems, they are about one-fourth as likely as whites to receive heart bypass surgery, even when the need for the surgery and the possession of health insurance to pay for it is the same for both groups. In the rural Southeast, researchers found that elderly black patients received one heart bypass for every seven given to whites ("Fewer Heart Bypasses," 1992). Even though controversy exists over whether all of the more than 200,000 heart bypass operations performed annually in the United States are necessary, such racial differences in surgery could well be affecting African American life expectancy.

Underrepresentation of African Americans in drug trials means that we may not know whether newly approved drugs have effects on blacks that they do not have on whites (Svensson, 1989). (Elderly persons and females are also underrepresented in drug trials.) For example, blacks and whites respond differently to drugs for hypertension, a cardiovascular disease to which African Americans are particularly prone. But most trials of new hypertension drugs do not ensure the inclusion of black subjects, nor do researchers report on results by race (Scott, 1989). Biased clinical trials undermine physicians' efforts to tailor therapies and dosages to individual patients. Prescriptions based on faulty trial data can prove ineffective or have dangerous side effects. One can only speculate on the role this situation may play in the health status of African Americans.

In sum, the disproportionate presence of people of color in the lower levels of the U.S. class structure has a negative impact on their health status. However, one's location in the system of racial inequality may affect one's health independently of class membership. The day-to-day treatment of people of color by the dominant white majority and its institutions, including the health-care system, appears to contribute to health-status differences along the lines of race, although a great deal more research is necessary. As we shall see, the system of sex inequality in the United States also plays an important role in influencing one's health status.

GENDER AND HEALTH STATUS

The U.S. health-care system has long been male-dominated—from physicians to researchers to executives and administrators. While still underrepresented, more and more women have begun to move into such central positions. At the same time, the women's movement has encouraged women to speak out against biases and shortcomings in how the health-care system treats them.

Women in general are in a weaker position in the labor market than men. They are thus more likely to be unemployed or employed part-time and less likely to occupy jobs that offer adequate employer-provided health insurance, even when they work full-time. This situation most adversely affects women who are living alone, as well as women who are the sole or principal wage earners for their families. Many of these women have experienced a broken marriage or the loss of their partners through death.

Because a high percentage of female-headed households occupy positions in the lower reaches of the class structure, they face serious problems in affording and gaining access to health care. As the number of women in poverty has increased in recent years, many female-headed households have become dependent on the government-sponsored health-care program known as Medicaid. The limitations and shortcomings of this program, discussed in the next section, leave those who are eligible for it chronically underserved (Muller, 1988).

Biases and shortcomings in the health-care system's treatment of women contribute to the problems women face in getting adequate care (Muller, 1990). Research bearing on women's health problems chronically lacks funding. For years women have been largely excluded as research subjects in studies sponsored by the federal National Institutes of Health (NIH). In 1988 a study revealed that taking small doses of aspirin regularly can reduce the probability of heart attacks. Unfortunately, the only subjects used in the study were 22,000 male physicians (Cimons, 1990). In 1990 researchers reported findings showing that heavy consumption of coffee was unrelated to increased risk of heart attacks and strokes. All of the 45,600 subjects were men. The effects of small doses of aspirin or heavy coffee consumption on the health of women—helpful, harmful, or none at all—remain unknown. What *is* known is that cardiovascular disease is the number-one cause of death among women, that more women than men suffer fatal heart attacks and strokes each year, and that more women than men die from their first heart attack (U.S. Congress: House of Representatives, 1991: 40).

Criticizing sex bias in research procedures, one U.S. senator observed:

Drugs are developed with incomplete data on metabolic differences between men and women. Diseases are studied without an understanding of the effects of hormones and reproduction. Even preliminary animal studies are usually done only with male rats (Cimons, 1990).

In responding to researchers' claims that the use of male research subjects is justifiable because women's bodies are more "complicated" than men's, one critic stated:

Saying that women's bodies are complicated is saying that there is a norm out there and that norm is the male body. It's such blatant sexism ("Our Bodies, Their Selves," 1990).

Sexism in the health-care arena also means that there are health problems pertaining to women on which little research is even being done. One example is osteoporosis, which afflicts some 25 million Americans. This is a highly preventable condition involving loss of bone tissue which leads to fractures of the wrist, hip, and spine. Twice as many women as men over the age of 65—one in three women—develop osteoporosis. While the condition is responsible for 1.3 million bone fractures annually, resulting in physical disability, anguish, and substantial expense, relatively little money goes toward research and education on this major public health problem (U.S. Congress: House of Representatives, 1991: 40–41). While experts posit that proper nutritional and exercise habits begun early in life could contribute significantly to prevention of osteoporosis in women's later years (Worcester and Whatley, 1992), much more research on causes and treatment remains to be done.

The list goes on. Little is known about menopause, even though many women have difficulties with it and place themselves at great risk for cancer if they must control its symptoms with hormone therapy. The sexually transmitted disease called chlamydia—which affects only women, can be difficult for those infected to detect, and leaves many women sterile—remains largely a mystery to scientists.

Breast cancer preponderantly strikes women and can cause death if not diagnosed early and treated, yet it has received relatively little research

Most breast cancer occurs in women. Despite the fact that such cancer can cause death unless detected and treated in its earliest stages, it has not received as much research attention as cancers that men frequently experience. This patient is undergoing mammography, x-ray photography of the breast, an important diagnostic tool and an early warning device that many women use to supplement self-examination.

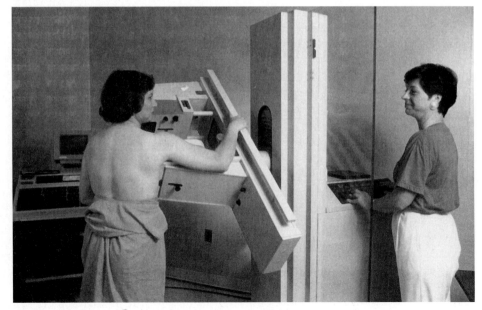

funding and attention in comparison to other forms of cancer that men are more likely to experience. In the United States most persons who have died from AIDS have been male, and most research on symptoms and treatment regimes has been directed toward men. Yet healthy women are fourteen times more likely than healthy men to be infected by the AIDS virus during heterosexual intercourse, an increasingly common form of transmission of the disease ("Our Bodies, Their Selves," 1990).

In response to growing outcries over such matters, the NIH promised to devote greater attention and more resources to research on women's health issues (Gladwell, 1990). It announced its intention to launch the largest federally funded study ever conducted on women's health, the Women's Health Initiative. The study is expected to cost $625 million over fourteen years, ending in the year 2007 (Schwartz, 1993). The Women's Health Initiative focuses on causes and treatment of a host of illnesses including breast, colon, and rectal cancer, heart disease, and osteoporosis. Women will be asked about their sexual behavior in order to gain knowledge for the first time about how health problems and treatment needs differ among heterosexual, lesbian, and bisexual women (Laurence, 1993).

Some mainstream male medical professionals criticize the Women's Health Initiative as being unnecessarily lengthy in duration, underestimated in costs, and faulty in design. Federal officials and women's health organizations have rejected the validity of such criticisms (Schwartz, 1993). The project is going forward, yet it will be quite a while before this reversal of research neglect begins to have a positive impact on the health status of women.

We have seen that the health status of people in the United States differs along the lines of class, race, and gender. Part of the explanation for these differences in health status rests with inadequacies in the U.S. health-care system itself. In the next section we shall discuss some of this system's features.

THE U.S. HEALTH-CARE SYSTEM

The United States spends more money on health care each year than any other nation in the world. Yet, as we saw earlier in this chapter, the United States does not fare as well in comparison with many other nations on commonly used measures of health status. In this section we shall look at inadequacies in the health-care system that help account for this (Abramson, 1990).

Inadequate Coverage

First of all, the system does not embrace all citizens. The United States is almost alone in this regard among industrialized nations (the only other is South Africa). Other nations provide either a system of national health insurance or a system of national health services that covers everyone. People are not denied care because they cannot afford it. In our society, on the other hand, health care is treated like other commodities in a market economy: you get what you are able to pay for.

Most people in the United States, approximately 160 million of those under age 65, receive some type of private health-care insurance coverage through employers. However, only two states (Hawaii and Washington) *require* employers to provide such insurance; in other states many employers do not do so. The coverage provided varies widely. For example, sometimes an employee's dependents are included; sometimes they are not. Policies vary in the range of health problems they cover, the nature and extent of services allowed, and the allocation of costs between employer and employee.

With rising health-care costs, insurance rates have gone up dramatically in recent years. Employers have responded by demanding that employees accept less comprehensive coverage and take on more of the burden of paying for the insurance. In one national survey, 31 percent of the respondents said they worried a great deal that their current benefits will be substantially cut back, while 39 percent were greatly worried that health insurance will become too expensive for them to afford (Commonwealth Fund, 1993).

Those who receive health-care insurance through their employers have been experiencing growing out-of-pocket health-care costs. Moreover, millions are covered by insurance that proves to be inadequate in the event of catastrophic illness. In such an event, many workers have no choice but to exhaust all their assets and go into heavy debt to pay medical and hospital bills. The fear of losing health-care benefits puts pressure on employees to think twice about moving to other jobs. Worse yet is the fear of how one will cope with health problems in the event of job loss, since having insurance is so dependent on one's employment status.

Today some 39 million Americans, more than one in six, have no health-care insurance at all. The figure would be even higher if we included many more who lack coverage at one or another point during the calendar year. Many uninsured persons are unemployed, moving between jobs, or searching for their first jobs (new college graduates included). But for the most part the uninsured are working people and their families. Some of these workers are employed by small firms that do not provide health benefits; others are self-employed and simply cannot afford the high costs of private insurance for themselves and their families. The 39 million Americans who are uninsured, over 10 million of whom are children, are also ineligible for the two main government-financed programs of health care, Medicare (for the elderly and people with disabilities) and Medicaid (for persons who are extremely poverty-stricken).

People who lack insurance but do not qualify for one of the government programs often put off seeking health care unless and until a problem becomes acute and disabling. Pregnant women do without prenatal care, and their infants and children have little contact with doctors. Income earners are reluctant to lose badly needed income by taking time off from work when they do not feel well. Symptoms of health difficulties that would send the more affluent, well-insured individual to the doctor immediately tend to be ignored or downplayed in importance. Many people may be affected by the uninsureds' failure to seek prompt treatment for infectious diseases. Thus, the health-care system often does not address the health problems of the uninsured until they end up in a state of extreme distress in overcrowded, understaffed hospital emergency rooms.

In an effort to meet some of the health-care needs of the elderly, the federal government began the health insurance plan called *Medicare* in 1965. Medicare covers about 30 million people age 65 and older and another 3 million people with disabilities. The program has proved to be a lifesaver for people who otherwise would have to go without health care, but it is not comprehensive enough for many people. It does not pay the full costs of care and limits the services it does cover. For example, Medicare policies allow payment for only a limited number of days of hospital care and physician visits. This has meant rising out-of-pocket health-care expenses for people who often have chronic health problems and typically must exist on fixed incomes.

Some elders are victims of "patient dumping," so-called because hospitals at times prematurely discharge patients whose health insurance does not adequately cover costs. Many are affected by Medicare's restrictions on payment for long-term skilled nursing-home care, important to the very old and their families. Such practices and restrictions may put adult children who must "parent their parents" under a great deal of stress and expense; they frequently must provide their parents with home care while juggling employment and child-rearing responsibilities. While elders may have some money of their own, Medicare policies tend to force the elderly to use up their assets to the point of poverty before they are eligible for government assistance in paying the bills for full-time, long-term care.

Medicaid is the other governmental health-care plan. It was begun as a cooperatively financed venture by federal and state governments in 1965 to help the poor, especially families that qualify for welfare. Yet today, as a consequence of various rules, regulations, and cost containment policies, barely over 40 percent of those living under the official poverty line are covered by Medicaid. And those in poverty who are covered often find the coverage inadequate.

For example, by law only certain amounts will be paid to physicians for the services they provide to Medicaid patients. Since these amounts tend to be about half of what the physicians customarily charge, many doctors have a policy of not taking Medicaid patients. The latter are put into the position of either begging for care or hunting around until a willing physician can be found. Moreover, each state sets its own standards for the depths of poverty that must be reached before persons are eligible for Medicaid. Thus, it is possible to be living well below the official federal poverty line and still be "too well off" to qualify by state standards, a stance adopted by many states to help slow their increasing benefit costs. Excluded by health-care providers and deemed ineligible by state programs, millions of the poor find themselves facing barriers to care.

We know that the poverty population disproportionately consists of women and children and that people of color are also overrepresented. These are the categories of people who are most likely to have either no health-care insurance or the inadequate coverage provided by Medicaid. The fact that people in other nations experience lower rates of infant mortality and greater life expectancies reflects in large part the failure of the U.S. health-care system to serve all its citizens.

Health Care: A Market Commodity

Other inadequacies of the system stem from the treatment of health care as a commodity to be bought and sold in a market system. In the United States physicians have always been independent entrepreneurs. While much of the cost of medical education is subsidized by the taxpayer through grants to medical schools and student loans, newly graduated doctors still find themselves burdened with educational debts, high costs of starting up and maintaining a new practice, and payments for malpractice insurance. Doctors also expect to receive personal incomes high enough to compensate for the effort and sacrifices associated with their chosen profession. Most do what astute businesspeople have always done—locate in, and cater to, that segment of the market that is likely to be most stable and lucrative.

In this case, the preferred market segment is made up of dense population centers containing relatively affluent, and well-insured, households. Physicians thus tend to migrate to metropolitan areas and their sprawling suburbs. In such communities, they can affiliate with high-quality medical

Millions of low-income people and people without health insurance lack access to private physicians and may have no place to take their health problems except busy hospital emergency rooms. Once there, those who are ill or injured must wait—until someone on the medical staff can find the time to help them.

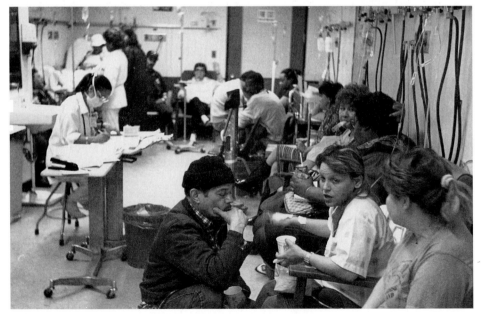

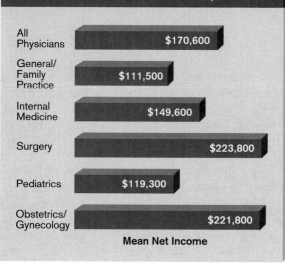

FIGURE 13.1 PHYSICIAN INCOMES BY SPECIALTY, 1991

	Mean Net Income
All Physicians	$170,600
General/Family Practice	$111,500
Internal Medicine	$149,600
Surgery	$223,800
Pediatrics	$119,300
Obstetrics/Gynecology	$221,800

Physicians who choose to become specialists have incomes that are often substantially higher than those received by general or family practitioners. Annual mean net incomes are highest for specialists in surgery and in obstetrics and gynecology. (*Source:* U.S. Department of Commerce, Bureau of the Census, *Statistical Abstract of the United States, 1994*, Washington: U.S. Government Printing Office, 1994, p. 123.)

facilities whose services such households can afford. But this means that people living in rural areas of the country, in small towns, and in the segregated ghettos and barrios of the nation's inner cities are not served as well.

The market effect on health-care delivery also is seen in the ever-increasing tendency toward specialization within the medical profession. This tendency, underway since World War II, is expressed in the declining proportion of newly trained doctors who go into general practice or family medicine. In part, specialization is a function of the generation of new knowledge and advanced technology. But it can also be understood as one way in which physicians have sought to capture and control the most lucrative share of the market for their services.

In the last 20 years the number of doctors in the United States has almost doubled. Many physicians become specialists in an attempt to control the competition with other physicians for patients. Another motivating force is the ability of specialists to command high levels of compensation for their services, which are not routinely available from every doctor. (See Figure 13.1.) Increased specialization has reduced the number of primary-care physicians, doctors who provide routine and continuing care and who know when it is necessary and appropriate to refer patients to more expensive specialists.

The net result of inadequate coverage and increasing specialization is that tens of millions of people in the United States are uninsured or underinsured, have difficulty paying for health care and put off seeking it as long as possible, and then face a system of providers who are either uninterested in serving them or simply inaccessible. What are the consequences? For many people, the hospital emergency room has become a substitute for the primary-care physician, and a desperate one at best. But the emergency room is likely to see patients whose conditions are more serious precisely because these people have not been seen by a primary-care physician. Ill and suffering adults and children wait for hours while life-and-death cases—severe burns, gunshot wounds, car accident injuries—receive first priority.

Rapid, impersonal, assembly-line processing by unknown and unchosen emergency room staff stands in sharp contrast to methods of private physicians serving the more affluent. Persons who must be hospitalized often find themselves shunted off to crowded, overtaxed, public charitable institutions where, because of overburdened budgets, the quality of care may not be the best. In some instances, uninsured people have been refused admission by upscale private hospitals and have been taken by ambulance to several different hospitals until one agreed to admit them. Those treated but not hospitalized can be offered little in the way of routine follow-up care. Unless one is well insured and able to take care of the bills, encounters with the health-care system are likely to be confusing, alienating, and dehumanizing.

The Corporatization of Medicine

In a relatively new trend within the health-care system, large private firms have been entering the health-service delivery field in a search for profits. This trend, termed the **corporatization of medicine,** has served to move health care even further away from the traditional approach of private practice by an individual physician (Starr, 1982; Light, 1989). Corporatization also represents a move away from the provision of services by nonprofit health-care facilities, whose main financial concern is only that income come close to matching expenses.

Nonprofit health maintenance organizations (HMOs), which provide comprehensive care to a designated population for a set fee, are a case in point. In a typical HMO, members and their employers pay a monthly premium, and members may then use the services of the HMO whenever and as often as they want. Since doctors in HMOs are usually salaried and get paid the same amount no matter how many patients they treat, they are more likely to emphasize *prevention* of health problems. Since their salaries and continued employment depend upon keeping costs down within the HMO's budget, physicians have an incentive to avoid ordering unnecessary tests and hospitalization of patients. HMOs have at times been criticized for the quality of care they provide and for reluctance to pay for non-HMO medical services that some patients may need or desire.

Corporatization represents a somewhat different approach. Clinics, hospitals, nursing homes, and home health services are increasingly owned by private investors seeking to provide services for profit. Ever-larger investor-owned firms run such facilities as chains, much like department stores and fast-food restaurants. Physicians themselves have become increasingly involved as owners and participants, understandably attracted by the lucrative returns such firms promise in a nation that spends hundreds of billions of dollars on health care each year.

The concentration of health-care services in the hands of large investor-owned corporations has its critics (Abramovitz, 1987; Relman, 1987). The main danger stems from the fact that these firms are profit-oriented. Owner-physicians may order tests and medical procedures that are lucrative but unnecessary, thereby pushing health-care costs up. Such firms are also likely to steer away from providing services to the public that are incompatible with their profit goals and to avoid low-income populations whose insurance status and ability to pay for services may be inadequate. Corporatization of medicine thus may ignore many people's actual health-care needs as firms provide only those services that guarantee the greatest return to investors. The specter of investors reaping financial benefits from the selective servicing of health misfortunes is not an attractive one. Nor does this trend bode well for improving the well-being of those who are not served by the present health-care system.

The U.S. health-care system is now undergoing strains that are unprecedented in magnitude and that promise to grow worse. These strains stem mainly from two factors: first, the AIDS epidemic, viewed by most people in the United States as the most serious health problem we face; and second, the health-care needs of those who are reaching old age, an ever-increasing proportion of the population. If the U.S. system of health care undergoes significant reform, it is likely to be spurred along by these two phenomena. Let us examine the problems posed by each of them.

STRAINS ON THE U.S. HEALTH-CARE SYSTEM

The Impact of AIDS

AIDS was unknown as a health problem prior to 1981. In little more than a decade or so it became a **pandemic,** a disease that can be found throughout the world. The most concentrated outbreaks of AIDS at present appear to be located in parts of Asia and Oceania, sub-Saharan Africa, and Latin America and the Caribbean (Global AIDS Policy Coalition, 1992: 4), but the United States leads all other nations in the number of officially documented cases. Between 1981 and 1994, more than 400,000 cases of AIDS were reported to the U.S. Centers for Disease Control. More than 243,000 people with AIDS have already died (Pollack, 1994). In addition, it is estimated that at least a million people in the United States are carrying the human immunodeficiency virus (HIV) by which AIDS is spread (U.S. Department of Health and Human Services, 1992: 34). Left unchecked, AIDS could kill millions of people in the United States alone, and tens of millions worldwide.

Outside the United States the picture is very frightening. According to the World Health Organization, between 1981 and 1994 about 17 million people in the world were found to be infected with HIV. Four million people (including those who died) have developed AIDS (Pollack, 1994). The Global AIDS Policy Coalition has noted that AIDS is spreading to new countries and communities around the world; no part of the globe is immune. The spread is rapid: in 1992 the coalition estimated that "the number of cumulative AIDS cases by the year 2000 would reach nearly 25 million" (Global AIDS Policy Coalition, 1992: 4). Such estimates may be conservative since many AIDS cases may go undiagnosed or misdiagnosed in underdeveloped nations, where health-care systems are typically very poorly equipped and understaffed.

AIDS is affecting a wide range of people in the United States, all of whom are desperate to survive (Russell, 1991). Those affected include heterosexuals, homosexuals, and bisexuals; women and men; white persons and people of color; adults, teenagers, children, and infants. While stereotyped as a "gay disease," in reality HIV and AIDS are well established in the general population. Survey results suggest that as many as 18 million people in the United States know or have known a person with AIDS (Russell, 1991: 2–3). In the future, more people in the United States will come to be affected as a result of little more than a single episode of unprotected sex, the sharing of a needle, a transfusion of infected blood, or birth with an HIV-positive mother.

As AIDS has taken on epidemic proportions within the United States, the health-care system has been faced simultaneously with finding a cure and caring for the many thousands who have been struggling against this fatal disease. Currently there is no known cure or preventive vaccine, although some breakthroughs have occurred in the discovery of drugs that seem to slow the appearance and initial severity of AIDS symptoms. Such drugs, and the medical care necessary to extend the lives of people with AIDS, are

Quality health care for people with AIDS is imperative, but not all members of the medical profession are willing to work with AIDS patients. This man is fortunate to have a supportive and compassionate physician to help him in his struggle against this fatal disease.

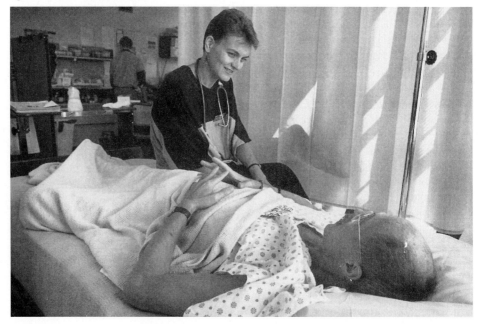

extremely expensive. For example, in the United States the average annual cost of treating a patient with AIDS (inpatient and outpatient) is $32,000, and treatment of an HIV-positive patient is $5,150. It is estimated that the total cost of treating people with AIDS and with HIV was $5.8 billion in the United States in 1991 (Global AIDS Policy Coalition, 1992: 495).

Some 60 percent of AIDS patients have no private health-care insurance and either are uninsured or must rely upon assistance under Medicaid. Since the medical bills can be substantial, and physicians are unlikely to treat individuals for whom they will receive very limited, if any, compensation, people with AIDS are often forced to depend on public hospitals. These hospitals tend to lack the funds and facilities needed to keep up with the enormous demands placed on them by the poor, including persons with AIDS.

Even persons who are well employed and covered under private insurance at the time AIDS enters their lives may face problems. When they become too ill to work and leave their jobs, they usually lose their health insurance. The cost of purchasing such insurance on their own is ordinarily so high as to be prohibitive. An individual health insurance policy with a private insurer can cost $4,500 a year or more, depending upon the comprehensiveness of the coverage desired. But, regardless of cost, firms that sell health insurance are not likely to insure individuals with AIDS. Paying for treatment on their own, such persons may spend their way down into abject poverty—and only then are they eligible for assistance from Medicaid.

Physicians, nurses, and others involved directly with patients have been engaged in debate over their professional responsibilities toward people with AIDS. Some are unwilling to work with AIDS patients at all, noting that there may be unknown risks to themselves that could endanger other patients. Others have taken on the care of AIDS patients as a personal crusade, risking physical and emotional burnout as they struggle to keep people alive in the hope that a cure will be discovered. As the number of people with AIDS steadily increases and ever more persons desperately seek help, the debate over who will provide the needed care is bound to intensify.

People with AIDS tend to be young (see Figure 13.2). Death rates from AIDS are highest for persons between the ages of 25 and 44 (U.S. Department of Health and Human Services, 1992: 179). The strain that these young people are placing on the health-care system is compounded by that being placed on it by their elders, as we will now see.

The Impact of Our Aging Population

Aging is accompanied by a variety of chronic health conditions, some of which are disabling. Given that the proportion of the U.S. population that is 65 or older is projected to increase from the current 12.5 percent to almost 20 percent by the year 2020, the number of elderly persons placing demands on the health-care system will escalate rapidly.

As people age, they are vulnerable to a host of problems, including heart conditions, rheumatism and arthritis, vision and hearing problems, and

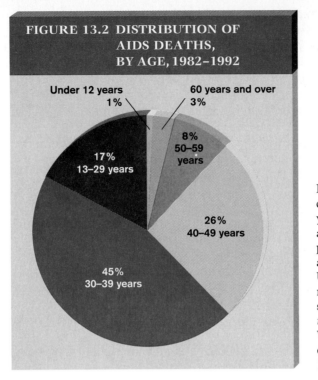

FIGURE 13.2 DISTRIBUTION OF AIDS DEATHS, BY AGE, 1982–1992

People who die as a consequence of AIDS tend to be young. Forty-five percent are in their thirties, and 17 percent are in their teens and twenties. (*Source:* U.S. Department of Commerce, Bureau of the Census, *Statistical Abstract of the United States, 1994*, Washington, DC: U.S. Government Printing Office, 1994, p. 98.)

numerous other maladies. One of the most serious health conditions, and one for which there is currently no effective treatment or cure, is Alzheimer's disease. A leading cause of death for the elderly in the United States, Alzheimer's involves the physical deterioration of the brain. As the brain deteriorates, people with Alzheimer's become progressively disabled—emotionally, cognitively, and physically. More than 100,000 of our elders die from the disease each year, many after lengthy and costly care in hospitals and nursing homes. So many are afflicted, particularly in the age category of 85 and older, that Alzheimer's disease has taken on the dimensions of a crisis.

Most elderly persons with Alzheimer's disease are cared for at home, rather than in a hospital or nursing-home setting. But they pose a major burden of responsibility for spouses, who are usually elderly themselves, or for their middle-aged offspring, who may be struggling to care for their own children at the same time. Whoever does the caretaking, the demands can be enormous. The physical and emotional stress accompanying caretaking can undermine the health of people who are well, causing them to need care themselves.

A real and growing need exists for quality, affordable nursing-home settings for people with Alzheimer's disease. Yet the U.S. health-care system seems paralyzed in the face of this crisis. One of the principal reasons so much home care occurs at all is the failure of Medicare, the government plan for the elderly, to provide adequate coverage for those who need long-term care in an institutional setting. Again, it is often necessary for the

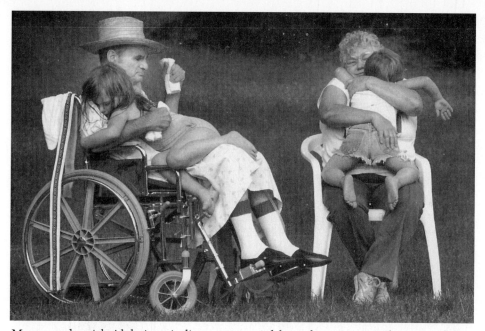

Most people with Alzheimer's disease are cared for at home, in part because of the high costs of nursing home or hospital care. This woman not only provides the daily care needed by her husband; she also works a second factory shift just to be able to afford the health insurance necessary to pay for his at-home medical expenses. Hugs from grandchildren lighten this couple's daily burdens.

elderly to divest themselves of all their savings and assets before they can be eligible for government programs. In the absence of a national health-care policy, the prospects awaiting the millions of people in the United States who will turn 65 in the next couple of decades, and who may live to face Alzheimer's, are not encouraging.

FIXING THE U.S. HEALTH-CARE SYSTEM

As we approach the year 2000, a broad public consensus has begun to emerge regarding the need to change our approach to health care in the United States. In one survey, 84 percent of those polled felt the system needs "fundamental change or complete rebuilding" (Commonwealth Fund, 1993). This sentiment reflects the fact that many people's needs are going unmet, as evidenced by the families in the accompanying boxed article. Yet there does not seem to be much agreement on the directions in which we should go. Let us briefly outline some ideas on how the system could be fixed (Eckholm, 1991; National Issues Forum, 1992).

One idea is to keep the existing system and look for ways to make it better. Advocates of this position suggest that we now have a health-care system that is the envy of much of the world. The system allows people a great deal of freedom to choose their physicians and take advantage of con-

Some of the problems people face due to lack of or inadequate health insurance are illustrated by the stories of the families that follow. In one case, a single mother who cannot afford health insurance must rely on public assistance and services of a free clinic. In another case, a financially comfortable elderly couple faces the prospect of going into poverty if they require long-term care.

The Weirathers: Part-Time Work, Full-Time Worry
One Tuesday night, Maria Weirather and her spirited little girls arrive 40 minutes early for an 8:30 appointment at the Iowa City Free Medical Clinic. The bus they take from their trailer park passes once an hour, and the next would have made them late. The children, Beverly, who is 4, and Andrea, 3, need physical examinations and immunizations, and here, there is no charge.

Ms. Weirather uses the clinic even though she works. Twenty-five years old and divorced, she transcribes researchers' notes in the psychology laboratory at the University of Iowa and cleans the cages of mice, cats and chimpanzees. The job is only 20 to 30 hours a week and ends in late May, when she hopes to get another. She earns $5.50 an hour.

Health insurance does not come with the job, and Ms. Weirather (pronounced WY-rather) cannot afford to buy it herself. She collects $260 a month in child support from her former husband, Mark Weirather, and her grandmother pays for her telephone. But with expenses like the $360-a-month rent for her trailer, she still qualifies for $247 a month in food stamps—"something I'm not very proud of," she said.

Ms. Weirather is 5 feet tall, a compact and vigorous, thoroughly engaged mother who boasts of the strength she has gained from chasing after buses and her kids. She finished high school at 17, married at 20, dropped out of college and had her two children.

She is among 56 percent of the 37 million uninsured Americans under 65 who have jobs, according to the Employment Benefit Research Institute in Washington. And Beverly and Andrea are among another 26 percent of the uninsured who are children. Typically, the wages of working people who lack insurance, however low, are not low enough to allow them access to Medicaid, the Federal-state health program for the poor.

Free clinics are often their principal recourse. The Iowa City clinic's mostly volunteer doctors, nurses and students provide outpatient services only, mostly shots, physicals, treatment of minor illnesses, some lab tests and prescriptions. It refers more serious cases to specialists, some of whom take the patients for free, more of whom charge a fee at the door or request monthly payments.

Ms. Weirather thinks she can find a job that would provide health insurance if she can get her bachelor's degree in microbiology, and by taking occasional courses, she has just one semester to go. But she is trapped in trying to work and arrange child care with friends, so making time for college and saving to pay for it seem beyond her grasp.

Once Ms. Weirather's care was simple and automatic. Her former husband had insurance through his job as a mechanic at a Chrysler dealership when, in October 1990, a malignant tumor was found on her left ovary. "I went in, and they said, 'Surgery,'" she said. "Within a week, I had surgery."

After the divorce, Mr. Weirather left his job for another without insurance in Keokuk, Iowa, a two-hour drive southeast of Iowa City. Her eyes welling up, Ms. Weirather said that a year after her operation, doctors spotted another growth on the same ovary. They removed it last October.

Public assistance paid for the operation and her chemotherapy, she said. "But I was left owing $5,000 to the hospital," she said. That is why Ms. Weirather takes the bus.

"Typically, the wages of working people who lack insurance, however low, are not low enough to allow them access to Medicaid."

"I had a 1990 Dodge Spirit turbo," she said. "It was essential transportation." She sold it for $4,000 to pay the bill. "It was the one really nice thing that I had," she said, "and the only new car that I ever owned."

The Coens: Cradled, for Now, by Medicare
Married for 57 years, William and Gertrude Coen talk about their health like a team, with more amusement than complaint.

"His liver enzymes went up," said Mrs. Coen, who is 76.

"Liver hepatitis, they called it," said Mr. Coen, 79.

"He lost about 35 pounds," she said.

"The enzymes are about normal now," he said.

"Gained 9 pounds," she said.

Only with prodding does the cost of Mr. Coen's treatment arise.

"He went to a doctor's office so they could take blood," Mrs. Coen said.

"Then we get a statement from Blue Cross saying how much they paid," Mr. Coen said.

The statement says, "Specimen transportation, $9."

"You got to pay the doctor to take the blood," Mrs. Coen said. "Now they even charge for carrying the blood."

For the Coens, health care is effective and gentle on their finances. Like 99 percent of the population 65 and older, they are covered by Medicare, the Government's health insurance program for the elderly, and they also have private insurance that covers most of what Medicare does not. "For us," Mr. Coen said, "it's O.K. the way it is. I know it's not for a lot of other people."

Mr. Coen worked for the post office for 37 years, the last 13 as Iowa City's postmaster. Mrs. Coen, who stopped work after their marriage to raise a daughter, is now a professor of nursing at the University of Iowa.

They have paid off the mortgage on their compact split-level house in an Iowa City subdivision. They have a pension, Social Security and savings that give them an income of more than $40,000 a year.

Their sole significant out-of-pocket health expenses last year were $1,939 for medicine and $1,828 for insurance for hospitalization costs not covered by Medicare. This year they expect to pay much less for medicine because they have joined a program for Federal workers and retirees that pays 80 percent of the cost of prescriptions.

The Coens, however, wonder about long-term care, which can eat up $30,000 a year or more and is not covered by Medicare. Mr. Coen's mother died at 93 of Alzheimer's disease after seven years in a nursing home. She was indigent by then, having exhausted proceeds from the sale of her four-unit apartment house that was also her home.

But much as they think about long-term care, they said they are not worried enough to submit to the blandishments of salesmen who pitch them insurance to pay for it. It could cost them $1,000 or more a month, and they say the policies are riddled with exclusions. "When you need it most," Mrs. Coen said, "it doesn't do you any good."

Many retirees want the Government to help pay for long-term care, but the Coens say they just have not given much thought to that. "As long as we're able to pay, we should pay," Mrs. Coen said. But rather than hold onto their assets only to lose them all to a nursing home, they have been thinking about giving some to their grandchildren. They would slide into poverty that much sooner, when Medicaid would pay.

Source: Peter T. Kilborn, "American Voices on Health Care: Even in Security, Anxiety," *New York Times,* May 9, 1993, p. 20.

stant advances in technology. The costs of health care are, however, rising too rapidly. And we could be doing more to provide some health insurance coverage for the 15 percent or so who lack any. Thus it has been suggested that all elements of the health-care system cooperate in searching for ways to reduce waste, eliminate duplication, and contain administrative costs. In addition, government should use tax incentives to encourage smaller firms to provide some health insurance coverage for their employees. Such measures, it is argued, will lead to a more affordable and more inclusive health-care system.

A second idea, which has been successful in Hawaii for a number of years and is in the process of being implemented in the state of Washington, more directly addresses the plight of those without adequate coverage. Under this idea, if adopted nationwide, the government would *require* employers to provide health insurance coverage to all employees and their families. All other persons would be eligible for expanded versions of government programs (such as Medicaid) from which they are now excluded. Employers would be encouraged to channel their employees into health-care programs that promise to help keep costs down. Such measures, it is argued, will address the need for all citizens to have some basic coverage while minimizing the burden on taxpayers. Clearly, however, government would play a greater role in this approach than in the first set of proposals mentioned.

A third idea, which calls for a more ambitious reform, is modeled after the health-care system operating in Canada. The U.S. government would guarantee health care for all citizens, paid for with new taxes. Under what is called a **single-payer plan,** employers and employees would no longer have to pay money to the approximately 1,500 insurance firms that provide coverage. The government would initiate strict controls over health-care fees (a policy that physicians initially strongly resisted in Canada) and streamline administrative procedures by having all bills submitted to it for payment. Advocates of this plan note that it allows everyone to receive the health care he or she needs, regardless of ability to pay. The plan also separates health care from employment status, since the government would make the same health-care benefits available to everyone, whether employed or not. Health care would become a right, not a privilege reserved for persons with money. Moreover, it would make sense within such a system to promote preventive care, since this would save taxpayers a great deal of money in the long run. The role of government would be greatest in this set of proposals.

The prospect of a universal, tax-supported health-care system inevitably raises the question of how comprehensive it would be. Can we afford to provide every citizen with all the health-care services that are now available to the wealthy and well-insured? Or will we have to reach a consensus on the conditions under which certain services will be provided, in effect rationing services that are extremely expensive or likely to be in short supply? (An attempt to introduce a detailed rationing policy is under way in Oregon. See Pear, 1993, and "Home Cures," 1993. The ethics of rationing are examined in Churchill, 1987.)

After all, some might argue, there must be outer limits to what can be spent on health. Other areas, from schools to highways, require heavy expenditures too that cannot go ignored. And don't all nations' health-care systems practice some type of rationing in the face of limited resources? For example, in most health-care systems people may be placed on a waiting list for surgery that is not considered urgent. In nations with the technological capabilities for organ transplants, rationing occurs whenever surgeons make decisions on who will receive replacement organs as they become available from newly deceased donors.

The debate about changing the existing system of health care in the United States, and the kinds of changes that should occur, takes place within a political and economic context. The United States is a class-divided capitalist society in which the most property-rich groups exercise a disproportionate amount of political power. Physicians, pharmaceutical and medical technology corporations, hospitals, and health insurers employ powerful lobbying and public relations firms to work on their behalf. They are capable of spending a great deal of money to make sure that the changes adopted are not against their collective self-interests.

In the absence of a strong groundswell of grass-roots sentiment and widespread political activism, it is unlikely that radical changes in the U.S. health-care system will occur. Moderate reforms that seek to minimize the worst features of the status quo seem more likely. Because of the powerful special interests that profit from the current health-care system, the medical model will no doubt continue to play the dominant role in shaping any adopted reforms, as opposed to a more proactive model that stresses social, economic, and political changes intended to prevent and protect people from risks to their health. Changes in the health-care system pursued by the Clinton administration represent such moderate reforms ("Clinton Solution," 1993; "Clinton Cure," 1993). In 1994, Congress failed to act on the administration's proposals in the face of highly partisan political opposition and fierce lobbying by various interest groups both inside and outside of the health-care system. Many experts predicted that Congress would eventually pass an extremely modest, scaled-down package of health-care reform legislation that would be phased in slowly, thus mollifying those groups concerned with threats reform might pose to the status quo.

CONCLUSION

If we look only at U.S. society and assess changes in its members' health status since the turn of the century, it is fair to say progress has been made. Improvements in such measures as infant mortality rates or rates of life expectancy have been rapid and substantial.

Yet this is only part of a larger reality. Despite our progress, and the fact that the United States spends more on health care today than any other nation, many other countries are doing better than the United States in terms of their citizens' health status. Even more, of course, are doing much worse—particularly the underdeveloped nations, in which the vast majority of the earth's population resides. Data comparing nations tell us that the world's populations differ greatly in their likelihoods of health-care needs and life expectancy.

Since the United States is one of the richest developed nations in the world, it is important to ask why we do not fare better than we do on measures of health status. Much of the answer lies in the way we have organized our health-care system. Rather than recognizing health care as a service all citizens deserve by right—just as we are in consensus that citizens deserve fire and police protection—we have relegated health care to the level of a purchasable commodity. If you need health care, you may purchase it, if you have enough money.

Since health care is very expensive and since wealth and income in the United States are so unequally distributed, tens of millions of people cannot afford it. Because people of color, women, and children are disproportionately represented among the economically disadvantaged in our society, their health-care needs tend to go unmet. Higher-than-necessary rates of infant mortality and lower-than-necessary rates of life expectancy in the United States are in part a reflection of gross economic inequalities and a system of health care that works in concert with them.

Various inadequacies of our health-care system seem to be out of sync with human needs. The system seems incapable of responding humanely to the massive AIDS epidemic or to the chronic health problems of our expanding population of elders. Although it is technologically sophisticated, the system tends to reflect many of the biases that prevail in the larger society, such as sexism, racism, and even homophobia. It is a system that both performs miracles and excludes people, saves lives and allows unnecessary suffering. Recognition of these kinds of inadequacies and contradictions is helping to stir demands for change and reform. The nature of the reforms will impact the biographies of us all.

THINKING CRITICALLY

1. Throughout this chapter our focus has been on physical health and not mental health. How important do you think it is that the U.S. health-care system address the mental health of society's members? In your own view, in what ways does the current system fall short? What changes do you think should be made, and why?

2. For many years the U.S. medical profession has resisted any type of national health-care system. Professional associations have condemned "socialized medicine," the idea that government should exert increased control over doctors and the services they deliver. Now many members of the medical profession are willing to accept some sort of reform. Why do you think this is the case?

3. What types of problems with the existing health-care system have you personally encountered? Were these problems somehow linked to your class membership, race, or gender? How so? What do you think it would take to eliminate such problems?

4. Discussion of health-care reform generally assumes that large, private insurance companies must continue to play a central role in the U.S. health-care system. Critics argue that the profit-seeking orientation of such companies drives up health-care costs; they point out that the Canadian system, in which private insurers do not play a role, is much

more inexpensive to administer. What keeps private companies in the picture in the plans for U.S. health-care reform?

5. The boxed article in this chapter highlighted some of the problems faced by a young divorced mother who cannot afford health-care insurance. If you and all your family members were, like 39 million other Americans, without any health insurance at all, what problems would you confront?

KEY WORDS

medical model, *431*

proactive health-care system, *432*

reactive health-care system, *432*

life expectancy, *432*

infant mortality, *432*

maternal mortality, *432*

corporatization of medicine, *452*

pandemic, *453*

single-payer plan, *460*

SUGGESTED READINGS

Bunyan Bryant and Paul Mohai (eds.), *Race and the Incidence of Environmental Hazards.* Boulder, CO: Westview Press, 1992. A collection of articles emphasizing the increased health risks to which people of color are exposed because of the disproportionate placement of hazardous waste and other toxic facilities in communities where they reside.

Peter Conrad and Rochelle Kern (eds.), *The Sociology of Health and Illness*, 3d ed. New York: St. Martin's Press, 1990. A collection of articles that bring a sociological perspective to a wide range of health issues, including the impact of class and racial inequality on health care.

Ray H. Elling, *The Struggle for Workers' Health: A Study of Six Industrialized Countries.* Farmingdale, NY: Baywood, 1986. A comparative analysis of policies toward worker health and safety and the reasons the policies protecting workers are vastly different in countries such as the United States and Sweden.

Randy Shilts, *And the Band Played On: Politics, People, and the AIDS Epidemic.* New York: Penguin, 1987. An analysis of the reasons why government and health institutions responded haltingly and inadequately to the appearance of AIDS in the early 1980s, thereby placing people in the United states at great risk.

Paul Starr, *The Social Transformation of American Medicine.* New York: Basic Books, 1982. A historical account of the development of health care in the United States, with special emphasis on the changing nature of the medical profession and the position of doctors in the health-care system.

Howard Waitzkin, *The Second Sickness: Contradictions of Capitalist Health Care.* Chicago: University of Chicago Press, 1982. A critical analysis of the U.S. health-care system and the ways in which it generates great profits for some people while failing to meet the needs of many.

FAMILIES

*C*onsider the various images of families we have seen on television over the years. In Leave It to Beaver, *the 1950s television program, mom is a full-time homemaker, dad works at an office in an unspecified occupation, they have two children, and they live in a comfortable suburban home. In* The Honeymooners, *a full-time homemaker is married to a bus driver, they have no children, and they live in a cramped, working-class walk-up apartment in New*

York City. By the 1980s these images began to change. In The Cosby Show, *mom and dad both have lucrative and satisfying professional careers; their five children live with them in a large-city brownstone house, although at various times the children move out or return to their parents' home with spouses and offspring. In* Punky Brewster *the family consists of a young foster child and the elderly man who adopted her. During the 1990s, the images continued to change. In* Blossom, *a single father raises his children alone. In* Murphy Brown, *a single, successful professional woman decides to maintain her pregnancy and raise her child alone. In* The Golden Girls, *four middle-aged and elderly women, including one woman's mother, live together in a Florida condominium.*

These television families are a limited array of the various forms that the institution of the family may take. Despite the variety of forms, they are all, in some fashion, families. Your own family situation may differ significantly from the families seen on television. What, then, is a family? In this chapter we will examine what we mean by "family." What family forms prevail in our society, and why? What factors make some forms more advantageous than others? Who benefits and who is hurt by different family forms? Does the variety of family forms, and the troubles afflicting many families, mean the family is breaking down as an institution?

Beyond being aware of the structural forms families may take, we need to understand the dynamics among family members and the forces that might affect those dynamics. In this chapter we will explore the factors that can create problems and stress for families. How do developments in other institutions affect the creation, alteration, and dissolution of family ties? For example, what roles do the state and economy play in encouraging and rewarding some family forms but not others?

Let's turn first to the meaning of family.

DEFINING FAMILY

In 1949, George Murdock defined family, on the basis of an analysis of nearly 500 societies, as "a social group characterized by common residence, economic cooperation, and reproduction" (1949: 1). Murdock's definition, which he believed to be universally applicable to all societies, stated that a family consisted of "adults of both sexes, at least two of whom maintain a socially approved sexual relationship, and one or more children, own or adopted, of the sexually cohabiting adults" (1949: 1). He believed this family form was widespread because it was functional to society: it fulfilled societal needs.

While many sociologists accept Murdock's definition, others frequently criticize it for what it omits. For example, Murdock's definition does not include the realities of many families today: single-parent families, married couples without children, gay male and lesbian couples, multigenerational families without sexual relationships, and elderly couples with no children. It also does not include cohabiting couples. Since 1970, according to the U.S. Bureau of the Census, the number of couples who live together without marriage has increased by more than 400 percent. By 1992, almost 3 million of the 93 million households documented in the United States consisted of cohabiting couples (Ames et al., 1992).

Murdock's definition of family seems to confuse *family* (defined by a set of principles determining relatedness) with **household** (a common residential unit in which related and nonrelated individuals may live) (Rapp, 1982; Gerstel and Gross, 1987; Andersen, 1990; Ferree, 1990). However, a family and a household are not necessarily the same thing. Consider, for example, slaves in colonial America. While they contributed to the slave owner's family as an economic unit, and were often considered part of the household, they would not be accepted as legitimate family members according to the conventional definition (Jones, 1987). Consider, too, the case of children of a divorce: they may live in a separate household without at least one of their parents, but the children often still consider both parents to be their family.

Sociologists who accept Murdock's functional definition of family often recognize that there may be different types of family, based on the role it plays for the individual. These sociologists have differentiated families on the basis of biological factors. **Families of orientation** are the families into which we are born or adopted, while **families of procreation** are those into which we marry and in which we produce our own offspring. This differentiation of family by the role it plays for the individual assumes that all individuals will marry into a heterosexual relationship that will produce offspring.

But this is a very shaky assumption. Many people enter into cohabitation relationships, both heterosexual and homosexual, and a growing number of couples (both married and cohabiting) are choosing not to have children. Individuals in many gay male and lesbian couples have increasingly come to refer to their relationships with their partners and their partners' relatives as **families of choice,** reflecting a family form not defined by biology (Weston, 1991). In this form, family and kinship are defined by stable relationships based on shared economic and emotional ties in one or more households.

Sociologists have also differentiated between nuclear and extended families. A **nuclear family** is composed of two parents and their offspring, while an **extended family** includes the nuclear family plus other members of one or both parents' families of orientation (such as grandparents, aunts and uncles, siblings). Some sociologists link these types of family to class: the nuclear family typifies the middle class, because the breadwinner earns enough to support that unit without the financial help of other family members; the extended family is more commonly found among the working class and poor, since several generations or members of the same generation tend to live together out of economic necessity. Such a differentiation of family forms not only continues to confuse households with families but also is historically inaccurate. Many middle-class families in the 1950s and 1960s in the United States lived in some form of extended family (particularly those including two married members, their children, and one or more grandparents) (Sussman and Burchinal, 1962; Litwak, 1965).

Research also indicates some racial differences in the prevalence of extended families. African Americans are twice as likely as whites to live in extended families (Tienda and Angel, 1982; Farley and Allen, 1987; Beck and Beck, 1989). One reason for this is that many African American women have grandchildren living with them (Beck and Beck, 1989). Moreover, Angel and Tienda (1982) found that while white families' household income tended to derive primarily from the incomes of one or both partners of a marriage, African American families' income was likely to be based primarily on the combined incomes of both partners, adult children, and extended relatives. Given the lower average annual earnings of African Americans compared with those of whites, as noted in Chapters 6 and 11, there are clear economic pressures to pool relatively limited financial resources as a means of escaping extreme poverty.

Economic pressures are contributing to a more general resurgence of extended families in the United States as well. Many middle-class families with aging parents in the 1990s are returning to a form of extended family. As reliable, adequate nursing-home care becomes increasingly expensive and inaccessible to the middle class, elderly parents are moving in with their children. The woman typically engages in the caretaking, regardless of whether the elderly parent is hers or her partner's (Taeuber, 1991). Stone and her colleagues (1987) found that in the mid-1980s more than one-third of the 1.2 million "frail elderly" in the United States lived with their adult children. In 1987, according to the National Survey of Families and Households, 8 percent of women younger than 65 lived with (and presumably cared for) an individual who was disabled or chronically ill, including parents and partners (McLanahan and Monson, 1989; see also Ferber, O'Farrell, and Allen, 1991).

Furthermore, as housing costs soar and jobs become scarce even for college graduates, an increasing number of middle-class offspring are returning home as adults to live with their parents. In 1990, almost 52 percent of young adults 18 to 24 years old and 11 percent 25 to 34 years old were living with their parents, up from 42 percent and 6 percent, respectively, in 1960 (U.S. Bureau of the Census, 1992b). So the extended family appears to be widespread among the population, reflecting a variety of social and economic circumstances.

Even though the divorce rate in the United States remains relatively high (nearly half of all marriages end in divorce), most divorced people remarry (U.S. Bureau of the Census, 1992b). Since many remarriages involve part-

Although the nuclear family is often assumed to be the "normal" family form, there are in fact a variety of family forms. Here we see just three of the types of families that are common in the United States (clockwise, top left): blended families, created when previously married people remarry and bring their offspring to the new family; families of choice, consisting of gay partners and their children; and families created by adoption.

ners with children from previous marriages, there are an increasing number of "blended" stepfamilies consisting of two new partners and their respective children. When these new marriages produce children as well, they create a family consisting of stepsiblings, half-siblings, stepparents, and parents. While only a minority of noncustodial parents actually maintain contact with their children after divorce (Furstenberg, Nord, Peterson, and Zill, 1983; Dudley, 1991), joint-custody arrangements can mean that remarriage to a new partner does not necessarily sever the relationship between a parent and his or her children. Thus, the children may live primarily with one parent but remain part of the other parent's household as well. The blended family, like the new extended family, challenges the conventional definition of family since it often involves several households.

How, then, are we to define family and still capture the wide diversity of forms which constitute that institution? We base our definition on that offered by Carol D. Stack (1974: 31), which reflects a variety of situations, including those contoured by race, class, and gender: **Family** is an organized, ongoing network of kin and nonkin who interact daily, sharing economic and household responsibilities and obligations, providing for domestic needs of all members, and ensuring their survival. The family network may span several households that may be based on biology or on choice.

DIVERSITY OF FAMILY FORMS

Given that the family may be structured in different ways at different times, which forms of the family are most prevalent today in the United States, and why? As shown in Figure 14.1 (based on data for 1991), the conventional understanding of the nuclear family, composed of a breadwinning father, a full-time homemaker mother, and two or more young offspring living in the same residence, describes less than 7 percent of U.S. households (U.S. Bureau of the Census, 1992b). Almost three times as many households consist of two income-earning adults and their children. U.S. households consisting of married couples with no children total just under 20 percent. Single-parent households are also common. Among these, female-headed households are almost four times more frequent than male-headed households (U.S. Bureau of the Census, 1992b).

Unmarried couples living together also are on the rise, increasing by over 80 percent in the 1980s to 3 million households in 1990 (Ames et al., 1992). In 1990 less than one-third of these households included children under 15 years of age (U.S. Bureau of the Census, 1991c).

Unfortunately, the Census Bureau does not have data for many household arrangements, such as homosexual couples living together, multigenerational households, and so on. However, even with these limitations, the data do tell us that the conventional nuclear family is no longer the typical U.S. family.

Are the proportions of family types similar for white, African American, and Latino families in the United States? According to Figure 14.2, in 1991 white families were more likely to be married-couple households than

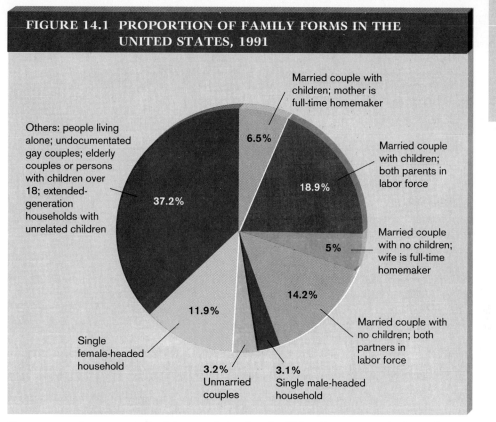

FIGURE 14.1 PROPORTION OF FAMILY FORMS IN THE UNITED STATES, 1991

Married couple with children; mother is full-time homemaker — 6.5%

Others: people living alone; undocumented gay couples; elderly couples or persons with children over 18; extended-generation households with unrelated children — 37.2%

Married couple with children; both parents in labor force — 18.9%

Married couple with no children; wife is full-time homemaker — 5%

Married couple with no children; both partners in labor force — 14.2%

Single female-headed household — 11.9%

Unmarried couples — 3.2%

Single male-headed household — 3.1%

Contrary to the stereotypical image of the "typical" family as a married couple with children living at home, families are actually quite diverse in the forms they assume. What is the structure of your own family? (*Source:* U.S. Bureau of the Census, *Money Income of Households, Families, and Persons in the United States, 1991,* Current Population Reports, Series P60-180, Washington, DC: U.S. Government Printing Office, 1992.)

were African American or Latino families. Wives in African American married-couple families were more likely to work in the formal labor force than Latino or white wives. African American families were also more likely to be headed by single mothers with no husband present than either Latino or white families. Let's take a closer look at the diversity of family forms in the United States.

Family Forms: Cultural Choice or Institutional Response?

In a controversial speech given in June 1992, Vice President Dan Quayle argued that single-parent families were largely responsible for much of what was wrong in the United States. He insisted that "appropriate" family values call for a two-parent family, in which one of the parents (pre-

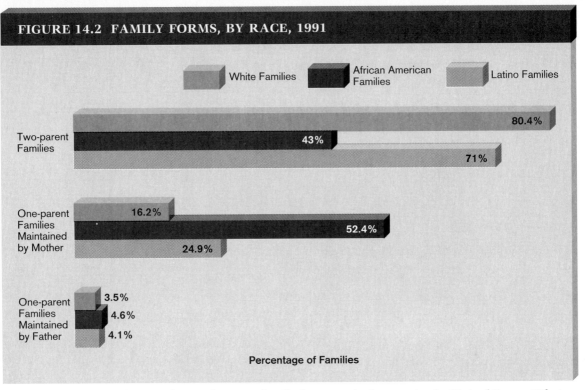

FIGURE 14.2 FAMILY FORMS, BY RACE, 1991

White Families — African American Families — Latino Families

Two-parent Families: 80.4% · 43% · 71%

One-parent Families Maintained by Mother: 16.2% · 52.4% · 24.9%

One-parent Families Maintained by Father: 3.5% · 4.6% · 4.1%

Percentage of Families

The prevalence of various family forms varies by race in the United States. What factors might affect this variation? (*Source:* U.S. Bureau of the Census, *Household and Family Characteristics: 1991,* Current Population Reports, Series P20-458, Washington, DC: U.S. Government Printing Office, 1992.)

sumably the mother) assumes primary responsibility for taking care of the children. He urged a return to such wholesome family values as the answer to most of today's social problems.

This attitude suggests that family forms other than the traditional nuclear family structure represent conscious choices on the part of individuals or reflect different cultural norms within the population. But what about institutional forces that might influence the form a given family may assume? Institutional forces may not only be responsible for diversity in family forms but might also influence the experiences within these forms.

Reasons for the Rise in Single-Parent Families

Several forces help account for the growing number of single-parent families. Many such families are the result of divorce. The divorce rate in the United States (measured as the number of divorces per 1,000 married women) has increased from 17 divorces per 1,000 married women in 1963–1965 to 37 per 1,000 in 1987–1989 (U.S. Bureau of the Census, 1992b).

Divorce has become easier to achieve since 1970 with the advent of **no-fault divorce** laws in many states. Prior to this legislation, couples were required to demonstrate that one of the partners was responsible for the destruction of the marriage, usually on the grounds of adultery or severe mistreatment. Under no-fault divorce laws, it is no longer necessary to attribute blame for misconduct in order to dissolve the marriage. One or both of the partners may simply apply to the courts for a divorce, citing irreconcilable differences. Such a significant change in legal requirements for divorce indicates substantial changes in society's values and cultural norms regarding marriage, the declining influence of religious institutions, and the increasing influence of the state in family affairs.

Another factor increasing the divorce rate is widespread access to effective contraception, which lessens the risks involved in marital infidelity (a leading cause of divorce). Moreover, while the presence of children reduces the probability of divorce, having *fewer* children may increase the viability of divorce as an option for unhappily married couples. Indeed, the average number of children involved per divorce has declined from 1.22 in 1970 to 0.89 in 1987 (U.S. Bureau of the Census, 1991c).

Economic conditions may also contribute to the divorce rate. Participation in the formal labor market provides some women with greater economic independence from their husbands, thereby making divorce a more viable option. A weak economy, including high rates of unemployment and inflation and a significant decline in the value of wages, may introduce serious stresses into a marriage, leading to divorce. The availability of welfare assistance to poverty-stricken female-headed households also makes divorce an option in some cases. Taken together, the forces of economic stress contribute to divorce; thus, divorce rates (as well as rates of marital separation and abandonment) are highest among the lowest-income groups (Neubeck, 1991: 378).

Divorce is not the only factor contributing to single-parent families. Many such families *begin* with a single parent. Unmarried mothers accounted for 38.9 percent of all births in the United States in 1989, up from 4 percent in 1950 (U.S. Bureau of the Census, 1991c). Almost one-fourth of all never-married women in the United States in 1992 became mothers, up from slightly more than 15 percent just a decade earlier (De Parle, 1993). Part of the reason for this increase is that cultural sanctions against out-of-wedlock births are changing: fewer people refer to children of unwed mothers as "illegitimate." And an increasing number of affluent, over-30 single women are choosing to have babies, without plans of marriage. However, apart from this trend, teenagers constitute a significant group among unwed mothers. Why should we see such an increase in births to single females, especially teenagers?

One factor is that girls are becoming capable of reproduction at increasingly younger ages, in part because of improved nutrition and health. An earlier onset of menstruation means that a greater percentage of females are able to become pregnant. Moreover, the proportion of teenagers who are sexually active has been increasing since at least the 1960s. According to the Alan Guttmacher Institute, in 1990, 56 percent of teenage women and 73 percent of teenage men were sexually active. Although such teenagers may have access to contraceptives, many do not use them. In 1988, 35 percent of sexually active young unmarried females did not use contraceptives during their first intercourse (Forrest and Singh, 1990). Many pregnancies result from females' first sexual experiences, when use of contraceptives is often neglected.

Why do so many teenagers neglect using contraceptives? Part of the problem is lack of knowledge and misinformation concerning birth control and pregnancy. Sex education in the schools takes place to some extent, but it is mired in controversy. The programs often fail to provide information about what leads to pregnancy and how to use and obtain contraceptives. Some parents fear that disseminating such information will only make teenagers more sexually active. But studies have found that sex education does *not* increase the rate of sexual activity among teenagers, and it may actually increase the probability that those who are sexually active will use contraceptives (Zelnick and Young, 1982; Hillman et al., 1991).

Religious and state institutions may also discourage use of contraceptives. The Roman Catholic church, for example, does not approve of the use of contraceptives for anyone. While most U.S. married couples tend to ignore the church's disapproval, teenagers who are active members of the church may be discouraged from using this protection. State and federal laws restrict access to certain types of contraceptives (birth-control pills, diaphragms, and intrauterine devices) by requiring a physician's prescription. Since many teenagers may be reluctant to admit sexual activity to a family doctor, or are unable to afford to see one, they may have limited access to prescribed contraceptives. Planned Parenthood and other clinics do offer free exams and contraceptives, but they are not necessarily located in places easily accessible to teenagers (especially in rural areas). Thus, policies of such institutions as education, religion, and the state contribute to high rates of teenage pregnancy and single parenthood.

In addition, gender socialization may contribute to teenage pregnancies. Traditional gender roles assume male aggression and sexual expertise and female docility and sexual purity. These gender roles often suggest that a "good girl" does not *plan* for a sexual encounter (Kisker, 1985). Guilt over sexual activity, coupled with the **cultural myth of romanticism,** may thus lead some females to avoid contraception: being prepared for sexual intercourse by having contraceptives amounts to admitting that one is sexually active; but a female's sexual activity may be understood or excused if she was "swept off her feet" in the heat of a romantic moment. In this way our cultural definitions of gender-specific appropriate behaviors contribute to single parenthood.

Reasons for the Rise in Other Nontraditional Family Forms

Institutional and cultural arrangements may also encourage other nontraditional family forms in the United States. For example, the lack of paid parental-leave policies and government-supported child-care programs may encourage single-parent households and multihousehold extended families. Other countries, such as Sweden, use income-tax revenues to provide for parental leave during the first year of a child's life, with minimal loss of income for the parents who elect to take such leave. And many governments in Europe at least partially support day-care facilities for children over age 1, thereby ensuring adequate institutional support for parents who must work outside the home but do not want to jeopardize the care and education of their children (Ferber, O'Farrell, and Allen, 1991: 170–171).

Clearly, then, varying family forms to some extent respond to such institutional forces as the dynamics of the economy and state policies, rather than merely reflecting individual choice and diversity in cultural norms. In fact, we can see how institutional changes and arrangements over the past half century have influenced the structure of the family in the United States. In particular, the decline in the value of wages and earnings has forced both parents in a household to participate in the formal labor market to maintain the family income and in many cases just to remain above poverty. Increasing divorce rates have also sent many women to work in order to provide for themselves and their children. But wage inequalities in the formal labor market mean that more women, especially those who are the sole providers for their families, will struggle to avoid poverty and many will not succeed. The lack of affordable dependent care for young children, persons with disabilities, and the elderly means that many families (and most often women) have to assume responsibility for kin from outside the traditional nuclear family, whether in one or more households. For example, the U.S. Bureau of the Census (1990) found that in 1987 almost 13 percent of children under age 15 whose mothers were employed in the formal labor market were cared for by relatives other than their parents; more than half of these children were cared for by their grandparents (Ferber, O'Farrell, and Allen, 1991: 78). The proportion was even higher among children under age 5: 24 percent were cared for by relatives other than their parents (Ferber, O'Farrell, and Allen, 1991: 80). Finally, because most state and local governments, as well as most corporations, do not recognize the legitimacy of cohabiting couples, such couples must increasingly rely on extended networks or communities of friends and kinship ties for financial help to cover medical costs and living expenses during retirement.

Does the diversity of family forms mean that the institution of the family in the United States is in a state of crisis? We don't think so. The impact of powerful institutions such as the economy make the traditional nuclear family untenable for many people. Yet other family forms develop to ensure the survival and well-being of societal members. The institution of the family is not breaking down, but it is undergoing substantial change. Whether all the changes are to the good is a matter of considerable debate and a worthy subject for social science research.

POVERTY AND FAMILIES

Institutional forces not only influence family forms but also affect the experiences of families. We see this most clearly in the different patterns of poverty shown in Figure 14.3. The U.S. Bureau of the Census (1994) found that in 1993 single-parent families, especially those headed by a female, were far more likely than married couples to be poor. And families of color were more likely than white families to be poor. Why do such patterns exist? How can we understand them in the context of our current economic climate?

The Effect of State Policies

Wage inequality (see Chapters 6 and 11) makes it more difficult for women of all races than for married couples and men to provide for their families and rise above poverty levels. For the same reason, African American and Latino married couples and single parents find doing so more difficult than their white counterparts. The inadequacy of the minimum wage means that even when a father works full-time, year-round, he may not earn enough money to provide adequately for his family. His spouse must also participate in the formal labor market. Even when both parents work, it is not always possible for the family to remain above poverty. Unfortunately, most social welfare programs that provide assistance to the poor are specifically designed to aid *single mothers* and their children. Such a policy

Not all family forms are equally susceptible to poverty in the United States. Which are more likely to be stricken by poverty? Why? (*Source:* U.S. Bureau of the Census, *Poverty in the United States: 1990,* Current Population Reports, Series P60-175, Washington, DC: U.S. Government Printing Office, 1991.)

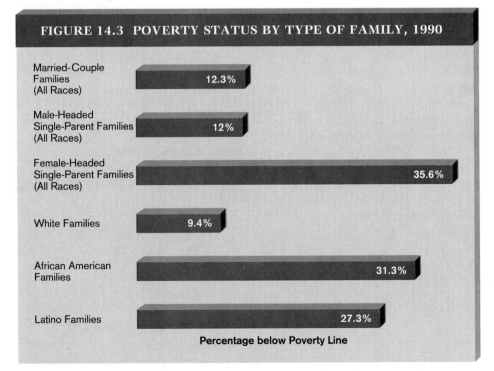

FIGURE 14.3 POVERTY STATUS BY TYPE OF FAMILY, 1990

Married-Couple Families (All Races) — 12.3%

Male-Headed Single-Parent Families (All Races) — 12%

Female-Headed Single-Parent Families (All Races) — 35.6%

White Families — 9.4%

African American Families — 31.3%

Latino Families — 27.3%

Percentage below Poverty Line

discourages partners from remaining together during serious economic hardship.

State policy may, on the other hand, improve rather than aggravate the economic circumstances of some families. Although African American and Latino families are more likely than white families to be in poverty, not all families of color are poor. In fact, the number of African American middle-class families has grown since 1988 (U.S. Bureau of the Census, 1994). Such growth suggests that state programs aimed at providing equal educational opportunities and prohibiting discrimination in employment are having an impact.

Other research demonstrates the effect of state policies on the economic well-being of various family forms. Federal economic policies of the 1970s and 1980s that reduced support for women and children, for example, heralded an era of **feminization of poverty** (Pearce, 1978), in which an increasing proportion of the poor were female-headed families (see also Stallard, Ehrenreich, and Sklar, 1983). The term "feminization of poverty" has been commonly used in the mass media to describe the increased presence of women in poverty, but its usage has come to suggest that women have either chosen to be poor (by electing to stay on welfare to remain home with their children, for example) or somehow brought poverty on themselves (by leaving their marriages, for instance). An increasing number of observers prefer instead to refer to the **pauperization of motherhood,** a concept that more accurately points to the *institutional* forces that have impoverished women (Folbre, 1985; see also Amott, 1993).

In an analysis of federal economic policies since World War II, Judith Treas (1983) found that supply-side policies emphasizing economic expan-

State policies and a culture of patriarchy often combine to impoverish single mothers. Here a single mother prepares for work while her teenage daughter prepares her own lunch for school. Not unlike many other single mothers, this office worker may find it difficult to afford many of the things that two-parent, dual-income families take in stride, such as the cost of her child's education.

sion as a solution to poverty (such as those implemented by the Reagan and Bush administrations) were advantageous only to traditional two-parent (particularly middle-class) families. In contrast, policies that emphasized transfers of wealth through welfare programs (such as those that began during the New Deal under Franklin Roosevelt) or opened up economic opportunities (the War on Poverty under Lyndon Johnson) tended to benefit single-parent families and the poor. The state, then, can play an influential role in determining the economic viability of various family forms. Under certain policies family forms other than the traditional two-parent nuclear family may be economic liabilities.

The Effect of Marital Dissolution

Marital dissolution provides another glimpse into the economic effect of institutional forces on family forms. Marriages are dissolved either by divorce or by death of one of the partners. Research shows that in both cases, women tend to suffer long-term negative economic consequences while men do not (Holden and Smock, 1991). Poverty rates for women, for example, have a strong tendency to be higher after divorce than during marriage (Duncan and Hoffman, 1985; Morgan, 1989). Many studies demonstrate that female-headed households have a much greater tendency than male-headed households to be poor (see Figure 14.3). This is true regardless of the age of the head of household (Sawhill, 1988; McLanahan et al., 1989). Other studies have found a range of erosion in women's standard of living following divorce, from about a 30 percent economic decline (Mott and Moore, 1978; Duncan and Hoffman, 1985) to as much as a 50 percent decline (Weiss, 1984; Weitzman, 1985).

In contrast, marital dissolution tends to *improve* men's standard of living. While women's ratio of income to needs drops by at least 50 percent following divorce (Burkhauser and Duncan, 1989), the ratio for men increases by 42 percent, even after deductions for child support and alimony (Weitzman, 1985). Why does this happen? Research suggests that institutional forces are at work here, particularly in state policies and labor-market practices. For example, on the assumption that women are more appropriate caregivers than men, courts tend to award women physical custody of children in a divorce, thereby reducing the economic responsibility fathers must bear. Even when courts order that fathers pay child support, few fathers comply fully, particularly after the first year. In any case, the amounts of the payments tend to be less than the actual costs of raising children (Weitzman, 1988; Seltzer, 1989). In addition, sex inequalities in the formal labor market help generate greater incomes for husbands than for wives (Sorensen and McLanahan, 1987; Treas, 1987). Together, these factors produce a situation in which "men retain a larger share of the family's income, while their economic needs decrease more than their income" (Holden and Smock, 1991).

The extent of a woman's decline in economic status after divorce seems to be related to class and race. The greatest decline following divorce occurs for women whose predivorce family incomes were highest. Weitzman (1985) found that these women suffered a 71 percent drop in income, while those with the lowest predivorce family incomes suffered a drop of 23 percent. Duncan and Hoffman (1985) found that the income of families of African American women dropped by almost 50 percent following divorce. They also showed that while the poverty rate for white women with above-median family incomes during marriage was only about 4 percent after divorce, the comparable rate for African American women was over 30 percent (Duncan and Hoffman, 1985).

The factors that seem to intensify the negative economic consequences of marital dissolution for women, then, appear to be related to gender roles in traditional nuclear families and to wage inequities based on sex and race in the formal labor market.

Research demonstrates that the economic effects of widowhood are often just as disadvantageous for women as divorce. For example, in one study poverty rates for women increased from 9 to 42 percent following the death of their husbands (Hurd and Wise, 1989). And while higher prewidowhood incomes may offer greater protection from postwidowhood poverty, women in higher-income groups are more likely to suffer a significant decline in their ratio of income to needs than women whose prewidowhood incomes were lower (Smith and Zick, 1986; Holden, 1990).

The age of the wife at the onset of widowhood significantly affects her chance of poverty: widows younger than 60 are more likely to fall into poverty (Zick and Smith, 1986; Holden et al., 1988). This is because in many insurance policies greater benefits accrue to an older widow and because younger widows with children may face restrictions and inequalities in the formal labor market (Holden and Smock, 1991). Also, federal social security policy tends to penalize younger widows with no children; they are not eligible for the survivor benefits normally extended to children, and they are too young to collect social security benefits themselves (Holden, 1990; Holden and Smock, 1991).

Some husbands may provide their surviving wives with protection from possible poverty through their pension funds, but only if the husbands are vested (that is, they have paid into the insurance for a long enough period of time, usually five to ten years). However, some pension funds do not extend any benefits to the surviving spouse; others may offer only a one-time lump-sum payment; and still others may deny the surviving partner any benefits until such time as the deceased would have become eligible to collect benefits as a retiree (Holden, 1990; Holden and Smock, 1991). Provisions that deny benefits altogether for widows or delay benefits for younger widows push women into poverty at the time of widowhood. In addition, while husbands may try to protect their partners from poverty in widowhood through private life insurance, research shows that they tend to seriously underinsure themselves (Auerbach and Kotlikoff, 1987).

Certain state policies can aggravate the economic disadvantages women confront. For example, the state may not enforce child-support payments or allow for the transfer of property following the death of a partner. And private-sector inequalities (such as wage inequalities, insurance policy inequalities based on age, and inadequate pension provisions) add to the institutional forces that penalize women in such circumstances.

Poverty in Nontraditional Families

State policies and market forces also affect workers' benefits and thus their families' economic well-being, particularly if the workers have adopted a nontraditional family form. Some policies, for example, penalize families that are based on cohabitation rather than marriage. Workers in gay male and lesbian couples, as well as in cohabitating heterosexual couples, often find that their partners are not covered as dependents under health insurance policies or as beneficiaries on pension and life insurance policies. Similarly, individuals in such relationships are frequently denied the right to participate in decision-making concerning care and continued life support of their partners in times of serious illness.

Some of this may be changing, however. Dozens of municipalities, including Hartford, San Francisco, Seattle, and Tacoma Park, recognize relations between cohabitants as legitimate and, upon application, will certify them as licensed domestic partnerships, much like licensed marriages. The city of Atlanta recently extended medical insurance coverage for "domestic partners" of its employees. Moreover, a small, but growing, number of corporations recognize the legitimacy of cohabitation in their policies. Ben and Jerry's Homemade, Inc., extends the same benefits, including health and pension benefits, to cohabitants that married partners enjoy at the firm. The Lotus Development Corporation has a domestic-partners plan for gay male and lesbian couples (but not for heterosexual cohabitants) so that they may receive family benefits. The firm's reasoning behind its homosexuals-only plan is that heterosexuals can marry to receive family benefits whereas gays and lesbians cannot. And Levi-Strauss has recently become the largest U.S. corporation to recognize the need to extend benefits to cohabitants (Ames et al., 1992). Such policies may help prevent poverty in nontraditional families in the event of a serious illness or retirement.

FAMILY DYNAMICS AND FAMILY ISSUES

We have seen how economic and state institutions can affect the economic well-being of various family forms. Those institutions also affect what occurs between family members. How do institutional forces affect the internal dynamics of families? For example, how do changes in the labor market affect the domestic division of labor within families? How might changes in the economy affect the role of children within families? How do state policies and the economy affect violence within families? And how might state policy affect reproductive and parenting rights of young women, gay males and lesbians, and people with disabilities?

Family Violence

We like to think of the family as providing a safe, satisfying and secure "haven in a heartless world" (Lasch, 1977). Unfortunately, this is not always the case: all too often the family is an arena in which people experience severe violence. Until recently, we assumed that only the mentally ill physically abused their spouses or children and that such abuse occurred only in poor families. However, research by Gelles and Straus (1988) has challenged these beliefs. Interviews with adults in 6,002 families revealed startling evidence that family violence and abuse are widespread: within one year, violence between marital partners occurred in one in six families; and 70 percent of parents used some form of physical violence against their children. Although most of the violence against children took the form of spanking, 14 percent of the children were victims of more severe attacks. In addition, 20 percent of the children hit their parents, including elderly parents; 10 percent of these attacks carried a high risk of physical injury to the victim. And children inflicted physical violence on one another more frequently than on any other member of the family. Although *reported* rates of family violence are highest among low-income people, violence was, in fact, common in families of all income levels. Mental illness was linked to only 10 percent of the acts of family violence.

If poverty and mental illness are not the principal causes of family violence, then how do we explain it? Gelles and Straus (1988) noted that family violence is not a new phenomenon. They argued that violence is related to the institution of the family itself, for it is a structure that puts individuals in close and constant contact with one another. Such a structure is likely to foster emotionally intense relationships simply because of the unrelenting proximity of family and household members. Constant contact may also increase the chances that some household members will become easy or convenient targets against whom other members unleash their everyday frustrations. The roles given to members of a family according to their age and sex also play a part in domestic violence. For example, conflicts between children and adults, or husband and wife, may reflect differences in power among members and may be a natural outcome of family roles built around age and gender inequalities. Using violence to resolve conflicts may also derive from social and cultural influences that encourage or reinforce violence. Many violent abusers were themselves abused or observed abuse in their families. Such experiences may lead them to see violence as an acceptable and normal way to resolve conflict. Furthermore, books, television, movies, and videos often treat the use of force as an understandable and acceptable form of behavior. Violence is a standard component of media entertainment, including sports. And the national jubilation that accompanies military victories such as the U.S. defeat of Iraq relates the use of violence to heroic acts. Gelles and Straus concluded that this combination of direct and indirect socialization experiences contributes to an atmosphere in which many forms of family violence are viewed as "normal" violence, because they are accepted and given legitimacy in the larger culture.

Another problem is that much family violence in the United States occurs out of public view. Americans value their privacy, so behaviors within the family such as physical violence and abuse are far less subject to public scrutiny and control than the same behaviors in many nonfamily settings. For example, we do not tolerate a teacher beating a student, an employer beating an employee, or a religious leader abusing followers (whether children or adults). Thus, using physical violence against another person in most institutional settings outside the family is construed as assault and battery. But within the family, violence is often viewed as a way for parents to discipline their children or as an adjunct to everyday marital conflicts. The reluctance of courts and local police to interfere in domestic disputes leaves family victims of physical violence unprotected and reinforces the legitimacy of violence as a means of coping with or resolving conflicts.

Finally, Gelles and Straus pointed to the many sources of mounting stress confronting families in the United States that may contribute to violent behavior. The ravages of poverty and unemployment increase stress in families; as a result, rates of violence tend to be highest among poor families. However, Straus and his colleagues (1980) emphasized that violence is not restricted to poor families alone. Stress factors other than poverty afflict higher-income families, including performance of household responsibilities while balancing two jobs or careers, lack of adequate day care for children, responsibility for aging or ailing parents or dependents with disabilities, and conflicting schedules. Let's examine these stresses and their effects on the family.

Sources of Stress in Families   Many families must depend on two incomes in order to maintain a middle-class standard of living. In a 1988 survey, 51

Assault and battery and other forms of physical violence are often treated by police as a private family affair when it occurs behind closed doors in a domestic setting. An increasing number of police departments, however, are beginning to treat violence in the home as they would if it occurred on the streets between strangers. Here, police are arresting a man accused of assaulting his partner, who is clearly shaken by the attack.

percent of the respondents felt they were working harder than they had been five years earlier, and 20 percent said they were working harder because things had gotten more expensive and they were trying just to maintain their standard of living (Research and Forecasts, 1988). And as we noted in Chapter 11, in a 1991 survey, 54 percent of the respondents said they worried "a great deal" about having their standard of living decline, and another 30 percent said they worried "a little" (Time/Cable News Network, 1991). A 1992 Harris poll found similar results (Harris and Associates, 1992). Such anxieties concerning their ability to maintain their standard of living often leads both partners in a two-parent middle-class family to enter the paid labor market.

Changes in the work force and the increasing frequency of dual-income couples has led to another, sometimes stressful situation: women earning higher salaries than their partners. In a society that grants the male status for being the family provider, this situation creates **status inconsistency.** Status inconsistency can also occur when one's educational level of achievement is much greater than one's occupational status, a source of stress for both men and women. This stress becomes increasingly likely in an economy in which jobs are relatively scarce and competition is high, since people with higher education credentials find themselves unemployed or underemployed. Gelles and Straus (1988) found that status inconsistency was a major factor in the profile of the battering husband.

How do two-earner families cope with domestic responsibilities? When both parents work, they frequently arrange their employment schedules so that they can take shifts caring for their children. While such an arrangement reduces the expense of day care, it also means that the parents rarely see each other. One study in the United States found that about one-third of the parents in families with young children work opposite shifts to accommodate child care (Presser, 1988). This arrangement produces stress because it severely reduces the partners' ability to interact as a couple and their ability to interact together with their children as a family. Such stress is likely to intensify for some families in the United States: recent trends suggest an increase in the three-income family, in which one parent takes one job while the other moonlights at two.

Most families know how stressful it is to balance employment with child care. In one survey, 82 percent of the respondents believed that middle-class U.S. families could no longer survive with just one paycheck, and most agreed that "child care facilities are indispensable if families are going to continue to maintain their standard of living" (Harris and Associates, 1989). Yet the high expense of daily child care, and the relative scarcity of adequate care facilities, can only add to the stress of families.

Child-care difficulties become particularly acute in single-parent families, where something of a vicious cycle occurs. Single-parent families tend to have lower incomes relative to two-parent families, and the parent has greater difficulties securing and paying for adequate child care that would enable him or her to maintain a job. One study found that in 1988 the annual cost of care for at least 30 hours per week for a child under the age of 5 averaged $1,820 (Hofferth, 1988). The study also found that low-income families paid almost one-fourth of their incomes, while higher-income families spent an average of one-tenth. Single-parent families spent higher proportions of their family incomes for child care, on average, than two-earner families. Of course, higher-quality child-care arrangements cost more than less-than-adequate child care.

In the absence of good alternatives, low-income families and single-parent families have little flexibility in the care they can choose for their children. Almost 12 percent of the children whose parents work in the formal labor force are cared for by relatives, usually grandmothers (Waite et al., 1988). This arrangement, while cheaper than day-care centers, may introduce conflict in families, since it extends the dependence of grown children on their aging parents even as they are now raising their own children.

Many families in all classes may suffer the added stresses of caring for elderly relatives or family members with disabilities. A 1991 panel on employer policies and working families found that 22 percent of people in the United States over the age of 65 were disabled, and 9 percent of the elderly were severely disabled to the point of needing help with many daily activities (such as preparing meals and eating, shopping for groceries, and bathing). The study found that most of the elderly with disabilities were cared for by their families and friends: "Of the 1.2 million 'frail elderly' . . ., 10.7 percent lived alone, 40 percent lived with only a spouse, and 35.7 percent lived with their children, with or without a spouse" (Ferber, O'Farrell, and Allen, 1991: 66). Other studies found that only one-fifth of the elderly with disabilities and half of the elderly with severe disabilities were cared for in nursing homes (Stone et al., 1987; Rivlin and Wiener, 1988).

Nursing-home care does not mean that family members are free from responsibilities: they visit relatives in nursing homes, and many often assist with chores such as laundry, shopping, financial management, management of medical appointments, and supervision of nursing-home care. And such care is not inexpensive: the average annual cost of nursing-home care per person in 1988 ranged between $22,000 and $25,000 (Price and O'Shaughnessy, 1988). Such costs influence families to assume greater and greater burdens of at-home care for the elderly, including the elderly with disabilities. One study noted that "a major conflict in work-family relations is the number of working-age relatives who work part-time or do not seek employment because of the need to care for elderly relatives" (Ferber, O'Farrell, and Allen, 1991: 66–68). In the absence of adequate, affordable nursing-care facilities, caring for elderly family members can easily become a major source of stress in families, contributing to increasing family violence in homes at all income levels.

It is easy to see that there are a variety of serious pressures on families in the United States. Any one of these pressures, or a combination of several, could raise a family's stress level so high that violence becomes increasingly possible. Gelles and Straus (1988) found that the greater the number of stressful factors present in a family, the greater the rate of child abuse in that family. In more than one-third of the families in their study that experienced ten or more stressful factors, parents admitted using violence against children in the previous year; this rate was "100 percent greater than the rate for households experiencing only one stressful event"

(Gelles and Straus, 1988: 86). Violence, then, is not something that occurs only in poor families or in families where mental illness prevails.

Another interesting and important finding by Gelles and Straus confounds conventional assumptions concerning domestic violence: there was no difference between the rates of child abuse in African American and white homes. Although African Americans do have higher rates of unemployment and lower average incomes than whites (both contributing factors to family violence), Gelles and Straus found a critical mitigating factor: extensive social networks and ties to the community. As a group, African Americans were more involved in family and community activities than whites, maintained greater contact and ties with family, and relied more on relatives for child care and financial help. "It was apparent that the extensive social networks that black families develop and maintain insulate them from the severe economic stresses they also experience, and thus reduce what otherwise would have been a higher rate of parental violence" (Gelles and Straus, 1988: 86).

Power Differentials in the Family In addition to the stress factors associated with institutional arrangements in the economy and the labor market and those connected with state policies, there is another element that contributes to domestic violence. Gelles and Straus (1988) noted a factor long emphasized by feminist analyses of family violence: power differentials in the home were one of the most important factors affecting spouse abuse and violence (see Walker, 1984, 1989; Browne, 1987, 1993). "The risk of intimate violence is the greatest when all the decision making in a home is concentrated in the hands of one of the partners. Couples who report the most sharing of decisions report the lowest rates of violence" (Gelles and Straus, 1988: 92). Thus, gender roles that reinforce power differentials, vesting males with greater power and control in decision-making, contribute to the likelihood of domestic violence.

Analyzing domestic violence in terms of power structures offers new insights into gender relations. For example, observers on all sides of the controversy concerning family violence agree that while women do sometimes batter their partners, the vast majority of batterers are men. Why should that be so? Conventional explanations suggest a biological or psychological answer, which might lead us to think of men as simply more innately aggressive than women. But such explanations do not address why men are more likely to vent their frustrations and anger against their female partners than against other potential targets, such as male friends and colleagues or male authority figures. Nor do they address why stress on women is not as likely to escalate into physical violence against male partners. A power structure analysis leads us to issues of dominance and power differentials based on gendered social structures (see Gordon, 1988): men more commonly attack women because women are more often socially perceived as subordinate, weaker, and less likely to strike back. In a society that ordains men as "naturally" more powerful and dominant, and in which most social institutions are dominated by men, it is likely that battering by men will be accepted as unfortunate but normal. This analysis suggests a route to change that doesn't depend on psychological explanations: to reduce domestic violence, particularly as it victimizes women, we must address gendered power differentials.

Reducing Violence in Families   Taken together, the studies by Gelles and Straus (1988), Walker (1984, 1989), and Browne (1993) cite important influences that the culture, the state, and the economy have on family violence. But their research also provides encouraging insights into the role these factors may play in *reducing* that violence. In a comparative analysis of family violence between 1975 and 1985, Gelles and Straus (1988: 109) found that child abuse had declined by 47 percent in 1985 and that wife abuse had declined by 27 percent. Several areas of change in that ten-year period helped reduce family violence, including changes in family structure, the economy, alternatives for abused women, treatment programs, and deterrence. Let's look at these changes.

The structure of the U.S. family has changed since 1975: the average age upon marriage and that upon the birth of one's first child have increased. The older one is when one marries, the older one is likely to be when bearing children. Such factors are associated with reduced rates of child abuse. In addition, many families in the United States are becoming more egalitarian: decision-making and power are becoming increasingly shared by partners, rather than being concentrated in the hands of one (usually the male). This change is associated with reduced rates of spouse abuse.

Furthermore, the economy in 1985 was somewhat healthier than that in 1975, with higher median family income. Since limited economic means to support a family is a stress factor associated with family violence, it is not surprising to find that a healthier economic environment produces lower rates of domestic violence. The warning signal in the 1990s is the nation's rising unemployment rates, which increase the likelihood of rising rates of domestic violence as well. So improving the economy is an important measure for reducing domestic violence.

Gelles and Straus cited the competing demands facing dual-occupation families as a stress factor that can lead to violence. However, other research suggests otherwise. Women may sometimes derive a greater sense of self-worth from juggling multiple roles simultaneously, while men may benefit from being less pressured about the family's financial well-being as well as having more opportunities to care for and spend time with their children (Crosby, 1991; Gerson, 1993). This finding calls into question Gelles and Straus's emphasis on psychological stress as an explanation for family violence. Indeed, female participation in the paid labor force may reduce power differentials based on income within the family and therefore may reduce the potential for family violence. Providing more support for women's participation in the paid labor force could be an important way to reduce family violence.

Other social changes have also contributed to women's empowerment in the home. Women no longer need to resign themselves to abuse. Since 1975 battered women have more alternatives, such as programs and shelters for both abuse victims and their children. While these projects still cannot support all who need them, their increased availability encourages women to realize that abuse need not be tolerated. Moreover, women's increased participation in the formal labor market provides them with an economic alternative to reliance on an abusive partner for financial support.

Since 1975 there have also been more innovative treatment programs for both abuse victims and their abusers. Most states now have laws that mandate reporting of cases of suspected child and partner abuse by teachers, health practitioners, and social workers. Findings of abuse often lead to mandatory attendance in a treatment program. More of these programs are needed, but at least their increased availability has helped reduce domestic violence.

Legal mandates for protection of abuse victims are far from perfect, however. A false accusation by an ignorant or vindictive teacher, for example, can tear a family apart. And given what we know about race and class assumptions in evaluating children in the classroom, the chances that even a well-meaning teacher may define poor and racial minority families as abusive are strong. Moreover, laws governing child abuse frequently tread a fine line between legal protection for abuse victims and civil liberties concerning parental rights and the right to privacy. All too often these laws still offer inadequate protection for victims of domestic violence.

Despite these difficulties, changes in the laws have increasingly made it clear that abuse will no longer be tolerated simply because it occurs behind closed doors. Many states now treat violence in the home as they would any other case of assault and battery, with arrest and jail time for offenders. Such was not the case in 1975.

As Gelles and Straus have shown, the same cultural and institutional factors that can greatly influence the acceptance of family violence can also serve to reduce that violence. Hence, policies that reinforce a healthy economy, that challenge conventional and unequal gender roles, and that provide social and economic supports to abuse victims are important in curbing and perhaps eliminating violence within families.

Reproductive and Parenting Rights and Issues

The choice to reproduce is largely understood to be a private matter, but for some families this decision is controlled or limited by the state. In such cases, the tension between the institutions of state and family affect decision-making dynamics between family members. For example, some people with disabilities must struggle against state laws or state agencies that interfere with their decision to bear and raise children. State agencies may encourage sterilization of people with severe mental or physical disabilities or refuse to extend social welfare benefits for children born of parents with disabilities (see Ames et al., 1992).

Several myths prompt this social and legal resistance to reproduction and parenting by people with disabilities. These myths include the notions that disabilities are inherited or contagious, that the presence of persons with disabilities is depressing and should not be inflicted on the children, and that physical mobility is critical for adequate child rearing (Shaul, Dowling, and Laden, 1985). None of these myths is supported by evidence. The vast majority of physical disabilities are not inherited. Even those that are inherited do not necessarily cause offspring to lead less-than-full lives. We base assumptions about the limitations posed by disabilities and the fear of their inheritance on the false notion that people with disabilities are unhealthy or sick. But those who have disabilities do not see themselves in that way; disability is viewed as the master status more by able-bodied observers than by persons with disabilities themselves. People with disabilities tend to focus their lives, much as everyone else does, on the demands posed by work, family, and a productive and full life. Finally, many people with physical disabilities and mobility restrictions are able to raise children through creative adjustments to the challenges posed by the disabilities (Shaul, Dowling, and Laden, 1985). Institutional supports, such as access ramps to buildings and streets, wheelchair-accessible public transportation, brail notations in public areas, and so forth, can make these adjustments easier. Thus, any restrictions posed by physical disabilities for raising children appear to be based more on cultural assumptions and the failure to provide institutional supports than on any intrinsic limitations posed by the disabilities themselves.

Another issue of reproductive rights involves the right to end unwanted pregnancies. State-imposed restrictions on this right can affect decision-making processes between family members. For example, some states, such as Pennsylvania, have restricted access to abortions for minors. The laws in such states require parental notification when teenagers seek abortions and parental permission before they can receive abortions. These

Many people with disabilities find they must struggle against state laws and agencies to preserve and protect their rights to parent. Although state laws and agencies often assume that people with disabilities are unable to give children proper care, many such persons creatively adjust to the disability to become quite competent as parents. This partially blind woman is taking her baby for a walk with the stroller in one hand and a seeing-eye dog in the other.

laws may pose problems for teenagers whose pregnancy is the result of incest or rape. Incest victims, for example, may face extreme danger in seeking permission for abortion from an enraged incestuous father. Thus, these laws can contribute to an increase in family violence.

Gay males and lesbians often find that the state interferes in their rights to parent. In custody battles, the courts often resist the right of gay and lesbian parents to retain custody of their children, regardless of their parenting abilities. Most custody decisions are made in state domestic relations courts, where the judge (rather than a jury) acts as fact finder and determines what is in "the best interest" of the child. While some state statutes require the demonstration of the existence of harm to the child in order to wrest custody from the parent, other statutes allow the judge to consider *future* potential harm to the child. In the latter situation, the bias of the judge regarding the "fitness" of gay males and lesbians to parent becomes a major influence in custody determinations (Rivera, 1987). In the accompanying box, a lesbian mother poignantly describes the personal consequences of such bias. There are some indications that gay and lesbian parents are winning significant custody battles, particularly in Delaware, Vermont, Maine, New Jersey, New York, Massachusetts, California, Washington, Oregon, and Alaska. In these states, supreme courts have determined that a parent's sexual orientation should not be a factor in determining parental fitness (Rivera, 1987).

Some adoption agencies have allowed gays and lesbians to adopt openly gay adolescent children, but only when the child has expressed "a clear and definite sense of his or her sexual identity" (Raymond, 1992: 119). Such a requirement limits the possibilities of children who need caring adoptive homes, since "clear and definite" sexual identities tend to occur relatively late in adolescence (on average, age 17 for men and age 22 for women). Adoption agencies erroneously assume that gay males and lesbians can be effective parents only of gay children, thereby focusing solely on the sexual identity of the prospective adoptive parents and ignoring the possible parenting talents they may have.

Such challenges to parental rights also confront heterosexuals. Take, for example, the case of Jennifer Ireland, a single mother in Michigan, who lost custody of her preschool-age daughter in 1994 because she enrolled the child in day care to attend college full-time. The judge in this case awarded custody of the child to the father, who was also a full-time student, because his mother could provide child care.

These statutes, agency practices, and legal precedents challenge our definition of family and parent. But they also highlight the role of the state and of social service agencies as institutions influencing the outcome of issues such as reproduction and parenting rights.

Contradictions between Work and Family

Conflicting demands between participation in the formal labor market and family responsibilities may produce tensions, particularly for women. When family responsibilities mount, adding care of the elderly, for example, to child care and housework, it is largely women who must balance them with the demands of work in the formal labor market. A survey of

In this excerpt, a Native American lesbian parent records her feelings after losing her child in a custody battle with her former husband. Her domestic partner, Ellen, supports her in her grief.

1978

I am awakened by the dream. In the dream, my daughter is dead. Her father is returning her body to me in pieces. He keeps her heart. I thought I screamed . . . Patricia! I sit up in bed, swallowing air as if for nourishment. The dream remains in the air. I rise to go to her room. Ellen tries to lead me back to bed, but I have to see once again. I open her door . . . she is gone. The room empty, lonely. They said it was in her best interests. How can it be? She is only six, a baby who needs her mothers. She loves us. This is not happening. I will not believe this. Oh god, I think I have died. Night after night, Ellen holds me as I shake. Our sobs stifling the air in our room. We lie in our bed and try to give comfort. My mind can't think beyond last week when she left. I would have killed him if I'd had the chance. He took her hand and pulled her to the car. The look in his eyes of triumph. It was a contest to him. I know he will teach her to hate us. He will! I see her dear face. Her face looking out the back window of his car. Her mouth forming the word over and over . . . Mommy Mama. Her dark braids tied with red yarn. Her front teeth missing. Her overalls with the yellow flower on the pocket, embroidered by Ellen's hands. So lovingly she sewed the yellow wool. Patricia waiting quietly until she was finished. Ellen promising to teach her the designs . . . chain stitch, french knot, split stitch. How Patricia told everyone that Ellen made the flower just for her. So proud of her overalls. I open the closet door. Almost everything is gone. A few little things hang there limp, abandoned. I pull a blue dress from a hanger and take it back to my room. Ellen tries to take it away from me, but I hold on, the soft, blue cotton smelling like her. How is it possible to feel such pain and live? Ellen?! She croons my name . . . Mary . . . Mary . . . I love you. She sings me to sleep.

1978

When I get home from work, there is a letter from Patricia. I make coffee and wait for Ellen, pacing the rooms of our apartment. My back is sore from the line, bending over and down, screwing the handles on the doors of the flashy cars moving by at an incredible pace. My work protects me from questions. The guys making jokes at my expense. Some of them touching my shoulder lightly and briefly, as a sign of understanding. The few women, eyes averted or smiling at me in sympathy. No one talks. There is no time to talk. There is no room to talk, the noise taking up all space and breath. I carry the letter with me as I move from room to room. Finally I sit at the kitchen table, turning the paper around in my hands. Patricia's printing is large and uneven. The stamp has been glued on half-heartedly and is coming loose. Each time a letter arrives, I dread it, even as I long to hear from my child. I hear Ellen's key in the door. She walks into the kitchen, bringing the smell of the hospital with her. She comes toward me, her face set in new lines, her uniform crumpled and stained, her brown

the effect of elder-care responsibilities on women workers found that, in 1987, 12 percent of the women quit their jobs to care for elderly family members; another 23 percent reduced their work hours; 25 percent took time off from their jobs without pay; and 35 percent rearranged their work hours (Stone et al., 1987).

Sometimes a woman's attempt to balance the competing demands of work and family threatens her livelihood. One study describes a woman

> **"Lesbian. The word that makes them panic, makes them afraid, makes them destroy children. The word that dares them."**

hair pulled back in an imitation of a french twist. She knows there is a letter. I kiss her and bring mugs of coffee to the table. We look into each others' eyes. She reaches for my hand, bringing it to her lips. Her hazel eyes are steady in her round face. I open the letter. Dear Mommy. I am fine. Daddy got me a new bike. My big teeth are coming in. We are going to see Grandma for my birthday. Daddy got me new shoes. She doesn't ask about Ellen. I imagine her father standing over her, watching the words painstakingly being printed. Coaxing her. Coaching her. The letter becomes ugly. I frantically tear it in bits and scatter them out the window. The wind scoops the pieces into a tight fist before strewing them in the street. A car drives over the paper, shredding it to mud and garbage. Ellen makes a garbled sound. "I'll leave. If it will make it better, I'll leave." I quickly hold her as the dusk swirls around the room and engulfs us. "Don't leave. Don't leave. . . ."

1979

After taking a morning off work to see my lawyer, I come home, not caring if I call in. Not caring, for once, at the loss in pay. Not caring. My lawyer says there is nothing more we can do. I must wait. As if we have done anything else. He has custody and calls the shots. We must wait and see how long it takes for him to get tired of being mommy and daddy. So . . . I wait. I open the door to Patricia's room. Ellen keeps it dusted and cleaned, in case she will be allowed to visit us. The yellow and bright blue walls are a mockery. I walk to the windows, begin to systematically tear down the curtains. I

slowly start to rip the cloth apart. I enjoy hearing the sounds of destruction. Faster and faster, I tear the material into long strips. What won't come apart with my hands, I pull at with my teeth. Looking for more to destroy, I gather the sheets and bedspread in my arms and wildly shred them to pieces. Grunting and sweating, I am pushed by rage and the searing wound in my soul. Like a wolf, caught in a trap, gnawing at her own leg to set herself free, I begin to beat my breasts to deaden the pain inside. A noise gathers in my throat and finds the way out. I begin a scream that turns to howling, then turns to hoarse choking. I want to take my fists, my strong fists, my brown fists, and smash the world until it bleeds. Bleeds! And all the judges in their flapping robes, and the fathers who look for revenge, are ground, ground into dust and disappear with the wind. The word . . . lesbian. Lesbian. The word that makes them panic, makes them afraid, makes them destroy children. The word that dares them. Lesbian. *I am one.* Even for Patricia, even for her, I will not cease to be! As I kneel amidst the colorful scraps, Raggedy Anns smiling up at me, my chest gives a sigh. My heart slows to its normal speech. I feel the blood pumping outward to my veins, carrying nourishment and life. I strip the room naked. I close the door.

Source: Beth Brant, "A Long Story," excerpted in Virginia Cyrus (ed.), *Experiencing Race, Class, and Gender* (Mountain View, CA: Mayfield, 1993), pp. 304–307; originally published in Beth Brant (ed.), *A Gathering of Spirit: A Collection of North American Indian Women* (Ithaca, NY: Firebrand Books, 1984).

who tried working reduced hours in order to care for her small child, only to find her boss implying that she may not have her job for very long under this arrangement. She noted, "If I go back [to my job] full time pretty soon, I'll be okay. But if I keep this up much longer, I won't be. I may already be out. My boss says, 'You're walking alone right now. You're not committed here'" (Hochschild and Machung, 1989: 91). Another woman in the study, struggling with the needs of her young child (who had an ear infection) and her job, felt the pressure to reconcile the conflict by quitting her job: "I'm on the verge of quitting. . . . I'm supposed to go on a business trip tomorrow, and I have a strong urge to say, 'I'm not going.' . . . The worst thing I could possibly do [at work] is to acknowledge that my children have an impact on my life" (Hochschild and Machung, 1989: 95–96).

Why do the demands of work and family collide as they do, and why do women bear the brunt of that antagonism? Although African American women and white working-class women have a history of working outside the home for pay (see Eisenstein, 1983), the world of the formal labor market was, until the end of World War II, largely defined as a male domain, and women's work was said to belong in the home. The formal labor market has been slow to recognize the permanent presence of women in the labor force, and so it has failed to take steps to resolve the contradictions between their roles on the job and their roles at home. So has the state: few state policies help reconcile those contradictions.

The same assumptions about women's and men's "appropriate" roles in the labor market also affect the division of labor in the family. After a full day in the formal labor market women frequently come home to work full-time on domestic responsibilities (see Chapter 11). Hochschild and Machung (1989) refer to the household responsibilities facing women after a full day on the job as the *second shift*. Families use a variety of strategies to deal with these conflicting demands, but most of them disadvantage women. Some women, like those we just described, are pressured to quit their jobs or reduce their hours in order to maintain the household, conventionally defined as women's responsibility. Others attempt to negotiate shared responsibilities within their families, with mixed and often unsatisfactory results. At the very least, such attempts frequently create tensions within the family. Men often resent being asked to assume greater responsibilities in the home and share the problems of balancing the competing demands between work and family. One couple in Hochschild and Machung's study tried to define spheres of responsibility by dividing the household chores between upstairs and downstairs; the wife explained:

> I do the upstairs and Evan [her husband] does the downstairs and the dog. So the dog is my husband's problem. But when I was getting the dog outside and getting Joey [their child] ready for childcare, and cleaning up the mess of feeding the cat, and getting the lunches together, and having my son wipe his nose on my outfit so I would have to change—then I was pissed! I felt that I was doing everything. All Evan was doing was getting up, having coffee, reading the paper, and saying, "Well, I have to go now," and often forgetting the lunch I'd bothered to make (Hochschild and Machung, 1989: 44).

We are making some progress toward redefining household responsibilities so that men share these burdens as partners with women, but there is still a long way to go before the notion of the second shift applies to men as well as women.

Of course, the gender inequalities in balancing home and work demands do not necessarily reflect all families in the United States. Research shows that these inequalities are less pronounced among African American couples than white couples (Beckett and Smith, 1981). Part of the reason for this may be that African American women have historically been more likely to participate in the formal labor market than white (and, particularly, middle-class) women. African American families may be more likely to view such participation as a matter of course and as an economic fact of life and therefore more likely to have adjusted to sharing responsibilities more equitably (Huber and Spitze, 1981). Research also shows that the greater likelihood of egalitarian divisions of household labor in African American families is not simply a function of economic necessity: compared with white families, African American families maintain this pattern regardless of the woman's employment status, income, and gender role values (Ross, 1987). However, despite these greater levels of egalitarianism, African American women, like their white counterparts, still remain responsible for most of the more traditionally female-relegated household chores like cooking, cleaning, and doing laundry (Broman, 1988).

A few changes slowly occurring in the workplace are beginning to address the tension between work and family. For example, an increasing number of firms have been instituting **flextime** to allow workers to maintain full-time job status while paying attention to shared responsibilities at home. Some flextime programs enable workers to arrive at their jobs earlier or later than is customary, as long as a full workday is put in. Other arrangements allow employees to work four days for ten hours each day, with three days off to care for family. These flextime arrangements are available to both men and women, facilitating greater sharing of the demands of work and family. However, evidence indicates that affluent professional women, many of whom are childless, use flextime most often. For a variety of reasons, flextime is less viable for others. Some people have jobs that are not time-flexible and cannot be altered, such as teaching or shift work. Others simply don't have the power to negotiate such options with their employers. For example, according to Cynthia Fuchs Epstein (1993), law firms provide flextime, and even emergency child-care assistance, for women attorneys but not for legal secretaries. Thus, flextime arrangements have great potential for easing some tensions between work and family responsibilities for both men and women, but their implementation has been less than perfect and still needs much work.

FUTURE TRENDS

As we have seen, institutions such as the state and the economy are influential factors affecting the family. Not only do these institutions influence the diversity of family forms we observe in the United States; they also affect the relationships between family members as well as the economic and social well-being of the family. Thus, the great diversity of families in the United States does not necessarily indicate a breakdown of traditional values and of the healthy family in the United States; rather, it indicates the broad variety of ways that people cope with pressures from the state and the economy. Since these institutions are such important influences on the family, what future policies are needed to ensure the efficacy of the family, regardless of the form it takes?

One way to answer this question is to examine the experiences of other countries. Many European countries spend freely on social welfare programs that support the family. While the United States devoted only 21.6 percent of its gross domestic product to such expenditures in 1989, European expenditures ranged from 23.3 percent in Italy to 33.7 percent in the Netherlands (Ferber, O'Farrell, and Allen, 1991: 157). On the other hand, the United States devoted the highest proportion of its gross domestic product, 25.8 percent, to military expenditures in 1989, while European countries' military expenditures ranged from 3.1 percent in Italy to 13.2 percent in the United Kingdom (Ferber, O'Farrell, and Allen, 1991: 159). Thus, different priorities affect each country's ability to support the family as an institution.

Many programs that are provided in the United States on a voluntary basis by private corporations are mandated by law in Europe and Canada. Such programs include universal health insurance and pensions for retirement. The reliance on voluntary private coverage in the United States generates inequality in access to benefits: only people who work in the formal labor market are likely to have access to such programs, and since these programs are voluntary for employers, not all workers will in fact receive benefits. Although federal programs (such as Medicaid and social security) provide some benefits to the poor, many people who need these programs are not eligible for them (see Chapter 11). This is an important issue in the United States today, because the labor market is increasingly dominated by service sector, minimum-wage, and (involuntary) part-time jobs (see Chapter 11). It is not surprising that the debate over universal health-care coverage has increasingly dominated our political process over the past decade.

Many European countries also provide parental-leave benefits through national health insurance programs, unemployment insurance, or special parental-leave programs. Employers themselves do not directly pay workers on leave; instead, the state provides parents with pay while they are on leave to care for newborn infants. State payments relieve small employers of an economic burden. Importantly, many of these programs provide leaves for fathers as well as mothers. Of course, the taxpayer ultimately pays for such programs, but the existence of these programs and the willingness of most citizens to pay for them indicates that the family is a political and social priority. Setting such priorities and convincing the population that they are worth paying for continues to be one of the most controversial issues facing elected officials in the United States.

European countries differ a great deal in the amount of benefits they provide. Sweden allows for the most generous benefits: if both parents have been gainfully employed, both may share 270 days of parental leave at 90 percent of their regular salary. They are not required to use all their parental leave at once; rather, it can be spread out over the first four years of the child's life and can be used to care for a sick child. Parents are entitled by law to the same position they had prior to taking parental leave or to an equivalent position (U.S. Department of Health and Human Services, 1985). At the other end of the continuum are Greece and the Netherlands, where maternity leaves are mandated for twelve weeks (Ferber, O'Farrell, and Allen, 1991).

Despite their diversity, all parental-leave policies in Europe are more generous than those provided in the United States, where, despite new laws, parental leave is still provided only on a voluntary and limited basis by many private (especially small-business) employers. Typically, such leaves are unpaid and do not necessarily ensure that parents will still have their jobs when they are ready to return to work. The lack of federal support for paid parental leave, coupled with the scarcity of affordable, adequate day-care facilities, undermines the ability of U.S. families to maintain a middle-class standard of living while caring for their children. The European approach is not perfect, however: it does not provide family-leave policies for workers to care for sick partners or elderly family members. In the face of inadequate affordable nursing-home care, and with increasing numbers of families assuming the care of sick or elderly family members themselves, such programs are clearly needed.

In the area of child care, many European countries provide greater state subsidies for facilities than the United States does. However, like the United States, no European country fully subsidizes child care, and none provides adequate, affordable care for *all* children from infancy on. Thus, child care remains a poorly funded aspect of the tension between family and work, both in Europe and in the United States. In an increasing number of families, single parents and both parents in two-parent families must earn wages in order to survive economically, and they clearly need state support for child care.

CONCLUSION

We all live in structures we refer to as families. The meaning of family, however, may be very different to each of us. What, then, is a family? It is an organized, ongoing, and enduring network of people whose daily interactions provide for the needs and survival of members, regardless of age or gender. Family networks may be confined to a single household or stretch over several households and may be defined by biological ties as well as by ties of choice. They contain one or more adults and may or may not include children.

Despite cultural and media depictions of the conventional nuclear family (consisting of two children and two parents, with the female parent as full-time homemaker-mother and the male parent as sole provider), the typical U.S. family is quite different. In fact, according to U.S. Bureau of the Census figures, the most common family form in the 1990s is the dual-earner family. This is partly because the economy necessitates that both partners work in the paid labor force in order to maintain even a modest middle-class standard of living. In addition, single-parent families (especially female-headed households) have become increasingly common, in part because of relatively high divorce rates, unwed parenthood, and state laws that discourage the presence of male partners in families supported by public welfare programs. Moreover, many couples set up households and maintain a marriagelike relationship despite the absence of state endorsement of that relationship. And, given the disruptive dynamics of the economy, it is not unusual to find multigenerational households or families that extend over several households. Thus, the structure of institutions like the economy and the state greatly influence the structure of the family in the United States.

These institutions also differentially reward or support various family forms. For example, dual-earner families often have an economic advantage over single-earner families; this, of course, depends upon the amount of income each earner gets. For example, an executive making over $200,000 per year can clearly support a family on the basis of that income alone, while two earners working part-time at minimum wage will be unable to manage the same standard of living. Given the growth in low-wage service sector jobs and involuntary part-time work, it is conceivable that even a dual-earner family will have difficulty providing for itself. Moreover, pressures from the economy can introduce stress factors that encourage such dynamics as family violence.

State policies have different effects. Transfer-of-payment state policies favor single-parent families, while trickle-down policies tend to favor two-parent families and males. State policies that do not support day care or dependent care provide greater advantages to two-parent families in which one parent earns enough money to support the entire family, thereby enabling the other parent to remain home and care for dependents. Health insurance and retirement benefits that are extended only to dependents or partners in state-sanctioned relationships may exclude cohabiting couples, both homosexual and heterosexual.

Patterns of institutional discrimination in the labor market also reward some family forms and disadvantage others. For example, income differences based on gender mean that female-headed households suffer more than male-headed households or two-parent households. Income differences based on race mean that African American and Latina female-headed households are likely to be less advantaged than white female-headed households.

Institutional influences from the economy and the state are also likely to affect the internal dynamics of various family forms. Family violence, for example, is most likely to occur when pressures increase. The stress of trying to maintain a single-parent family is increased under conditions of low pay; the stress of insufficient income is likely to be heightened when state policies do not support dependent care, health care, and so forth, in all family forms. Hence, violence can occur even in dual-earner families, particularly when the wage earners work part-time and/or at minimum-wage jobs. Even in families of higher income, family violence can be precipitated by increased stress, such as the fear of losing one's job or the necessity of working additional hours to maintain one's position. The state and the economy, then, not only contribute to the diversity of family forms but also influence the relative advantages and internal dynamics of these forms.

1. Families do not exist in a social vacuum: social institutions can affect family forms as well as their daily experiences. What effect does the state have on family structures? How does the dominant definition of family affect families whose structures depart from that definition? Consider the family in the boxed excerpt in this chapter. From what dominant norms does that family depart? How would you define the structure of that family? What effect does the state have on the structure of your own family?

2. An old African proverb suggests that it takes an entire village to raise a child. What does this mean? What institutions and people might be important for raising a child? Think of your community or state. What supports exist for child rearing? What is lacking? Now think of your own family. What people or institutions besides your parents participate or have participated in raising you or your siblings? What does the African proverb suggest about the definition of family?

3. Look at the wedding-announcements section of a newspaper. What sorts of information are included in these announcements? Are there race, class, and gender differences in the information or the way it is provided? What is not included in the information given? What social message might the existence of wedding-announcement sections be promoting? What social arrangements are *not* being promoted?

4. In 1993, advances in reproductive technology enabled several postmenopausal women in Europe to bear children. What implications does this ability have for the definition of family? How might it alter the structure and dynamics of families? What are the advantages and disadvantages of bearing children late in life? What are some social implications of this technology and the changes it might bring?

5. How would you define the structure of your own family? What factors influence that structure? Consider who performs each of the various roles of provider and homemaker: What are the sources of family income, and who contributes the income? Who handles the household responsibilities? What factors influence who performs these roles? Have the structure and division of labor in your family always been the same as they are now? If not, what prompted the change?

KEY TERMS

household, *467*

families of orientation, *467*

families of procreation, *467*

families of choice, *467*

nuclear family, *467*

extended family, *467*

family, *470*

no-fault divorce, *473*

cultural myth of romanticism, *474*

feminization of poverty, *477*

pauperization of motherhood, *477*

status inconsistency, *483*

flextime, *493*

SUGGESTED READINGS

Naomi Gerstel and Harriet Engel Gross (eds.), *Families and Work.* Philadelphia: Temple University Press, 1987. A selection of readings on the intersection of the institutions of family and work, including readings exploring concerns about race, class, and gender.

Lillian Rubin, *Families on the Fault Line: America's Working Class Speaks about the Family, the Economy, Race, and Ethnicity.* New York: Harper Collins, 1994. An exploration of specific working-class families who are struggling to carve out an existence in an increasingly difficult economic environment. Rubin examines how the intersection of race and ethnicity, gender, and class may affect these families' experiences.

Arlene Skolnick, *Embattled Paradise: The American Family in an Age of Uncertainty.* New York: Basic Books, 1991. A critical analysis of the "culture of nostalgia," which romanticizes the family of the 1950s and implies a modern breakdown of the U.S. family in the 1990s.

Carol B. Stack, *All Our Kin: Strategies for Survival in a Black Community.* New York: Harper Collins, 1974. An examination of the organization of kinship in an African American community in the United States and the effect it has on the everyday existence of individuals. The analysis of the positive and creative strategies such networks may develop offers implications for the meaning of family, gender, and community.

Judith Stacey, *Brave New Families: Stories of Domestic Upheaval in Late Twentieth Century America.* New York: Basic Books, 1991. An exploration of the great variety of family forms that have replaced the traditional nuclear family, including many that are defined by choice rather than by blood and that may not conform to traditional gender roles.

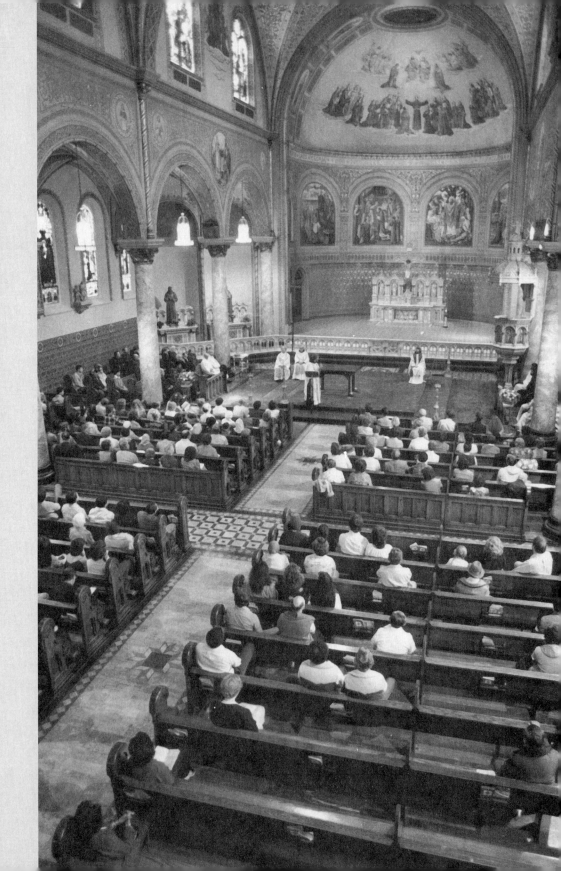

RELIGION

Since the Industrial Revolution, humanity has become ever more knowledge-able and sophisticated in its collective scientific and technological accom-plishments and capabilities. The evidence for this is all around us. Some prod-ucts of science, such as medicines and machinery, help make our lives longer

15

and easier; other products, such as toxic wastes and nuclear weapons, threaten our health or even our very existence.

Sociologists, theologians, and others have commented on the sharp contrast between the rational, calculating style of thinking required by modern science and the reliance on faith that has traditionally accompanied the belief systems of many religions. Some have argued that the great wave of modern scientific and technological advances has eroded the significance of religion as a framework for viewing the world. The term used to characterize this process of decline is secularization, *a concept to which we shall turn later in the chapter.*

Yet for people throughout the world—whether they reside in core, semiperipheral, or peripheral nations—religion is often of great significance even today (see Sahliyeh, 1990; Shupe, 1990). Consider the following numerous and varied developments:

- *In Bosnia, Muslims are terrorized, hunted down, raped, tortured, and massacred by Serbs, many of whom are members of the Eastern Orthodox church, in a wave of "ethnic cleansing."*
- *In Latin America, a cadre of priests and nuns in the Roman Catholic church preaches a gospel of liberation theology that calls upon poor people to organize and seek a more just distribution of economic rewards from land and factory owners.*
- *In Mideast Arab nations, devout followers of Islam participate in a fundamentalist religious movement, one which revolutionarily transforms and militarily emboldens Muslim leadership in such countries as Iran.*
- *In the United States, New Right Christian religious leaders and media televangelists call upon their followers to oppose the teaching of moral relativism in public schools, condemn legalized abortion, reject the acceptability of gay and lesbian lifestyles, and demand that candidates take positions on these issues in state and national political campaigns.*
- *In South Africa, black Christian churches encouraged their members to become activists in the struggle to end racial apartheid, a role similar to that played by the black church in the United States during the civil rights movement.*

- In Northern Ireland, Roman Catholics and Protestants have engaged in violence against each other.

- In India, the political domination, economic adversity, and social persecution experienced by the Sikh religious minority contributes to the emergence of a militant Sikh religious movement and terrorist attacks aimed at Hindus and the Hindu-controlled state.

These events and trends, many of which have been the focus of media attention, suggest that even now religion is having a dramatic impact on the biographies and life chances of people across the globe. Religion can play a key role in the emergence and perpetuation of serious social tensions and conflcts, both within and between societies. It can be a catalyst for large-scale social change.

While less newsworthy, religion can also be an important component of the shared cultural values that contribute to stability and harmony among members of a society. In the United States, groups such as the Mennonites, the Amish, and the Society of Friends (or Quakers) serve as models of the ways in which religion can inform a lifestyle of cooperation and nonviolent actions. Even when there is more than one religion within a society, harmony may prevail on the basis of societal members' willingness to accept or at least tolerate religious diversity. This is certainly the case at present in the United States.

In this chapter we shall address several questions. What is religion? Why is religion universal in human societies? What functions can religion be said to play? In what ways can religion contribute to societal harmony and stability? In what ways can it contribute to conflct? What are the characteristics of religion in the United States? What links exist between religion in the United States and class, race, and gender? Is there a general worldwide trend toward secularization?

Before we address these questions, it is important to stress that by bringing the sociological imagination to bear on religion, sociologists do not aim to prove the validity of their own religious beliefs or to disprove the validity of any others. For example, determining whether there is a higher power or an afterlife is beyond the scope of sociology. These are not matters that can be pursued empirically. Rather, sociologists are interested in religion because it is a universal *phenomenon that affects people's thinking and behavior. In short, sociologists are interested in understanding the social significance of religion. We invite you to share this interest.*

WHAT IS RELIGION?

Sociologists have reached a broad consensus about the meaning of religion. **Religion** has the following characteristics (see Johnstone, 1992: chap. 1):

1. *Sociologists regard religion as essentially a* **group phenomenon.** While religion is certainly a very personal matter, and while many people pray, contemplate, or meditate in solitude, religion is typically something that is shared with other people. In the United States expressions of religion include rituals involving family and friends in the home; church, mosque, or synagogue services; revival meetings; and the appearances of ministers from television's "electronic churches," communicating to vast viewing audiences. In each case, religion is a collective experience.

2. *Religion is concerned with the* **sacred.** French sociologist Émile Durkheim, in his studies of religion, made a distinction between the **sacred**—objects, beings, and situations considered so special as to inspire awe, reverence, or fear—and the **profane**—ordinary objects, beings, and situations that are a routine part of everyday life. When Muslims make their obligatory pilgrimage to Mecca in Saudi Arabia, where Islam had its origins, or when Christians take communion to commemorate the body and blood of Jesus Christ, they are expressing reverence for the sacred.

3. *Religion is commonly concerned with the* **supernatural.** People may hold certain things or matters as sacred because they associate them with higher forces, powers, or beings. Such supernatural elements, while not readily observable, are believed to play a role in the workings of the universe. For example, people may believe that there is one god **(monotheism),** as in Judaism, Christianity, and Islam; that there are many gods and goddesses **(polytheism),** as in Hinduism; or that spirits can be found in other people or in the natural environment **(animism),** as is the case with many African and Native American groups.

4. *Religion, then, is characterized by a* **body of beliefs.** The beliefs typically include a systematic set of accepted facts concerning the sacred and the workings of the supernatural. This body of beliefs provides a set of norms to guide the thinking and behavior of the group's members. Hindus, for example, hold to a doctrine of reincarnation, which views the life span as endless: people are born and eventually die, but they return to exist in a different life whose nature and level of good fortune or suffering depend upon their actions in the earlier life. Muslims and Christians believe that God's judgment of a person's actions can condemn the person to eternal suffering in hell or eternal bliss in paradise or heaven. Jews who follow the teachings of the Torah (the first five books of the Old Testament) believe

God has designated Jews as a chosen people to show others how to live in his image.

5. *The norms accompanying religion prescribe and sanction a particular set of* practices.   Religions typically involve the conduct of a set of rituals, dictated by or otherwise linked to the body of beliefs members share. Rosh Hashanah, a high holy day in the Jewish New Year, is a festival accompanied by the blowing of the ram's horn, a rite said to celebrate God's handing down of the teachings contained in the Torah. Unlike most Christian churches, the Seventh-Day Adventists observe Saturday as the day of rest and worship, believing it to be the original sabbath day and the one observed by Christ and his apostles. Some fundamentalist Protestant groups handle rattlesnakes and drink poisonous strychnine in the course of their religious services, believing themselves protected from harm by God.

6. *Finally, religion provides group members with* moral prescriptions.   In accordance with their accepted system of beliefs, group members embrace a morality that dictates "good" and "bad" ways of thinking and behaving. The moral prescriptions act as a form of social control. Members must avoid the bad or suffer the consequences of, perhaps, offending a deity or creating disharmony with a higher power. The Roman Catholic clergy warn against committing serious "mortal sins" that violate the Ten Commandments (e.g., "Thou shalt not kill"). Violating these laws denies a person admission to heaven. Buddhists, who follow the teachings of Buddha, known as the "Enlightened One," are exhorted to abstain from destroying life, stealing, impurity, lying, and alcohol if they wish to transcend this world and enter the absolute peace of nirvana.

In sum, religion exists when a social group embraces a body of beliefs and practices that are concerned with the supernatural and the sacred and encourages its members to conduct themselves in accordance with moral prescriptions associated with these beliefs. Clearly, religion can take many different forms. In the next section we shall examine some ways in which sociologists categorize religions.

FORMS OF RELIGION

Churches, Sects, Denominations, and Cults

Sociologists generally characterize religions as sects, churches, cults, or denominations (McGuire, 1992: chap. 5). These categories are models. No one religious group necessarily fits perfectly into any one of the categories. But they provide sociologists with a way to think about the differences and similarities among religious groups, which often vary along such lines as size, openness to membership, doctrine, degree of commitment expected, authority structure, and relationship to the larger society (Johnstone, 1992: 83–89).

The sociological categorization of forms of religion was heavily influenced by Ernst Troeltsch (1931), whose writings on Christian churches posed a dichotomy between two forms, the church and the sect. Since his time, sociologists dissatisfied with the church-sect dichotomy, which did not seem to address the full range and diversity of religious groups, have expanded the categories.

The term **church** is used in a generic sense to refer to religions whose membership is open to everyone. Persons are often born into church membership. Churches are somewhat conservative institutions in that they exist comfortably with and within the prevailing order, functioning in cooperation with the state and other social institutions. Indeed, the membership of churches includes people who hold key positions in such institutions and are themselves supportive of the church. Thus, churches tend to be part of the prevailing social order.

Internally, church organization is hierarchical, with substantial authority over religious affairs granted to trained clergy. Churches view their own doctrines as the only legitimate ones, hold a position of religious dominance to the point of monopoly, and actively discourage competitors. They can be quite large, encompassing the population of an entire society or set of societies. The Roman Catholic church in medieval Europe fit these characteristics closely. While some religious groups in the United States contain many churchlike characteristics, including the contemporary Roman Catholic church, none exercises the level of dominance called for in this definition. The major religious groups in the United States, as will be discussed shortly, are perhaps best categorized as denominations.

A **sect,** in contrast, is a religious group formed by people in protest of their social environment, including other religious groups. Sects thus tend to exist, to varying degrees, in a state of negative tension with the larger society. Sects typically are small and are organized along informal democratic lines that maximize members' involvement. The membership of sects is more exclusive than that of churches, which essentially consider all persons or citizens to be eligible for full membership. Groups such as the Mormons and the Jehovah's Witnesses have many sectlike characteristics.

Sect members consider themselves to have been specially selected for salvation; as members of an elect, they pride themselves on being the "true believers." Their insistence on doctrinal purity often leads them to revive doctrines associated with an earlier religious group; accordingly, they dismiss any other doctrines as wrong. Lay members play a major role in sect leadership, and new members are formally admitted through a process involving religious conversion or adult baptism. Sects demand strict membership conformity to their teachings regarding moral principles and behavior.

A **denomination** is a religious group that lies somewhere between churches and sects in terms of characteristics. Denominations lack the religious dominance of churches and seek to coexist with other religious groups. This requires that denominations accept the legitimacy of—or at least be willing to tolerate—other groups' doctrinal claims. Like churches, denominations generally accept the status quo and experience little tension with the larger society. Most of the major religious groups in the United States today are considered denominations, such as the Lutherans,

Methodists, Presbyterians, Episcopalians, Roman Catholics, American Baptists, and Reform and Conservative Jews (McGuire, 1992: 140).

Finally, sociologists use the term "cult" to refer to some religious groups. Among members of the general public this term has taken on negative connotations since the early 1970s because of such developments as the "brainwashing" charges made against religious groups like the Hare Krishna and the Unification church; the horrifying mass suicide and murder involving the Reverend Jim Jones and over 900 members of the People's Temple in Guyana in 1978; and the controversial 1993 tragedy in which religious leader David Koresh and his community of more than 80 Branch Davidians suffered death from fire and gunshots in Waco, Texas.

As sociologists use the term, however, a **cult** is simply another form of religious group. Like denominations, cults are willing to live with or tolerate the religious claims of other groups. At the same time, cults retain a sectlike negative tension with their social environment. The cult, like the sect, emerges as an alternative to dominant ways of thinking and is a form of dissent against religious mainstream doctrines. However, the dissent is typically far less encompassing and rigid than it is in sects, and cult adherents may even simultaneously participate in other religious groups or share in other groups' belief systems.

Unlike the sect, the cult does not call for going back to original doctrines, but often organizes its beliefs around *new* revelations or rediscoveries of forgotten doctrinal lore. Cults, more so than other religious groups, may be organized around a leader who is believed to have special insights or gifts pertaining to the supernatural and the interpretation of truths. While many cults are short-lived, some go on to thrive and eventually take on the characteristics of a denomination, as in the case of Mary Baker Eddy's Christian Science and Elijah Mohammed's Nation of Islam, popularly called the Black Muslims (Johnstone, 1992: 99–100).

Official versus Nonofficial Religion

Our discussion of forms of religion has focused on what some sociologists call **official religion,** involving organized religious groups such as those to which we referred above (McGuire, 1992: 99). But many people—including many who are adherents of an official religion—hold to beliefs and engage in practices that depart from the religious norms of such groups. Such beliefs and practices may be thought of as expressions of **nonofficial religion,** also often termed *popular* or *folk* religion (McGuire, 1992: 104). Nonofficial religious beliefs and practices are part of many people's lives, but they are not authorized by or under the control of organized religious groups.

Nonofficial religion takes a wide variety of forms (see McGuire, 1992: 104–111). Many people are followers and fans of the popular religion provided by independent evangelists and religious entertainers who appear on radio and television. Such media personalities provide inspirational messages to huge audiences. They seek to stimulate and guide spiritual thinking among those exposed to their showmanship, but they do so outside the auspices of official religion (Frankl, 1987).

Nonofficial religion also includes everyday folk practices that reflect common superstitious and magical beliefs, such as carrying special charms and amulets, avoiding walking under ladders, throwing salt over one's shoulder, and knocking on wood for luck. Many people believe in a world of the unknown that is responsible for paranormal occurrences, those that go beyond what we typically understand to be reality. Some people claim, for example, that they or others have detected spirits or ghosts, communicated with deceased persons, or traveled out of their bodies. Others believe in unseen laws and forces that govern the predictive powers of palmistry and astrology, faith healing, or the practice of witchcraft. All these practices may be considered expressions of nonofficial religion.

From a sociological perspective, nonofficial religion may be different from official religion, but it is not inferior to it. Indeed, as mentioned earlier, persons may readily hold to both. Sociologists view both official and nonofficial religion as socially significant and worthy of study. Nonofficial religion, for example, can provide important roles for women (palm reader, faith healer, astrologer, medium, witch), in contrast to official religion, which often excludes women from key positions and responsibilities. Women's celebration of "feminist spirituality," to be discussed later in this chapter, is an important form of nonofficial religion that offers an alternative to the male domination in most organized religious groups in the United States.

Religion, in one form or another, has existed in virtually all known societies. But why? We address this question in the next section.

WHY IS RELIGION UNIVERSAL?

Some sociologists have posited that religion exists because it helps meet people's psychological needs. Others have suggested that religion makes important social contributions, such as contributing to the order and stability that are necessary for societies to operate. Let us examine different views on the functions of religion.

Psychological Functions

Explaining the existence of religion as a means of serving certain psychological needs of humanity requires that we make assumptions about just what these psychological needs are, a topic that is certainly debatable.

One might argue, for example, that religion helps people explain various important events that occur in their lives—from weather and environmental changes to loss in war to childbirth. The causes of many events and situations that inspire awe, terrify, or generate great joy may be beyond the boundaries of rational understanding for the people who experience them. Religion may help people "make sense" of events that are mysterious.

Consider, for example, the phenomenon of suicide. In the United States more than 30,000 persons take their own lives annually, according to official statistics (U.S. Department of Commerce, 1993: 91). (The statistics are widely believed to underestimate the actual numbers.) Despite many decades of research by social scientists and others, the reasons people kill themselves still remain highly speculative. Theories abound (see Neubeck, 1991: chap. 15). The official doctrines of some religions, such as Roman Catholicism, tend to view the act of suicide negatively. But religious clergy may help persons most directly affected by a suicide to understand and accept the event, may endow the death (and the life) of the deceased with meaning, and may assist them in the grieving process. In this way, religion may provide people with an understanding of events not otherwise understandable.

Religion may also provide answers to fundamental questions about human existence that can be anxiety-provoking: Where did I come from? Why am I here on this earth? What is the meaning or purpose of my life? What happens to me after I die? Religious belief systems offer guidance in answering such questions, giving people meaning and purpose to their lives, especially when they are suffering. Indeed, the system of beliefs characterizing a religion often psychologically sustains people who are struggling to change the shape of their world (and thus of the world of those who will follow them).

Any debate about what the universal psychological needs of humanity are, and how religion meets these needs, would have to take into account the fact that some people are not religious or reject religion. This suggests either that there are no universal psychological needs or—perhaps more likely—that people may at times construct or adopt nonreligious belief systems that function to meet some of the kinds of needs we have been discussing.

The doctrine of the Communist party of the Soviet Union is sometimes cited as an example. The party officially outlawed religious expression and persecuted such groups as Jews. Yet the party's members embraced a very encompassing nonreligious belief system regarding the revolutionary origins, changing nature, and future of Soviet and world socialism. This belief system presumably provided answers to many of the party members' questions about conditions in the Soviet Union and elsewhere, justified their own existence, and helped provide them with a mission in life.

Ultimately, the beliefs and actions of the Communist party proved unable to cope with the fundamental dissatisfaction of growing segments of the population, and the political domination of the party entered its dramatic decline. But for a brief historical period, it can be argued, a belief system other than that provided by religion met important psychological needs of many people in the Soviet Union. During this same period, other citizens of the Soviet Union hid their religiosity and moved their outlawed religious practices underground. Since the Communist party's fall from power and the breakup of the Soviet Union, many people in the newly independent republics have begun to openly practice their religion.

Social Functions

While acknowledging the probable significance of religion in helping meet people's psychological needs, sociologists seeking to explain why religion exists have been more interested in addressing its social significance. This involves looking at the possible functions that religion plays in society and the benefits that accrue to society as a whole, or to particular groups within society, from its presence. Two approaches to religion, the functionalist and the Marxist, will be used as illustrations.

A Functionalist Approach to Religion　Earlier, we mentioned the French sociologist Émile Durkheim, who, in drawing a distinction between the sacred and the profane, emphasized the importance of the sacred as a key element of religion. Durkheim's *Elementary Forms of Religious Life* (1954), which first appeared in print in 1915, has had an important influence on sociological thinking about religion.

Durkheim was fascinated by the fact that religion, in one form or another, seemed to be a feature of all societies. He explained its universal presence by hypothesizing that religion made important social contributions. In the absence of religion, societies would fall into disorder and decline. Durkheim's *functionalist approach* thus posited that religion was "functional" to society as a whole. Let us briefly examine his logic.

Durkheim believed that a system of moral values serves as the cement that binds the individual members of a society together. A society cannot operate unless its members live in relative harmony and cooperation with one another to accomplish all the tasks necessary for its survival. Therefore, people must agree on what they will consider "good" and "evil" behavior. Religion provides a society's members with a system of moral values that help define and discourage deviant behavior within the society. Without such a system of values, individuals would be likely to behave in ways that would bring them into conflict with one another, thus undermining social order and threatening societal survival.

According to this view, commonly held beliefs, as expressed and reaffirmed through religious practices, bring people together, remind them of their shared identity, and strengthen their interpersonal bonds. The rituals surrounding important life events—baptisms, weddings, and funerals—contribute to group solidarity. The traditions of religion remind people that they share a history and, by implication, possess the opportunity to share a common destiny. In times of hardship and disappointment, religious rituals can ease despair and provide a sense of hope that energizes the group and keeps it going until times get better.

Durkheim based much of his thinking about the functional nature of religion on his knowledge of non-Western preliterate societies. He recognized that his ideas were not as applicable to industrial societies of his day, which were characterized by outbreaks of crime and other forms of deviant behavior, as well as civil disorder and labor unrest. In Durkheim's view, the influence of traditional religion declined in industrializing societies. As such societies grew in size, heterogeneity, and complexity, it became more difficult for societal members to hold on to a shared set of moral values. The increasingly interdependent division of labor, which he thought was an important element of the modern industrial order, could not maintain harmony and stability. Thus, Durkheim championed the forging of revitalized systems of morality that would increase the stability of industrial societies (Durkheim, 1964).

Religious ceremonies and rituals surrounding important life events bring people together, involve them in a shared experience, and are thought to contribute to increased group solidarity. The fathers of the bride and groom touch their heads in blessing at a Reform Jewish wedding.

Durkheim's functionalist approach to religion helps us see how religion may contribute to societal cohesiveness and solidarity. But his analysis ignores one key factor: societal inequalities. Some would argue that in many societies religion plays an important role in justifying or legitimizing, and thus perpetuating, the unequal distribution of power. Let us consider this argument in more detail.

A Marxist Approach to Religion   Karl Marx was just as interested in the social problems associated with industrializing societies as was Durkheim. But the interpretation Marx gave to the origins of such phenomena as civil disorder and labor unrest was very different. While Durkheim held that social instability and class conflict arose from the loss of a shared set of moral values in industrial societies, Marx believed that class conflict was a natural outcome of capitalism, the economic system around which industrialization was organized in Europe and the United States.

In Marx's view, class conflicts were not only natural but also inevitable. Interclass warfare would ultimately lead to a revolutionary overthrow of capitalism by the working class and thus to the creation of a new economic system organized around production to meet the needs of workers: socialism. Understanding what capitalism was doing to them, many workers realized the desirability of joining with others to struggle against the capitalist class. In Marx's terminology, these workers possessed **class consciousness.**

Yet not all workers thought at this level. Many members of the working class possessed what Marx called **false consciousness.** They failed to understand that the sources of their collective alienation and misery—and the limitations on their life chances due to bouts of unemployment, poverty, poor housing, hunger, and ill health—lay within the capitalist economic system to which they sold their labor power. Instead of condemning capitalism, the victims of false consciousness tended to blame themselves for their hardships, to think their suffering was a matter of bad luck or fate, or to believe that it must somehow be a part of God's master plan.

To Marx (1964), religion was a form of false consciousness. Many Christian churches, for example, preached acceptance of one's life burdens because they were simply God's will. One might suffer in this life, but by observing the moral prescriptions accompanying the church's system of religious beliefs, it was possible to be rewarded in the afterlife. In Marx's view, this way of thinking led workers to look for happiness after death rather than to create happiness now by changing the society in which they were living.

Marx believed that religion functioned to benefit the capitalist class. It counseled members of the working class to go along with the capitalist economic system, a system that redistributed wealth upward and left workers very little in return for all their labor. It was in this sense that Marx referred to religion as "opium":

> Religion is the sigh of the oppressed creature, the sentiment of a heartless world, and the soul of soulless conditions. It is the opium of the people (Marx, 1964).

In Marx's view, workers in capitalist society who possessed false consciousness would suffer until they developed class consciousness—casting aside religious and other beliefs that undermined the potential for change.

RELIGION, SOCIAL CONTROL, AND SOCIAL CONFLICT

Religion may help legitimize systems of inequality. Elites may use religion to exert control over potentially disruptive or rebellious groups. On the other hand, sometimes religion provides such groups with ideas that inspire them to struggle against inequalities and resist unjust treatment by elites. In this section we shall examine ways in which religion can play a role in maintaining social control as well as in generating social conflict.

Religion and Social Control

Sociologists influenced by Marx's ideas on religion point out that people in power are likely to enjoin the powerless to embrace beliefs that portray the existing situation as natural and just. In many societies, a dominant religion performs exactly this function. Its belief system mutes and blunts social conflict to the advantage of the privileged. In effect, religion acts as a form of social control.

For example, Christian doctrines provided the basis for belief in the divine (God-ordained) right of kings to rule, legitimizing the power of the monarchy during the European feudal era. Early Protestants, such as the puritanical Calvinists, held to religious doctrines that interpreted material success and the accumulation of business assets as a sign that one was among God's chosen people and destined for heaven; those who were poor, despite their hard work, could only try harder and accept God's decision as to their destination. Hindu religious doctrine maintains a hierarchy of castes in part by forbidding adherents to change to a higher caste than the ones into which they were born, lest they come back in their next lives at a much lower level of existence. In South Africa, missionaries of the Dutch Reformed church helped build a religious justification for apartheid by preaching that white minority rule is part of God's plan and converting many black Africans to this belief.

When one group of people is conquered by another, use of military force is often only the first step in their subjugation. As in the case of black South Africans, the religions of the native peoples may be supplanted by that of the conqueror. European colonial powers often used Christianity as a key part of their strategy to control indigenous populations. Mexico is a case in point. Mexico City was once the site of Tenochtitlán, the capital city of the Aztecs. After the Spanish colonial forces conquered the Aztecs in 1521, they systematically tore down Aztec religious temples and destroyed or buried other material evidence of the Aztec religious belief system. The grand Roman Catholic Metropolitan Cathedral in Mexico City's main square was built by the Spanish on the site of razed Aztec tem-

Religion may at times function as a form of social control, enabling some groups to dominate others. Spanish colonization of Mexico included a combination of military force and Roman Catholic missionary activity to gain control of the native peoples. Mexican muralist Diego Rivera depicts this feature of his nation's history in his work entitled "The Constitution."

ples; it stands today as a symbol of the long history of Spanish colonial rule.

Over the course of centuries, throughout Mexico and the rest of Latin America, the military put down rebellions while the Catholic church proselytized and sought to convert and baptize as many members of the indigenous population as possible. The peoples of Latin America were confronted by the sword *and* the cross, a powerful combination that enabled the occupying colonial powers to undermine the autonomy and traditional beliefs of native groups. Clearly, however, the social control functions of religion are not always wholly successful. For example, the military continues to play an important role in protecting the system of political and economic inequality found in most Latin American nations.

Moreover, while it may seem contradictory, religion may at times inspire groups to actively challenge the status quo. For example, in recent years, with the development of the liberation theology movement within the Roman Catholic church in Latin America, clergy and church members have challenged patterns of inequality there. Thus, religious groups may play an important role in existing social conflicts or may provoke new conflicts. In the discussion below, we shall examine some of these groups.

Religion and Social Conflict

Religion is not always a system of beliefs that can be used to justify the status quo. Religion can be a source of inspiration for oppressed peoples to struggle against inequality and injustice. In this section we shall look at ways in which religion has played a role in social conflict that arose in connection with issues of justice and human rights.

Church Involvement in the U.S. Civil Rights Movement In the antebellum (pre-Civil War) period some white churches in the United States were important defenders of slavery. Later, as in South Africa (Villa-Vicencio, 1978), many white churches in the United States accepted or actively backed racial segregation (Jaynes and Williams, 1989: 91–95). Yet white churches ultimately played an important role in the struggle to overturn segregation during the civil rights movement of the 1950s and 1960s. Many white churches joined with African American churches in supporting civil rights activities in this period, even while other white churches, most prominently in the South, continued to support segregation (Morris, 1984).

African American churches and individual black clergy were at the forefront of the civil rights movement from the beginning. These churches supplied an already organized constituency of activists, trained leaders, financial assistance, political savvy, and important moral and spiritual support (Lincoln and Mamiya, 1990: chap. 8). The churches also served as major points of mobilization for meetings and demonstrations and helped feed and house traveling civil rights workers from various political organizations and religious groups. Black women, as well as black men, played valuable leadership and supportive roles (Barnett, 1993). Realizing the importance of the African American churches, segregationist whites attacked

In many instances religion has provided people with the inspiration, strength, and resources to carry on struggles against inequalities and injustice. The black church played a crucial role in the U.S. civil rights movement. Here, police attempt to stop ministers from leading a protest march to the city hall in Birmingham, Alabama, in 1963.

hundreds of them during the civil rights era. Fires and bombings destroyed many church buildings.

African American clergy forged important ties and coalitions with one another and with their white counterparts. Alliances with white clergy were possible because in the post-World War II period some of the largest white religious groups slowly began to denounce segregation (Jaynes and Williams, 1989: 91–92). One of the most important organizations to come out of racially integrated coalitions was the Southern Christian Leadership Conference (SCLC), formed in 1957.

The SCLC, which was dominated by African American clergy, gained acclaim under the activist leadership of the Reverend Dr. Martin Luther King, Jr. (Blumberg, 1991). It played a significant role in attacking ideas of white racial supremacy and dismantling racial segregation by helping to organize freedom rides, sit-ins, and protest marches across the southern states, as well as the historic "March on Washington" on August 28, 1963. The accompanying boxed excerpt is from King's famous "I Have a Dream" speech, which he delivered in Washington in front of the Lincoln Memorial.

Religious participants in SCLC, and in the civil rights movement more generally, held that reward in the afterlife requires people to treat one another nonviolently and with justice while on earth. They viewed racial segregation—a system of injustice often enforced by violence—as contrary to God's will and believed it was one's religious duty to oppose it. Such

The excerpt below is from the famous speech that the Reverend Dr. Martin Luther King, Jr., delivered before hundreds of thousands of people of color and white people who were participating in the March for Jobs and Freedom in Washington, D.C., in 1963. Members of the clergy like King linked religious ideas to the goal of racial equality and thus helped broaden the base of citizen support for civil rights legislation in the 1960s.

I am happy to join with you today in what will go down in history as the greatest demonstration for freedom in the history of our nation.

Five score years ago a great American in whose symbolic shadow we stand today signed the Emancipation Proclamation. This momentous decree is a great beacon light of hope to millions of Negro slaves who had been seared in the flames of withering injustice. It came as a joyous daybreak to end the long night of their captivity. But 100 years later, the Negro still is not free. One hundred years later the life of the Negro is still badly crippled by the manacles of segregation and the chains of discrimination. One hundred years later the Negro lives on a lonely island of poverty in the midst of a vast ocean of material prosperity. One hundred years later the Negro still languished in the corners of American society and finds himself in exile in his own land. So we've come here today to dramatize a shameful condition. . . .

Now is the time to make justice a reality for all of God's children. It would be fatal for the nation to overlook the urgency of the moment. This sweltering summer of the Negro's legitimate discontent will not pass until there is an invigorating autumn of freedom and equality—1963 is not an end but a beginning. Those who hope that the Negro needed to blow off steam and will now be content will have a rude awakening if the nation returns to business as usual. . . .

We must forever conduct our struggle on the high plane of dignity and discipline. We must not allow our creative protests to degenerate into physical violence. Again and again we must rise to the majestic heights of meeting physical force with soul force. The marvelous new militancy which has engulfed the Negro community must not lead us to distrust all white people, for many of our white brothers, as evidenced by their presence here today, have come to realize that their destiny is tied up with our destiny.

They have come to realize that their freedom is inextricably bound to our freedom. We cannot walk alone. And as we walk we must make the pledge that we shall always march ahead. We cannot turn back.

I say to you today, my friends, though, even though we face the difficulties of today and tomorrow, I still have a dream. It is a dream deeply rooted in the American dream. I have a dream that one day this nation will rise up, live out the true meaning of its creed: "We hold these truths to be self-evident, that all men are created equal."

beliefs also helped inspire many black and white South African clergy and churches to struggle against apartheid. South African leader Bishop Desmond Tutu, like Martin Luther King, Jr., was awarded the Nobel Peace Prize for his role in nonviolent struggles for racial equality.

Liberation Theology: The Case of Latin America   Liberation theology in Latin America provides yet another example of religion acting as an agent to challenge inequality. In this case a segment of the Roman Catholic church has helped mobilize its followers in a struggle against the huge gap

> **"Again and again we must rise to the majestic heights of meeting physical force with soul force."**

I have a dream that one day on the red hills of Georgia sons of former slaves and the sons of former slave-owners will be able to sit down together at the table of brotherhood. I have a dream that one day even the state of Mississippi, a state sweltering with the heat of injustice, sweltering with the heat of oppression, will be transformed into an oasis of freedom and justice.

I have a dream that my four little children will one day live in a nation where they will not be judged by the color of their skin but by the content of their character. I have a dream . . . I have a dream that one day in Alabama, with its vicious racists, with its governor having his lips dripping with the words of interposition and nullification, one day right there in Alabama little black boys and black girls will be able to join hands with little white boys and white girls as sisters and brothers.

I have a dream today . . . I have a dream that one day every valley shall be exalted, every hill and mountain shall be made low. The rough places will be made plain, and the crooked places will be made straight. And the glory of the Lord shall be revealed, and all flesh shall see it together. This is our hope. This is the faith that I go back to the South with. With this faith we will be able to hew out of the mountain of despair a stone of hope. With this faith we will be able to transform the jangling discords of our nation into a beautiful symphony of brotherhood. With this faith we will be able to work together, to stand up for freedom together, knowing that we will be free one day.

This will be the day when all of God's children will be able to sing with new meaning, "My country, 'tis of thee, sweet land of liberty, of thee I sing. Land where my fathers died, land of the pilgrim's pride, from every mountain side, let freedom ring." And if America is to be a great nation, this must become true. So let freedom ring from the prodigious hilltops of New Hampshire. Let freedom ring from the mighty mountains of New York. Let freedom ring from the heightening Alleghenies of Pennsylvania. Let freedom ring from the snow-capped Rockies of Colorado. Let freedom ring from the curvaceous slopes of California.

But not only that. Let freedom ring from Stone Mountain of Georgia. Let freedom ring from Lookout Mountain of Tennessee. Let freedom ring from every hill and molehill of Mississippi, from every mountain side. Let freedom ring. . .

When we allow freedom to ring—when we let it ring from every city and every hamlet, from every state and every city, we will be able to speed up that day when all God's children, black men and white men, Jews and Gentiles, Protestants and Catholics, will be able to join hands and sing in the words of the old Negro spiritual, "Free at last, Free at last, Great God a-mighty, We are free at last."

Source: Dr. Martin Luther King, Jr., "I Have a Dream," in Lenwood G. Davis, *I Have a Dream . . . The Life and Times of Martin Luther King, Jr.* (Westport, CT: Negro Universities Press, 1969), pp. 261–264.

between the rich and the poor that exists in much of Latin America.

Latin America, as we noted earlier, was conquered and colonized with the help of the Catholic church. Over the centuries colonial powers, especially Spain and Portugal, drained the vast wealth and natural resources of this region of the world. When the various Latin American nations finally achieved independence, they were among the poorest and most underdeveloped nations in the world. The colonial powers' withdrawal left intact masses of people in poverty, as well as a relatively small group of landowners and other capitalists who had been able to accumulate great wealth under the protection of the state. This economic and political situation continues to characterize much of Latin America today.

The origins of liberation theology are thought to lie with a meeting of dissident Latin American Catholic bishops in Medellín, Colombia, in 1968. At this meeting, the bishops condemned all forms of institutionalized violence, including poverty and economic exploitation by employers. Their ideas were given form and popularized by Peruvian priest and theologian Gustavo Gutiérrez in his book, *A Theology of Liberation* (1973; see also Gutiérrez, 1983). The focus of his work is liberation of the poor as a class from their position of oppression. In Gutiérrez's view, this liberation requires a society built around the principles of socialism,

> a society in which private ownership of the means of production is eliminated, because private ownership of the means of production allows a few to appropriate the fruits of the labor of many, and generates the division of society into classes, whereupon one class exploits another (Gutiérrez, 1983: 37).

Proponents of **liberation theology** demand that the Catholic church end its historic support of the existing order and cease teaching that people should simply resign themselves to their fates and hope for rewards in the afterlife. In Gutiérrez's words, "The first step is for the church as a whole to break its many ties with the present order, ties that it has maintained overtly or covertly, wittingly or unwittingly, up to now" (1983: 29). Gutiérrez believed that the church must side with the "poor of this world—the exploited classes, despised ethnic groups, and marginalized cultures" (1983: 37). It cannot be neutral, a position that allows economic exploitation and poverty to continue to exist.

Needless to say, the governing hierarchy of the Roman Catholic church, headquartered at the Vatican, has not welcomed liberation theology (Gismondi, 1988; Scherer-Warren, 1990). The new theology calls for political activism in the face of inequalities, and its groundings in Marxist class analysis call for the Catholic church—traditionally conservative and anti-socialist—to take a position on the political left. It has criticized traditional church teachings and the role of the church in Latin America. Nonetheless, liberation theology has proved popular among poor people in Latin America. (See the accompanying box for the words of Oscar Romero, former archbishop of San Salvador.) Its teachings have provided the foundation for a growing number of *comunidades eclesiáis de base* (local community-based churches) that serve important religious, social, and economic needs of the rural and urban poor. These local churches may have been important contributors to the social movement that overthrew the U.S.-backed Somoza dictatorship in Nicaragua in 1979, and they have provided a vehicle for grass-roots political organizing aimed at change in other Latin American nations as well.

The Sanctuary Movement in the United States   In the United States, as well as in many other countries, religious groups have had a long history of being open to people fleeing persecution and seeking refuge. Indeed, many of us have ancestors who came to the United States as refugees from other countries and who looked to churches for aid in their efforts at resettlement. Churches in the United States, moreover, have had a tradition of providing sanctuary to individuals fleeing persecution by the state. They played a role in hiding and protecting runaway slaves and, more recently, provided sanctuary to conscientious objectors resisting the military draft in the Vietnam war era. When poor peasants from Guatemala and El Salvador began to seek sanctuary in the United States in the 1970s, churches opened their doors to provide protection. In 1982, a religious movement known as the Sanctuary Movement emerged to protect the growing stream of refugees. By 1987, some 600,000 Central American refugees had entered this country (Kowalewski, 1990).

Popular movements against the policies of dictatorial governments had been met with harsh oppression in both Guatemala and El Salvador, turning many of the poorest people into armed guerrillas and revolutionaries. Many people were caught in the middle. Those thought to be supportive of the state were open to threats and violence from the revolutionary forces, while those thought to be supporting the insurgents were subject to persecution and violence from the state's police and military apparatus. U.S. government, which had long supported the ruling elites in both countries,

The Sanctuary Movement, begun in the early 1980s, sheltered and protected some of the hundreds of thousands of refugees who illegally entered the United States to escape political repression and violence in nations such as El Salvador and Guatemala. Religious groups formed the base of the Sanctuary Movement. These refugees, masked to hide their identities, are attending Easter religious services in Washington, D.C.

Oscar Romero, Roman Catholic archbishop of San Salvador, El Salvador, was assassinated by political enemies on March 24, 1980, while celebrating mass. He was outspoken on issues of economic justice and beloved by poor people in Latin America.

Our Salvadoran world is no abstraction. It is not another example of what is understood by "world" in developed countries such as yours. It is a world made up mostly of men and women who are poor and oppressed. And we say of that world of the poor that it is the key to understanding the Christian faith, to understanding the activity of the church and the political dimension of that faith and that ecclesial activity. It is the poor who tell us what the world is, and what the church's service to the world should be. It is the poor who tell us what the *polis* is, what the city is and what it means for the church really to live in that world.

Allow me, then, briefly to explain from the perspective of the poor among my people, whom I represent, the situation and the activity of our church in the world in which we live. . . .

In its pastoral work, our archdiocese in recent years has been moving in a direction that can only be described and only be understood as a turning toward the world of the poor, to their real, concrete world.

Just as elsewhere in Latin America, the words of Exodus have, after many years, perhaps centuries, finally resounded in our ears: "The cry of the sons of Israel has come to me, and I have witnessed the way in which the Egyptians oppress them" (Exod. 3:9). These words have given us new eyes to see what has always been the case among us, but which has so often been hidden, even from the view of the church itself. We have learned to see what is the first, basic fact about our world and, as pastors, we have made a judgment about it at Medellín and at Puebla. "That misery, as a collective fact, expresses itself as an injustice which cries to the heavens." At Puebla we declared, "So we brand the situation of inhuman poverty in which millions of Latin Americans live as the most devastating and humiliating kind of scourge. And this situation finds expression in such things as a high rate of infant mortality, lack of adequate housing, health problems, starvation wages, unemployment and underemployment, malnutrition, job uncertainty, compulsory mass migrations, etc." Experiencing these realities, and letting ourselves be affected by them, far from separating us from our faith has sent us back to the world of the poor as to our true home. It has moved us, as a first, basic step, to take the world of the poor upon ourselves.

It is there that we have found the real faces of the poor, about which Puebla speaks. There we have met landworkers without land and without steady employment, without running water or electricity in their homes, without medical assistance when mothers give birth, and without schools for their children. There we have met factory workers who have no labor rights, and who get fired from their jobs if they demand such rights, human beings who are at the mercy of cold economic calculations. There we have met the mothers and the wives of those who have disappeared, or who are political prisoners. There we have met the shantytown dwellers, whose wretchedness defies imagination, suffering the permanent mockery of the mansions nearby.

It is within this world devoid of a human face, this contemporary sacrament of the suffering servant of Yahweh, that the church of my archdiocese has undertaken to incarnate itself. I do not say this in a triumphalistic spirit, for I am well aware how much in this regard remains to be done. But I say it with immense joy, for we have made the effort not to pass by afar off, not to circle round the one lying wounded in the roadway, but to approach him or her as did the good Samaritan.

This coming closer to the world of the poor is what we understand both by the incarnation and by

"It is the poor who tell us what the world is, and what the church's service to the world should be."

conversion. The changes that were needed within the church and in its apostolate, in education, in religious and in priestly life, in lay movements, which we had not brought about simply by looking inward upon the church, we are now carrying out by turning ourselves outward toward the world of the poor.

Our encounter with the poor has regained for us the central truth of the gospel, through which the word of God urges us to conversion. The church has to proclaim the good news to the poor. Those who, in this-worldly terms, have heard bad news, and who have lived out even worse realities, are now listening through the church to the word of Jesus: "The kingdom of God is at hand; blessed are you who are poor, for the kingdom of God is yours." And hence they also have good news to proclaim to the rich: that they, too, become poor in order to share the benefits of the kingdom with the poor. Anyone who knows Latin America will be quite clear that there is no ingenuousness in these words, still less the workings of a soporific drug. What is to be found in these words is a coming together of the aspiration on our continent for liberation, and God's offer of love to the poor. This is the hope that the church offers, and it coincides with the hope, at times dormant and at other times frustrated or manipulated, of the poor of Latin America.

It is something new among our people that today the poor see in the church a source of hope and a support for their noble struggle for liberation. The hope that our church encourages is neither naive nor passive. It is rather a summons from the word of God for the great majority of the people, the poor, that they assume their proper responsibility, that they undertake their own conscientization, that, in a country where it is legally or practically prohibited (at some periods more so than at others) they set about organizing themselves. And it is support, sometimes critical support, for their just causes and demands. The hope that we preach to the poor is intended to give them back their dignity, to encourage them to take charge of their own future. In a word, the church has not only turned toward the poor, it has made of the poor the special beneficiaries of its mission because, as Puebla says, "God takes on their defense and loves them."

The church has not only incarnated itself in the world of the poor, giving them hope; it has also firmly committed itself to their defense. The majority of the poor in our country are oppressed and repressed daily by economic and political structures. The terrible words spoken by the prophets of Israel continue to be verified among us. Among us there are those who sell others for money, who sell a poor person for a pair of sandals; those who, in their mansions, pile up violence and plunder; those who crush the poor; those who make the kingdom of violence come closer as they lie upon their beds of ivory; those who join house to house, and field to field, until they occupy the whole land, and are the only ones there.

Amos and Isaiah are not just voices from distant centuries; their writings are not merely texts that we reverently read in the liturgy. They are everyday realities. Day by day we live out the cruelty and ferocity they excoriate. We live them out when there come to us the mothers and the wives of those who have been arrested or who have disappeared, when mutilated bodies turn up in secret cemeteries, when those who fight for justice and peace are assassinated. Daily we live out in our archdiocese what Puebla so vigorously denounced: "There are the anxieties based on systematic or selective repression; it is accompanied by accusations, violations of privacy, improper pressures, tortures, and exiles. There are the anxieties produced in many families by the disappearance of their loved ones, about whom they cannot get any news. There is the total insecurity bound up with arrest and detention without judicial consent. There are the anxieties felt in the face of a system of justice that has been suborned or cowed."

521

In this situation of conflict and antagonism, in which just a few persons control economic and political power, the church has placed itself at the side of the poor and has undertaken their defense. The church cannot do otherwise, for it remembers that Jesus had pity on the multitude. But by defending the poor it has entered into serious conflict with the powerful who belong to the monied oligarchies and with the political and military authorities of the state.

Source: Oscar A. Romero, "The Political Dimension of the Faith from the Perspective of the Option for the Poor," in *Voices of the Voiceless* (Maryknoll, NY: Orbis Books, 1985), pp. 179–181.

took their side in the fight against the insurgents, providing training and assistance in intelligence gathering and in low-intensity warfare tactics.

Clergy from U.S. churches and synagogues not only harbored and counseled the refugees, who were illegal immigrants, but began speaking out against the government policies that had created the need for refuge. The U.S. government responded by actively seeking to deport the refugees it could find and by harassing the activists in the Sanctuary Movement who were fighting the deportations and speaking out against the government. Some religious activists were imprisoned.

In taking such steps, argued supporters of the Sanctuary Movement, the U.S. government violated traditional understandings regarding sanctuary by religious groups. Even so, the government's actions, far from intimidating those involved, actually increased support for the Sanctuary Movement in the United States and abroad. They also gave momentum to the domestic political pressures that were building for the United States to change its foreign policies, end its role in the widespread violence, and assist the governments of El Salvador and Guatemala in adopting democratic reforms.

These examples illustrate some ways in which religion may play an active role in social conflict, helping to inspire movements that challenge religious and civil authority that supports oppression. An interesting area of research for sociologists has involved exploring the conditions under which religion serves this function versus the conditions under which it justifies the status quo.

RELIGION IN THE UNITED STATES

Religion plays a major role in the lives of people in the United States. The evidence for this lies in data on people's affiliation with organized religious groups, participation in religious services, exercise of religious beliefs, and

Table 15.1

RELIGIOUS PREFERENCE AND CHURCH MEMBERSHIP AND ATTENDANCE IN THE UNITED STATES, 1957–1990 (IN PERCENT)

| YEAR | RELIGIOUS PREFERENCE | | | | | CHURCH/ SYNAGOGUE MEMBERS | PERSONS ATTENDING CHURCH/ SYNAGOGUE* |
	PROTESTANT	CATHOLIC	JEWISH	OTHER	NONE		
1957	66	26	3	1	3	73[†]	47
1967	67	25	3	3	2	73[‡]	43
1975	62	27	2	4	6	71	41
1980	61	28	2	2	7	69	40
1985	57	28	2	4	9	71	42
1989	56	28	2	4	10	69	43
1990	56	25	2	6	11	65	40

*In previous week.
[†]1952 data.
[‡]1965 data.
Source: U.S. Bureau of the Census, *Statistical Abstract of the United States, 1992* (Washington, DC: U.S. Government Printing Office, 1993), p. 58.

prayer behavior. Religion may even influence how we view our nation and its purpose or mission. Religion also tends to reflect existing systems of class, race, and sex inequality in the United States. Let us discuss these features of religion in more detail.

The United States as a Denominational Society

While statistics on religious preference are somewhat limited in their detail, they do provide a rough picture of the U.S. population's orientation. Among the people surveyed in 1990, most named one of the major denominational families as their religious preference: Protestant, 56 percent; Catholic, 25 percent; and Jewish, 2 percent. Another 6 percent were classified as "other," while 11 percent of those polled did not identify a preference (U.S. Department of Commerce, 1993: 58). Over the last three decades the percentage of Protestants has slipped while that of persons claiming no preference has increased (see Table 15.1). In 1989 Protestants outnumbered Roman Catholics, 79 million to 57 million, in terms of actual membership in religious bodies (U.S. Department of Commerce, 1993: 58). However, membership in the Roman Catholic church far surpasses that of any *single* Protestant religious group in the United States.

The United States has been called a **denominational society** because it is characterized by religious pluralism, rather than the presence of a dominant church (Greeley, 1972). While there are major denominational families, well over a thousand different religious groups exist in the United States (Melton, 1989). The emergence and coexistence of denominations, sects, and cults are facilitated by constitutionally guaranteed rights to freedom of association and freedom of religion and by a historic consensus that one's religion is a personal and private matter. Thus, in the United States people tend to tolerate even groups whose beliefs and practices seem unusual or extreme.

Civil Religion in the United States

The diverse collection of religious groups exists within a larger cultural context that sociologist Robert Bellah (1967) has called **civil religion.** According to Bellah, a set of widely held beliefs, akin to a national religion, holds that the nation and its institutions, particularly its political institutions, are under the special favor of God. Civil religion is said to provide the nation with an ideal view of itself and to promote national cohesion among heterogeneous groups. It is accompanied by its own rituals, through which people reaffirm commitment to their nation and its divine mission (McGuire, 1992: 179–185).

Thus, we pledge allegiance to "one nation, under God." Memorial Day ceremonies celebrate the sacrifices of the deceased with prayer, while presidential inaugurations call upon God's blessings and ask for his guidance. The notion that the United States exists for purposes ordained by God, and is carrying out his will, was a major theme in justifying our participation in World Wars I and II. Politicians portrayed the Korean war and the Cold War as wars against "atheistic communism." In the nation's history, many immigrants have come seeking relief from religious persecution, a fact we use to support the view that the United States is the "Promised Land." When political dissenters desecrate "sacred" symbols—for example, by burning the flag in protest of the Vietnam war—they are considered "heretics."

Religious Participation and Belief

Religion has long been and continues to remain a strong institution in U.S. society. We can see the strength and social significance of religion today, for example, in the political debates that take place over issues such as legalized abortion, the death penalty, the availability of sex education and contraceptives in the public schools, gun control, and the rights of gay males and lesbians. Religious groups are usually major participants in debates on these controversial issues, and they often influence public policy.

Key indicators of religious activity provide evidence that religion is important in the lives of millions of people in the United States. As Table 15.1 shows, nearly two-thirds of the adults surveyed belonged to a church or synagogue in 1990, a figure that has not varied much in the last few decades. Membership, of course, is not the same as attendance, which is somewhat lower. In 1990, 40 percent of the adults surveyed said they had attended religious services in the previous week, a figure that has also been relatively stable in polls over the years. New research, however, suggests that the actual attendance rates may be half that reported by pollsters (Hadaway, Marler, and Chaves, 1993). People may want to appear more religious than they are. While this research is based upon very limited data from a single state, it does remind us that we should be cautious in accepting poll data until their validity is clarified.

But membership and attendance are only part of the picture. Polls pertaining to beliefs also point to the importance of religion in people's lives. For example, 89 percent of persons surveyed believe there is a God; 10 percent say they don't know; and only 1 percent say they do not believe a God exists (Anti-Defamation League, 1992). Eighty percent of poll respondents say they feel "extremely close" or "somewhat close" to God most of the time (National Opinion Research Center, 1991b). Sixty-two percent of those polled say they believe in the devil (National Opinion Research Center, 1991b). Finally, 72 percent believe there is a life after death (National Opinion Research Center, 1991a).

The National Opinion Research Center (1991c) reports that 78 percent of those polled pray at least once a week and almost 60 percent pray at least once a day. Prayer is a more common behavior among women (91 percent) than men (85 percent), and it is more likely to be engaged in by African Americans (94 percent) than whites (87 percent). Andrew M. Greeley, a sociologist and priest, has examined patterns of prayer behavior over time and believes that, by this measure, people in the United States may be becoming more, rather than less, religious ("Talking to God," 1992: 41).

Class, Race, Gender, and Religion

Religion, like other institutions, reflects, and in some cases reinforces, systems of inequality that prevail across U.S. society as a whole. In this section we explore some of the links between religion and class, race, and gender.

Religion and Class   Different religious groups tend to draw more members from some social classes than from others. Using such indicators of class position as income level, educational attainment, and occupational prestige, we find that people who are Jews, Episcopalians, and Presbyterians tend to be among the more successful and affluent members of society, while those who belong to the Southern Baptist church, the Nazarenes, and Churches of God are more likely to occupy positions in the lower and working classes (Roof and McKinney, 1987).

Moreover, the mode of religious expression favored by people tends to differ by class. According to Stark and Bainbridge (1985: 10–11), the upper classes are more likely than the poor to be church members, to attend church, and to participate in church ritual observances. Poor people are more likely to pray in private, to hold strong beliefs based on the doctrine of their religion, and to have highly intense religious experiences. One's position in the class structure, then, may determine what meaning religion has and what rewards it provides for participation.

Religion and Race: The Case of African Americans   Earlier we pointed out that white churches in the United States historically chose to ignore, and in some cases actively supported, racial segregation. Many religious groups did not become actively involved in antiracism activities until the era of the civil rights movement. But the widespread activism of the civil rights era has retreated into history, and the movement's goal of societywide racial integration has been only partially achieved. As we have seen in other chapters, in a variety of subtle and not-so-subtle ways, racism and racial segregation are still very much alive.

A major characteristic of religion in the United States today is the separation of African Americans from whites in practices of religious worship (Jaynes and Williams, 1989: 92). In contrast to other areas of life in which substantial racial desegregation has occurred since World War II (such as employment and higher education), most U.S. churches tend to be either predominantly white or predominantly black. The degree of racial separation in religious worship is revealed by the results of a 1991 survey of church attendance (National Opinion Research Center, 1991a). Whites and blacks were asked, "Do (blacks/whites) attend the church that you yourself attend most often, or not?" Almost half the respondents said no; only 39 percent responded in the affirmative. (Another 11 percent volunteered that they did not attend church.) Surveys during the 1980s showed similar results.

This separation is not simply a matter of differences in accustomed and preferred ways of worshiping. It reflects past and present effects of racial discrimination, current patterns of residential segregation along racial lines, and denominational loyalty (Jaynes and Williams, 1989: 92). Many African Americans worship at black churches that are part of denominations to which their families have belonged for generations, such as the African Methodist Episcopal Church. Some 80 percent of African Americans who are church-affiliated belong to one of seven major black denominations (Lincoln and Mamiya, 1990: xii).

The black church has always been an important institution for African Americans, for it is one of the few institutions in the United States over which they can exercise control and in which they can conduct themselves autonomously. The church has served a number of functions for African Americans. Besides providing a key forum for religious expression, the black church has been an important center of community social life, group communication, and information exchange. The black church has served important economic functions for African Americans, providing charitable aid to the needy, support for the ill, and assistance with burial costs. It has played an active role in education of black children, in many cases raising funds for and operating schools. Finally, the black church has been central to political activity on the part of African Americans, providing an environment within which people can develop useful political skills and from which they can act collectively against racism and segregation. Mobilization of people and finances by black churches was crucial to the success of the civil rights movement.

Black churches continue to serve many of these important functions. For millions of African Americans today the black church remains a place of respite from a white-dominated society.

Religion and Gender Like race and class, gender plays a role in religion in the United States. Judaism, Christianity, and Islam are patriarchal in orientation, with adherents worshiping a male God or father figure. These religious traditions have historically accorded men a higher spiritual status and more important religious leadership roles than women. Moreover, elements of their belief systems have been used to legitimize female subordination (Renzetti and Curran, 1992: chap. 11).

Orthodox Jews comprise a small, but significant, segment of the U.S. Jewish community. In the Orthodox Jewish tradition, men engage in communal worship, daily prayer, and religious studies; women attend to the religious training of children and the maintenance of religious rituals in the domestic realm. Orthodox women may not serve as rabbis, and at synagogue services the women sit behind the men and cannot take part in significant rituals. Religious laws prohibit married women from bequeathing property to others without their husbands' consent. While men can divorce women, women are not free to divorce men. Beliefs and practices bearing on gender are somewhat more egalitarian among Conservative Jews, and much more so among Reform Jews. Among the latter, women may participate fully in services and a growing number are serving as rabbis.

Within Christianity women have traditionally been relegated to a secondary status. Some observers trace the rationale for this back to the writings of St. Paul, which can be used to justify gender subordination. For example:

> Let the wives be subject to their husbands as to the Lord; because a husband is head of the wife, just as Christ is head of the Church, being himself savior of the body. But just as the Church is subject to Christ, so also let wives be to their husbands in all things (Ephesians 5:22–24).

Among Christian denominations the degree to which patriarchy plays a role varies, just as it does among Jewish denominations. Its presence is strong in fundamentalist Protestant denominations that tend to be guided by literal interpretations of the Bible. But the Roman Catholic church, by far the largest of the Christian religious groups in the United States, is also heavily invested in doctrinal rules affecting male-female relations.

Under Catholic doctrine sex before or outside marriage is prohibited, and within marriage sexual intercourse is to take place only for the purpose of procreation. Births are to occur only within marriage. The use of artificial methods of birth control is outlawed, as is abortion. Marriage is a sacrament, and divorce is not recognized as legitimate. The norm of heterosexuality is emphasized: gay males and lesbians may be Catholics in good standing as long as they do not engage in homosexual behavior, which is sinful.

The fact that there are gay priests and lesbian nuns has contributed to debate within the church over its doctrine regarding homosexuality (see Curb and Manahan, 1985; Grammick, 1989). Until recently there was little acknowledgment that many clergy members themselves were violating church doctrine. Similar debate over church doctrine has been occurring in many other religious groups that view homosexuality negatively (Sheler, 1990; Ostling, 1991).

Participants in the Muslim faith of Islam often adhere to strict rules pertaining to male-female relations. The men and women attending a college in Pakistan are separated in their classroom by a privacy screen. The women's clothing is designed to shield their faces and bodies from the eyes of men.

Finally, from the pope to the parish priest, the most important religious leaders are male. Female nuns play a supportive and auxiliary role through church institutions such as schools, hospitals, and social services organizations. Unlike other Christian denominations, and some Jewish denominations as well, the Catholic church has remained quite inflexible in its position of prohibiting females from performing the religious roles of male clergy.

Islam is the fastest-growing religious group in the United States, largely as a consequence of immigration from nations heavily populated with Muslims, such as those of the Middle East. The Muslim faith also has a major impact on male-female relations, particularly among those who adhere to strict fundamentalist beliefs. Men are the heads of their households, and women are to be obedient to their wishes. Women are expected to bear children for their husbands and confine themselves to duties as wives and mothers within the home, while men fulfill religious obligations and serve as breadwinners. Women are prohibited from entering mosques, and most religious rituals involve only males. Female confinement to the home in part reflects a moral issue. Muslims believe that women are so sexually alluring to men that it is best to keep them hidden away. Women may not travel without an appropriate male companion, generally a relative. When appearing in public, they must dress modestly; many Muslim women use a veil and drape themselves to hide their faces and figures. In public life, every effort is made to segregate women from men and avoid any social contact between them, lest men be sexually tempted.

Earlier we mentioned the concept of nonofficial religion, beliefs and practices that depart from those of organized religious groups. Influenced by their own dissatisfactions with the treatment of women by official religion, informal groups of women across the United States have begun to create and experiment with beliefs and practices based on principles of **feminist spirituality** (see Plaskow and Christ, 1989; Christ and Plaskow, 1992). Feminist spirituality revolves around ecological sensitivity and the view that we are part of nature and its cycles; images or symbols of the divine, such as the Goddess, that derive from and speak to female experiences; and close interpersonal bonding and sharing of power with others as equals (Martin, 1993: 117).

The principles of feminist spirituality promote positive views of women. In Judith G. Martin's words,

> The primary source of feminist spirituality is *women's experiences*—their experiences of joy and anguish, of connectedness and alienation, of anger expressed and confidence restored; experiences that teach us to attune ourselves to the waxing and waning of opportunities; experiences that simultaneously help us appreciate how our lives are woven into the process of creation and the events of history, and how holistic participation in them liberates by bringing us into touch with our deepest selves (Martin, 1993: 18).

Often, gatherings coincide with particular cycles of nature or important historical events. The women create their own rituals at these gatherings, which may include inspirational readings, storytelling, music, and prayer or meditation. Participants at times borrow from or reinterpret aspects of existing religious traditions (see MacNichol and Walsh, 1993).

In sum, there are a variety of links between religion and patterns of class, race, and sex inequality in the United States. Religious groups tend to vary in their class composition. Many places of religious worship are largely racially segregated. Most African Americans, for example, are members of predominantly black churches. And religious doctrines often place strictures on the roles deemed appropriate for women. The latter situation has been undergoing some change in recent years. Yet the emergence of gatherings of women practicing feminist spirituality suggests that official religion in the United States still does not treat women as equals to men or speak adequately to women's spiritual needs.

THE SECULARIZATION THESIS: A REEXAMINATION

In the introduction to this chapter we mentioned the concept of **secularization,** a decline in the significance of religion in people's lives. For many years social scientists and other social thinkers accepted the secularization thesis, which predicted that religion would progressively play a less important role in societies around the world. Religious institutions would come to exercise less control over people's thinking and behavior, as other institutions (science, education, the state) would progressively take over functions traditionally performed by religion.

The secularization thesis can be traced back to some of the original contributors to sociological thinking about religion. As we have seen, Marx believed that religion was a form of false consciousness. It would, he believed, be cast aside as more and more people came to understand that they could transform their existence here on earth by making radical changes in capitalist society. To Durkheim, the increasing size, heterogeneity, and complexity of industrial societies were undermining religion, as they made it more and more difficult for societal members to cling to a shared set of moral values. Finally, the German sociologist Max Weber (whose work we discussed in Chapter 3) believed that modern societies were increasingly becoming organized around large-scale bureaucratic work and governmental organizations that emphasized human rationality, calculability, and efficiency. This approach superseded traditional modes of thinking and thus diminished the role of religion in the conduct of daily life.

Influenced by such thinking, for many years social scientists accepted the idea that "reason" would progressively vanquish "superstition" and religious beliefs would be supplanted by knowledge generated by science and technology. "God Is Dead" became a popular slogan in the 1960s to symbolize the assumed ascendance of the secularization process over religious faith. Proponents of the secularization thesis took the position that "science is expected to make religion implausible" (Stark and Bainbridge, 1985: 430).

In the words of anthropologist Anthony F. C. Wallace:

> The evolutionary future of religion is extinction. Belief in supernatural beings and in supernatural forces that affect nature without obeying nature's laws will erode and become only an interesting historical memory. . . . [As] a cultural trait, belief in supernatural powers is doomed to die out, all over the world, as a result of the increasing adequacy and diffusion of scientific knowledge . . . the process is inevitable (Wallace, 1966: 264–265).

In recent years the secularization thesis has undergone a major reexamination by social scientists, largely because the predictions of religion's demise have simply not proved true (Shupe, 1990). Sociologists have concluded that secularization is not a master trend occurring around the world in a unidimensional manner; the situation is much more complex. As two sociologists explained, commenting on the possible extinction of religion:

> There is growing evidence to indicate that such forecasts were premature. . . . This is not to deny the dramatic secularizing forces in the world. But in the United States and around the world, the religious factor is thriving. Religion has not disappeared even in those societies that have sought vigorously to suppress faith and organized religion (Shupe and Hadden, 1988: viii).

Statistics on the world population cannot tell us how intensely people hold on to religious beliefs or how significant religion is in their everyday lives. But such statistics do reveal that people adhere to a wide array of religions and that massive numbers of people around the world share common religious beliefs (see Table 15.2). Of the world's 5.4 billion people, fewer than 1 billion profess to be nonreligious. Of the remaining 4.5 billion who do adhere to a religion, 3.8 billion belong to the largest religious groups. For example, there are 1.8 billion Christians (including over 1 billion Catholics and more than 368 million Protestants). The other large religious groups are Muslims (951 million), Hindus (719 million), and Buddhists (309 million). Smaller groups, but still with significant numbers, are adherents of Chinese folk religion, tribal religionists, Sikhs, Jews, Shamanists, Confucians, Baha'is, Jains, Shintoists, and followers of new religions of various kinds (U.S. Department of Commerce, 1993: 60).

How can we account for the persistence, and in some cases the revival or resurgence, of religion in the face of secularization? Sociologists have been struggling with this question in recent years. One idea being explored is that religion may in some cases actually be *stimulated* by secularization processes. This is the position taken by sociologists Rodney Stark and William Sims Bainbridge (1985: 429–456; see also Finke and Stark, 1992). Let us briefly look at their analysis.

Stark and Bainbridge begin with the premise that religion assures people of highly desired rewards that cannot be achieved through any other

Table 15.2

RELIGIOUS ADHERENTS IN THE WORLD POPULATION, 1991

RELIGION	TOTAL (IN THOUSANDS)	PERCENT DISTRIBUTION
Total population	**5,385,330**	**100.0**
Christians	1,783,660	33.1
Roman Catholics	1,010,352	18.8
Protestants	368,209	6.8
Orthodox	168,683	3.1
Anglicans	73,835	1.4
Other Christians	162,581	3.0
Muslims	950,726	17.7
Nonreligious	884,468	16.4
Hindus	719,269	13.4
Buddhists	309,127	5.7
Atheists	236,809	4.4
Chinese folk-religionists	183,646	3.4
New-religionists	140,778	2.6
Tribal religionists	93,996	1.7
Sikhs	18,461	0.3
Jews	17,615	0.3
Shamanists	10,302	0.2
Confucians	5,917	0.1
Baha'is	5,402	0.1
Jains	3,724	0.1
Shintoists	3,163	0.1
Other religionists	18,268	0.3

Source: U.S. Bureau of the Census, *Statistical Abstract of the United States, 1992* (Washington, DC: U.S. Government Printing Office, 1993), p. 60.

means. Religion offers the possibility of an afterlife, thus helping people to endure tragedy by promising an end to their suffering. Indeed, *only* religion can offer people the possibility of an afterlife, which means they will not simply become extinct. The existence of an afterlife is something science can neither prove nor disconfirm. Stark and Bainbridge state: "We see no reason to suppose that the diffusion of science will make humans in the future less motivated to escape death, less affected by tragedy, less inclined to ask 'What does it all mean?' " (1985: 431). They thus posit that religion assumes important psychological functions for people that other institutions cannot replicate.

In modern times, religion has found itself in tension with the growing influence of other institutions. Forced to compete for people's attention and allegiance with such institutions as education, science, and the state, religion has *itself* in many instances become secularized. That is, many religions have progressively shed their traditional character. They have made changes in their practices and rituals and modified their belief systems in an attempt to reduce the tensions between themselves and other institutions and to broaden their appeal for membership. But in seeking to become more modern and relevant, such religious groups may make fewer claims about the powers of the supernatural. Indeed, they may place less emphasis on the supernatural altogether. In Stark and Bainbridge's view, the secularization of religion diminishes its effectiveness in assuring people that it can deliver the much-desired rewards of the afterlife. This being the case, why should people involve themselves in secularized religious groups?

Stark and Bainbridge suggest that typically the secularization process is uneven among religions. Thus, people in a religious group that is becoming secularized may simply shift to more traditional religious groups that relieve their existential anxieties and reassure them of a rewarding afterlife. But the secularization process may also produce two other reactions: revival and innovation (Stark and Bainbridge, 1985: 435–439). In the case of **revival,** efforts are made to renew and revitalize the traditional orientations of secularizing religions, as in the case of the Catholic charismatic movement and Protestant evangelicism in the United States. An alternative reaction, **innovation,** involves establishing entirely new religious traditions or new religions, such as the Mormons and the Unification church. The appearance of sects and cults, discussed earlier, is a form of innovation, as is the emergence of feminist spirituality and other forms of nonofficial religion.

Stark and Bainbridge's ideas also shed light on why societies dominated by nonreligious belief systems, such as the system that existed in the Soviet Union, are unsuccessful in stamping out religion. In their view, the secular character of these societies' belief systems fails to address the highly desired rewards that only religion can promise. Only religion can address people's unmet psychological needs. Thus, some form of traditional religion continues within such societies, even if it is in an underground capacity.

Other sociologists have been struggling to come up with a more global understanding of the relationship between secularization and religion. This approach reflects sociologists' increased interest in analyzing societies as parts of a larger environment that influences what goes on within them. Sociologists Anson Shupe and Jeffrey Hadden (1988) draw attention to the possible usefulness of the world-system perspective in this regard (see Chapter 2). In this view, individual societies are progressively becoming more globally integrated with one another. The development and growth of the world-system involves

> processes by which the world becomes a single place, both in respect to recognition of a very high degree of interdependence between spheres and locales of social activity across the entire globe and to the growth of consciousness pertaining to the globe as such (Roland Robertson, quoted in Shupe and Hadden, 1988: x–xi).

Sociologists influenced by the works of Marx have articulated this perspective.

However, Shupe and Hadden point out that the processes involved in the continued evolution and development of the world-system create "opposing trends." As governments pursue various political and economic arrangements associated with global integration, they make decisions that often pose challenges to religion-related cultural values within their societies. Earlier we saw that the Sanctuary Movement arose in the 1980s in response to U.S. cooperation with repressive governments in Guatemala

Religious movements may be energized by the political elite to change familiar traditional institutions and practices. Supporters of fundamentalist Islamic religious leader Ayatollah Khomeini overthrew the government of the shah of Iran partly for such reasons. Here, thousands of Iranian citizens gather for the tenth anniversary celebration of the 1979 revolution.

and El Salvador and U.S. policies on deportation of refugees from those countries. More recently, efforts by Arab and Israeli leaders to forge peaceful ties between their nations have outraged some segments of the Jewish and Arab Muslim communities, in some instances leading to additional violence.

Other governmental decisions may pose unwanted changes in traditional ways of life of societal members. The shah of Iran's efforts to modernize the institutions of Iranian society in the 1960s and 1970s are thought to have helped promote the rise of Islamic fundamentalism, which fueled the historic Iranian revolution and led to his overthrow. In periods of social change and uncertainty, when all that is familiar seems subject to transformation, traditional religion can provide people with moorings to hold on to. The Shah was replaced by a religious leader, the Ayatollah Khomeini, who created a state governed by Islamic clergy in 1979.

Thus, some groups or populations may view secularization processes as inappropriately crossing over into domains of thinking and behavior traditionally occupied by religion:

> As a result, any secularization that accompanies globalization, insofar as it involves culture conflict and challenges to the truth claims of various traditional religions, is self-limiting. In other words, secularization turns in on itself and creates the very conditions for a resurgence of religious influence. . . . At some point, globalization sets in motion the dynamic for a search for ultimate meaning, values, and resacralization [a return to the sacred] (Shupe and Hadden, 1988: xi).

Yet another opposing trend to secularization, according to Shupe and Hadden, is the globalization of electronic mass communications. People in even the most underdeveloped nations increasingly have instantaneous access to news of events all around the world. Yet the biases in coverage and superficiality in analysis associated with the mass media may well help fan misunderstandings and conflicts between religious groups and between religious groups and the state. Shupe and Hadden argue that the shortcomings of the mass media may also stimulate religious hostility between nations and even between entire geographic regions (1988: xii).

Thus, what had long been considered a truism, the demise of religion in the face of secularization, has come under active reexamination. Sociologists are now pursuing the challenge of understanding the conditions under which secularization energizes or reduces the social significance of religion.

CONCLUSION

Clearly, the continuing significance of religion in many, if not most, people's lives cannot be ignored. While our scientific and technical knowledge has expanded exponentially, people continue to harbor traditional religious beliefs or develop new ones that guide their thinking and behavior. In some cases these beliefs buttress the existing order, legitimizing even the most extreme differences in wealth, power, and prestige. In other cases religious beliefs inspire oppressed people to challenge the status quo, providing a powerful rationale for social movements aimed at transforming society.

We have also seen that religion, like other social institutions, often reflects the systems of class, race, and sex inequality that characterize our society. One's race and class background may influence one's religious-group membership and religious practices. The secondary role women play in many religious denominations reflects the pervasiveness of patriarchy and male dominance in U.S. society as a whole. The relationship between religion and such systems of inequality, and the impact of this relationship on people's biographies, deserves much more sociological inquiry.

The hold that religion has over people does not appear to be dwindling, either in the United States or worldwide. On a rapidly changing planet, where the emergence of new discoveries and new issues seems to constantly challenge our taken-for-granted lives, the solace and inspiration provided by religion may be humanly indispensable. If this is the case, we can only conclude that religion—in all its variety of forms—is here to stay.

THINKING CRITICALLY

1. Consider your own religion or that of a friend or relative. What were its origins? Is it closest today to the category of church, sect, denomination, or cult? Why?

2. Many people, even those who are members of organized religious groups, hold to beliefs or engage in practices that might be called nonofficial religion. What are some examples from your own life or from the lives of others you know?

3. In recent years there has been a great deal of controversy in the United States over such issues as women's legal right to abortion and discrimination against gay males and lesbians. Discuss the different positions taken on these topics by various religious groups with which you are familiar.

4. Sociologists have detected among people a wave of interest in new religions and various forms of nonofficial religion in recent years. How would you explain this, based upon your reading of this chapter?

5. Feminist spirituality reflects the feeling of women that they have been demeaned or treated unequally by conventional organized religious groups. Why is there at times so much resistance, as in the case of the Roman Catholic church, to making changes in this regard?

KEY TERMS

religion, *504*
sacred, *504*

profane, *504*
monotheism, *504*

polytheism, *504*
animism, *504*
church, *506*
sect, *506*
denomination, *506*
cult, *507*
official religion, *507*
nonofficial religion, *507*
class consciousness, *511*

false consciousness, *511*
liberation theology, *518*
denominational society, *523*
civil religion, *524*
feminist spirituality, *529*
secularization, *529*
revival, *532*
innovation, *532*

SUGGESTED READINGS

Carol P. Christ and Judith Plaskow (eds.), *Womanspirit Rising: A Feminist Reader in Religion.* San Francisco: Harper, 1992. A classic set of articles dealing with a wide range of issues in feminist theology and spirituality.

C. Eric Lincoln and Lawrence H. Mamiya, *The Black Church in the African American Experience.* Durham, NC: Duke University Press, 1990. A comprehensive overview of the black church that traces its history from its origins to the present and raises questions about its future.

J. Gordon Melton, *The Encyclopedia of American Religions.* Detroit, MI: Gale Research, 1989. A key work that provides detailed information on the beliefs and practices of the amazing array of religious groups that have operated in the United States since the sixteenth century.

Rodney Stark and William Sims Bainbridge, *The Future of Religion: Secularization, Revival, and Cult Formation.* Berkeley, CA: University of California Press, 1985. An overview of religion in the United States which posits that secularization may actually stimulate new religious activity.

Mary Jo Weaver, *New Catholic Women: A Contemporary Challenge to Traditional Religious Authority.* San Francisco: Harper & Row, 1985. An exploration of women's historical role in the Roman Catholic church and an analysis of the present controversy over the male monopolization of authority.

THINKING ABOUT THE FUTURE

EMERGING ISSUES

A sociological imagination enables us to grasp issues as they develop, not only in our own neighborhood or country but around the world. It empowers us to recognize the relationship between these issues and our own daily existence, even if their implications are not well developed. It also helps us identify questions that need to be examined in order to better understand the world around us. Using a sociological imagination enables us to play a part in shaping our existence and to take an active role in the decisions that affect our lives.

In this chapter we will introduce four emerging issues to demonstrate how one might use sociological insights to analyze such issues. What seems to be an isolated development in one sector of social life in fact sends ripples throughout the social system and illuminates the complex webs of social relationships and structures that form our society. The first issue concerns alternatives to funding schools with property-tax revenues. One alternative is the use of vouchers, or state-subsidized tuition allowances, whereby parents would pay for schools of their own choosing. The use of vouchers implies increasing privatization of a public service that is mandated by law for all persons until at least 15 years of age. While the media emphasize that vouchers can increase all parents' ability to choose the kind of education they want for their children, they have said little about the implications of privatizing such an important public service. Will everyone, indeed, benefit from privatizing education through vouchers? Will we all benefit equally? What are the costs of using vouchers for each of us and for society? Are there alternatives other than vouchers that could address the educational inequalities created by funding schools with property-tax revenues? If so, what are they?

The second emerging issue we will examine is the impact of the graying of America. We are living longer, and more of us are entering our senior years now than ever before. What does this mean for society and for the quality of life that we can each expect to have during retirement? Will we all face the same issues and challenges as we age, or are there differing patterns based on gender, race, and class? As the baby-boom generation enters middle age and looms as the largest cohort of elderly people in our society, we must begin to untangle the implications of an aging population.

We will also look at the issue of the future of military production in the aftermath of the Cold War. Industries that have been devoted to defense contracting must now find a way to survive without such contracts or with drastically reduced military production. What choices do they have? Must they continue to produce arms, or are there other alternatives? What are the implications—for each of us, for society, and for the world—of the choices these industries make? Since the end of the Cold War has eliminated the justification for continued mili-

tary production, it is increasingly important for us to explore the possible alternatives.

Finally, we will explore the issue of environmental racism. Few analyses concerning the environment examine the roles of race and racism in decisions on where to put toxic waste or what to do with pesticides and other toxic substances that are banned in the United States. Yet patterns indicate that pollutant and toxic waste sites are selected on the basis of race. That such patterns exist, and why, is important for each of us, because they affect such fundamental issues as health and life span. They also suggest significant insights about power and decision-making.

The sociological imagination you have by now developed invites you to examine the social context in which these issues continue to evolve. We should ask questions concerning the structural arrangements, institutional processes, and social relationships that help define these emerging issues as public issues rather than simply personal troubles. Armed with sociological concepts and a sociological imagination, we can begin to explore how our own and others' biographies may be affected by emerging issues.

VOUCHERS FOR EDUCATION

As we noted in Chapter 12, funding schools with revenues from property taxes produces unequal educational opportunities and institutionalized discrimination. What other resources for school budgets can we use that would not create racially segregated schools or educational inequality based on the economic class of the local community members?

Connecticut Governor Lowell Weicker offered a bold proposal in 1993. His proposal was in response to a lawsuit filed by an African American parent who charged that her son was denied his constitutional rights to an education equal to that provided to whites in the suburbs. The National Association for the Advancement of Colored People (NAACP) agreed, arguing that the state had the responsibility to reduce racial and economic inequality in education. Weicker's proposal would divide the state into several large school districts, each containing poor communities as well as wealthier towns and including school systems composed primarily of people of color as well as systems composed almost entirely of whites. Each new school district would pool its property-tax revenues for education in one large fund, and children would be assigned to schools within that large district. The idea is to retain the current method of raising money for schools but to redistribute the funds more equitably. The proposal would promote greater racial integration in schools, because it would override patterns of racial discrimination in housing that produce racially segregated local community schools.

Needless to say, Weicker's proposal created controversy. Residents in affluent towns do not want to pay higher property taxes than residents in poorer towns, only to have their children sent to school elsewhere. Some critics of the proposal have also noted that it preserves reliance on property-tax revenues as the basis for funding schools and increases the likelihood of busing children to schools outside their own neighborhoods, a practice that has been highly controversial.

The Arguments for a Voucher System

Are there alternatives to using property-tax revenues to fund schools? An increasing number of observers and critics assert that *privatizing* the school system, or at least resorting to funding schools through a voucher system, will solve the problem. The debate has centered around the notions of *choice* and *competition*: schools will "earn" their budgets in a competitive marketplace in which parents choose the schools they want their children to attend. Families will not be restricted to schools in their local community: poor parents may send their children to schools in more affluent communities, and people of color may send their children to schools in all-white or integrated neighborhoods. The schools parents select will receive vouchers from the parents as payment for the children's tuition.

School vouchers are certificates given to families that authorize the government to use public funds to pay their children's tuition at the school of their choice. Vouchers are for a specified amount of money. Parents may augment this stipend with their own funds to pay tuitions that are more expensive than the amount the vouchers provide, but everyone will receive an equal value in a voucher. There are varying proposals concerning how the vouchers could be used. For example, conservative economist Milton Freidman suggests a *laissez-faire* approach, involving few, if any, governmental controls over which schools could receive the funds. In contrast, educators Christopher Jencks and John Coons suggest that the government carefully monitor the types of schools that could receive the funds (Doyle, 1983). In either case, supporters of the use of vouchers insist that they will offer parents choice and control over their children's education (Kirkpatrick, 1990).

Vouchers are not the same as **tax credits,** another mechanism often touted as a means of facilitating parental choice of education. Tax credits allow parents to simply deduct the costs of their children's education from their annual federal tax burden (Doyle, 1983). Although both vouchers and tax credits could involve the use of public funds to support private schools, tax credits are meaningful only for wealthy and middle-class families who have significant tax burdens; the poor generally do not have high-enough income-tax burdens to need deductions.

Hence, supporters of school vouchers argue that vouchers would be more egalitarian than tax credits and would promote greater equal opportunity than currently exists. They believe that the present system of governmentally funded public schools and privately funded private schools reinforces inequality, since the wealthy have always had the economic means to send their children to schools providing better education. The poor have had to rely on public schools, which do not have sufficient resources to provide adequate education or to address problems such as drug abuse, violence, and teenage pregnancy (Nathan, 1985). The use of school vouchers, supporters argue, would give economically disadvantaged parents the same ability that wealthy parents have to choose the education they want for their children (Coons and Sugarman, 1991).

Supporters also argue that vouchers would promote improvements in public schools by creating a competitive education marketplace: because increasing enrollments would also mean increased funds, public schools would naturally compete with private schools for students. Thus, public schools would have a greater incentive to provide evidence of their effectiveness—such as improved scores on achievement tests, increased motivation of students, higher graduation rates, and improved literacy rates—particularly in regard to children of color and low-income students (most of whom are white), who currently seem to benefit least from public education (Nathan, 1989).

Proponents of school vouchers believe that the voucher system will encourage schools to experiment with their settings and curricula. Relying on a common structure and common curriculum, as public schools do, does not recognize that many students have individual learning needs: "Some will blossom, for example, in a strict traditional school, or one that emphasizes performing arts along with basic skills. Others will do better in a Montessori program" (Nathan, 1989: 24). The use of vouchers would encourage schools to specialize in particular curricula or learning structures to attract students and maximize their learning. Proponents of vouchers, then, see the invisible hand of the market in education as a stimulus for effective reform.

The Arguments against a Voucher System

Critics of school vouchers raise several objections. First, they take issue with the assumption that competition among schools will increase the quality of education. They point out that competition in the business world does not guarantee higher-quality products; profit, not quality, motivates corporate activity. Corporate competition occasionally enables consumers to save money (as a result of price wars, for instance), but the products purchased at a lower price may still be of poor quality (Evans, 1990). The same may be said about schools. Competition stimulated by the use of school vouchers does not guarantee greater quality of education. Rather, schools may compete through price wars, lowering tuitions in order to attract students. Keeping tuitions low may force schools to decrease wages of faculty, skimp on facilities and resources, increase class sizes, and reduce programs. Indeed, colleges and universities throughout the United

States have faced just this problem in the 1990s. All have acknowledged the extreme difficulty of keeping tuition increases under control without sacrificing quality. Critics believe that elementary and high schools will face the same problems under the competitive marketplace created by the use of vouchers.

Moreover, the incentive to keep tuitions low could mean that the less expensive, and therefore perhaps lower-quality, schools would be economically attractive to low-income families. These families lack the resources to add to their vouchers to pay for more expensive, higher-quality schools. Vouchers thus may very well re-create the inequality that currently characterizes education in the United States: high-quality private schools for the wealthy, and low-quality, overburdened public education for the poor.

Furthermore, the notion of school choice is premised on the assumption of equal access to information about the educational programs from which parents may choose. However, studies of underparticipation in several social welfare programs suggest that there is inequality in access to information, creating an environment in which poor, minority, or uneducated parents will be making choices on the basis of inadequate information (Love, 1970; Piven and Cloward, 1971; Welch, Steinman, and Comer, 1973; Taylor-Gooby, 1976). For example, researchers have long acknowledged that minorities, particularly bilingual groups, tend to use more informal methods of information gathering than do majority populations (Olivas, 1981). These informal methods frequently include networks of word-of-mouth, often non-English, sources, as opposed to printed material from outreach programs and advertisements that require literacy skills or a working command of the English language. But information transmitted through informal networks is often based on the limited experiences or knowledge of the persons involved. Because voucher proposals are designed to generate a complex array of choices, complete and accurate information about them is crucial for decision-making. Voucher plans, then, would be more likely to decrease informed participation by low-income or bilingual families, "as oral and informal communication networks would be inadequate to convey the complicated data on school characteristics or parental prerogatives to organize and establish new schools" (Olivas, 1981: 450).

Supporters of the use of vouchers often point to the success of private and parochial schools, which tend to have higher test scores and graduation rates than public schools (Nathan, 1985). This argument, however, does not acknowledge the important fact that private and parochial schools are *selective* and may siphon off the high-performance students from the public schools. Moreover, they often reject or expel students with behavioral or scholastic problems. This selectivity leads to higher aggregate test scores and fewer problems with drug abuse, teenage pregnancy, and violence, explaining why the private and parochial schools seem to be more successful or efficient than public schools.

Another problem with school vouchers is that they may in fact use public money to subsidize better education for the already-privileged in society, thereby increasing inequality. Since private schools are under less governmental scrutiny and regulation than public schools, vouchers may encourage "circumvent[ion of] laws and regulations governing such issues as equal employment opportunity, due process, desegregation, religious activities, licensure" (Finch, 1985: 11). For example, private schools are under few regulations regarding equal opportunity or affirmative action compliance, in both hiring personnel and selecting students. They may elect to expel students or fire personnel without evidence of the use of due process. Moreover, they are under no obligation to provide remedial programs to address the needs of learning-disabled, disadvantaged, or bilingual students (Stimson, 1986). Indeed, a study of the Milwaukee Parental Choice Plan, an experiment in the use of school vouchers to support school choice, found that students with disabilities were not accommodated well at all (Underwood, 1991).

This last issue raises the question of the influence of budget sources on school policy. What, or who, influences educational approaches? Under a voucher program, such decisions have great potential to be driven more by what is profitable in the marketplace than by what is most educationally sound. For example, educational professionals have long debated the most effective learning environment for students with disabilities: Are they best educated in classes segregated from the rest of the student population, or are they better served by being "mainstreamed" and integrated into this population? Currently, continuing research into the effectiveness of each approach and professional educators' analyses drive this issue. But the competitive marketplace created by the use of vouchers could become the influential factor, instead, thereby potentially subsidizing and aggravating increasing inequality by ignoring the educational needs of some populations of students such as the disabled, the bilingual, and people of color.

The battle lines concerning school choice and school vouchers have clearly been drawn. Before we rally to the appeal of this alternative to inequitable locally funded schools, we must ask many pointed questions: What evidence exists to suggest that vouchers would decrease the racial and economic inequality that current methods of funding schools create? How would vouchers address the issue of tracking within schools? What safeguards would guarantee adequate education of populations such as non-English-speaking groups and the disabled? How can we guarantee equal access to information for informed decision-making? How would we ensure diversity and integration in the curriculum under a school-choice and voucher program? Might the competitive marketplace created by vouchers introduce the development of "point-of-view" schools that would limit a student's exposure to a variety of ideas and create gross inconsistencies in curriculum? How can we monitor such a possibility, and how do we ensure that it does not happen? Does the use of vouchers for parochial and other religious schools mean state subsidization of religious education; and, if it does, does this violate the constitutional separation of church and state? These are some of the policy questions we must answer in order to make an informed decision on the use of school vouchers as an alternative source of school budget funding. They arise as a consequence of applying the sociological imagination to the study of education and its relationship to the larger society.

How these questions are handled will affect your children. If schools become increasingly privatized through the use of vouchers, will your chil-

The use of school vouchers to give parents choices concerning their children's education introduces several controversial issues. For example, critics argue that using vouchers for parochial or religious schools, such as the one pictured here, would violate the constitutional separation of church and state.

dren benefit, or will they be among those who are shortchanged? Can you be certain that you will have enough economic resources to add to the value of your voucher so that you can purchase the best education possible for your children? And even if you can, will the shift in education to a market-oriented voucher system ensure the best education for your children? Or will market forces introduce factors that reduce the quality of your children's education? We must entertain such concerns as we listen to and participate in the national debate about school vouchers.

THE GRAYING OF AMERICA

Imagine walking down the street in 30 or 40 years and noticing that more than one-third of the people you see have gray hair. Within the next few decades such a scenario will be a reality. The age distribution in the United States will have shifted so dramatically toward the elderly that society as we know it is likely to look quite different. Imagine the impact an aging population will have on institutions such as the family, the economy, and the government. Many of our social institutions will have to change in order to accommodate the pressure of a large elderly cohort.

The Demographic Facts

Demographers and the U.S. Bureau of the Census have noted that the population of the United States is aging. The average life span has been steadily increasing since the 1950s, largely as a result of advances in nutrition, exercise, and medicine. Children born in 1990, for example, can expect to live an average of 75.4 years (U.S. Bureau of the Census, 1992b). In addition, the baby-boom generation (persons born between 1946 and 1964) has begun to enter middle age. But while the birth rate since the 1980s has been increasing somewhat, in an "echo boom" of the baby boom, it is not as large an increase as that following World War II. This means that by the turn of the century, the **population pyramid** will be decidedly top-heavy. A population pyramid is a bar graph composed of age groups arranged from the youngest at the bottom to the oldest at the top (see Figure 16.1). By the year 2000, the number of people age 65 and over will be larger than it has ever been, and the bars of the population pyramid depicting the oldest age groups will be longer than the bars of the youngest groups.

Estimates vary about exactly how many people will be in this older group, but there is wide consensus that the increase will be rather dramatic. In 1990, 3.3 million people in the United States were 85 years old or older; by the year 2080, according to Census Bureau estimates, there will be 18.7 million people in this age group (Kolata, 1992). Meanwhile, the growth of the younger segments of the population is slowing down. In 1960, for example, 16.5 million children were 5 years old or younger; by 1990, the number had grown only slightly, to 19.2 million. The growth in the 65-and-older age group was far more pronounced: in 1960 there were 16.7 million people in this group, roughly the same as the youngest age group; but by 1990, the number had almost doubled, to 31.2 million (U.S. Bureau of the Census, 1991c). Observers agree that this age group will continue to increase rapidly. What are the implications of this graying of America?

The Experience of the Elderly

We can anticipate some of the effects of this population bulge by examining the experiences of today's elderly and applying a sociological imagination. As we noted in Chapter 6, our elders' experiences are affected both by social constructions of age and by combinations of age and other statuses, particularly race, class, and gender. For example, not everyone born in the United States in the same year can expect to have the same life span. As Figure 16.2 indicates, one's sex and race affect one's life expectancy. White females born in 1990 have a life expectancy four years greater than the average life expectancy of all children born in that year; African American females have a life expectancy a year lower than the average. The life expectancy of males born in 1990 is lower than that of females, regardless of race, but white males can expect to live six years longer than African American males (U.S. Bureau of the Census, 1992b). What effects do these differential life expectancies have?

Gender Differences Since females on average live longer than males, women outnumber men in the older bands of the population pyramid. By age 75, the present sex ratio is 55 men for every 100 women. Since the cultural trend in the United States runs against older women marrying sub-

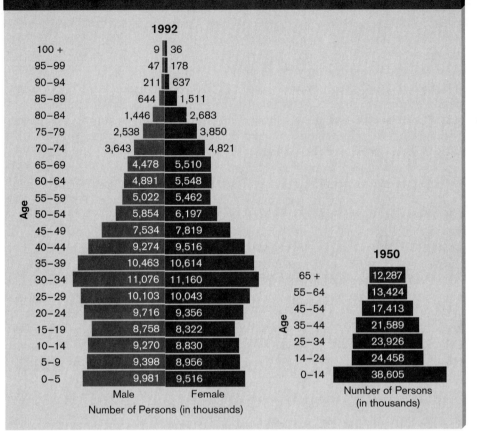

FIGURE 16.1 POPULATION PYRAMID, 1992 AND 1950

Population pyramids demonstrate how age groups are distributed throughout the population, as shown here for both 1950 and 1992. While the 1950 data were not reported by sex, the 1992 data were. Note that the 1950 pyramid has only a few, broad age groups, with the last group including everyone over age 65. Why does the 1992 pyramid divide persons over 65 into a number of specific age groups? What are the implications of an aging population? What are the implications of the sex distributions of various age groups? (*Source:* U.S. Bureau of the Census, *Population Projections of the United States, by Age, Sex, Race, and Hispanic Origin: 1992 to 2050*, Current Population Reports, Series P25-1092, Washington, DC: U.S. Government Printing Office, 1992.)

stantially younger men, it is likely that many older women will live for years without partners. Indeed, 80 percent of the widowed elderly in the United States are women (Neubeck, 1991).

What does this mean? How do institutions such as the family, the economy, and the state affect the social construction of being an elderly female? As we noted in Chapter 14, studies show that the detrimental economic consequences of widowhood for many women are as serious as

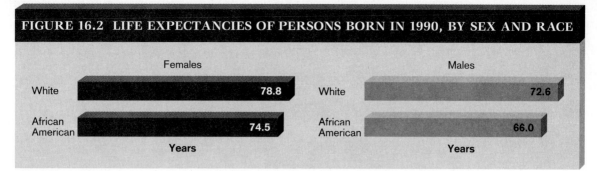

FIGURE 16.2 LIFE EXPECTANCIES OF PERSONS BORN IN 1990, BY SEX AND RACE

Females		Males	
White	78.8	White	72.6
African American	74.5	African American	66.0
Years		**Years**	

While population pyramids provide information about age distributions by sex, they do not tell us anything about such distributions by race. This figure shows that life expectancies vary significantly by race. Why might this be the case? (*Source:* U.S. Bureau of the Census, *Statistical Abstract of the United States, 1993,* Washington, DC: U.S. Government Printing Office, 1993, p. 76.)

those of divorce. Women suffer significant declines in their economic well-being as a result of widowhood, partially because men frequently do not provide adequate survivor's insurance benefits to their partners (see Holden and Smock, 1991). Since women either are full-time unpaid workers at home or are paid less on average than men in the formal labor force (see Chapter 11), it is likely that they will suffer serious declines in income after widowhood. Thus, as women outlive men, they will spend a significant proportion of their elderly years most likely alone and possibly poor (or at least much poorer than they were accustomed to).

Race Differences Since the life span of people of color tends to be shorter than that of whites, the older bands in the population pyramid are likely to be disproportionately white. If we couple this probability with the gender differentials in both life expectancy and labor-force incomes, we can develop an understanding of the meaning of quality of life among various categories of the elderly.

How well one lives in retirement depends a great deal on one's income while a member of the formal labor force. Thus, while overall the poverty rate has been declining among older groups, the picture changes when we examine the distribution of poverty by race and gender. As Figure 16.3 shows, in 1990 the poverty rate for whites 65 and older was 10.1 percent, while the rate for African Americans in this age group was more than three times as high, at 33.8 percent. Women in this age group were more than twice as likely as men to be poor (15.4 percent of elderly women were poor, compared to 7.6 percent of elderly men). And while white men in this age group had a poverty rate of 5.6 percent, African American women were almost *seven* times more likely to be poor (at 37.9 percent); almost half (48.1 percent) of African American female-headed households with no husbands were in poverty (U.S. Bureau of the Census, 1991b). This disparity occurs because, as we pointed out in Chapters 6 and 11, the incomes of women and people of color are lower than those of white males during

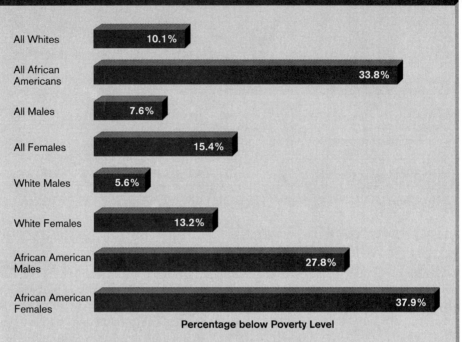

FIGURE 16.3 POVERTY STATUS OF PERSONS 65 YEARS AND OVER, BY RACE AND SEX, 1990

	Percentage below Poverty Level
All Whites	10.1%
All African Americans	33.8%
All Males	7.6%
All Females	15.4%
White Males	5.6%
White Females	13.2%
African American Males	27.8%
African American Females	37.9%

Not all elderly people are poor. However, among those 65 and older, the distribution of poverty varies greatly by race and sex. Why might these factors affect poverty in the elderly? (*Source:* U.S. Bureau of the Census, *Poverty in the United States: 1990,* Current Population Reports, Series P60-175, Washington, DC: U.S. Government Printing Office, 1991, p. 24.)

their years in the formal labor force; since women tend to live longer than men, the likelihood that they will live out their later years in poverty is increased. Thus, groups that are disadvantaged in the formal labor market (women, people of color) continue to be disadvantaged in retirement. The wage differential in the labor market forces these groups to place increased pressure on federal and state programs that already are inadequate to aid the aging poor.

The Effect of the Elderly on Social Institutions

An aging population in general increases pressures on the institution of the state, particularly on programs designed to address the issues and needs of the elderly. As was discussed in Chapter 13, we become more vulnerable to illnesses and disease as we age; thus we require greater and more extensive medical care. Of course, aging does not necessarily entail becoming frail, feeble, or senile, but the older we get the more susceptible we become to chronic or long-term illnesses such as arthritis, heart disease, Alzheimer's, and various types of cancer. Some chronic conditions are exacerbated by extended exposure to environmental toxins or by other ongoing factors such as smoking, alcohol abuse, lack of exercise, or high-fat diets; the longer we live, the more these factors are affecting us. Chronic illnesses typically are among the most expensive to treat, which means that the more elderly there are in the population, the greater the expense of health care for the nation.

By some estimates, the medical expenses of people over age 85 are two and a half times greater than the expenses of those between 65 and 69 (Samuelson, 1993). Thus, Medicare costs will increase significantly as the baby-boom bubble of the population ages in increasingly longer life spans. Samuelson (1993) estimates that taxes will have to increase by about $120 billion by the year 2010 in order to cover the increased health costs. Such tax hikes can create antagonism between the smaller population of taxpaying younger workers and the larger (and growing) population of the nonworking elderly.

The government is considering including nursing-home and other long-term care (such as visiting nurses and caretakers) in an expanded Medicare package. This is because many older persons in the United States face the terrifying prospect of being bankrupted by the costs of nursing-home care. The annual cost of such care per person in 1988 averaged between $22,000 and $25,000 (Price and O'Shaughnessy, 1988). The elderly and their families pay slightly more than half of that cost, with the remainder currently paid by Medicaid. Between 1986 and 1990, when the total national bill for nursing-home care was $33 billion, Medicaid and Medicare paid out $14.6 billion of that bill (Rivlin and Wiener, 1988). Estimates suggest that the annual cost of extended home health care and nursing-home care is $45 billion (Samuelson, 1993). Adding the full cost of nursing-home care and home health care to the government bill would significantly increase the tax burden on the younger working population.

The institution of the family is greatly affected by these pressures on health-care systems. In Chapter 14 we noted that the high cost of nursing-home care was causing more families to care for their frail or disabled elderly members themselves. Indeed, in 1985, most of the elderly with disabilities were cared for by their own families, either in the elders' own homes in the same community or in their children's homes (Liu et al., 1986; Macken, 1986). More than one-third of the elderly with disabilities lived with their children, compared with only 21 percent in nursing-home care (Stone et al., 1987). The impact this has on families is important. The children of elderly parents with disabilities are often ill-equipped to care for them, since many of the children either are working couples or are unemployed or underemployed. Some 30 percent of the caregivers had incomes in the poor or near-poor categories in one study (Stone and Kemper, 1989; see also Ferber, O'Farrell, and Allen, 1991). In this way class influences the impact of aging on families.

Gender also figures prominently in the effects of elder care. Studies indicate that women are more often the caregivers than men, with 2.6 million women performing that role, compared with 1.6 million men (Stone and Kemper, 1989; see also Ferber, O'Farrell, and Allen, 1991). Such women spend an average of 12 to 35 hours per week on elder care, depending on the severity of the dependence (Creedon, 1989). Research also shows that 12 percent of the *full-time* working women in the United States are responsible for elder care in their families (Stone and Kemper, 1989; see also Ferber, O'Farrell, and Allen, 1991). In addition, 3.5 percent of the women working full-time in the formal labor force were responsible for caring for both elderly family members *and* children (McLanahan and Monson, 1989). How do they cope with the role conflicts introduced by such tremendous burdens on their time and energy?

One study, noted in Chapter 14, found that 12 percent of women workers responsible for elder care quit their jobs in the formal labor force, while another 25 percent took time off without pay, and another 23 percent reduced their work hours. Only 35 percent were able to rearrange their work schedules to accommodate their elder-care responsibilities (Stone et al., 1987; see also Freidman, 1991). These data show that 60 percent of the women in the formal labor force who were responsible for elder care in their families had to accept reductions in their family incomes in order to provide that care. Thus, an aging population puts financial strains on both federal budgets and family incomes.

An aging population also places pressures on the social security system. Originally designed as a social contract with America's workers, the social security system relies on payments from current workers to pay the benefits of current retirees; the assumption is that when these current workers retire and begin to collect their entitlements, enough workers will fill their vacated places in the labor market to support them throughout retirement. However, the shift in the population pyramid suggests that this may not be the case after the turn of the century. If more elderly peo-

Retirement often means a seriously reduced income. For many retirees it also means being forced out of the labor market at a time when they are still capable of being productive. While some retirees engage in volunteer work to continue making important contributions to society, others find they can be productive and earn much-needed income by working in places like the fast-food restaurant pictured here.

ple in the United States are living longer after they retire, and fewer younger and middle-aged people are in the labor force to pay their entitlements, pressures on the social security system could mount to crisis proportions. Indeed, over the past decade many people have debated whether or not the system is already bankrupt or in danger of becoming so.

Such fears raise the question of the social construction of retirement. Currently, most workers retire between 62 and 65 years of age. Most of them retire willingly, but for as much as 40 percent of retirees, retirement is involuntary (Neubeck, 1991). Because of improvements in health care and health awareness, many people in the United States are still quite healthy physically and mentally when they retire, and they can expect to live 20 more years. This creates a role strain, in which a person may want to fulfill the obligations of a productive citizen but may not have the opportunity to do so. What does retirement mean, then, when a retiree is still able and willing to be productive? And how is a retired person to live for 20 or more years on an income that is just a fraction of that to which he or she may have been accustomed?

Some retirees resolve their role strain by seeking employment after retirement. Fast-food firms such as McDonald's have made a point of hiring retirees as counter workers. Retirees who do not necessarily need the income of a paying job but want to continue making positive contributions to their communities often perform important volunteer services; many donate time and skills as day-care workers, hospital aides, soup-kitchen aides, cancer-care volunteers, and so forth, as did the people described in the accompanying boxed excerpt. All these pursuits suggest that our social construction of retirement may indeed be based on antiquated stereotypes of elderly fragility, senility, and declining productivity. Yet a shrinking labor market encourages continuation of these stereotypes, as younger workers pressure older workers to retire to make room for them.

In addition to its effects on the institutions of the economy, the state, and the family, the aging of America also affects the political process. As the baby-boom generation ages and lives longer, it has a greater impact on voting and the legislative process, in part because it represents one of the largest age cohorts in the voting population. Studies show that political participation rates increase with age (Dobson, 1983). As we saw in Chapter 10, politicians are paying increasing attention to the issues and needs of older people in the United States because there is a significant and growing number of them and because they vote.

Of course, political clout among the aged is dependent upon the development of **age consciousness,** the awareness of common interests based on age. Older people can have a tremendous political impact by organizing and mobilizing their collective effort for change (see Chapter 9). Opportunities for increasing age consciousness are growing as a result of such trends as segregated housing for the elderly in retirement communities and federal and state programs that stimulate interaction among the elderly, such as senior day-care arrangements (Neubeck, 1991).

Their potential for organized political clout has not been lost on aging persons in the United States. They have been organizing into powerful

I n her book on aging, The Fountain of Age, *Betty Friedan describes how retired persons have maintained their vitality through mindful, not mindless, activity. In this excerpt she provides first-person accounts of the Peace Corp experiences of retirees.*

A funny thing has been happening to the Peace Corps: more and more of the volunteers now have gray hair. The average age was twenty-three when John F. Kennedy started the Peace Corps in 1961. Today, over 500 of the 6,300 recruits are from fifty to seventy-eight years old, and someone recently retired at eighty-six. Odi Long joined the Peace Corps at sixty-five after he retired from his job as a lineman at Illinois Bell. Patricia "Sam" Udall went in at fifty-seven, and came out at sixty-one to start a new career as Senior Volunteer Facilitator. She told me:

> The Peace Corps was designed for people fresh out of college; they'd get this vigorous Outward Bound physical training, and be sent off to Mozambique to dig wells. Many had never held jobs before, they wanted this adventure before going into their careers or professional training. Now we get the older persons at the end of their careers, with enormous experience profession-

ally and in life. Their business skills are more and more what's needed in the Third World countries, where most people live in cities now and the problems are more complex than digging wells.

> We've discontinued that vigorous physical training because it isn't appropriate any more. The major difference with the older volunteers is that they have the skills and experience the young don't have, and they insist on being constructive. At sixty-five, they've been pushed out of the American job market, and the Peace Corps offers an opportunity for them to be very productive and continue using their skills in society. It seems to revitalize older people, though physically it's still hard, and harder still to learn a new language, like Swahili.

> One big thing we've got going for us is the respect for age in most of the countries we go to. We hear and learn a lot that younger people don't because people in other countries aren't that comfortable talking to younger people. The worst problem is that older people want to see results, because they recognize their time is finite, how they use their time is vital, they're not as willing to just be laid back, hang out. They take more risks too, if they've had to sell their homes, or quit their jobs, or have a health condi-

political groups ever since Maggie Kuhn founded the Gray Panthers in the 1970s. Currently enjoying a membership of over 70,000, the Gray Panthers organization has frequently challenged ageist stereotypes and age discrimination in the workplace and society. It also helps increase awareness among legislators of the need for policies for the elderly. Other groups, such as the American Association of Retired Persons (AARP), have also had an impact on the political process. As the bulk of the population pyramid shifts to the elderly, and these people find their voice in influential political organizations, the political process will pay more and more attention to issues and interests affecting the elderly.

The shift in the population pyramid has an interesting effect on a culture that has focused primarily on youth since the 1960s, when baby

"They assigned me to Tonga and my daughter was vehemently opposed: 'You may never see your grandchildren alive.'"

tion. But people over fifty don't seem to get "separated" from the Peace Corps at any higher rate than at thirty-five. The problems of placing an older person with a history of high blood pressure aren't any greater than a young one with a history of asthma.

At sixty-six, Bernie Lovitsky, an executive search consultant in Atlanta, recalled his depression, and deterioration of confidence, in his years of early retirement before he joined the Peace Corps. He had sold his discount store in Michigan after his wife died, and moved to a California beach community:

I wasn't working, and got very depressed, just sitting around in that beach lifestyle. Everyone seemed to be running away, living on the surface. I thought of starting a new business, but I was losing confidence I could do it again. Driving down the freeway, I heard a public service announcement about joining the Peace Corps, age didn't matter. Maybe the yuppies weren't volunteering enough.

They assigned me to Tonga and my daughter was vehemently opposed: "You may never see your grandchildren alive." The language training was hard, but I was determined to understand these people and have them understand me. I'd join their wedding processions, clap when they did, eat what they ate. I went to their feasts and fireworks, and danced with the women and men. I was supposed to help them set up a wholesale grocery distribution system. I found out they were being taken advantage of, high prices, bad merchandise. In two years their cooperative went from $20,000 a year to $2 million. Today they're doing $4 million and the business is being run by the Tongan people themselves.

Today, in my mid-sixties, I have more energy than I've ever had in my life. After my two and a half years as a Peace Corps volunteer, I got myself a job in an executive search firm, met my second wife who'll never stop either—we set up the only couples' shelter for the homeless, we've got fourteen hundred volunteers. I'll never retire again. But what's important to me now is not the work I do for money but what I do that isn't just materialistic, that really touches people's lives and makes a difference.

Source: Betty Friedan, *The Fountain of Age* (New York: Simon and Schuster, 1993), pp. 222–224.

boomers became relatively affluent and the largest and most vocal segment of the population. Films, television, advertising, and subject matter have tended to strongly favor the young. Over the past several years, however, more commercials have been appearing for products pitched to an aging population, such as adult disposable diapers for incontinence, vitamins designed for older people, electric light switches that operate at the clap of a hand, emergency alert systems that are voice-activated, and life insurance programs that will not deny policies no matter how old the applicant. Where we once saw only young models in advertisements and fashion magazines, we now occasionally see older, gray-haired models. Television programs such as *The Golden Girls* and *Golden Palace* contain older actors, who are depicted as vibrant, sexually active, and productive.

On the other hand, our culture's emphasis on the desirability of youth has hardly disappeared. As the population ages, advertisements offer hair dyes to cover the gray, products to replace hair on balding heads, facial creams to smooth out wrinkles, and senior citizen exercise videotapes promising to make their users look and feel young. While we may be living longer, the advertisers emphasize that we need not look "old." The population shift to older cohorts, then, also increasingly affects the culture, simultaneously celebrating and resisting the aging process.

Why is this population shift of concern to you now? First, you probably have parents or other relatives who are currently elderly, and thus you are learning firsthand what the population shift already means to their existence (and to your own if you are their primary caretaker). Second, if current trends continue, we will all eventually become part of those increasingly larger older bands of the population pyramid. Who will support the social security program on which we will depend? How will decisions we make now concerning the federal budget and the deficit affect our ability to count on programs such as Medicare, social security, and elder care when we are eligible for them? How will current decisions regarding a national health-care policy affect our quality of life in retirement? How can we improve our economic well-being while we are in the labor force so as to increase our life chances when we retire? It is important not to frame our questions and our analysis in terms of a pitched battle between the young and the elderly; rather, we should frame them in terms of our life-cycle relationship to such macro-level social structures as the economy, the state, and the intersection of race, class, gender, and age within institutions.

THE FUTURE OF MILITARY PRODUCTION

By the 1990s, the Cold War between the East (represented by the communist bloc countries of the Soviet Union and Eastern Europe) and the West (represented by the capitalist economies of the United States and Western Europe) had come to an end. The Berlin Wall had been torn down, and the German Democratic Republic and the Federal Republic of Germany reunited after existing separately since World War II; the Soviet Union had ceased to exist following the restructuring of Soviet society, or *perestroika,* and its republics became independent nations. Despite evidence of a rise of neofascist, ultra-right-wing parties and candidates in Russia and other European countries, the threat from the communist bloc essentially disappeared for the Western countries. They were left with the question of how to deal with huge industrial production efforts focused on supporting the military. Since World War II, the U.S. economy has been military-industrial-based. Should it now convert to peacetime production or continue engaging in military production and export arms elsewhere? How do we make such decisions, and what do they entail? And, in the light of our discussion in Chapter 10, what role can the military-industrial complex be expected to play in the decision-making process? These decisions affect jobs, levels of global violence, and even levels of interpersonal violence domestically (through sales of weapons at home, for example).

We need to consider the sociological questions concerning conversion and apply a sociological imagination to answer some of them. For example, who benefits and who is hurt by conversion? What sorts of jobs are created by conversion, and what sorts are lost because of cutbacks in defense contracts? How do the new jobs compare with the lost jobs in terms of employees' hours, wages, benefits, rights to organize in a union, and work conditions? Who gets the new jobs created by conversion, particularly relative to race and gender? Will persons displaced by the loss of contracts be retained in the newly converted industries, or will new workers be hired? If new workers are hired, where do they come from and who are they? Usually, males, especially white males, benefit from military expansion; they are commonly the ones hired by aerospace and defense contractors to build weapons systems and vehicles. When jobs previously held by white males are lost, are industries in fact converting in part to the use of lower-cost female and racial minority workers?

Importantly, we need to ask questions about the power structures involved. Who owns and controls the new or converted plants? Are they the same as those who owned and controlled defense industries? Does conversion alter the power structure of the plant or the local community? For example, does conversion produce any increase or decrease in ownership and control by the local community, labor, the state, plant managers, stockholders, and finance-capital interests?

The question of what to do with massive sectors of the economy devoted to defense production is not simply a question of U.S. foreign policy and the future of our military. It is inextricably linked to the structure of the entire military-industrial complex, as well as to the health and future of our economy. Indeed, the end of the Cold War raised debates about what to do with the anticipated "peace dividend" presumed to derive from that momentous change in global politics. Although the Cold War was presumably over, an estimated $95 billion continued to be spent fighting it out of a total Department of Defense budget of $295 billion in 1992 (Friedman, 1993: 29). What pressing domestic problem should become the beneficiary of the billions of dollars previously spent on military needs? Moreover, since many people attributed the bloating deficits in the federal budget to military expenditures, they expected to see the economy begin a strong recovery following the Cold War. Yet the economy continued to slump, with unemployment stubbornly refusing to improve significantly and the gross domestic product stagnant. Some observers blamed the sluggish economy on the burden of debt, a collapsing real estate market, and failing banks, but many acknowledged that the real problem was the aftermath of the Cold War (Farrell and Mandel, 1992; Lynch, 1992). Why is this the case?

Part of the problem was the cut in defense spending. Although less than 5 percent of the jobs in the United States are directly related to defense spending, cutbacks in defense industries accounted for 25 percent of industrial job loss in two years in the early 1990s (Farrell and Mandel, 1992:

78–79). The jobs lost included not only those directly involved in military production but also service sector jobs in businesses that supply and support defense contractors, such as department stores, supermarkets, and banks in communities with military bases, shipyards, and defense contractors (Lynch, 1992). Moreover, job loss related to military and defense spending typically occurs in manufacturing, the very sector of the economy that was already hard-hit by foreign competition. The electronics and aerospace industries have been the main victims. Military spending had insulated these industries from the effects of foreign competition. Now they will have to find new ways to offset the losses incurred by the end of the Cold War.

Of course, the end of the Cold War has benefits of its own. Winding down the arms race in and of itself may make the world a more secure place. A decline in the constant drumbeating about communist threats may allow more attention to be focused on severe domestic problems such as hunger and homelessness, unemployment, deteriorating infrastructure, inadequate education facilities, and racial inequality. Moreover, as military spending declines, so too will federal expenditures (assuming no increases in other spending), a decline which often serves to reduce interest rates and inflation. And an improved economy means that eventually we will have more money to devote to pressing domestic needs; research and development monies previously allocated to military projects can then be turned

The transition from reliance on military production in the aftermath of the Cold War can often mean a serious loss of jobs in many communities. Here, completed tanks are waiting to be tested and shipped at the Army's tank plant operated by General Dynamics in Warren, Michigan. When that plant closed in 1992, 1,400 workers lost their jobs at the facility, and countless others lost theirs in support industries such as restaurants and stores that could not survive the loss of these customers.

to civilian needs. Finally, workers being laid off from defense contractors are highly trained and educated; such workers can fill an anticipated shortage of skilled labor by the end of the century.

However, it may be at least a decade before we see these benefits. Why? Because a shift in the economy's focus has the potential to temporarily stall economic growth (Lynch, 1992). Estimates as to how many jobs will be lost in the transition from a military-industrial economy to peacetime production vary, depending on how much will be cut from the military budget. "If Congress lops off [$75 billion], as many expect, real GDP [gross domestic product] growth could be less than 2% annually over the next five years. By 1996, some 1.8 million jobs could be lost" (Farrell and Mandel, 1992: 78). If federal defense spending cuts are doubled to $150 billion, which some congressional leaders insist should be the case, job loss could reach 3.3 million.

What these scenarios suggest is that the U.S. economy will have to find new ways to stimulate growth. How do we do that? Basically, there are two main choices: federal support for transition of defense contractors to peacetime production, based on existing labor in those industries, or exportation of arms abroad. Evidence indicates that the military-industrial complex in general and defense contractors in particular have adopted the latter course.

Choice 1: Export of Arms

In 1991, U.S. arms manufacturers sold or issued licenses to sell $62.9 billion in weapons to 153 countries, making the United States the leading arms-exporting nation in the world. In that year some 21 countries engaged in war were using U.S. weapons and defense services (see Figure 16.4). Arms makers in the United States account for "more than half of all global sales. No other country is close" (Bixby, 1992: A1). The exports included a General Dynamics Corporation sale of F-16 fighter jets to Taiwan for $6 billion and a $5 billion sale of F-15 fighter jets to Saudi Arabia (total sales of arms to Saudi Arabia topped $13 billion in 1991). In fact, the United States became the top exporter of arms to the Middle East, where increases in arms served to increasingly destabilize the region. According to the Congressional Research Service, between 1988 and 1991, the United States sold $36.5 billion in arms to the Middle East, compared with $11.1 billion from the Soviet Union (the second-largest arms exporter to the region) (Bixby, 1992: A1, A7).

These exports occurred even as the Bush administration publicly spoke of a "new world order" stimulated by arms restraint, and lectured other countries to join the United States in such restraint. How is it possible to have one position in the international arena and another at home? The rationale for allowing such exports is that we must save jobs that would otherwise be lost through dramatic cuts in defense spending in the United States. Indeed, in a tight battle for his reelection in 1992, President Bush tried the unsuccessful political alchemy of turning jobs into votes by approving several new foreign arms sales, including those to Saudi Arabia and Taiwan. And although Congress has the constitutional power to veto these sales, the fact is that it did not. Why? Each senator and congressperson has constituents who desperately need jobs, and it would be political suicide to refuse arms sales that give them employment.

Who has benefited and who has been hurt by this strategy of arms export? The main beneficiaries of arming the world have been the weapons-manufacturing corporations themselves, not the workers and not the world. The Congressional Office of Technology Assessment found that such corporations have indeed reaped great profits from international arms sales: "One large contractor claimed that although foreign sales were only 11 percent of revenues, they accounted for 25 percent of profits. . . . For another firm the figures were 15 and 33 percent; while an executive in the electronics group of one large firm asserted that international sales accounted for 40 percent of the group's profits, about 20 percent of total business" (Bixby, 1992: A7). In many ways, the Gulf war against Iraq in 1991 became a live commercial for arms manufacturers such as Raytheon (the manufacturer of

When the United States sells weapons abroad, the transactions affect more than just economics. Some would argue that such sales also fuel increased potential for conflicts throughout the world.   (Source: Adapted from the *Hartford Courant*, October 25, 1992, p. A1.)

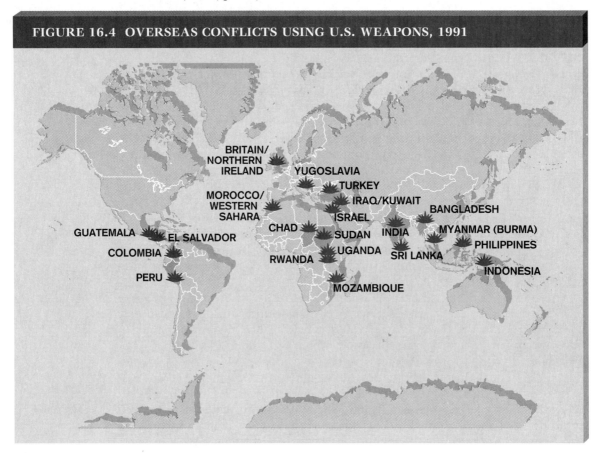

FIGURE 16.4 OVERSEAS CONFLICTS USING U.S. WEAPONS, 1991

the Patriot missile), as potential international buyers saw dramatic videos purporting to show evidence of the efficiency and kill-power of U.S. weapons systems.

Not surprisingly, given the organization of work and production we discussed in Chapter 11, the story is quite different for workers. They are still losing jobs. For the arms manufacturers, exports in a competitive world market are not as profitable as production in the noncompetitive market for the Department of Defense. For example, United Technologies Corporation, the eighth-largest arms exporter in the United States, decided to downsize because of defense cutbacks and announced the layoff of 14,000 workers; its Pratt & Whitney division eliminated 7,500 jobs, even as it seemed it would be the likely manufacturer of the engines for the jets sold to Saudi Arabia and Taiwan (Bixby, 1992: A7).

Further, increased arms exports are not making the world any safer. In fact, they are increasing the likelihood of armed conflicts and arms buildups everywhere. According to Lora Lumpe, a research analyst for the Federation of American Scientists, U.S. sales of arms to Saudi Arabia are encouraging Iran to import arms from Russia. Said Lumpe, "We're not in a position to tell the Russians, who are in such dire financial straits, not to sell this stuff to Iran when we're selling this equipment to Saudi Arabia" (Bixby, 1992: A7). Arms have become a key commodity traded in the world system. With everyone becoming ever more heavily armed in regions of the world where tensions are traditionally quite high, the probability of future armed conflicts increases immeasurably.

Choice 2: Conversion to Peacetime Economy

What is the alternative, then, to exporting arms as a way to reduce the impact of decreases in military expenditures? Many critics have suggested federal support of transition to peacetime consumer production, a significant shift in the focus of the economic institutions of the United States, and a shift in the relationship between economic and state institutions. The process of converting military contractors from defense-related manufacturing to civilian manufacturing is called **economic conversion.** In order to promote this conversion, we must reduce the economic incentives for arming the world, and manufacturers must be able to convert their facilities to civilian production without losing profits or workers (Cassidy, 1990).

Researchers have found that economic conversion may, in and of itself, carry incentives. According to one study, for example, an annual federal investment of $14.3 billion in railroads, mass transit, solid waste disposal, and solar energy could create more than 750,000 jobs each year. Furthermore, the jobs generated in these industries would rely on the skills already mastered by workers in military production (Webre, 1979). Another study showed that the skills of machinists, engineers, technicians, craftspersons, and semiskilled assembly workers are well suited for work in solar energy industries (DeGrasse et al., 1978). Conversion to these four key industries would eliminate or greatly reduce the need to invest in retraining workers or in hiring new, untrained workers. And it would preserve the jobs of those already working in military production, thereby avoiding the displacement of thousands of workers as conversion takes place.

Economic conversion is not new. Similar efforts have worked in other countries. For example, Swedish labor and community organizations have cooperated to convert a military shipyard into a place where 50 new firms now manufacture a broad range of consumer goods. Gordon and McFadden noted that more than 2,300 workers were originally laid off when the shipyard discontinued military production but that 1,650 have been rehired in the new companies doing business in the old shipyard (1984: 112). In England, workers crafted a civilian focus for Lucas Aerospace, a military contractor; that focus included production of oceanic instruments, kidney machines, and railroad cars (Wainwright and Elliott, 1982). Such examples indicate that it is technically possible, as well as profitable, for economic conversion from military production to civilian manufacturing to take place.

These international endeavors illustrate two of several possible models of conversion (see Hill, Deitrick, and Markusen, 1991). One model focuses on converting the company as a business-adjustment strategy. Here, firms attempt to diversify their activities away from military production and toward consumer manufacturing. A common strategy to achieve diversification involves merging with or acquiring another firm that already manufactures consumer goods. For example, Raytheon, the Patriot missile manufacturer, spent 20 years anticipating diversification by acquiring two appliance producers and one plane manufacturer, as well as a publishing firm and an oil exploration concern. These purchases reduced Raytheon's reliance on military production to less than 50 percent by the mid-1980s, allowing the company to survive the end of the Cold War in the 1990s (Stevenson, 1991). Unfortunately, Raytheon's strategy of acquisition did not result in any transfer of expertise from the company's military production activities, nor did it save any jobs; when military cutbacks hit Raytheon, thousands of workers lost their jobs (Massachusetts State Department of Employment and Training, 1989). Also, while the strategy ensured Raytheon's corporate survival despite military cutbacks, it did nothing to cushion the communities in which its military-related employees lived. Raytheon grew as an economic institution at the expense of workers, local communities, and the larger economy because of its power structure of work and production. Workers for firms like Raytheon are thus losing their jobs not because they are incompetent or unskilled but because corporate decisions are affecting the organization of work.

A better success story of company conversion occurred at Frisby Airborne Systems on Long Island, New York, where military production was shifted to production of commercial aircraft. Frisby's conversion strategy not only helped the company survive military cutbacks but also saved jobs by transferring the technological skills and training of its work force to commercial activities. And the company's dependency on Department of Defense contracts fell from 95 percent in 1985 to 35 percent in 1990 (McNeilly, 1990).

A second conversion strategy involves converting the local economic base by co-opting elements of the military-industrial complex, for example, by converting usage of a closed military base, manufacturing plant, or, as in our Swedish example, shipyard. In nearly three decades, more than 100 military bases have been converted to schools, businesses, residential housing, and a variety of other uses, producing a net gain of 64,680 civilian jobs (President's Economic Adjustment Committee, 1986, 1990). While this model of conversion may be quite promising, local communities must approach it with caution. Since economic planners tend to focus on development and improvement of the business climate, such conversions may occur at the expense of workers' rights (such as collective bargaining). As we discussed in Chapter 11, the costs to the local community and the state of securing a positive business climate (with such incentives as tax abatements and cheap or free infrastructural support) may be greater than the benefits received by the community from the businesses attracted.

A third model of conversion involves converting the workers themselves. In this approach, companies close plants and leave the community, but workers are retrained, counseled throughout the dislocation, and offered placement services (often resulting in the relocation of workers to other communities). Federal income support programs may aid the dislocated workers. Such programs, however, have thus far been few and small, and they have tended to benefit technical and professional workers in war-

Many communities address the economic loss created by cuts in the military with a variety of conversion strategies. In Alexandria, Louisiana, a former Air Force base was converted to accommodate several new businesses. J. B. Hunt Transport, Inc., one of the largest trucking companies in the country, was the first tenant to occupy the base, using its space as a school to train truck drivers.

related industries rather than blue-collar workers on these industries' assembly lines (Kulik and Fairchild, 1987). This is unfortunate, as well as unfair, since engineers and scientific workers are likely to have a somewhat easier time finding new employment in the civilian market. Evidence indicates that blue-collar workers are typically unemployed for longer periods and confront sharper declines in their incomes following the close of defense plants than engineers and scientists (Howland, 1988). Moreover, worker retraining efforts assume that jobs will be there for workers once they have undergone retraining, a questionable assumption in the short run: substantial military cuts are likely to contribute to overall economic recession, which means fewer jobs available, even for retrained workers (Hill, Deitrick, and Markusen, 1991).

A fourth economic conversion strategy involves a shift in the power structure of production: conversion of the facilities results from a coalition of community, labor, and management rather than from a unilateral effort by management or government. The Lucas Aerospace conversion effort in Great Britain, described earlier, used this approach. These coalitions do not occur easily, and their processes of conversion are not smooth and problem-free, but they do seem the most promising way to accomplish community-based conversions that capitalize on local labor and address local needs, as well as the need for businesses to survive and profit. Moreover, these coalitions offer the greatest opportunity for more democratic conversions. As Hill, Deitrick, and Markusen (1991) found, conversion efforts tend to fail when management resists them, thus suggesting the necessity of including management in a conversion effort. Their study also suggested the need for an activist state to support conversion efforts, such as passing early-warning legislation to give local communities and workers sufficient time to develop conversion coalitions when plant closings are likely. Thus, as we noted in Chapter 10, the institution of the state intersects in important ways with the institution of the economy. (See Table 16.1 for a summary of the four conversion strategies we have discussed.)

If economic conversion is possible and can be profitable, why does it not occur more often? For one thing, defense contractors are reluctant to give

---

Table 16.1

ECONOMIC CONVERSION OF MILITARY PRODUCTION FACILITIES

Model 1 Diversification of business activities from military production to consumer manufacturing

Model 2 Conversion of closed local military bases by the government and conversion of manufacturing plants by management to civilian facilities such as schools, housing, business premises, and prisons

Model 3 Conversion of workers by retraining them, placing them in new jobs, and sometimes relocating them

Model 4 Conversion of the power structure of production by coalitions of workers, community governments, community groups, and management that take over facilities and convert them to meet community-defined needs

up the enormous profits derived from defense contracting and the protected market provided by the Department of Defense. They may resist conversion and instead spend much time and money on convincing the Department of Defense and Congress to continue contract expenditures. This is because it is cheaper and easier for a firm to become proficient in the skills required to produce the specific products ordered by the military than to acquire a broad range of skills and the production flexibility required to produce civilian goods in a competitive market (Dumas, 1982; Melman, 1983). Studies have indeed shown that military contracting provides not only a significantly higher profit rate than does civilian production but also significantly higher cost overruns (Gerth, 1985).

In addition, the relationships of the military-industrial complex, noted in Chapter 10, play an important role. Incredible (and commonplace) cost overruns notwithstanding, "more and more weapons systems are produced not because they correspond to rational defined military need but because they benefit defense contractors who have lobbied effectively or because jobs will go to voters whose Congresspersons support the weapons" (Cassidy, 1990: 783–784; see also Alperovitz and Faux, 1984). The structure of the military-industrial complex fuels firms' resistance to converting production to civilian goods. Yet a survey of chief executives at 125 major defense contractors found that most were planning to study or to begin civilian production alternatives to military contracting. Moreover, these executives viewed almost half of the conversion efforts begun since 1986 as successful (Hughes, 1991). The findings of this survey contradict the horrible scenarios of economic disaster that some observers predict will result from conversion efforts. How, then, do we encourage economic conversion?

One important factor is federal support. The Defense Authorization Bill of 1991 granted $200 million in economic assistance to communities and individuals, to be spent over three years; 75 percent of the grant was earmarked for job retraining and 25 percent for economic development projects in those communities hard-hit by cutbacks in Department of Defense contracting (Pennar, 1992). Unfortunately, only $2 million of the grant has thus far been deployed. Unless the full grant is actually allocated and used, the intent of federal help is meaningless.

In addition to this grant, aimed at communities and individuals, Congress authorized $1.5 billion in 1992 to aid corporate conversion and job retraining programs (Bixby, 1992: A7). With these aid programs the federal government has assumed some responsibility for helping the economy shift from military to civilian and consumer production while limiting the harmful effects on individuals, local communities, and the national economy. Those groups and institutions most affected by economic conversion need to cooperate: federal, state, and local levels of government, along with labor, community action groups, and corporations.

Some state and local governments have already begun to move in this direction. In Los Angeles, for example, there is a push to shift from aerospace defense manufacturing to production of transportation and railcar products. In Connecticut, the Office of Defense Diversification, funded with $12.5 million from defense firms themselves, is aiding conversion. Textron Lycoming, for example, is shifting from manufacturing jet and tank engines for the military to producing commercial jet engines for British Aerospace PLC (Farrell and Mandel, 1992: 80).

It is important for the United States to develop a long-term industrial policy to stimulate economic growth in combination with these conversion efforts. For example, the Pentagon has been a major source of military research and development funds in universities and private laboratories; federal policy could redeploy that expenditure for civilian and consumer research and development. The 1992 federal budget offered a tiny step in that direction: whereas 60 percent of all federal research funds once went to military research and development, 59 percent of the 1992 federal research budget of $74 billion was earmarked for civilian projects (Pennar, 1992). Accelerated increases in such shifts in federal research monies could eventually offer the kind of stimulation to the economy once provided by military spending.

Furthermore, the government is showing signs of recognizing the need for a federal industrial policy. Both the Clinton administration and corporations, as well as organized labor, are increasingly aware of the need to aid conversion to peacetime production and of the limitations and problems of arming the world. This awareness could form the basis of a consensus for developing a national industrial policy that supports economic growth with *viable* jobs (not just the minimum-wage, service sector, and involuntary part-time jobs that have been the hallmark of economic "growth" in the past decade).

Our analysis has explored only some of the questions raised at the beginning of this section. A continued sociological analysis must pursue the remaining questions, particularly as more conversion attempts take place and provide us with greater data to analyze their effects. Moreover, we must develop and apply the insights we gain so that we can participate more fully in the changes that will undoubtedly take place as we enter the next century. How these questions are answered will affect each of us. What kind of world can we look forward to in the aftermath of the Cold War? What kind of economy can we expect in the United States by the turn of the century? And what kinds of jobs, if any, await us, whether we convert our military production to peacetime production or insist on an emphasis on arms production for export?

TOXIC IMPERIALISM AND ENVIRONMENTAL RACISM

National and worldwide attention has focused on environmental concerns since the first Earth Day celebration in 1970. Increasing awareness of the effects our daily actions have on the health and stability of the environment has caused many of us to modify our lifestyles and patterns of consumption. Political action has increasingly focused on industrial production and on ways to curb corporate contributions to environmental instability. However, the sociological imagination leads us to ask: Do we all suffer the consequences of environmental pollution equally? How are toxic waste sites selected and pollution cleanups assigned? Are they distributed equitably throughout the world and in this country? How do power relationships and processes affect the selection of sites for toxic waste dumps?

Toxic Imperialism

We have paid scant attention to exploring the possible intersection of environmental issues and issues of inequality. Yet evidence suggests that this question warrants close scrutiny. For example, there are indications that corporations and core countries like the United States have been dumping toxic wastes and polluting products in peripheral countries such as Nigeria, Guinea, and Haiti, as well as in black townships in South Africa (Marks and Brown, 1990; see also Alston, 1990: 32–33). American Cyanamid and Thor Chemicals of Great Britain have been dumping mercury wastes in the South African black township of KwaZulu (deMause, 1990). And South Pacific countries and islands, such as Johnston Atoll, have been the storage sites of chemical and nerve gas weapons since the early 1970s (Glenn, 1990). The Earth Day/Wall Street Action Group has referred to international toxic dumping in underdeveloped countries by major corporations and industrialized countries as **toxic imperialism** (Cohen, 1990: 78).

Why are underdeveloped countries targeted as viable sites for toxic waste dumping? Part of the answer can be understood in the context of world-system relations: underdeveloped countries are far less powerful and much poorer economically than developed countries like the United States. Indeed, overwhelming debt has prompted some underdeveloped nations to accept toxic waste in exchange for payments as a way of raising money to reduce debt burdens. The Chamorro government in Nicaragua has actively supported a proposal to accept ash wastes from Florida-based Alqui Distributors in exchange for $1.2 million per shipment in order to pay off the $6 billion debt it owes to private banks. That ash is heavily laced with toxic substances and carcinogens such as lead, cadmium, dioxins, arsenic, and mercury (Cohen, 1990: 78).

Loopholes in U.S. federal laws regulating toxic materials, especially the Federal Insecticide, Fungicide and Rodenticide Act (FIFRA), have encouraged exports of toxic materials, even when these substances have been banned in the United States as unsafe. Legislative efforts since 1978 to close the loopholes have failed. Thus, federal policy initiatives and lax enforcement of regulatory laws have made it profitable for corporations to export products that are deemed unsafe for people in the United States (Isaac, 1990).

Few underdeveloped countries have regulatory policies governing toxic substances and pesticides. Those that do often do not adequately enforce them. This gives the large international pesticide producers and toxic waste producers the freedom to export these substances without restriction (Weir and Schapiro, 1981).

The governments of many developing countries do not wish to publicly acknowledge the level of chemical poisoning caused by toxic imports. Press reports of contaminated food, water, and land could severely depress tourism in these countries. Furthermore, many governments are understandably reluctant to admit that their lack of legal controls or inability to enforce them has aided and abetted the poisoning of their own citizens. And finally, any admission that toxic substances are present in the land or water invites investigation by the U.S. Food and Drug Administration (FDA) of all food imports into this country, thereby potentially damaging the developing countries' source of trade income (Weir and Schapiro, 1981). Taken together, these factors make it easy for corporations to dump unsafe substances and toxic wastes in underdeveloped countries.

Environmental Racism

A growing body of research has begun to focus on the issue of inequality and toxic pollution within the United States (Asch and Seneca, 1978; Bullard, 1983; Gelobter, 1992; West et al., 1992). In a 1987 study of the relationship between toxic wastes and racial composition of communities, the Commission for Racial Justice (under the auspices of the United Church of Christ) noted that there were "clear patterns which show that communities with greater minority percentages of the population are more likely to be the sites of commercial hazardous waste facilities. The possibility that these patterns resulted by chance is virtually impossible" (Chavis and Lee, 1987: 23).

Toxic waste dumps and industries are frequently located in racial minorities' communities, a practice some refer to as environmental racism. These children are playing basketball in the shadow of highly toxic oil refineries and pesticide-producing industries in North Richmond, a community of racial minorities in the San Francisco Bay area.

In particular, Commission for Racial Justice researchers found "an inordinate concentration of uncontrolled toxic waste sites in Black and Hispanic communities, particularly in urban areas" (Chavis and Lee, 1987: 23). Indeed, they found that communities in which commercial waste sites existed had twice the proportion of people of color as communities that did not have any such sites. And communities that had two or more commercial toxic waste sites had more than three times the proportion of people of color than those that had no such sites. Moreover, racial composition correlated with the location of a commercial toxic waste site more strongly than any other variable, including socioeconomic variables such as average household income and average home values (see Bullard, 1990). Researchers came to similar conclusions regarding air pollution (Freeman, 1972; Gianessi, Peskin, and Wolff, 1979; Gelobter, 1992), as well as the effects of toxic waste dumping on people who consume fish caught in dump site waters (West, Fly, Larkin, and Marans, 1992).

Some researchers refer to this pattern as a problem of **environmental racism** (Lee, 1992). Why have minority communities become the disproportionate recipients of toxic waste sites? Various studies have begun to unravel this issue. The sociological imagination alerts us to at least four important factors related to social arrangements.

First, land values in minority and heavily integrated communities are often depressed. This is because white communities are frequently defined by real estate agencies and mortgaging banks as "more desirable." In fact, banks often **redline** minority and heavily integrated communities, a practice that defines these areas as ineligible for mortgages and small-business loans (Foley, 1973; Squires, DeWolfe, and DeWolfe, 1979; Leahy, 1985; Logan, 1988). Redlining also frequently makes it difficult for small businesses to obtain insurance, a situation which can escalate the flight of businesses from communities in transition. Land is consequently readily available and cheap, with owners eager for a buyer (Asch and Seneca, 1978; Bullard and Wright, 1987; Chavis and Lee, 1987).

Second, the combination of racial discrimination in housing and poverty often means that both poor and middle-class people of color have far less mobility than middle-class whites. They may not be able to afford to move from a community where toxic waste sites are located (Bullard and Wright, 1987; Chavis and Lee, 1987).

Third, people of color often have few political and economic resources and are not politically organized. When commercial toxic waste sites are targeted for their communities, they are not able to respond with the strong, organized opposition that white middle-class communities typically put together (Bullard and Wright, 1987; Chavis and Lee, 1987).

Finally, those promoting the toxic waste facilities often promise jobs for the host communities, thereby mitigating some of the opposition that might develop. Minority communities may have unemployment rates that are two to three times higher than those of white communities. Economically depressed communities are vulnerable to promises of much-needed jobs (Bullard and Wright, 1987; Chavis and Lee, 1987). Waste companies have attempted to negotiate agreements with at least 30 Native American

These residents of the Torres Martinez Indian Reservation southeast of Los Angeles are demonstrating outside the Los Angeles County Hall of Administration in 1994 to protest the dumping of Los Angeles and Orange Counties' sewage sludge on reservation lands. Although the protesters have won cease-and-desist orders issued by the Bureau of Indian Affairs and the tribal council, the two counties continue to send their sludge to private processors on the reservation. Clearly, the struggle against environmental racism will be a long one.

communities to use their land as dump sites in exchange for jobs and money (Wei, 1991). Financial incentives are intended to make local residents perceive the benefits of agreeing to a toxic waste facility as greater than the risks and costs (O'Hare, Bacow, and Sanderson, 1983).

It should not be assumed that people of color are unconcerned about dump sites in their neighborhoods. Indeed, evidence suggests that African Americans are just as concerned about the environment as are whites (Mohai, 1990). Native Americans have organized an environmental action group, Citizens Against Ruining Our Environment, which helps residents on tribal lands resist toxic waste dumping in their communities. This task is complicated by the fact that Native lands are not subject to the same state and federal regulations as non-Native lands (Wei, 1991). And the National Association for the Advancement of Colored People (NAACP) increasingly links civil rights issues to the issue of environmental racism.

Despite these resistance efforts, patterns of toxic waste dumping suggest that sitings continue to be overwhelmingly located in minority communities. One reason may be lack of information. Even when grass-roots activists attempt to resist these facilities, they often find it difficult to obtain the key information necessary to organize their efforts. In one study, 88 percent of the 110 community groups surveyed "perceived obstacles to obtaining information. Almost half (45 percent) claimed that government agencies blocked their learning process" (Freudenberg, 1984; Bullard, 1993). Chavis and Lee (1987) noted that such "institutional resistance" to providing access to information is likely to increase when agencies deal with groups that they believe are less powerful (see also Gould, 1993).

It is crucial for all of us to understand environmental racism and toxic imperialism as a public issue. Why? First, when toxic wastes and other unsafe materials are exported to underdeveloped countries, they can return to the United States in imports. For example, a 1990 study by the General Accounting Office (GAO) revealed that 90 percent of U.S. pesticides are exported to the five countries that together provide more than half of all our fruit and vegetable imports (Chile, Costa Rica, the Dominican Republic, Guatemala, and Mexico) (Isaac, 1990). The GAO also reported that more than 15 percent of the peppers imported from Mexico exceeded the Food and Drug Administration's limits on pesticide residue; almost half of the coffee beans imported contained pesticides banned as unsafe in the United States; and an estimated 14 percent of the beef imported from Central America was contaminated with illegal levels of pesticide residues (Weir and Schapiro, 1981). Thus, U.S. consumers may be ingesting the very pesticides that were banned here because of their toxicity or carcinogenic dangers. Similarly, waterways that are polluted by toxic waste dumping may be the source of much of the fish and seafood consumed in the United States (Weir and Schapiro, 1981). Toxic wastes and carcinogenic materials such as mercury, dioxins, and lead dumped in other countries still find their way into the food chain, and they may return to the United States through the economics of imports and exports.

Moreover, the factors uncovered by the studies of the relationship between inequality and pollution suggest that *all* communities can be potentially at risk. That is, any community that is not well organized or does not have access to political and economic resources may be vulnerable. Furthermore, as we noted in Chapter 11, in an economy where jobs are continuing to disappear, many communities that are stable now could change and become susceptible to the appeal of jobs and financial compensation in exchange for the risks and hazards of toxic waste facilities. Similarly, a recessionary economy frequently attacks the real estate values of many communities, including previously stable middle-class white neighborhoods. Such depreciated areas become increasingly vulnerable to hazardous waste sitings. Together, these factors suggest that we all would benefit from an understanding of how the processes of power and economic inequality relate to toxic pollution. While this relationship currently manifests itself as toxic imperialism and environmental racism, it could extend to other inequalities as well.

Finally, we may be relieved that such hazards and risks occur in someone else's neighborhood and not our own, but the fact is that we all may lose a great deal in increased health-care costs related to illnesses from toxic waste locations. Furthermore, tolerating toxic waste sites in anyone's community ultimately cedes power to those who produce hazardous and toxic substances. As long as these proponents believe that jobs and cash can appease communities, and as long as governmental agencies can hinder efforts to secure adequate information to fend off unwanted risks, we will all be less able to struggle against these forces.

CONCLUSION

Our discussion concerning emerging issues suggests that, armed with a sociological imagination, we may begin to frame questions concerning new issues and concerns as they develop. We do not need to wait for someone else to do the research in order to ask questions. A well-developed sociological imagination should provide us with the tools to analyze aggregate statistics and averages; who benefits and who is hurt by certain relationships and processes; and what implications changes might have for a variety of different members of our society and of other societies around the world. Armed with a tool kit of sociological concepts such as those we have introduced in this text and applied in our analysis of emerging issues, we can anticipate future trends and understand new developments in terms of institutional arrangements rather than just individual choices. In short, we can learn to link our personal, individual biographies to the larger institutions in society and thereby discover the patterns and processes that might affect us. Doing so leads us to an analysis of how *we* might affect those institutions and thus gives us the greater freedom of being actors in our world, not just people who are acted upon.

THINKING CRITICALLY

1. Suppose you were put in charge of developing a new plan to pay for education in the United States. Suggest an alternative to the present use of property-tax revenues, and offer a sociological impact assessment: Who will likely benefit and who will likely be hurt by your proposal, and why? What social issues does your proposal address? What social consequences might your proposal cause? How would you deal with these consequences? How might your own education experiences have been different had your proposal been the actual policy when you were in elementary school and high school?

2. Increasing longevity is causing more people to reconsider the meaning of retirement and "old age." Look at the accounts of the people in the boxed excerpt in this chapter. What did these people do to redefine their retirements? Perhaps some people you know are currently retired. What have they done to redefine their retirements? How do their experiences compare with those of the people in the excerpt? What factors may explain the differences, if any, between the people in the excerpt and the people you know? Which institutions affect the retirement experiences of the people in the excerpt and the people you know? How? How might these institutions need to change in the future in order to accommodate the presence of a larger elderly cohort?

3. What sorts of peacetime uses can you envision for military bases and defense production facilities? What social factors would you consider important in your decision, and how would you address them? What institutions do you think might be affected by your suggestions, and how? What other social consequences might your suggestions have?

4. Suppose you were asked to offer a plan for toxic waste disposal that addresses the problem of environmental racism. What factors would you consider in the development of your plan? Why? Who is likely to benefit and who is likely to be hurt by your proposal? Are there things that you can do to minimize or eliminate the differential impact of your plan? What institutional changes, if any, would have to take place in order to accommodate your plan?

5. Select an emerging issue that has not been covered in this chapter (perhaps reproductive technology, privatization of public services like prisons, gays in the military, decriminalization of drugs, or any other that you may find interesting). Using a sociological imagination, explore the institutional arrangements that might contribute to the issue. Examine who benefits and who is hurt by the issue as it currently stands, and try to assess why. What alternative arrangements would you suggest to deal with the issue? Are there race, class, and gender factors to be considered when examining this emerging issue? Be specific.

KEY TERMS

school vouchers, *542*
tax credits, *542*
population pyramid, *547*
age consciousness, *553*
perestroika, *556*

economic conversion, *561*
toxic imperialism, *567*
environmental racism, *569*
redline, *569*

SUGGESTED READINGS

Vern L. Bengston and W. Andrew Achenbaum (eds.), *The Changing Contract across Generations.* New York: Aldine de Gruyter, 1993. A collection of readings that explore the question of generational equity as an important consideration of policy formation during the 1990s. Many of the readings examine the role of race, class, and gender in evaluating the effect of an aging population on social policy.

Robert D. Bullard (ed.), *Confronting Environmental Racism: Voices from the Grassroots.* Boston: South End Press, 1993. A collection of readings concerning the emerging grass-roots movement for environmental justice. The focus of the readings is an analytical shift from mainstream environmental groups and the government to African American, Latino, and Native American environmental groups.

Betty Friedan, *The Fountain of Age.* New York: Simon and Schuster, 1993. An examination of the many ways people confront and celebrate growing older in the United States, including stories of how they have redefined the meaning of being elderly.

Ann Markusen and Joel Yudken, *Dismantling the Cold War Economy.* New York: Basic Books, 1992. An examination of the effect of a military economy on society and an exploration of the possibility of a society that does not depend so heavily on Department of Defense contracts. The analysis is based in part on interviews not only with defense industry executives and spokespersons and military officials but also with community activists and union leaders.

Michael Renner (ed.), *Economic Adjustments after the Cold War: Strategies for Conversion.* Geneva: U.N. Institute for Disarmament Research, 1992. A collection of readings focusing on the complexities of converting a military economy to a peacetime economy and offering a wide array of perspectives on conversion strategies.

GLOSSARY

ableism Prejudice and discrimination against a group of people because of their physical or mental disability. (Chapter 6)

absolute deprivation The state of being unable to purchase the things related to basic survival. (*Compare with* relative deprivation.) (Chapter 9)

achieved status Social status acquired through a person's application of resources, talent, effort, and opportunity. (*See also* status; *compare with* ascribed status.) (Chapter 3)

affirmative action Regulations requiring that employers not discriminate in hiring and that they take positive steps to increase the number of members of racial minority groups and women in their job applicant pools. (Chapter 6)

age consciousness The awareness of common interests based on age. (Chapter 16)

age inequality A system of inequality in which members of a particular age group are thought of and treated as less worthy than those of another; usually refers to older people. (Chapter 6)

ageism Prejudice and discrimination against a group of people because of their age; usually directed against older people. (Chapter 6)

alienation A withdrawing or separation from something; for example, in Marxist theory, workers experience a sense of estrangement from their work. (*Compare with* apathy.) (Chapters 8 and 10)

alterative movement A type of social movement that focuses on changing individuals' thinking and behavior in a specific, limited way; for example, Students Against Drunk Driving. (*Compare with* redemptive movement, reformative movement, and transformative movement.) (Chapter 9)

animism The belief that spirits exist in other people or in the natural environment. (*Compare with* monotheism and polytheism.) (Chapter 15)

anticipatory socialization Preparation for future roles in society; for example, parents prepare their children for the world of work they are likely to be a part of when they are adults. (Chapter 5)

antithesis According to Marx and Engels, the contradictions and antagonisms within the structure of society that challenge that structure. (*See also* dialectic, thesis, and synthesis.) (Chapter 9)

apathy Indifference or lack of interest or concern. (*Compare with* alienation.) (Chapter 10)

appearance norms Standards of attractiveness, often applied to women. (Chapter 8)

ascribed status Social status over which a person has no control, such as race, sex, and class. (*See also* status; *compare with* achieved status.) (Chapter 3)

basic needs What a country's population requires for survival, including health, education, food, water, and sanitation. (Chapter 9)

bureaucracy An organization characterized by clear-cut division of labor, hierarchy of authority, adherence to formal rules, impartiality, and rewards based on merit. (*See also* secondary group.) (Chapter 3)

business dominance theory (also known as **instrumentalism**) The view that the state is not a neutral arbiter of the common good because capitalists have captured it and use it to further their own interests. (Chapter 10)

capital-accumulation interests Individuals and organizations that benefit from amassing and maintaining private profits. (Chapter 10)

capitalists Those who have capital invested in business and therefore own the means of production. (*Compare with* proletariat.) (Chapter 9)

church In the generic sense, religion or religious membership. (Chapter 15)

civil religion According to Bellah, a set of widely held beliefs, akin to a national religion, that a nation and its institutions are under the special favor of God, thus promoting national cohesion among heterogeneous groups. (Chapter 15)

class consciousness According to Marx, workers' understanding of what capitalism was doing to them and their realization that it would be desirable to join others in a struggle against the capitalist class. (*Compare with* false consciousness.) (Chapter 15)

class dialectic perspective The view that the conflict between the working and capitalist classes results in compromises in state policy that are not necessarily in the best interests of the capitalists. (Chapter 10)

class identity The sense of belonging to a particular economic class, resulting from shared life experiences, as, for example, that experienced by members of an elite. (Chapter 10)

competitive individualism The belief that individuals are completely responsible for their own economic condition so that economic success (wealth) or failure (poverty) is the result of individual effort. (Chapter 4)

competitive sector A part of the formal labor market in which production is medium- to small-scale and which relies primarily on human labor rather than machinery for production. (*Compare with* monopoly sector and state sector.) (Chapter 11)

concessional loans Loans to peripheral countries from core nations and international develop-

ment agencies, such as the World Bank; the loans have below-market interest rates and do not have to be repaid for a relatively long time. (*Compare with* nonconcessional loans.) (Chapter 9)

conflict perspective The view that social divisions and struggles characterize society; also the belief that social change is a result of conflict. (*Compare with* order perspective; *see also* cyclical perspective, evolutionary perspective, and equilibrium perspective.) (Chapters 1, 5, and 9)

containment theory A social-psychological explanation that suggests that deviant behavior is limited in society because of internal (personal) and external (societal) controls that contain the behavior of individuals. (*See also* social-psychological explanations; *compare with* differential association theory, control theory, and social reinforcement theory.) (Chapter 8)

control group In research, a group of subjects that does not receive the special treatment designed for an experimental group. The control group serves as a baseline of comparison for the experimental group. (*Compare with* experimental group.) (Chapter 1)

control theory A social-psychological explanation for deviant behavior that suggests that such behavior results from the absence of social control or constraints. (*See also* social-psychological explanations; *compare with* differential association theory, containment theory, and social reinforcement theory.) (Chapter 8)

co-optation The socialization of prospective and new members of the power elite so that they come to share the world view of that elite. (*See also* power elite.) (Chapter 10)

core nations In a world-system, countries in which production is based on technology that relies more on machinery than on human labor and in which human labor is relatively skilled and highly paid; they are usually relatively wealthy nations. (*See also* world-system; *compare with* peripheral nations and semiperipheral nations.) (Chapter 2)

corporate culture The relationships and structures created in societies by corporate ideologies that promote and enhance the production of private profit; corporations in the core frequently export these ideologies to peripheral countries. (Chapter 4)

corporatization of medicine A trend in health care in which large private firms have entered the health-care services field for the purpose of making a profit. (Chapter 13)

cottage industry A business whose labor force consists of family members who work at home using their own equipment. (Chapter 9)

counterculture A subculture whose members embrace values, norms, rituals, and lifestyles that directly challenge those of the dominant culture. (Chapter 4)

critical analysis A view that challenges the structural functional perspective that all of society's members benefit from the way society is structured and from the ways it adjusts to its environment. (*See also* structural functional perspective.) (Chapter 2)

cult A religious group that generally accepts the legitimacy of other religious groups but has a negative tension with its social environment. (*Compare with* sect and denomination.) (Chapter 15)

cultural capital Material and nonmaterial goods that are socially valued, such as education or important social connections. (Chapter 12)

cultural deprivation A general lack of knowledge and intellectual skills, usually ascribed to people from poor and working-class backgrounds. (Chapter 1)

cultural diffusion The sharing and incorporation of a diversity of cultures from one society to another, or of subcultures within the dominant culture. (Chapter 4)

cultural hegemony A situation in which the ideas and values of the dominant members of society are diffused throughout society's institutions and imposed on less powerful members. (Chapter 4)

cultural lag The time it takes from the point at which a new subculture, technology, or idea is introduced to the point at which it is accepted or incorporated into the dominant culture. (Chapter 4)

cultural myth of romanticism Ideology that explains female sexual activity as the result of being "swept off her feet" in the heat of a romantic moment. (Chapter 14)

cultural relativity A perspective that considers other cultures and their points of view as worthy of respect and understanding. (*Compare with* multiculturalism.) (Chapter 4)

cultural synchronization A condition in which people have shared cultural values and traits; according to Irvine, for example, many African Americans have cultural traits not shared by the dominant "Eurocentric" majority, and the two groups therefore lack cultural synchronization. (Chapter 12)

culture The social construction of reality of society's dominant groups, often imposed as a shared way of life among members of a society; it is sometimes shared and frequently challenged by subordinate groups. (Chapter 4)

culture of poverty The belief that poor people are poverty-stricken because of a shared lack of motivation to work hard, earn a living, or gain an education. (Chapter 4)

culture shock A feeling of confusion, uncertainty, surprise, or anxiety experienced when people are exposed to a different culture or behavior that does not conform to the prevailing norms. (Chapter 4)

cyclical perspective The view that society is like a natural organism and that each society passes naturally and inevitably through the same life cycle phases as individual biological organisms, so that ultimately social change may be viewed as part of a natural cycle. (*Compare with* evolutionary perspective, equilibrium perspective, and conflict perspective.) (Chapter 9)

de facto segregation Segregation as if by law; for example, schools may be segregated because neighborhoods are segregated, and it is "unwritten law" that neighborhoods will remain segregated. (*Compare with* de jure segregation.) (Chapter 12)

de jure segregation Segregation as a matter of law; for example, in the South before the 1964 Civil Rights Act was passed, there were laws to segregate schools. (*Compare with* de facto segregation.) (Chapter 12)

debt dependency A strategy of development based on reliance on aid and loans from other countries, international aid agencies, and banks. (*Compare with* dependent development and trade dependency.) (Chapter 9)

debt-for-nature swaps Arrangements in which debt-ridden governments agree to purchase or set aside land to conserve as state-owned parks and to protect the land's natural resources in exchange for debt cancellation. (Chapter 9)

declining significance of race The belief that because of changes in attitudes, passage and enforcement of civil rights laws, and efforts to promote educational and occupational opportunities, one's race is no longer a key social determinant in the United States. (Chapter 7)

definition of the situation *See* Thomas theorem.

degradation ceremony The process in which socialization agents attack and devalue an individual's existing identity in an effort to break it down and build a new one. (Chapter 5)

deindustrialization A state of decline in a nation's manufacturing activity; for example, goods may be produced in other countries and only assembled domestically. (Chapter 11)

democracy A government, organization, or group ruled and controlled by the people, usually the majority. (Chapter 3)

denomination A religious group that accepts the legitimacy of other religious groups and coexists peacefully with its social environment. (*Compare with* sect and cult.) (Chapter 15)

denominational society A society characterized by religious pluralism rather than by one dominant church. (Chapter 15)

dependent development A dual strategy combining import substitution and export processing adopted by peripheral nations in order to combat the drain on their resources and the unequal benefits of trade dependency. (*See also* import substitution and export processing; *compare with* trade dependency and debt dependency.) (Chapter 9)

deregulation The process of removing or significantly relaxing government restrictions on an industry. (Chapter 10)

desegregation The elimination of the barriers separating or isolating the members of a racial minority group from the rest of society. (Chapter 12)

deviance Behavior or a condition of being that is in violation of or departs from social norms. (Chapter 8)

dialectic According to Marx and Engels, the ongoing process of social change marked by conflict. (*See also* thesis, antithesis, and synthesis.) (Chapter 9)

differential association theory A social-psychological explanation for deviant behavior that suggests that such behavior results from an individual associating with people who are already disposed toward deviant behavior. (*See also* social-psychological explanations; *compare with* containment theory, control theory, and social reinforcement theory.) (Chapter 8)

direct democracy A government, organization, or group in which all members participate in decision-making. (*See also* democracy; *compare with* representative democracy.) (Chapter 3)

direct interlock A structural tie that exists between two corporations that have one person serving on both boards of directors. (*Compare with* indirect interlock.) (Chapter 10)

direct observation A type of field research in which the researcher enters the research site and observes the group members' thinking and behavior. (*See also* field research; *compare with* passive observation and participant observation.) (Chapter 1)

disengagement theory The view that it is natural for all elderly people to withdraw from the social roles they occupied when they were younger because of inevitable biological and psychological decline. (Chapter 6)

domestic labor Work done to maintain the home and family, usually unpaid. (*Compare with* formal labor market and informal labor market.) (Chapter 11)

double day A situation in which women who work full time also perform most or all of the domestic chores at home; also called **double shift** or **second shift**. (*Compare with* triple shift.) (Chapters 5, 7, 11, and 14)

double shift See double day.

dual labor market Segregation in the labor market on the basis of race or sex; for example, many jobs are defined as those that should be held by men or by women. (Chapter 6)

economic conversion The process of converting military contractors to producers of goods and services for civilian markets. (Chapter 16)

economic inequality A system of inequality characterized by a vast difference in wealth and income possessed by families and individuals. (Chapter 6)

economy The institution made up of structures, relationships, and activities whose manifest function is to produce and distribute goods and services throughout society. (Chapters 2 and 10)

education The institution whose manifest function is to transmit the knowledge and skills that all young members of society need to become productive members of the economy as adults. (Chapter 2)

elite pluralism A perspective in which competing elites coexist and compromise to achieve a balanced government for the common good. (*Compare with* interest-group pluralism.) (Chapter 10)

environmental racism The dumping of toxic wastes in racial minority communities to a disproportionate degree compared to dumping in other areas. (Chapter 16)

equilibrium perspective The view that society is like a biological organism such as the human body; according to this notion all systems in the organism are interdependent, and any disturbance or alteration in one of the systems requires adjustments in the other systems in order for the organism to maintain its equilibrium. (*Compare with* cyclical perspective, evolutionary perspective, and conflict perspective.) (Chapter 9)

ethnic groups People with a shared racial, religious, or national heritage who possess the same cultural traits and sense of community. (Chapter 7)

ethnocentrism The view that one's culture is the standard against which other cultures should be evaluated. (Chapter 4)

evolutionary perspective The view that society is like a biological organism that evolves to a higher life form with each change, so that social change is viewed as evolutionary. (*Compare with* cyclical perspective, equilibrium perspective, and conflict perspective.) (Chapter 9)

experimental group In research, a group of subjects that receives special treatment designed by the researcher so that the effects of that treatment may be studied. (*Compare with* control group.) (Chapter 1)

experimental research Research conducted to determine how a particular organism or object is affected by different types of treatment selected by the researcher. (*Compare with* field research and historical research.) (Chapter 1)

export processing The strategy adopted by peripheral nations of manufacturing goods for sale abroad in order to combat the drain on their resources and the unequal benefits of trade dependency. (*See also* trade dependency.) (Chapter 9)

extended family A family that includes the nuclear family plus other members of one or both of the parents' families of orientation, such as grandparents or aunts and uncles. (*See also* families of orientation; *compare with* nuclear family.) (Chapter 14)

false consciousness According to Marx, the failure of workers to understand that capitalism and not themselves is to blame for their alienation and misery. (*Compare with* class consciousness.) (Chapter 15)

false universalism The belief that all persons with a given status experience life in the same ways; for example, that all women have the same life experiences regardless of their race, class, or age. (Chapter 7)

families of choice A family form not defined by biology but by choice, marked by stable relationships based on shared economic and emotional ties in one or more households, such as those found where heterosexual or homosexual couples live together but are not married. (*Compare with* families of orientation and families of procreation.) (Chapter 14)

families of orientation Families into which people are born or adopted. (*Compare with* families of procreation and families of choice.) (Chapter 14)

families of procreation Families into which people marry and produce offspring. (*Compare with* families of orientation and families of choice.) (Chapter 14)

family An organized ongoing network of kin and nonkin who interact daily, sharing economic and household responsibilities and obligations, providing for domestic needs of all members, and ensuring their survival. (Chapters 2 and 14)

feminist A person who believes in the political, economic, and social equality of the sexes. (Chapter 6)

feminist spirituality An unofficial religion that supports the beliefs that people need to be ecologically sensitive and that they are part of nature and its cycles. (*See also* unofficial religion.) (Chapter 15)

feminization of poverty A situation in which a growing percentage of the poor live in female-headed households; subtly suggests that women choose to be poor and stay on welfare or somehow bring poverty on themselves. (*Compare with* pauperization of motherhood.) (Chapter 14)

field research Research conducted at the place where the subjects are located so that the researcher may gain information through first-hand observation. (*Compare with* experimental research and historical research.) (Chapter 1)

finance capital A combination of money, stocks, bonds, loans, and pension funds and the social relationships of the owners and controllers of these resources (often banks). (Chapter 10)

flex time An arrangement of work hours that allows more free time for the worker so long as a full day or week of work is performed; for example, some workers work four-day weeks with ten hours of work a day so that they can have three days off to take care of their families. (Chapter 14)

folkways The least formal or important norms, usually involving conventional routines such as how many meals a day we eat. (*See also* norms; *compare with* mores and laws.) (Chapter 4)

formal labor market Consists of people who are paid for their work, usually performed outside the home. (*Compare with* informal labor market and domestic labor.) (Chapter 11)

functional imperatives According to functionalists, the social needs that must be met in order for a society to survive. (Chapter 2)

functionalist theory of deviance The belief that deviant behavior is a necessary and possibly even desirable thing; for example, criminals perform a service to society in that their crimes anger and upset members of society who then come together and become more cohesive as a group. (Chapter 8)

functionalist theory of stratification The belief that economic inequality is the result of beneficial forces and that different occupational levels in society should receive markedly different rewards. (Chapter 6)

gatekeepers Schools that open different doors of opportunity for different student populations through such policies as tracking, thus depriving students from economically disadvantaged backgrounds of knowledge and school credentials that could facilitate their future upward mobility. (*See also* tracking.) (Chapters 1 and 12)

gender The category of masculine or feminine, determined by societal expectations for behavior and ways of relating to others based on sex. (*Compare with* sex.) (Chapter 6)

generalized other A concept developed by George Herbert Mead to refer to the attitude of the larger community assumed by an individual to be important. (*Compare with* significant other.) (Chapter 5)

genocide The systematic extermination of a group of people by those who consider themselves racially superior. (Chapter 6)

glass ceiling A level in a company or bureaucracy above which women or racial minorities rarely are able to rise. (Chapter 11)

government The politicians who occupy the structure of the state. (*See also* state.) (Chapter 10)

greenhouse effect An increase in the earth's temperature that results when carbon dioxide is released and trapped in the atmosphere; occurs, for example, when fossil fuels are burned. (Chapter 2)

group A collection of individuals who have regular interaction. (Chapter 3)

heterosexism The belief that homosexuality is unnatural and immoral. (Chapter 6)

historical research A type of research that is concerned with establishing facts about the past. (*Compare with* experimental research and field research.) (Chapter 1)

homogenization of news A single perspective and analysis of news stories resulting from a few large conglomerates owning several media outlets. (Chapter 5)

household A common residential unit in which related and nonrelated individuals may live. (Chapter 14)

hubs The most central corporations in a network of interlocking corporations. (Chapter 10)

hypothesis A carefully formulated proposition that may be either verified or discarded on the basis of the examination of relevant data. (Chapter 1)

ideological hegemony The dominance of a set of ideas that govern actions and make other options appear not to make sense. (Chapter 6)

ideology A systematic body of ideas (for example, doctrines or myths) held by members of a class, institution, or group. (Chapters 4 and 6)

immigrant minorities Groups who came to the United States voluntarily, such as Asians and Latin Americans. (*Compare with* involuntary minorities.) (Chapter 12)

import substitution The strategy adopted by peripheral nations of substituting locally produced goods for imported goods in order to combat the drain on their resources and the unequal benefits of trade dependency. (*See also* trade dependency.) (Chapter 9)

imposter syndrome The feeling of people from the lower classes who succeed in life that they have fooled others into thinking that they are deserving of recognition, respect, and acceptance. (Chapter 5)

indirect interlock The relationship that exists between two corporations when one member of yet another corporate board is also a member of both boards of directors.

inequality based on able-bodiedness A system of inequality in which members with physical or mental disabilities are thought of and treated as less worthy than others. (Chapter 6)

inequality based on sexual orientation A system of inequality in which members with a particular sexual orientation are thought of and treated as less worthy than others. (Chapter 6)

infant mortality The number of infants who die within the first year of life per 1,000 live births. (Chapter 13)

informal labor market Consists of people who are not paid for their work; may include both voluntary and involuntary work. (*Compare with* formal labor market and domestic labor.) (Chapter 11)

informal organization A social structure that emerges spontaneously as people interact in bureaucratic or formal organizational settings. (Chapter 3)

innovation With respect to religion, the establishment of new religious rituals or entirely new religions as a response to the secularization of a religion. (*See also* secularization; *compare with* revival.) (Chapter 15)

institutional racism Racial prejudice or discrimination embedded in the routine functioning of societal institutions. (*Compare with* personal racism.) (Chapter 6)

institutional sexism Prejudicial or discriminatory practices that foster advantages for males that accompany the routine operations of societal institutions. (Chapter 6)

institutions The social structures societies possess to fulfill fundamental social needs; five institutions are found in all societies—family, religion, economy, education, and the state. (Chapter 2)

instrumentalism *See* business dominance theory.

interchangeability of elite The mobility of members of the power elite to progress from one institutional sphere of influence to another; for example, someone may be a leader in a corporation and then move to a position of power in the state. (*See also* power elite.) (Chapter 10)

interest-group pluralism A perspective in which a variety of competing interest groups coexist and compromise to produce a balanced government for the common good. (*Compare with* elite pluralism.) (Chapter 10)

interlocking board of directors *See* interlocking corporate directorate.

interlocking corporate directorate A relationship between two corporations formed when one person serves on the board of directors of both corporations. (Chapter 10)

inventions New practices and objects developed out of existing knowledge. (Chapter 9)

involuntary minorities Groups who were incorporated into U.S. society through colonization, conquest, or slavery; for example, Native Americans and African Americans. (*Compare with* immigrant minorities.) (Chapter 12)

iron law of oligarchy The inevitable tendency for organizations to be ruled by a few people, even those organizations that purport to be democratic. (Chapter 3)

label An identifying or descriptive word or phrase, often with a negative connotation when applied to people; for example, a "label of deviance" or "labeled an outcast." (Chapter 8)

language Patterns of written symbols, audible sounds, and gestures that convey meanings. (Chapter 4)

latent function An unintended and sometimes unrecognized result that is produced as institutions carry out their manifest functions. (*See also* institutions; *compare with* manifest function.) (Chapter 2)

latent social change Social change that is largely unrecognized and unintended; for example, the effects of the baby boom in the United States. (*Compare with* manifest social change.) (Chapter 9)

laws The most formal and important norms, which are considered so vital that they are written as legal formalizations. (*See also* norms; *compare with* folkways and mores.) (Chapter 4)

learned helplessness The learned lack of confidence in one's abilities, usually resulting as a response to how one is treated. (Chapter 12)

lending consortium A group of banks that pool their resources in order to meet the large borrowing needs of major corporations and governments. (Chapter 10)

liberation theology Religious teaching that stresses nonacceptance of poverty, challenge of authority if it is oppressive or punitive, civil disobedience, and the legitimacy of nontraditional lifestyles. (Chapters 5 and 15)

life expectancy The average number of years a group of people all born in the same year are expected to live. (Chapter 13)

longitudinal study   A type of research in which the researcher studies the same people over an extended period of time. (Chapter 1)

looking-glass self   People's evaluation of themselves based on how they imagine others perceive and react to them. (Chapter 5)

macro-level social structures   The large-scale social structures that organize and distribute individuals into social positions, for example, institutions, societies, and the world-system. (*See also* social structure; *compare with* mid-level social structures and micro-level social structures.) (Chapter 2)

male chauvinism   A form of sexism through which men express the belief that males are superior to females and have a right to insist on the subordination of females. (*See also* sexism.) (Chapter 6)

managerial revolution   The separation of the functions of ownership and control in corporations, with the power of corporate decision-making going to managers. (Chapter 11)

manifest function   The basic social need an institution is intended to address. (*See also* institutions; *compare with* latent function.) (Chapter 2)

manifest social change   Social change resulting from a deliberate organized effort on the part of one group; for example, the American Revolution or the women's movement. (*Compare with* latent social change.) (Chapter 9)

Marxist theory of deviance   A sociological explanation for deviant behavior that suggests that such behavior within the lower class results from a sense of alienation, low wages, and unemployment. (*See also* sociological explanations and alienation; *compare with* opportunity structure theory.) (Chapter 8)

master status   The one status (among several that each individual has) that overrides all others, thus dictating how a person is treated. (*See also* status.) (Chapter 3)

material culture   Physical artifacts that define a society; for example, a flag, style of dress, or housing. (*Compare with* nonmaterial culture.) (Chapter 4)

maternal mortality   The number of women who die as a result of pregnancy and birthing per 100,000 infants born. (Chapter 13)

medical model   The perspective that health consists of the absence of illness or disease. (*See also* proactive health-care system and reactive health-care system.) (Chapter 13)

merger   The takeover or absorption of one company by another, often accomplished by the purchase of the company that is taken over. (*See also* merger mania.) (Chapter 11)

merger mania   A situation in which many mergers or company takeovers occur. (*See also* merger.) (Chapter 11)

meritocracy   A system that rewards people based on their merit. (Chapter 12)

micro-level social structures   Social structures through which individuals relate to one another, such as an individual's status or role in society. (*See also* social structure; *compare with* mid-level social structures and macro-level social structures.) (Chapter 3)

mid-level social structures   Medium-sized social structures such as groups and organizations. (*See also* social structure; *compare with* macro-level social structures and micro-level social structures.) (Chapter 3)

military-industrial complex   A group, composed of the uniformed military, the aerospace-defense industry, the civilian national security managers, and the U.S. Congress, that works to advance the interests of its members while simultaneously promoting and reinforcing the interests of the others. (Chapter 10)

minority group   An inferior status assigned by the dominant group in a society to another group of people regardless of their numbers within the society. (Chapter 6)

modernization theory   The view that poor countries can move from traditional to industrial economies by adopting the value systems of industrialized Western nations. (Chapter 9)

monopoly sector   A part of the formal labor market in which production is large-scale and capital-intensive and in which production is done by large national or transnational corporations that rely more on machinery than on human labor. (*Compare with* competitive sector and state sector.) (Chapter 11)

monotheism   Belief in one god. (*Compare with* polytheism and animism.) (Chapter 15)

mores   Norms specifying behaviors that must or must not occur, and to which strong feelings may be attached, such as those relating to the selection of a marriage partner. (*See also* norms; *compare with* folkways and laws.) (Chapter 4)

motherhood norms   A standard of behavior holding that normal women want and have children; in contrast, women who do not have children or who choose not to have children are exhibiting a form of deviant behavior. (Chapter 8)

multiculturalism A perspective that acknowledges the heterogeneity of societies, examines the contributions and the intersection of many different groups at crucial moments in history, and explores the factors that affected the experiences of each group. (*Compare with* cultural relativity.) (Chapter 4)

multinational (or **transnational**) **corporations** Companies that operate production and trade facilities in countries other than their own. (Chapter 10)

nations Political entities with clearly defined geographic boundaries usually recognized by neighboring nations and characterized by the viewpoint and interests of their dominant groups or societies. (Chapter 2)

natural differences Elements, usually physical, that differentiate one person from another. (Chapter 6)

nature versus nurture debate Disagreement among social scientists concerning whether genetics (nature) or environment (nurture) exerts a stronger influence on human behavior. (Chapter 5)

negative sanctions Social control in the form of punishment meted out to those who violate the norms of society by exhibiting deviant behavior. (*See also* sanctions; *compare with* positive sanctions.) (Chapter 8)

New Federalism A political philosophy that endorses the belief that the federal government should be involved only in taxation and national defense and that all else is the responsibility of state or local governments. (Chapter 10)

no-fault divorce The dissolution of a marriage in which neither party must attribute blame or misconduct to the other in order to be granted the divorce. (Chapter 14)

nonconcessional loans Loans made by private banks to peripheral countries; the loans do not have special interest rates or payback periods. (*Compare with* concessional loans.) (Chapter 9)

nonmaterial culture The body of abstractions that defines the way a society's members live; abstractions include knowledge, beliefs, values, customs, rituals, and symbols. (*Compare with* material culture.) (Chapter 4)

normative indoctrination The teaching of norms to individuals. (*See also* norms.) (Chapter 4)

norms Rules or standards of proper behavior that are formed by interacting individuals. (Chapters 3, 4, and 8)

nuclear family A family consisting of two parents and their offspring. (*Compare with* extended family.) (Chapter 14)

official religion A formal, organized religious group. (*Compare with* unofficial religion.) (Chapter 15)

open-ended questions In research, exploratory questions that leave the sociologist flexibility in deciding what should be considered relevant data. (Chapter 1)

opportunity structure theory A sociological explanation for deviant behavior that suggests that such behavior results from a society that stresses the importance of material success but does not provide all members with the same means to achieve that success. (*See also* sociological explanations; *compare with* Marxist theory of deviance.) (Chapter 8)

order perspective The belief that human society is a naturally stable, harmonious social system held together by a culture made up of values, rules, and practices that are widely shared. (*Compare with* conflict perspective.) (Chapter 1)

outside director A person who is a member of a corporation's board of directors but whose primary affiliation is not with that corporation. (Chapter 10)

pandemic A disease found throughout the world and affecting a large number of people. (Chapter 13)

participant observation A type of field research in which the researcher plays an active role in the group to the point where he or she becomes an active participant. (*See also* field research, direct observation, and passive observation.) (Chapter 1)

passive observation A type of field research in which the researcher observes the group and records the events for later analysis and interpretation. (*See also* field research, direct observation, and participant observation.) (Chapter 1)

patriarchy A social system in which male dominance is considered a natural, inalienable right. (Chapters 4 and 6)

pauperization of motherhood A situation in which a growing percentage of the poor have female-headed households; subtly suggests that women are impoverished as a result of institutional forces. (*Compare with* feminization of poverty.) (Chapter 14)

perestroika The restructuring of the Soviet Union. (Chapter 16)

peripheral nations In a world-system, countries in which production is based on technology that relies more on inexpensive human labor than on expensive machinery; such countries are usually economically poor. (*See also* world-system; *compare with* core nations and semiperipheral nations.) (Chapter 2)

personal racism The racial prejudice or discrimination expressed by individuals or small groups of people. (*Compare with* institutional racism.) (Chapter 6)

personal troubles Matters involving a person's character and his or her relations with others over which the individual has control. (*Compare with* public issues.) (Chapter 1)

physiological explanations Within the context of explaining deviant behavior, explanations that attribute such behavior to a physical peculiarity or malfunction or to heredity. (*Compare with* psychological explanations, social-psychological explanations, and sociological explanations.) (Chapter 8)

pluralism The theory that competing interest groups or elites coexist, cooperate, and maintain a balance of power to create government in the common good. (Chapter 10)

political socialization The process through which people internalize a political identity that defines who they are and how they should behave in the political and economic institutions of society. (Chapter 5)

polytheism Belief in more than one god. (*Compare with* monotheism and animism.) (Chapter 15)

positive sanctions Social control in the form of rewards given to those who conform to the norms and abide by the rules of society. (*See also* sanctions; *compare with* negative sanctions.) (Chapter 8)

power elite People who fill the command positions of strategically important institutions, such as the state, the corporate economy, and the military, and who come from a single group and share a single world view. (Chapter 10)

primary group A collection of individuals who interact frequently and share important connections that bring the members together; for example, family, friends, and coworkers. (*See also* group; *compare with* secondary group.) (Chapter 3)

primary source A source of information used in historical research that has not been interpreted, evaluated, or analyzed by others, for example, original records, diaries, official documents, eyewitness accounts, and oral histories. (*Compare with* secondary source.) (Chapter 1)

proactive health-care system A preventive system of health care aimed at enhancing people's overall well-being and potential. (*See also* medical model; *compare with* reactive health-care system.) (Chapter 13)

profane Ordinary, everyday, or nonreligious. (*Compare with* sacred.) (Chapter 15)

proletariat The working class; those who do not own the means of production and must therefore sell their labor power in order to live. (*Compare with* capitalists.) (Chapter 9)

psychological explanations Within the context of explaining deviant behavior, explanations that attribute such behavior to emotional problems or unusual personality traits that often result from experiences with family members or other people in a position to influence one's psychological development. (*Compare with* physiological explanations, social-psychological explanations, and sociological explanations.) (Chapter 8)

public issues Societal conditions that transcend the individual and lie beyond his or her personal environment and control, such as rising unemployment. (*Compare with* personal troubles.) (Chapter 1)

racial formation According to Omi and Winant, the process in which the dominant groups establish the content and importance of racial categories. (Chapter 6)

racial inequality A system of inequality in which members of one race are thought of and treated as less worthy than members of another, resulting in discrimination and exploitation. (Chapter 6)

radical elite theory The view that the state is not neutral and that it favors the power elite. (*See also* power elite.) (Chapter 10)

reactive health-care system A health-care system organized to respond to existing illness or disease rather than prevent it. (*Compare with* proactive health-care system.) (Chapter 13)

recidivism A tendency to relapse into a previous mode of behavior; for example, people who have gone to prison more than once are recidivists. (Chapter 8)

redemptive movement A type of social movement directed at totally changing individuals rather than society as a whole; often a religious movement. (*Compare with* alterative movement, reformative movement, and transformative movement.) (Chapter 9)

redline A banking practice that defines certain areas, such as those with a large minority population, as ineligible for mortgages and small business loans. (Chapter 16)

reductionism A process that reduces complex ideas or information to simple terms; for example, people who attribute deviant behavior to physiological or psychological reasons only and do not consider larger societal influences are practicing reductionism. (Chapter 8)

reference group A group to whom people look for approval, guidance, and role models; for example, peer groups. (Chapter 5)

reformative movement A type of social movement that aims to make limited but specific changes in society rather than just in individuals; for example, the civil rights movement. (*Compare with* redemptive movement, alterative movement, and transformative movement.) (Chapter 9)

relative deprivation According to Davies, the state in which people's understanding of deprivation is relative to the conditions around them, to conditions they expect, or to conditions that previously existed. (*Compare with* absolute deprivation.) (Chapter 9)

religion A body of beliefs and practices (embraced by a social group) concerned with the supernatural and the sacred that encourages followers to conduct themselves in accordance with moral prescriptions associated with the beliefs. (Chapters 2 and 15)

representative democracy A government, organization, or group in which people choose or elect others to make decisions for them. (*See also* democracy; *compare with* direct democracy.) (Chapter 3)

resocialization The process in which an individual's previous self is replaced with a new, more acceptable social identity. (Chapter 5)

resource mobilization theory The view that social movements, and revolutions, will not occur unless human and supportive resources are available and deployed for use regardless of how strong the feelings of the people may be. (Chapter 9)

reverse discrimination Discriminatory practices of employers against members of the majority resulting from efforts to follow affirmative action. (*See also* affirmative action.) (Chapter 6)

revival With respect to religion, an effort to renew and revitalize the traditional orientations of religions that are becoming secularized. (*See also* secularization; *compare with* innovation.) (Chapter 15)

role conflict The distress individuals experience when the demands of two or more roles they play are at odds. (*Compare with* role strain.) (Chapter 3)

role strain The distress individuals experience when one of the roles they play contains contradictory demands. (*Compare with* role conflict.) (Chapter 3)

rolelessness The absence of socially sanctioned roles. (Chapter 7)

runaway shops Work facilities that are moved to locations where labor is inexpensive and often nonunionized and taxes and laws favor business interests. (Chapter 11)

sacred Relating to religious objects, beings, and situations that inspire awe, reverence, or fear. (*Compare with* profane.) (Chapter 15)

sanctions Social control in the form of punishment meted out to those who exhibit deviant behavior or rewards given to those who conform to the norms of society. (Chapters 4 and 8)

school vouchers Certificates given to families authorizing the government to use a specific amount of public funds to pay for their children's tuition at the school of their choice. (Chapter 16)

second shift *See* double day.

secondary group A collection of individuals who come together for a specific purpose such as accomplishing a task or achieving a goal; primary groups may form as a result of people's participation in secondary groups. (*See also* group; *compare with* primary group.) (Chapter 3)

secondary source A source of information used in historical research that has been interpreted, evaluated, or analyzed by others, for example, publications of scholars. (*Compare with* primary source.) (Chapter 1)

sect A religious group formed by people protesting their social environment, including other religious groups. (*Compare with* denomination and cult.) (Chapter 15)

secularization The decline in significance of religion in people's lives. (Chapter 15)

segmented labor market A divided labor market resulting from the fact that men and women, and people in different racial categories, compete in different labor markets for different jobs. (Chapter 11)

self-fulfilling prophecy The phenomenon in which people achieve to the level expected of them rather than to the level of which they may actually be capable. (Chapters 1, 5, and 12)

semiperipheral nations In a world-system, countries in which production is based on a mixture of intermediate levels of machinery and human labor and in which human labor is semiskilled and paid intermediate levels of wages. (*See also* world-system; *compare with* core nations and peripheral nations.) (Chapter 2)

sex The category of male or female, determined by fundamental biological characteristics. (*Compare with* gender.) (Chapter 6)

sex inequality A system of inequality based on the belief that biological differences between the sexes require that members of each sex play different roles in society; one sex (usually women) is thought of and treated as less worthy.

sexism The systematic subordination of people on the basis of their sex. (Chapter 6)

sexual division of labor A division of responsibilities for women and men based on biological differences; for example, because women bear children, it is often the custom that they stay home and be caretakers. (Chapter 6)

significant other An individual who serves as the most important person, and therefore a crucial role model, in another individual's life. (*Compare with* generalized other.) (Chapter 5)

single-payer plan A system of health care in which the government controls fees, streamlines administration, and has all bills submitted to it for payment. (Chapter 13)

social aggregate A collection of individuals with no real interpersonal ties or patterned relationships, such as people who attend a concert or sporting event. (Chapter 3)

social change Significant variations or alterations in social structures and cultures over time. (Chapter 9)

social construction (of deviance) The definition of an act (as deviance) within the context of society's norms for acceptable behavior. (Chapter 8)

social control Means of minimizing socially deviant behavior. (Chapter 8)

social Darwinism An extension of the evolutionary perspective which holds that as societies evolve and change, only the fittest will survive and those that are less fit will die out. (*See also* evolutionary perspective.) (Chapter 9)

social movements Large-scale, persistent efforts in which individuals working together may alter how institutions and whole societies operate. (Chapters 2 and 9)

social-psychological explanations Within the context of explaining deviant behavior, explanations that attribute such behavior to conditions in people's immediate social environment that influence their thinking and actions. (*Compare with* physiological explanations, psychological explanations, and sociological explanations.) (Chapter 8)

social reform An adjustment in the content of cultural patterns of behavior or normative systems that does not fundamentally alter the social structure. (*Compare with* social revolution.) (Chapter 9)

social reinforcement theory A social-psychological explanation for deviant behavior that suggests that such behavior results from the belief that the rewards of deviant behavior outweigh the punishments. (*See also* social-psychological explanations; *compare with* differential association theory, containment theory, and control theory.) (Chapter 8)

social reproduction Maintenance rather than change of existing social systems; for example, by conserving the status quo, schools perpetuate racism and sexism. (Chapter 12)

social revolution A fundamental and radical upheaval of existing social structures. (*Compare with* social reform.) (Chapter 9)

social role The behavior expected of individuals in the various positions or statuses they hold. (Chapter 3)

social stratification The system in which people occupy different social positions from high to low. (Chapter 6)

social structure The way in which recurring patterns of relationships within a social system are organized. (Chapter 2)

socialization The ongoing process of learning the ways of a culture. (Chapter 5)

socialization agents Elements that bring about the process of socialization; the agents can be grouped into seven categories—family; peers;

school; religion; work; media; and toys, games, and recreational activities. (Chapter 5)

socially constructed Ideas or relationships that are created and given meaning by members of a social group; for example, the idea that there are biologically distinct races, some of which are inferior to others. (Chapter 6)

society An organization of people who share a common territory, govern themselves, and cooperate to secure the survival of the group. (Chapter 2)

sociobiology The study of the biological basis of social behavior. (*See also* nature versus nurture debate.) (Chapter 5)

sociological explanations Within the context of explaining deviant behavior, explanations that attribute the behavior to societal factors outside the control of individuals. (*Compare with* physiological explanations, psychological explanations, and social-psychological explanations.) (Chapter 8)

sociological imagination A way of thinking that enables individuals to understand how they are affected by broad features of the society and the times in which they live. (Chapter 1)

sociology The study of people as participants in and creators of society. (Chapter 1)

state The institution made up of political positions and the structure of political relations whose manifest function is to protect society's members from internal and external threats. (Chapters 2 and 10)

state sector A part of the formal labor market in which the government is the employer and work tends to be service-oriented. (*Compare with* monopoly sector and competitive sector.) (Chapter 11)

status The position a person occupies in a group or organization; for example, in a family a person may have the status of son and brother. (Chapter 3)

status inconsistency A situation in which one indication of a person's standing in society is out of sync with the others; for example, someone with an advanced academic degree working at a blue-collar job. (Chapter 14)

stigma A negative mark that discredits a person's worth. (Chapters 6 and 8)

structural functional perspective The view that societies are adaptive social structures which help human beings adjust to their physical, political, economic, and social environments. (Chapter 2)

structuralist theory The view that the state shapes its policies in ways that are consistent with capital-accumulation interests because its fate rests on the health of the economy. (*See also* capital-accumulation interests.) (Chapter 10)

subculture A group whose members participate in the larger society and its institutions but who share values, norms, a heritage, and rituals that differ from those of the dominant culture. (Chapter 4)

supply-side economics An economic philosophy that supports the belief that benefits to capitalists will trickle down to benefit labor and ultimately to benefit everyone; also called trickle-down economics. (Chapter 10)

surrogate mother A woman, usually hired by a married couple, who carries a fertilized egg and gives birth to a child but then turns over the baby to the other woman who will be the child's legal mother. (Chapter 9)

survey A type of research in which the participants fill out a questionnaire or answer questions in person or over the phone. (Chapter 1)

symbolic interaction An interpersonal process that uses language, symbols, and sanctions to create, maintain, and alter culture and society. (Chapter 5)

synthesis According to Marx and Engels, the result of the conflict between the thesis and the antithesis; a whole new social structure containing elements of both the thesis and the antithesis. (*See also* dialectic, thesis, and antithesis.) (Chapter 9)

systems of inequality Sets of social relationships built around an attribute, such as wealth or sexual orientation, to which members of society accord a great deal of meaning and importance in everyday life. (Chapter 6)

tax credit A mechanism that allows parents to deduct the cost of their children's education from their annual federal tax payments. (Chapter 16)

thesis According to Marx and Engels, the current or temporary state of existence of a society. (*See also* dialectic, antithesis, and synthesis.) (Chapter 9)

Thomas theorem The view that if a situation is defined as real, the consequences of actions based on that definition are quite real, regardless of whether the definition is accurate; for example, if women are defined as inferior to men, they will be treated as inferior regardless of the reality; also called definition of the situation. (Chapter 4)

total institutions Institutions in which individuals are completely isolated from the rest of society for an extended period of time; for example, mental institutions. (Chapter 5)

toxic imperialism Toxic dumping in underdeveloped countries by major corporations and industrialized or core nations. (Chapter 16)

tracking A policy in many schools wherein students are grouped for instruction on the basis of the presumption that their past classroom performance and standardized test scores are valid indicators of their ability and potential; for example, schools may divide students into academic (college-bound) and vocational (employment-bound) tracks. (*See also* gatekeepers.) (Chapters 1 and 12)

trade dependency A relationship between nations characterized by limited numbers of core trade partners for peripheral countries. (*Compare with* dependent development and debt dependency.) (Chapter 9)

transformative movement A type of social movement that aims to make sweeping, rather than limited, changes in society; for example, revolution. (*Compare with* redemptive movement, alterative movement, and reformative movement.) (Chapter 9)

trickle-down economics *See* supply-side economics.

triple shift A situation in which women work in the formal labor market and the informal labor market in addition to working at domestic labor. (*See also* formal labor market, informal labor market, and domestic labor; *compare with* double day.) (Chapter 11)

underdeveloped nation A peripheral nation that has experienced historically disadvantageous relationships with more powerful industrialized or core nations and thus has been limited in its development opportunities. (*See also* peripheral nation and core nation.) (Chapter 9)

unofficial religion A departure from the beliefs and practices of official religion; also called popular or folk religion. (*Compare with* official religion.) (Chapter 15)

values Assumptions and judgments made about the goods, goals, or states of existence that are deemed important, desirable, and worth striving for. (Chapter 4)

whistle-blowers People, usually workers, who speak out against unfair, unethical, unsafe, or illegal practices of the institution for which they work. (Chapter 8)

white-skin privilege Social advantages, usually unearned, provided to members of the white majority. (Chapter 7)

work Any activity that produces something of value for other people. (Chapter 11)

worker cooperative A company that is owned and operated by its workers. (Chapter 11)

world-system An international social system of cultural, normative, economic, political, and military relations organized around the exchange of goods and services; the most complete macro-level social structure which encompasses all other levels of social structure. (*See also* social structure and macro-level social structure.) (Chapter 2)

REFERENCES

ABC News/Washington Post. 1991. "National Adult Voter Attitudes." Telephone survey (October 24).

Aberle, David. 1966. *The Peyote Religion among the Navaho.* Chicago: Aldine.

Abramovitz, Mimi. 1987. "Privatizing health care." *The Nation* (October 17):410–412.

Abramson, Leonard. 1990. *Healing Our Health Care System.* New York: Grove Weidenfeld.

Ackerman, Frank. 1982. *Reaganomics: Rhetoric vs. Reality.* Boston: South End Press.

Acuña, Rodolfo. 1988. *Occupied America,* 3rd ed. New York: Harper & Row.

Adam, Barry D. 1978. *The Survival of Domination.* New York: Elsevier.

———. 1987. *The Rise of the Gay and Lesbian Movement.* Boston: Twayne.

Adams, Gordon. 1982. *The Iron Triangle: The Politics of Defense Contracting.* New Brunswick, NJ: Transaction Books.

Adizes, Ichak. 1971. *Industrial Democracy: Yugoslav Style.* New York: Free Press.

Akers, Ronald L. 1985. *Deviant Behavior,* 3rd ed. Belmont, CA: Wadsworth.

Alan Guttmacher Institute. 1981. *Teenage Pregnancy: The Problem That Hasn't Gone Away.* New York: The Alan Guttmacher Institute.

———. 1994. *Sex and America's Teenagers.* New York: The Alan Guttmacher Institute.

Alba, Richard D., and Gwen Moore. 1982. "Ethnicity in the American elite." *American Sociological Review* 47(3):373–383.

Alexander, Karl L., Martha A. Cook, and Edward L. McDill. 1978. "Curriculum tracking and educational stratification: Some further evidence." *American Sociological Review* 43:47–66.

——— and Edward L. McDill. 1976. "Selection and allocation within schools: Some causes and conse-quences of curriculum placement." *American Sociological Review* 41:963–980.

Allen, Michael Patrick, and Philip Broyles. 1989. "Class hegemony and political finance: Presidential campaign contributions of wealthy capitalist fami-lies." *American Sociological Review* 54(2):275–287.

Almanac of Higher Education, The. 1993. Chicago: University of Chicago Press.

Almquist, Elizabeth M. 1979. *Minorities, Gender, and Work.* Lexington, MA: Lexington Books.

———. 1989. "The experience of minority women in the United States." Pages 414–445 in Jo Freeman (ed.), *Women: A Feminist Perspective,* 4th ed. Mountain View, CA: Mayfield.

Alperovitz, G., and J. Faux. 1984. *Rebuilding America.* New York: Pantheon.

Alston, Dana (ed.). 1990. *We Speak for Ourselves: Social Justice, Race and Environment.* Washington, DC: Panos Institute.

Alwin, Duane F. 1984. "Trends in parental socializa-tion values: Detroit, 1958–1983." *American Journal of Sociology* 90:359–382.

American Association of University Women and the Wellesley College Center for Research on Women. 1992. *How Schools Shortchange Girls.* Washington, DC: AAUW Educational Foundation.

American Sociological Association. 1989. *Code of Ethics.* Washington, DC: ASA.

Ames, Katherine, with Christopher Sulavik, Nadine Joseph, Lucille Beachy, and Todd Park. 1992. "Domesticated bliss: New laws are making it official for gay or live-in straight couples." *Newsweek* (March 23):62–63.

Amott, Teresa. 1993. *Caught in the Crisis: Women and the U.S. Economy Today.* New York: Monthly Review Press.

——— and Julie A. Matthaei. 1991. *Race, Gender, and*

Work: A Multicultural Economic History of Women in the United States. Boston: South End Press.

Andersen, Margaret L. 1990. "Feminism and the American family ideal." *Journal of Comparative Family Studies* 22:35–46.

——— and Patricia Hill Collins (eds.). 1992. *Race, Class, and Gender: An Anthology*. Belmont, CA: Wadsworth.

Anderson, Elijah. 1976. *A Place on the Corner*. Chicago: University of Chicago Press.

Angel, Ronald, and Marta Tienda. 1982. "Determinants of extended household structure: Cultural pattern or economic model?" *American Journal of Sociology* 87:1360–1383.

Anti-Defamation League of B'nai B'rith. 1992. *Anti-Semitism and Prejudice in America*. New York: ADL.

———. 1993. *Highlights from an Anti-Defamation League Survey on Racial Attitudes in America*. New York: ADL.

Asch, Adrienne, and Michelle Fine. 1988. "Introduction: Beyond pedestals." Pages 1–37 in Michelle Fine and Adrienne Asch (eds.), *Women with Disabilities*. Philadelphia: Temple University Press.

Asch, Peter, and Joseph J. Seneca. 1978. "Some evidence on the distribution of air quality." *Land Economics* 54:278–297.

Asher, Carol. 1992. *Successful Detracking in Middle and Senior High Schools*. New York: ERIC Clearinghouse on Urban Education, Columbia University.

Atchley, Robert C. 1985. *Social Forces and Aging*, 4th ed. Belmont, CA: Wadsworth.

Auerbach, A. J., and L. J. Kotlikoff. 1987. "Life insurance of the elderly: Its adequacy and determinants." Pages 229–267 in G. Burtless (ed.), *Work, Health, and Income among the Elderly*. Washington, DC: Brookings Institute.

Babbie, Earl. 1992. *The Practice of Social Research*, 6th ed. Belmont, CA: Wadsworth.

Bahr, Howard M., Bruce A. Chadwick, and Joseph H. Strauss. 1979. *American Ethnicity*. Lexington, MA: Heath.

Baker, David P., and Doris R. Entwisle. 1987. "The influence of mothers on the academic expectations of young children: A longitudinal study of how gender differences arise." *Social Forces* 65(3)(March):670–694.

Baker, Therese L. 1988. *Doing Social Research*. New York: McGraw-Hill.

Ball-Rokeach, Sandra J., Milton Rokeach, and Joel W. Grube. 1984. *The Great American Values Test: Influencing Behavior and Belief through Television*. New York: Free Press.

Bane, Mary Jo, and David T. Ellwood. 1991. "Is American business working for the poor?" *Harvard Business Review* (September–October):58–66.

Banfield, Edward, and James Q. Wilson. 1963. *City Politics*. New York: Vintage.

Baratz, Steven S., and Joan C. Baratz. 1970. "Early childhood intervention: The social science base of institutional racism." *Harvard Educational Review* 40:29–50.

Barnet, Richard J. 1969. *The Economy of Death*. New York: Atheneum.

Barnett, Bernice McNair. 1993. "Invisible southern black women leaders in the civil rights movement: The triple constraints of gender, race, and class." *Gender & Society* 7(June):162–182.

Barnett, Mark A. 1977. "The role of play and make believe in children's cognitive development: Implications for social class differences and education." *Journal of Education* 159(4)(November):38–48.

Barringer, Felicity. 1993. "School hallways as gantlets of sexual taunts." *New York Times* (June 2):B7.

Barry, David S. 1993. "Growing up violent." *Media and Values* 62(Summer):8–11.

Barthel, Diane. 1988. *Putting on Appearances: Gender and Advertising*. Philadelphia: Temple University Press.

Bayat, Assef. 1991. *Work, Politics, and Power: An International Perspective on Workers' Control and Self-Management*. New York: Monthly Review Press.

Beauchamp, Tom L., et al. (eds.). 1982. *Ethical Issues in Social Science Research*. Baltimore: Johns Hopkins University Press.

Beck, Ruby W., and Scott H. Beck. 1989. "The incidence of extended households among middle-aged black and white women: Estimates from a 5-year panel study." *Journal of Family Issues* 10:147–168.

Becker, Howard S. 1963. *Outsiders: Studies in the Sociology of Deviance*. New York: Free Press.

Beckett, Joyce O., and Audrey D. Smith. 1981. "Work and family roles: Egalitarian marriage in black and white families." *Social Service Review* 55:314–326.

Bell, Daniel. 1973. *The Coming of Post-industrial Society*. New York: Basic Books.

Bellah, Robert N. 1967. "Civil religion in America." *Daedalus* 96:1–21.

Benedict, Ruth. 1959. *Race: Science and Politics*. New York: Viking.

Benjamin, Lois. 1991. *The Black Elite: Facing the Color Line in the Twilight of the Twentieth Century*. Chicago: Nelson-Hall.

Benokraitis, Nijole, and Joyce A. Griffin-Keene. 1982. "Prejudice and jury selection." *Journal of Black Studies* 12(4):427–449.

Bensman, David, and Robert Lynch. 1987. *Rusted Dreams: Hard Times in a Steel Community*. New York: McGraw-Hill.

Berch, Bettina. 1982. *The Endless Day: The Political Economy of Women and Work*. New York: Harcourt Brace Jovanovich.

Berger, Peter L. 1963. *Invitation to Sociology: A Humanistic Perspective*. New York: Doubleday.

——— and Thomas Luckmann. 1966. *The Social Construction of Reality*. Garden City, NY: Doubleday.

Berk, Sarah Fenstermaker. 1985. *The Gender Factory: The Apportionment of Work in American Households*. New York: Plenum Press.

Berle, Adolph, and Gardiner C. Means. 1932. *The Modern Corporation and Private Property*. New York: Harcourt, Brace & World.

Bernstein, Aaron, with David Woodruff, Barbara Buell, Nancy Peacock, and Karen Thurston. 1991. "What happened to the American dream? The under-30 generation may be losing the race for prosperity." *Business Week* (August 19):80–85.

Billy, John O. G., et al. 1993. "The sexual behavior of men in the United States." *Family Planning Perspectives* 25 (March–April):52–60.

Bixby, Lyn. 1992. "Peace dividend: More markets for arms makers." *Hartford Courant* (October 25):A1, A6–A7.

Blauner, Robert. 1964. *Alienation and Freedom*. Chicago: University of Chicago Press.

Block, Fred. 1987. *Revising State Theory*. Philadelphia: Temple University Press.

Bluestone, Barry, and Bennett Harrison. 1982. *The Deindustrialization of America*. New York: Basic Books.

Blumberg, Rhoda Lois. 1991. *Civil Rights: The 1960s Freedom Struggle*, rev. ed. Boston: Twayne.

Blumenfeld, Warren J. (ed.). 1992. *Homophobia: How We All Pay the Price*. Boston: Beacon Press.

Boggiano, A. K., and M. Barrett. 1991. "Strategies to motivate helpless and mastery-oriented children: The effect of gender-based expectancies." *Sex Roles* 25:487–510.

Bonavoglia, Angela. 1992. "The sacred secret." *Ms.* (March–April):40–45.

Boorstin, Daniel J. 1961. *The Image, or, What Happened to the American Dream?* New York: Atheneum.

———. 1991. "What happened to the American dream?" *Business Week* (August 19):80–85.

Bornschier, Volker, and Thanh-Huyen Ballmer-Cao. 1979. "Income inequality: A cross-national study of the relationship between MNC penetration, dimensions of the power structure and income distribution." *American Sociological Review* 44(3):487–506.

——— and Christopher Chase-Dunn. 1985. *Transnational Corporations and Underdevelopment*. New York: Praeger.

———, ———, and Richard Rubinson. 1978. "Cross-national evidence of the effects of foreign investment and aid on economic growth and inequality: A survey of findings and a reanalysis." *American Journal of Sociology* 84:651–683.

Boserup, Esther. 1970. *Women's Role in Economic Development*. New York: St. Martin's Press.

Bourdieu, Pierre, and Jean-Claude Passeron. 1991. *Reproduction in Education, Society, and Culture*, rev. ed. Newbury Park, CA: Sage.

Bowen, Ezra. 1987. "Bad news about math." *Time* (January 26):65.

Bowker, Lee H. 1972. "Red and black in contemporary history texts: A content analysis." Pages 101–110 in Howard M. Bahr, Bruce A. Chadwick, and Robert C. Day (eds.), *Native Americans Today: Sociological Perspectives*. New York: Harper & Row.

Bowlby, John. 1973. *Attachment and Loss*, vol. 2. New York: Basic Books.

Bowles, Samuel, and Herbert Gintis. 1976. *Schooling in Capitalist America: Educational Reform and the Contradictions of Economic Life*. New York: Basic Books.

Bowman, Philip, and Cleopatra Howard. 1985. "Race-related socialization, motivation, and academic achievement: A study of black youth in three-generation families." *Journal of the American Academy of Child Psychiatry* 24:134–141.

Bowser, Benjamin P., Gale S. Auletta, and Terry Jones. 1993. *Confronting Diversity Issues on Campus*. Thousand Oaks, CA: Sage.

Boyle, Sarah Patton. 1962. *The Desegregated Heart: A Virginian's Stand in Time of Transition*. New York: William Morrow.

Braddock, Jomills Henry. 1990. "Tracking the middle grades: National patterns of grouping for instruction." *Phi Beta Kappan* 71(February):445–449.

Brint, Steven, and Jerome Karabel. 1989. *The Diverted Dream*. New York: Oxford University Press.

Broman, Clifford L. 1988. "Household work and family life satisfaction of blacks." *Journal of Marriage and the Family* 50:743–748.

Brophy, Jere E. 1983. "Research on the self-fulfilling prophecy and teacher expectations." *Journal of Educational Psychology* 75:631–661.

Brown, J. Larry. 1987. "Hunger in the U.S." *Scientific American* 256(February):37–41.

Brown, Michael. 1980. *Laying Waste: The Poisoning of America by Toxic Chemicals*. New York: Pantheon.

Brown, Tina A. 1993. "Police seek motive in murder-suicide." *Hartford Courant* (August 8):B1.

Browne, Angela. 1987. *When Battered Women Kill*. New York: Macmillan/Free Press.

———. 1993. "Family violence and homelessness: The relevance of trauma histories in the lives of homeless women." *American Journal of Orthopsychiatry* 63(3):370–384.

Browne, Susan E., Debra Connors, and Nanci Stern (eds.). 1985. *With the Power of Each Breath: A Disabled Women's Anthology*. Pittsburgh: Cleis Press.

Bryant, Bunyan, and Paul Mohai (eds.). 1992. *Race and the Incidence of Environmental Hazards*. Boulder, CO: Westview Press.

Bullard, Robert D. 1983. "Solid waste sites and the Houston black community." *Sociological Inquiry* 53(Spring):273–288.

———. 1990. *Dumping in Dixie: Race, Class, and Environmental Quality*. Boulder, CO: Westview Press.

———. 1993. *Confronting Environmental Racism: Voices from the Grassroots*. Boston: South End Press.

Bullard, Robert, and Beverly Hendrix Wright. 1987. "Environmentalism and the politics of equity: Emergent trends in the black community." *Mid-American Review of Sociology* 12(2):21–38.

Burawoy, Michael. 1982. *Manufacturing Consent: Changes in the Labor Process under Monopoly Capitalism*. Chicago: University of Chicago Press.

Burkhauser, R. V., and G. J. Duncan. 1989. "Economic risks of gender roles: Income loss and life events over the life course." *Social Science Quarterly* 70:3–23.

Burnham, James. 1941. *The Managerial Revolution*. New York: John Day.

Burns, Ailsa, and Ross Homel. 1989. "Gender division of tasks by parents and their children." *Psychology of Women Quarterly* 13(1)(March):113–125.

Burris, Val. 1992. "Elite policy-planning networks in

the United States." *Research in Politics and Society* 4:111–134.

Business Week. 1980. "Industry's schoolhouse clout." (October 13):156–160.

———. 1984. *The Reindustrialization of America.* New York: McGraw-Hill.

———. 1991. *The Business Week 1,000: America's Most Valuable Companies.* New York: McGraw-Hill.

Calavita, Kitty, and Henry Pontell. 1991. "'Other people's money' revisited: Embezzlement in the savings and loan insurance industries." *Social Problems* 38(1):94–112.

Campbell, Anne. 1984. *The Girls in the Gang: A Report from New York City.* New York: Basil Blackwell.

Cannon, Carl M. 1993. "Honey, I warped the kids." *Mother Jones* 18(July–August):16–17.

Caplan, Arthur L. 1979. *The Sociobiology Debate.* New York: Harper & Row.

Carter, Bill. 1991. "Children's TV, where boys are king." *New York Times* (May 1):A1, C18.

Cashmore, Ellis, and Eugene McLaughlin (eds.). 1991. *Out of Order?: Policing Black People.* New York: Routledge.

Cassidy, Kevin J. 1990. "Economic conversion: Industrial policy and democratic values." *Policy Studies Review* 9(4):775–786.

Castellani, Paul J. 1987. *The Political Economy of Developmental Disabilities.* Baltimore: Paul H. Brookes.

CBS News/New York Times. 1991. "CBS News/New York Times Poll" (June 17).

Chase-Dunn, Christopher. 1989. *Global Formation: Structures of the World Economy.* Cambridge, MA: Basil Blackwell.

Chavis, Benjamin F., Jr., and Charles Lee. 1987. *Toxic Wastes and Race in the United States: A National Report on the Racial and Socio-Economic Characteristics of Communities with Hazardous Waste Sites.* New York: United Church of Christ Commission for Racial Justice.

Cherry, Robert, and Susan Feiner. 1992. "The treatment of racial and sexual discrimination in economics journals and economics textbooks: 1972–1987." *Review of Black Political Economy* 21(Fall):99–118.

Chesler, Mark, Joseph Sanders, and Debra S. Kalmus. 1988. *Social Science in Court: Mobilizing Experts in the School Desegregation Cases.* Madison: University of Wisconsin Press.

Christ, Carol P., and Judith Plaskow (eds.). 1992. *Womenspirit Rising: A Feminist Reader in Religion.* San Francisco: Harper-SanFrancisco.

Chronicle, The. 1991. "Study shows poor, middle class hit hardest by taxes." (April 22):1, 7.

Churchill, Larry R. 1987. *Rationing Health Care in America.* Notre Dame, IN: University of Notre Dame Press.

Cimons, Marlene. 1990. "GAO cites bias in health research." *Los Angeles Times* (June 19):A20.

Clark, Charles S. 1991. "Youth gangs." *Congressional Quarterly Researcher* 1(22):753–776.

Clark, Kenneth B., and Mamie P. Clark. 1947. "Racial identification and preferences in Negro children." Pages 169–178 in Theodore M. Newcomb and Eugene L. Hartley (eds.), *Readings in Social Psychology.* New York: Holt, Rinehart and Winston.

Clawson, Dan. 1980. *Bureaucracy and the Labor Process: The Transformation of U.S. Industry, 1860–1920.* New York: Monthly Review Press.

Clinard, Marshall B., and Robert F. Meier. 1992. *Sociology of Deviant Behavior,* 8th ed. Fort Worth, TX: Harcourt Brace Jovanovich.

Clinton cure, the." 1993. *Newsweek* (October 4):36–38 ff.

"Clinton solution, the." 1993. *Newsweek* (September 20):30–32 ff.

Cockburn, Alexander. 1992. "Stalking the poor." *New Statesman and Society* 5(December 4):17.

Cohen, Albert K. 1955. *Delinquent Boys: The Culture of the Gang.* New York: Free Press.

Cohen, Mitchell. 1990. "Toxic imperialism: Exporting Pentagonorrhea." *Z Magazine* (October):78–79.

Coleman, James S., et al. 1966. *Equality of Educational Opportunity.* Washington, DC: U.S. Government Printing Office.

Coleman, James William. 1989. *The Criminal Elite.* New York: St. Martin's Press.

Collins, Patricia Hill. 1990. *Black Feminist Thought.* Boston: Unwin Hyman.

Collins, Randall. 1979. *Credential Society.* New York: Academic Press.

Commonwealth Fund. 1993. "The Kaiser/Commonwealth Fund Health Insurance Survey."

Comstock, George, and Haejung Paik. 1991. *Television and the American Child.* San Diego, CA: Academic Press.

Comte, Auguste. 1966. *System of Positive Polity,* vol. 3. New York: Burt Franklin.

Connecticut Department of Education. 1991. *Connecticut Public Schools: Town and School District Profiles.* Hartford: State Department of Education.

Cookson, Peter W., and Caroline Hodges Persell. 1985. *Preparing for Power: America's Elite Boarding Schools.* New York: Basic Books.

Cooley, Charles Horton. 1902. *Human Nature and the Social Order.* New York: Scribner.

———. 1929. *Social Organization.* New York: Scribner.

Coons, John E., and Stephen D. Sugarman. 1991. "The private school option in systems of education choice." *Educational Leadership* 48(4):54–56.

Corcoran, Katherine. 1991. "Openly gay candidates winning more elections." *Washington Post* (March 12):A3.

Corm, Georges. 1982. "The indebtedness of the developing countries: Origins and mechanisms." Pages 15–110 in J. C. Sanchez Arnau (ed.), *Debt and Development.* New York: Praeger.

Cose, Ellis. 1993. *The Rage of a Privileged Class.* New York: Harper Collins.

Council on Competitiveness. 1991. "National Adult Population Attitudes toward Economics." Telephone survey. (September).

Council of Great City Schools. 1992. *National Urban*

Education Goals: Baseline Indicators, 1990–91. Washington, DC: Council of Great City Schools.

Cowgill, Donald O. 1986. *Aging around the World.* Belmont, CA: Wadsworth.

Creedon, Michael A. 1989. "The corporate response to the working caregiver." *Aging Magazine* 358:16–19 ff.

Crosby, Faye J. 1991. *Juggling: The Unexpected Advantages of Balancing Career and Home for Women and Their Families.* New York: Macmillan/Free Press.

Crystal, Graef S. 1991. *In Search of Excess: The Overcompensation of American Executives.* New York: Norton.

Culver, John. 1992. "Capital punishment, 1977–1990: Characteristics of the 143 executed." *Sociology and Social Research* 76(2):59–61.

Cumming, Elaine, and William E. Henry. 1961. *Growing Old: The Process of Disengagement.* New York: Basic Books.

Cummings, Scott (ed.). 1988. *Business Elites and Urban Development.* Albany: State University of New York Press.

—— and Del Taebel. 1978. "The economic socialization of children." *Social Problems* 26(December):198–210.

Curb, Rosemary, and Nancy Manahan (eds.). 1985. *Lesbian Nuns: Breaking Silence.* Talahassee, FL: Naiad Press.

Curtiss, Susan R. 1977. *Genie: A Psycholinguistic Study of a Modern World "Wild Child."* New York: Academic Press.

Cutler, James Elbert. 1969. *Lynch-Law: An Investigation into the History of Lynching in the United States.* Montclair, NJ: Patterson Smith.

Cyrus, Virginia (ed.). 1993. *Experiencing Race, Class, and Gender in the United States.* Mountain View, CA: Mayfield.

Dagnoli, Judann. 1990. "Consumers Union hits kids' advertising." *Advertising Age* 61(30)(July 23):4.

Dahl, Robert A. 1961. *Who Governs? Democracy and Power in an American City.* New Haven: Yale University Press.

Dale, Richard S., and Richard P. Mattione. 1983. *Managing Global Debt.* Washington, DC: Brookings Institute.

Daniels, Arlene Kaplan. 1988. *Invisible Careers: Women Civic Leaders from the Volunteer World.* Chicago: University of Chicago Press.

D'Augelli, Anthony R. 1989. "Lesbians' and gay men's experiences of discrimination and harassment in a university community." *American Journal of Community Psychology* 17(June):317–321.

Davies, James. 1962. "Toward a theory of revolution." *American Sociological Review* 27(1):5–19.

——. 1969. "The J-curve of rising and declining satisfactions as a cause of some great revolutions and a contained revolution." Pages 671–709 in H. D. Graham and T. R. Gurr (eds.), *Violence in America.* New York: Signet.

——. 1974. "The J-curve and power struggle theories of collective violence." *American Sociological Review* 39:607–610.

Davis, Angela Y. *Women, Race and Class.* 1983. New York: Vintage.

Davis, D. M. 1990. "Portrayals of women in prime-time network television: Some demographic characteristics." *Sex Roles* 23(5–6):325–332.

Davis, George, and Glegg Watson. 1982. *Black Life in Corporate America.* Garden City, NY: Doubleday/Anchor.

Davis, Kingsley. 1949. *Human Society.* New York: Macmillan.

—— and Wilbert Moore. 1945. "Some principles of stratification." *American Sociological Review* 10:242–249.

Davis, Nanette J., and Clarice Stasz. 1990. *Social Control of Deviance.* New York: McGraw-Hill.

Debt Crisis Network. 1985. *From Debt to Development: Alternatives to the International Debt Crisis.* Washington, DC: Institute for Policy Studies.

DeCecco, John P. (ed.). 1985. *Bashers, Baiters, and Bigots: Homophobia in American Society.* New York: Harrington Park Press.

Deere, C., and M. Leon deLeal. 1981. "Peasant production, proletarianization, and the sexual division of labor in the Andes." *Signs* 7(2):338–360.

——, J. Humphries, and M. Leon deLeal. 1982. "Class and historical analysis for the study of women and economic change." Pages 87–116 in R. Anker, M. Buvinic, and N. Youssef (eds.), *Women's Roles and Population Trends in the Third World.* London: ILO.

DeGrasse, R., Jr., et al. 1978. *Creating Solar Jobs: Options for Military Workers and Communities.* Mountain View, CA: Center for Economic Conversion.

Delacroix, Jacques, and Charles C. Ragin. 1981. "Structural blockage: A cross-national study of economic dependency, state efficacy, and underdevelopment." *American Journal of Sociology* 86:1311–1347.

De La Rosa, Mario. 1989. "Health care needs of Hispanic Americans and the responsiveness of the health care system." *Health and Social Work* (May):104–113.

deMause, Neil. 1990. "Cyanamid slips mercury to South Africa." *Guardian* (April 25):13.

Dennis, Rutledge M. 1981. "Socialization and racism: The white experience." Pages 71–85 in Benjamin P. Bowser and Raymond G. Hunt (eds.), *Impacts of Racism on White Americans.* Beverly Hills, CA: Sage.

DePalma, Anthony. 1990. "A house divided." *New York Times* (April 8):ED31.

DeParle, Jason. 1990. "War, class divisions, and burden of service." *New York Times* (November 13):A14.

——. 1993. "Big rise in births out of wedlock." *New York Times* (July 14):A1, A9.

——. 1994. "Report to Clinton sees vast extent of homelessness." *New York Times* (February 14):A1.

Deutsch, Martin. 1963. "The disadvantaged child and the learning process: Some social and developmental considerations." In A. H. Passow (ed.), *Education in Depressed Areas.* New York: Teachers Press.

De Witt, Karen. 1992a. "The nation's schools learn a

4th R: Resegregation." *New York Times* (January 19):E5.

———. 1992b. "Rising segregation is found for Hispanic students." *New York Times* (January 9):A15.

Diebel, Linda. 1993. "Unions not welcome: That's the message workers get as they try to organize to defend themselves in North Carolina." *Toronto Star* (June 6):F1.

Dill, Bonnie Thornton. 1983. "Race, class, and gender: Prospects for an all-inclusive sisterhood." *Feminist Studies* 9(1):131–150.

———. 1988. "'Making your job good itself': Domestic service and the construction of personal dignity." Pages 33–52 in Ann Bookman and Sandra Morgen (eds.), *Women and the Politics of Empowerment.* Philadelphia: Temple University Press.

Dines, Gail. 1992. "Pornography and the media: cultural representation of violence against women." *Family Violence and Sexual Assault Bulletin* 8(3):17–20.

Dobash, R. E., and R. Dobash. 1979. *Violence against Wives.* New York: Free Press.

——— and ———. 1991. *Women, Violence, and Social Change.* London: Routledge.

Dobson, Douglas. 1983. "The elderly as a political force." Pages 123–144 in William P. Brown and Laura Katz Olson (eds.), *Aging and Public Policy.* Westport, CT: Greenwood Press.

Dohrenwend, Bruce P., et al. 1980. *Mental Illness in the United States: Epidemiological Estimates.* New York: Praeger.

Dolbeare, Kenneth M. 1986. *Democracy at Risk: The Politics of Economic Renewal,* rev. ed. Chatham, NJ: Chatham House.

Domhoff, G. William. 1970. *The Higher Circles.* New York: Random House.

———. 1979. *The Powers That Be: Processes of Ruling Class Domination in America.* New York: Vintage Books.

———. 1983. *Who Rules America Now?* New York: Simon & Schuster.

———. 1990. *The Power Elite and the State: How Policy Is Made in America.* New York: Aldine de Gruyter.

Dougherty, Kevin. 1981. "After the fall: Research on school effects since the Coleman report." *Harvard Educational Review* 51(2):301–308.

Doyle, Bertram Wilbur. 1971. *The Etiquette of Race Relations in the South: A Study in Social Control.* New York: Schocken Books.

Doyle, Denis P. 1983. "Private interests and the public good." *College Board Review* 130(Winter):6–11.

Duberman, Martin. 1993. *Stonewall.* New York: Dutton.

Dudley, James R. 1991. "Fathers who have infrequent contact with their children." *Family Relations* 40:279–285.

Dumas, L. (ed.). 1982. *The Political Economy of Arms Reduction.* Boulder, CO: Westview Press.

Duncan, G. J., and S. D. Hoffman. 1985. "Economic consequences of marital instability." Pages 427–467 in M. David and T. Smeeding (eds.), *Horizontal Equity, Uncertainty, and Economic Well-Being.* Chicago: University of Chicago Press.

Duneier, Mitchell. 1992. *Slim's Table: Race, Respectability, and Masculinity.* Chicago: University of Chicago Press.

Dunning, Eric. 1993. "Sport in the civilising process: Aspects of the development of modern sport." Pages 39–70 in Eric G. Dunning, Joseph A. Maguire, and Robert E. Pearton (eds.), *The Sports Process: A Comparative and Developmental Approach.* Champaign, IL: Human Kinetics Press.

Durkheim, Émile. 1954. *The Elementary Forms of Religious Life.* Trans. Joseph W. Swain. Glencoe, IL: Free Press.

———. 1964. Trans. George Simpson. *The Division of Labor in Society.* New York: Free Press.

Durning, Alan Thein. 1994. "Redesigning the forest economy." Pages 22–40 in Lester R. Brown (ed.), *State of the World, 1994.* New York: Norton.

Dutton, Diane B. 1986. "Social class, health, and illness." Pages 31–62 in Linda H. Aiken and David Mechanic (eds.), *Applications of Social Science to Clinical Medicine and Health Policy.* New Brunswick, NJ: Rutgers University Press.

Dye, Thomas R. 1979. *Who's Running America?* Englewood Cliffs, NJ: Prentice-Hall.

———. 1983. *Who's Running America? The Reagan Years.* Englewood Cliffs, NJ: Prentice-Hall.

———. 1990. *Who's Running America? The Bush Era.* Englewood Cliffs, NJ: Prentice-Hall.

Eccles, Jacquelynne S., Janis E. Jacobs, and Rena D. Harold. 1990. "Gender role stereotypes, expectancy effects and parents' socialization of gender differences." *Journal of Social Issues* 46(2):183–201.

Eckholm, Erik. 1991. "Rescuing health care." *New York Times* (May 2):A1 ff.

Eckholm, Erik P. 1982. *Down to Earth: Environment and Human Needs.* New York: Norton.

Economist, The. 1990. "Doing what comes naturally." (November 17):29.

Economist Book of Vital World Statistics, The. 1990. New York: Times Books/Random House.

Edelman, Marion Wright. 1988. "Growing up black in America." Pages 143–162 in Jerome H. Skolnick and Elliott Currie (eds.), *Crisis in American Institutions,* 7th ed. Glenview, IL: Scott, Foresman.

Eder, Donna, and Stephen Parker. 1987. "The cultural production and reproduction of gender: The effect of extracurricular activities on peer-group culture." *Sociology of Education* 60(July):200–213.

Edgerton, Robert B. 1978. *Deviance: A Cross-Cultural Perspective.* Menlo Park, CA: Cummings.

Edsall, Thomas B., and Mary D. Edsall. 1992. *Chain Reaction: The Impact of Race, Rights, and Taxes on American Politics.* New York: Norton.

Edwards, Richard. 1979. *Contested Terrain: The Transformation of the Workplace in the Twentieth Century.* New York: Basic Books.

Ehrenreich, Barbara. 1986. "Is the middle class doomed?" *New York Times Magazine* (September 7):44 ff.

———. 1992. "Stamping out a dread scourge." *Time* (February 17):88.

Ehrlich, Isaac. 1975. "The deterrent effect of capital

punishment: A question of life and death." *American Economic Review* 48:397–417.

Eisenstein, Sarah. 1983. *Give Us Bread but Give Us Roses: Working Women's Consciousness in the United States, 1890 to the First World War.* London: Routledge & Kegan Paul.

Eitzen, D. Stanley, and Maxine Baca Zinn. 1989a. "The forces reshaping America." Pages 1–18 in D. Stanley Eitzen and Maxine Baca Zinn (eds.), *The Reshaping of America: Social Consequences of the Changing Economy.* Englewood Cliffs, NJ: Prentice Hall.

——— and ——— (eds.). 1989b. *The Reshaping of America: Social Consequences of the Changing Economy.* Englewood Cliffs, NJ: Prentice-Hall.

——— and ———. 1991. *In Conflict and Order,* 5th ed. Boston, MA: Allyn and Bacon.

Elias, Norbert, and Eric Dunning. 1986. *Quest for Excitement: Sport and Leisure in the Civilizing Process.* Oxford: Blackwell.

Elias, Robert. 1986. *The Politics of Victimization: Victims, Victimology, and Human Rights.* New York: Oxford University Press.

Elling, Ray H. 1986. *The Struggle for Workers' Health: A Study of Six Industrialized Countries.* Farmingdale, NY: Baywood.

Enloe, Cynthia. 1989. *Bananas, Beaches, and Bases: Making Feminist Sense of International Politics.* Berkeley: University of California Press.

Epstein, Cynthia Fuchs. 1993. *Women in Law,* 2nd ed. Urbana: University of Illinois Press.

Erikson, Erik. 1963. *Childhood and Society.* New York: Norton.

Erikson, Kai T. 1966. *Wayward Puritans.* New York: Macmillan.

Errington, Frederick Karl, and Deborah Gewertz. 1987. *Cultural Alternatives and a Feminist Anthropology: An Analysis of Culturally Structured Gender Interests in Papua, New Guinea.* New York: Cambridge University Press.

Evans, Dennis L. 1990. "The mythology of the marketplace in school choice." *Education Week* (October 17):32–34.

Evans, Peter, and Michael Timberlake. 1980. "Dependence, inequality, and the growth of the tertiary: A comparative analysis of less developed countries." *American Sociological Review* 45(4):531–552.

Ewen, Stuart. 1976. *Captains of Consciousness: Advertising and the Social Roots of the Consumer Culture.* New York: McGraw-Hill.

"Excerpts from school poll: What administrators think." 1988. *New York Times* (January 20):B9.

Farber, Susan L. 1981. *Identical Twins Reared Apart.* New York: Basic Books.

Farkas, George, and Paula England (eds.). 1988. *Industries, Firms, and Jobs.* New York: Plenum Press.

Farley, Reynolds, and Walter R. Allen. 1987. *The Color Line and the Quality of Life in America.* New York: Russell Sage Foundation.

Farrell, Christopher, and Michael J. Mandel. 1992. "The Cold War's grim aftermath." *Business Week* (February 24):78–80.

Feagin, Joe R. 1991a. "The continuing significance of race: Antiblack discrimination in public places." *American Sociological Review* 56(February):101–116.

———. 1991b. *The Continuing Significance of Race: The Black Middle-Class Experience.* Unpublished manuscript, Department of Sociology, University of Florida.

——— and Clairece B. Feagin. 1986. *Discrimination American Style,* 2nd ed. Malabar, FL: Krieger.

——— and Melvin P. Sikes. 1994. *Living with Racism: The Black Middle-Class Experience.* Boston: Beacon Press.

Federal News Service. 1993. White House press briefing: Secretary of the Treasury Lloyd Bentsen (March 10).

Feiner, Susan F., and Bruce B. Roberts. 1990. "Hidden by the invisible hand: Neoclassical economic theory and the textbook treatment of race and gender." *Gender & Society* 4(2):159–181.

Fennema, Elizabeth. 1987. "Sex-related differences in education: Myths, realities, and interventions." Pages 329–347 in Virginia Richardson-Koehler (ed.), *Educators' Handbook: A Research Perspective.* New York: Longman.

Ferber, Marianne A., Brigid O'Farrell, and La Rue Allen. 1991. *Work and Family: Policies for a Changing Work Force.* Washington, DC: National Academy Press.

Ferraro, Kathleen J. 1993. "Cops, courts, and woman battering." Pages 165–176 in Pauline B. Bart and Eileen Geil Moran (eds.), *Violence against Women: The Bloody Footprints.* Newbury Park: Sage.

Ferree, Myra Marx. 1990. "Beyond separate spheres: Feminism and family research." *Journal of Marriage and the Family* 52(November):866–884.

——— and Elaine J. Hall. 1990. "Visual images of American society: Gender and race in introductory sociology textbooks." *Gender & Society* 4(4)(December):500–533.

——— and Beth B. Hess. 1994. *Controversy, Coalition, and Consolidation: The New Feminist Movement across Three Decades of Change.* Boston: Twayne.

"Fewer Heart Bypasses for Blacks on Medicare." 1992. *New York Times* (March 18):B6.

Finch, Lew. 1985. "Voucher/choice battle heats up: Con: Public school vouchers jeopardize equal opportunity." *School Administrator* 42(8):10–12.

Fine, Gary Alan. 1986. "The dirty play of little boys." Pages 171–179 in Michael S. Kimmel and Michael A. Messner (eds.), *Men's Lives.* New York: Macmillan.

———. 1987. *With the Boys: Little League Baseball and Preadolescent Culture.* Chicago: University of Chicago Press.

Fine, Michelle. 1992. "Sexuality, schooling, and adolescent females: The missing discourse of desire." Pages 31–59 in Michelle Fine, *Disruptive Voices.* Ann Arbor: University of Michigan Press.

——— and Adrienne Asch. 1985. "Disabled women: Sexism without the pedestal." Pages 6–22 in Mary Jo Deegan and Nancy A. Brooks (eds.), *Women and Disability: The Double Handicap.* New Brunswick, NJ: Transaction Books.

Finke, Roger, and Rodney Stark. 1992. *The Churching*

of America, 1776–1990. New Brunswick, NJ: Rutgers University Press.

Fischer, David H. 1978. *Growing Old in America*. New York: Oxford University Press.

Fischer, Frank, and Carmen Sirianni (eds.). 1984. *Critical Studies in Organization and Bureaucracy*. Philadelphia: Temple University Press.

Fishbein, Diane H. 1990. "Biological perspectives in criminology." *Criminology* (28):27–72.

Fisher, William A., and Guy Grenier. 1994. "Violent pornography, antiwoman thoughts, and antiwoman acts: In search of reliable effects." *Journal of Sex Research* 31(1):23–38.

Fitzgerald, Joan, and Peter B. Meyer. 1986. "Recognizing constraints to local economic development." *Journal of the Community Development Society* 17(2):115–126.

Folbre, Nancy. 1985. "The pauperization of motherhood: Patriarchy and public policy in the U.S." *Review of Radical Political Economics* 16(4):72–88.

Foley, Donald L. 1973. "Institutional and contextual factors affecting the housing choices of minority residents." Pages 85–147 in Amos H. Hawley and Vincent P. Rock (eds.), *Segregation in Residential Areas*. Washington, DC: National Academy of Sciences.

Foner, Phillip S. 1965. *The Case of Joe Hill*. New York: International Publishers.

Forbes. 1986. "The 100 largest multinationals." (July 28):207.

Ford, Clellan S., and Frank A. Beach. 1951. *Patterns of Sexual Behavior*. New York: Harper & Row.

Ford, Ramona L. 1988. *Work, Organization and Power*. Boston: Allyn and Bacon.

Forrest, Jacqueline Darroch, and Susheela Singh. 1990. "The sexual and reproductive behavior of American women, 1982–1988." *Family Planning Perspectives* 22(5):206–214.

Frahm, Robert A., and Theresa Sullivan Barger. 1993. "Four of five teens sexually harassed in school, survey says." *Hartford Courant* (June 2):A1, A6.

Frank, Andre Gunder. 1967. *Capitalism and Underdevelopment in Latin America: Historical Studies of Chile and Brazil*. New York: Monthly Review Press.

Frank, Francine, and Frank Anshen. 1983. *Language and the Sexes*. Albany: State University of New York Press.

Frankl, Razelle. 1987. *Televangelism: The Marketing of Popular Religion*. Carbondale: Southern Illinois University Press.

Franklin, Barry M. 1986. *Building the American Community: The School Curriculum and the Search for Social Control*. Philadelphia: Falmer Press.

Franklin, Raymond S. 1991. *Shadows of Race and Class*. Minneapolis: University of Minnesota Press.

Frazier, Nancy, and Myra Sadker. 1973. *Sexism in School and Society*. New York: Harper & Row.

Freeman, A. Myrick. 1972. "The distribution of environmental quality." Pages 243–278 in Allen V. Kneese and Blair T. Bower (eds.), *Environmental Quality Analysis*. Baltimore: Johns Hopkins University Press for Resources for the Future.

Freiberg, P. 1991. "Separate classes for black males?" *APA Monitor* (May):1, 47.

Freidman, Dana E. 1991. *Linking Work-Family Issues to the Bottom Line*. New York: Conference Board.

Freudenberg, Nicholas. 1984. "Citizen action for environmental health: Report on a survey of community organizations." *American Journal of Public Health* 74(5):444–448.

Friedman, Thomas L. 1993. "Cold War without end." *New York Times Magazine* (August 22):28–30, 45.

Frodi, A., et al. 1977. "Are women always less agressive than men?" *Psychological Bulletin* 84:634–660.

Furstenberg, Frank F., Jr., Christine Winquist Nord, James L. Peterson, and Nicholas Zill. 1983. "The life course of children of divorce: Marital disruption and parental contact." *American Sociological Review* 48(10):656–668.

Gallup, George, Jr., and Jim Castelli. 1989. *The People's Religion: American Faith in the 90's*. New York: Macmillan.

Gallup Organization. 1985. "Gallup/Newsweek Poll" (August).

———. 1988. "Gallup Poll" (July).

———. 1989. "Gallup/Newsweek Poll" (October).

———. 1993. "Gallup/CNN/USA Today Poll" (July).

Gamoran, Adam, and M. Berends. 1987. "The effects of stratification in secondary schools: Synthesis of survey and ethnographic research." *Review of Educational Research* 57:415–435.

——— and Robert D. Mare. 1989. "Secondary school tracking and educational inequality." *American Journal of Sociology* (March):1146–1183.

Gans, Herbert. 1982. *The Urban Villagers*, rev. ed. New York: Free Press.

Garfinkel, Harold. 1956. "Conditions of successful degradation ceremonies." *American Sociological Review* 61:420–424.

Garson, Barbara. 1980. *All the Livelong Day*. New York: Penguin.

Gaskell, Jane. 1984. "Gender and course choice: The orientation of male and female students." *Journal of Education* 166(1)(March):89–102.

Gelles, Richard J., and Murray A. Straus. 1988. *Intimate Violence*. New York: Simon & Schuster.

Gelobter, Michel. 1992. "Toward a model of environmental discrimination." Pages 64–81 in B. Bryant and P. Mohai (eds.), *Race and the Incidence of Environmental Hazards: A Time for Discourse*. Boulder, CO: Westview Press.

Gerbner, George, Larry Gross, Michael Morgan, and Nancy Signorielli. 1982. "Charting the mainstream: Television's contributions to political orientation." *Journal of Communication* 32(2):100–127.

Gerson, Kathleen. 1993. *No Man's Land: Men's Changing Commitments to Family and Work*. New York: Basic Books.

Gerstel, Naomi, and Harriet Engel Gross. 1987. "Introduction and overview." Pages 1–12 in Naomi Gerstel and Harriet Engel Gross (eds.), *Families and Work*. Philadelphia: Temple University Press.

Gerth, Hans, and C. Wright Mills (eds.). 1968. *From Max Weber: Essays in Sociology*. New York: Oxford University Press.

Gerth, J. 1985. "U.S. weapons makers ring up health profits." *New York Times* (April 9).

Gianessi, Leonard, Henry M. Peskin, and Edward Wolff. 1979. "The distributional effects of uniform air pollution policy in the US." *Quarterly Journal of Economics* (May):281–301.

Gibbs, Jewel Taylor (ed.). 1988. *Young, Black and Male in America: An Endangered Species.* Dover, MA: Auburn.

Gibson, Paul. 1989. *Gay Male and Lesbian Youth Suicide.* Report of the Secretary's Task Force on Youth Suicide, vol. 3. Washington, DC: U.S. Department of Health and Human Services.

Gilbert, Dennis, and Joseph A. Kahl. 1993. *The American Class Structure,* 4th ed. Belmont, CA: Wadsworth.

Gilligan, Carol, Nona P. Lyons, and Trudy J. Hanmer (eds.). 1990. *Making Connection: The Relational Worlds of Adolescent Girls at Emma Willard School.* Cambridge, MA: Harvard University Press.

Giloth, Robert, and Susan Rosenblum. 1987. "How to fight plant closings." *Social Policy* 17(3)(Winter):20–26.

Girvan, Norman. 1984. "Swallowing the IMF medicine in the seventies." Pages 169–181 in Charles K. Wilber (ed.), *The Political Economy of Development and Underdevelopment,* 3rd ed. New York: Random House.

Gismondi, Michael. 1988. "Conceptualizing religion from below: The Central American experience." *Social Compass* 35(2–3):343–370.

Glaberson, William. 1990. "One of four in New York custody are young blacks, study says." *New York Times* (October 4):B6.

Gladwell, Malcolm. 1990. "Women's health research to be new priority at NIH." *Washington Post* (September 11):A17.

Glasberg, Davita Silfen. 1987. "International finance capital and the relative autonomy of the state: Mexico's foreign debt crisis." *Research in Political Economy* 10:83–108.

———. 1989. *The Power of Collective Purse Strings: The Effect of Bank Hegemony on Corporations and the State.* Berkeley: University of California Press.

——— and Michael Schwartz. 1983. "Ownership and control of corporations." *Annual Review of Sociology* 9:311–332.

——— and Daniel Skidmore. 1992. *State Policy Formation and Unintended Consequences: Bank Deregulation and the Savings and Loan Crisis.* Paper presented at the annual meeting of the American Sociological Association, Pittsburgh.

——— and Kathryn B. Ward. 1993. "Foreign debt and economic growth in the world system." *Social Science Quarterly* 74(4):703–720.

Glassner, Barry. 1988. *Bodies.* New York: Putnam.

Glazer, Nona Y. 1987. "Servants to capital: Unpaid domestic labor and paid work." Pages 236–255 in Naomi Gerstel and Harriet Engel Gross (eds.), *Families and Work.* Philadelphia: Temple University Press.

Glazer, Sarah. 1990. "Why schools still have tracking." *Editorial Research Reports* (December 28):746–759.

Glenn, Alcalay. 1990. "U.S. toxic arms dumping angers South Pacific." *Guardian* (September 26):15.

Glenn, Evelyn Nakano. 1985. "Racial ethnic women's labor: The intersection of race, gender, and class oppression." *Review of Radical Political Economics* 17(3):86–108.

———. 1988. "A belated industry revisited: Domestic service among Japanese-American women." Pages 57–75 in Anne Statham, Eleanor M. Miller, and Hans O. Mauksch (eds.), *The Worth of Women's Work.* Albany: State University of New York Press.

Gliedman, John, and William Roth. 1980. *The Unexpected Minority.* New York: Harcourt Brace Jovanovich.

Global AIDS Policy Coalition. 1992. *AIDS in the World.* Cambridge, MA: Harvard University Press.

Goffman, Erving. 1961. *Asylums: Essays on the Social Situation of Mental Patients and Other Inmates.* Chicago: Aldine.

———. 1963. *Stigma: Notes on the Management of Spoiled Identity.* Englewood Cliffs, NJ: Prentice-Hall.

Goldberg, Alan D., and Timothy J. L. Chandler. 1989. "The role of athletics: The social world of high school adolescents." *Youth and Society* 21(2)(December):238–250.

Goode, Erich. 1984. *Deviant Behavior,* 2nd ed. Englewood Cliffs, NJ: Prentice-Hall.

Goodlad, John I. 1984. *A Place Called School.* New York: McGraw-Hill.

Goodwin, Donald W. 1988. *Is Alcoholism Hereditary?* New York: Ballantine.

Goodwin, M. H. 1980. "Directive-response sequences in girls' and boys' task activities." Pages 157–173 in S. McConnell-Ginet, R. Borker, and N. Furman (eds.), *Women and Language in Literature and Society.* New York: Praeger.

Gopaul-McNicol, Sharon-Ann. 1988. "Racial identification and racial preference of black preschool children in New York and Trinidad." *Journal of Black Psychology* 14(February):65–68.

Gordon, Linda. 1988. *Heroes of Their Own Lives.* New York: Viking Penguin.

Gordon, Richard A. 1990. *Anorexia and Bulimia: Anatomy of a Social Epidemic.* Cambridge, MA: Basil Blackwell.

Gordon, Robert A. 1945. *Business Leadership in the Large Corporation.* Washington, DC: Brookings Institution.

Gordon, S., and D. McFadden. 1984. *Economic Conversion: Revitalizing America's Economy.* Cambridge, MA: Ballinger.

Gordon S. Black Corporation. 1989. "Gordon S. Black/U.S.A. Today Poll" (September).

———. 1990. "National Adult Voter Attitudes." Telephone survey. (August 26).

Gossett, Thomas F. 1965. *Race: The History of an Idea in America.* New York: Schocken Books.

Gould, Kenneth A. 1993. "Pollution and perception: Social visibility and local environmental mobilization." *Qualitative Sociology* 16(2):157–178.

Gould, Stephen J. 1981. *The Mismeasure of Man.* New York: Norton.

Gouldner, Alvin W. 1954. *Patterns of Industrial Bureaucracy.* Glencoe, IL: Free Press.
———. 1970. *The Coming Crisis of Western Sociology.* New York: Avon.

Grammick, Jeannine (ed.). 1989. *Homosexuality in the Priesthood and Religious Life.* New York: Crossroad.

Gramsci, Antonio. 1971. *Selections from the Prison Notebooks.* New York: International Publishers.

Grant, Carl A., and Christine F. Sleeter. 1988. "Race, class and gender and abandoned dreams." *Teachers College Record* 90(1)(Fall):19–40.

Gray, Susan. 1982. "Exposure to pornography and aggression toward women: The case of the angry male." *Social Problems* 29(4)(April):387–398.

Greeley, Andrew. 1972. *The Denominational Society.* Glenview, IL: Scott, Foresman.

Green, Gary. 1987. *Finance Capital and Uneven Development.* Boulder, CO: Westview Press.

Green, Philip. 1985. *Retrieving Democracy: In Search of Civic Equality.* Totowa, NJ: Rowman & Allenheld.

Greenberg, David F. 1988. *The Construction of Homosexuality.* Chicago: University of Chicago Press.

Greenwald, John. 1992. "Why we're so gloomy." *Time* (January 13):34–38.

Griffin, Keith. 1979. "Underdevelopment in history." Pages 77–90 in Charles K. Wilber (ed.), *The Political Economy of Development and Underdevelopment,* 2nd ed. New York: Random House.

Gutiérrez, Gustavo. 1973. *A Theology of Liberation.* Maryknoll, NY: Orbis Books.
———. 1983. *The Power of the Poor in History.* Maryknoll, NY: Orbis Books.

Gutman, Herbert G. 1977. *Work, Culture, and Society in Industrializing America.* New York: Vintage.

Hacker, Andrew. 1992. *Two Nations: Black and White, Separate, Hostile, and Unequal.* New York: Scribner.

Hacker, Sally. 1989. *Pleasure, Power, and Technology: Some Tales of Gender, Engineering, and the Cooperative Workplace.* Boston: Unwin Hyman.

Hadaway, C. Kirk, Penny Long Marler, and Mark Chaves. 1993. "What the polls don't show: A closer look at U.S. church attendance." *American Sociological Review* 58(December):741–752.

Hagan, John. 1994. *Crime and Disrepute.* Thousand Oaks, CA: Pine Forge Press.

Hagedorn, John M. 1988. *People and Folks: Gangs, Crime, and the Underclass in a Rustbelt City.* Chicago: Lake View Press.
———. 1991. "Gangs, neighborhoods, and public policy." *Social Problems* 38(4):529–542.

Hall, Elaine J. 1988. "One week for women: The structure of inclusion of gender issues in introductory textbooks." *Teaching Sociology* 16(October):431–442.

Hamilton, Richard. 1972. *Class and Politics in the United States.* New York: Wiley.

Hamper, Ben. 1991. *Rivethead: Tales from the Assembly Line.* New York: Warner Books.

Handleman, David. 1990. "ACT UP in Anger." *Rolling Stone* (March 8):80 ff.

Harris, Adella J., and Jonathan Feinberg. 1978. "Television and aging: Is what you see what you get?" *Gerontologist* 18(5).

Harris, Louis, and Associates. 1986. "The ICD Survey of Disabled Americans: Bringing Disabled Americans into the Mainstream." (March).
———. 1989. "Family Survey II: Child Care." Telephone survey (December–February).
———. 1991. "Harris Poll" (April 21).
———. 1992. "Kaiser/Commonwealth Health Insurance Survey." Telephone survey (January–February).

Hart, Peter D., Research Associates. 1972. *World Poverty and Development.* Overseas Development Council.

Harty, Sheila. 1979. *Hucksters in the Classroom: A Review of Industry Propaganda in Schools.* Washington, DC: Center for the Study of Responsive Law.

Harvard Law Review. 1988. "Developments in the law: Race and the criminal process." 101:1472.

Harvey, D. G., and G. T. Slatin. 1975. "The relationship as hypothesis." *Social Forces* 54:140–159.

Hauser, Robert M., William H. Sewell, and Duane F. Alwin. 1976. "High school effects on achievement." Pages 309–341 in William H. Sewell, Robert M. Hauser, and David L. Featherman (eds.), *Schooling and Achievement in American Society.* New York: Academic Press.

Hayes, Thomas C. 1991. "Earnings soar 75% at Exxon." *New York Times* (April 25):D1, D10.

Hearn, Frank (ed.). 1988. *The Transformation of Industrial Organization.* Belmont, CA: Wadsworth.

Henry, Jules. 1963. *Culture against Man.* New York: Vintage Books.

Henry, William A. 1990. "Beyond the melting pot." *Time* (April 9):28–31.

Herman, Edward S. 1981. *Corporate Control, Corporate Power.* Cambridge, England: Cambridge University Press.
——— and Noam Chomsky. 1988. *Manufacturing Consent: The Political Economy of the Mass Media.* New York: Pantheon.

Hesse-Biber, Sharlene. 1985. "Male and female students' perceptions of their academic environment and future career plans: Implications for higher education." *Human Relations* 38(February):91–105.

Hill, Catherine, Sabina Deitrick, and Ann Markusen. 1991. "Converting the military industrial economy: The experience at six facilities." *Journal of Planning Education and Research* 11:19–36.

Hillman, E., M. F. Hovel, L. Williams, et al. 1991. "Pregnancy, STDs, and AIDS prevention: Evaluation of new image teen theatre." *AIDS Education and Prevention* 3(4):328–340.

Hilts, Philip J. 1992. "FDA restricts use of implants pending studies." *New York Times* (April 17):A1.
———. 1993. "Why whistle-blowers can seem a little crazy." *New York Times* (June 13):E6.

Hirschi, Travis. 1969. *Causes of Delinquency.* Berkeley: University of California Press.

Hochschild, Arlie, and Anne Machung. 1989. *The Second Shift: Working Parents and the Revolution at Home.* New York: Viking Penguin.

Hodson, Randy. 1978. "Labor in the monopoly, competitive, and state sectors of production." *Politics and Society* 8:429–480.

———— and Teresa A. Sullivan. 1990. *The Social Organization of Work.* Belmont, CA: Wadsworth.

Hofferth, Sandra. 1988. *The Current Child Care Debate in Context.* Paper presented at the annual meeting of the American Sociological Association, Atlanta.

Holden, Constance. 1980. "Twins reunited." *Science* 80(1):55–59.

————. 1986. "Homelessness: Experts differ on root causes." *Science* 232(May 2):569.

Holden, Karen C. 1990. *Social Security Policy and the Income Shock of Widowhood.* Working Paper No. 3, Madison, WI: University of Wisconsin, Institute of Public Affairs.

————, R. V. Burkhauser, and D. J. Feaster. 1988. "The timing of falls into poverty after retirement and widowhood." *Demography* 25:405–414.

———— and Pamela J. Smock. 1991. "The economic costs of marital dissolution: Why do women bear a disproportionate cost?" *Annual Review of Sociology* 17:51–78.

Hollinger, Richard C., and John P. Clark. 1982. "Formal and informal controls of employee deviance." *Sociological Quarterly* 23:333–343.

"Home Cures." 1993. *The Nation* (April 12):29–30.

hooks, bell. 1981. *Ain't I a Woman: Black Women and Feminism.* Boston: South End Press.

Horowitz, Irving Louis (ed.). 1967. *The Rise and Fall of Project Camelot.* Cambridge, MA: M.I.T. Press.

Hoselitz, Berthold Frank. 1960. *Sociological Aspects of Economic Growth.* Glencoe, IL: Free Press.

Hossfeld, Karen. 1988. *Divisions of Labor, Divisions of Lives: Immigrant Women Workers in Silicon Valley.* Unpublished doctoral dissertation, University of California at Santa Cruz.

————. 1989. "The triple shift: Immigrant women workers and the household division of labor in Silicon Valley." Paper presented at the annual meeting of the American Sociological Association, Atlanta.

Houston, Brant, and Jack Ewing. 1991. "Justice jailed." *Hartford Courant* (June 16):A1, A10–A11.

———— and ————. 1992. "Racial inequity still evident in setting of bail." *Hartford Courant* (May 17):A1, A6.

Howland, M. 1988. *Plant Closings and Worker Displacement: The Regional Issues.* Kalamazoo, MI: Upjohn Institute for Employment Research.

Huber, Joan, and Glenna Spitze. 1981. "Wives' employment, household behaviors, and sex-role attitudes." *Social Forces* 60:150–169.

Hughes, David. 1991. "Survey on defense firm commercial efforts shows surprising success rate, activity." *Aviation Week and Space Technology* (December 9):21–22.

Humphreys, Laud. 1970. *Tearoom Trade.* Chicago: Aldine.

Hurd, M., and D. A. Wise. 1989. "The wealth and poverty of widows: Assets before and after the husband's death." Pages 177–260 in D. Wise (ed.), *The Economics of Aging.* Chicago: University of Chicago Press.

In These Times. 1986. "Cost of jobs rising for Illinois taxpayers." (February 26–March 11):4.

Inkeles, A., and D. Smith. 1975. *Becoming Modern.* Cambridge, MA: Harvard University Press.

"Insanity defense, the." 1985. Special issue of *Annals of the American Academy of Political and Social Science* (January).

Irvine, Jacqueline Jordan. 1990. *Black Students and School Failure.* New York: Greenwood Press.

Isaac, Katherine. 1990. "Stopping poison exports." *Multinational Monitor* (June):7–8.

Iyengar, Shanto. 1990. "The accessibility bias in politics: Television news and public opinion." *International Journal of Public Opinion Research* 2(1):1–15.

Jackall, Robert. 1988. *Moral Mazes: The World of Corporate Managers.* New York: Oxford University Press.

———— and Henry M. Levin (eds.). 1984. *Worker Cooperatives in America.* Berkeley: University of California Press.

Jackman, Robert. 1987. "Political institutions and voter turnout in the industrial democracies." *American Political Science Review* 81(2)(June):405–425.

Jackson, James, Wayne McCullough, and Gerald Gurin. 1988. "Family, socialization environment, and identity development in black Americans." Pages 242–256 in Harriette McAdoo (ed.), *Black Families,* 2nd ed. Beverly Hills, CA: Sage.

Jaynes, Gerald David, and Robin M. Williams, Jr. (eds.). 1989. *A Common Destiny: Blacks and American Society.* Washington, DC: National Academy Press.

Jenkins, J. Craig. 1983. "Resource mobilization theory and the study of social movements." *Annual Review of Sociology* 9:527–553.

———— and Charles Perrow. 1977. "Insurgency of the powerless: Farm workers movements, 1946–72." *American Sociological Review* 42(2):249–268.

Jessop, Bob. 1990. *State Theory: Putting the Capitalist State in Its Place.* University Park: Pennsylvania State University Press.

Jewell, K. Sue. 1993. *From Mammy to Miss America and Beyond.* New York: Routledge.

Johnson, Allan G. 1991. *The Forest for the Trees.* San Diego, CA: Harcourt Brace Jovanovich.

Johnson, Bradley. 1989. "California moves to ban Whittle's 'Channel One.'" *Advertising Age* 60(May 29):1, 48.

Johnson, Dirk. 1990. "More prisons using iron hand to control inmates." *New York Times* (November 1).

Johnstone, Ronald L. 1992. *Religion in Society,* 4th ed. Englewood Cliffs, NJ: Prentice-Hall.

Jones, E. F., et al. 1985. "Teenaged pregnancy in developed countries: Determinants and policy implications." *Family Planning Perspectives* 17:53–62.

Jones, Edward W. 1986. "Black managers: The dream deferred." *Harvard Business Review* (May–June):84–93.

Jones, Jacqueline. 1987. "Black women, work, and the family under slavery." Pages 84–110 in Naomi Gerstel and Harriet Engel Gross (eds.), *Families and Work.* Philadelphia: Temple University Press.

Jones, M. Gail. 1989. "Gender bias in classroom interactions." *Contemporary Education* 60(Summer): 216–222.

———— and Jack Wheatley. 1989. "Gender influences in classroom displays and student-teacher behaviors." *Science Education* 73(5):535–545.

Jones, Woodrow, Jr., and Mitchell F. Rice (eds.). 1987. *Health Care Issues in Black America.* Westport, CT: Greenwood Press.

Joppke, Christian. 1993. *Mobilizing against Nuclear Energy: A Comparison of Germany and the United States.* Berkeley: University of California Press.

Jordan, Mary. 1992. "Big-city schools become more segregated during 1980s, study says." *New York Times* (January 9):A3.

Judson, George. 1993. "In Hartford, data portray schools in crisis of poverty." *New York Times* (January 2):26.

Kagan, Jerome, J. Steven Resnick, and Nancy Snidman. 1988. "Biological bases of childhood shyness." *Science* 240(April 1):167–171.

Kane, Michael B. 1970. *Minorities in Textbooks: A Study of Their Treatment in Social Science Texts.* Chicago: Quadrangle.

Kane, Parsons and Associates. 1989. "*Parents* Magazine Poll, Wave 10" (October).

Kanfer, Stefan. 1993. *The Last Empire: De Beers, Diamonds, and the World.* New York: Farrar Straus Giroux.

Kanter, Rosabeth Moss, and Barry Stein (eds.). 1979. *Life in Organizations: Workplaces as People Experience Them.* New York: Basic Books.

Kaplan, Howard B., Robert J. Johnson, and Carol A. Bailey. 1987. "Deviant peers and deviant behavior: Further elaborations of a model." *Social Psychology Quarterly* 50(4):227–252.

Kaufman, Robert L. 1986. "The impact of industrial and occupational structure on black-white employment allocations." *American Sociological Review* 51:310–322.

Kelly, Delos H., and William T. Pink. 1982. "Crime and individual responsibility: The perpetuation of a myth?" *Urban Review* 14(1):47–63.

Kelly, Ed, and Lee Webb (eds.). 1979. *Plant Closings: Resources for Public Officials, Trade Unionists and Community Leaders.* Washington, DC: Conference on Alternative State and Local Policies.

Kennedy, Paul. 1987. *The Rise and Fall of the Great Powers.* New York: Random House.

Kerbo, Harold R. 1991. *Social Stratification and Inequality,* 2nd ed. New York: McGraw-Hill.

Kilbride, Howard W., David L. Johnson, and Ann Pytkowicz Streissguth. 1977. "Social class, birth order, and newborn experience." *Child Development* 48(4)(December):1686–1688.

Kimball, Meredith M. 1986. "Television and sex-role attitudes." In Tannis M. Williams (ed.), *The Impact of Television: A Natural Experiment in Three Communities.* Orlando, FL: Academic Press.

King, David R. 1978. "The brutalization effect: Execution publicity and the incidence of homicide in South Carolina." *Social Forces* 57:683–687.

King, Deborah. 1988. "Multiple jeopardy, multiple consciousness: The context of a black feminist ideology." *Signs* 14(1):42–72.

King, Wesley C., Jr., Edward W. Miles, and Jane Kniska. 1991. "Boys will be boys (and girls will be girls): The attribution of gender role stereotypes in a gaming situation." *Sex Roles* 25(11–12):607–623.

Kinsey, Alfred, Wardell Pomeroy, and Clyde Martin. 1948. *Sexual Behavior in the Human Male.* Philadelphia: Saunders.

————, ————, ————, and Paul Gebhard. 1953. *Sexual Behavior in the Human Female.* Philadelphia: Saunders.

Kirk, Marshall, and Hunter Madsen. 1989. *After the Ball: How America Will Conquer Its Fear & Hatred of Gays in the 90's.* New York: Penguin.

Kirkpatrick, David W. 1990. *Choice in Schooling: A Case for Tuition Vouchers.* Chicago: Loyola University Press.

Kirschenman, Joleen, and Kathryn M. Neckerman. 1991. "'We'd love to hire them, but': The meaning of race for employers." Pages 203–232 in Christopher Jencks and Paul E. Peterson (eds.), *The Urban Underclass.* Washington, DC: Brookings Institution.

Kisker, E. E. 1985. "Teenagers talk about sex, pregnancy, and contraception." *Family Planning Perspectives* 17(2):83–90.

Kluegel, James R., and Eliot R. Smith. 1986. *Beliefs about Inequality: Americans' Views of What Is and What Ought to Be.* Hawthorne, NY: Aldine.

Knowles, Louis L., and Kenneth Prewitt (eds.). 1969. *Institutional Racism in America.* Englewood Cliffs, NJ: Prentice-Hall.

Kochman, Thomas. 1981. *Black and White Styles in Conflict.* Chicago: University of Chicago Press.

Kohn, Melvin. 1977. *Social Competence, Symptoms and Underachievement in Childhood: A Longitudinal Perspective.* Washington, DC: Winston.

Kolata, Gina. 1992. "New views on life spans alter forecasts on elderly." *New York Times* (November 16):A1, A15.

Konner, Melvin. 1982. *The Tangled Wing: Biological Constraints on the Human Spirit.* New York: Holt, Rinehart and Winston.

Kowalewski, David. 1990. "The historical structuring of a dissident movement: The sanctuary case." *Research in Social Movements, Conflict and Change* 12:89–110.

Kozol, Jonathan. 1991. *Savage Inequalities.* New York: Crown.

Krecker, Margaret L., and Angela M. O'Rand. 1991. "Contested milieux: Small firms, unionization and the provision of protective structures." *Sociological Forum* 6(1):93–117.

Kulik, J., and C. Fairchild. 1987. "Worker assistance and placement experience." In J. Lynch (ed.), *Economic Adjustment and Conversion of Defense Industries.* Boulder, CO: Westview Press.

Kusterer, Ken C. 1978. *Know-How on the Job: The Important Working Knowledge, of "Unskilled" Workers.* Boulder, CO: Westview Press.

Lacayo, Richard. 1989. "Between two worlds." *Time* (March 13):58–68.

R-12

————. 1990. "Why no blue blood will flow: On the front lines, a disproportionate number of troops hail from minorities and the working class." *Time* (November 26):34.

Lacey, Marc. 1992. "Death toll from L.A. riots is lowered to 51." *Los Angeles Times* (August 12):A1.

Lamb, Michael E. (ed.). 1981. *The Role of the Father in Child Development*, rev. ed. New York: Wiley.

————, Joseph H. Pleck, and James A. Levine. 1986. "Effects of increased paternal involvement on children in two-parent families." Pages 141–158 in Robert A. Lewis and Robert E. Salt (eds.), *Men in Families*. Beverly Hills, CA: Sage.

Landry, Bart. 1987. *The New Black Middle Class*. Berkeley: University of California Press.

Lareau, Annette. 1989. *Home Advantage: Social Class and Parental Intervention in Elementary Education*. Philadelphia: Falmer Press.

Lasch, Christopher. 1977. *Haven in a Heartless World: The Family Besieged*. New York: Basic Books.

Laurence, Leslie. 1993. "Issues of lesbians are mostly ignored." *Orlando Sentinel Tribune* (December 7):E3.

Lawson, Steven F. 1990. *Running for Freedom: Civil Rights and Black Politics in America since 1941*. Philadelphia: Temple University Press.

Leahy, Peter J. 1985. "Are racial factors important for the allocation of mortgage money?" *American Journal of Economics and Sociology* July:185–196.

Lederman, Douglas. 1992. "Men get 70% of money available for athletic scholarships at colleges that play big-time sports, new study finds." *Chronicle of Higher Education* 38(March 18):A1, A45–46.

Lee, Charles. 1992. "Toxic waste and race in the United States." Pages 10–27 in B. Bryant and P. Mohai (eds.), *Race and the Incidence of Environmental Hazards: A Time for Discourse*. Boulder, CO: Westview Press.

Lee, Felicia R. 1994. "Grappling with how to teach young speakers of black dialect." *New York Times* (January 5):A1.

Lee, Jim, and Eric Bates. 1992. "Who owns the media?" *Southern Exposure* 20(4):11–17.

Lenart, Silvo, and Kathleen M. McGraw. 1989. "America watches 'Amerika': Television docudrama and political attitudes." *Journal of Politics* 51(3):697–712.

Lens, Sidney. 1970. *The Military-Industrial Complex*. Philadelphia: Pilgrim Press.

Lenski, Gerhard. 1966. *Power and Privilege*. New York: McGraw-Hill.

————, Jean Lenski, and Patrick Nolan. 1991. *Human Societies: An Introduction to Macrosociology*. New York: McGraw-Hill.

Lever, J. 1976. "Sex differences in the games children play." *Social Problems* 23:478–487.

Levin, Jack, and William C. Levin. 1980. *Ageism: Prejudice and Discrimination against the Elderly*. Belmont, CA: Wadsworth.

Levin, Murray B. 1960. *The Alienated Voter*. New York: Holt, Rinehart and Winston.

Levine, Rhonda. 1988. *Class Struggle and the New Deal: Industrial Labor, Industrial Capital and the State*. Lawrence: University Press of Kansas.

Levy, Emanuel. 1989. "The democratic elite: America's movie stars." *Qualitative Sociology* 12(1):29–54.

Lewis, Neil A. 1994. "Prize in an unusual lottery: A scarce experimental drug." *New York Times* (January 7):A1.

Lewis, Oscar. 1959. *Five Families: Mexican Case Studies in the Culture of Poverty*. New York: Basic Books.

————. 1961. *The Children of Sanchez*. New York: Random House.

————. 1966. *La Vida: A Puerto Rican Family in the Culture of Poverty: San Juan and New York*. New York: Random House.

Lichtensztejn, Samuel, and Jose Manuel Quijano. 1982. "The external indebtedness of the developing countries to international private banks." Pages 185–265 in J. C. Sanchez Arnau (ed.), *Debt and Development*. New York: Praeger.

Liddle, Joanna, and Rama Joshi. 1986. *Daughters of Independence: Gender, Caste and Class in India*. London: Zed Books.

Liebert, Robert M., and Joyce Sprafkin. 1988. *The Early Window: Effects of Television on Children and Youth*, 3rd ed. New York: Pergamon Press.

Liebow, Elliot. 1967. *Tally's Corner: A Study of Negro Streetcorner Men*. Boston: Little, Brown.

Liem, Ramsey, and Paula Rayman. 1982. "Health and social costs of unemployment." *American Psychologist* 37(October):1116–1123.

Light, Donald W. 1989. "Corporate medicine for profit." Pages 294–308 in Phil Brown (ed.), *Perspectives in Medical Sociology*. Belmont, CA: Wadsworth.

Lincoln, C. Eric, and Lawrence H. Mamiya. 1990. *The Black Church in the African American Experience*. Durham, NC: Duke University Press.

Lindsey, Linda L. 1994. *Gender Roles: A Sociological Perspective*, 2nd ed. Englewood Cliffs, NJ: Prentice-Hall.

Link, Bruce G., et al. 1987. "The social rejection of former mental patients: Understanding why labels matter." *American Journal of Sociology* 92(May):1461–1500.

Linton, Ralph. 1936. *The Study of Man*. New York: Appleton-Century-Crofts.

Lipset, Seymour Martin. 1960. *Political Man: The Social Bases of Politics*. Garden City, NY: Doubleday.

Liska, Allen E. 1987. *Perspectives on Deviance*, 2nd ed. Englewood Cliffs, NJ: Prentice-Hall.

Litwak, Eugene. 1965. "Extended kin relations in an industrial democratic society." Pages 290–323 in Ethel Shanas and Gordon T. Strieb (eds.), *Social Structure and the Family: Generational Relations*. Englewood Cliffs, NJ: Prentice-Hall.

Liu, Korbin, Kenneth Manton, and B. M. Liu. 1986. "Home care expenses for the disabled." *Health Care Financing Review* 7(2):51–58.

Logan, John R. 1988. "Fiscal and developmental crises in black suburbs." Pages 333–356 in Scott Cummings (ed.), *Business Elites and Urban Development: Case Studies and Critical Perspectives*. Albany: State University of New York Press.

Long, Robert Emmet (ed.). 1991. *The State of U.S. Education*. New York: Wilson.

Lonsdale, Susan. 1990. *Women and Disability*. New York: St. Martin's Press.

Love, Harold. 1970. "The reasons participants drop out of the food stamp program: A case study of its implications." *American Journal of Agricultural Economics* 52(3):387–394.

Lowe, Marcia D. 1994. "Reinventing transport." Pages 81–98 in Lester R. Brown (ed.), *State of the World, 1994*. New York: Norton.

Luker, Kristin. 1984. *Abortion and the Politics of Motherhood*. Berkeley: University of California Press.

Luria, Dan, and Jack Russell. 1981. *Rational Reindustrialization: An Economic Development Agenda for Detroit*. Detroit: Widgetripper Press.

Lynch, Brian. 1992. *No Swords into Plowshare, No Tridents into Breadboxes: The Local Meaning of U.S. Military Budget Cuts in Southern New England*. Unpublished doctoral dissertation, University of Connecticut.

Mabry, Marcus. 1992. "New hope for old unions?" *Newsweek* (February 24):39.

MacArthur, John R. 1992. *Second Front: Censorship and Propaganda in the Gulf War*. Berkeley: University of California Press.

Macken, Candace L. 1986. "A profile of functionally impaired elderly persons living in the community." *Health Care Financing Review* 7(4):33–49.

MacNichol, Sally Noland, and Mary Elizabeth Walsh. 1993. "Feminist theology and spirituality: An annotated bibliography." *Women's Studies Quarterly* 21(Spring–Summer):177–196.

Madrid, Arturo. 1992. "Missing people and others." Pages 6–11 in Margaret L. Andersen and Patricia Hill Collins (eds.), *Race, Class, and Gender*. Belmont, CA: Wadsworth.

Maio, Kathi. 1990. "Hooked on hate? Unfunny comedians, MTV, tabloid television, fright films, and other media invasions." *Ms.* 1(2):42–44.

Majoribanks, Kevin. 1987. "Gender/social class, family environments and adolescents' aspirations." *Australian Journal of Education* 31(1)(April):43–54.

Maltz, D. N., and R. A. Borker. 1983. "A cultural approach to male-female miscommunication." Pages 195–216 in J. J. Gumperz (ed.), *Language and Social Identity*. New York: Cambridge University Press.

Malveaux, Julianne. 1985. "The economic interests of black and white women: Are they similar?" *Review of Black Political Economy* 14(Summer):5–27.

———. 1990. "Gender difference and beyond: An economic perspective on diversity and commonality among women." Pages 226–238 in Deborah L. Rhode (ed.), *Theoretical Perspectives on Sexual Difference*. New Haven and London: Yale University Press.

Marable, Manning. 1983. *How Capitalism Underdeveloped Black America*. Boston: South End Press.

Marcus, Ruth. 1992. "Court cuts federal desegregation role, schools' anti-bias obligations eased." *New York Times* (April 1):A1.

Marger, Martin N. 1991. *Race and Ethnic Relations*. Belmont, CA: Wadsworth.

Mariano, Ann. 1988. "Is it a mortgage deduction, or a housing subsidy for the wealthy?" *Washington Post National Weekly Edition* (October 24–30):20.

Marks, Donovan, and Nicole Brown. 1990. "The next link in the dumping chain." Pages 32–33 in Dana Alston (ed.), *We Speak for Ourselves: Social Justice, Race and Environment*. Washington, DC: Panos Institute.

Marschall, Dan (ed.). 1979. *The Battle of Cleveland: Public Interest Challenges Corporate Power*. Washington, DC: Conference on Alternative State and Local Policies.

Martin, D. 1976. *Battered Wives*. San Francisco: Glide Word Press.

Martin, Judith G. 1993. "Why women need a feminist spirituality." *Women's Studies Quarterly* 21(Spring–Summer):106–120.

Martin, M. Kay, and Barbara Voorhies. 1975. *Female of the Species*. New York: Columbia University Press.

Marx, Karl. 1844/1964. *Economic and Philosophic Manuscripts of 1844*. Trans. Martin Milligan. New York: International Publishers.

———. 1964. *Selected Writings in Sociology and Social Philosophy* (edited by T. B. Bottomore and Maximillian Rubel). Baltimore: Penguin.

——— and Friederich Engels. 1967. *The Communist Manifesto*. Baltimore: Penguin.

——— and ———. 1970. *The German Ideology*. New York: International Publishers.

Massachusetts State Department of Employment and Training. 1989. *Defense Industry Profile*. Boston: Field Research Services.

Mater, Gene P. 1989. "Monday memo." *Broadcasting* 117(July 10):23.

Mazzocco, Dennis W. 1994. *Networks of Power: Corporate TV's Threat to Democracy*. Boston: South End Press.

McAdam, Doug. 1982. *Political Process and the Development of Black Insurgency, 1930–1970*. Chicago: University of Chicago Press.

———. 1988. *Freedom Summer*. New York: Oxford University Press.

McClain, Leanita. 1992. "The middle-class black's burden." Pages 120–122 in Margaret L. Andersen and Patricia Hill Collins (eds.), *Race, Class, and Gender*. Belmont, CA: Wadsworth.

McCrary, Teresa. 1993. "Getting off the welfare carousel." *Newsweek* (December 6):11.

McCutcheon, Gail, Dian Kyle, and Robert Skovira. 1979. "Characters in basal readers: Does 'equal' now mean 'same'?" *Reading Teacher* 32:438–441.

McFadden, Robert D. 1991. "Degrees and stacks of résumés yield few jobs for class of '91." *New York Times* (April 22):A1, B6.

McGuire, Meredith B. 1992. *Religion: The Social Context*, 3rd ed. Belmont, CA: Wadsworth.

McGuire, Patrick, and Donald McQuarie (eds.). 1994. *From the Left Bank to the Mainstream: Historical Debates and Contemporary Research in Marxist Sociology*. Chicago: Nelson Hall.

McIntosh, Peggy. 1992. "White privilege and male privilege." Pages 70–81 in Margaret L. Andersen and Patricia Hill Collins (eds.), *Race, Class, and Gender*. Belmont, CA: Wadsworth.

McKinlay, John B., and Sonja M. McKinlay. 1990. "Medical measures and the decline of mortality." Pages 10–23 in Peter Conrad and Rochelle Kern (eds.), *The Sociology of Health and Illness*, 3rd ed. New York: St. Martin's Press.

McLanahan, Sara, and Rene Monson. 1989. *Caring for the Elderly: Prevalence and Consequences*. Paper prepared for the Panel on Employer Policies and Working Families, Committee on Women's Employment and Related Social Issues, Commission on Behavioral and Social Sciences and Education, National Research Council, Washington, DC.

———, Annemette Sorensen, and Dorothy Watson. 1989. "Sex differences in poverty, 1950–1980." *Signs* 15:102–122.

McNeilly, M. 1990. *Braving the New World*. Mountain View, CA: Plowshare Press.

McQuiston, John T. 1990. "Dozens are injured in further outbreak of Rikers Island unrest." *New York Times* (August 22):A1.

Mead, George Herbert. 1934. *Mind, Self, and Society*. Chicago: University of Chicago Press.

Mead, Lawrence M. 1992. *The New Politics of Poverty*. New York: Basic Books.

Meier, Kenneth J., et al. 1989. *Race, Class, and Education: The Politics of Second-Generation Discrimination*. Madison: University of Wisconsin Press.

Melman, Seymour. 1983. *Profits without Production*. New York: Knopf.

Melton, J. Gordon (ed.). 1989. *The Encyclopedia of American Religions*, 3rd ed. Detroit: Gale Research.

Merton, Robert K. 1957. *Social Theory and Social Structure*. New York: Free Press.

———. 1968. *Social Theory and Social Structure*, enlarged ed. New York: Free Press.

Meyer, David S. 1993. "Institutionalizing dissent: The United States structure of political opportunity and the end of the nuclear freeze movement." *Sociological Forum* 8(2):157–180.

Michels, Robert. 1962. *Political Parties: A Sociological Study of Oligarchical Tendencies of Modern Democracy*. New York: Free Press.

Michelson, Stephan. 1972. "The political economy of school finance." Pages 140–174 in Martin Carnoy (ed.), *Schooling in Corporate Society*. New York: McKay.

Mickelson, Roslyn Arlin. 1987. "Education and the struggle against race, class, and gender inequality." *Humanity and Society* 11(4):440–464.

Miliband, Ralph. 1969. *The State in Capitalist Society*. New York: Basic Books.

Miller, Casey, and Kate Swift. 1991. *Words and Women Updated: New Language in New Times*. New York: Harper Collins.

Mills, C. Wright. 1957. *The Power Elite*. New York: Oxford University Press.

———. 1959. *The Sociological Imagination*. New York: Oxford University Press.

Mintz, Beth, and Michael Schwartz. 1985. *The Power Structure of American Business*. Chicago: University of Chicago Press.

Mishel, Lawrence, and Jacqueline Simon. 1988. *The State of Working America*. Washington, DC: Economic Policy Institute.

Mitchell, Emily. 1991. "Do the poor deserve bad schools?" *Time* (October 14):60–61.

MLR Publishing. 1991. *Mergers and Acquisitions*. Philadelphia: MLR.

Mohai, Paul. 1990. "Black environmentalism." *Social Science Quarterly* 71(4):744–765.

Monaghan, Peter. 1993. "Facing jail, a sociologist raises questions about a scholar's right to protect sources." *Chronicle of Higher Education* (April 7):A10.

Monagle, Katie. 1990. "The killing numbers." *Ms.* 1(2)(September–October):45.

Montagu, Ashley. 1974. *Man's Most Dangerous Myth: The Fallacy of Race*, 5th ed. New York: Oxford University Press.

Moore, Joan, and Harry Pachon. 1985. *Hispanics in the United States*, 2nd ed. Englewood Cliffs, NJ: Prentice-Hall.

Moore, Molly. 1990. "Crossing the culture gulf: For female soldiers, different rules." *Washington Post* (August 23):D1–D2.

Moore, Thomas. 1990. "The nature and unequal incidence of job displacement costs." *Social Problems* 37(2):230–242.

Morgan, L. A. 1989. "Economic well-being following marital termination." *Journal of Family Issues* 10:86–101.

Morgan, Michael, and James Shanahan. 1991. "Television and the cultivation of political attitudes." *Journal of Communication* 41(1):88–103.

Morris, Aldon D. 1984. *The Origins of the Civil Rights Movement: Black Communities Organizing for Change*. New York: Free Press.

Morrisey, Marietta. 1987. "Female-headed families: Poor women and choice." Pages 302–314 in Naomi Gross and Harriet Engel Gross (eds.), *Families and Work*. Philadelphia: Temple University Press.

Morrison, Toni (ed.). 1992. *Race-ing Justice, En-gendering Power: Essays on Anita Hill, Clarence Thomas, and the Social Construction of Reality*. New York: Pantheon.

Mortimer, Jeylan T., and Roberta G. Simmons. 1978. "Adult socialization." Pages 421–454 in Ralph H. Turner, James Coleman, and Renee C. Fox (eds.), *Annual Review of Sociology*, vol. 4. Palo Alto, CA: Annual Reviews.

Mott, F. L., and S. F. Moore. 1978. "The causes and consequences of marital breakdown." Pages 113–135 in F. Mott (ed.), *Women, Work and Family*. Lexington, MA: Lexington Books.

Mueller, L. 1977. "Women and men, power and powerlessness in Lesotho." *Signs* 3(1):154–166.

Muller, Charlotte. 1988. "Medicaid: The lower tier of health care for women." *Women and Health* 14(2):81–103.

———. 1990. *Health Care and Gender*. New York: Russell Sage Foundation.

Muller, Ronald. 1979. "The multinational corporation and the underdevelopment of the third world." Pages 151–178 in Charles Wilber (ed.), *The Political Economy of Development and Underdevelopment*. New York: Random House.

Murdock, George. 1949. *Social Structure*. New York: Macmillan.

Nardi, Peter M., David Sanders, and Judd Marmor. 1994. *Growing Up before Stonewall: Life Stories of Some Gay Men.* New York: Routledge.

Nasar, Sylvia. 1992. "Employment in service industry, impetus to boom in 80s, falters." *New York Times* (January 1):A1, D4.

Nathan, Joe. 1985. "Voucher/choice battle heats up: Pro: Families should have choice." *School Administrator* 42(8):10–12.

———. 1989. "Interdistrict programs offer 'expanded opportunities.'" *Education Week* (April 19):24, 32.

National Advisory Commission on Civil Disorders. 1968. *Report of the National Advisory Commission on Civil Disorders.* Washington, DC: U.S. Government Printing Office.

National Center for Education Statistics. 1984. *Digest of Education Statistics, 1983–84.* Washington, DC: U.S. Government Printing Office.

———. 1990. *Digest of Education Statistics: 1989.* Washington, DC: U.S. Government Printing Office.

———. 1992. *Digest of Education Statistics, 1992.* Washington, DC: U.S. Government Printing Office.

National Center for Health Statistics. 1989. *Vital and Health Statistics, Current Estimates from the National Health Interview Survey, 1988.* Hyattsville, MD: U.S. Department of Health and Human Services.

National Commission on Excellence in Education. 1983. *A Nation at Risk.* Washington, DC: U.S. Government Printing Office.

National Education Association. 1990. *Academic Tracking.* Washington, DC: NEA.

National Institute on Drug Abuse. 1991. *National Household Survey on Drug Abuse: 1991.* Washington, DC: U.S. Government Printing Office.

National Issues Forum. 1992. *The Health Care Crisis: Containing Costs, Expanding Coverage.* New York: McGraw-Hill.

National Journal, The. 1989. "AFL-CIO calls for legislation to control mergers, ease impact on workers, communities." 21(February 18):395.

National Opinion Research Center. 1991a. *General Social Survey, 1990.* Chicago: NORC.

———. 1991b. *General Social Survey, 1991.* Chicago: NORC.

———. 1991c. *General Social Survey, 1991.* International Social Survey, 1991, Module on Religion. Chicago: NORC.

Navarro, Mireya. 1992. "Far away from the crowded city, tuberculosis cases increase." *New York Times* (December 6):L49, L58.

Navarro, Vincente. 1990. "Race or class versus race and class: Mortality differentials in the United States." *Lancet* 336(November 17):1238–1240.

———. 1991a. "The class gap." *The Nation* (April 8):436–437.

———. 1991b. "Class and race: Life and death situations." *Monthly Review* 43(September):1–13.

Neff, Robert, and Joyce Barnathan. 1992. "How much Japanese CEOs really make." *Business Week* (January 27):31.

Neubeck, Kenneth J. 1991. *Social Problems: A Critical Approach,* 3rd ed. New York: McGraw-Hill.

Neustadtl, Alan, and Dan Clawson. 1988. "Corporate political groupings: Does ideology unify business political behavior?" *American Sociological Review* 53(2):172–190.

"New era of segregation, a." 1993. *Newsweek* (December 27):44.

Newman, Katherine S. 1989. *Falling from Grace: The Experience of Downward Mobility in the American Middle Class.* New York: Vintage.

Newton, Barbara J., and Elizabeth B. Buck. 1985. "Television as significant other: Its relationship to self-descriptors in five countries." *Journal of Cross-Cultural Psychology* 16(3)(September):289–312.

North, Liisa. 1988. "The women poor of Peru." *ISIS: International Women's Journal* 17(March):12–14.

Northeast Utilities. 1990. *Let's Explore Electricity.* South Deerfield, MA: Channing L. Bete.

"Not enough for all: Oregon experiments with rationing health care." 1990. *Newsweek* (May 14):53.

"Not just for nerds." 1990. *Newsweek* (April 9):52–57.

Novak, Viveca. 1991. "Why workers can't win." *Common Cause Magazine* (July–August):28–32.

Nussbaum, Bruce, with Ann Therese Palmer, Alice Z. Cuneo, and Barbara Carlson. 1992. "Downward mobility: Corporate castoffs are struggling just to stay in the middle-class." *Business Week* (March 23):56–63.

Oakes, Guy. 1990. *The Soul of the Salesman: The Moral Ethos of Personal Sales.* Atlantic Highlands, NJ: Humanities Press International.

Oakes, Jeannie. 1985. *Keeping Track: How Schools Structure Inequality.* New Haven: Yale University Press.

———. 1990. *Multiplying Inequalities: The Effects of Race, Social Class, and Tracking on Opportunities to Learn Mathematics and Science.* Santa Monica, CA: Rand Corporation.

O'Connor, James. 1987. *The Meaning of Crisis: A Theoretical Introduction.* New York: Basil Blackwell.

Ogbu, John U. 1978. *Minority Education and Caste: The American System in Cross Cultural Perspective.* New York: Academic Press.

———. 1991. "Immigrant and involuntary minorities in comparative perspective." Pages 3–33 in Margaret A. Gibson and John U. Ogbu (eds.), *Minority Status and Schooling.* New York: Garland.

Ogburn, William F. 1964. *On Culture and Social Change: Selected Papers* (edited by Otis Dudley Duncan). Chicago: University of Chicago Press.

O'Hare, Michael, Lawrence Bacow, and Debra Sanderson. 1983. *Facility Siting and Public Opposition.* New York: Van Nostrand Reinhold.

O'Hare, William. 1989. "In the black." *American Demographics* (November):25–29.

Olivas, Michael A. 1981. "Information access inequities: A fatal flaw in educational voucher plans." *Journal of Law and Education* 10(4):441–465.

Olson, Jon, and Jon Miller. 1983. "Gender and interaction in the workplace." *Research in the Interweave of Social Roles* 3:35–58.

Olson, Laura K. 1982. *The Political Economy of Aging.* New York: Columbia University Press.

Olson, Susan. 1984. *Clients and Lawyers: Securing the Rights of Disabled Persons.* Westport, CT: Greenwood Press.

Omi, Michael, and Howard A. Winant. 1986. *Racial Formation in the United States from the 1960s to the 1980s.* New York: Routledge, Chapman & Hall.

Orcutt, James D. 1983. *Analyzing Deviance.* Chicago: Dorsey Press.

Orfield, Gary, and Franklin Monfort. 1988. *Racial Change and Desegregation in Large School Districts.* Washington, DC: National School Boards Association.

———— et al. 1989. *Status of School Desegregation, 1968–1986.* Washington, DC: National School Boards Association.

Ornstein, Allan C. 1988. "State financing of public schools." *Urban Education* 23(July):188–207.

Ostling, Richard N. 1991. "What does God really think about sex?" *Time* (June 24):48–50.

Ostrander, Susan A. 1984. *Women of the Upper Class.* Philadelphia: Temple University Press.

Oullette, Laurie. 1993. "Class bias on campus." *Utne Reader* (September–October):19, 22–24.

"Our bodies, their selves." 1990. *Newsweek* (December 17):60.

Oxford Analytica. 1989. "The new technologies and economic productivity." Pages 24–32 in D. Stanley Eitzen and Maxine Baca Zinn (eds.), *The Reshaping of America: Social Consequences of the Changing Economy.* Englewood Cliffs, NJ: Prentice-Hall.

Page, Reba Neukom. 1991. *Lower Track Classrooms.* New York: Teachers College Press.

Page, Stewart, Daniel Linz, and Edward Donnerstein. 1990. "The turnaround on pornography research: Some implications for psychology and women." *Canadian Psychology* 31(4):359–367.

Papanek, H. 1979. "Development planning for women: The implications of women's work." Pages 170–201 in R. Jahan and H. Papanek (eds.), *Women and Development.* Dacca: Bangladesh Institute of Law and International Affairs.

Parcel, Toby L. 1979. "Race, regional labor markets and earnings." *American Sociological Review* 44:262–279.

———— and Charles W. Mueller. 1983. *Ascription and Labor Markets: Race and Sex Differences in Earnings.* New York: Academic Press.

Parenti, Michael. 1986. *Inventing Reality: The Politics of the Mass Media.* New York: St. Martin's Press.

Pareto, Vilifredo. 1963. *Treatise on General Sociology.* New York: Dover.

Park, Jeannie, and Susan Schindehette. 1989. "Thousands of women, fearing for their lives, hear a scary echo in Tracey Thurman's cry for help." *People Weekly* 32(October 9):112–116.

Parkin, Frank. 1971. *Class Inequality and Political Order: Social Stratification in Capitalist and Communist Societies.* New York: Praeger.

Parsons, Jacquelynne Eccles, et al. 1982. "Sex differences in attributions and learned helplessness." *Sex Roles* 8(4):421–432.

Parsons, Talcott. 1951. *The Social System.* New York: Free Press.

Passell, Peter. 1991. "Washington offers mountain of debt to save forests." *New York Times* (January 22):C1, C9.

Pear, Robert. 1992. "55% voting rate reverses 30-year decline." *New York Times* (November 5):B4.

————. 1993. "Oregon's health plan for covering all poor people." *New York Times* (March 20):8.

Pearce, Diana. 1978. "The feminization of poverty: Women, work, and welfare." *Urban and Social Change Review* (February):28–36.

Pearl, David. 1982. *Television and Behavior: Ten Years of Scientific Research.* Washington, DC: U.S. Government Printing Office.

Peltz, William H. 1990. "Can girls + science – stereotypes = success?" *Science Teacher* (December): 44–49.

Pennar, Karen. 1992. "Defense cuts don't have to wound the economy." *Business Week* (February 24):82.

Perrow, Charles. 1986. *Complex Organizations: A Critical Essay,* 3rd ed. New York: Random House.

Persell, Caroline Hodges. 1977. *Education and Inequality: A Theoretical and Empirical Synthesis.* New York: Free Press.

Personick, Martin E., and Ethel C. Jackson. 1992. "Injuries and illnesses in the workplace, 1990." *Monthly Labor Review* 115(April):37–38.

Peters, Marie. 1985. "Racial socialization of young black children." Pages 159–173 in Harriette McAdoo and John McAdoo (eds.), *Black Children.* Beverly Hills, CA: Sage.

Petersilia, Joan. 1985. "Racial disparities in the criminal justice system." *Crime and Delinquency* 31:15–34.

Peterson, Gary W., and Boyd C. Rollins. 1987. "Parent-child socialization." In Marvin B. Sussman and Suzanne K. Steinmetz (eds.), *Handbook of Marriage and the Family.* New York: Plenum Press.

Peterson, Ruth C., and L. L. Thurstone. 1933. *Motion Pictures and the Social Attitudes of Children.* New York: Macmillan.

Pfouts, Jane H. 1980. "Birth order, age spacing, IQ differences, and family relations." *Journal of Marriage and the Family* 42(3)(August):517–531.

Philadelphia Daily News. 1986. "Putting the squeeze on banks." (October 7):29, 36.

Phillips, Kevin. 1990. *The Politics of Rich and Poor: Wealth and the American Electorate in the Reagan Aftermath.* New York: Random House.

Phoenix Gazette. 1986. "Law pushes banks toward community involvement." (September 12):1, 6G.

Pilisuk, Marc, and Thomas Hayden. 1965. "Is there a military-industrial complex which prevents peace? Consensus and countervailing power in pluralistic society." *Journal of Social Issues* 21(July):67–117.

Pisko, Valena White, and Joyce D. Stern. 1985. *The Condition of Education, 1985 Edition.* Statistical report, National Center for Educational Statistics. Washington, DC: U.S. Government Printing Office.

Piven, Francis Fox, and Richard Cloward. 1971. *Regulating the Poor: The Functions of Public Welfare.* New York: Pantheon.

———— and ————. 1977. *Poor People's Movements: Why They Succeed, How They Fail.* New York: Vintage.

———— and ————. 1982. *The New Class War: Reagan's Attack on the Welfare State and Its Consequences.* New York: Pantheon.

———— and ————. 1988. *Why Americans Don't Vote.* New York: Pantheon.

Plaskow, Judith, and Carol P. Christ (eds.). 1989. *Weaving the Vision: New Patterns in Feminist Spirituality.* San Francisco: Harper & Row.

Pogatchnik, Shawn. 1990. "7000 hate crimes on gays reported in '89." *Los Angeles Times* (June 8):A22.

Polit, Denise F., and Janet R. Kahn. 1987. "Teenage pregnancy and the role of schools." *Urban Education* 22(July):131–153.

Pollack, Andrew. 1994. "Meeting lays bare the abyss between AIDS and its cure." *New York Times* (August 12):A1.

Pollitt, Katha. 1992. "Implants: Truth and consequences." *The Nation* 254(March 16):325, 329.

Portes, Alejandro. 1985. "The informal sector and the world economy: Notes on the structure of subsidized labor." Pages 53–62 in Michael Timberlake (ed.), *Urbanization and the World-System.* New York: Academic Press.

———— and Saskia Sassen-Koob. 1987. "Making it underground: Comparative material on the informal sector in Western market economies." *American Journal of Sociology* 93(1):30–61.

Possley, Maurice. 1986. "All-white juries draw focus." *Chicago Tribune* (January 3):E13.

Poulantzas, Nicos. 1968. "The problem of the capitalist state." Pages 238–253 in Robin Blackburn (ed.), *Ideology in Social Science.* New York: Pantheon.

————. 1973. *Political Power and Social Classes.* London: New Left Books and Sheed and Ward.

Powell, Richard R., and Jesus Garcia. 1985. "The portrayal of minorities and women in selected elementary science series." *Journal of Research in Science Teaching* 22:519–533.

Powell-Hopson, Darlene, and Derek Hopson. 1988. "Implications of doll color preferences among black preschool children and white preschool children." *Journal of Black Psychology* 14(February):57–63.

Pratt, W. F., W. D. Mosher, C. A. Bachrach, and M. Horn. 1984. "Understanding U.S. fertility: Findings from the national survey of family growth." *Population Bulletin* 39(5):1–41.

President's Economic Adjustment Committee. 1986. *25 Years of Civilian Reuse: Summary of Completed Military Base Economic Adjustment Projects.* Washington, DC: U.S. Government Printing Office.

————. 1990. *Civilian Reuse of Former Military Bases.* Washington, DC: U.S. Government Printing Office.

Presser, Harriet B. 1988. "Shift work and child care among young dual-earner American parents." *Journal of Marriage and the Family* 50:133–148.

Price, Richard J., and Carol O'Shaughnessy. 1988. *Long-Term Care for the Elderly.* Issue Brief IB88098, Education and Public Welfare Division, Congressional Research Service, Washington, DC.

Princeton Survey Research Associates. 1990. "Reflections of the Times #1." (May).

Public Law 101-335, an Act to Establish a Clear and Comprehensive Prohibition of Discrimination on the Basis of Disability. 1990. Washington, DC: U.S. Government Printing Office.

Quadagno, Jill S. 1984. "Welfare capitalism and the Social Security Act of 1935." *American Sociological Review* 49(5):632–647.

———— and M. H. Meyer. 1989. "Organized labor, state structures and social policy development: A case study of old age assistance in Ohio, 1916–1940." *Social Problems* 36(2):181–196.

Quindlen, Anna. 1991. "Women warriors." *New York Times* (February 3).

Quinn, Peggy. 1994. "America's disability policy: Another double standard?" *Affilia* 9(Spring):45–59.

Quinney, Richard. 1979. *Criminology: Analysis and Critique,* 2nd ed. Boston: Little, Brown.

"Race: Can we talk?" 1991. *Ms.* (July–August):34–39.

"Racial harm is found in schools' 'tracking.'" 1990. *New York Times* (September 20):A14.

"Racial link described in infant deaths." 1992. *Hartford Courant* (June 4):A14.

Radelet, Michael L. 1981. "Racial characteristics and the death penalty." *American Sociological Review* 46:918–927.

Raffalli, Mary. 1994. "Why so few women physicists?" *New York Times,* Education Life (January 9):26 ff.

Rapp, Rayna. 1982. "Family and class in contemporary America." Pages 168–187 in Barrie Thorne and Marilyn Yalom (eds.), *Rethinking the Family: Some Feminist Questions.* New York: Longman.

Rayman, Paula. 1982. *The Kibbutz Community and Nation Building.* Princeton, NJ: Princeton University Press.

Raymond, Diane. 1992. "'In the best interests of the child': Thoughts on homophobia and parenting." Pages 114–130 in Warren J. Blumenfeld (ed.), *Homophobia: How We All Pay the Price.* Boston: Beacon Press.

Reckless, Walter C. 1961. *The Crime Problem.* New York: Appleton-Century-Crofts.

Reece, Ray. 1980. "The solar blackout: What happens when Exxon and DOE go sunbathing together?" *Mother Jones* (September–October):28–37.

Reich, Robert B. 1991. "Secession of the successful." *New York Times Magazine* (January 20):16, 42–45.

Reiman, Jeffrey H. 1984. *The Rich Get Rich and the Poor Get Prison,* 2nd ed. New York: Wiley.

Relman, Arnold S. 1987. "The new medical-industrial complex." Pages 597–608 in Howard D. Schwartz (ed.), *Dominant Issues in Medical Sociology,* 2nd ed. New York: Random House.

Renchler, Ron. 1992. *Financial Equity in the Schools.* Eugene, OR: ERIC Clearinghouse on Educational Management, University of Oregon.

Renzetti, Claire M., and Daniel J. Curran. 1992. *Women, Men, and Society,* 2nd ed. Boston: Allyn and Bacon.

Research and Forecasts. 1988. "Working Americans: Emerging Values." Telephone survey (October).

Reskin, Barbara F., and Heidi I. Hartmann (eds.). 1986. *Women's Work, Men's Work: Sex Segrega-*

tion on the Job. New York: National Academy Press.

———— and Patricia A. Roos. 1990. *Job Queues, Gender Queues: Explaining Women's Inroads into Male Occupations*. Philadelphia: Temple University Press.

Rifkin, Jeremy, and Randy Barber. 1978. *The North Will Rise Again: Pensions, Politics, and Power in the 1980s*. Boston: Beacon Press.

Rist, Ray C. 1970. "Student social class and teacher expectations." *Harvard Educational Review* 40 (August):411–451.

————. 1973. *The Urban School: A Factory for Failure*. Cambridge, MA: M.I.T. Press.

Ritzer, George. 1992. *Sociological Theory*, 3rd ed. New York: McGraw-Hill.

Rivera, Rhonda R. 1987. "Legal issues in gay and lesbian parenting." Pages 199–227 in Frederick W. Bozett (ed.), *Gay and Lesbian Parents*. New York: Praeger.

Rivlin, Alice M., and Joshua M. Wiener, with Raymond J. Hanley and Denise A. Spence. 1988. *Caring for the Disabled Elderly: Who Will Pay?* Washington, DC: Brookings Institution.

Robinson, Eugene. 1993. "Rupert Murdoch: Global gatekeeper; tycoon makes series of deals in effort to expand reach with new technologies." *Washington Post* (October 2):C1.

Roethlisberger, Frederick J., and William J. Dickson. 1939. *Management and the Worker*. Cambridge, MA: Harvard University Press.

Rollins, Judith. 1985. *Between Women: Domestics and Their Employers*. Philadelphia: Temple University Press.

Romero, Mary. 1992. *Maid in America*. New York: Routledge.

Romo, Frank P., Hyman Korman, Peter Brantley, and Michael Schwartz. 1989. "The rise and fall of regional political economies: A theory of the core." *Research in Politics and Society* 3:37–64.

Roof, Wade Clark, and William McKinney. 1987. *American Mainline Religion*. New Brunswick, NJ: Rutgers University Press.

Roper Organization. 1990. "Human Sexuality Poll." (September).

Rose, Arnold. 1967. *The Power Structure*. New York: Oxford University Press.

Rose, Mike. 1989. *Lives on the Boundary*. New York: Penguin.

Rosenbaum, James E. 1976. *Making Inequality: The Hidden Curriculum of High School Tracking*. New York: Wiley.

Rosenfeld, Rachel A. 1980. "Race and sex differences in career dynamics." *American Sociological Review* 45:583–609.

Rosenhan, David L. 1973. "On being insane in insane places." *Science* 179(January 19):250–258.

————. 1975. "The contextual nature of psychiatric diagnosis." *Journal of Abnormal Psychology* 84 (October):462–474.

Rosenthal, Marilynn M., and Marcel Frenkel (eds.). 1992. *Health Care Systems and Their Patients: An International Perspective*. Boulder, CO: Westview Press.

Rosenthal, Robert, and Lenore Jacobson. 1968a. *Pygmalion in the Classroom*. New York: Holt, Rinehart and Winston.

———— and ————. 1968b. "Teacher expectations for the disadvantaged." *Scientific American* 218(April): 19–23.

Ross, Catherine E. 1987. "The division of labor at home." *Social Forces* 65:816–833.

Rostow, W. W. 1960. *The States of Economic Growth: A Non-Communist Manifesto*. London: Cambridge University Press.

Rothenberg, Paula S. (ed.). 1992. *Race, Class, and Gender in the United States: An Integrated Study*. New York: St. Martin's Press.

Rothman, Barbara Katz. 1989. *Re-creating Motherhood: Ideology and Technology in a Patiarchal Society*. New York: Norton.

Rothman, Robert A. 1993. *Inequality and Stratification*, 2nd ed. Englewood Cliffs, NJ: Prentice-Hall.

Rothschild, Joyce, and J. Allen Whitt. 1986. *The Cooperative Workplace: Potentials and Dilemmas of Organizational Democracy and Participation*. New York: Cambridge University Press.

Rowland, Robyn. 1992. *Living Laboratories: Women and Reproductive Technologies*. Bloomington: Indiana University Press.

Rude, George F. E. 1964. *The Crowd in History: A Study of Popular Disturbances in France and England, 1730–1848*. New York: Wiley.

————. 1985. History from Below: *Studies in Popular Protest and Popular Ideology in Honour of George Rude* (edited by Frederick Krantz). Montreal: Concordia University.

Rule, James, Douglas McAdam, Linda Stearns, and David Uglow. 1980. *The Politics of Privacy*. New York: New American Library.

Russell, Charles. 1991. *AIDS in America*. New York: Springer-Verlag.

Russell, George. 1987. "Rebuilding to survive." *Time* (February 16):44–45.

Ryan, Jake, and Charles Sackrey. 1984. *Strangers in Paradise: Academics from the Working Class*. Boston: South End Press.

Ryan, William. 1976. *Blaming the Victim*, rev. ed. New York: Vintage.

Sadker, David, and Myra Sadker. 1988. *Teachers Make the Difference*, 2nd ed. New York: McGraw-Hill.

———— and ————. 1994. *Failing at Fairness: How America's Schools Cheat Girls*. New York: Scribner.

Sahliyeh, Emile (ed.). 1990. *Religious Resurgence and Politics in the Contemporary World*. Albany: State University of New York Press.

St. Louis Post Dispatch. 1986. "ACORN gets bankers to sit at attention." (September 28):1, 6G.

Samuelson, Robert J. 1993. "What Clinton isn't saying: As America ages, spending will explode—which is why we need to cut more now." *Newsweek* (March 15):38.

Sawhill, I. V. 1988. "Poverty in the U.S.: Why is it so persistent?" *Journal of Economic Literature* 26: 1073–1119.

SCAM (Southern Counties Action Movement). 1986. "Bank of Zeigler Update." *SCAM Report* (January):2.

Scarr, Sandra. 1982. "Development is internally guided, not determined." *Contemporary Psychology* 27:852–853.

Schaefer, Richard T. 1990. *Racial and Ethnic Groups*, 4th ed. Glenview, IL: Scott, Foresman/Little, Brown.

Schaffer, H. Rudolph, and Peggy E. Emerson. 1964. "The development of social attachments in infancy." *Monographs of the Society for Research in Child Development* 29(Serial No. 94).

Schatan, Jacobo. 1987. *World Debt: Who Is to Pay?* London and New Jersey: Zed Books.

Scherer-Warren, Ilse. 1990. "'Recovering our dignity'—An appraisal of the utopia of liberation in Latin America." *International Sociology* 5(March):11–25.

Schilling, Bradley R. 1989. *The Economics of Poverty and Discrimination*, 5th ed. Englewood Cliffs, NJ: Prentice-Hall.

Schmalz, Jeffrey. 1993. "Survey stirs debate on number of gay men in U.S." *New York Times* (April 16):A20.

Schofield, J. W. 1981. "Complementary and conflicting identities: Images and interaction in an interracial school." Pages 53–90 in S. R. Asher and J. M. Gottman (eds.), *The Development of Children's Friendships*. New York: Cambridge University Press.

Schur, Edwin M. 1984. *Labeling Women Deviant: Gender, Stigma, and Social Control*. New York: Random House.

Schwartz, Joe. 1988. "Learning and earning." *American Demographics* (February):12.

Schwartz, John. 1993. "Federal women's health study faulted." *Washington Post* (November 2):A10.

———— and Todd Barrett. 1992. "Can you top this? The war between the states—for new business—rages on." *Newsweek* (February 17):40–41.

Scott, Janny. 1989. "Study suggests racism may affect health care." *Los Angeles Times* (January 13):1, 26.

Seeman, Melvin. 1959. "On the meaning of alienation." *American Sociological Review* 24:783–791.

Seers, Dudley. 1969. *The Meaning of Development*. Paper presented at the Eleventh World Conference of the Society for International Development, New Delhi.

Seiber, Marilyn J. 1982. *International Borrowing by Developing Countries*. New York: Pergamon Press.

Seidman, Gay. 1993. *Manufacturing Militance: Workers' Movements in Brazil and South Africa, 1970–1985*. Berkeley: University of California Press.

Seltzer, J. A. 1989. *Relationships between Fathers and Children Who Live Apart*. NSFH Working Paper No. 4, University of Wisconsin–Madison, Center for Demographic Ecology.

Serrin, William. 1970. *The Company and the Union*. New York: Vintage.

Sexton, Patricia Cayo. 1991. *The War on Labor and the Left: Understanding America's Unique Conservatism*. Boulder, CO: Westview Press.

Seybold, Peter. 1987. "Beyond the veil of neutrality."

Pages 175–193 in Rhonda F. Levine and Jerry Lembcke (eds.), *Recapturing Marxism*. New York: Praeger.

Shapiro, Joseph P. 1993. *No Pity: People with Disabilities Forging a New Civil Rights Movement*. New York: Times Books/Random House.

Shapiro, Thomas M. 1985. *Population Control Politics*. Philadelphia: Temple University Press.

Shaul, Susan, Pamela J. Dowling, and Bernice F. Laden. 1985. "Like other women: Perspectives of mothers with physical disabilities." Pages 133–142 in Mary Jo Deegan and Nancy A. Brooks (eds.), *Women and Disability: The Double Handicap*. New Brunswick, NJ: Transaction Books.

Sheler, Jeffrey L. 1990. "Homosexuality doctrines." *U.S. News & World Report* (July 16):55.

————. 1992. "The unpardonable sin." *U.S. News & World Report* (November 16):94–96.

Shupe, Anson. 1990. "The stubborn persistence of religion in the global arena." Pages 17–26 in Emile Sahliyeh (ed.), *Religious Resurgence and Politics in the Contemporary World*. Albany: State University of New York Press.

———— and Jeffrey K. Hadden. 1988. *The Politics of Religion and Social Change*. New York: Paragon House.

Sidel, Ruth. 1990. *On Her Own: Growing Up in the Shadow of the American Dream*. New York: Viking Penguin.

Sidel, Victor W., and Ruth Sidel. 1983. *A Healthy State*, rev. ed. New York: Pantheon.

Siegel, Jessica. 1991. "What Army ads don't say." *New York Times* (January 18):A31.

Signorielli, Nancy. 1991. *A Sourcebook on Children and Television*. New York: Greenwood Press.

Silberman, Charles. 1970. *Crisis in the Classroom*. New York: Vintage.

Simon, Barbara Levy. 1988. "Never-married old women and disability." Pages 215–225 in Michelle Fine and Adrienne Asch (eds.), *Women with Disabilities*. Philadelphia: Temple University Press.

Simon, David R., and D. Stanley Eitzen. 1990. *Elite Deviance*, 3rd ed. Boston: Allyn and Bacon.

Simon, Rita J., and Gloria Danziger. 1991. *Women's Movements in America: Their Successes, Disappointments, and Aspirations*. Westport, CT: Praeger.

Slavin, Robert E. 1990. "Achievement effects of ability grouping in secondary schools: A best-evidence synthesis." *Review of Educational Research* 60 (Fall):471–499.

Small, Meredith F. 1993. "The gay debate: Is homosexuality a matter of choice or chance?" *American Health* 12(March):70.

Smith, Dorothy E. 1984. "The deep structure of gender antitheses: Another view of capitalism and patriarchy." *Humanity and Society* 8(4)(November):395–402.

Smith, K. R., and C. D. Zick. 1986. "The incidence of poverty among the recently widowed: Mediating factors in the life course." *Journal of Marriage and the Family* 48:619–630.

Smith, Lillian. 1961. *Killers of the Dream*. New York: Norton.

Sokoloff, Natalie J. 1992. *Black Women and White*

Women in the Professions: Occupational Segregation by Race and Gender, 1960–1980. New York and London: Routledge.

Sommers, Evelyn K., and James V. P. Check. 1987. "An empirical investigation of the role of pornography in the verbal and physical abuse of women." *Violence and Victims* 2(3)(Fall):189–209.

Sorensen, A., and S. McLanahan. 1987. "Married women's economic dependency, 1940–1980." *American Journal of Sociology* 93:659–687.

Sorokin, Pitirim A. 1957. *Social and Cultural Dynamics,* rev. abridged ed. Boston: Porter Sargent.

Sorrels, Bobbye D. 1983. *The Nonsexist Communicator: Solving the Problems of Gender and Awkwardness in Modern English.* Englewood Cliffs, NJ: Prentice-Hall.

Spelman, Elizabeth. 1988. *Inessential Women.* Boston: Beacon Press.

Spengler, Oswald. 1926. *The Decline of the West.* New York: Knopf.

Spergel, Irving A., and G. David Curry. 1990. "Strategies and perceived agency effectiveness in dealing with the youth gang problem." Pages 288–309 in C. Ronald Huff (ed.), *Gangs in America.* Newbury Park, CA: Sage.

Spitz, Rene A. 1946. "Hospitalism: A follow-up report." *Psychoanalytic Study of the Child* 2:113–117.

Sprouse, Martin (ed.). 1992. *Sabotage in the American Workplace: Anecdotes of Dissatisfaction, Mischief, and Revenge.* San Francisco, CA: Pressure Drop Press.

Squires, Gregory D., Ruthanne DeWolfe, and Alan S. DeWolfe. 1979. "Urban decline or disinvestment: Uneven development, redlining and the role of the insurance industry." *Social Problems* 27(1):79–95.

Stack, Carol D. 1974. *All Our Kin: Strategies for Survival in a Black Community.* New York: Harper & Row.

Stack, Steven. 1987. "Publicized executions and homicide, 1950–1980." *American Sociological Review* 52:532–540.

Stallard, Karen, Barbara Ehrenreich, and Holly Sklar. 1983. *Poverty in the American Dream: Women and Children First.* Boston: South End Press.

Stallings, Barbara. 1982. "Euromarkets, Third World countries, and the international political economy." Pages 193–230 in Harry Makler, Alberto Martinelli, and Neil Smelser (eds.), *The New International Economy.* Beverly Hills, CA: Sage.

Stanley, Julia P. 1977. "Paradigmatic woman: The prostitute." Pages 303–321 in David L. Shores (ed.), *Papers in Language Variation.* Birmingham: University of Alabama Press.

Stark, Rodney, and William Sims Bainbridge. 1985. *The Future of Religion: Secularization, Revival and Cult Formation.* Berkeley: University of California Press.

Starr, Paul. 1982. *The Social Transformation of American Medicine.* New York: Basic Books.

Steelman, Lala Carr, and Brian Powell. 1985. "The social and academic consequences of birth order: Real, artifactual, or both?" *Journal of Marriage and the Family* 47(1)(February):117–124.

Steinberg, Stephen. 1981. *The Ethnic Myth: Race, Eth-nicity, and Class in America.* New York: Atheneum.

Stephenson, Patricia, and Marsden G. Wagner (eds.). 1993. *Tough Choices: In Vitro Fertilization and the Reproductive Technologies.* Philadelphia: Temple University Press.

Stevenson, R. 1991. "Contractor plans cutback of 27,000 jobs." *New York Times* (May 2).

Stimson, Jim. 1986. "Battlelines on vouchers are drawn clearly." *School Administrator* 43(2):25–26.

Stolberg, Sheryl. 1994. "For MS victims, fate deals their medication." *Hartford Courant* (January 7):A1.

Stone, Robyn I., Gail Lee Cafferata, and Judith Sangl. 1987. *Caregivers of the Frail Elderly: A National Profile.* Report No. 181-345:60026, National Center for Health Services Research and Health Care Technology Assessment, Public Health Service, U.S. Department of Health and Human Services. Washington, DC: U.S. Government Printing Office.

——— and Peter Kemper. 1989. *Spouses and Children of Disabled Elders: Potential and Active Caregivers.* Paper prepared for the National Center for Health Services Research and Health Care Technology Assessment, Public Health Service, U.S. Department of Health and Human Services. Washington, DC: U.S. Government Printing Office (January).

Stone, Sharon. 1989. "Marginal women unite! Organizing the disabled women's network in Canada." *Journal of Sociology and Social Welfare* 16(1):127–145.

Straus, Murray A., Richard J. Gelles, and Suzanne K. Steinmetz. 1980. *Behind Closed Doors: Violence in the American Family.* Garden City, NY: Anchor.

Streeten, Paul, with Shahid Javed Burki, Mahbub ul Haq, Norman Hicks, and Frances Stewart. 1981. *First Things First: Meeting Basic Human Needs in Developing Countries.* New York: Oxford University Press.

Stroman, Duane F. 1982. *The Awakening Minorities: The Physically Handicapped.* Washington, DC: University Press of America.

Strouse, Jeremiah, and Richard A. Fabes. 1985. "Formal versus informal sources of sex education: Competing forces in the sexual socialization of adolescents." *Adolescence* 20(78):251–263.

Sullivan, Brenda. 1993. "Students gain hand in drafting schedule." *Willimantic Chronicle* (February 8:3).

Sullivan, Harry Stack. 1953. *The Interpersonal Theory of Modern Psychiatry.* New York: Norton.

Sussman, Marvin B., and Lee Burchinal. 1962. "Kin family network: Unheralded structure in current conceptualizations of family functioning." *Marriage and Family Living* 24:231–240.

Sutherland, Edwin H., and Donald R. Cressey. 1974. *Criminology,* 9th ed. Philadelphia: Lippincott.

Sutton, Terri. 1992. "Bustin' loose: Why big breasts are back." *Utne Reader* (May–June):60–61.

Svensson, C. K. 1989. "Representation of American blacks in clinical trials of new drugs." *Journal of the American Medical Association* 261(January 13):258.

Swedberg, Richard. 1987. "The impact of an exogenous event: The oil shocks, the private banks and the origin of the debt crisis." *International Social Science Journal* 39(3):323–335.

Syme, S. Leonard, and Lisa F. Berkman. 1976. "Social class, susceptibility, and sickness." *American Journal of Epidemiology* (104):1–8.

Szekely, Eva. 1988. *Never Too Thin*. Toronto: Women's Press.

Taeuber, Cynthia. 1991. *Statistical Handbook on Women in America*. Phoenix, AZ: Oryx Press.

"Talking to God." 1992. *Newsweek* (January 6):39–44.

Tanenbaum, Sandra. 1989. "Medicaid and disability: The unlikely entitlement." *Milbank Quarterly* 67(Suppl. 2, Pt. 2):288–310.

Taylor, Ian, Paul Walton, and Jock Young. 1973. *The New Criminology*. New York: Harper & Row.

———, ———, and ———. 1975. *Critical Criminology*. London: Routledge & Kegan Paul.

Taylor-Gooby, Peter. 1976. "Rent benefits and tenants' attitudes: The Batley rent debate and allowance study." *Journal of Social Politics* 5(1):33–48.

Thomas, W. I. 1928. *The Child in America*. New York: Knopf.

Thompson, E. P. 1966. *The Making of the English Working Class*. New York: Vintage.

Thompson, Larry. 1991. "Examining the Health Status of Hispanics." *Washington Post* (January 15):7.

Thorne, Barrie. 1989. "Girls and boys together . . . but mostly apart: Gender arrangements in elementary schools." Pages 138–153 in Michael S. Kimmel and Michael A. Messner (eds.), *Men's Lives*. New York: Macmillan.

———. 1993. *Gender Play: Girls and Boys in School*. New Brunswick, NJ: Rutgers University Press.

Thornton, Michael, et al. 1990. "Sociodemographic and environmental influences on racial socialization by black parents." *Child Development* 61: 401–409.

Tienda, Marta, and Ronald Angel. 1982. "Headship and household composition among blacks, Hispanics, and other whites." *Social Forces* 61:508–531.

Time. 1982a. "Countdown on the ERA: As the deadline nears, supporters mount last-gasp drives." (June 14):25.

———. 1982b. "ERA dies: But its backers will try again." (July 5):29.

Time/Cable News Network. 1991. "National Adult Population Attitudes toward Financial Problems." Telephone survey. (December).

———. 1992. "National Adult Population Perspectives Comparing Current Standards of Living with Previous Generations'." Telephone survey (January).

Tobias, Sheila, et al. 1982. *What Kinds of Guns Are They Buying for Your Butter?* New York: Morrow.

Todaro, Michael P. 1985. *Economic Development in the Third World*, 3rd ed. New York: Longman.

Tomaskovic-Devey, Donald. 1993. *Gender and Racial Inequality at Work: The Sources and Consequences of Job Segregation*. Ithaca, NY: ILR Press.

"Tracking and civil rights." 1990. *Editorial Research Reports* (December 28):748.

Treas, Judith. 1983. "Trickle down or transfers? Postwar determinants of family inequality." *American Sociological Review* 48:546–559.

———. 1987. "The effect of women's labor force participation on the distribution of income in the United States." *Annual Review of Sociology* 13:259–288.

Troeltsch, Ernst. 1931. *The Social Teaching of the Christian Churches*. Trans. Olive Wyon. New York: Macmillan.

Truman, David B. 1951. *The Governmental Process*. New York: Random House.

Tudor, Keith. 1989. "The politics of disability in Italy: *La lega per il diritto al lavero digli handicappati.*" *Critical Social Policy* 9(1):37–55.

Tumin, Melvin. 1966. "Some principles of stratification: A critical view." Pages 53–58 in Rheinhard Bendix and Seymour Martin Lipset (eds.), *Class, Status and Power*, 2nd ed. New York: Free Press.

Turner, Jonathan H., et al. 1989. *The Emergence of Sociological Theory*, 2nd ed. Chicago: Dorsey Press.

"20 million in U.S. said to go hungry." 1987. *New York Times* (October 27):A33.

Underwood, Julie K. 1991. "The financial toll of choice." *School Administrator* 48(8):16, 18–19.

United Nations, Department of Social and Economic Development. 1992. *1991 Demographic Yearbook*. New York: United Nations.

United Nations Children's Fund. 1988. *The State of the World's Children, 1988*. New York: Oxford University Press.

U.S. Bureau of the Census. 1988. *Money, Income of Households, Families, and Persons in the United States, 1987*. Current Population Reports, Series P60, No. 162. Washington, DC: U.S. Government Printing Office.

———. 1989. *Money, Income and Poverty Status in the United States: 1988*. Washington, DC: U.S. Government Printing Office.

———. 1990. *Who's Minding the Kids? Child Care Arrangements: 1986–87*. Current Population Reports, Series P70, No. 20, Washington, DC: U.S. Government Printing Office.

———. 1991a. *Pensions: Worker Coverage and Retirement Benefits, 1987*. Current Population Reports, Series P70, No. 25, Washington, DC: U.S. Government Printing Office.

———. 1991b. *Poverty in the United States: 1990*. Current Population Reports, Series P60, No. 175, Washington, DC: U.S. Government Printing Office.

———. 1991c. *Statistical Abstract of the United States, 1991*. Washington, DC: U.S. Government Printing Office.

———. 1991d. *The Black Population in the United States: 1990 and 1989*. Current Population Reports, Series P20, No. 448, Washington, DC: U.S. Government Printing Office.

———. 1992a. *Poverty in the United States, 1991*. Current Population Reports, Series P60, No. 191, Washington, DC: U.S. Government Printing Office.

———. 1992b. *Statistical Abstract of the United States, 1992*. Washington, DC: U.S. Government Printing Office.

———. 1992c. *Money Income and Poverty Status in*

the United States, 1991. Washington, DC: U.S. Government Printing Office.

———. 1993a. *Money Income of Households, Families, and Persons in the United States: 1992.* Current Population Reports, Series P60, No. 184, Washington, DC: U.S. Government Printing Office.

———. 1993b. *Money Income and Poverty Status in the United States, 1992.* Washington, DC: U.S. Government Printing Office.

———. 1994. *Income, Poverty, and Valuation of Non-cash Benefits: 1993.* Current Population Reports, Series P60, No. 188, Washington, DC: U.S. Government Printing Office.

U.S. Bureau of Labor Statistics. 1984. *Employment and Earnings, January.* Washington, DC: U.S. Government Printing Office.

———. 1991. *Employment and Earnings, January.* Washington, DC: U.S. Government Printing Office.

———. 1992a. *Employment and Earnings.* Washington, DC: U.S. Government Printing Office.

———. 1992b. "Worker displacement increased sharply in recent recession." *News* (August 19):1–3.

U.S. Centers for Disease Control. 1991. "Premarital sexual experience among adolescent women: United States, 1970–1988." *Morbidity and Mortality Weekly Report* (39):929–932.

U.S. Central Intelligence Agency. 1993. *The World Fact Handbook, 1992.* Washington, DC: CIA.

U.S. Congress: House of Representatives, Select Committee on Aging. 1991. *Women Health Consumers: Short-Changed on Medical Research and Treatment.* Washington, DC: U.S. Government Printing Office.

U.S. Congress: Senate. 1980. *Structure of Corporate Concentration*, 2 vols. Hearings before the Senate Committee on Governmental Affairs. Washington, DC: U.S. Government Printing Office.

———. 1989. *Americans with Disabilities Act of 1989.* Hearings before the Committee on Labor and Human Resources and the Subcommittee on the Handicapped, 101st Congress, 1st Session. Washington, DC: U.S. Government Printing Office.

U.S. Congress: Senate Committee on Banking, Housing, and Urban Affairs. 1991. *Roundtable Hearing on Problems of African-American Males in Urban America.* Washington, DC: U.S. Government Printing Office.

U.S. Department of Commerce. 1990. *Survey of Current Business* 70(8). Washington, DC: U.S. Government Printing Office.

U.S. Department of Commerce, Bureau of the Census. 1993. *Statistical Abstract of the United States, 1993.* Washington, DC: U.S. Government Printing Office.

U.S. Department of Defense. 1992. *Prime Contract Awards.* Washington, DC: U.S. Government Printing Office.

U.S. Department of Education. 1987. *The Condition of Education.* Washington, DC: U.S. Government Printing Office.

U.S. Department of Health, Education, and Welfare. 1973. *Work in America.* Report of a Special Task Force to the Secretary of Health, Education, and Welfare. Washington, DC: U.S. Government Printing Office.

U.S. Department of Health and Human Services. 1985. *Social Security Programs throughout the World.* Washington, DC: U.S. Government Printing Office.

———. 1989. *Health, United States, 1988.* Washington, DC: U.S. Government Printing Office.

———. 1992. *Health, United States, 1991.* Washington, DC: U.S. Government Printing Office.

U.S. Department of Justice, Bureau of Justice Statistics. 1992. *Sourcebook of Criminal Justice Statistics, 1991.* Washington, DC: U.S. Government Printing Office.

U.S. Department of Labor. 1985. *Displaced Workers, 1979–83.* Washington, DC: U.S. Government Printing Office.

———. 1989. *Handbook of Labor Statistics.* Washington, DC: U.S. Government Printing Office.

———. 1990a. *Employment and Earnings.* Washington, DC: U.S. Government Printing Office.

———. 1990b. *Hourly Average Wages.* Washington, DC: U.S. Government Printing Office.

———. 1991a. *Employment and Earnings.* Washington, DC: U.S. Government Printing Office.

———. 1991b. *International Comparisons of Hourly Compensation Costs for Production Workers in Manufacturing, 1990.* Washington, DC: U.S. Government Printing Office.

———. 1991c. *A Report on the Glass Ceiling Initiative.* Washington, DC: U.S. Government Printing Office.

———. 1992. *Monthly Labor Review.* Washington, DC: U.S. Government Printing Office (January).

U.S. News & World Report. 1990. "Getting slim." (May 14):56–64.

Upchurch, Dawn M., and James McCarthy. 1990. "The timing of first birth and high school completion." *American Sociological Review* 55(April):224–234.

Useem, Michael. 1984. *The Inner Circle: Large Corporations and the Rise of Business Political Activity in the U.S. and U.K.* New York: Oxford University Press.

Utne. 1991. "The top ten censored stories of 1990." *Utne Reader* (July–August):61–64.

Vernon, Raymond. 1986. "Multinationals are mushrooming." *Challenge* 29(May–June):41–47.

Villa-Vicencio, Charles. 1978. "The theology of apartheid." *Christianity and Crisis* (March 13): 45–49.

Vloebergh, Assomption. 1979. "Does pornography incite violence?" *Recerche* 10(101)(June):682–684.

Wainwright, H., and D. Elliott. 1982. *The Lucas Plan.* New York: Alison and Busby.

Waite, Linda J., Arleen Leibowitz, and Christina Witsberger. 1988. *What Parents Pay For: Quality of Child Care and Child Care Costs.* Santa Monica, CA: Rand Corporation (March).

Walker, Lenore E. 1984. *The Battered Woman Syndrome.* New York: Springer.

———. 1989. *Terrifying Love: Why Battered Women*

Kill and How Society Responds. New York: Harper & Row.

Wall Street Journal. 1991. "Noted . . . Media." (April 5):B2.

Wallace, Anthony F. C. 1966. *Religion: An Anthropological View.* New York: Random House.

Wallace, Michael, Larry J. Griffin, and Beth A. Rubin. 1989. "The positional power of American labor, 1963–1977." *American Sociological Review* 54(2): 197–214.

Wallerstein, Immanuel. 1974. *The Modern World System: Capitalist Agriculture and the Origins of the European World-Economy in the Sixteenth Century.* New York: Academic Press.

———. 1980. *The Modern World System II: Mercantilism and the Consolidation of the European World Economy, 1600–1750.* New York: Academic Press.

Walsh, Mark. 1990a. "N.C. board sues to block the use of 'Channel One.'" *Education Week* 9(February 28):1, 21.

———. 1990b. "Shanker quits 'Channel One' advisory panel." *Education Week* 19(November 21):4.

——— and Peter Schmidt. 1990. "Amid furor, 'Channel One' to debut in 400 schools." *Education Week* 9(February 21):4.

Walton, John, and Charles Ragin. 1990. "The debt crisis and political protest in the Third World." *American Sociological Review* 55(6):876–890.

Ward, Kathryn. 1984. *Women in the World System.* New York: Praeger.

———. 1987. "The impoverishment of U.S. women and the decline of U.S. hegemony." Pages 275–290 in Terry Boswell and Albert Bergesen (eds.), *America's Changing Role in the World System.* New York: Praeger.

———. 1990. "Introduction and overview." Pages 1–24 in Kathryn B. Ward (ed.), *Women Workers and Global Restructuring.* Ithaca, NY: ILR Press.

——— and Charles Mueller. 1985. "Sex differences in earnings." *Work and Occupations* 12(4):437–463.

Warshaw, Robin. 1988. *I Never Called It Rape.* New York: Harper & Row.

Washington, James M. (ed.). 1986. *A Testament of Hope: The Essential Writings of Dr. Martin Luther King, Jr.* San Francisco: Harper & Row.

Washington Post. 1991. "Survey on Women and Family" (April).

Waters, Harry F. 1993. "Black is bountiful: Fox focuses on African-American shows—but at what cost?" *Newsweek* (December 6):59–61.

Watson, Bill. 1971. "Counter-planning on the shop floor." *Radical America* 5(May–June).

Weber, Max. 1947. *The Theory of Social and Economic Organization.* Trans. A. M. Henderson and Talcott Parsons. New York: Free Press.

Webre, P. 1979. *Jobs to People: Planning for Conversion to New Industries.* Washington, DC: Alternatives.

Wei, Ann. 1991. "Dumping on Native Americans." *Multinational Monitor* (October):7.

Weigman, O., M. Kuttschreuter, and B. Baarda. 1992. "A longitudinal study of the effects of television viewing on aggressive and prosocial behaviours." *British Journal of Social Psychology* 31(2):147–164.

Weinstein, James. 1968. *The Corporate Ideal in the Liberal State, 1900–1918.* Boston: Beacon Press.

Weir, David, and Mark Schapiro. 1981. *Circle of Poison: Pesticides and People in a Hungry World.* San Francisco: Institute for Food and Development Policy.

Weiss, Lois. 1986. "'Thirty years old and I'm allowed to be late': The politics of time at an urban college system." *British Journal of Sociology of Education* 7(3)(September):241–263.

Weiss, R. 1984. "The impact of marital dissolution on income and consumption in single-parent households." *Journal of Marriage and the Family* 46:115–127.

Weiss, Rick. 1991. "Implants: How big a risk?" *Science* 252(May 24):1060.

Weitzman, Lenore J. 1985. *The Divorce Revolution: The Unexpected Social and Economic Consequences for Women and Children in America.* New York: Free Press.

———. 1988. "Child support: Myths and reality." Pages 251–276 in A. Kahn and S. Kammerman (eds.), *Child Support: From Debt Collection to Social Policy.* Newbury Park, CA: Sage.

Welch, Susan, Michael Steinman, and John Comer. 1973. "Where have all the clients gone? An examination of the food stamp program." *Public Welfare* 31(2):48–54.

Wellesley College Center for Research on Women. 1992. *How Schools Shortchange Girls.* Washington, DC: American Association of University Women Educational Foundation.

West, Patrick C., J. Mark Fly, Francis Larkin, and Roberts Marans. 1992. "Minority anglers and toxic fish consumption: Evidence from a state-wide survey of Michigan." In B. Bryant and P. Mohai (eds.), *Race and the Incidence of Environmental Hazards: A Time for Discourse.* Boulder, CO: Westview Press.

Weston, Kath. 1991. *Families We Choose: Lesbians, Gays, Kinship.* New York: Columbia University Press.

Wheeler, David L. 1993. "Study of lesbians rekindles debate over biological basis for homosexuality." *Chronicle of Higher Education* (March 17):A6.

"Whistle-blowing nuclear worker gains." 1993. *New York Times* (June 10):A18.

Whitam, Frederick L., and Robin M. Mathy. 1985. *Male Homosexuality in Four Societies: Brazil, Guatemala, the Philippines, and the United States.* New York: Praeger.

Whitt, J. Allen. 1982. *The Dialectics of Power: Urban Elites and Mass Transportation.* Princeton, NJ: Princeton University Press.

Whyte, William Foote, and Joseph R. Blasi. 1982. "Worker ownership, participation, and control: Toward a theoretical model." *Policy Sciences* 14:137–163.

——— and Kathleen King Whyte. 1988. *Making Mondragon: The Growth and Dynamics of the Worker Cooperative Complex.* Ithaca, NY: ILR Press.

Wiatrowski, M., et al. 1982. "Curriculum tracking and delinquency." *American Sociological Review* 47: 151–160.

R-24

Wilkinson, Louis Cherry, and Cora B. Marrett (eds.). 1985. *Gender Influences in Classroom Interaction.* Orlando, FL: Academic Press.

Williams, Juan. 1987. *Eyes on the Prize.* New York: Penguin.

Williams, Norma. 1990. *The Mexican American Family: Tradition and Change.* Dix Hills, NY: General Hall.

Williams, Robin M., Jr. 1965. *American Society: A Sociological Interpretation,* 2nd ed. New York: Knopf.

Willie, Charles V. 1983. *Race, Ethnicity, and Socioeconomic Status.* Bayside, NY: General Hall.

———. 1989. *Caste and Class Controversy on Race and Poverty,* 2nd ed. New York: General Hall.

Willis, David P. (ed.). 1989. *Health Policies and Black Americans.* New Brunswick, NJ: Transaction Books.

Wilson, Edward O. 1978. *On Human Nature.* Cambridge, MA: Harvard University Press.

Wilson, John. 1992. "Cleaning up the game: Perspectives on the evolution of professional sports." Pages 65–95 in Eric Dunning and Chris Rojek (eds.), *Sport and Leisure in the Civilizing Process: Critique and Counter Critique.* Toronto: University of Toronto Press.

Wilson, William Julius. 1978. *The Declining Significance of Race.* Chicago: University of Chicago Press.

———. 1987. *The Truly Disadvantaged.* Chicago: University of Chicago Press.

Wolf, Naomi. 1991. *The Beauty Myth.* New York: Morrow.

Women's International League for Peace and Freedom. 1991. "Victory or defeat for people of color?" *Questions and Answers about the Gulf War* 3(April):1–4.

Wood, Robert E. 1985. "The aid regime and international debt." *Development and Change* 16(2): 179–212.

———. 1986. *From Marshall Plan to Debt Crisis: Foreign Aid and Development Choices in the World Economy.* Berkeley: University of California Press.

Worcester, Nancy, and Marianne H. Whatley. 1992. "The selling of HRT: Playing on the fear factor." *Feminist Review* (Summer):1–26.

World Bank. 1991. *World Development Report, 1991.* New York: Oxford University Press, 1991.

Wright, James D., and Sonia R. Wright. 1976. "Social class and parental values for children: A partial replication and extension of the Kohn thesis." *American Sociological Review* 41:527–537.

Yankelovich Clancy Shulman. 1991. "Telephone Survey on Attitudes toward Problems in the United States" (December). Time/CNN/Yankelovich Clancy Shulman.

———. 1992. "Survey on Family Values" (August).

Zavella, Patricia. 1984. "The impact of 'sun belt industrialization' on Chicanas." *Frontiers* 8(1):21–27.

———. 1987. *Women's Work and Chicano Families.* Ithaca, NY: Cornell University Press.

Zeitlin, Irving M. 1990. *Ideology and the Development of Sociological Theory,* 4th ed. Englewood Cliffs, NJ: Prentice-Hall.

Zelnick, Melvin, and John F. Kantner. 1977. "Sexual and contraceptive experience of young unmarried women in the United States, 1976 and 1971." *Family Planning Perspectives* 9(March–April): 55–71.

——— and J. Kim Young. 1982. "Sex education and its association with teenage sexual activity, pregnancy, and contraceptive use." *Family Planning Perspectives* 14(May–June):117–126.

Zick, C. D., and K. R. Smith. 1986. "Immediate and delayed effects of widowhood on poverty: Patterns from the 1970s." *Gerontologist* 26:669–675.

Zinn, Howard. 1980. *A People's History of the United States.* New York: Harper Colophon.

Zinn, Maxine Baca, and Bonnie Thornton Dill (eds.). 1993. *Women of Color in United States Society.* Philadelphia: Temple University Press.

Zweigenhaft, Richard L., and G. William Domhoff. 1991. *Blacks in the White Establishment?: A Study of Race and Class in America.* New Haven: Yale University Press.

Zwerdling, Daniel. 1984. *Workplace Democracy.* New York: Harper & Row.

Zwerling, L. Steven. 1976. *Second Best.* New York: McGraw-Hill.

CREDITS AND ACKNOWLEDGMENTS

NAME INDEX

SUBJECT INDEX